# A WORLD OF TROUBLE

# A WORLD OF TROUBLE

*The White House and the Middle East—from the Cold War to the War on Terror*

# PATRICK TYLER

FARRAR STRAUS GIROUX • NEW YORK

Farrar, Straus and Giroux
18 West 18th Street, New York 10011

Distributed in Canada by Douglas & McIntyre Ltd.
Printed in the United States of America
First edition, 2009

Library of Congress Cataloging-in-Publication Data
Tyler, Patrick.
    A world of trouble : the White House and the Middle East—from the Cold
War to the War on Terror / Patrick Tyler.— 1st ed.
        p.   cm.
    Includes index.
    ISBN-13: 978-0-374-29289-8 (hardcover : alk paper)
    ISBN-10: 0-374-29289-2 (hardcover : alk. paper)
    1. Middle East—Foreign relations—United States.   2. United States—
Foreign relations—Middle East.   3. Middle East—Politics and government—
20th century.   4. United States—Politics and government—20th century.
5. Middle East—Politics and government—21st century.   6. United States—
Politics and government—21st century.   I. Title.

DS63.2.U5 T95   2008
327.7305609'045—dc22

                                                                    2008041261

Designed by Debbie Glasserman

www.fsgbooks.com

1   3   5   7   9   10   8   6   4   2

To Linda . . .

# CONTENTS

List of Illustrations ix

Prologue: America in the Middle East 3

1. The Arab Awakening: Eisenhower, Nasser, and Suez 19

2. The Six-Day War: Johnson and Israel 64

3. Nixon and Brezhnev: Cold War and International Terror 107

4. Nixon and Kissinger: Yom Kippur—The October War 135

5. Jimmy Carter: Camp David and the Struggle with
    Menachem Begin 176

6. Carter and the Shah: Khomeini's Revolution 210

7. The Shame of Lebanon: Reagan's Warriors in the Middle East 249

8. The Iran-Contra Affair: The Clash of Saudi and
    Israeli Influence 308

9. Nebuchadnezzar-Land: Saddam Hussein and the
    Persian Gulf War 352

10. Bill Clinton: Tilting at Peace, Flailing at Saddam 402

11. Clinton: Flight from Terror; Lost Peace 457

12. George W. Bush: A World of Trouble 525

Notes 557

Acknowledgments 607

Index 611

# ILLUSTRATIONS

10 George W. Bush with George Tenet (© Eric Draper/ The White House/Reuters/Corbis)

26 Gamal Abdul Nasser with Edward R. Murrow in Cairo (Popperfoto/Getty Images)

69 Lyndon Johnson with King Faisal of Saudi Arabia (Francis Miller/Time Life Pictures/Getty Images)

110 Richard Nixon with Golda Meir (AFP/AFP/Getty Images)

174 Henry Kissinger with Anwar Sadat (David Hume Kennerly/Getty Images)

212 Jimmy Carter with Mohammed Reza Pahlavi, the shah of Iran (Archive Photos/Getty Images)

240 Ayatollah Khomeini in Tehran, 1979 (© Alain DeJean/ Sygma/Corbis)

260 Ronald Reagan and Saudi Arabia's King Fahd (AP Photo/Barry Thumma)

309 Hezbollah hijackers in Lebanon (Joel Robine/AFP/ Getty Images)

365 George H. W. Bush with Brent Scowcroft (AP Photo/ Barry Thumma)

406 Bill Clinton with Yasser Arafat (© Gary Hershorn/ Reuters/Corbis)

468 Osama bin Laden (© EPA/Corbis)

496 Saddam Hussein (© Jacques Pavlovsky/Sygma/Corbis)

539 George W. Bush, May 2002, in the War on Terror (© Brooks Kraft/CORBIS)

# A WORLD OF TROUBLE

# PROLOGUE

## America in the Middle East

**N**ight had long since fallen over central Saudi Arabia in early 2004 when George Tenet came trudging out of his bedroom in Prince Bandar bin Sultan's palace and asked for scotch whiskey.

In Riyadh, the capital of a conservative Islamic monarchy where alcohol was banned and women were not allowed to drive, it was possible in the cloister of the Saudi royal family to grant this wish to the American director of Central Intelligence.

Tenet had retired for the evening, or so the household thought. His security detail was bedded down.

It was unusual for a CIA director to have such a close relationship with a foreign envoy, but Prince Bandar was an unusual figure, having served for more than two decades in Washington as ambassador to four American presidents, having traveled the globe on discreet missions for his king, and having nurtured long-standing friendships—almost familial in character—with George H. W. Bush and his son, George W. Bush.

The CIA delegation had arrived late and eaten sumptuously from a buffet of lamb, salad, and sweets that Bandar's staff laid out. A CIA bodyguard and two senior officers, the director of the CIA's Near East Division and the agency's general counsel, had accompanied Tenet for the overnight. The CIA station chief, based in the kingdom, had joined them, as had Prince Salman, Bandar's younger half brother. But Tenet's group was tired and groggy from a tough itinerary that included a high-security stop in Iraq. The next morning, they were headed for Amman, Jordan.

Tenet took a sleeping pill and Bandar walked him down the hall to the guest room and said good night. But fifteen minutes later, the door to Tenet's room opened and closed. The director was stalking the elegant corridors in search of the prince. Bandar and his closest aide, Rihab Massoud, were still up watching television in the family room, which offered an inviting splay of well-stuffed divans oriented toward a wall covered with large-screen televisions. This high-tech array, with nine news channels on display at once, was a feature of Prince Bandar's villas, manor houses, and chalets around the world.

One wall of the broad living area was glass, which opened onto a large veranda paved with the blond native stone of central Arabia and overlooking a sparkling pool and a grove of date palms. Each year, the dates were harvested and sealed in vacuum packs to be delivered as gifts to friends of Prince Bandar and his wife, Princess Haifa, the youngest daughter of the late King Faisal.

On one wall, a portrait of Bandar's grandfather, King Abdul Aziz al-Saud, the tall and powerfully built warrior who had unified modern Saudi Arabia and who had cast the country's lot with America, looked down on them with a stern visage.

The prince had just suggested to Massoud that he, too, stay over because it was already 1:00 a.m. They were talking about Iraq and the troubles that had befallen the administration of George W. Bush when Tenet reappeared, disheveled in his boxers and T-shirt and with thunder in his mood.

"I can't sleep," he said.

A servant appeared with a bottle. Tenet knocked back some of the scotch. Then some more. They watched with concern. He drained half the bottle in a few minutes.

"They're setting me up. The bastards are setting me up," Tenet said, but "I am not going to take the hit."

The prince understood what Tenet was talking about. Someone had to take the blame for the missing weapons of mass destruction—the overarching pretext for the war in Iraq—and Tenet was raging against the realization that the White House expected him to fall on his sword to protect the president.

As the scotch melted what was left of his restraint, Tenet began to flail verbally at his enemies: the "assholes" in the Pentagon, the "crazies" and sneering ideologues in the White House, especially around Vice President Dick Cheney.

According to one witness, he mocked the neoconservatives in the Bush administration and their alignment with the right wing of Israel's political establishment, referring to them with exasperation as, "the Jews."[1]

More scotch. More invective.

After arriving in Riyadh, Tenet had spent part of his time on his secure phone back to Langley, sometimes shouting over the instrument to his deputy, John McLaughlin. "Fuck you . . . no, no, no, we are not going to take this . . . we've picked enough shit off our backs." Those were the lines that echoed in Bandar's ears, and it seemed that Tenet was spitting mad, negotiating, indirectly, with the White House on what would be said about the intelligence meltdown.

"I am going to protect the agency and my ass," Tenet had stated emphatically.*

Tenet was going to need a lot of protection, because by early 2004 the sham of the prewar intelligence had been revealed. David Kay, the veteran United Nations weapons inspector and chief of the Iraq Survey Group in Baghdad, had abruptly resigned and stated publicly that he didn't think Saddam Hussein had possessed any stockpiles of chemical or biological weapons.

---

*The scene at Prince Bandar's palace is taken from the accounts of three people who witnessed it, including the CIA Near East division chief, who was responsible for writing the trip report and who was not drinking. Tenet, in an interview, initially suggested he had not stayed at Prince Bandar's palace. He then denied that he had said anything during his midnight foray to the pool, which he asserted was of short duration. He disputed the remarks attributed to him and denied that his memory might have been affected by the amount of alcohol he was reported to have consumed on top of a sleeping pill. The CIA general counsel who accompanied Tenet to Saudi Arabia also disputed the account of the other witnesses, saying that he was with Tenet every moment during the evening; he asserted that Tenet did not make the remarks attributed to him by others.

"We were almost all wrong, and I certainly include myself," he told the Senate Armed Services Committee on January 28. Kay had seen enough to conclude that "it is highly unlikely that there were large stockpiles of deployed militarized chemical and biological weapons there." Not only Americans were shocked. Many Iraqis—scientists, military men, and Baath Party officials—had assumed, as the CIA had, that Saddam maintained hidden stockpiles of weapons.

"We weren't smart enough to understand that the hardest thing in intelligence is when behavior remains consistent but underlying reasons change," Kay told the senators. Though Saddam had built a terrifying military mystique based on chemical warfare in the 1980s, the Iraqi dictator's desire to end United Nations sanctions impelled him to destroy his arsenal. Apparently, it was as simple as that. Even Saddam, after his capture, admitted he had kept up the pretense that he was armed with weapons of terror: "You guys just don't understand. This is a rough neighborhood."[2]

After Kay's bombshell, Secretary of State Colin Powell said that he, too, was having second thoughts about the war based on Kay's testimony. "The absence of a stockpile [of chemical or biological weapons in Iraq] changes the political calculus," he told the editors at *The Washington Post*, pointing out that the Americans had overwhelmingly supported the war "with the understanding that there was a stockpile and there were weapons" that posed significant threat to the United States and its allies. Powell all but retracted his remarks the next day, but the damage had been done.

For many Americans, such candor from inside the intelligence establishment was both illuminating and devastating. It didn't matter that the Survey Group had reaffirmed Saddam's capacity to reconstitute his illicit weapons program, or that he had been developing ballistic missile systems that might deliver new weapons in the future. It didn't matter that Saddam had killed or scarred tens of thousands of Kurds and Iranians with nerve agents or mustard gas, or that he had been twice discovered developing nuclear weapons. Hadn't the Israelis destroyed Iraq's Osirak reactor in 1981 to block one effort at getting an atomic bomb? And a decade later, UN inspectors discovered and destroyed a second and more advanced nuclear program.

All that mattered in the winter of 2004 for many Americans—and Britons as well, for they had been mobilized for war by the same intelligence claims—was that they had been colossally misled. Kay said that it was "important that we acknowledge failure," but acknowledging failure was not something that came easily to the Bush administration when so many lives had been taken and so many billions spent on a war that had bogged down into a costly, low-intensity conflict against Iraqi insurgents and an influx of al-Qaeda operatives.

The White House had begun erecting its defense: Bush had relied on Tenet and the CIA in making the final decision for war based on the unambiguous CIA assessment that Iraq possessed weapons of mass destruction—the "slam dunk" case, as Tenet had famously referred to it.[3] Tenet knew that, in the end, he bore responsibility for the final intelligence judgments on Iraq that were presented to Bush. The National Intelligence Estimate that the CIA had produced and that had served as the foundation of the administration's case for war was Tenet's product. And it was wrong.

Tenet had tried to defend himself in public. "In the intelligence business, you are almost never completely wrong or completely right," he said in a speech at Georgetown University days after Kay's testimony. The CIA "painted an objective assessment for our policy-makers of a brutal dictator who was continuing his efforts to deceive and build programs that might constantly surprise us and threaten our interests."

Now the flaws in the CIA's analysis, its deductive leaps, the unreliable sources were coming back to haunt Tenet's doorstep, and the sulfurous tone that was filling Bandar's spacious family room suggested to the prince that his friend had made up his mind to leave the administration.

"My run is done," Tenet had told his top aides on the plane coming out to Saudi Arabia. "We did our job. We called it like we saw it, but this is going to be a rough period and I think I want to get out."

The lines of loyalty and trust that had sustained Tenet in the Bush circle had snapped. Now the question was whether Tenet would leave with a modicum of dignity, or whether his enemies in the White House would drive him out unceremoniously, because Tenet had always had detractors among the neoconservatives. It was also an election year. The 9/11 Commission Report was due out, and Tenet knew that the CIA was going to get blasted for having withheld critical information from the FBI about two of the 9/11 hijackers who had been in the country for eighteen months before the attacks.

Bush had been one of Tenet's defenders. "Tenet's under lots of pressure, but I am going to stick with him—I like him," Bush had confided to one of his Iraq advisers the previous October.[4]

To Bandar, Tenet was a lot like Powell: instinctively loyal, protective of the boss, and a strong member of the team. Neither was martyr material. They might remonstrate privately, but that was just part of the process of giving in to the inevitable realization that they would have to leave.

"I would like to go swimming," Tenet suddenly announced.

Bandar and Massoud exchanged looks of alarm; Tenet was clearly too drunk to swim. All that scotch on top of a sleeping pill: How long would he be conscious? They followed closely out into the warm midnight air of Riyadh as Tenet rumbled down the stairs, still in his underwear, and threw himself into the water.

Somehow Tenet managed to hold on to a Havana cigar and a glass of scotch. But his watch flew off and CIA aides dove to the bottom of the pool to retrieve it. There was the director of U.S. intelligence, bobbing up and down, trying to recover his mood with humor and defiance. He did impressions of Yasser Arafat and of Omar Suleiman, the Egyptian intelligence chief who loved to make sport of how fat Ariel Sharon, the Israeli prime minister, had become.

Tenet gazed down at his own mountainous girth. He had gained thirty-five pounds during his directorship. "I'm a pig!" he shouted into the night.

Bandar watched from a stool by the bar where a Pakistani servant was mixing drinks. Let the guy have a swim; it was the least he could do for Tenet. Bandar had observed five American presidents from close quarters and he recognized the political excision that was under way.

There was nothing Bandar could do to save the best friend he had ever had in a CIA director. Though the antiterror war had gotten brutal, Bandar believed that Tenet had performed a great service to the United States and to its allies. No CIA director—not even the legendary William Casey of the Reagan era—had worked as effectively in the Middle East to build an intelligence alliance that actually worked behind the veil. Tenet had a gift for personal relations. He laid on hands, he shared gossip about despots and potentates, and he kept secrets. He had won the confidence of the Arabs as well as the Israelis. He demonstrated American trust by presenting key foreign leaders with CIA secure phones that enabled them to speak to the president or his aides without risk of interception. Among the first to receive them had been the Saudi royal court and the Israeli prime minister's office. Bandar had his own CIA phone that traveled with him. These intelligence relationships continued to function even when diplomatic channels were roiled by George W. Bush's hard edges or the unilateral bent of his foreign policy.

Tenet had done an unparalleled job of organizing America's allies against Osama bin Laden and al-Qaeda in the wake of the September 11 attacks. He had dispensed hundreds of millions of dollars to the intelligence services of moderate Arab states—Egypt, Jordan, and Morocco—and to allies in Eastern Europe and Asia. He had built a formidable coalition and expanded agent networks in the Muslim world; he had shared technologies to put terror suspects under surveillance. He had broken down barriers, sharing raw "voice cuts"—conversations intercepted by the National Security Agency—with foreign intelligence services so native Arabic speakers could help identify them.

Tenet had been especially attentive to Saudi Arabia. He had traveled personally to the kingdom the year before to present the evidence to Crown Prince Abdullah, the day-to-day ruler, that al-Qaeda was planning to assassinate members of the royal family and that al-Qaeda cells were shopping for Russian-made nuclear weapons. Tenet's warning, delivered with Prince Bandar at his side, had led to a broad crackdown on al-Qaeda in the kingdom.

Tenet and the CIA had taken the gloves off in the war on terror.

He had overseen the "rendition" of terror suspects who were dispatched on CIA planes to secret prisons or interrogation facilities in Europe, the Middle East, and Asia. He had overseen the development of controversial interrogation methods, such as waterboarding, a simulated drowning that incites gagging and panic. It had been approved by Bush for use in these secret chambers. To any reasonable person, it was torture, but Tenet had been prepared to employ and defend such techniques because he and the president believed—they later said as much—that they could preempt new terror attacks with the information.

Those were the days when the American public overwhelmingly supported taking strong measures to prevent another attack on the U.S. homeland. The details of the CIA interrogation techniques were highly classified; the public was unaware until long afterward that George W. Bush had sanctioned torture in 2002 and 2003 against major al-Qaeda operatives in captivity.[5] In April 2004, when the Abu Ghraib prisoner abuses were documented in Iraq, public revulsion set in; the instinct to take the gloves off dissipated when Americans saw what it had led to.

George W. Bush with George Tenet: one an idealist, one a pragmatist—and both called it wrong in the Middle East.

Tenet's case had to be handled carefully. Bandar, too, knew that the president had very specifically and graphically instructed the CIA to do what was necessary to extract information about possible terrorist attacks. Bush had expressed himself brutally in meetings that Bandar had attended because Saudi Arabia was a full partner in the American coalition to destroy al-Qaeda in the wake of the 9/11 attacks.

"Why can't we send them to be tortured?" Bush had asked in one such conversation about al-Qaeda suspects.

"Stick something up their ass!" Bush had said. America was at war. Bush was willing to authorize tough tactics, even torture.

"Look, I just can't afford to see any more people in America die," he rationalized.[6]

Some of the scenes involving Bush that Bandar and Tenet had witnessed in the wake of 9/11 had been Strangelovian, and there were going to be court cases, maybe even criminal charges over the treatment of detainees. Bandar felt that the White House would be making a big mistake if it assumed that allegations of torture and detention in secret CIA prisons were going to be "George's problem." Tenet had made it clear to Bandar that he was not going to be the fall guy—everything the CIA had done, it had done with the authorization of the president, with review by the attorney general and briefings to key members of Congress. They both knew who had authorized the CIA to do what.[7]

Now, Tenet was going down.

Bandar deeply regretted his departure from the CIA because Tenet, along with Colin Powell, the secretary of state, and Tony Blair, the British prime minister, represented an informal cabal during the George W. Bush years. They understood the Middle East in the way Bandar did—that it was essential to work for peace in the Holy Land because the tragedy of Palestinians living under occupation for forty years represented an open wound that profoundly affected attitudes not just in the Middle East but throughout the world as a reservoir of grievance, passion, and anger. It fed the psychology of righteous retribution—the terrorist instinct—on the streets of Gaza, Ramallah, and Jenin, but also among those Islamic clerics throughout the world who preached an extremist course to impressionable young Muslims.

The four of them—Blair, Powell, Tenet, and Bandar—had worked in different ways and, at times, in concert to encourage George W. Bush to pursue a more pragmatic policy in the Middle East, one that balanced a determination to use military force to protect American interests with a humanistic agenda to bring an end to the Israeli occupation of Palestinian territories and to establish a viable Palestinian state.[8]

Their energy was arrayed against an equally formidable policy cabal that also had the president's ear, including Vice President Dick Cheney, his chief of staff Lewis "Scooter" Libby, Elliott Abrams of the National Security Council (NSC) staff and, in the Pentagon, Paul Wolfowitz, the deputy defense secretary, and Douglas Feith, the deputy secretary for policy. This neoconservative group of senior officials and their aides appealed to the president's idealism in the wake of the 9/11 attacks. They urged him to think of his presidency as a mission to expand the boundaries of freedom while ruthlessly attacking terrorism. The Palestinian cause was a sideshow and Arafat had discredited himself by playing the terror card when it suited him.

They defined terror as an all-encompassing evil in the Orwellian sense that ignored historic grievance or local political context; in this worldview, any state or political movement whose most militant adherents resorted to violence was the enemy.

Tenet might be taking the fall, justifiably, for the prewar intelligence blunders, but he also was walking away from the larger struggle to define America's interests more pragmatically in the Middle East, and that was a struggle that connected him and his like-minded colleagues back through the line of American officials to Eisenhower and Dulles, to Truman and Roosevelt, each of whom laid down foundation stones of American policy based on self-interest, a strong sense of justice, and a magnanimous American spirit.

Tenet believed that Bush had the strength, the vision, and the will for great achievement in the Middle East. He could use those strengths to do what was necessary to close the deal—to create a viable Palestinian state that had been put on the table during Clinton's final days in office. And both he and Bandar were disappointed by Bush's delay and prevarication.

The prince was the most reluctant to give up on Bush. Over twenty-five years, the former F-15 pilot had become a phenomenon of Saudi-American relations, with unparalleled access to the White House, but also to European and Asian capitals. He was rumored to maintain a private dialogue with the director of Mossad, Israel's intelligence service, about the requirements for Middle East peace; he lobbied both Bill Clinton and George W. Bush on a secret nuclear initiative: Would Washington consider putting moderate Arab nations under a NATO nuclear umbrella as a hedge against the growth of Iran's power? And he used his private channel to Bush to make the case for setting a time line for creating a Palestinian state at peace with Israel before he left office.

The White House was seven thousand miles away across desert and ocean, but its wires were still intimately connected to Bandar, the Westernized prince of the House of Saud, and to Tenet, the beefy son of Greek immigrants from Little Neck, Queens, who was now wrestling with the beast of his disappointment in Bandar's pool. It was tragic, and the intensity of the scene inspired surreal fantasy: What on earth would they do if he drowned?

In the annals of U.S. foreign policy, Tenet's last night in Riyadh in April 2004 was not unprecedented. Other powerful men had been unhorsed or come unglued in the bureaucratic wars fought over policies forged confidently in Washington but played out disastrously overseas. Tenet was not the first or the last senior member of the Bush administration to suddenly recognize the cleavage between traditional American ideals and the ideological cant and whimsy emanating from the White House. Powell would follow him out the door by the end of the year. The collapse of the intelligence underpinning the invasion of Iraq, Tenet's political demise, and the bloody insurgency that has claimed tens of thousands of lives and inflicted an incalculable cascade of destruction during the U.S. occupation of Iraq was the most current expression of a half century of costly miscalculations in the Middle East, the sum of which has deepened the American predicament.

This book is a history of the American experience in the Middle East over the past half century. It is a story of ten U.S. presidents and how they engaged or confronted the region and its leaders. The particulars are taken primarily from the declassified record of successive administrations buttressed by interviews with key players, recollections drawn from memoirs, oral histories, and other accounts. My aim is to understand—and to help the reader understand—the chaotic and very human perspective with which our presidents look out at the world while remaining tethered to politics at home.

It is essential to say at the outset that this narrative leads to a surprising conclusion about U.S. foreign policy. After nearly six decades of escalating American involvement in the Middle East, it remains nearly impossible to discern any overarching approach to the region such as the one that guided U.S. policy through the cold war. And, after endless cycles of conflict, an alarming buildup of arms, civil strife, and an escalation of religious confrontation, American leaders have been unable to agree on a firm set of principles, a consistent set of goals, or a course of action that could bring peace and stability to the Middle East. What stands out is the absence of consistency from one president to the next, as if the hallmark of American diplomacy were discontinuity.

Dwight Eisenhower, when confronted with a crisis, liked to say "the fat is in the fire," and it often was in the Middle East. Arab-Israeli wars broke out in 1956, 1967, 1969, 1973, and 1982. Islamic revolution in Iran was followed by the eight-year Iran-Iraq War (1980–88). Libya invaded Chad. Saddam Hussein invaded Kuwait. Israel pummeled Lebanon in 2006 following a Hezbollah incursion. Each catastrophe blindsided or flummoxed presidents who wondered how, given the billions of dollars spent on American spy satellites and the most extensive intelligence apparatus in the world, surprise was the most frequent denominator in the Middle East equation. War, for the most part, triggered escalating interventions by superpowers, whose arms deliveries were fueled by the run-up in Arab oil-producing wealth. Presidents found themselves reacting to events, or flailing at the last minute to head off the violence, as Jimmy Carter did in the face of Ayatollah Khomeini's return to Tehran and the Soviet army's march into Afghanistan.

Given the extent of American commitment in the region today—in response to the aftermath of war in Iraq, the rise of Iran's power, devastation in Lebanon, and the ongoing struggle between Israelis and Palestinians in the Holy Land—it is surprising to look back and realize that for most of the last century the Middle East was not a crucial region for the United States. When Eisenhower and Richard Nixon captured the White House in 1952, the Middle East was considered a backwater. Israel had been a state for only four years and most Americans had only a passing familiarity with the history of the region. But with the declaration of Jewish statehood in 1948, together with the rise of Arab nationalism, the advent of oil politics, and Islamic revivalism, ignorance gave way to curiosity and, eventually, to the near obsession with which America now seeks to manage its affairs in the region. If anything mattered more than religion for many Americans—because the Middle East was synonymous with the Holy Land—it was oil. Oil had won the world wars. Access to Middle Eastern oil was essential for America's postwar development. In the event of renewed world war, the control of oil would be pivotal to Western security.

Because of this, the victorious powers that emerged from World War II—Great Britain, France, the Soviet Union, and the United States—came to see the Middle East as a zone of competition. British and French colonial armies withdrew, abandoning possessions and protectorates that had been secured for centuries; they gave up bases along the Suez Canal and in Algeria and Bahrain. It was not surprising that America would come to the fore, if only to block Moscow's opportunities. But it was far from inevitable that America would prevail, and what is most striking about the half century of U.S. effort is the record of vacillation, of shifting policies, broken promises, and misadventures, as if America were its own worst enemy. The Middle East would never have been an easy region to master for the purpose of protecting U.S. national interests, but our mistakes have made it progressively harder to do so. The cumulative effect of American diplomacy has fed the anti-American rhetoric that is heard on the streets in Middle Eastern capitals, even in countries nominally allied with the United States. While it would be overstatement to say that John F. Kennedy reversed Eisenhower's approach, Lyndon Johnson reversed Kennedy's, Nixon reversed Johnson's, and so on, the most prominent feature of this chronicle of presidential thought and action is how much each leader sought to distinguish himself from his predecessor—a very human trait—and in doing so injected a permanent element of instability to Middle East policy.

Kennedy, for example, thought it was crucial for the United States to prevent Israel from obtaining nuclear weapons; he was certain such an eventuality would give rise to a nuclear arms race in the region, or could prompt the Soviets to place a nuclear umbrella over Israel's Arab foes. But by the time Nixon entered the White House, the focus had shifted to building up regional allies like Israel and Iran with massive infusions of conventional weapons and a studied silence about their secret nuclear ambitions.[9] Thirty years later, Bill Clinton's frenetic and undisciplined peacemaking efforts in the Middle East were abandoned by an incoming George W. Bush, who rebelled against the notion of spending political capital in endless negotiations with Arab and Israeli leaders at Camp David, the site of previous Middle East breakthroughs. The intensity of partisanship that flowed out of the 2000 presidential election called forth a hubristic mantra among the Bush advisers, who insisted that the new president would be very *un*-Clintonian, and Bush himself said he would be unlike his father in dealing with the Middle East.

Some historians argue that history is shaped by tectonic forces among nation-states seeking a balance of power or a kind of equilibrium. But this chronicle of American involvement in the Middle East is rooted in the conviction that history arises chaotically from the scrum of human events, where the tactical maneuvering of leaders, local politics, and the seemingly random eruptions of war, revolution, and natural disaster drive the human narrative more profoundly, and unpredictably. Tectonic forces count. Playing the balance-of-power game is one path along which heads of state may proceed, but this can cause them, fatally at times, to ignore the finer mesh of social, religious, and intellectual upheaval where the turns of history take place.

America's engagement with the Middle East demonstrates just how dramatically history goes its own way. It also reveals how outsized personalities and freewheeling intellects arrogate unto themselves the prerogatives of power, putting self-interest ahead of national interest with willful and history-changing acts. Witness the conspiracy of allies to deceive Eisenhower in the Suez crisis, or Anwar Sadat's amazing decision to go to Jerusalem to break the psychological barrier to peace. Consider Kissinger's breathtaking deceptions during the 1973 Arab-Israeli War; or Nixon's betrayal of his own desire to engage Leonid Brezhnev for comprehensive peace in the Middle East. Witness the depth of Alexander Haig's contempt for Ronald Reagan, who was so little prepared for Israel's invasion of Lebanon in 1982 that he had to spend the next two years zigzagging across a burning landscape to find an adequate American response. All the while, the death toll mounted for American civilians, diplomats, and the marines in Beirut.

Though many analysts believe that American foreign policy is heavily influenced by the pro-Israeli lobby in Congress, and others assert that the great economic power of the Arab oil-producing states weighs heavily on presidents, it is startling how quickly these salients of leverage and political influence, which are real, sometimes are swept aside.

When Saddam Hussein's army overran Kuwait in August 1991, George H. W. Bush and his secretary of state, James A. Baker III, built a coalition of Arab states—including Syria and excluding Israel—to oppose Saddam on the premise that Arab cooperation was critical if the Iraqi dictator was to be defeated. Bush was firm that Israel not be allowed to participate in the war, or even in the search for Scud missiles that Saddam's forces fired against the Jewish state, because Israeli involvement would have split the American-Arab coalition.

But after the Persian Gulf War cease-fire, Bush pushed Israel's interests back to the fore. He convened a Middle East peace conference in Madrid that afforded respect to all the parties, most particularly for Yitzhak Shamir, the Israeli prime minister, who became the first Israeli leader since 1948 to sit with the Arab leadership and debate their rival national claims. Even so, the competition between Jews and Arabs to sway U.S. presidents in order to gain the upper hand in congressional debates or to seize the moral high ground in public opinion is now a permanent aspect of American foreign policy. And this fact reaffirms the contours of the core dispute.

The creation of a Jewish state in the heart of the Arab world has proved to be one of the great rifts of history brought about by an equally great confluence of events at the end of World War II. Ever since the Zionist brief to establish a Jewish homeland was elevated to the level of moral imperative by the Holocaust, the Arab-Israeli dispute has loomed over every American effort in the region. It arises, of course, from two competing national claims on the same land, where the Bible documents the birth of Hebrew nationalism that was crushed and dispersed by Rome, though never extinguished. Islamic conquerors supplanted Rome in the Middle East, and when the Zionists returned in numbers in the late nineteenth century, a population that was predominantly Arab and Muslim was still in charge of the Holy Land. The dispute has animated politics, diplomacy, and war since the first stirrings of Arab nationalism in the early twentieth century and Arab passions were vented against Jewish pioneers living under Ottoman rule. The depth of this conflict is so profound that some modern political figures have sought to escape its power over the diplomatic agenda by denigrating its importance, arguing that America has a larger stake and a broader portfolio in the region. During the presidency of George W. Bush, the conflict was shunted aside by neoconservative strategists who reassigned the conflict as a "local" issue, one not worthy of the president's attention and not worth investing political capital in, as Bill Clinton had done painfully and without substantial results over his eight-year term. Some even argued that the road to Palestine lay through Baghdad—in other words, that once America had toppled the region's worst dictator and established a democratic model in the Arab world, resistance to a Pax Americana would melt and old conflicts would settle under the force of American will or military coercion. When these chimeras fade, the core conflict reemerges, more complex and more deeply felt than ever. And if history has revealed anything, it is that it takes American leadership, robust leadership that galvanizes the Congress and world opinion, to bring the two sides—Arab and Israeli—into a position where they have a chance to solve it.

Many historians have produced insightful portraits of postwar American leaders, but even the best of them lack extensive familiarity with the Middle East and its personalities. This book attempts to join the two worlds to show that it is not enough to perceive Eisenhower's or Nixon's or Clinton's Middle East outlook without also understanding Nasser's zeal for the Arabs, Ayatollah Khomeini's rage against the West, Saddam Hussein's ruthless ambition, or Osama bin Laden's alienation from the modern world.

The United States still stands as the indispensable power in the Middle East. Yet American leadership, especially during the eight years of George W. Bush's presidency, has measurably declined. The security of the West, including that of the continental United States, has steadily eroded in the face of intensifying enmities and grievances directed at Washington. American policy mistakes have cost countless thousands of lives. They have sundered landscapes once vibrant with diverse cultures, and they have squandered hundreds of billions of dollars of resources.

Most distressing for America today, and for a new American president, is the task of untangling the policies of the past, of addressing the acute hostility that has developed toward a country once trusted as an honest broker, of containing an unrelenting arms race that has introduced nuclear weapons and ballistic missiles to the region, and of bridging the intractable differences that lie at the heart of the Middle East's most long-standing conflict.

It is high time Americans reached a consensus—both at home and with our allies in Europe and Asia—on the next steps toward peace and security. To achieve this, a new president will need help—from a bipartisan congressional leadership, from academia, and from trusted allies. Above all, he will have to reestablish America's standing as a benevolent and magnanimous power capable of engendering trust and exercising leadership—with continuity.

These requirements may appear self-evident, but they can be fulfilled only when Americans gain a fuller understanding of their own history in the region that was not always apparent in the making because so much was shielded by the strictures of classification, diplomatic artifice, or just blatant concealment and obfuscation. The foreign policy of great powers is difficult to distinguish or separate from domestic politics, and because of this, Americans will have to protect any consensus from the tactical maneuvering of politicians, domestic grandstanding, and demagoguery. They will have to distinguish among sound national strategy, interest-group lobbying, and propaganda, all of which are part of the background noise and of the occasional foolishness of modern media. As Americans, we may know who we are, but we may not understand how we are regarded or how our policies are perceived in the Middle East. And so we must learn who we are in fuller dimension if we hope to succeed in the region that is critical to our future. That is the story that this book aims to tell and the question it hopes to answer.

# 1

# THE ARAB AWAKENING

*Eisenhower, Nasser, and Suez*

J ohn Foster Dulles, Dwight Eisenhower's secretary of state, had a bloodless and terrifying manner when conveying American disquietude. He was a righteous man—his critics said self-righteous—and his formidable intellect, honed by practicing diplomacy and international law for nearly half a century, radiated a Calvinist certitude that could be unsettling, if not pompous. On the last weekend in October 1956, it was this very tone that was emanating from the secretary's chair as he looked out from the edifice of his discontent and demanded from Abba Eban some kind of explanation for what was happening in the Middle East.

Why, the secretary of state wanted to know, was the Eisenhower administration receiving intelligence reports by the hour indicating that a full military mobilization was under way in Israel?[1]

Eban, Israel's ambassador to the United States, was prone to sit as erect as a British schoolboy. A charming studiousness animated every muscle in his face and was meant to show Dulles how seriously he took the secretary's concern. There was also, perhaps, a slight furrow of puzzlement to signal that Dulles was not likely to get a real answer because Prime Minister David Ben-Gurion was not prepared to surrender details at this most sensitive moment of conspiracy.

Born in Cape Town, South Africa, and raised in England as Aubrey Meir, Eban changed his name as Ben-Gurion and others had changed theirs to accentuate their Jewishness. Educated at Cambridge University, Eban represented the British intellectual school of Diaspora Jews, whose number included many scientists and academics whose contribution to the nation-building process would prove crucial.

Eban had served with British forces during the war as a liaison to the Jewish Agency before rushing to Palestine in 1948 and then to the just-established United Nations, where he assisted in marshaling the votes needed for the creation of the Jewish state. For the first eight years of Israel's existence, he had been serving as its ambassador in America, working to expand its recognition internationally and voraciously defending its prerogatives as a sovereign and independent nation.

These were years during which Israel was a tenuous outpost of a million or so Jews in a sea of fifty million Arabs. People, not least the Arab leaders, were betting that the Zionist enterprise would not survive. Its budget consisted of loans and donations. The achievements of each year were measured by hectares cleared, meters of irrigation pipe laid—in other words, the full metrics of anchoring a state on the Mediterranean shore. While some toiled, others rescued displaced persons, survivors of Hitler's extermination campaign, and still others opened camps for Jews arriving from Iraq, Egypt, Morocco, and Yemen. The Zionist dream was now a frenetic, day-to-day task of breaking rocks on barren landscapes to build up an agricultural base, seize and channel water resources, lay out a plan for industry, and construct housing for the flood of immigrants.

Sitting there in Dulles's intimidating presence, his dark hair combed neatly back above black-framed glasses in the style of the times, Eban was ever the London sophisticate, though given what he knew, he had every reason to be nervous. He had quick eyes and an impressive expanse of jowl. Put Eban at a podium, stand him in the pit of diplomacy, and he could call down the heavens with a ringing oration. His voice had become one of Israel's most powerful weapons.

In the midst of the War of Independence, when Israel had existed barely a fortnight and was under Arab attack, Eban had taken the rostrum at the United Nations to warn the Arab leaders of their folly: "Israel is the product of the most sustained historic tenacity which the ages recall," he told the delegates. "The Jewish people [have] not striven towards this goal for twenty centuries in order that, having once achieved it, it will now surrender it in response to an illegitimate and unsuccessful aggression. Whatever else changes, this will not. The State of Israel is an immutable part of the international landscape. To plan the future without it is to build delusions on sand."[2] Words flew out of Eban as if he were tearing them from Scripture.

Dulles's aides had tracked Eban down at Congressional Country Club in the Washington suburbs where he had been enjoying a round of golf with Congressmen Sidney Yates of Illinois and the journalist Martin Agronsky. Israel's mobilization looked opportunistic to most analysts in the State Department. The Jewish state faced no immediate provocation, yet it had summoned its population to arms. Men and women dismounted their tractors and reported for military duty—but what duty?

Now, pinned to his chair like an insect before the secretary, Eban was desperately short of a strategy. Dulles had handed him a copy of President Eisenhower's letter to Ben-Gurion of the previous day warning against any precipitous military action by Israeli forces. Eban had to think fast. He studied the letter for a few moments, then pointed out that the secretary had placed him in a position that made it difficult to respond. If he had been given a copy of the president's letter on Friday, he might have had the opportunity to cable home, before the Sabbath, for some instructions or elucidation about the mobilization that was of such great concern.

Next, he parried the limited facts that were in Dulles's possession.

Israel might be overreacting with this mobilization, he said, but it had very good reason to fear that the Arab nations were "concerting together" in preparation for an attack on Israel. Gamal Abdul Nasser, the Egyptian leader, had whipped up the Arab world to a crescendo. A joint command had been established among Egyptian, Jordanian, and Syrian forces. Preparations for attacks by Arab fedayeen—self-sacrificing martyrs with guns—against Israel had been detected by Israeli intelligence; also detected were Iraqi troops near the Jordanian border. Israel had to be prepared, Eban said, and so it should be no surprise to the secretary that some reserve battalions had been called up.

Instead of allaying Dulles's suspicions, Eban only incited them.

"Some reserve units had been called up," Dulles repeated Eban's words. No, no, no. That was not what Dulles was talking about. According to his information, Israel's armed forces were totally mobilized. *Totally.* Hundreds of thousands of able-bodied men and women had dropped their civilian routines and reported to military units, bringing the economy to a virtual standstill. Of course, Israel had a right to call up its reserves, Dulles said, but he wondered why Eban would minimize the extent of this vast mobilization. According to the information he possessed, Israel had called up *all* of its reserves.

What could be the purpose? Was it the situation in Jordan?

Dulles knew that Jordan's monarch, the twenty-year-old King Hussein, was shaky on the throne. His grandfather, King Abdullah, was one of the Hashemite princes whose line had long ruled in Mecca as descendants of the Prophet Muhammad. Both Iraq and Jordan were unique British protectorates owing to the fact that they were created to reward the progeny of Sherif Hussein, the Hashemite patriarch in western Arabia who had thrown in with the British to defeat the German-Ottoman axis in World War I.

Abdullah and his older brother, Faisal, had fought with Colonel T. E. Lawrence—Lawrence of Arabia—against the Ottoman Turks because they believed imperial Britain would allow the Arabs to reclaim the glory that had existed under the caliphate, the early Islamic empire, by reestablishing its realm on the Arabian Peninsula, in Mesopotamia, and across the Levantine crescent to include Damascus, Beirut, and Jerusalem.[3] But the British had broken most of their promises, allowing the French to kick Faisal out of Damascus and standing pat as Sherif Hussein himself was driven out of Mecca by Abdul Aziz al-Saud, the upstart desert warrior from central Arabia who was unifying a state that would take his name, Saudi Arabia. As a consolation, Winston Churchill had put Faisal on the throne in Iraq; Abdullah was imposed on the Arab population of a new state that the British colonial office had dubbed Transjordan (later, simply Jordan), a wedge of desert that would come to include East Jerusalem and the Old City, where the holy mosques al-Aqsa and the Dome of the Rock stood on ancient Jewish foundations.[4] This artificial desert kingdom was facing the threat of overthrow by pro-Nasser students and Palestinians, who made up the bulk of Jordan's population.

King Hussein's cousin in Iraq, King Faisal II, had marched Iraqi troops westward to bolster the loyal elements of Jordan's armed forces. Ben-

Gurion suspected that Iraq was positioning itself to take over the eastern half of Jordan if Jordan's monarchy collapsed.

The United States and Britain had taken pains to consult with Ben-Gurion over the Iraqi troop movements—meant to stabilize Jordan—but the Israeli mobilization seemed to give the lie to Ben-Gurion's reply that Israel was not threatened by the Iraqi force.[5]

Did Israel fear an attack from Jordan? Dulles asked.

Yes, Eban replied, it did—he was now on the verge of blatantly deceiving the secretary of state. Given Israel's fears, Eban continued, he understood that its mobilization might raise the question of whether Israel's intentions were defensive or offensive. But all of his information, Eban said, indicated that Israel's mobilization was for defensive purposes.

This was a lie, of course. Eban knew more about the mobilization than he was allowed to say. He had just returned from Israel. Ben-Gurion had called home his ambassadors as a way to signal that he was preparing to take action against Jordan. It was a grand deception, for it had been plain for some time that if Jordan fell apart, Israel would be tempted to seize all of the territory west of the Jordan River that had been part of the historic land of Israel.[6]

That would leave nothing for any future Palestinian Arab state as envisioned by the UN's partition resolution of 1947, and the presumption was that Israel would push the Arabs across the Jordan River where they could take over the remnants of King Hussein's realm.

Since coming out of retirement the previous year, Ben-Gurion had been pursuing an activist military strategy against the Arabs, staging large-scale raids on Jordan and Egypt in retaliation for attacks against Jewish settlements. A raid at Qalqilya on the night of October 10 had turned into a ferocious battle in the densely populated Arab town, and when dawn broke nearly one hundred Palestinians lay dead with as many wounded. The Israeli paratrooper force, under the command of Ariel Sharon, a brash young practitioner of the punitive strike, limped home with eighteen dead and sixty wounded.

Eban had come to understand—he wasn't fully informed—that the border tension with Jordan was more calculated charade than real invasion. When he arrived home that October, Ben-Gurion pulled him aside and whispered conspiratorially that he was about to fly secretly to France to confer with Prime Minister Guy Mollet on a plan that would have "sensational results."[7] The real target was Egypt, not Jordan. The conspiracy—

with Eisenhower and Dulles kept in the dark—was to seize the Suez Canal, overthrow the Egyptian regime, and expand Israel's frontiers into the Sinai Peninsula and thereby bolt Jewish foundations even more firmly on the Mediterranean shore where the Hebrew nation had been born.

Eisenhower was campaigning for reelection against Adlai Stevenson. The war hero president was riding a wave of popularity—he had ended the Korean War—and not even an incipient uprising in Hungary against Soviet tyranny was going to induce him to betray his political instinct that, above all, America needed a period of peace and prosperity. He was dedicated to building up institutions (the United Nations) and alliances (NATO) that would avert war in the future.

"The sum of our international effort," he said in his State of the Union address that year, "should be this: the waging of peace, with as much resourcefulness, with as great a sense of dedication and urgency, as we have ever mustered in defense of our country in time of war. In this effort, our weapon is not force. Our weapons are the principles and ideas embodied in our historic traditions, applied with the same vigor that in the past made America a living promise of freedom for all mankind."

Eisenhower looked at the Middle East with the eyes of a military strategist and saw a fulcrum that joined continents, a nexus where lines of communication crossed and, crucially for the future, a basin that held the world's most bountiful oil supply.

"There is no more strategically important area in the world," he had said, and whoever controlled it in a world war would have an enormous advantage.[8] After Korea, Eisenhower had no illusions about the Soviet Union or Mao Zedong's China. America had entered a long struggle against international communism. Eisenhower and Dulles believed that the Kremlin leadership was itself seeking to minimize the risk of war, but a global competition for influence and power would be intense. In the Middle East, the American leaders saw the potential for collaboration with the British in erecting a new alliance to block Soviet attempts to encroach on the oil-producing region or to secure warm-water ports for the Soviet fleet. In this competition, Gamal Abdul Nasser of Egypt, the rising star of Arab politics, figured prominently. The British distrusted him. So did Israel, whose national emergence represented a completely new kind of challenge for the United States: here was a state whose very existence was deeply resented by its neighbors.

Truman, who was both emotionally and politically attuned to the Jewish community in the United States—his friend and business partner Eddie Jacobson had been a passionate Zionist—infuriated the British and his own State Department in 1945 by supporting Jewish immigration to Palestine.[9]

Unlike Truman, Eisenhower was not beholden to Jewish votes or the Jewish community's nascent political fund-raising machine. Eisenhower struck some people as uncomfortable around Jews, though not anti-Semitic. Eban had met him in Paris in 1952, when Eban accompanied Moshe Sharett, the foreign minister, on a trip to Europe. They had been surprised when the general, the amiable war hero running for president, explained unabashedly how he had come to consciousness about the Jewish experience in history. He told them that as a boy in Abilene, Kansas, he had believed that Jews—he called them the "Israelites"—were creatures of mythology and legend, like angels or cherubs. He confessed to being surprised and disconcerted to discover upon reaching a certain age that they existed outside the Bible.[10]

Eisenhower's easy confession may have seemed strange and inscrutable to a Cambridge man, but Ike's awkward Midwestern naïveté masked the calculating politician who had contested and maneuvered among the great egos of the world war. And he had come out on top.

It had again surprised the Israelis—indeed, it alarmed them—that from the outset of the administration, Eisenhower and Dulles worked diligently and creatively to find solutions in the Middle East. The alarm went up because most of these schemes required Israel to give up land or share water resources with the Arabs. Eisenhower's motivation was straightforward and certainly not hostile to Israel. He was out to protect and expand American interests in the region.

In their first year in office, Eisenhower and Dulles concerted with the British to overthrow Mohammad Mossadegh, the nationalist prime minister of Iran, who had taken the first steps to nationalize British Petroleum's assets in Iran, Britain's largest single investment abroad. Eisenhower and Churchill agreed that Mossadegh was a demagogue who would drive Iran into the Communist camp, upending the pro-Western monarchy of the young shah, Mohammed Reza Pahlavi.

The CIA's Operation Ajax to bring down Mossadegh was touch-and-go. Mossadegh stood his ground when the shah issued a decree dismissing him. The fate of Iran teetered when the shah lost his nerve in midplot and fled the country. The CIA was looking at failure until Iranian mobs—

Gamal Abdul Nasser with Edward R. Murrow in Cairo: America's anticommunist in the Middle East

with some inducements from American and British intelligence agents—
rallied the populace for the shah. The army did the rest. The shah returned to Tehran, and Iran (along with British oil assets) was saved for
the West.

Then came Nasser as the new Arab leader. In the postwar order,
Eisenhower understood that ideological loyalty—communism versus
democratic capitalism—was the new geopolitical currency in the competition with Moscow for hearts and minds in the so-called third world.
Nasser's appeal was an organizing force and in Washington there was
great excitement when he turned against Egypt's Communists. Washington wanted him to lead the opposition against international communism
in the Middle East.

Dulles was getting nowhere with Eban over the military buildup in Israel
as Eisenhower's campaign swung into its final weekend. But he wanted
to send a signal to Ben-Gurion. Israel was safer than at any previous time
in its short history, he told Eban. There was no need to contemplate war.

To the east, King Hussein's position in Jordan was extremely weak. To the west, Israel had nothing to fear from Nasser because Egypt was locked in a dispute with Britain and France over control of the Suez Canal.

Thinking out loud, Dulles wondered whether Israeli leaders had concluded that the region was so distracted by other confrontations that Israel might take advantage of the chaos and strike out. He did not specify a target, but Dulles knew that Ben-Gurion considered Jordan a "nonviable" state ripe for the plucking.

Eban said nothing to allay Dulles's other concern: if Israel attacked Jordan, Britain and France could then seize the moment to attack Egypt.[11] Dulles had no idea that a significant conspiracy still was hidden from Washington's view.

The secretary needed some answers. He told Eban that even the American ambassador in Tel Aviv had not been able to see Ben-Gurion, who was avoiding him by saying he was endlessly tied up in cabinet meetings. This was Eban's cue to escape Dulles's glare. He would get through to Ben-Gurion and relay all that Dulles had said and then he would report to the secretary as soon as possible, probably the next day, Monday.

But Monday was the day of the attack.

Eban had deceived Eisenhower's secretary of state on a crucial matter of war and peace. Ben-Gurion had taken a calculated risk that America would understand (or at least tolerate) the duplicity and deception. But his relationship with Eisenhower never really recovered. Both men knew that America was, potentially, Israel's most important protector. If world war should ever engulf the Middle East, only America could save Israel from Soviet and Arab aggression aimed at extinguishing the Jewish state. Eisenhower was thus livid when reports of war breaking out reached him in the final days of the presidential campaign.

Israeli tanks and artillery sundered the calm with explosive percussion, causing the Egyptian garrison in the Gaza Strip to dive for cover, returning fire as best it could. But the main attack was deep in Sinai, where paratroopers commanded by Ariel Sharon leaped from transports and caught the Egyptian defenders, who were guarding the passes just a few dozen miles from the Suez Canal, by surprise.

The principle of nonaggression, deeply imbedded in the postwar efforts to stabilize the Middle East after the armistice of 1949, lay in tatters. Another Arab-Israeli war was under way. In Eisenhower's view, Israel was in brazen violation of the armistice.

The president was so worked up on that Monday that he was ready to call a special session of Congress and throw America's weight behind the victim, Egypt, a prospect that he did not "fancy" but felt compelled to consider if anyone was going to take American policy seriously in the future. In the Cabinet Room at the White House, Dulles wondered aloud whether the Israeli assault might touch off a wave of anti-Semitism in the United States, and there was a chorus of muttered agreement among Eisenhower's advisers.[12]

On the second day, however, all talk of bringing back Congress or of taking immediate action to defend principles ended when British warplanes started bombing Egypt, destroying camps and airfields and brutally killing more than one thousand civilians living in the canal zone.[13] British and French troops landed with tanks and artillery on the Egyptian coast.

With this unilateral act by America's closest allies—not only Israel but also Britain and France had deceived him—Eisenhower stood humiliated on the eve of his reelection. Their conspiracy violated everything that bound them to America as allies. And under all that Midwestern affability, Eisenhower's vanities had been sorely abused. His best friends had torn up the Tripartite Declaration[14] and ignored the greatest power in the alliance. He was flummoxed: How could America confront its own allies militarily? The Western alliance would dissolve. The Soviets would achieve a great victory. What was he to do?

The conspiracy had been finalized just six days earlier, when Ben-Gurion flew secretly from Tel Aviv to Paris. In those days, that required a seventeen-hour entombment in a DC-4. When his plane touched down on a rain-soaked runway in the French capital, an unobtrusive motorcade whisked his party to a villa in the Paris suburb of Sèvres. With him were his military chief of staff, Moshe Dayan, and Shimon Peres, a young Defense Ministry aide to the prime minister. Greeting them in secret was the Socialist prime minister, Guy Mollet.

With the whole group arrayed before the French leaders, Ben-Gurion spoke in Hebrew of his fervent desire to tap the power of France, Britain and, he hoped, the United States to redraw the boundaries of the Middle East. The current boundaries did not make sense, he argued. The armistice lines of 1949 did not augur well for long-term security. And Israel, in his view, the newest state with the greatest potential, already felt confined.

David Ben-Gurion, at seventy, had been fighting for the Zionist cause for much of the century. He had arrived in Palestine from Poland in 1906, was expelled by the Ottoman Turks at the onset of World War I, and returned to Palestine in 1918 to eventually head the Jewish Agency as the indispensable organizer of military, political, and social institutions that would provide the structure of the future state.

Excepting Chaim Weizmann, playing the role of Zionist elder from London, there was no one on the Israeli scene like Ben-Gurion, a leader prone to volcanic outbursts, an admirer of Lenin, and a militarist driven by an exaggerated sense of threat. ("I am a quarrelsome, obstreperous man," he often said.[15]) He was the founding architect, the military strategist, and the political master at once. His judgment could be questioned and some of his judgments were questionable, but he dominated with energy, vision, and an intimidating aura of authority. Moshe Sharett, who disagreed with Ben-Gurion on policy toward the Arabs, was so intimidated that he had a nightmare of being arrested for high treason and sentenced to the gallows for disagreeing with the "old man."[16] Ben-Gurion's torrent of grey hair swirled around his pumpkin-shaped noggin that was stuck on a high-waisted frame, giving him an elfish countenance. He was born with the rabbinical inclination for exhaustive argument, and it required some patience to hear him out because, at times, he began at the Book of Genesis.

He told the French prime minister and his colleagues that he would like to make the case for a new Middle East order, something that only the great powers could accomplish and more effectively so with Israel's connivance. What he had in mind might seem "fantastic," he said, but he really believed it was feasible. First he would propose the dissolution of Jordan as a state, giving all the land west of the Jordan River to Israel and all the land east of the river to Iraq. That would unite the Hashemite kingdom under one roof in Baghdad and give Israel some vital strategic depth. Next he would propose the dismemberment of Lebanon, giving Syria the eastern quarter and Israel the southern quarter up to the Litani River and consolidating what remained as a Christian state under the Maronite majority of Mount Lebanon. The Western powers could then install a pro-Western ruler in Damascus in exchange for expanding Syria's territory. Egypt would be forced to give up the Suez Canal, which would be placed under international control. Israel would also take Egyptian territory at the mouth of the Gulf of Aqaba to guarantee its access to Asia through the Red Sea. Ben-Gurion confided that he would really like to annex Sinai altogether because it appeared that there were significant oil deposits in western Sinai, and he solicited Mollet's support for the idea by suggesting joint exploration.

Ben-Gurion knew that he was straining French tolerance; the agenda of the meeting had been limited to deciding whether and how Britain, France, and Israel would agree to invade Egypt, then seize the Suez Canal and overthrow Nasser, with whom they had effectively been engaged in low-intensity warfare for several years. Nasser supported Algeria's FLN (Front de Libération Nationale) revolutionaries against the French; he had evicted the British army from Egypt, and Egyptian-backed militants in the Gaza Strip conducted a guerrilla-style campaign against Israeli villagers. Nasser had also infuriated the West by purchasing Soviet arms and by recognizing "Red" China. The British tabloids were calling Nasser "Hitler on the Nile," a dangerous Arab nationalist whose appeasement the West could not afford. Ben-Gurion told Mollet that Israel, too, wanted what they wanted: "Before all else, naturally, the elimination of Nasser."[17]

The Israeli leader was heartened by the fact that two of the great powers seemed more than ready to perform surgery in the Middle East. It was worth exploring whether the conspiracy could be expanded. He saw the potential—the necessity, really—to bring in the United States to secure the outcome from any threatening intervention by the Soviet Union.

But Mollet stopped him cold and brought Ben-Gurion back to earth. France had to decide whether to act on the plan that was on the table. France needed Israel's reply: Are you in or out?

Ben-Gurion was not ready to answer. The plan as it stood had one outrageous element. The French and British leaders expected Israel to attack Egypt with no warning. That would set up a pretext for an intervention by Britain and France, who would appear to be coming to the rescue to reestablish peace in the face of Israeli aggression. The British needed a clear and convincing "act of war," or so Prime Minister Anthony Eden had told his French colleagues, or Britain would not participate. The plan called for Israel to make a credible thrust across the Sinai Peninsula toward the canal zone, engaging Egyptian forces along the way. Britain and France would demand a cease-fire and, failing to get one, they would bombard Egyptian military bases and send their own military forces ashore to seize the canal and, if all went as planned, drive Nasser from power, although the precise mechanism for Nasser's removal remained vague.

The outrage for Ben-Gurion was that Israel was getting set up as the aggressor, a lightning rod that would suffer the world's indignation. Ben-Gurion said that he could not accept a division of labor whereby "Israel volunteered to mount the rostrum of shame so that Britain and France could have their hands in the waters of purity."[18]

Ben-Gurion also wanted to delay the attack so as not to disrupt the American presidential election, where Eisenhower was running on his record of enforcing the peace after an era of war. There had been an endless stream of private communications from Eisenhower warning Israel not to take advantage of the crisis in the Middle East by making precipitous military moves.

Mollet, the determined French leader, kept repeating that the plan on the table was the only plan that would draw the British in, and the French defense minister said that without Israeli acceptance, the French military would pull out because winter storms would soon be sweeping the eastern Mediterranean, making a beach landing too dangerous. Ben-Gurion was faced with the question of whether the ends might justify the ignoble means for Israel.

When Selwyn Lloyd, the British foreign secretary, arrived at the villa that evening, the atmosphere darkened. He was sullen, and to the Israeli leaders he seemed embarrassed to be closeted with them in a distasteful plot against the Arabs. Lloyd was condescending to Ben-Gurion. Mollet briefed him on the deadlock in the talks, and when Lloyd wheeled on Ben-Gurion, his tone indicated that Israel had better jump on the train or it would lose an opportunity. Israel should consider, he said, that Britain might be able to solve the whole dispute through diplomatic negotiations. Therefore, the only reason for considering the military option now under discussion was that it promised the additional benefit, aside from reclaiming the canal, of overthrowing Nasser. But if Israel wasn't game, they could go the diplomatic route.

Neither Lloyd's lack of enthusiasm nor Ben-Gurion's sense that he was being treated as a subordinate—and that Israel would be forced to "lie to the world" to "make the matter easier and more convenient for Britain"— overcame the more compelling desire to destroy Nasser.

By the fall of 1956, Europe lay exhausted, still climbing out of the rubble of world war while the Middle East was a smoldering landscape, seething with national ambition and historic grievances at the end of the colonial era. Peoples of the region looked out to horizons profoundly altered by the realignment of great powers. Intense expectations made for explosive politics. The defeat of Germany and the Axis, and the rise of America and the Soviet Union as the arbiters of the postwar world order had changed the matrix of control, shifted lines of commerce and national capacities for coercion. The war had smashed the old architecture where small states existed under the protection of colonial powers whose treasuries were now depleted or bankrupt and whose armies were spent. The system that had dominated for more than a century was collapsing.

The British mandate in Palestine was an early casualty. Conferred after World War I, it had put the most contested remnant of the Ottoman Empire—Jerusalem and the Holy Land—under London's administration until the great powers could reconcile the conflicting demands of the local Arab population and the Zionists, whose vision to create a Jewish homeland in Palestine had sprung from the intellectual ferment of nineteenth-century Europe and from the persecution of Jews across the continent. In 1894, a mob in France had shouted "Death to Jews!" when the military high command had prosecuted Captain Alfred Dreyfus, a Jew, on trumped-up treason charges. The tribunal stripped Dreyfus of his rank and dispatched him to Devil's Island. (Dreyfus was finally exonerated in 1906 and served in World War I with distinction.)

Theodor Herzl, Zionism's founder, wrote that "the Dreyfus case contains more than a miscarriage of justice, it contains the wish of the vast majority in France to damn one Jew and through him all Jews." That this could occur in "Republican, modern, civilized France, 100 years after the Declaration of the Rights of Man" was worse than tragic.[19]

Herzl, a journalist in Vienna, had awakened the Jewish Diaspora in 1896 with his *Der Judenstaat* (The Jewish State), in which he made the revolutionary argument that Jews themselves could end their long exile, that an independent state in Palestine was the best defense against Europe's anti-Semitism and the confinement of Jewish communities—the Pale of Settlement—in czarist Russia and in Eastern Europe.

Few thought Zionism would succeed, yet Herzl's idealism proved inspirational beyond any expectation when early waves of pioneers, backed by wealthy Jewish financiers, purchased farmland in Palestine for Zionist immigrants who were prepared to brave hardship and attack to build their communities.

In the aftermath of World War I, the Zionist leaders leaped at the opportunity presented by the Ottoman collapse. Suddenly, most of Arabia—from Aleppo to the Empty Quarter—was a land without boundaries. The rise of nation-states in Europe suggested a new template for organizing the Old World. The great powers maneuvered to create new national identities under their patronage—a lighter form of colonial rule that sought to protect economic interests, oil being the most prominent.

The great betrayal started here for the Arabs. Having thrown in with the British, under Colonel T. E. Lawrence, to fight the Ottoman Turks, Arab leaders expected—some were told as much—that the great powers would re-create a unified Arab nation after the war. The failure to meet Arab expectations was just the beginning of the long humiliation that stained Western honor. Syria, Iraq, Lebanon, and Jordan—all took shape in a Middle Eastern carve-up that followed the Paris Peace Conference of 1919. But the disposition of Jerusalem and the Holy Land—the old Ottoman province of Palestine—was complex beyond any national consideration.

"You cannot ignore all history and tradition in the matter," Lord Alfred Milner, the former high commissioner in South Africa, had told the British parliament in the early 1920s. "You cannot ignore the fact that this is the cradle of three of the greatest religions of the world. It is a sacred land to the Arabs, but it is also a sacred land to the Jew and Christian; and the future of Palestine cannot be left to be determined by the temporary impressions and feelings of the Arab majority in the country of the present day."[20]

Many stalwarts of the British establishment had embraced the Zionist cause and the Balfour Declaration of 1917 (named for British Foreign Secretary Arthur James Balfour), which stated that "His Majesty's Government view with favor the establishment in Palestine of a national home for the Jewish people." It wasn't just skillful lobbying by Chaim Weizmann, the Zionist leader in Britain. Winston Churchill also advanced the cause, joining the long parliamentary battle in support of an equitable division of the land and its resources so that both peoples—Arab and Jew—might fulfill their destinies.

In a visit to Jerusalem in 1921, Churchill told a gathering at the Hebrew University on Mount Scopus that "personally my heart is full of sympathy for Zionism." The establishment of a Jewish national home in Palestine "will be a blessing to the whole world" including to "all the inhabitants of this country without distinction of race and religion." But he admonished them that "this last blessing depends greatly upon you.

"Our promise is a double one. On the one hand we promised to give our help to Zionism, and on the other, we assured the non-Jewish inhabitants that they should not suffer in consequence. Every step you take should therefore be also for the moral and material benefit of all Palestinians."[21]

The promise had not been fulfilled, and both sides were to blame. Jewish immigration had incited the Arab population during the interwar years. Arab rioting, violence, and demagoguery were followed by Jewish reprisals and British crackdowns until World War II, when the Holocaust and the exodus of displaced Jews from Europe overwhelmed the mandatory authority and mobilized international support for a Jewish state while the Jewish underground fomented terrorist attacks on British troops, thus rendering the mandate unsustainable. Public opinion in Britain would no longer tolerate casualties.

In 1946, Harry Truman, running to succeed Roosevelt, publicly endorsed the Zionist call to allow one hundred thousand Jews into Palestine that year over howls of protest from the British government that was struggling to keep order. For Truman, it was good politics. He had influential Jewish constituents and financial backers and, fundamentally, he was sympathetic to the Zionist cause, up to a point. The next year, the United Nations crafted a partition resolution to create Arab and Jewish states in Palestine, but in the aftermath of world war, no international authority—including the United Nations—stood ready to enforce a new boundary regime as the great powers had done after World War I.

As the British marched out, a community of six hundred thousand Jews—the *yishuv*—declared itself a nation in May 1948. Truman immediately recognized it, as did the Soviet Union. From town to village, Arabs and Jews fought an intense civil war, and then Arab armies from Egypt, Jordan, and Syria invaded to try to extinguish the "Zionist entity." The Israeli militias, not yet under a single command, fought the Arabs to a standstill along boundaries that gave shape to a new country. The Arab defeat, especially for King Farouk's forces on the Egyptian front, helped to stoke revolutionary fires among the young officers who felt Egypt's shame, whose ranks included Gamal Abdul Nasser and Anwar Sadat.

Jerusalem was left divided, the Old City still in the hands of the Arabs, who trashed and looted the Jewish Quarter. Egypt occupied the Gaza

Strip, but the new state of Israel established frontiers that ranged well beyond the contours that the United Nations had prescribed in its partition plan. In fact, the Palestinians would thereafter point out that Israel had taken 78 percent of a land that was to have been equitably divided.

As many as 750,000 Palestinian Arabs, out of a population of 1.3 million, had been displaced by the war of 1948–49, many of them driven out of their homes by Israeli militias and others stampeded by fear. Atrocities had taken place. At Deir Yassin, the Irgun (the militant underground national military organization) under Menachem Begin slaughtered most of the inhabitants of an Arab village on the road to Jerusalem. The Irgun fighters trucked the bullet-riddled corpses of men, women, and children through Jewish West Jerusalem in a "victory parade" and then dumped the bodies in Arab East Jerusalem.[22]

The Arabs responded in kind. A few days after the Deir Yassin massacre, Arabs assaulted an Israeli convoy of doctors, nurses, and faculty members on their way to Hebrew University. They doused some of the vehicles with gasoline to flush the passengers and killed more than seventy Jews in the attack.

But in the end, the battle was a catastrophe for Palestinian Arabs and, thereafter, that's how they referred to what happened: *yom al-naqba*, the day of catastrophe. They lost their homes, lands, businesses, and pastures, and there was no court of redress. Those who remained within the new state's borders became Arab Israelis, an unassimilated minority whose loyalty to the Jewish state would always be an open question.

Many Zionist leaders had romanticized the creation of Israel as a moral beacon to the world. They had not foreseen the protracted civil conflict their enterprise would engender. Realists like Ben-Gurion had foreseen it, as had Vladimir (Ze'ev) Jabotinsky, the founder of the revisionist movement, whose adherents believed Jews would have to fight the Arabs—and the British—to get their state, and would have to keep fighting until the Arabs accepted the legitimacy of Zionism, or until they so feared being completely vanquished that they would acquiesce peacefully.

Zionist legitimacy rested on the claim that history conferred on the Jews the right to build a modern state in the lands of the ancient Hebrew kingdom. The latter-day Zionists, the ones who were preparing to seize any opportunity to nail their destiny to the land in Palestine at long last, understood that the two communities, Arab and Jew, might never be reconciled. The revisionist thinking shaped Menachem Begin, the Polish army private who led the Irgun. It had also shaped Yitzhak Shamir, leader of the Stern Gang, another Zionist extremist organization in Palestine.

Eisenhower and Dulles both were pragmatists about the creation of Israel, and Eisenhower had taken the first serious steps to work for reconciliation in the Middle East.

His idea had been a Marshall Plan for the region to develop the water resources of the Jordan Valley—as the Tennessee Valley Authority had done in the United States—and use hydroelectric power and new reservoirs to build an agricultural belt throughout the West Bank. Palestinian refugees could move out of their squalid camps and into new farming communities. Peace would follow.

But neither the Israelis nor the Palestinians were ready for compromise. The Arab camp was in the grip of a pan-Arab awakening, a new pulse of Arab power. Grievance and humiliation rendered the Arabs susceptible to the charismatic leadership of Nasser, who had overthrown the vestiges of colonial control in the Nile Valley and kicked the British army out. The Arabs dedicated themselves to arming for a climactic battle that would destroy the "imposed" Jewish state.

The Israelis, meanwhile, were busy constructing their nation. Every citizen was a soldier ready to rush to the border to repel an Arab attack. They built their own national water carrier to divert the flow of the Jordan River and the Sea of Galilee to Israeli farms, triggering even deeper Arab resentment. Yet the Zionist enterprise seemed fragile and reversible, dependent on loans and donations from Jews abroad and on backbreaking agriculture to survive.

The effect over time was that the idealism with which so many Jews had embraced Zionism eroded as it ran hard up against resistance and enmity from the Arab community. Moshe Dayan, the one-eyed general who personified so much of the self-reliance of the founding generation, gave voice to the cruel reality that faced the pioneers in his eulogy for Ro'i Rothberg, a young Israeli security officer ambushed near Gaza in 1956.

"Yesterday, Ro'i was murdered," he began. "The quiet of the spring morning blinded him, and he did not see those who sought his life hiding behind the furrow. Let us not today cast blame on the murderers. What can we say against their terrible hatred of us? For eight years now, they have sat in the refugee camps of Gaza, and have watched how, before their very eyes, we have turned their lands and villages, where they and their forefathers previously dwelled, into our home. It is not among the Arabs of Gaza, but in our own midst that we must seek Ro'i's blood. How did we shut our eyes and refuse to look squarely at our fate and see, in all its brutality, the fate of our generation?

"Beyond the border surges a sea of hatred and revenge; revenge that looks toward the day when the calm will blunt our alertness, the day when we shall listen to the envoys of malign hypocrisy who call upon us to lay down our arms . . . We are a generation of settlement, and without the steel helmet and the gun's muzzle we will not be able to plant a tree or build a house. Let us not fear to look squarely at the hatred that consumes and fills the lives of . . . Arabs who live around us . . . That is the fate of our generation. This is our choice—to be ready and armed, tough and harsh—or to let the sword fall from our hands and our lives be cut short."[23]

Looking back much later, Nadav Safran, who was born in 1925 to a Jewish household in Egypt, who fought for Israel's independence in 1948, and died in 2003 after a scholarly career at Harvard, said, "Because of my background people will question my qualification to speak objectively on this issue. Let me state my belief. I happen to believe that both the Arabs and Israelis have unassailable moral arguments, and anyone who does not understand how this is true, cannot understand the true nature of tragedy."[24]

Dulles's service to American diplomacy went all the way back to Woodrow Wilson, who had been more spectator than participant in the drawing of the new Middle East map. Dulles did not question the historic forces that had given birth to Israel, but he allowed in private conversations that the Zionists had been afforded too much influence in the previous administration, where Truman had pandered to the Jewish community when it was politically expedient to do so.

Dulles was not known for humor, warmth, or flexibility. Churchill had dismissed him as "dull, duller, Dulles." But he and Eisenhower kept close counsel on how to prevent another spasm of violence in the Middle East. The problem was that both men were overstretched in late 1956: Eisenhower was a sixty-five-year-old heart attack victim and Dulles was sixty-eight, overtaxed by months of crisis management that followed Nasser's seizure of the Suez Canal.

In July, the Egyptian leader had struck a painful blow against the West by nationalizing the Anglo-French company that operated the canal, and Nasser's assault on the artery of British commerce had opened a rift across the Atlantic. There was a strong war camp in Britain and France to overthrow Nasser and take back the canal. Eisenhower, campaigning for reelection on his peacemaking record, was having none of that kind of talk.

Nasser had come from nowhere as an avatar of Arab indignation. He stood as the first Arab leader to rise after the war with a political voice that carried across borders with a message of pan-Arab power and unity. He and a band of "free officers"—most of them colonels—had burst into Egyptian politics just as Eisenhower and Dulles were coming into office. Nasser was the ringleader of the group that had forced the abdication and exile of the corrupt and dissolute King Farouk in 1952. Within a very few years, Nasser had become the lion of the Middle East. He had not invented Arab nationalism, but in the cauldron of postwar politics, out among the detritus of empire, it had invented him, and his clarion was soon pulsating on Radio Cairo and on the medium that radiated to every corner of the region as the "Voice of the Arabs." He was among the first to speak of the latent power of the Arab control of oil, a resource critical to rebuilding the postwar economies of the West.

"I wish to conquer no foreign land in the name of the Arab nation," Nasser said. "I want only to assemble the members of this nation, who once gathered," he added, would reach a state of "self-awareness" about their power.

Nasser had read broadly if not deeply. The conspirator in him understood the nexus of politics, strategy, and war. He had come to the conclusion that the United States had secured a foothold in the Arab region because half the world's oil reserves were concentrated there and because the cost of extraction was far lower than in the United States. He observed America's obsession with containing Soviet expansion, and he admired America's economic strength while mistrusting its intentions. The strategist in Nasser knew that as the leader of Egypt, he faced a hopeless task of trying to outrun poverty and population growth, but to lead the Arabs was to cast the shadow of a leviathan in the Middle East and, more than anything, Nasser craved that.

"I have an exact knowledge of the frontiers of the Arab nation," Nasser told a French interviewer. "I do not place it in the future for I think and I act as though it already existed. These frontiers end where my propaganda no longer rouses an echo. Beyond this point, something else begins, a foreign world which does not concern me."[25]

Gamal Abdul Nasser was born in 1918 in a poor and dusty village of Upper Egypt, the son of an itinerant postal clerk from the Saidi clan, known for producing male offspring who were generally taller, darker, and intellectually fiercer than the more languid Egyptians of the Nile Delta. As a young man he already was a fervent nationalist and briefly read law. At age seventeen, he wrote, "Egypt . . . is in a state of hopeless despair. Who can remove this feeling? The Egyptian Government is based on corruption and favors . . . Who can cry halt to the imperialists?" In the letter to a friend, he said there were men in Egypt "who do not want to be allowed to die like dogs. But where is . . . the man to rebuild the country?"[26]

Nothing held his interest until he entered the national military academy in 1937. His formative years tracked the period of Egypt's humiliation as a protectorate of Great Britain. The history Nasser observed revealed the European powers as giants loosed on his native landscape, exercising their prerogatives along the Nile as if Egypt were just another colonial plantation. After the completion of the Suez Canal in 1869, Britain and France had consolidated their ownership over the critical artery and thus staked a proprietary interest in Egypt, where the commerce of Europe, Asia, and Africa intersected. The canal generated tens of millions of dollars in revenues a year and served as the imperial bridge between Britain's colonies in Asia and markets in Europe. In the geographical argot of the time, "east of Suez" was one way to divide the world. As Nasser said, the canal made Egypt part of the British Empire.

As Britain lost colonies, its trade cargoes from the East declined, but the demand for crude oil began to boom and tanker traffic through the canal surged. The Allies had used seven billion barrels of oil to defeat Germany and Japan. Six billion had come from the United States, but that era was ending. After the war, a new era of Middle East oil was dawning, and the canal was a critical highway for its delivery to the West. By 1956, two-thirds of the shipping tonnage that passed through the canal comprised crude oil in tankers bound for Europe, and about a third of those deliveries went to Britain.[27]

Nasser grew up in an Egypt that had nominally achieved its independence. But the onset of World War II had proved otherwise. When General Rommel marched the German Afrika Corps across the rim of the continent toward Suez in 1942, the faltering loyalty of King Farouk impelled the British to send an armored column to Cairo, where it surrounded Abdin Palace and Farouk. London dictated a change in prime ministers to ensure Egypt's alignment against Hitler, but what the Allies saw as pragmatism, the Egyptians regarded as an assault on their sovereignty, which fired the passions of military cadets that included Nasser and Sadat. They were in the streets, like so many Egyptian youth, demonstrating and engaging in assassination conspiracies against Egyptian politicians whom they considered to be co-opted by the British.

Nasser had fought in Gaza in 1949 with decrepit arms. "We were fighting in Palestine but our dreams were in Egypt," he recounted. And when he and his comrades returned from the front, they acted on their dreams. Nasser spoke the idiom of the Egyptian peasantry, of the Nile Delta village and rice paddy, of the camel market and bedouin camp; he evoked the plowman's struggle and the plight of peasants—the fellahin—whose lives were poised precariously in the narrow band of Nile River cultivation hard up against the unsustaining desert. In 1952, Egypt was a country of twenty million people. Virtually all the land and wealth was in the hands of the elite. Peasants lived in servitude on the land. The birthrate was exploding at 4 percent a year and there was little prospect that Egypt would ever build an economy that could provide for the demands of its population.

It takes a rebel to lead a revolution, and Nasser looked out across the hopelessness with a genuine zeal. His disillusionment was theirs; his conversion to revolutionary fervor was pure Egyptian, at once self-deprecating and proud: "Formerly I believed neither in the Arabs or Arabism," he said in 1953. "Each time that you or someone else spoke to me of the Arabs, I laughed at what you said. I could not believe that Arab peoples were capable of anything. The Palestine War strengthened even more my conviction concerning the powerlessness of the Arabs. But when I realized all of the potential possessed by the Arab states, that is what made me change my mind!"[28]

Nasser helped himself to power and then helped Egyptians purge themselves of the shame of poverty and subjugation, if not the fact of it. The greatest obstacle to a revolutionary Egypt, he told them, was the lassitude of Egyptians. When he and his vanguard of rebels had stormed the palace in 1952 to eject Farouk, he said he had turned around to see if the Egyptian "masses" would follow. "We needed discipline but found chaos behind our lines. We needed unity but found dissension. We needed action but found nothing but surrender and idleness."[29]

Nasser would change that. His first target was the British military presence that remained in Egypt, a massive base that straddled the canal and represented the largest concentration of British troops—eighty thousand of them—in the region. The maritime commerce along the canal still beat as the heart of British dominion, and its revenues, $100 million annually in gross receipts, had become a critical revenue stream to Britain's fragile postwar economy. But the hostility of the Egyptians was evident. British patrols and the base itself were subjected to harassment and random sniper fire. Islamic nationalists—the Muslim Brotherhood— joined the anti-British fray, as did Egyptian Communists.

Nasser demanded a full British withdrawal from Egypt; the British government pressed for a "Turkish clause" that would allow British forces to return in the event of an attack by an outside power on the Middle East.[30] Nasser accepted this condition (for seven years) in order to get the British out, but it led to his first confrontation with the Muslim Brotherhood. One of their number fired a pistol at Nasser—eight shots from close range—during an address in Alexandria's main square. The drama was captured live on an October 26, 1954, broadcast and Nasser shouted defiantly, after one bullet shattered a lightbulb above his head, "They can kill Nasser but another will take his place!"

Though he seemed invincible to the West, it took Nasser until the fall of 1954 to consolidate his power by suppressing the Muslim Brotherhood and the Communists, and though he spoke admiringly of parliamentary democracy, he maneuvered away from it toward his own dictatorial rule. Not since Napoleon landed in Egypt had a leader made such an impact on the Nile Valley and the world around it. For centuries, the land of the pharaohs was known only for its crumbling monuments and the gilded traces of a civilization that had slipped into somnolent decrepitude. Then Bonaparte sloshed ashore borne by the tide of the Age of Reason and lay the foundations of science and technology. Nasser wanted to build them anew. He was tall, with sharply chiseled features. In uniform he stood as a bronze centurion, but he said Egypt needed tractors more than tanks. His lively eyes flashed over a politician's envy of a smile and he spoke

English well. He was hypersensitive to threats and displayed a bent for conspiracy and intrigue. He trusted Anwar Sadat as an unthreatening younger comrade, a gifted schemer with a sense of theater. Sadat had aspired to be an actor and, incomprehensibly, had gone to the movies the day of the revolution.

The CIA under Allen Dulles, the younger brother of the secretary of state, was first to see Nasser as a new-style Arab leader who might assist the Eisenhower administration to create a stable structure—ideally, an alliance—against Soviet encroachment in the Middle East. The CIA, more than the State Department, was in charge of the American relationship with Nasser. Kermit Roosevelt, the head of CIA operations in the Middle East and grandson of President Theodore Roosevelt, had sent Nasser suitcases full of cash, literally several million dollars, as a personal gift dressed up as funds for "leadership security" or the like. But the transparent bribery had offended Nasser, who lived simply and viewed himself as incorruptible. To him, the money reeked of imperial arrogance: Did they think they could buy Nasser? With the suitcases of cash, he ordered a tower to be built in the center of Cairo with a revolving restaurant on top. Within the leadership circle—and later in all of Egypt—it was known as "Roosevelt's erection."[31]

The Egyptians believed that Nasser could not be bought. They may have feared the concentration camps he built to contain the Communists and Islamic extremists, but Nasser's revolutionary commitment seemed as solid as the pyramids. Jefferson Caffery, the American ambassador who had seen King Farouk off to exile from the Alexandria pier, described the revolution as "honest, sincere, progressive and intelligent" in "its goal to raise the living standards of the Egyptian people."[32]

In this period of seduction, 1953–55, the Americans provided Nasser with a powerful radio transmitter to beam his voice to the Arabs, never imagining that he would turn it against them, and they imported propaganda experts to show him how to shape a message. They sent secret delegations to discuss arms sales, an extremely sensitive subject because Israel would be opposed. And they sent him development aid. Everything had seemed possible in those early years. The CIA station in Cairo was the most powerful in the region. With the hubris of the times, its officers asserted that they had "invented" Nasser.[33]

In November 1954, a team of CIA and Pentagon officers flew to Cairo to parlay secretly with Nasser about the future. They met at a safe house in the Cairo suburb of Maadi, the leafy enclave developed by the British to insulate them from the masses of the Egyptian capital.[34] Nasser arrived with Abdel-Hakim Amer, his corevolutionary and the chief of staff of the Egyptian army. Nasser placed two packets of Kent cigarettes on the table. The Americans had come to determine whether Nasser could be coaxed into a military relationship, perhaps an alliance, with America. They described to him an aid package of $20 million for weaponry as a down payment, but they explained that Nasser would have to accept an American military mission to administer the aid program. Nasser smoked and listened. He expressed surprise that they did not seem to understand Egyptian politics. Having just fought tooth and nail to force eighty thousand British troops out of Egypt, how could he open the door to American military advisers? Nasser did not need to remind them that he had just survived an assassination attempt by the Muslim Brotherhood.

One of the Americans, a Pentagon colonel, said the Soviet threat made regional defense essential. Nasser said he saw no signs of Russian hostility, except to the Americans, who were trying to surround the Soviet Union with regional defense pacts. Besides, the common enemy in the region was not Russia, Nasser said, but Israel. There it was. The differences in outlook now crowded the table between them.

"A regional arrangement might serve your purpose," General Amer told the Americans, but how were they going to define the enemy? The Pentagon colonel said that for planning purposes, the enemy was the Soviet Union. But a common defense with the Arabs could confront any enemy that appeared, and "we would take our chances that you and we would recognize a common enemy when the moment of real danger appears."[35]

That's when Nasser interrupted. He had already asked for food while the debate was going on and he was working his way through the cigarettes in front of him. All this planning was fine, he said, but the Arabs would know that their enemy was Israel and the Americans would be focused on Russia.

"The Arabs will say you are trying to get them to unite against your enemy while they know that if they show any intention of fighting their enemy, you would quickly stop all aid. Any regional military agreement that did not take this attitude into account would be a fraud." And any attempt to stir up the Arabs against the threat of Soviet invasion in the Middle East would fail because no such threat was remotely visible to the Arabs. The Americans would look foolish. In the long run, Nasser said,

Egypt must be free and independent. America would see a greater interest in providing assistance to an independent Egypt rather than one sub-
jugated as an American satellite. Nasser wanted unconditional American
aid, including $100 million for heavy weapons. A stronger Egypt, he told
the Americans, could afford to work for peace.

"Only when you are in a strong position can you afford to take unpopular decisions," he told the American ambassador a few months later.[36] If
the United States wanted Egypt to reach an accommodation with Israel,
Nasser would have to act from a strong domestic position, especially
within the military, which was the source of his power. American
weapons would ensure that.

The minuet between the United States and Nasser was viewed with
deep suspicion in Israel, where the prevailing view was that Nasser was
out to dominate the Arab world and destroy the Jewish state. In the summer of 1954, Israel's military intelligence chiefs activated an eleven-
member unit that started setting off bombs against American and British
targets in Cairo and Alexandria. The goal of the sabotage was to drive a
wedge between Nasser and the Americans, and halt the withdrawal of
British forces from Egypt. The saboteurs were captured and their Israeli
intelligence connections discovered. Two of the Israeli agents were
hanged. Nasser was sobered by how relentlessly the Israelis were out to
thwart him.[37]

At the outset of 1955, Dulles conceived the Alpha Project to draw
Nasser into peace negotiations with Israel. But Nasser was a hard sell.
He ridiculed Dulles's effort to create a land bridge that would connect
Egypt with Jordan through the Negev Desert. Dulles proposed giving Egypt
and Jordan each a finger of Israeli land. At the place where the fingers
met, a highway overpass would connect the Arab salients and an under-
pass would connect Israel's northern Negev with the southern Negev.
Nasser told American diplomats the plan would lead to war the first time
"nature" called: an Arab truck driver would stop to relieve himself from
the overpass, urinating onto Israeli traffic below. Nasser called it the
"pee-pee bridge."

Still, it was a time of unparalleled creativity. Eisenhower and Dulles
were in search of a grand design, like dam building and agricultural development, that might divert Arab anger and create a sense of common
interest with the Jewish state. Eisenhower sent a personal envoy, Eric
Johnston, to broach his idea: Jews and Arabs could irrigate the barren

hills of the West Bank, creating new farms and permanent homes for the 750,000 Palestinian refugees.[38]

Nasser had his own visions. He wanted to build a high dam on the Nile in Upper Egypt, create the largest lake in Africa, and use its waters to regulate the Nile flood. Doing so would increase land under cultivation by a third or more. The $500 million engineering project rivaled, in scale, the construction of the Suez Canal, and it promised to feed an expanding population.

There are many reasons why Eisenhower's idealism failed in the Middle East. Not the least was the gulf between political expectations and culture. Israel had its national infrastructure plans; it would not share resources with the Arabs for fear of jeopardizing national security. The Arabs felt the same way, but the Arab mind still seemed like terra incognita for American leaders, perhaps because the Judeo-Christian experience was a boundary of history that had rendered the Islamic experience remote; few Americans had penetrated the other world, certainly not Eisenhower or Dulles. The world war had brought Europe and America closer, but the Middle East remained a region of Oriental complexity whose leaders felt a deep nostalgia for a triumphal Islamic past. Islamic pieties bolstered emerging nationalisms and fed on the bitterness of the colonial era. The political culture in the Middle East saw America as an anticolonial power, idealistic and glamorous through the projection of Hollywood but still tainted by alliance with Europe's colonial masters.

Eisenhower's prescriptions for an American-imposed settlement in the Middle East alarmed Ben-Gurion, who aspired to expand the young Jewish state's borders, to give it more depth and make its frontiers more defensible. Egypt, with its huge population, was the greatest threat to Israel's existence, and the rise of Nasser had brought Ben-Gurion out of retirement in 1955 with a missionary's fervor. The Holocaust was barely a decade past when Nasser appeared, to many Israelis, as fascism reincarnated. And there was a desperate pressure of time. Israel had to arm itself; the population had to stay mobilized because Nasser was riding a wave of Arab grievance and hatred. It was going to be a race for weapons, and Israel's only hope was to build the best-armed and most nimble military in the region. It was during this period, according to a number of sources, that Ben-Gurion resolved to acquire atomic weapons to ensure that what had happened to the Jews could never happen again.[39] In great secrecy, Ben-Gurion pushed forward his plan. Shimon Peres was his agent to the French, whose Socialist leaders were inclined to help Israel join the nuclear club.

It is surprising that Nasser's honeymoon with America lasted as long as it did, given the pressures. In February 1955, Israel attacked the Egyptian military headquarters in Gaza, blew up the building, and killed thirty-eight Egyptian soldiers in a large-scale incursion. Then the British announced the formation of the Baghdad Pact, which was aimed as much at countering Nasser's growing influence as at blocking the Soviets. The Israeli raid ostensibly was conducted as a reprisal for the death of an Israeli bicyclist ambushed by Arabs, but Nasser viewed it as an attempt to humiliate him and to demonstrate Egypt's military weakness. It convinced him that he had to find a major arms supplier to defend his country.

Nasser made his debut as a world leader at the Bandung Conference in Indonesia in April 1955. There he stood on a stage with Zhou Enlai and Jawaharlal Nehru, the Chinese and Indian premiers, for the birth of the Non-Aligned Movement. From Washington's perspective, the image could not have been more negative: Zhou was the personification of totalitarian menace on earth. The wounds of the Korean War were still fresh. Dulles had refused to shake Zhou's outstretched hand at the Geneva Conference the previous year. Yet Zhou had a transcendent effect on Nasser, sharing midnight dinners, revolutionary philosophy, and pragmatic advice on how Nasser might get the arms he wanted from Russia or from China. With Zhou's encouragement, Nasser turned Bandung into a rally for Palestinian rights and a pulpit against Israel. When he returned to Cairo, he was talking about a new policy of "positive neutralism" and the need to strengthen Egypt's armaments. The American and British ambassadors refused to meet his plane, as was diplomatic protocol. After all the blasts against the West, the British envoy, Humphrey Trevelyan, told his American colleague that Nasser would surely understand if "we white folks sat this one out." The racial tinge of his remark reflected how deeply the West had been cut by the Bandung performance.[40] When Nasser did see the American ambassador, he said very pointedly that if he couldn't get weapons from the United States, he would get them somewhere else.

The paradox of Nasser was that in private, he was still the most compelling personality of all the Arab leaders. Those who knew him marveled at his potential. He would slam America on Radio Cairo and then explain his demagogic excesses as an imperative of Arab politics. It was public relations, Nasser told them. Eisenhower's envoy, Eric Johnston, said that he sounded like the French revolutionary leader who said, "The mob is in the streets. I must find out where it is going, for I am its leader."

Nasser had flashed a big smile at Johnston and exclaimed, "Exactly! The first task of the leader is to be the leader; only after you have ensured that you are the leader can you start thinking about becoming a good leader."[41]

Ben-Gurion came back from retirement with a dark view of Egypt's rise and of Eisenhower's clumsy proposals for a peace. The Israeli leader was a pessimist who had long since lost hope for a peaceful settlement between Arabs and Jews. He could never countenance, as Dulles had suggested, giving up territory for an Arab land bridge across the Negev. The Negev split the Arab world. It drove a geographical wedge between Egypt and the armies to the east in Jordan, Syria, and Iraq. The desert provided land for Israeli settlement and agriculture. Its remoteness provided a hiding place for Israel's nuclear complex. It was difficult for Eisenhower to perceive the Jewish state's concept of deterrence and how that would drive Israeli leaders toward a goal of becoming the dominant military power in the Middle East. Such a power would be less interested in reaching transitory accommodations with the Arabs than in achieving military and economic superiority over them.[42] Peace with the Arabs was relegated to some utopian future, but the realists who controlled Israel's security establishment believed that unrivaled military power and its forceful application against any threat was the only certain path to long-term security.

Thus Israel rejected Eisenhower's ideas for joint development of water resources with the Arabs as Israel pursued a unilateral course to tap the water flow through the Jordan Valley, building a national pipeline that could irrigate the coastal plain and the southern desert.

Word that Nasser was talking to the Russians about bartering Egyptian cotton for Russian arms reached the new American ambassador, Henry Byroade, in July 1955. Nasser sent a private message to Kermit Roosevelt telling him that the Americans had a very short time to talk him out of making the deal with Moscow, but in fact the decision had already been made. Eisenhower left Washington for a golfing vacation in Fraser, Colorado, where, on the afternoon of September 23, he was called back twice to the clubhouse at the Cherry Hills course to confer with his secretary of state. The phone connection was terrible, but the unwished-for news from the Middle East likely dominated the conversation. Shortly after midnight, chest pains hit Eisenhower, and when Mamie, the first lady, got a look at him, she called the doctor. That was it: Eisenhower was out of action with a major heart attack, and no one knew whether it would be for good.

It is difficult to know whether the prospect of losing Egypt—the largest and most important Arab state—contributed to the stress that leveled the president. Kermit Roosevelt's report back to Washington that the Soviets had scored a big gain—$100 million in Soviet tanks and planes would soon be paraded through the streets of Cairo—must have been profoundly troubling, given all of Eisenhower's efforts. To add to the tension, the CIA was reporting that Syria was discussing a similar arms pact with Moscow.

The heart attack had one positive political effect. It diverted attention from the Middle East and focused it on the president's health and the turmoil over whether he would even be able to return to office. So when Nasser made his big announcement about the arms deal, it did not set off the storm it might have. The fig leaf Nasser employed publicly was that he was purchasing arms from Czechoslovakia, something that even Israel had done. Nasser told his people that he had appealed to the Western powers for arms, "but all we got were demands." He said he would always refuse arms that came "at the expense of our freedom."[43]

There was too much at stake for Eisenhower to abandon the troublesome Arab leader. The Soviet arms deal mobilized American support for the Aswan Dam project as the centerpiece of U.S. foreign policy toward Egypt. By December, Dulles had won the agreement of Anthony Eden, who had succeeded Churchill as prime minister, and from Eugene Black, the World Bank president, to commit $400 million in grants and loans to Egypt.

Despite Eden's willingness to take this step, Britain remained deeply suspicious of Nasser and had pushed ahead with the Baghdad Pact alliance as a hedge against a Soviet-armed Egypt. When Eden tried to bring Jordan into the Baghdad Pact, Nasser called on Jordanians to riot and bring down King Hussein's government until the king backed out. Eisenhower wrote in his diary that Eden had "blindly" overreached in challenging Nasser's influence. And Eden, livid over Jordan's decision to back out, wheeled on an aide and said Nasser had to go.

"It's either him or us, don't forget that!"[44] To another aide, he said, "I want him destroyed, can't you understand? I want him removed . . . ; I don't give a damn if there's anarchy and chaos in Egypt."[45]

Anthony Eden had made his mark in British politics by resigning as a junior minister from Neville Chamberlain's cabinet after the appeasement of Hitler and Mussolini at Munich in 1938. After one of the longest apprenticeships in British politics, Churchill had finally stepped aside for Eden in 1955, praising his successor and thereafter calling himself an "Anthony man." But in private, Churchill expressed the same doubts that others harbored.

"Courage—Anthony has courage. He would charge," Churchill allowed, "but would he charge at the right time and in the right place?"[46]

Doubt also surrounded Eisenhower's struggle to define an American strategy for the Middle East. In his diary entry of March 8, 1956, the president worried that "chaos" was "rapidly enveloping" the region. "We have reached a point where it looks as if Egypt, under Nasser, is going to make no move whatsoever to meet the Israelites in an effort to settle outstanding differences. Moreover, the Arabs, absorbing major consignments of arms from the Soviets, are daily growing more arrogant and disregarding the interests of Western Europe and of the United States in the Middle East region." At a minimum, Eisenhower wrote, it was necessary to further isolate Nasser by splitting off Saudi Arabia, which was beginning to fall under his spell, inducing the Saudis to "see that their best interests lie with us," and to enter into a defense treaty with Israel to protect its territory. Dulles was thinking along similar lines. It was time the United States joined the Baghdad Pact, in which Britain had taken the lead, and to begin selling arms to Iraq, Saudi Arabia and, in small consignments, Israel.[47]

Nasser saw it coming: Eisenhower and Dulles were going to disappoint him, and the British were out to topple him. Fortunately, from his perspective, the Kremlin's eagerness to help Egypt gave him leverage. If Eisenhower reneged on the Aswan Dam, the Soviets might be willing to step in. American financing depended on Congress, and three critical constituencies had turned against the dam project: a "cotton lobby" of Southern farm states that did not want to see Egyptian production expand; the Israeli lobby that feared Egypt's latent power; and the Free China lobby, which turned on Nasser when Egypt established diplomatic relations with China in May 1956. For Dulles, recognition of Communist

China was the worst betrayal. The timing, in an election year, could not have been worse.

The moment of truth was orchestrated for July, as the World Bank moved forward to qualify Egypt for the Aswan financing package. Nasser was on the beach at Burg el-Arab, where the Mediterranean is a turquoise sheet and the desert is radiant gold. The Egyptian leader was in shorts. He and his family romped on the shore and enjoyed lunch together. Afterward, Nasser set aside time for his ambassador to Washington, Ahmed Hussein, and for Mohamed Heikal, Nasser's close adviser, chief propagandist, and editor of *Al-Ahram*, the national daily newspaper that dispensed Nasserism to the world. Nasser drove the party in his Chevrolet to another bungalow that looked out to the sea. He listened to Hussein's report on the opposition in the American Congress.

"I'm not going to go into details," Nasser said to his ambassador. "I have concrete evidence that even if you went back and accepted all their conditions, they will not give us the Aswan Dam."[48] Nasser instructed his ambassador to return to Washington and tell Dulles that Egypt accepted all the conditions that Washington had laid down: Egypt would stop buying arms from the Soviets and it would make peace with Israel. Heikal was the only witness to this conversation, but it seems plausible that Nasser also instructed his ambassador to play the Soviet card by informing Dulles of the Kremlin's willingness to finance and build the dam, because that is what he did.

Eisenhower was absent from the drama. He had once again fallen ill. His long recovery from the heart attack was followed in the summer of 1956 by a debilitating six-week bout of ileitis, an inflammation of the intestine, which had required surgery on June 5. He was convalescing in Pennsylvania. Dulles drove up to Gettysburg to get a decision on the Aswan question. The choice had become painfully obvious: they would have to jettison Nasser, admit the failure of their long effort to win him over. He had returned every favor with an insult. The British were ready to bring him down. The French accused him of supporting the Algerian nationalists. Congress was in no mood to placate a potential Hitler on the Nile by granting massive foreign aid when, as Senator Wayne Morse of Oregon kept harping on, there were dams to be built in America. And it *was* an election year. Could a tottering Eisenhower, a sixty-five-year-old heart attack survivor down with yet another illness, fight a tough reelection battle while embracing this Soviet-armed menace in the Middle East?

Dulles drove back to Washington with Eisenhower's instructions. Within days, there were new intelligence reports that Nasser was contemplating a second large arms deal with Moscow. The secretary called Nasser's ambassador to the State Department on July 19 and told him that the United States did not think Egypt's economy was strong enough for Nasser both to build the dam and buy Soviet arms. Ambassador Hussein protested, perhaps employing a tone that offended Dulles. He said he had the Russian offer to build the dam in his breast suit pocket. That's when Dulles lost his temper and summoned that righteous voice to say that the United States did not submit to blackmail. The Egyptian ambassador fled the building and telephoned American friends, saying Dulles had insulted Nasser and impugned Egyptian honor.

Nasser waited only a week before calling a huge rally in Alexandria and unfurling his defiance to more than one hundred thousand Egyptians. The physical takeover of the canal was planned as a military operation, timed to be executed during Nasser's speech when he mentioned the code words "Ferdinand de Lesseps."

"The canal belongs to us," he called out to the masses, and Egypt was seizing its property to use the $100 million a year in revenue to build the Aswan Dam. "We shall rely on our own strength, our own muscle, our own funds," he said, adding to the delight of the crowd, "And it will be run by Egyptians! . . . Egyptians! . . . Egyptians!"[49]

The West, he said, could choke on its fury.


The nationalization of the canal was a declaration of independence that electrified the Arab world. For Britain and France, it was a declaration of war. Neither government thought it could survive the political blowback at home if it failed to stand up for the national interest. For Britain particularly, the loss of canal revenues threatened to seriously weaken the British pound. Churchill, still the dean of the Conservative Party that was watching over Anthony Eden's shoulder, was heard to say of Nasser, "We can't have that malicious swine sitting across our [lines of] communications." America had failed to listen to British warnings about Nasser, but now that the dictator had made his move, "We don't need Americans for this!" Churchill exclaimed. For his part, Eden, having made his career by taking a stand against "appeasement" at Munich, could do no less in the face-off with Nasser.[50] French emotion ran just as high, even higher since the public had learned that Nasser was also shipping arms to Algeria's revolutionaries, who were engaged in the violent overthrow of French rule.

For many historians, the Suez crisis was the last gasp of crumbling empires in the Middle East and Eisenhower's finest hour, but this kind of postcolonial intervention would be repeated over and over in the region. Looking at the Suez crisis as the end of the colonial era is an exercise of exaggerated merit. It is more important in what it revealed about Eisenhower, Dulles, Eden, and Mollet as leaders. Eisenhower came to the fore, but only because Britain and France failed so miserably to execute a viable plan. Had they succeeded quickly in reclaiming the canal and toppling Nasser, there is little Eisenhower could—or likely would—have done to reverse the fait accompli.

For all the talk about ending colonial meddling in the Middle East, America and Britain in late 1956 were deeply engaged in plotting a pro-Western coup in Syria in Operation Straggle,[51] something that Allen Dulles was at pains to remind the president during the first hours of the war council over Suez. Both Eisenhower and Dulles told the British in the course of 1956 that if they could not get Nasser to play ball with the West, they would have to change policy and, perhaps, work for his removal. Though Eisenhower opposed military action to topple Nasser, he had shown sympathy for a broader and more subtle program to undermine him by turning the Egyptian people against him and building up Saudi Arabia. Dulles also favored this approach.[52]

When the Suez crisis flared, there was a strong consensus in Washington that the kingdom of Jordan might disintegrate, and, if that was the case, it was expected that Iraq, with British backing, and Israel, with general acquiescence, would both seize the bits of Jordan that were strategically important to them. Eisenhower and Dulles voiced no opposition to various contingency plans on how to allocate Jordanian territory; Jordan, after all, had been created by Britain when it carved up the region with France following the San Remo conference of 1920, and King Hussein, like King Faisal II in Baghdad, owed his throne to British imperial sufferance. The Suez crisis was just three years on from the Anglo-American toppling of Mossadegh's government in Iran, and two years on from the toppling of the Arbenz government in Guatemala, both of which could be described as acts of intervention on behalf of colonial era economic interests. In Iran it was oil; in Guatemala, bananas. Another attempt to overthrow the Syrian government would be orchestrated by the CIA in 1957;

in 1958 Eisenhower, after authorizing the CIA to spend millions of dollars to prevent pro-Nasser candidates from winning in Lebanon's elections, sent nineteen thousand American soldiers ashore to stabilize the Middle East after the bloody nationalist coup in Baghdad. Eisenhower explained that he was saving Lebanon and its president, Camille Chamoun, from international communism under the Eisenhower Doctrine: the United States would send military aid to any country in the Middle East fighting Communist aggression. In fact, he was saving them from Nasser.[53] But Nasser's agents cheered the toppling in Baghdad of the British-backed monarchy. It brought an end to the Baghdad Pact, which had been more anti-Nasser than anti-Communist.

The Suez crisis was certainly connected to the colonial era in the Middle East—and to the rise of America's global leadership—but Suez was a war conceived by Europe's stalwarts to destroy the rising power of Arab nationalism. Suez marked the death of the 1949 armistice in the Middle East and the eruption of the fierce and, at times, desperate armed struggle that has continued in cycles of war and terrorism through five decades. To understand the crisis, it is crucial to understand how much Eisenhower and Dulles did *not* know as it unfolded—and how that infuriated them. The columnist James Reston wrote, "The White House rang with barracks-room language that had not been heard at 1600 Pennsylvania Avenue since the days of General Grant."[54]

For the first twenty-four hours, Eisenhower simply did not understand the scale of the conspiracy. Israel had attacked alone on October 29, crashing into Gaza with tanks and sending a large force under Ariel Sharon to seize the overland approaches to the Suez Canal. Eisenhower's first instinct was to invoke the Tripartite Declaration, which opposed the use of force in the region, as a way to stop the Israeli aggression. In those early hours, it seemed possible that Eisenhower might employ American military forces to block Israel.[55] There were consultations with the Joint Chiefs, and their chairman, Admiral Arthur Radford, told the president that it was best to take swift action to stop the Israeli advance. But on the day British and French troops joined the invasion, when Eisenhower finally understood what was afoot, the president just stood back. America needed to adopt a "hands-off" attitude until the air cleared, he told Dulles. Eisenhower abandoned any thought of defending Egypt or of calling Congress into session. He waited to see whether the British and French would succeed or fail. He was angry at being double-crossed, and he could see nothing good coming from the invasion; he was concerned about Muslim rage and Soviet intervention on Egypt's side. That would put the "fat in the fire"—one of Ike's pet phrases. He also paused because, as a seasoned commander, he respected military power and understood that when it was employed, it implied a great commitment and the highest resolve of leaders. In a letter to Anthony Eden the day of the invasion, Eisenhower said nothing to exclude the possibility that this ill-considered enterprise might succeed, or that America might find a way to support a felicitous outcome. After laying out what might go wrong, he concluded that America had missed the takeoff, but, as an ally, he wanted to be there for the landing: "Because of all these possibilities, it seems to me of first importance that the UK and the US quickly and clearly lay out their present views and intentions before each other, and that, come what may, we find some way of concerting our ideas and plans so that we may not, in any real crisis, be powerless to act in concert because of [our] misunderstanding of each other."[56]

Crucially, Eisenhower held back the next day at the National Security Council session when John Foster Dulles and Harold Stassen, the former governor of Minnesota and political aide to Eisenhower, debated how to position the United States. Dulles was all fire and brimstone, asserting that America was on the fault line between eras, and the men in that room would be "deciding today whether we think the future lies with a policy of reasserting by force colonial control over the less developed nations, or whether we will oppose such a course of action by every appropriate means." Dulles impaled them with his rectitude: "We should be forced to choose between following in the footsteps of Anglo-French colonialism in Asia and Africa, or splitting our course away from their course."

The tension was considerable, but Eisenhower temporized. His mind seemed to be sputtering because, while he absorbed Dulles's point—that he had to draw a sharp distinction between U.S. objectives and those of Britain and France, America's closest allies—Eisenhower was having trouble figuring out "what we are going to do."[57] It was Stassen who pulled him back from Dulles's abyss. Like a terrier against the hulking frame of Dulles, Stassen argued for a simple cease-fire and an avoidance of condemnation. While the British had committed a terrible error, "our real enemy" was the Soviet Union, he said, and, therefore, America had to act cautiously, holding the alliance together at all costs. Dulles "emphatically" disagreed, stating that "what the British and French had done was nothing but the straight old-fashioned variety of colonialism of the most obvious sort." He appeared to favor the maximum rebuke, arguing that to do less would risk losing the entire third world to the Soviet camp.[58] Stassen's simple pragmatism was compelling and trumped Dulles's histrionics. Stassen turned toward Eisenhower repeatedly and explained that if America acted brutally toward Israel, Britain, and France, it would divide public opinion in the United States. Eisenhower, who faced the prospect of a Democratic Congress even if he won reelection, would lose support for his policies in the Middle East. "We must keep the [American] people united, and we would certainly not succeed in doing this if we split away from Britain and France" and acted on the assumption (which Stassen said he did not believe) that these two allies were headed for the dustbin of history.

Eisenhower revealed what was on his mind in a private note to Alfred M. Gruenther, the four-star general who had succeeded him as the supreme allied commander in Europe. The letter indicates that Eisenhower had been canvassing "British friends" for intelligence about how much support Eden retained in parliament, a shrewd bit of reconnaissance. He wrote that most of the unnamed British "friends" he spoke with "are truly bitter about the action taken by their government. One man said, 'This is nothing except Eden trying to be bigger than he is.' I do not dismiss it that lightly." Eisenhower continued, "I believe that Eden and his associates have become convinced that this is the last straw and Britain simply *had* to react in the manner of the Victorian period." Eisenhower's political antennae and his personal military assessment were pointing toward a disaster for Eden, but in this chatty private note to a military confidant, Eisenhower described Eden's errors as political, without saying whether removing Nasser by more subtle strategies might have been a goal that he shared and would have been willing to join in, as he was in Syria.

"If one has to fight, then that is that," he said. "But I don't see the point in getting into a fight to which there can be no satisfactory end, and in which the whole world believes you are playing the part of the bully and you do not even have the firm backing of your entire people."[59]

By late 1956, Eisenhower was leaning toward the view that the Middle East would be less dangerous and more peaceful without Nasser, but his private opinion was that Eden had misread the politics of how and when to act. Eisenhower correctly deduced that there was no war mood in America or in Britain as a response to Nasser's seizure at Suez. The canal had always belonged to Egypt, and the canal company—the moneymaking enterprise that operated it—was due to revert to Egyptian ownership by 1968 in any case.

After a cease-fire, after the smoke cleared to reveal dozens of ships that Nasser had ordered sunk in the canal, many with concrete poured into their cargo holds, after Anthony Eden fell ill and swanned off to Jamaica, and after British and French soldiers, stoic in the face of the failure of their leaders, trooped back aboard ship and sailed home, Eisenhower was left facing one player still on the field—Ben-Gurion—and he would prove the most reluctant to back down.

Israeli troops had routed the Egyptian forces in Sinai but at substantial cost in lives, because Ariel Sharon was prone to exceed his orders and he had charged into one heavily defended pass only to see his men mauled under withering Egyptian fire. Victory, nonetheless, incited ambition. In a speech to the Knesset, Israel's parliament, Ben-Gurion seemed to lose control of his enthusiasm. ("I was too drunk with victory," he would later state.[60]) He called it "the greatest and most glorious operation in the annals of our people and one of the most remarkable in world history." He also claimed—absurdly, according to Eban—that Sharm el-Sheikh had been the seat of an ancient Jewish kingdom, and thus there might be a legal precedent for Israel's claim to the land at the tip of Sinai. Israel would resist "with the full force of unflinching determination" any foreign attempt to enter the captured territory.[61] Canadian prime minister Lester Pearson heard of Ben-Gurion's speech and told Eban, "If you people persist with this, you run the risk of losing all your friends." It was true. Arab, African, and Asian countries at the United Nations were preparing to impose sanctions on Israel. Eisenhower let the pressure build on Ben-Gurion. Without allies and facing sanctions, the Israeli leader had no hope to annex the Sinai. So he decided on a delaying strategy, laying down tough conditions: he wanted assurance that the Gulf of Aqaba would never again be closed to Israeli shipping and that Gaza would not be allowed to become a base of attack for fedayeen guerrillas.

Ben-Gurion sent his foreign minister, Golda Meir, to Washington just after Christmas 1956 to conduct reconnaissance on Dulles's thinking. Meir was a powerful weapon in Israeli diplomacy. Never as glib as Eban, she nonetheless was a matriarch who spoke with the weight of Jewish suffering and projected a metallic self-reliance. Born in Kiev, she compellingly bridged the distance between the Middle East and America, where she had lived as an immigrant (in Milwaukee and Denver) from 1906 to 1921 before moving to Israel with her husband, Morris Meyerson. A chain-smoker, she had grandmotherly looks before her time, and Bogart toughness. Her wit stirred audiences to the Israeli cause and she could level an adversary with a Yiddish barb or freeze him with a glint of immovable willpower. She looked out from the dark eyes of a sage, but her imposing aura masked a doctrinaire stubbornness, which was her weakness as well as her strength.

Dulles was impervious to Meir's appeal for time and sympathy. She apologized for the lack of consultation over Suez and said Israel had been forced by circumstances to act. She hoped that Dulles, at the United Nations, would oppose those pressing for Israel's withdrawal from Sharm el-Sheikh, the promontory that overlooked the Strait of Tiran, the entrance to the Gulf of Aqaba. The waterway led to the newly established Israeli port of Eilat, a crucial outlet to the Red Sea and the markets east of Suez. Meir invoked "Israeli public opinion" when she said her government could not withdraw from this strategic outpost that controlled all shipping into Israel from the Red Sea. If the Egyptian army was allowed to return to Sharm el-Sheikh, Nasser could reinstate the blockade at any time.

Dulles stopped her there. He told her that the American misunderstanding with Britain, France, and Israel was not based on the fact that the United States had not been informed in advance, but "on our disapproval of the nature of the action taken by them." Three months prior to the attack, America had "conveyed fully our view" to the British and the French "that the United States would have to oppose a resort to force in Egypt or we would face virtual destruction of the United Nations with the resulting breakdown of world order and risk of World War III. We had not had an equal opportunity to express these views to Israel," he continued, "because we had not known that Israel contemplated forceful action."

He lectured Meir on the virtues of the new era of the United Nations, which had been created to prevent the resort to war as a means to resolve conflict. Of course that meant that there had to be processes for addressing injustice in the world, he said, but their inadequacy was not a justification for war. Dulles was "perplexed as to how Israel regarded its long term future." It seemed to him the epitome of pragmatism to consider that Israel was surrounded by hostile Arab states and that the best path to security would be to work on building amicable relations with the Arabs; in the end, "there was no military strength which could protect" Israel if it embarked on a policy of militarism. Surprisingly, Dulles said, there was "more hatred" directed at Israel in 1957 than in 1948 when the state was formed and, though most of the blame for the failure of peace-making lay elsewhere—with the Arabs, he meant—"Israel's retaliatory policies," mounting large-scale attacks against Arab towns in response to small-scale border incidents, was escalating the tension. Diplomacy could not work when emotions ran high over raids that humiliated Arab leaders by showing them not to be in control of their borders. Militarism just engendered more hatred.

Meir could hold her own. If you added up all the Israelis who had been killed or wounded during Arab attacks since 1948, she said, and multiplied that number to make it proportionate in the American population, you would be looking at 150,000 casualties. Imagine attacks from enemies camped on the Mexican and Canadian borders inflicting those kinds of casualties in America, she said. "What would the United States have done in such a situation?" She said the reason there was so much hatred among the Arabs was that they hated the idea that Israel existed. Existence was the only condition that the Jewish state insisted on for peace, and peace had failed because the Arabs would not accept this condition. Nasser, she said, was using the passions of the Arabs to achieve his ambition. In her disarming way, she told Dulles that she was not going to insist that Israelis were angels, but Israel's conscience was clear. Dulles could see he was up against a lioness. He got to his feet, but as he walked Meir to the door, he could not let her have the last word. He said there was no lack of sympathy for Israel in the United States, but Israel's future could be secured only in a friendly Middle East and, for now, Israel's policies were not inclined in that direction.[62]

Israel's refusal to abandon Sinai led to a confrontation that stands as a low point in America's relationship with the Jewish state. Eisenhower was determined to break Israel's resistance to giving up newly conquered territory. He was standing on the fresh mandate of his electoral landslide. He had taken the least blame for the Suez crisis, though there were voices in Congress that complained that his decision to pull the plug on the Aswan Dam had triggered the whole mess: America had made a promise, then reneged, inciting Nasser to seize the canal and its revenues to build his dam. Yet Ike stood untrammeled as British and French prestige buckled. Who was holding together the Atlantic Alliance if not Eisenhower?

In January 1957, the president reasserted American leadership. In a dramatic address to a joint meeting of Congress, he announced what became the Eisenhower Doctrine, riveting the country with alarm that the Communist threat to the Middle East was now dire and required urgent action. He also sought unrestricted authority to spend $200 million on foreign aid to help states in the region meet their development goals and to defend themselves. With war powers and new funding, Eisenhower aimed this policy offensively at Moscow, but Nasser took the point that he was regarded as part of the Soviet camp.

In an act that would be repeated by subsequent cold war presidents, Eisenhower tapped the wellspring of Western mobilizing power—the global competition with the Soviet Union—to justify his actions. He reset the compass to navigate around Suez, an uncomfortable episode where the means failed before the ends were achieved—the end of Nasser, anyway. Of course the Arab leaders were baffled by the Eisenhower Doctrine because it identified "international communism" as the enemy at a time when Israel had just invaded the largest Arab state—with Western collusion—and was refusing to withdraw. Eisenhower seemed to have posed a classic non sequitur: the problem was the Israeli invasion; America would respond by fighting communism. Defending the doctrine in the Senate, Dulles asserted that the Communist menace in the Middle East was more dangerous than any threat that had appeared since the end of World War II. Senator J. William Fulbright responded that this seemed strange, given that Dulles had soothed the country's nerves the previous year by stating that the Russians had made very little progress in the Middle East. When Senator Richard Russell pressed Dulles to reveal what the administration would spend the $200 million on, Dulles turned red and cried out with a tone of indignation worthy of Joseph McCarthy that the administration could not be expected to "telegraph its punches" in front of Communist eyes that were watching the hearing. If Congress did not act, he warned them, the whole region could "be lost in a great and maximum disaster."[63]

The Eisenhower Doctrine befuddled the bureaucracy. The CIA reportedly did not want the task of briefing Arab heads of state because the new policy would appear to be a "lunatic scheme"[64] by an out-of-touch president. Nasser, however, confided to an American friend that he saw the "genius" of Eisenhower's strategy. It allowed the Suez disaster to slip beneath the waves and put the West back in order under Eisenhower's command. All that remained was the squeeze play to discipline Israel, and there Eisenhower faced contentious domestic opponents, most prominently Senator Lyndon B. Johnson, the majority leader, who was among Israel's staunchest defenders on Capitol Hill. Harry Truman came out of retirement to urge Congress to support the president, asking that it take steps to protect Israel from guerrilla attacks and to promote a diplomatic solution that would do justice to both sides.

"Israel is here to stay," Truman declared in a message to Washington, "and we might as well say so, and insist on its right to have access to its own ports free of blockade, and equal rights to use the canal with other nations."[65]

The demand that Ben-Gurion had made, and for which he had burgeoning support among Israel's allies in Congress, was that Israel must get something substantial and permanent for any pullback. The Israeli army had expended blood to acquire territory, and its commanders, backed by public opinion, expected Ben-Gurion to secure some tangible benefit.

Initially, Eisenhower had been focused only on forcing a withdrawal. In February, the president retreated to Augusta, Georgia, for a golf holiday and a little respite from Washington. But Dulles followed him there to consult on how they would handle Ben-Gurion. When Dulles returned to Washington, he called Eban to his home and showed him a document he had drafted. It stated that the Gulf of Aqaba and the Strait of Tiran were international waters and no nation had the right to prevent free and innocent passage there. On the question of Gaza, the source of guerrilla attacks on Israel, the United States would support the insertion of United Nations forces as part of a general deployment of UN peacekeepers along the Egyptian-Israeli frontier, including at Sharm el-Sheikh to monitor freedom of navigation through the adjoining Strait of Tiran. Dulles told Eban that Ben-Gurion must accept the terms quickly because Israel was "on the verge of a catastrophe."[66] The mood at the United Nations was building toward a sanctions motion. Israel was headed for pariah status before the world unless it made the deal that Dulles had set before him. But when Eban reached Israel, Ben-Gurion rejected the terms. He tried to buy more time by making an eccentric and impractical plea for Dulles to organize a panel of experts from disinterested states to come to the Middle East and suggest a solution.

On February 20, Eisenhower called the congressional leaders to the White House and asked them for their support in putting pressure on Israel to withdraw from Sinai and conclude a new peace. Lyndon Johnson led the resistance, arguing that it was unfair to bring such pressure on Israel when the Soviet Union had escaped similar sanction for its crushing blow against the rebellion in Hungary that had erupted at the same time as the Suez crisis. There was LBJ, stalwart of the Senate, taking on his commander in chief on a matter of foreign policy, as if Johnson were Israel's attorney. Eisenhower had already decided to go over their heads and speak directly to the American people, where there was overwhelming support for the high principles of the United Nations Charter. Television was a relatively new medium and the intimacy of Eisenhower's appearance before the nation magnified the impact of the message.

In the Middle East, "we are approaching a fateful moment," he told the public that evening, "when either we must recognize that the United Nations is unable to restore peace in this area, or the United Nations must renew with increased vigor its efforts to bring about Israeli withdrawal." He told the country that the United Nations had taken far-reaching measures to ensure Israel's safety after its withdrawal, including the creation of a UN force to protect the border and ensure freedom of navigation to Israel's port at Eilat. But, he added, "Israel seeks something more. This raises a basic question of principle. Should a nation which attacks and occupies foreign territory in the face of United Nations disapproval be allowed to impose conditions on its own withdrawal?

"If we agree that armed attack can properly achieve the purposes of the assailant, then I fear we will have turned back the clock of international order," he continued. "We will, in effect, have countenanced the use of force as a means of settling international differences and through this gaining national advantages.

"I would, I feel, be untrue to the standards of the high office to which you have chosen me," he went on, "if I were to lend the influence of the United States to the proposition that a nation which invades another should be permitted to exact conditions for withdrawal."

Egypt, he said, had been wrong to blockade Israeli shipping through the Suez Canal and in the Gulf of Aqaba, "but such violations constitute no justification for the armed invasion of Egypt which the United Nations is now seeking to undo." And to answer Lyndon's Johnson's complaint about fairness, given the Soviet rampage through Hungary, Eisenhower said, "It would indeed be a sad day if the United States ever felt that it had to subject Israel to the same type of moral pressure as is being applied to the Soviet Union."

Ben-Gurion knew that it was over. Eban arrived in Israel days after Eisenhower's speech with his ears ringing from the private admonitions of senators and leaders of the American Jewish community, who told him that Ben-Gurion had taken stubbornness to an extreme. It was time to withdraw. In the end, Israel did, however, extract a crucial condition by gaining a clear statement of U.S. support for its navigation rights in the Gulf of Aqaba, an achievement whose critical importance would be apparent a decade later.

The Suez crisis was Eisenhower's finest hour as president in the sense that every public step he took anchored America firmly within the principles of the United Nations Charter. He maneuvered cautiously and shrewdly, at times brutally, when he withheld oil shipments and loans, which Britain desperately needed, until Eden agreed to withdraw and restore Egypt's rights. In contrast, Eden had never seemed so lacking in all of the Churchillian qualities that he had observed as apprentice. Once parliament learned how fully he had deceived them, and Eisenhower as well, his own party brought him down and replaced him with Harold Macmillan, the hawk who had egged Eden on but who now had support in Washington to patch things up and move on. If Eden took any credit, it was for having adhered to a Hobbesian view learned at Churchill's knee. "The whole history of the world," Churchill had said, "is summed up in the fact that, when nations are strong, they are not always just, and when they wish to be just, they are no longer strong." Eden had sought to defend British interests, but he had failed in execution, in politics and, perhaps, in nerve.

Eisenhower emerged once again as the unrivaled Western leader, but his strategy of anchoring his Middle East policy to the fight against international communism was not enough, for it failed woefully to address the deep-seated grievances of the region. Middle Eastern leaders did not share America's perception of a Communist threat but rather seethed over borders, broken promises, lost resources, and development dreams that required intensive diplomatic engagement. The Arab-Israeli dispute in the Holy Land hung over everything, but Eisenhower had run out of initiative. Instead, the last years of his administration were marked by a series of clandestine maneuvers, coup plots, and payoffs as the CIA fought Nasserite networks (financed by Cairo, or by the KGB) for the allegiance of the region. Nasser's brand of Arab nationalism was gaining the upper hand; America was on the defensive as Israel's patron and defender, even as Washington struggled to maintain a balance.

In 1958, Arab nationalists inspired by Nasser overthrew the Hashemite monarchy in Iraq in a bloody coup that ended British influence there. Nasser stepped up pressure on Saudi Arabia, where King Saud, the feckless elder son of King Abdul Aziz, was caught trying to purchase a pro-American uprising in Damascus with $5 million in cash. In that same year, Egypt and Syria formed the United Arab Republic, a new powerhouse that so threatened the pro-American regime in Lebanon that Eisenhower sent troops ashore along with bundles of CIA cash to save Lebanese president Camille Chamoun's government. Eisenhower was out to demonstrate that American power—and his leadership—still counted, but at the end of the decade there was no discernible U.S. policy addressing the region's principal conflicts. Instead, there was an escalatory dance of arms under the framework of the cold war as Nasser recruited German scientists to build ballistic missiles and Israel began construction of its secret nuclear weapons complex at Dimona.

The first CIA "special" national intelligence estimate on Dimona arrived on Eisenhower's desk in early December 1960, just after John Kennedy defeated Vice President Richard Nixon in the presidential election. Allen Dulles told Eisenhower that the CIA had concluded that Dimona "cannot be solely for peaceful purposes." Christian Herter, the secretary of state who succeeded after John Foster Dulles's death, called in the Israeli ambassador, Avraham Harman, and demanded some answers. By the end of that month, Ben-Gurion had issued a statement confirming the existence of the Dimona project but insisting that it was "designed exclusively for peaceful purposes." Any allegation that Israel was making an atomic bomb was a "deliberate or unwitting untruth." Eisenhower could do nothing but punt the issue to Kennedy.

The journalist Arthur Krock asked John McCone, the chairman of the Atomic Energy Commission, whether the discovery of Israel's secret nuclear program offered "a very perfect opportunity" for Israel "to agree to be the model for an inspection system whereby the benevolence of intent could be proved, not only to us but to the world."[67]

McCone agreed that it could. But it was not to be.

# 2

# THE SIX-DAY WAR

*Johnson and Israel*

The first reports of an Israeli air attack on Egypt reached the duty officer at the White House Situation Room at 2:38 a.m. on June 5, 1967. They came from news agencies whose correspondents could hear the bombs going off at air bases on the outskirts of Cairo.

The duty officer called the National Security Agency, which monitors communications around the world, but the NSA could not confirm the reports.

At 2:50 a.m., the duty officer woke Walt Rostow, the president's national security adviser, but Rostow told him to call back when there was confirmation and hung up.

At 2:55 a.m., a flash message from the United States embassy in Tel Aviv spewed out of the encrypted teletype confirming that the war had begun. Rostow got to the White House at 3:25 and waited an hour before he woke the president at 4:35 and told him that Israel and Egypt were at war. The official Situation Room log recorded that in the Middle East "all hell broke loose."[1]

The entire Israeli air force had taken off—nearly two hundred planes, save for a few left behind for defense. They had flown west out over the Mediterranean so that the pilots could approach Egyptian air bases from the north or west. The Egyptians, who had been on a high state of alert for weeks, were nonetheless creatures of habit. They flew their first patrols at dawn and then all the pilots reported for breakfast. That's when the Israelis struck. Egyptian radar systems were oriented toward the east and, in any case, could not detect planes approaching at low altitudes. The swarm of Israeli warplanes roared in from the sea, first dropping bombs that cratered the runways. Then they pounced on the trapped Egyptian warplanes, shredding them at will. On Egypt's eastern frontier, three columns of tank-led Israeli infantry crashed into Sinai and began to pummel the Egyptian army, which was heavily dug in.

At 5:00 a.m., President Lyndon Johnson telephoned Dean Rusk, his secretary of state, who was at his desk, probably reading the overnight messages from Vietnam. Between 6:00 and 6:30, the president, still in bed, conferred with Rostow and press secretary George Christian about a statement for the wire services calling for a speedy end to hostilities. Sometime before the president showered, shaved, and ate a breakfast of chipped beef, grapefruit, and tea, he knocked on a door on the third floor. White House records indicate that Mathilde Krim, a former member of the Irgun, the Jewish underground, and wife of Arthur Krim, the head of the entertainment conglomerate United Artists and Johnson's top fund-raiser, was staying there as a guest. The president's diary does not record, but Mrs. Krim vividly recalls, that Johnson came to her door and, finding her in her nightgown, told her that the war was on and soon departed.

In the weeks leading up to the war, Johnson had spent many hours in conversation with the Krims, in Washington and at Johnson's ranch in Texas, where the Krims were frequent guests.[2] He had granted them top secret security clearances. They sat in on Robert McNamara's briefings on Vietnam. LBJ shared his frustrations with them about the war that was consuming his presidency and about his rivalry with the Kennedys— the legacy of John Kennedy, and Senator Robert Kennedy, who was being urged to challenge Johnson for the party's presidential nomination in 1968.

The siege of Johnson's presidency was growing with each day's casualty figures, but among his personal stalwarts were the friends and advisers, a number of them Jewish, who reinforced the liberal domestic agenda that he had pursued throughout his political life and that extended to his unconditional support for Israel. By the time his relationship with the Krims blossomed, Johnson had put himself in the service of Israel like no previous president, selling the Jewish state tanks and warplanes that allowed the Israeli military to build a fighting force that was unmatched by any combination of Arab foes.

The contrast with President Kennedy's approach was marked. Kennedy had clashed repeatedly with David Ben-Gurion over Israel's secret nuclear weapons program. The Cuban missile crisis had so lifted Kennedy's stature and invested his presidency in the struggle to contain the spread of nuclear weapons—to China, most ominously—that he was adamant about heading off Israel's atomic development, which threatened to undermine the credibility of his foreign policy. How could he halt the spread of nuclear weapons to China, India, and the Arab states if he could not stop tiny Israel from going nuclear? The American public had been largely unaware of the tension in the relationship. It played out in secret diplomatic channels until Ben-Gurion gave Kennedy written assurance—not ironclad; far from it—that Israel was not out to join the nuclear club. This was strong enough that Kennedy stepped back from the brink of a public confrontation over Israel's nuclear intentions. Israel accepted American "visits"—but not inspections—to the Dimona nuclear reactor complex in the Negev and the CIA continued to monitor the facility because its very size and configuration suggested that Ben-Gurion's assurances that it had no military purpose were false. As an inducement, Kennedy sold Israel advanced antiaircraft missiles, and this opened the door that Eisenhower had kept mostly shut, preferring to send the Israelis to Europe for their defense needs.[3]

Kennedy had an extensive and probably more balanced view than Johnson of the Middle East conflict. He had visited what was then Palestine during the British mandate years and witnessed its complexities firsthand. He had no illusions about the dangers of the Arab-Israeli dispute, or of its repercussions on American domestic politics. As president, he had carried on an extensive correspondence with both Ben-Gurion and Nasser. He saw Nasser as part of the new generation of postwar leaders whose loyalty was up for grabs. Nasser had power and influence over a region that was critical to Western security. Kennedy followed a pragmatic course of increasing food shipments to Egypt to entice Nasser toward the West even as Nasser attacked Yemen and brought down another monarchy, challenging the Saudis in their own backyard.

Johnson was far less worldly, a creature of the Senate and of American domestic politics. He saw Nasser and his allies as a cat's-paw of Soviet expansion, a dangerous destabilizer and a threat to Israel. Johnson did not know the Middle East, but he had long been committed to Israel's cause through the convergence of liberal ideology, money politics, and the deep friendships he had forged with Jewish intellectuals, who populated the ranks of the civil rights movement and who raised prodigious amounts of money for the Democratic Party to champion a liberal agenda. The Krims, along with New York banker Abe Feinberg, and David Ginsburg, a Washington lawyer, comprised an unofficial circuit between Johnson and the Israeli leadership and through which he sent political messages that he did not want to share with the State Department or the Pentagon. He received back, through the same channel, requests for arms and other assistance for the Jewish state.[4]

As a senator, Johnson had once asked his political aide Harry McPherson whether he was Jewish. (He was not.) Johnson wanted to know because McPherson had been pestering Johnson to bring up an immigration bill in the Senate. "The only people who want this bill that you keep putting on here are Jews, and I'm not going to take it up until I get something for it," Johnson had told him. At that moment, McPherson understood that Johnson's relationship with the Jewish community involved more than sentimentalism for Israel. Johnson was sympathetic, all right, but politics was about leverage, compromise, and reciprocity. The circle extended to Arthur Goldberg, Johnson's ambassador to the United Nations, and to Supreme Court Justice Abe Fortas. Jews also comprised the synaptic connection between Johnson's political brain and a moneyed class of Democratic elites—New York investment bankers and Hollywood moguls—dedicated to a social liberalism that would give shape to Johnson's Great Society programs. In foreign policy, they were anti-Soviet, progressive, and humanistic in the support of expanding freedom and fiercely protective of Israel as the fulfillment of Zionist aspirations. Johnson was the maestro of intellectual and political synergy, and this informal trust of advisers connected the lines—policy, politics, money, and friendship—that defined his presidency and, really, his life. Liberalism had converted Johnson to the Zionist cause, even if he confessed to Mathilde Krim that he did not fully understand Zionism and its origins. He admired Israel, he knew that. Everything else was horse trading.

When the Middle East suddenly erupted in May 1967, Johnson hoped that Prime Minister Levi Eshkol would show some patience, given all that Johnson had done for the Jewish state.[5] The Middle East, like Vietnam, was for Johnson a battleground against Soviet expansion and subversion. He regarded Israel as an outpost of democracy and liberalism in a sea of hostility. One of the few times he had clashed privately with Eshkol, who had succeeded Ben-Gurion as prime minister, was over selling American arms to Jordan's King Hussein.

"We oughtn't to let this little king go down the river . . . We ought to keep him as far away from the Soviet [Union] and Nasser as we can," the president once told Abe Feinberg in a telephone call, knowing that Feinberg would take the message directly to Eshkol.

"We won't sell [King Hussein] a damn thing. But we want it to be clear, it's their [Israel's leaders'] decision, and we want to be clear we are doing it so that we can satisfy the Jews, and not irritate them." If Jordan fell to the Soviet bloc, Johnson said Israel would have to take the responsibility.

"If anybody is [pro-Israel], I am," Johnson told Feinberg. "When they were in real problems [during the Suez crisis] and they [Eisenhower's administration] were getting ready to impose sanctions . . . I stopped it. But . . . I'm not going to . . . have one of them leak it on me that I want to join up with the Arabs."[6]

Johnson's tactic had worked. His support for Israel was nestled intricately with America's other interests in the region. Israel did not oppose the tank sale to Jordan. When a prominent rabbi in New York came out against the Vietnam War, Johnson called in the Israeli ambassador and demanded that he get the Jewish community under control.

"I have three Cohens in my Cabinet!" he shouted at the diplomat. No president had ever done as much for the Jews, he said.[7]

Eshkol was grateful for Johnson's support. Raised in Ukraine, Eshkol had immigrated to Palestine in 1914 and was among the founding generation of party apparatchiks and technocrats who supported Ben-Gurion in almost everything he did until the old man's final years. Eshkol was an affable consensus builder who spent most of his career developing water and agricultural resources before taking over the Ministry of Finance and finally, with Ben-Gurion's blessing, the premiership in 1963. Short on

Lyndon Johnson with King Faisal: "I'm not going to . . . join up with the Arabs."

charisma and military experience, Eshkol was quick to find a Yiddish joke to break the tension of debate, and though he was prone to long-windedness, it seemed to be his way of searching for the right phrase—he repeated himself endlessly—that met with the approval of his audience. Although he wore berets, he could never muster military bearing or command much respect from the generals, who distrusted his instinct for compromise. But he had made a favorable impression on Johnson during long discussions in 1964.

The Middle East had been low on Johnson's list of priorities. The president had shown little interest in the Arab world and, unlike Eisenhower and Kennedy, Johnson betrayed no fascination for the currents of Arab nationalism or the phenomenon of Nasser's power. In reality, Johnson and Rusk had given up on Nasser, whose alignment with the Soviet camp, while far from satisfactory from Moscow's viewpoint because Nasser did not tolerate Communists at home, was still a major feature of cold war rivalry in the region. Besides, for Johnson, Vietnam had overtaken everything else.

The president had taken pains to shield his close relationship with the Krims from the news media. Mathilde Krim was a blond beauty who was born in Switzerland and raised a Calvinist, and she spoke elegant French. While studying genetics at the University of Geneva, she had married an Irgun fighter from Palestine, a protégé of Menachem Begin's, who had arrived in the Swiss capital in 1947. She had become a kind of "groupie" to "these guys who were fighting for the survival of their country."[8] In the aftermath of world war, she had joined the Irgun and helped to run guns to Israel, converting to Judaism and then settling there until she divorced at the end of the 1950s. That's when she met Arthur Krim, who had come to Israel to visit the Weizmann Institute, where he was on the board of directors and Mathilde worked as a researcher. Everyone knew, as she claims she did, that the institute was supporting the secret nuclear weapons work at Dimona.

Mrs. Krim had a very hawkish view of what fate should befall Nasser. The Egyptian leader had thrown his army menacingly into Sinai in mid-May, sending a United Nations buffer force packing. Then Nasser had done the one thing that he should have known was a casus belli—he had closed the Strait of Tiran. In the decade since the Suez crisis, Israel and

Egypt had lived at peace under terms that had guaranteed the free passage of shipping through the strait into the Gulf of Aqaba, where Israel's
port at Eilat had become a bustling oil terminal for trade with Iran.[9] As
soon as Nasser closed the strait, the State Department reminded Johnson
of a point that he probably remembered quite well: Eisenhower and
Dulles had committed themselves in writing in 1957 to the principle of
freedom of navigation in the Gulf of Aqaba and pledged to support Israel's right of passage. Their statement of policy was the event that finally
dislodged Ben-Gurion from Sinai. Nasser had now put the fat back in the
fire.

All Johnson asked was that Eshkol give the United States a few weeks
to organize a group of maritime nations willing to dispatch a flotilla of
warships to the Middle East to steam through the Strait of Tiran. If Egyptian troops fired on the flotilla, the maritime powers would retaliate and
teach Nasser a painful lesson. But Eshkol had disappointed Johnson. He
launched a full-scale attack without waiting.

On the morning of June 5, as the Middle East convulsed with war,
Johnson was trying to convince himself that he had a clear conscience.
The Israelis made their own decision, against his strong advice, to attack.
Johnson had gotten every indication from Eshkol that Israel was willing
to wait for at least another week. De Gaulle, too, had warned the Israelis
not to fire the first shot. But all of these admonitions had been overcome
by an apoplectic mood in Israel and by a concerted assault on Eshkol by
the leaders of Israel's military. The generals demanded a prompt decision
to go to war. Eshkol had resisted until there literally was talk of locking
him in a room and starting the war without him. Eshkol had hurt himself,
too. At a key moment on May 28, during an address on national radio, he
stuttered and stammered like a man who had lost his nerve. His performance undermined public confidence. Ben-Gurion privately denounced
him as too weak to lead, and Eshkol was forced to take Moshe Dayan into
his cabinet as defense minister, a step that meant war was almost certain,
since Dayan was a leader of the war camp. Eshkol's wife, Miriam, felt afterward as if she had witnessed a coup of sorts against her husband.[10]
Others agreed that it was the closest Israel had come to overturning civilian rule.[11]

On May 26, Johnson had summoned Abba Eban, Golda Meir's successor as foreign minister, to the White House and told him emphatically
that "your nation [must] not be the one to bear responsibility for any out-

break of war." And then Johnson had spoken very slowly and deliberately
the words that Rusk had formulated: "Israel will not be alone unless it decides to go alone."[12]

It was a war that in many respects should not have been fought. It
came at a time of extraordinary distraction for Johnson and of public dis-
enchantment with his leadership. But more, Johnson's diplomacy was not
nearly as vigorous as it should have been given the cost, the death toll,
and the war's long-term consequences. The United Nations, particularly
Secretary-General U Thant, failed to mobilize the international community to head off war. The Burmese diplomat, who may have been susceptible to Nasser's flattery, badly fumbled his own mission to Cairo in an
attempt to deter the Egyptian leader from a disastrous course. When
Egypt requested that UN peacekeepers be withdrawn, India and Yugoslavia, whose leaders were strong Nasser supporters in the Non-
Aligned Movement, conspired to pull their UN troops out precipitously.
U Thant failed to stall—he could have called an emergency UN session—and allow Johnson's diplomacy to gain some traction. And Johnson
seemed more spectator than leader as these shoes were dropping. He
seemed unwilling to engage Nasser personally in a manner that might
have induced the Egyptian leader to climb down, as he had after a similar military feint into Sinai in 1960. Nasser's delusion that he could somehow prevail in a war with Israel may well have been stoked by a stream of
Soviet assurances delivered by Marshal Andrei A. Grechko, the hard-line
but somewhat dim-witted Soviet defense minister. Moscow would stand
with Nasser even in a confrontation with America, Grechko told Nasser's
envoys.[13]

In the midst of the crisis, Johnson went to Texas for Memorial Day, ca-
vorting at the ranch with the Krims and other friends while massive
armies maneuvered in the desert. Johnson retreated to a level of caution
that accentuated his weakness, and it was this, more than anything, that
allowed Hobbesian impulses to take over. Looking back later, some
quoted Thucydides on the Peloponnesian War to explain it: "What made
war inevitable was the growth of Athenian power and the fear which this
caused in Sparta."

When Johnson got to the Oval Office at 8:15 a.m. on June 5, he leaned
over one of the wire service teletype machines he had installed there to

monitor the news. But soon, his secretary noticed that he had pulled open its doors. There was the president of the United States, sticking his head inside the machine so he could read each line of news as it came off the printer head. Then Johnson went to the study off the Oval Office where he watched the news on three television sets, one for each of the major networks. Before long, he called out to the secretaries and said that he wanted the best television technician to fix the audio, pronto. He put down his diet root beer and stuck his thumbs in his lips to show them that he was getting a "mumbly, foggy sound" and not the "clear, sharp sound" he wanted, and then he imitated the precise staccato of an anchorman. Johnson sent word to the press secretary to provide him with the transcripts of all news briefings that day "page by page" as they came out of the secretarial pool. He wanted to read the questions from the press.

At 11:37 a.m., Johnson went down the hall of the West Wing to the Cabinet Room, where he met an expanded group of national security advisers that included not only Rusk and Robert McNamara, the defense secretary, but also former secretary of state Dean Acheson, the American ambassador to Moscow, Llewellyn Thompson, and McGeorge Bundy, who had been Kennedy's national security adviser. Walt Rostow was there, as was Clark Clifford, the presidential counselor. The gathering of wise men reflected the magnitude of risk this new war posed to Johnson's Vietnam policy—magnifying the political rebellion that Johnson already was facing at home. That was the first concern. Clifford was harsh in his judgment against Israel: Eshkol had "jumped off on minimum provocation in a very purposeful effort" to destroy the Egyptian air force. There was a political subtext to his anger. Clifford knew that Johnson was hoping to orchestrate a diplomatic or military breakthrough in Vietnam that would enable him to stand for reelection. What if the Israelis got into trouble and asked for help? Clifford might well have thought that Israel owed Johnson a little more consideration, as no other president had been a more loyal friend. Dean Acheson, in his dotage, reminded everyone at the table that.he had not shared President's Truman's enthusiasm for the creation of Israel. The implanting of a million Jews in the heart of the Middle East was a formula for endless conflict. Clifford had supported Truman's decision, but Clifford shared Acheson's frustration with the Jewish's state's preemptive action.

Johnson wasn't interested in the old ghosts and historical recriminations. He had a problem and he needed a solution. By the spring of 1967, more than 450,000 American troops were fighting in Vietnam; in April, marines holding the hills around Khe Sanh clashed with Vietnamese regulars in a series of battles that served as the prelude to the Tet offensive. Back home, a group of young men founded Vietnam Veterans Against the War. They would soon join the protesters who were turning university campuses into battlegrounds. Crucially, the Senate, long the base of Johnson's power, was turning against him, and when he heard that Senators Fulbright and Symington were speaking in opposition to his policies, Johnson told himself that he was being tested in a great struggle, like Roosevelt in the darkest days of World War II. Such things could have a volcanic effect on him. One night at Camp David, he raged for hours when John Chancellor, then director of the Voice of America (and later anchorman of NBC News), made fun of Jack Valenti, who had been quoted in the press saying that he slept better at night knowing that Lyndon Johnson was in the White House.[14] Johnson stormed, lectured, and scolded, according to Arthur Krim's account, working his way through a bottle of whiskey to purge his anger. McPherson would later say that Johnson was a "clean tube man—that is, he cleans out his tubes constantly. He blows everything out: good, bad, fears, rages, all of it. And he has got more to blow out than most people do."[15]

Small wonder that Johnson was so agitated as he waited for news from the Middle East. He was not so much hurt that Eshkol had ignored his plea for patience as he was anxious to know how the war was going to turn out—for him as much as for the Arabs and the Israelis. He incessantly watched television and seemed, to the White House staff, a little more obsessive than usual. He called one secretary into the presidential study and, over the noise from the three televisions, debriefed her in detail about her weekend in New York with a new boyfriend, but all the while she could tell that he was watching the news over her shoulder. At lunch with George Christian and Tom Johnson from the press office, he ate four pimento cheese sandwiches and two Jell-O custard deserts and then told Christian that he was still starving. That's what happened when he was upset, he explained. A half hour later, Marvin Watson, another presidential assistant, called the secretaries and said the president had just directed him to move the gold ashtrays from one set of end tables to the other in the Oval Office. The president "wanted them to know that they had been moved and placed in their present position at the president's direction."

These manifestations were rattling through the West Wing just before the governor of Colorado, John Love, came in to tell Johnson that, after spending eight days in Vietnam, he did not see how a military victory could be won.

At 3:21 p.m., Johnson went upstairs to have a nap, but instead he made twenty-four phone calls over the next two hours, obsessively canvassing advisers and friends about what he should do. By the time he again assembled his national security team that evening, Richard Helms, the CIA director, was able to convey just how successful the Israeli air force's attack had been that morning. Rostow was calling it a "turkey shoot."[16] Yet the battlefield still was murky and many prominent American Jews were seething with resentment over the Johnson administration's public stance. That first morning, Robert McCloskey, the State Department spokesman, had responded to a question about U.S. support for Israel by saying, "Our position is neutral in thought, word and deed."

Jewish leaders had expected some expression of support, but Johnson was trying to avoid taking sides. That evening, Johnson and Lady Bird watched the war on television. He seemed amused by one CBS *Special Reports* segment, exclaiming to Lady Bird that "it was easy to tell there was some Jewish background in the commentator by the slanted method in which he was reporting." Johnson called George Christian to say that he thought Dan Rather "had been rather mean." It was the end of a long day, Lady Bird reminded him. The president rang for "the chief," a tall and powerfully built African American who laid the president out on a massage table for his nightly "rub." On this night, Johnson called Justice Fortas, who served, despite the separation of powers, as one of Johnson's closest political advisers. There was the president, half naked, one arm dangling from the massage table and the other holding the phone. They talked about the war and, at one point, Johnson put Fortas on hold and called the secretaries to say, "Bring me the folder I just gave you on the statistics on the airplanes downed in the Middle East today."

Maybe the Israelis would not be the ruin of him.


No one had been expecting a war that spring. Israel was suffering from economic troubles and rising unemployment. In Egypt, Nasser had sent a third of his army to Yemen to fight a costly proxy war against Saudi Arabia that was really about who would lead the Arabs. Nasser's war in

Yemen had divided the Arab world and undermined the vision of Arab unity that Nasser had championed. The strain on Egypt's economy was extensive. The country was grinding toward bankruptcy, its foreign currency reserves nearly exhausted. Nasser had suffered a cutoff of wheat shipments from the United States because Congress was in a mood to punish him for his constant verbal assaults on the West. A group of businessmen, all close to Johnson, had visited Nasser that spring and in a letter to the White House reported that Nasser was facing a "desperate food situation." Lucius Battle, the insightful American ambassador who had just completed two years in Cairo, was deeply troubled by the "ungovernable problem" of Nasser's demagoguery. Battle had worked Congress to get more wheat shipments for Egypt to head off bread riots. But then Nasser had gone on the radio and blasted Congress for criticizing him. Battle would ask him, "Why?"

"I was only talking to my people," Nasser would say, or "I have to answer back."

Battle, like almost all of the Americans who had had extensive personal contact with Nasser, knew him as intelligent, pragmatic, and likable. But "when he's in front of an audience," Battle said later, "Nasser becomes something quite different from what he is in private." Nasser with a microphone was a fount of paranoid ideation, delusional anger, and insults. He would call King Hussein the "whore" of Jordan and speak of the West in reptilian terms. Battle worried that there was some mental instability at the root of this behavior. He had organized a group of CIA psychiatrists to study "the nature of Nasser" and "his difficulties."[17] But it was really too late. Nasser had become almost the caricature of the shrieking Arab dictator seeking to bend the Middle East to his will, to topple "feudal" monarchies and destroy Israel. America, to Nasser, had become the imperial manipulator that was trying to undermine his power, or worse, assassinate him. Various emissaries had come to Cairo and told him that there was pressure on Johnson to "unleash" Israel against him. Meanwhile, the CIA was documenting Nasser's chemical weapons use against Yemen's royalist forces with the goal of formally exposing him, at a time of Johnson's choosing, before the United Nations. Relations had hit bottom. Nasser, foolishly, had refused further food shipments. In Yemen, his intelligence agents raided American offices and arrested three U.S. diplomats, accusing them of espionage and setting off yet another confrontation until the diplomats were released.

During their last conversation, Battle, perhaps in self-justification, told the Egyptian leader, "I want you to remember one thing: that you gave up before I did. You wrote off any further relationship before I wrote it off—before the United States wrote it off." With that, Battle left, and in his exit telegram to the secretary of state, he wrote that he feared Nasser would do something drastic to break out of his desperate circumstances. The three possibilities he thought most likely were: heating up the war in Yemen, attempting a takeover of Libya by toppling King Idris, or provoking another Arab-Israeli war. Any one of those might put him back on center stage.[18]

Nasser's mood was only part of the psychological tinderbox in the region. Israel's military power, too, had grown rapidly through the 1960s. Soviet arms sales to Syria and Egypt, and British and American arms sales to Jordan made it inevitable that pressure would build among Jewish Americans and in Congress for the United States to begin selling offensive weapons to Israel. Eshkol had convinced LBJ that with America tied down in Vietnam, Israel needed to be militarily self-reliant. "We cannot afford to lose. This may be our last stand in history," Eshkol told him.[19] Johnson agreed and colluded secretly with Germany to give Israel 150 American-made tanks that had been stationed in Europe. That was the start, and much more would follow in aircraft, artillery, and other battlefield weapons.

The buildup to war had begun in 1966. In Syria, a leftist military coup brought a Soviet-backed government to power inspired by the "Arab renaissance" ideology of the Baath Party. The new president, Nureddin Atassi, stood before his troops on the Golan Heights and said Syria would wage a "people's liberation war." Atassi looked out over Israel and said, "We want total war with no limits, a war that will destroy the Zionist state." His defense minister, General Hafez al-Assad, told the troops that Syria would never accept peace: "We have resolved to drench this land with our blood." Addressing the Israelis, he said Syria would "oust you aggressors and throw you into the sea for good."[20]

The arrival of the war party in Damascus coincided with another important development. The Soviet Union was more aggressively seeking gains in the Middle East. The tough new defense minister, Marshal Grechko, encouraged the radical Arab states to counter American and Israeli power. Another factor was growing Palestinian militancy. Young Palestinians, many of them radicalized during their university years in

Cairo and Amman, demanded that Arab heads of state take the fight to Israel. Among them were Yasser Arafat and an amalgam of former university radicals. Nasser tried to keep Palestinian politics under his control because, he believed, it would take another three to five years before the Arabs were ready to attack Israel. Nasser thus supported the creation of the Palestine Liberation Organization at a Cairo summit of Arab leaders, but he did not let the PLO operate from Egyptian territory. Instead, the Palestinians stepped up their attacks from Lebanon, Syria, and Jordan. Israel responded by pushing more aggressively into demilitarized zones along the armistice lines with Syria where control of water sources was in dispute.

This conflict had been simmering for months when an Israeli police patrol near Hebron hit a land mine, killing three soldiers. Within days, on November 13, 1966, the Israelis launched the largest reprisal raid in years, not against Syria, but against the village of Samu in the Jordanian-controlled West Bank, systematically destroying 125 civilian houses. The attacking Israeli force comprised four hundred soldiers and sixty armored vehicles, ten of them tanks. When a Jordanian military column raced forward to challenge the incursion, the Israelis leveled their guns on the Jordanians, killing fourteen and wounding more than fifty. The Samu raid triggered bitter recriminations among the Arabs. Nasser signed a mutual assistance pact with the new Syrian regime, pledging that Egypt would attack Israel from the south if Israel launched its forces against Damascus in the north. For the Arab in the street, it was as if the "union" of Syria and Egypt as the United Arab Republic were back.[21]

In early 1967, the attacks from Syria continued. On April 7, an Israeli tractor pushed into the demilitarized zone and Syrian gunners opened up. Soon there were exchanges of tank and mortar fire. Hundreds of mortar rounds rained down on Israeli farms and settlements. Eshkol authorized the Israeli air force to respond, and an air battle then erupted in which six Syrian MiGs were shot down. Israeli warplanes buzzed Damascus. Nasser was on the spot to exert some leadership and to defend the Arabs. Palestinians in Jordan rioted against King Hussein as a weakling in the face of Israeli aggression. The king, through Jordanian media, lashed out at Nasser for "hiding behind the skirts" of the United Nations force that had been sitting on the Egyptian-Israeli border since the Suez crisis. Why hadn't Nasser sent his air force to defend Syria? Jordanian radio asked.

On May 12, Eshkol said publicly that Israel was considering a major military operation to punish Syria. "We may well have to act against the centers of aggression and those who encourage it by means no less serious than those we used on April 7." General Aharon Yariv, chief of military intelligence, was more explicit, saying that it would probably take "a military operation of great size and strength" to thwart the Syrians, though he was careful to say none was planned. But he candidly explained that one option, however remote, was an "all-out invasion of Syria and conquest of Damascus." The remarks were broadly interpreted as Israel was preparing a major military strike.

Eshkol's threat to Syria had popped up on Johnson's CIA briefing that weekend. In Cairo, the Russians had taken the matter a step farther. Soviet Ambassador Dimitri Pojidaev had called for an "urgent" appointment at the Egyptian Foreign Ministry. He presented a detailed intelligence report: Israel, he said, was massing troops, ten to twelve brigades, near the Syrian border. The top KGB officer in Cairo repeated the warning to Salah Nasr, the chief of Egyptian intelligence. And in Moscow, where Anwar Sadat was leading an Egyptian delegation, a senior Soviet Foreign Ministry official, Vladimir Semenov, delivered the same warning. All three reports were rushed to Nasser. All three proved to be false, but an escalation psychology already was operating on Nasser.[22] If his pledges to defend the PLO and Syria from Israeli attack meant anything, Nasser had to act even though he knew that Egypt was not prepared for a military confrontation.

On the afternoon of May 13, he called a meeting of the supreme executive council and ordered the Egyptian army into the field. Nasser sent his chief of staff, General Muhammad Fawzi, to Damascus for urgent consultations. Suddenly, Egyptian troops were in the streets heading for Sinai. Tank carriers, mobile artillery, rockets, and endless lines of troop transports streamed through a delighted capital, along the Nile, and then out into the desert. Crowds poured out to cheer the convoys. Nasser was taking a stand that was wildly popular.

In Israel, Eshkol called in the Soviet ambassador, Dimitri Chuvakin, and offered to escort him to northern Israel so that he could see for himself that there were no concentrations of Israeli troops, but Chuvakin begged off with an Orwellian retort: "I am not here to observe facts in Israel, I am here to present the views of Moscow."

May 15 was Independence Day in Israel and Eshkol mounted the reviewing stand in Jerusalem with Yitzhak Rabin, the Israeli chief of staff.

Couriers arrived and handed both of them notes from military intelligence indicating that Egyptian forces were advancing into Sinai.

In Washington, the CIA told the president in his daily briefing that "Nasser is going all out to show that his mutual security pact with Syria is something which the Israelis should take very seriously." The agency reported scenes of widespread mobilization for war. "Nasser must be hoping desperately that there will be no need for him to fight the Israelis" but the briefing note added that "his prestige in the Arab world would nose dive if he stood idly by while Israel mauled Syria again."[23] This was the last thing Johnson wanted to hear. In Vietnam, some of the most ferocious battles of the war were under way around Khe Sanh in the central highlands. More than 150 marines had died defending their firebases and more than 750 had been wounded. Massive antiwar demonstrations pulsed in New York's Central Park, where two hundred young men burned their draft cards. On April 20, Johnson for the first time ordered U.S. bombers to strike Haiphong harbor in an attempt to close the route through which Hanoi got major arms shipments from the Soviet Union.

On the evening of May 15, Walt Rostow sent a note to Johnson in advance of his meeting the next day with two private emissaries from Eshkol, Abe Feinberg, the New York banker, and David Ginsburg, the Washington lawyer close to Johnson. Eshkol was using the two Americans to lobby for the sale of armored personnel carriers to Israel. Rostow said that no matter how much Washington sympathized with Eshkol's desire to stop the raids coming from Syria, "You would be justified in letting these gentlemen know that a miscalculation causing a Mid-East blow-up right now would make life awfully hard for you."[24] But events were moving fast. The Egyptian chief of staff notified the commander of the United Nations Emergency Force in Sinai that Egypt wanted him to withdraw his troops so that Egyptian forces could prepare to "go into action against Israel, in case and whenever it launches an act of aggression against any Arab country."[25] This was followed by a formal request by the Egyptian foreign minister to UN headquarters in New York. U Thant, the secretary-general, felt he had no choice but to order the UN force to withdraw, a questionable judgment at best.

American diplomats were caught off guard and were slow to react. With few choices, Johnson sent an urgent message to Eshkol, warning him off any idea of striking Syria. "I would like to emphasize in the strongest terms the need to avoid any action on your side which would add further to the violence and tension in your area." He told Eshkol that he expected close consultation and added, "I cannot accept any responsibilities on behalf of the United States for situations which arise as the result of action on which we are not consulted."[26]

The Israelis initially thought Nasser was grandstanding. As the first six Egyptian divisions streamed into Sinai, Nasser flew to the Abu Suweir air base just west of the Suez Canal and addressed the pilots in a speech that was broadcast to the Arab world. He told them that Israel was isolated. No major power stood with the Jewish state as Britain and France had in 1956. America might come to Israel's aid with arms, he said, "but the world will not accept a repetition of 1956.

"We are face to face with Israel," he went on. Egyptian forces were back at Sharm el-Sheikh after a decade and the United Nations peacekeepers were out.

"We shall on no account allow the Israeli flag to pass through the Gulf of Aqaba. The Jews threaten to make war. I reply: *ahlan wa-sahlan!*— Welcome! We are ready for war. Our armed forces and all our people are ready for war, but under no circumstances will we abandon any of our rights. This water is ours!"[27] And with that, Nasser closed the Strait of Tiran and threatened to blow any Israeli ship out of the water that attempted to pass.

The Israeli response was immediate. In the war room in Tel Aviv called "the pit"—a deep subbasement beneath the Defense Ministry—General Yariv briefed the leadership of the Israeli Defense Forces: "The post-Sinai Campaign period has come to an end. It's no longer just a matter of freedom of navigation. If Israel takes no action in response to the blockade of the straits, she will lose her credibility and the IDF its deterrent capability."[28] Yitzhak Rabin, the Israeli chief of staff, and Ezer Weizman, the air force chief, made the case for a preemptive strike against the Egyptian air force and a ground invasion of Sinai to destroy the Egyptian army. Later that day, May 23, Eshkol convened the Ministerial Defense Committee, which included members of his coalition as well as opposition leaders such as Moshe Dayan and Menachem Begin. Rabin laid out the risks. It was not going to be the walk in the park for Israel that 1956 had been. Israel would have to attack Egypt alone and then face attacks from Syria and Jordan and other Arab states. Eshkol evoked the militant mood, saying, "Any interference with freedom of passage in the straits constitutes a gross violation of international law, a blow at the sovereign rights of other nations and an act of aggression against Israel." It wasn't a question of responding; it was when and how, Eshkol told them, establishing a tough principle while giving himself time to maneuver.

Eban spoke in agreement, but he urged a pause to ensure American support and protection from Soviet intervention. He said there was a new letter from President Johnson, urging a forty-eight-hour delay. Johnson had approved their request for arms, and there was talk in Washington of using American warships to assert freedom of passage. It was decided that Eban should go urgently to Washington.

Dayan was last to speak. Israel could not afford to dally, he said. They could not risk losing a war. "We're not England here," he said. The Arabs had to win only once—that would be the end of Israel. Dayan said he would support a brief delay for diplomacy, but there was an opportunity for Israel to destroy hundreds of Egyptian tanks with a two- or three-day campaign, significantly reducing the threat posed to Israel by its main enemy. Dayan's words carried great weight. He and Ben-Gurion and Shimon Peres had broken with Eshkol and the Labor Party establishment over generational change and world outlook. They had formed a new political party, Rafi, that stood for an activist defense, and some members were questioning whether Eshkol was committed to the secret atomic bomb project. With Nasser's army in Sinai, what hung in the air for some was whether Eshkol was leader enough—man enough—to attack Egypt. Dayan was a formidable loner and a gifted military strategist, though he had failed to dominate politics the way he had dominated the military as the architect of the Suez attack in 1956. Eshkol sat as the rotund apparatchik of the Labor Party, but in contrast Dayan stood as the homegrown Israeli sabra in a dusty uniform fresh from the southern front. He looked back at Eshkol with that slash of an eye patch across his face and a sneer of self-assurance.[29] He was the personification of self-reliance and decisiveness, the very opposite of Eshkol.

The reaction in the Arab world to Egypt's sudden awakening was rapturous. Nasser calculated that he could achieve a significant political victory in a standoff. If Israel launched an unprovoked attack, Egypt would absorb the blow. It would reap international support for its stand against aggression, as it had in 1956. The mobilization also gave Nasser an opportunity to bring Egyptian forces home from Yemen, for his losses there had

suddenly been overtaken by the support he was reaping in the confrontation with Israel.

Johnson was boxed in. The State Department assembled the record of
the Eisenhower commitment to Israel. Within twenty-four hours, the
White House issued a statement affirming that the United States considered the Gulf of Aqaba to be an "international waterway and feels that a
blockade of Israeli shipping is illegal and potentially disastrous to the
cause of peace." Johnson characterized the right of passage there as a "vital interest of the entire international community."[30] Johnson could not
sleep that night. The Situation Room log says he called down at 3:10 a.m.
for a briefing on Vietnam and the Middle East. He had sent Rusk to
Capitol Hill to sound out the Senate leaders on support for American action to open the Strait of Tiran. Three powerful Democrats, Mike Mansfield, William Fulbright, and Stuart Symington, had forcefully stated that
the United States was stretched thin in Vietnam and going to war in the
Middle East, while justified perhaps by Nasser's act, might be a bridge
too far for American forces. A two-front war was dangerous for America.
Johnson bristled when he heard Rusk's report. This was a new tactic to
get him to pull out of Vietnam. They were throwing up a choice: Vietnam
or the Middle East.

The next day Johnson told Rusk to go back to Senator Mansfield, the
majority leader, and tell him that "this kind of music in the Senate is just
what [Soviet Premier Alexei N.] Kosygin wants to hear." In the long discussion that afternoon, Johnson returned over and over to the question of
what would happen if the Israelis couldn't hold out against the Arab
armies, if all the intelligence predictions that the Israelis would prevail
proved wrong. Hadn't they been wrong in Vietnam? General Earle G.
Wheeler, chairman of the Joint Chiefs, said that Israel had ammunition
and supplies for a thirty-day war. A long war would threaten its economy.
"At that point, we would have to decide whether we were going to send
in forces and confront Nasser directly," Wheeler said.

Nasser always left a door open for escape, Ambassador Battle interjected, but in this case he had slammed it.

CIA director Helms had said that he was "quite positive" that there
were no nuclear weapons "in the area," but General Wheeler had
quipped that although he was less well-informed than Helms on the subject, he was also "more skeptical."

There were long-standing American concerns that the Soviets might

put nuclear weapons in Egypt to deter Israel. Eisenhower had feared
such a turn of events in 1956. It was a hell of a thought, but the Soviets
had already provided Egypt with three different types of chemical
weapons, Wheeler pointed out. And Johnson knew that Israel was close
to producing its first atomic bomb. Johnson then looked at the worst
case: If the United States intervened, he asked, could the Russians avoid
doing likewise? Wheeler said he thought the Soviets would cut their
losses at that point and back out. But McNamara disagreed. He specu-
lated that there would be a massive initial air battle and both sides would
seek air support from their patrons. He felt the Soviets might send in
MiGs with Russian pilots to even up the air war. Helms thought the Soviets were in the game only to score political points with the Arabs and
they were not ready to rush into any general war. Isolating America, ensuring that it was "fully black-balled in the Arab world as Israel's supporter," was their strategy, he said.

Johnson was frustrated. He kept asking what was in Nasser's mind.
Helms ventured that Nasser had already achieved his objective. He had
rallied the Arab world. That would help him solve his problems at home.
But then Johnson turned to Luke Battle, who knew Nasser best and who
had puzzled over his contradictions.

"What is in Nasser's mind?"

Battle replied that up until the moment that Nasser blockaded the
Gulf of Aqaba, he would have agreed with Helms that all Nasser wanted
was a limited propaganda victory. Now, however, with this huge gamble
and provocation, Battle wondered whether Nasser "has more Soviet support than we know about, or had gone slightly insane."[31]


Eban had left Tel Aviv in the middle of the night. When he reached Paris,
de Gaulle said, "Don't make war." The French president's expression was
grave. "You have a case, but on no account should you shoot the first
shell." When Eban protested that it had been France a decade earlier
that had energetically supported Israel's rights in the Gulf of Aqaba, de
Gaulle replied that France's stand was correct at the time, but "that was
1957. It is now 1967." Only de Gaulle could make this simplistic point
sound profound. He urged Israel to hold back. Nasser's mobilization
could not last, and time was needed for the four great powers to act in
concert "to enable ships to pass through the straits." Eban flew to Lon-

don, where Prime Minister Harold Wilson told him that the British cabinet had met that morning and reached a consensus that the Egyptian blockade must not be allowed to triumph. Eban knew that it would all come down to Johnson.

As Eban made his way west, Rabin was caught in a vise back at home between his generals and a deeply conflicted civilian leadership. Ben-Gurion himself had upbraided Rabin for courting disaster. How could he go to war without a major power as an ally? Moshe Chaim Shapira, the interior minister, pulled Rabin aside after a meeting with Eshkol and rebuked him: "If we're attacked, of course, we'll fight for our lives. But to take the initiative? To bring this curse down on us with our own hands? Do you want to bear the responsibility for endangering Israel? I shall resist it as long as I draw breath!"[32] To Weizman, Rabin wondered whether they were headed for a military disaster. Maybe he should resign. He went home that evening and collapsed and was out of action until late the next day. When he finally reported to Eshkol, he offered to resign, explaining to the prime minister that he had suffered a breakdown. He blamed it on "nicotine poisoning" and lack of sleep, but it was clear that exhaustion had combined with a massive loss of self-confidence. Eshkol told Rabin to go back to work.

Dayan had moved into the office of Meir Amit, the Mossad chief, and the two men opened their own channel to Helms and, through him, to the White House. Amit was no admirer of Eshkol, either. The two men had clashed over Mossad's involvement with the assassination in Paris of Mehdi Ben Barka, the Moroccan dissident whose death King Hassan II had sought in return for all of his secret favors to Israel, most notably his protection of Morocco's Jewish community.[33] Amit asserted that he had received high-level approval for an assassination, while Eshkol stated he had given no approval. Now Amit found himself in opposition to Eshkol on a profound question of national security. Amit, too, believed that Nasser had made himself vulnerable by deploying the bulk of his army in Sinai and giving Israel the pretext to destroy it. Dayan and Amit came to the conclusion that the real issue was no longer the closure of the Gulf of Aqaba; it was Israel's right to attack Egypt and destroy the Egyptian army. The closure of Aqaba was ample pretext. Dayan and Amit were the first to articulate a new strategic imperative: Israel must act decisively—and, if necessary, alone. The implication was that in doing so, Israel would demonstrate that it no longer saw itself as a vulnerable outpost of Jews in

Arabia. If it succeeded, it would cross a threshold as the Middle East's dominant military power—soon to be a nuclear power. If Egypt's army was laid to waste, if Syria and Jordan were held in check, *that* would bring to an end the myth of collective Arab power. In Dayan's words, "The true purpose of the war for Israel lay not in reopening the straits, but in demonstrating to the Arabs that Israel would stand up for itself."[34] But it was more than that, and Dayan sensed it. War was a chance to change the paradigm of Israel's existence as an impermanent implant established in word by the declaration of statehood in 1948 but not in lasting deed. Dayan had been the chief of staff during the Suez War and Amit had been his chief of operations. There was no more formidable duo in Israel's security establishment, and they were now committed to war.

On May 25, after Israel received an intelligence report that Egypt might attack as soon as the next morning, Amit summoned John Hadden, the CIA station chief, for a midnight meeting at Amit's apartment in Ramat-Gan near Tel Aviv. Hadden arrived to find Amit with Efraim Halevy, a Mossad officer overseeing American relations, and Colonel David Carmon of military intelligence.

"We have reached a turning point that is more significant for you than for us," Amit told Hadden.[35] The Mossad chief described the huge formation of Egyptian forces and told Hadden they could go on the offensive at any moment.

"Time is working against us. Personally, I regret not responding immediately," Amit told him. "Look at what is happening in Jordan. Do you think Jordan and Saudi Arabia are interested in Nasser's success? They have been dragged into it and this is the result of [our] taking no action."

Hadden was treated as a member of the family in Mossad. They playfully called him the "bastard" after he was caught walking through the residential area near the Dimona nuclear complex copying down the names on mailboxes. Mossad had also boosted Hadden's career in 1966 when they turned a MiG-21 over to the CIA for a month of analysis after an Iraqi pilot defected with the plane. But this night, Hadden argued forcefully that Israel must wait. He asserted that if Israel attacked, the United States might have no alternative to landing forces to protect Egypt, just as it had threatened to do in the early hours of the Suez crisis.

"Do not create a situation in which we will have to go against you," Hadden argued. They were drinking whiskey and eating the snacks that Amit's wife, Yona, was ferrying in from the kitchen and, at times, they were nearly shouting at each other because the mood in Israel—on the radio (there was no television), in the press, and especially among the Holocaust survivors—was one of imminent annihilation. Amit said that President Johnson could propose only "cosmetic" steps focused on opening the Gulf of Aqaba, when the real issue was the Egyptian army in Sinai. Yes, Hadden agreed, Johnson's steps might be cosmetic, but Israel had to allow the president time to put on his "lipstick" and his "rouge" to show that he had done everything possible to avert war. Israel should respect Johnson's political requirements because in the short history of Israel, Johnson had been the Jewish state's most loyal ally. Hadden's report, the one that included the message to Johnson that Israel had reached a "turning point," was accompanied by a CIA analysis that undermined most of Amit's arguments, describing them as a clever attempt to force the United States to make a public commitment to Israel's security.

Johnson got angry over the CIA's denigration of Mossad's case and told Helms he wanted the CIA memo "scrubbed," which meant he wanted something smarter than just the CIA's reactive dismissal of the Mossad chief. A new CIA assessment arrived at the White House within hours. It said: "Nasser is gambling with possible hostilities in the hope of exacting heavy concessions from the United States as the price of his keeping the peace. He will try to obtain both wheat and money from the U.S. as the price for his avoiding war with Israel." It said Nasser would not attack unless he believed that the United States was not responding.[36]


As soon as Eban landed in Washington on May 25, he was handed a cable from Eshkol saying that Egyptian forces were now configured for offensive operations and an attack was imminent. Eshkol instructed him to go immediately to Rusk and seek a firm commitment from the United States to treat any attack on Israel as an attack on the United States. Were they nuts? Eban wondered. The United States had never extended such a commitment outside of NATO. Eban could only guess that Israeli leadership was seized with panic, but in reality Rabin and the military had stepped up their demand to strike.

"What is the point of waiting any longer?" Rabin asked Eshkol.

But Eshkol held firm. "The generals want to fight," he told his wife, Miriam. "That's what they were taught to do. They have to fight, but it doesn't mean that I have to let them."[37] Eshkol stayed focused on the importance of the relationship with Johnson. "The IDF will not attack before the political options have been exhausted," he said.

At dinner with Rusk, Eban learned that the United States had no information to "support the belief" that an attack on Israel was imminent. Also, a NATO-like commitment to Israel was not in the cards. But Rusk said Johnson had flown to Canada earlier in the day and had come back from talks with Lester Pearson, the prime minister, who indicated that Canada would pledge two ships to join with American, British, and other navies to challenge Nasser's blockade of the strait.

Johnson was unsettled by the Israelis' talk of imminent attack. On Friday morning, May 26, he fired off an urgent cable to Harold Wilson, the British prime minister, and told him that the Israelis were sounding an alarm.[38] Johnson asked "whether your intelligence people share our judgment that the Israeli assessment is overdrawn and, indeed, your estimate of Nasser's intentions." The president summoned his top advisers at midday. What should he tell Eban? He was due at the White House at seven o'clock that evening.[39]

General Wheeler laid out the tense military scene: Egypt had moved 50,000 troops into Sinai and established them along two defensive lines, one behind the other. Israel had mobilized 160,000 ground troops but was not fully mobilized. Neither side looked as if it were readying for attack, and he figured that Israel could stay mobilized for two months without harming its economy, whereas Egypt could probably sustain its deployment for only a month.

Rusk focused on what Eban "needed" to take back to Eshkol, something the prime minister could use to contain the "apocalyptic pressures" to launch a war. Rusk told Eban that during the Berlin crisis of 1961–62 he had told Andrei Gromyko, the Soviet foreign minister, that he could have a war "in five minutes," but that a peaceful solution would take time to work out. He tried to explain to Eban the importance of world opinion in fixing blame for which side started a shooting war. He said that Israel would not be alone unless it chose to go alone, and he emphasized that the United States could not be drawn into a war by unilateral actions in the Middle East. Congress and public opinion demanded that the parties exhaust all other means first, and therefore, "the Israelis must give our efforts a chance."

General Wheeler, Clark Clifford, and Abe Fortas all told Johnson that the United States had to give Eban some assurance that American warships would escort an Israeli vessel through the Strait of Tiran and force Nasser to back down or face the consequences. Johnson said he was not yet in a position to make such a commitment. Eban would not get all that he wanted, the president said, but he was under "unanimous pressure" from Congress to "try the UN and multilateral machinery."

"The big question was whether we will regret on Monday not having given him more," Johnson added.[40]

A few hours later, Eban took the elevator to the residence in the White House. In the Yellow Room, Johnson explained what he had done so far and what he was going to do to keep the strait open. "Our best judgment is that no military attack on Israel is imminent," he said, adding that Israel would prevail decisively in any war. The United States would take the issue of the blockade to the United Nations and pursue it vigorously, and if that failed, "Israel and its friends, including the United States, who are willing to stand up and be counted, can give a specific indication of what they can do." The tools were at hand—a public declaration by the maritime nations and an international naval force to assert freedom of navigation in the strait. But Israel had to give the diplomacy a little more time. Johnson suggested that Israel join in organizing the international effort. He said he was "fully aware" of the Eisenhower commitment on freedom of passage in the Gulf of Aqaba, "but this is not worth five cents if the people and the Congress do not support the president." He made his points forcefully and persuasively, and then read slowly from the sheet of paper that Rusk had prepared, and twice stated the line that "Israel will not be alone unless it decides to go alone."[41] He said he could not imagine that the Israeli cabinet could make such a decision.

"We are Israel's friend," Johnson said. "The straits must be kept open." He pledged to work full-time on the problem until it was solved, but they had to move in concert and whatever step they took "must have reasonable expectation of support at home and internationally." Johnson said he had been on the phone to members of Congress, and while the process was moving along, "Israel should not make itself the guilty party by starting a war."

The president could not have been clearer. Eban mounted no counterargument. His mind was surely racing on whether he had done everything he could to nail down the Americans on a course of action.

"I would not be wrong if I told the prime minister that your disposition is to make every possible effort to assure that the strait and the gulf will remain open to free and innocent passage?" Eban asked.

"Yes," Johnson replied. He signaled that this was as much as Eban could expect and to press no further. In any case, Johnson hoped that it was enough. That night at dinner, which didn't get under way until after 10:00 p.m., the president regaled Lady Bird about the Eban meeting in a tone of wild and misplaced self-satisfaction.

"They came loaded for bear, but so was I!"[42]

McNamara "just wanted to throw his cap in the air!"

He quoted George Christian, saying, "It was the best meeting of the kind he had ever sat in on."

Eban flew through the night and reached Israel late on Saturday, May 27. He found that Eshkol had been holding back the torrent of military pressure to launch an attack. Other shards of intelligence were reaching the prime minister: an intercepted message from the Egyptian embassy in Washington quoted an unidentified State Department official saying that the United States would not fight to open the strait; Abe Feinberg called Eshkol to say that in a brief exchange with Johnson, the president said Israel would have to decide itself what it must do.

On Friday, Rabin had interrupted a meeting of Eshkol and the Foreign Affairs Committee of the Knesset to say that for the second time since the crisis began on May 14, Egypt had staged a high-altitude intrusion of Israeli airspace in what appeared to be a reconnaissance mission over the Dimona nuclear reactor. Rabin said some very "worrying" signals had been intercepted indicating that Nasser was preparing to launch a strike force of forty bombers at Dimona. Eshkol had asked why the Israeli air force couldn't send planes aloft to protect Dimona and Rabin had replied that this would quickly exhaust the air force.

But Eshkol had refused to launch the war. "If the IDF goes into action while Eban is in Washington, the Americans will say, 'You pulled a Pearl Harbor on us! You sent an emissary to us to put us to sleep and then you did what you did.'"

Perhaps to demonstrate that he was willing to take the most drastic steps to defend the Jewish state, Eshkol, according to a number of Israeli sources, secretly ordered the Dimona scientists to assemble two crude nuclear devices. He placed them under the command of Brigadier General Yitzhak Yaakov, the chief of research and development in Israel's Defense Ministry. One official said the operation was referred to as Spider because the nuclear devices were inelegant contraptions with appendages sticking out. The crude atomic bombs were readied for deployment on trucks that could race to the Egyptian border for detonation in the event Arab forces overwhelmed Israeli defenses.[43]

Eban went straight to Eshkol's home and briefed the prime minister and his aides on the consultations with de Gaulle, Wilson, and Johnson. Eban said that Johnson's position was very convincing, but Eshkol deflated the importance of the message by pointing out that Johnson was focusing only on the strait issue. The situation, Eshkol said, had evolved: it was now a question of the Egyptian force massed in Sinai.

"If it was just the straits, we could have waited. But it is also deterrence," Eshkol said. It was now clear that Eban's mission was a failure because the pressure from Dayan and the military chiefs had changed the equation of war. Eshkol and his ministers argued until 4:00 a.m. The vote on whether to launch the war was nine to nine. He told his colleagues that they should get some sleep before they considered the matter further. One of them said it was a good idea not to act as soon as Eban returned since that would alienate the American president. Eshkol was edging toward war, but during the few hours he and his government slept that Sunday morning, a personal message from Johnson arrived informing Eshkol that Soviet Premier Kosygin reported from Moscow that Soviet intelligence had indications that Israel was about to attack. Johnson reiterated, "I repeat even more strongly than what I said yesterday to Mr. Eban: Israel just must not take pre-emptive military action and thereby make itself responsible for the initiation of hostilities." America was determined to open the strait and Israel must give diplomacy time to work.

Rabin was crestfallen. Eshkol told him that Israel could not ignore Johnson's message. When the cabinet reconvened, Rabin told Eshkol, "I don't believe the countries of the world will open the straits for us. I am sure that in 2–3 weeks, we will face the same problem but under harsher political and military conditions." Eshkol backed down the war camp, saying he was not going to push the ministers to the wall and force them to say yes or no to war. Even if they said yes, "I'm not interested in it!" They would wait, two to three weeks if necessary, for Johnson to complete the steps he had outlined for a naval challenge to Nasser. Eshkol said he would go to "the pit" with Rabin to explain the decision to the generals, but before that, he would make a radio address to the nation.

The Israeli general staff had been certain it would get the order to attack on May 28, and when Eshkol pulled the generals up short, some of them reacted so passionately as to seriously consider taking matters into their own hands. Exhaustion, the strain of the debate, and lack of sleep were now taking a toll on Eshkol. When he went live on national radio that day to address the nation, he faltered and stammered in front of the microphone. Some listeners gasped. The Israelis needed reassurance, and all they got was a prime minister who seemed befuddled or, worse, rattled by Nasser's threats. Was Eshkol coming unglued?[44]

Then he walked into the buzz saw that was waiting for him in "the pit."

"Today we shredded with our bare hands the deterrence power of the IDF," said General Ariel Sharon.[45] He ripped into Eshkol, and Rabin just stood there and let him. The reliance on diplomacy, Sharon said, made Israel appear weak and incompetent. "The IDF forces," he continued, "are ready like never before to totally destroy the Egyptian forces." It was now a moral question of whether the Israeli civilian leaders would opt to save lives and reduce casualties by acting quickly. Waiting for America, was "a first-degree mistake." The real goal, he said, was to make sure that with its army destroyed, Egypt would not have the stomach to take on Israel for twenty years or more. "Who if not us is authorized to come and tell you that the army is ready for war?" Sharon demanded.

One by one, as the generals took him on, Eshkol could not keep his emotions under control, especially after Sharon's attempt to humiliate him. "Nobody said we are a pre-emptive army," he admonished them in a tone that conveyed that they had better regain a sense of discipline, patience, and maturity. Had they not received from him, Eshkol asked, everything they requested to build the Israeli army, whose main goal was to deter war?

"You wanted one hundred aircraft. You got it. You got tanks as well. You got everything so that we can win if we have to. You did not get it so that one day we get up and say, 'Now we can destroy the Egyptian army,' and do it. I did not think that if there is a great Egyptian army near the border we will get up at night and destroy it. Deterrence does not mean we have to act. I'm saying deterrence needs to be the ability to wait and to allow exhaustion of all other means."[46]

Eshkol rebuked Sharon for denigrating diplomacy. "All we have in the material strength of our army comes from this running around [diplomatically]. Let us not forget that, and let us not see ourselves as Goliath. Say we broke the enemy today. Tomorrow we would have to start rebuilding.

Will we have an ally to help? It is important that Johnson will say that we did not deceive him, because we might need him—and I hope we will not need him in the middle of the campaign.

"Military victory will not end the conflict," Eshkol told them. "Because the Arabs will still be there." And finally, he asked, because this was the deeper psychological point: "Will we always live by our sword?"

No Israeli leader had ever been so blunt about the militarist instinct. Eshkol walked out of "the pit" and left the generals to sulk. Frustration poured forth. Weizman, the air force chief who had spent his entire career preparing for a surprise air attack on Egypt, said there had to be a way to force the government to act. "This forum must find a solution as to how to bring [the government] to decide," he said.

Rabin agreed. "In two or three weeks, there is no guarantee we can screw the Egyptians as we wanted."[47]

Sharon wheeled on Rabin and told him that this was the first time in Israel's history that there was not only the possibility of the army's taking control and forcing a decision on the civilian leaders but that also such a bold act would be welcomed by the public, which was in a state of panic as Arab armies continued to mass on its borders. Rabin didn't encourage them, but he didn't say no.

Israel is a small society. Word of the near revolt spread like an ill wind. When Ben-Gurion heard of it, he called a news conference at the Knesset and read a statement. "An army in a democratic country does not act by its own opinion and not by the opinions of its military commanders, but by the opinion of the civil government and its orders." He refused to take questions from journalists, but the newspaper *Haaretz* reported that the old lions of Israel were trying to tamp down an incipient putsch.

The impulse to overrule Eshkol was bleeding into the news media and infecting the whole country. Newspapers called on the prime minister to turn over his post to someone more decisive. But the Israeli public was ignorant, necessarily so, of Eshkol's decisive steps to prepare for war, including his activation of Israel's nuclear deterrent and his secret consultations with Johnson for coordinated naval action in the Strait of Tiran.

The generals shifted their focus, challenging the notion that America was going to live up to expectations and open the strait.

On morning of May 29, perhaps after some collusion, General Yariv, chief of military intelligence, suggested to Eshkol that he dispatch his Mossad chief, Meir Amit, to Washington to probe whether Johnson was serious. Amit flew to Washington on May 31 with a strong predisposition that Israel had to go to war. Amit's account of what he learned in Washington, given in interviews and a memoir, does not square with the U.S. declassified record. Amit later recounted that he went straight to see his close friends at the CIA, Richard Helms, the director, and James J. Angleton, the longtime counterintelligence chief of the agency and its official liaison with Israeli intelligence. From his conversations, Amit said he learned, "There is no [maritime] task force" working on getting the strait reopened, "there is no armada of maritime nations," and "there is no concrete action plan."

These statements were inaccurate. Amit's insistence that he could find no evidence that Johnson's pledge of maritime deployment was being translated into action is so at variance with the facts that it raises the question of whether the Mossad chief fabricated his most prominent account, published in Hebrew, to justify the preemptive war decision for a domestic Israeli audience.[48] It seems impossible that Helms told Amit that there was no task force or no plan when he was acutely aware of the intense efforts under way at the State Department, Pentagon, and White House to organize more than two dozen maritime nations to support both a declaration on the right of passage in the Gulf of Aqaba and a military plan to break Nasser's blockade.

A Middle East task force, called the Arab-Israeli Control Group, that reported to the president through his national security adviser, Rostow, had been established and was meeting on the days that Amit was in Washington. The Joint Chiefs of Staff had undertaken urgent planning to dispatch warships to the Red Sea and to bring an antisubmarine warship from the Pacific to cope with the two Egyptian submarines that had been detected in the area of the strait.[49] The record of this planning is extensive, and for Amit to assert, as he did at the time and in subsequent years, that the United States was not vigorously building an international maritime force to back Nasser down is an attempt at deception that masks the larger mission that Amit saw for himself: to break Eshkol's resistance to going to war immediately. Indeed, Helms's memo to Johnson on June 2 opens by saying that "Amit thinks the Israelis' decision will be to strike." He regarded Eban's mission as a "failure" for focusing too narrowly on reopening the Strait of Tiran and that Nasser's manipulation of the Arabs, "if left unimpeded" would "result in the loss of the area to the United States," as one "domino" after the other would fall.[50]

"It seems clear from Amit's remarks that the 'tough' Israelis, who have never forgotten that they are surrounded by hostile Arabs, are driving hard for a forceful solution, with us and with their own government," Helms wrote privately to Johnson, noting that Amit and Moshe Dayan were allied in leading the war camp—"both are Sabras—men born in Israel"—and that the time of decision was only a matter of days away.

Thus, Amit needed to go home with a report that discredited Johnson's pledge to Eban. During a visit to Israel in 2005, I met Amit, who was in his eighties, at his home near Tel Aviv, where he has lived since he was a boy. We sat in the same room where he and Dayan had discussed the need to go to war. He told me that when he went to see Robert McNamara, he didn't ask the secretary of defense a single question about the so-called task force. At his kitchen table, Amit held up his arm to show how he stopped McNamara from speaking. "Don't say a word," he told him. Amit said he was there for one reason: to explain why he was going to return to Israel and recommend that Eshkol unleash the army for war.

"We cannot go on like this," Amit recounted his words to McNamara. "The whole economy is standing still. People are mobilized. I am going back and I will recommend to them to start the war." He also explained that the crisis was rallying the Arab world behind Nasser, and the region was tipping toward a belief that Israel could be defeated. King Hussein of Jordan, one of Nasser's targets for many years, had flown to Cairo on May 30 and put Jordanian forces under Egyptian command. The Arabs were lining up. Now Israel was facing three fronts: Egypt to the south, Syria to the north, and Jordan to the east. Both men knew that Israel would prevail, but the question "At what cost?" was tearing Israel apart. The Israeli public heard alarming reports of Egyptian chemical weapons deployed in Sinai, and estimates were leaking out of "the pit" that the IDF expected ten thousand or more casualties.

No one would sit shiva (a seven-day period of mourning) if Israel got rid of Nasser, Amit reassured McNamara. All that McNamara could do was ask a few questions: How long did he estimate a war would last? How many casualties did he estimate? Amit said he thought the war would take three to four weeks and that Israel would suffer about four thousand combat losses among military personnel.

Amit flew back to Israel in a jetliner that had been chartered to carry twenty thousand American-made gas masks and crates of medical supplies, including plenty of morphine used for battlefield injuries, all of it approved by Johnson and McNamara as contingency supplies after a special request from the Israeli embassy in Washington.[51]

Amit went straight to Eshkol's home in Jerusalem. The prime minister looked like a broken man. He had been forced to take Dayan into his government as minister of defense. This had triggered its own kind of hysteria in the military command.

Weizman had burst into the prime minister's study during a private lunch. "The country is getting ruined! Everything is getting ruined!" Weizman shrieked. "What do you need Moshe Dayan for? Give us an order and we will win . . . and you will be the prime minister of a victorious government."[52] Weizman ripped the epaulets off his uniform and threw his general's stars at Eshkol's feet.

The war camp had won. In the Israeli system, the defense minister is almost as powerful as the prime minister and, on matters of national security, more influential unless the prime minister has a strong military background. Rabin recorded from this meeting that Eshkol's face was a palette of depression. The prime minister ended the discussion at 3:00 a.m., saying he would convene the cabinet first thing on June 4 to vote on war. Everyone knew the resolution would prevail this time.

Meanwhile in Washington, some of Johnson's key aides started wondering aloud whether it was time to turn the Israelis loose. Harold Saunders, the principal Middle East expert on the National Security Council staff, wrote to Rostow saying "we don't have a right" to restrain Eshkol further "while his enemy gets stronger unless we're willing to take on the Arabs ourselves." The plan for an American-led armada was complicated and risky. "Pretty soon we'll have Soviet warships in the Red Sea. We ought to consider admitting that we have failed and allow fighting to ensue." [53]

Then Walt Rostow, on June 4, just as the Israeli cabinet was voting in secret to go to war, penned a memorandum to Johnson that showed just how poorly he understood the historic forces in the Middle East. He told the president that the moderate Arab states, in fact, "all Arabs who fear the rise of Nasser as a result of this crisis—would prefer to have him cut down by the Israelis rather than by external forces." Rostow argued that "the radical nationalism represented by Nasser" was "waning" in the Middle East. "Just beneath the surface is the potentiality for a new phase in the Middle East of moderation," focusing on "economic development; regional collaboration, and an acceptance of Israel as part of the Middle

East if a solution to the refugee problem can be found. But all this depends on Nasser's being cut down to size." [54]

There is no evidence in the now extensive record that Johnson succumbed to any logic that it just might be better for America to let the Israelis sort things out in the Middle East with a preemptive strike on the Arab armies. The risks were far too great, given Vietnam. The president flew to New York on June 3 and stood before 1,650 Democratic loyalists at a major fund-raising dinner. Johnson looked out to the faces of American Jewish leaders and told them he was working day and night to prevent war in the Middle East.

"The position of your country, the United States, in this crisis is a bipartisan one. It bears the marks of President Eisenhower. It bears the mark of both of our national political parties. It is designed solely to serve the cause of freedom and to serve the cause of peace in the world . . . I have not come here to ask your blessings on the work we have finished," Johnson told the crowd. "I have come here to ask for your support for the work we have yet to do." He repeated his determination to keep the peace twice more before turning to domestic politics. He accepted a warm tribute and endorsement from Robert F. Kennedy, the man who would soon turn on him over Vietnam. But that night, Kennedy said of Johnson, "He has poured out his own strength to renew the strength of the country. He has sought consensus, but has never shrunk from controversy . . . he has gained huge popularity, but never hesitated to spend it on what he thought important."[55]

The next day, a smiling Johnson and Kennedy were on the front page of *The New York Times*. Johnson had great hopes for holding Kennedy's support, for keeping the peace, for getting a deal in Vietnam—the obvious political goals that the president obsessively was pursuing.

It was evident from this political context that Lyndon Johnson was not seeking to send (as some historians have argued) a green light or a yellow light to the Israelis to launch a war to destroy Nasser when the results of such a war were so unpredictable. When the new American ambassador to Egypt, James Nolte, announced in Cairo that the United States was prepared to challenge the blockade in the Gulf of Aqaba, Johnson blew his top, ordering Rusk to muzzle the ambassador and roll back the statement so as not to provoke Nasser or undermine the delicate canvassing of maritime nations and the consultations with Congress that were under way. Extreme caution was the hallmark of his every move. In secret diplomatic channels, Johnson had finally reached out to Nasser, sending the veteran Eisenhower envoy, Robert Anderson, to see the Egyptian leader and offer a high-level dialogue to defuse the crisis. And Nasser, in a series of private messages through various emissaries, had conveyed to Johnson that he would not initiate hostilities; he was engaged in a war of nerves, and it would soon be over. Johnson responded that he was willing to send Vice President Hubert Humphrey to Cairo, or receive the Egyptian vice president in Washington, and Nasser had agreed to send his vice president, Zakaria Mohieddin, to meet Johnson on June 7. But Johnson had waited too long. His last message to Eshkol on June 3, two days before Israel attacked, seemed a desperate attempt to buck up the embattled prime minister. Johnson praised Eshkol's "steadfastness" and "calm" and told him that the United States and Britain "on an urgent basis" were exploring the establishment of an "international naval presence in the area of the Strait of Tiran." Eshkol ignored these efforts. After the battles began, Johnson called Eshkol an "old coot" and complained, "I had a firm commitment from Eshkol [to wait] and he blew it."[56]

Nothing would ever be the same. The Six-Day War was a failure of American diplomacy—a costly failure whose consequences would bleed through decades marked by further outbreaks of war and unending strife. Unlike Eisenhower, who had invoked the United Nations Charter against Israeli's occupation of Sinai in 1956, Johnson would not demand that Israel give up its 1967 conquests. Johnson embraced what seemed to him a perfectly reasonable argument that Israel, having been provoked, should trade the conquered lands for a permanent peace with the Arabs. Johnson did not see how profoundly he had undermined the high principle of the United Nations Charter—the inadmissibility of conquest as a means of settling disputes—nor did he foresee the corrosive effects of military occupation on lands populated by more than one million Arabs.

Nonetheless, any immediate sense of failure was overshadowed by the scale of the Israeli victory. The Jewish state had shattered the Arab armies and buried, perhaps forever, the question of whether some combination of Arab nations could annihilate the Jewish state. Israel would never again be regarded as a vulnerable outpost. Not only had Sparta vanquished Athenian hegemony, but the great nations of the modern world had stood on the sidelines as the Jews had acted decisively and alone.

Johnson's political aide, Harry McPherson, was in Israel when the war erupted. He had stopped there on his way back from a depressing tour of Vietnam and had sent his impressions to Johnson: "The spirit of the army, and indeed of all the people, has to be experienced to be believed. After the doubts, confusions, and ambiguities of Vietnam, it was deeply moving to see people whose commitment is total and unquestioning. I was told that eight year olds went to the telegraph office Monday morning to deliver telegrams, as the regular force of messengers had gone off to military duty." [57]

He described a certain eroticism of victory: "I saw two good-looking girls in uniform riding in the back of a half-ton jeep, one with a purple spangled bathing cap on her head, the other with an orange turban. They were on their way to the front, driven by two burly sergeants." Israel at war destroyed the stereotype "of the pale, scrawny Jew," he observed. "The soldiers I saw were tough, muscular, and sunburned." They fought with "an extraordinary combination of discipline and democracy among officers and enlisted men." The latter, he said, "rarely salute and frequently argue, but there is no doubt about who will prevail."

Egypt's army had collapsed in the desert. Without air cover, it fled in a chaotic retreat in which ten thousand to fifteen thousand Egyptian soldiers were cut down by Israeli forces and another five thousand taken prisoner. Jordanian troops fought tenaciously around the Old City of Jerusalem, but when their ranks broke, the fallback turned into a rout and the West Bank tumbled into Israel's hands. The Israeli army controlled all of historic Palestine as well as the sacred Temple Mount—what the Arabs call Haram al-Sharif, the Noble Sanctuary—in the heart of the Old City in Jerusalem. They had taken all of Sinai up to the Suez Canal. And in the final battle of the war, Moshe Dayan, without bothering to consult with either Eshkol or Rabin, the chief of staff of the Israeli military, unleashed General David Elazar, the northern commander known as "Dado," to push Syrian forces off the Golan Heights, an act that was extremely popular among Israelis who had lived for two decades under the threat of Syrian gunners commanding the heights over Galilee.

There had been moments of high drama and near confrontation between the superpowers. On the fourth day of the war, Israeli aircraft and torpedo boats had attacked the USS *Liberty*, an electronic intelligence-gathering ship that was steaming sixty miles off the Egyptian coast in the Mediterranean Sea. It was a bright, sunny day. The *Liberty* was in international waters flying the American flag. Its hull markings were in English, yet Israeli pilots and gunners went after the American vessel as if it were an enemy. The attack left 34 officers and crew members dead and more than 170 wounded, and engendered bitter recriminations over Israel's claim that the attack had been a case of mistaken identity. Johnson, Rusk, CIA Director Helms, and other senior officials could not believe that the highly professional Israeli forces could have made such a huge blunder. But Israel was quick to assert that it was an innocent error and issued a profuse apology. The transcripts of the communications that day among Israeli pilots, their controllers, and their colleagues on the torpedo boats revealed the intense confusion in which the identification of the vessel was questioned and debated even as the attacks proceeded.[58] They also revealed the competitiveness between the Israeli navy and air force over which one would get the "kill" as they both tried to sink the suspected enemy vessel.

But the transcripts also established Israeli negligence, even incompetence, in failing to confirm the identity of the vessel before the attack began, and this failure persisted during repeated bombing and strafing runs in which the Israeli crews threw torpedoes, napalm, and machine gun fire against a noncombatant vessel that was not returning fire. The clear presumption expressed by the attacking pilots and torpedo men was that they were hitting an Egyptian target. What seemed appalling was that even after the pilots spotted English lettering on the hull— Egyptian ships are marked in Arabic—and read it out over the radio: "Charlie-Tango-Romeo Five"—Israeli air controllers continued to insist that the ship was an Egyptian supply boat. The fact that the attack continued for an hour after a serious question had been raised about its identity, including one controller's statement that it was "possibly American," left many resentful. U.S. navy commanders and the families of crew members were deeply affected, seeing the attack as a deliberate attempt by the Israeli military to interdict American intelligence gathering in a war zone where American interests were on the line.

Johnson may have been incredulous, but he did not allow the episode to affect relations. Many Americans, and certainly most Israelis, were willing to accept that it was a case of mistaken identity induced by the chaos that takes hold in high-adrenaline combat operations. Dean Rusk, one of those who felt a strong sense of outrage over the attack, drafted one of the toughest statements ever delivered by the United States to a friendly government. He said the attack was "quite literally incomprehensible" given that Israeli aircraft circled the vessel three times before they went in for bombing runs. "At a minimum, the attack must be condemned as an act of military recklessness reflecting wanton disregard for human life."[59]

The war had also given the hotline between Moscow and Washington its first extensive test in a crisis, allowing Johnson and Kosygin to gauge each other's intentions and to pass warnings and messages meant for the clients of each. But its use had not prevented more brutal displays of power, as occurred on June 10, when Moscow warned that it would take military steps if Israel did not adhere to a cease-fire and halt its attack on the Syrian army. The Soviet leadership feared that the Israeli army might go all the way to Damascus and topple the Moscow-backed regime. Johnson was groggy that morning, having failed to sleep most of the night.[60] He had just excused himself, perhaps to go to the bathroom, when the translators finished with Kosygin's hotline message, which threatened to resort to "military" means against Israel. McNamara looked around the table and suggested they order the Sixth Fleet to turn and steam toward Syria and the Soviet fleet. Helms agreed. He knew that Soviet submarines in the area would immediately alert Moscow of such a move. When the president returned, they filled him in.

"Go ahead and do it," Johnson said.[61] But Johnson was not looking for confrontation. He sent urgent messages to Eban in Israel and to the Israeli ambassador in Washington: "The United States government does not want the war to end as a result of a Soviet ultimatum. This would be disastrous for the future not only of Israel, but of us all. It is your responsibility to act now." The Israelis ceased firing.

In a war of amazing results, what was most astounding was that Nasser came out stronger.

"Hail the Conquered!" *Newsweek* declared on its cover.

On the fifth day of the fighting, the CIA reported that Nasser's prestige in the Arab world had suffered a severe blow, and Soviets were asking themselves, "How could we have gotten into such a mess?"[62] But then Nasser went on the radio to announce that he would resign "and return to the ranks of the public."

"The imperialist forces imagine that Nasser is their enemy," he said, "but I want it to be clear to them that it is the whole Arab nation, not just Abdul Nasser." Throngs of Egyptians rushed to the streets shouting, "We want Nasser!"

The demonstrations swept to Beirut and Baghdad, where the CIA reported huge crowds of weeping Arabs calling on Nasser to stay.[63] It was beyond Western comprehension. The first instinct was to suspect Nasser's secret police agents of whipping up the crowds, and that was undoubtedly true to some extent. But the scale of the outpouring in Egypt and across the region soon outstripped any notion of manipulation. Even in defeat, Nasser was still the heroic leader. He had stood up to Israel and to America. His rule may have been chaotic and his secret police hyperactive, but Nasser had become the Arab tribune who had restored the dignity of what it meant to be Egyptian and to be an Arab. The masses, at least at home, revered their pharaoh.

The next day, Anwar Sadat announced that Nasser had agreed to remain as president, but only "until all traces of aggression are eliminated." The immediate question was whether Israel would give up the Arab lands it had seized. One of the first messages that reached Johnson when the war broke out[64] came from Eban, who said Israel would soon state formally that it had no intention of "taking advantage" of the war "to enlarge its territory and hoped that peace could be restored with its present boundaries.[65] But when the cannons fell silent and Jews by the thousands rushed to the Old City to marvel at what their martial skills had returned to them—the Temple Mount, the Wailing Wall, all that connected them to their origins—a wave of Hebrew nationalism and religious fervor rolled through the population. Israel had trebled the size of its domain. The airwaves crackled with messianic statements about Zion revived. Israel suddenly had strategic depth. McPherson wrote in his cable to Johnson that "every Israeli I talked to said in effect that no government could survive" in Israel that gave up the Old City or control of Sharm el-Sheikh at the Strait of Tiran."

Eban changed his tune, too. He told the Americans that there was a "transformational strategy" afoot. He spoke of "opportunities which were inconceivable before." Withdrawal to the previous lines was now "inconceivable" and what was needed was a blueprint for new Arab-Israeli relations.[66] Dayan had said Israel was waiting for a phone call from the Arabs. If they wanted their land back, the price would be peace, real peace. He spoke of keeping Sinai and Eshkol corrected him, but not very convincingly.

Johnson, too, was astonished by the scale of the victory, but he told his advisers that there was nothing to celebrate because of all the problems that lay ahead. He had gotten very little credit for all his exertions, he felt, including his tough moves with the Sixth Fleet that kept the Soviets out of the fray. Mathilde Krim, who stayed at the White House for the duration of the war, had sent a steady stream of notes to the Oval Office, reporting on, among other things, the "anti-American feelings in Israel" over the State Department's posture of neutrality.

"The Jews are people with a persecution complex and they understood the statement of the State Department to mean that in an hour of gravest danger to them—before they knew the Israeli army would be victorious and therefore at a time when they thought they would be exterminated by Nasser—that this country disengaged itself, and the Jews and Israelis look at Nasser like a second Hitler."[67] She had dictated to Rostow a statement that she strongly recommended the president make, declaring Nasser a discredited leader. Johnson, she suggested, should refuse to "resume relations with the government headed by Mr. Nasser because he is responsible for useless and deplorable bloodshed." An hour later, Johnson put Dean Rusk on hold and asked his secretary to bring him Mrs. Krim's memo on Jewish anger so he could read portions to the secretary of state.

The big question, for Israel and for the United States, was what to do about Israel's conquest of Arab lands. Eshkol's government sputtered with contradictory impulses. With Dayan and Begin in the cabinet, the pressure to keep the West Bank—biblical Israel—plus Jerusalem and the eastern parts of Sinai and the Golan was intense. On June 19, deliberating in secret, the Israeli cabinet reached a consensus to offer—privately through the Americans—to withdraw from Sinai and the Golan Heights in return for negotiated peace treaties with Egypt and Syria. It seems almost certain that Eshkol's government knew the Arabs would reject such an offer, given that it conspicuously excluded the West Bank and Arab East Jerusalem. The exercise in secret diplomacy may have been conceived for its effect on Johnson as much as on the Arabs. The Arab demand was first and foremost for unconditional Israeli withdrawal from all of the lands occupied by Israel during the war. Ten thousand or more Arab soldiers had died. Hundreds of Arab towns and villages had fallen and were now under Israeli occupation. Johnson and Rusk faced a choice: support Israel's occupation strategy or demand a full withdrawal. There was very little debate, at least in the White House. Johnson believed that Nasser had provoked the war, and though Israel had ignored his pleas to avoid a rush to combat, Johnson acceded to Israel's desire on how to play the postwar diplomacy. Abe Fortas, Arthur Goldberg, Abe Feinberg, the Krims—all advised him to leave the next steps to Israel.

Radio Cairo called America and Israel "the pirate and the lackey, the speckled snake and its tail." America in the Middle East had "destroyed all man's values and ethics, applied the law of the jungle, and turned the human race back to primitive ages."[68]

As he had done in 1956, Nasser closed the Suez Canal and ordered ships sunk to block the channel. By October, four hundred thousand Egyptian refugees from the cities of the canal zone had flooded into Cairo.[69] Nasser put his army under new management, firing Field Marshal Abdel-Hakim Amer for incompetence. For the Soviets, the only way out of the humiliation was to rearm Egypt. Moscow sent a delegation of nearly one hundred officers to survey Cairo's military needs and to take control of training.

Hundreds of thousands of Palestinians also were uprooted. Many who had fled into the West Bank in 1948 now fled into Jordan. Dayan wanted to blow up the bridges across the Jordan River to demonstrate that the link between the West Bank and Jordan was being severed, but he agreed to delay so that more Palestinians could leave. These scenes of Palestinian suffering further radicalized the Arabs. Yasser Arafat and the leaders of his Al-Fatah organization announced that they were moving their headquarters into the occupied territories. Arafat made a secret journey to Cairo, where Nasser urged him to open a new front against Israel.

"Why not be our Stern [Gang]? Why not be our Begin?" Nasser asked him, referring to the leaders of the Jewish underground during the 1940s. "You must be our irresponsible arm," Nasser said, using a euphemism for terrorist or "resistance" operations. "On this basis, we will give you all the help we can."[70]

Throughout the summer, the United Nations debated resolutions calling for Israeli withdrawal. Nasser called the Arab leaders to a summit meeting in Khartoum, a safe distance from the front lines, and told them that the Arabs must prepare for "the liberation of our territories by force." Nasser was greeted like a hero in the Sudanese capital, where five hundred thousand people lined the route from the airport to the city center. King Faisal, the Saudi monarch who had fought Nasser's army in Yemen, declared him the leader of the summit. King Faisal won agreement from the oil-producing states to finance war preparations with hefty pledges of aid to the "frontline" states of Egypt, Syria, and Jordan, plus the Palestine Liberation Organization, which Nasser effectively controlled. The message that rang out from Khartoum was that there would be no negotiation, no recognition, and no peace with Israel. These would become known as the "Three No's" of Khartoum, and Israel used them to justify an indefinite occupation of the lands it had seized in war. The irony was that Nasser at Khartoum urged King Hussein to explore with the Israelis the possibility of a negotiated settlement that would return the West Bank and Gaza to the Palestinians as part of a comprehensive peace with the Jewish state.[71]

On November 22, diplomacy yielded UN Security Council Resolution 242, which emphasized "the inadmissibility of the acquisition of territory by war and the need to work for a just and lasting peace in which every state in the area can live in security." And in particular, it called for "withdrawal of Israeli armed forces from territories occupied during the recent conflict."[72] U Thant, the secretary-general who had done so little to prevent the war, appointed a special representative to implement the resolution, Gunnar Jarring, a former Swedish ambassador to Moscow.

The Arabs had hoped that Johnson would respond as Eisenhower had in 1957, insisting on the immediate return of conquered territory, but times had changed. Eisenhower's emphasis had been to win hearts and minds among the Arabs in order to keep the Soviets out, protect the region's oil, and advance American priorities. Johnson was hemmed in by Vietnam; he was losing the hearts-and-minds battle everywhere and he simply lacked the capacity to master the complexities of the Middle East. So he was inclined to accept the Israeli logic of keeping the land and trading it—or part of it—for peace.

After the war, Eshkol sent Johnson an extensive list of weaponry needed to replenish Israel's arsenal. Rusk urged Johnson to use the leverage of Israel's arms requirements to persuade Eshkol to sign the Nuclear Non-Proliferation Treaty of 1968. Israel wanted F-4 Phantoms for its air force and Rusk argued that signing the treaty and forswearing the development of nuclear weapons should be the price. But in his final days in office, Johnson undermined the State Department negotiators who sought to freeze Israel's incipient nuclear weapons program. Preventing Israel from becoming a full-fledged nuclear weapons state had been one of Kennedy's most pressing priorities. Rusk had shared the fervor, but

Johnson's commitment proved erratic. He had promised Eshkol the planes, and so he pulled the plug on Rusk's idea to use them as leverage.

After Richard Nixon won the election in November 1968, the lame duck Johnson pleaded again with Eshkol to sign the nonproliferation treaty. Johnson invited President-elect Nixon to the Oval Office, where Rusk laid it out: Nixon was facing the spread of nuclear weapons in the Middle East. Rusk warned that if Israel fielded a nuclear capability, the Soviet Union would most likely place nuclear weapons in Egypt.[73] Late that month, Johnson sent a private message to Nixon saying that he would call Congress into an extraordinary session in December and use the forum to bring pressure to bear on Israel and other allies to sign the treaty. Johnson emphasized that Nixon's public endorsement for this strategy would be essential. But Nixon responded that he would not endorse a special session of Congress. His excuse was that he had "problems with members of his own party" over the treaty.[74]

Johnson, unwilling to withhold the promised F-4 Phantoms, was left with little more than sentimentalism to gird his final arguments to Eshkol. "As I look back over my five years in office, I find that one endeavor overshadowed all those that have called upon my time and energy. This has been the search for peace," Johnson wrote in a letter. "Israel's failure to sign the NPT would be a severe blow to my Government's global efforts to halt the spread of nuclear weapons." He said the United States would be "deeply troubled if operational strategic missiles were to appear in the Near East. I hope you can give me an encouraging response."[75]

Eshkol disappointed him again.

# 3

# NIXON AND BREZHNEV

*Cold War and International Terror*

airo, the largest Arab capital, is a noisy horizon of dust-covered architecture: a mixture of glassy modernism, bulky Soviet-era masonry, Islamic style and, in the distance, the sublime contours of the ancients, all worn to the same texture and hue by sandstorms and sun. The city confronts the senses: the traffic moves as a surly orchestra of klaxons inching along the Nile; lines of boxy black-and-white taxis and buses of every size radiate along ribbons of pavement into a hazy urban sprawl; the air hangs with an acrid tinge of smoke that lingers as an unforgettable olfactory signature; and the dust-filled nimbus that envelops the place softens every surface with its gritty residue. Cairo and its hinterland fill the geological depression, almost imperceptible because of the scale, where the river arrives from Upper Egypt and divides into branches that run to the sea through the lush Nile Delta. The basin stretches from an eastern escarpment where the old citadel overlooks the city all the way to the edge of the Giza plateau in the west, where the sphinx guards the great pyramids.

The Nile's stately advance, regulated by the high dam at Aswan, makes for the smooth passage of water taxis that chug up and down the stream. Their commerce is interspersed with that of slow-moving feluccas, the brightly colored sailboats that vie for tourists seeking a silent foray out onto the meandering current to escape the din of the city. Along the corniche stand the faded hotels of colonial times grouped near the national museum, where the treasures of Egypt are on display.

In 1971, though, tourism had slowed to a crawl because the previous year, the Israeli air force, equipped with American-made F-4 Phantoms, had staged deep-penetration air raids throughout the Nile valley, killing hundreds of Egyptians. Golda Meir, who was elected prime minister following Levi Eshkol's death in 1969, hoped the bombing would convince the Egyptians that Nasser could not protect them and thus incite his overthrow. There would be no peace until Nasser was gone, she had declared. The new Israeli ambassador to the United States, Yitzhak Rabin, had implored Washington to speed the delivery of the Phantoms because, he argued, Nasser was vulnerable.[1] But, instead, the four-month bombing campaign had triggered a large Soviet mobilization and airlift to reinforce Nasser with arms, air defense systems, and thousands of military advisers. Then Nasser had died suddenly from a heart attack in September 1970 and still there was no peace.

Up to the moment of his death, Nasser stood athwart the main current of Arab politics, and under his successor, Anwar Sadat, Cairo remained the preeminent Arab capital, home to the Arab League, whose Joint Defense Council was the hub of Arab military planning to recover Arab lands. The war deliberations had brought the prime minister of Jordan, Wasfi al-Tal, to Cairo to help refine the Arab strategy of the "frontline" states—Egypt, Syria, and Jordan—that were receiving arms from Moscow and funding from Saudi Arabia and the other oil producers. Tal was a powerfully built man with a big brush mustache and a military bearing. He had spent the morning of November 28, 1971, in consultations with the Joint Defense Council. Tal's background made him well suited to the task. He had fought with the British army during World War II and had battled the Israelis in the 1948 war. He had briefly served in the Syrian army before moving to Jordan and entering the service of the crown.

Tal and Abdullah Salah, the Jordanian foreign minister, moved through Cairo traffic in a dark sedan escorted by an Egyptian security officer. They were returning to the Sheraton on the Giza side of the river where

Tal was to meet his wife. The hotel staff had noticed a man lingering near the entrance all morning.

The fifty-one-year-old prime minister was known as King Hussein's "crisis man," and the crisis for which he had been brought back to power for his fifth stint at the top of the king's government was the consolidation—or, more aptly, the rescue—of the monarchy. The previous year, Yasser Arafat and the PLO had been on a course to topple the thirty-six-year-old king in order to turn Jordan into a Palestinian base for subversion and guerrilla war against Israel. The civil conflict had exploded in September 1970—hence Black September—after a series of assassination attempts against the king and a string of airplane hijackings. In addition, three planes had been blown up at a desert airfield in Jordan and a Pan Am jumbo jet was incinerated on the tarmac in Cairo in the middle of the night, sending up a fireball as bright as dawn. King Hussein declared martial law and set loose the Jordanian army, which had been more than ready to bomb PLO bases and shell Palestinian refugee camps; now it did so, creating a new terror for the refugees. The crisis briefly engaged the Nixon White House when a Syrian tank brigade moved into Jordan in support of the Palestinians. Nixon and Kissinger, the national security adviser, consulted with the Israelis about joint action and Nixon alerted the Sixth Fleet—seeing the incursion, incorrectly, as some Soviet-backed move—but the Syrian threat quickly faded and the Jordanian armed forces prevailed.

The king had brought Tal back to head a government that would crush the Palestinian ministate in Jordan. Thousands of PLO militants and civilians were killed or wounded. Arafat was forced to flee, dressed as a woman and hidden among the Arab League delegation that had rushed to Amman to mediate. Not surprisingly, Tal was now one of the most hated men in the Arab world. He was disparaged as "Mr. Tal-Aviv" for his alleged collaboration with Israel in the suppression of the PLO. Thousands of refugees had fled the Palestinian camps in Jordan for Syria and Lebanon. But Tal's most distinguishing attribute was his intense loyalty to the Hashemite crown in Jordan. He seemed unflappable in the face of broad Arab world condemnation.

He stepped briskly out of the black sedan and, as he climbed the steps to the glass doors of the Sheraton lobby, a gunman lunged forward and opened fire on Tal at point-blank range. Two other gunmen burst out of the lobby and joined in the shooting. At least ten shots were heard by wit-

Richard Nixon with Golda Meir, as America makes a full entry into the Middle East

nesses. Mortally wounded, the prime minister fell backward as tourists screamed and bystanders ran for cover. Accounts of the shooting varied, but the most sensational and often quoted account said that one of the gunman kneeled over the dying Tal and licked the blood flowing from his wounds and then declared to the horrified onlookers, "We are Black September!"[2]

Those were the days of extraordinary rage in the Middle East. It was not just revenge, it was not just assassination and other feats of violence; it was political theater among emergent and competitive liberation movements that arose among the Palestinians to seek the support, loyalty, and funding from their people and from Arab leaders. They formed a new constellation of nonstate power.

With the defeat of Hubert Humphrey in 1968, Richard Nixon had finally emerged from the long shadow of his loss to Kennedy in 1960. The country had turned against the Democratic establishment that supported the costly escalations in Vietnam, where sanguinary guerrilla warfare had shredded American lives at a rate the public would no longer support. The Middle East had receded as a distant cauldron during the presidential campaign and so Yasser Arafat's debut on *Time* magazine's cover a month after Nixon's victory was only a passing reminder of the instability of the region.

Nixon had assumed the presidency with a self-image of an American de Gaulle—an old warrior called back to rescue the nation from strategic lassitude, foreign entanglement, and domestic strife.[3] His long conversations in March 1969 with the French president during Nixon's first journey to Europe had yielded moments of profound satisfaction because de Gaulle, the visionary who looked out across decades, had described the shifting forces in the world in terms similar to Nixon's thinking: Russia was preparing for global war while also contemplating peace; China was emerging; the West, distracted by domestic affairs and Vietnam, needed to organize its defenses. Nixon had found de Gaulle invigorating because in a world still dominated by the memory of titans—Roosevelt, Churchill and, need it be said, de Gaulle—here was a man of the older generation who took Nixon seriously.[4]

The former vice president styled himself as a cold war leader who would be tougher—brutal, if necessary—than Kennedy and Johnson had been in dealing with the Soviet Union because force was the language the Kremlin understood. At the same time, Nixon would stabilize relations and seek cooperation because that was the pragmatic thing to do, given the threat of mutual nuclear annihilation. One thing was certain when Nixon arrived at the White House: there would be no second term unless he found a way to get U.S. troops out of Vietnam. Nixon was determined to persuade the Communist camp—Hanoi and its backers in Moscow and Beijing—to allow America to make a dignified exit from Vietnam. It was not Nixon's war, and he was willing to end it so long as America was not humiliated.

Strangely, though Nixon warned publicly at the outset of his term that the Middle East was a "powder keg," the region otherwise was not on the presidential agenda. Yet Nixon's presidency marked America's full entry into the Middle East; the United States, for the first time, committed itself emphatically to arming Israel and Iran as major regional powers. Their mission was to counter the Arab rearmament after the Six-Day War, to deter Soviet-backed radicals among the Arab regimes, and to protect the flow of oil—more critical than ever to the American economy and the industrialized world. The commitments Nixon would make in the Middle East were not especially premeditated; indeed, like Eisenhower, Kennedy, and Johnson before him, Nixon would find himself reacting to events. His Middle East policies reflected his general belief that America could arm regional allies (Iran and Israel) and allow other emerging powers to develop unmolested (India and China) as a balancing act against Soviet power. Hence Nixon's quiet decision to drop American opposition to Israel's nuclear weapons program.[5] The American failure in Vietnam had triggered psychological and strategic retrenchment at home, and so Nixon's strength would depend on how well he played a weak hand.

In Henry Kissinger, Nixon had an unusually bright and activist national security adviser who would become the first Jewish secretary of state in 1973. Kissinger's ascension would have a profound impact on America's Middle East policy for two reasons: first, because from the beginning he set out to undermine the Middle East initiatives of his rival, William P. Rogers, secretary of state from 1969 to 1973; and second, because his own management of foreign policy tilted so markedly toward Israel's regional interests that American policy actually enhanced Israeli resistance to the peace overtures of Anwar Sadat. More than any other official, Kissinger authored the notion that without a disproportionate bias in American policy toward Israel, the Arab camp would sense a loss of American support for the Jewish state and rush in to annihilate it. He seemed deaf to the advice of his more knowledgeable peers that this was a military impossibility because of Israel's total mobilization of its society for defense, but also because the U.S. Sixth Fleet stood as Israel's ultimate security guarantor (not to mention the broader point that Americans in large proportion supported Israel's security). Yet, by the end of the Nixon administration in 1974, Israel would be straining under the load of American arms that Nixon and Kissinger authorized, and the sheer size of the arsenal would lead Israeli generals, and their political patrons, to contemplate offensive military operations to alter the balance of power in the region, the invasion of Lebanon being the most devastating example. And when the Watergate scandal drove Nixon to take even greater risks in the hope of bringing about peace in the Middle East, it would be Kissinger who pulled the plug on his president, refusing to execute Nixon's last major overture to Leonid Brezhnev in the era of détente.

Vietnam had brought Nixon into office, but just weeks after the inauguration in 1969, the Sinai thundered with artillery duels along the Suez Canal in a new round of combat. That's when Nixon said publicly that the Middle East was a "powder keg" that could explode at any time. Gamal Abdul Nasser, whom Nixon, as a private citizen, had met during his years out of office, was pursuing a strategy to bleed Israel in a war of attrition, forcing a sustained Israeli mobilization that would devastate Israel's economy. Golda Meir was presiding over—*ruling* would be too strong a word—a divided cabinet that included powerful hawks, such as Menachem Begin and Moshe Dayan, who were determined to strike back at Egypt. The Meir government responded by mounting deep-penetration bombing raids throughout the Nile Valley to shake the foundations of Nasser's regime. American-made Phantoms bearing the Star of David bombed Cairo and its suburbs in a strategy to topple the Egyptian leader. The Suez Canal itself was choked with the rusting hulks of ships Nasser had ordered sunk in 1967 to block the waterway until the Israelis agreed—or were forced—to withdraw from Sinai.[6] In the Egyptian rear area west of the canal, new Soviet weapons arrived to replace those lost during the Six-Day War.

Before he took the oath of office, Nixon had sent William Scranton, the former Pennsylvania governor, on a tour of the Middle East to see whether there were any opportunities for diplomacy. It was just a fact-finding mission, but Scranton set off Jewish Americans when he said he would recommend a more "evenhanded" approach in the region, one that took "into consideration the feelings of all persons and all countries in the Middle East and [did] not necessarily espouse [the views of] one nation over some other." His remarks were taken as code that Nixon might tilt toward the Arabs. The blowback was so intense that Nixon dropped Scranton instantly.

. . .

Terrorism, that is to say spectacular feats of violence meant to shock the international community and garner attention to a cause, had been largely absent from the Middle East since the days of the British mandate. But the catastrophe (for the Arabs) of the Six-Day War—the failure of Arab leadership—had given rise to a new Palestinian militancy that would astound and repulse. Yasser Arafat and his al-Fatah organization was but one of the militant groups seeking to lead the Palestinian resistance movement. Al-Fatah had been created in the early 1950s when Arafat and Salah Khalaf, both students at Cairo University, gathered a cell of like-minded Palestinian students and dedicated themselves to armed struggle against Israel. (*Fatah* is a reverse acronym for the Arabic rendering of Palestinian National Liberation Movement.)

Arafat came from a respected Jerusalem family on his mother's side and grew up among the Arab notables of the Holy Land who fought the creation of the Jewish state. He spent a lifetime concealing the details of his birth, perhaps because he had been born in Cairo and considered his Egyptian connection distracting to his Palestinian profile.[7] In 1948, he helped run guns into Gaza (where Nasser was a young officer serving in King Farouk's army), and by the time Arafat got to the university, he was a veteran of political agitation for the Palestinian cause.

Khalaf, known for most of his life as Abu Iyad, was Arafat's partner, adjutant, and intellectual foil. Five years younger, Khalaf was fourteen when his family fled Jaffa, the ancient port south of Tel Aviv, under fire from Jewish militia guns less than twenty-four hours before Israel proclaimed its statehood.

"I clambered onto a makeshift boat with my parents, my four brothers and sisters, and other relatives," he later wrote. "I was overwhelmed by the sight of this huge mass of men, women, old people and children, struggling under the weight of suitcases or bundles, making their way painfully down the wharfs of Jaffa in a sinister tumult. Cries mingled with moaning and sobs, all punctuated by deafening explosions."[8]

After the Arab defeat, Fatah emerged as the largest and most powerful of the resistance groups loosely affiliated under the PLO umbrella and its executive committee. Arafat built the first Fatah networks in the occupied West Bank to support guerrilla attacks on Israeli military outposts.

The Battle of Karameh, in March 1968, put Fatah and Arafat on the political map. The Israeli army sent an armored force into Jordan to wipe out the Fatah base in the town just a few miles from Jericho in the Jordan

Valley. Arafat had decided to make a stand against the superior force, and though the PLO guerrillas fought tenaciously, they were falling back when the battle was saved by Jordanian artillery units that moved forward and mauled the Israeli assault force.

Militarily, the Battle of Karameh inflicted significant losses on Fatah, but the combined PLO and Jordanian defense was so punishing to the Israelis—leaving thirty dead and several armored vehicles, including a tank, destroyed—that the Arab street rejoiced.

Here were young Palestinians fighting the Israelis to a standstill and reclaiming the dignity of the Arabs. All manner of exaggerations about the battle followed, and Arafat emerged as the face of Palestinian resistance. On the cover of *Time*, he was identified as a "fedayeen leader" under a headline that said "Arab commandos" were a "defiant new force in the Middle East." Young Palestinians swarmed to join Fatah's ranks.

Arafat's chief rival was the Popular Front for the Liberation of Palestine, founded by George Habash, a Christian Palestinian whose family had fled its home in Lydda (now Lod, Israel) in 1948 and walked forty miles to Jerusalem through raging gun battles and hordes of panicked refugees. Habash had grown up in Lebanon, where he studied medicine at the American University in Beirut. But instead of practicing, Habash pursued Arab nationalist politics as a Palestinian devotee of Nasser. He founded the PFLP after the 1967 war. Habash avoided frontal attacks on Israel. Instead, he embraced a concept of "revolutionary violence"—hitting Israel's vulnerable spots: its national airline, El Al; its embassies and offices in Europe; and civilian markets inside Israel.

In July 1968, as Arafat and his Fatah fighters were recovering from their "victory" at Karameh, PFLP gunmen hijacked an El Al flight from Rome to Tel Aviv and diverted the plane to Algiers, where after a month's standoff, the hijackers released the passengers and crew. Israel released sixteen Arab guerrillas two days later. Over the next two years, Habash's PFLP cut a swath of terror through the airline industry. His gunmen attacked El Al planes or passengers in Athens, Munich, and Zurich. They bombed the El Al office in Brussels and threw grenades at the Israeli embassies in Bonn and The Hague.

In Jordan, where two-thirds of the population was Palestinian, Arafat's popularity soared, but he was inexperienced in politics. He flirted with mutiny. He undermined King Hussein's authority even as the king sought to accommodate the PLO presence. PLO bases, safe houses, armories, and checkpoints dotted the hills of Amman. Fatah commanded a fifteen thousand-man militia that was bivouacked in neighborhoods and refugee camps. The PLO ran roughshod over the Jordanian army. Its gunmen humiliated the king's soldiers. There were PLO courts and gun-toting security men in leather jackets who gave Amman the ambience of a warlord encampment. Arafat had said that the PLO did not want the distraction of taking over Jordan, but events made a lie of his disclaimer. As time went on, hubris and growing PLO military power fueled ambition and delusion about the organization's ability to defeat the Jordanian army.

Nasser tried to mediate. In Egypt, he was under enormous strain from the Israeli bombing campaign meant to force him from office. In January 1970, he secretly traveled to Moscow, where he told Leonid Brezhnev, the new strongman of the Politburo, that unless the Soviet Union took over the air defense of Egypt, he would resign and install a pro-American successor. The Nixon administration had looked on helplessly as Brezhnev won Politburo approval to airlift fifteen thousand Soviet technicians, pilots, and air defense crews to Egypt. Dozens of new SAM (surface-to-air missile) installations were delivered along with 150 advanced aircraft. The Soviet deployment brought the Israeli bombing campaign to a halt.

Thus reinforced at home, Nasser summoned Arafat and King Hussein to Cairo. To Arafat, Nasser was harsher. The Egyptian leader had shut down the PLO radio station after the voice of the Palestinian resistance had called Nasser a "traitor" for engaging in cease-fire diplomacy with Israel. Nasser explained to Arafat that the Arabs needed time to build a "rocket wall" to stop the Israeli air force and to rebuild Arab armies for the resumption of the war against the Zionist state.

"Don't give me heroic speeches about resistance," Nasser had snapped. "I want to keep [King] Hussein. I am not asking your secrets, but I tell you: do not try to do such a thing [as toppling the monarchy]."

To King Hussein, Nasser said, "I oppose any action you may be contemplating against the [Palestinian] *fedayeen* [fighters]."

The king returned to Amman, where he learned that Nasser had collapsed and died from a heart attack after seeing off the Arab leaders who had come to help secure the truce. Sadat, never taken seriously as Nasser's understudy, was now in charge of Egypt, though perhaps only until a stronger figure emerged. With Nasser gone, Arafat threw down the gauntlet: "If the [Jordanian] government wants a showdown our revolution will be obliged to take action, but this showdown will be the last and our armed revolutionary masses will determine the result—inevitable victory."[9] The next night, King Hussein's motorcade was nearly hit by a rocket-propelled grenade in a blatant assassination attempt. The king publicly warned the PLO that he would brook no challenge to his authority. The Jordanian army moved into action against the PLO. Arab leaders warned the king not to strike. Iraq threatened to send its army into Jordan to protect the Palestinians, but the purge began nonetheless.

On September 6, George Habash's PFLP gunmen went on their hijacking rampage, seizing five airliners in three days and blowing up four of them in the desert. Arafat and the entire resistance movement faced condemnation. The PLO had been forced to criticize Habash's actions and suspend him from its executive committee, but on the Palestinian street, Habash was a hero who had internationalized the plight of Palestinians. Grand terrorism was now a new stage in the conflict.

Jordan's assault on the PLO unfolded in stages, with the first strikes in September 1970 and a final assault in July 1971. The PLO was forced to flee and regroup, moving its headquarters to Lebanon, where it could manage only limited attacks on northern Israel. It was not enough to slake the impulse for vengeance. The popular Arab reaction to Habash's terrorism infected Fatah's leaders and, thus, Black September was born, with Khalaf secretly overseeing its operations. Wasfi al-Tal had been its first target.

"By nature as well as by conviction, I am resolutely opposed to political assassinations and, more generally to terrorism," Khalaf later wrote in a memoir. "Revolutionary violence, on the other hand, is part of a large, structured movement. It serves as a supplementary force and contributes, during a period of regrouping or defeat, to giving the movement more impetus.

"Black September was never a terrorist organization," he asserted. "It acted as an auxiliary to the resistance when the resistance was no longer in a position to fully assume its military and political tasks."[10]

After the failed attempt on King Hussein's life, the next assassination target was Zaid Rifai, Hussein's boyhood friend and Jordan's ambassador to Great Britain. For anyone who has driven through the elegant Belgravia section of London, it is easy to imagine the sheer terror of seeing a man standing on a traffic island suddenly pull a submachine gun from under his coat and open fire from close range. This is what Rifai saw on December 15, 1971. He dove for the floor of his limousine. The gunman emptied his magazine on the car but, miraculously, Rifai suffered only a hand wound.

During the first half of 1972, Black September waged a bombing campaign against Jordanian embassies and airline offices in Europe. In May, four Black September terrorists hijacked a Sabena airliner flying from Brussels to Israel and brazenly landed near Tel Aviv, where they demanded the release of hundreds of Palestinians imprisoned there. Moshe Dayan, the defense minister, stalled for time and assembled a commando team, which stormed the plane and killed two hijackers and captured two others, losing only one passenger to a fatal gunshot wound.

Black September's day of infamy came on September 5, 1972, when it sent a squad of terrorists over the six-foot security wall of the Olympic Village at Munich and seized eleven Israeli athletes. Two of them were killed resisting their captors, who demanded the release of Palestinian prisoners. But the remaining nine died later that day in a hail of bullets and grenade explosions on an airport runway as German police executed a poorly prepared rescue operation. The Munich Massacre, as it came to be called, was the most dramatic hostage drama ever to unfold before a worldwide television audience. And for Israelis, thirty years after the Holocaust, here were Jews again being slaughtered in Germany, this time by Arabs. Almost everything that could have gone wrong in the attempts to save the Israeli athletes had gone wrong, down to the final moments when the ABC sports announcer Jim McKay got word the hostages had been rescued only to retract the statement moments later. "Our worst fears have been realized tonight—they're all dead," he said in a live broadcast.

The attack was said to have stirred Golda Meir to authorize Operation Grapes of Wrath, a combined military and intelligence campaign to track and kill PLO operatives throughout Europe and the Middle East. Some were connected to Black September and others not. Israeli forces hit PLO bases in southern Lebanon, and in a larger raid north of Beirut they destroyed the facilities where the military said "the murderers of Munich" had trained with Japanese terrorists who had attacked Tel Aviv's airport in May 1972, killing twenty-six people.

But Arafat stayed on the offensive in a campaign of blood that deeply troubled moderate Palestinians and some leading members of his movement. The PLO even singled out America for retribution. One of the Munich conspirators, a senior Fatah operative named Abu Daoud, was preparing a spectacular attack on the United States embassy in Amman when Jordanian intelligence officers arrested him in February. Jailed and subjected to torture, Abu Daoud gave a detailed accounting of his role in the Munich Massacre.

With Abu Daoud in prison in Jordan, Arafat and Khalaf shifted to an alternate plan.

On March 1, 1973, President Nixon and Kissinger were hosting Golda Meir in Washington. Seated in the Oval Office, Meir flattered Nixon on his success in Vietnam. Kissinger and Le Duc Tho had just achieved the breakthrough, arranging an interval for U.S. withdrawal that would spell the eventual collapse and defeat of South Vietnamese forces.

"I want to give you congratulations from the depth of my heart on your revolutionizing the world and creating for the first time hope in the hearts of people that we are approaching the end of wars," she said.

Nixon was a little ill at ease. Israel had just shot down a civilian Libyan airliner that lost its way in a dust storm while flying into Cairo. It had overshot the Egyptian capital and flown over the Israeli-occupied zone in Sinai, where an air defense battery shot it out of the sky, killing more than one hundred passengers and crew. Nixon said the United States would forgo any public condemnation.

Meir was still defensive. "I want you to know that at the UN in January, we got warnings from friends that the Black September Organization was planning a plane full of explosives to crash into an Israeli city," she said, foreshadowing a tactic that would be employed against the United States nearly thirty years later. "At Lod, we had Japanese kamikazes [referring to the May 1972 terrorist attack on the airport]. So we had to consider it a serious matter."

Despite the tension over the shoot-down, Nixon and Meir agreed on a deal to sell Israel more Phantoms and to do so in a manner that would minimize public disclosure. Nixon wanted Meir, in return, to "get off dead center" in negotiations with the Arabs and to rein in pro-Israel senators, like Henry Jackson, who was holding up trade benefits for Moscow that were needed to give substance to his policy of détente.

"For us to make progress here is in your hands," Nixon told her. "We can't face down the Soviet Union any more—it would mean mutual suicide.

"Let us develop a Soviet policy so we can influence them," he added, and then he stood up to show her out.[11]

That was just before noon. At 3:05 p.m. Kissinger sent Nixon an urgent message. Arab terrorists had seized the Saudi embassy in Khartoum, where most of the senior diplomats posted to Sudan were attending a reception. They included the American ambassador, Cleo A. Noel Jr., and the deputy chief of mission, George Curtis Moore. By the end of the afternoon, Nixon knew that it was Black September. They had stormed into the reception and were holding Noel and Moore as well as top Belgian, Jordanian, and Saudi diplomats, and some family members. They demanded the release of their comrade Abu Daoud in Jordan and seventeen other terrorists being held in Jordan, and they demanded the release of the Palestinian Sirhan Sirhan, the murderer of Robert F. Kennedy, from prison in California.

Cleo Noel, fifty-four, and Curt Moore, forty-seven, were foreign service veterans who had known each other since the 1950s, when they studied Arabic together at the Foreign Service Institute in Washington. They had traveled broadly in the Middle East and were part of the "Arabist" tradition in the foreign service. Noel had just arrived in Sudan in January, leaving Washington before he received Senate confirmation because the State Department wanted to reward Sudan's decision to reestablish formal diplomatic relations with the United States. Sudan, like most Arab countries, had broken relations with Washington over the war in 1967. Moore had kept the embassy open during the period of estrangement, and his six-foot figure was well-known in Khartoum, where he and his wife, Sally, were popular with the Sudanese and within the diplomatic corps. At a small ceremony at the embassy that day, Noel, with his wife Lucille holding the Bible, was sworn in by Moore, the Senate having voted its advice and consent. Moore was scheduled to depart Khartoum the following Monday after three and a half years, so the evening at the home of Abdullah al-Malhouk, the Saudi ambassador, had been both a welcome and a farewell.

Then the Black September team burst in. It was all over in twenty-four hours. The terrorists issued their demands and set a deadline. The Sudanese tried to stall. Nixon, during a news conference in Washington, foolishly said, "We will do everything that we can to get them released, but we will not pay blackmail." The terrorists heard his remarks, as did Black September's leaders monitoring events from other Middle Eastern capitals. A radio message was transmitted for them to carry out their orders. Some alleged that it came directly from Arafat.[12]

Noel was allowed to make a call to his embassy. "Is there any word from Washington on the demands?"

The embassy officer replied, "Negative."

Noel asked if *any* information had been received.

The embassy officer, knowing the terrorists were monitoring the call, said, "We expect somebody from Washington later tonight."

"That will be too late," Noel replied.[13]


At 8:15 p.m., the leader of the Black September squad telephoned a Sudanese official and told him that they were going to kill the three Western hostages, Noel, Moore, and Guy Eid, a Belgian diplomat. Moore cried out, "Untie my hands. If I am going to die, I want to talk with my wife first." Noel, too, asked to speak with his wife. But the gunmen gave them paper and said they could write a final message to their families. Eid, who had been beaten badly, did not have the strength to write and broke into tears.

"Cleo and I will die bravely and without tears as men should," Moore said in his note to Sally. Noel turned to the Saudi ambassador, who would be spared, and told him that he and Moore did not in any way hold their host responsible for the assault and for what was about to happen. He thanked al-Malhouk for his hospitality.

They were marched into a basement. An embassy lookout in a darkened building near the Saudi ambassador's residence heard five bursts of submachine gun fire.

The security officer at the embassy radioed, "We think they're dead."

The bodies were brought home for state funerals and, in May, Lucille Noel and Sally Moore visited Nixon at the White House. The president said he was pressing the United Nations to do something about terrorism. The Soviets and Israelis were doing the same.

Countries were getting torn apart "because of the damned terrorism," he said. "It's poisoning the whole Middle East.

"It gets down to the Arab-Israeli problem," Nixon told them. "I've talked to Mrs. Meir as strongly as possible. Egypt is tough; Jordan is reasonable. The best way to get at terrorism is to get at the Arab-Israeli dispute."

Nixon had asked if there was anything he could do.

"Everyone has been so helpful," Lucille Noel said.

"There's so little we can do," the president said. "We will work for a peaceful world—what your husbands worked for."

He asked them where they lived.

In Washington, they replied.

"Washington is pretty in the spring," Nixon said. "I also like it in the summer—the long evenings. I go out on the *Sequoia* after long days of work." He must have realized he was talking about himself instead of their grief.

"I can only thank you for your sacrifice," he concluded. "Be of good faith. This will pass. We are with you."[14]

In June of that year, Nixon traveled to San Clemente, California, where he was hosting Leonid Brezhnev at the Western White House as part of a superpower summit. On the night of the twenty-third, after a full day of meetings, Nixon went to bed early. At 10:30, Kissinger sent word that Brezhnev apparently wanted to have another meeting. Nixon roused himself and stepped sleepily out of his bedroom to see what it was all about. The pall of Watergate had been weighing on the president, but he was putting up a tough front. He would weather it, he said. He would protect the presidency from those who wanted to tear it all down.

A fire was lit in the study that overlooked the Pacific Ocean. Brezhnev arrived with Andrei Gromyko, his foreign minister, and Anatoly Dobrynin, the Soviet ambassador in Washington. When they were all settled, Nixon and Kissinger learned that Brezhnev wanted to talk about the Middle East.

"I could not sleep, Mr. President," Brezhnev began apologetically.

The U.S.-Soviet summit was in its final hours and the Middle East had not been on the agenda. Nixon and Brezhnev had completed work on a document with the high-sounding name "Agreement on the Prevention of Nuclear War," a set of guidelines the superpowers agreed to follow in crises. Nixon and Kissinger had wrestled with Brezhnev over China. The Soviets had been secretly weighing an attack on China since the summer of 1969, so it was relevant, to say the least, how the agreement's provisions bore on America's response to such an attack. Brezhnev feared Mao Zedong as a madman with a growing nuclear arsenal. Brezhnev was a man of big emotions and he showed a visceral hatred for the Chinese. The Chinese arsenal would be ten times larger in a decade. The superpowers had an opportunity—a responsibility—to disarm Mao, Brezhnev had argued.

Nixon had flirted with the idea of going along with a Soviet attack to strip Mao of his nuclear weapons complex if Brezhnev in return would help Nixon bring North Vietnam to the negotiating table. Brezhnev couldn't—or wouldn't—deliver, and that had put Nixon back on the road to China, seeking some leverage against both Moscow and Hanoi.[15]

Brezhnev had never given up on his China option, but the Middle East was now urgently on his mind. The failure of diplomacy since the Six-Day War—Israel's refusal to give up land, the Arabs' refusal to recognize or negotiate with the Jewish state—had created an inexorable military preparation on the Arab side for another round of war.

Kissinger had given the Soviets no hope that the White House was prepared to exert any political pressure on Israel. As he explained to Brezhnev, "It is hard to convince Israel why they should give up the territory in exchange for something they already have [a cease-fire], in order to avoid a war they can win." Kissinger's attitude reflected the hubris of the time about Israel's invincibility. The Arab states could not expect to reclaim through negotiation that which they had lost in combat. William Rogers, Nixon's secretary of state, had said as much to Nasser's foreign minister, Ismail Fahmy: "Don't forget that you have lost the war and therefore have to pay the price."[16]

Somewhere, a line had been crossed in America's relationship with Israel. The Jewish state had gone from being a tiny and troublesome power in the Middle East that the United States kept at arm's length despite strong sentimental bonds to the Jewish community in America to become a regional powerhouse equipped with American tanks and warplanes, and its own nuclear weapons. It had devastated the Arab armies in 1967, outgunning Soviet arms. Israeli leaders, Yitzhak Rabin among them, had seen that the cold war could transform the Jewish state into an indispensable U.S. ally, sharing intelligence from Mossad's Soviet bloc spy networks and passing on nuggets of secret information from the Arab world. America had benefited from Israeli intelligence coups, such as when Mossad delivered a Russian MiG fighter to the CIA at the height of the Vietnam War, and when Rabin handed over to Kissinger a complete transcript of a Brezhnev meeting in the Kremlin with Arab leaders.[17] The transformation of U.S.-Israeli relations was unmistakable: From the low point of the Eisenhower years and the wariness of John Kennedy, the relationship had warmed and matured significantly during the Johnson years and had evolved into a more calculated embrace by Nixon. Israel was becoming more fully identified in the Middle East as an American surrogate, though Washington still had only marginal influence over the Jewish state. The requirements of the cold war and Israel's skill at fund-raising and political lobbying were giving it an outsize influence in Washington, where major figures in the Senate—Henry "Scoop" Jackson, Jacob Javits, Hubert Humphrey, and Alan Cranston—became staunch advocates of an Israeli-centric view of the region.

Nixon tended to look at the Middle East in domestic political terms, which is why he was keeping the issue away from the White House. William Rogers, his first secretary of state, had been in charge of the Middle East while the president focused on Vietnam, the Soviets, China and, increasingly, the Watergate scandal. He had indulged Rogers's desire to float the first comprehensive Middle East peace proposal, the Rogers Plan, which had called on Israel to withdraw from the vast majority of Arab land taken in 1967 with only minor adjustments that would not "reflect the weight of conquest." But at the same time, Nixon had undermined Rogers by sending back-channel messages to Golda Meir that she was free to criticize the plan and that Washington would not pressure Israel into any settlement. Kissinger was also extremely wary of the Middle East. He had told the Iranian ambassador in 1973 that he would "get involved" in an attempt to broker some kind of limited peace treaty in the Middle East only "if it's worth it." He added that he didn't think it was worth the effort as long as the Arabs insisted that Israel withdraw from the territories they had occupied in 1967.

"It is also senseless for a country which lost a war to demand [its territory back] as a precondition," he told his Iranian friend. Given that kind of intransigence, Kissinger wondered whether the status quo was the least painful course for the United States since "no conceivable solution is going to be all that acceptable to the Arab governments. Why not let the Egyptians take the heat?"

In the summer of 1973, as the Senate Watergate hearings electrified the American public, and as he waited for Nixon to appoint him as secretary of state to replace the dispirited Rogers, Kissinger was not taking any career risks by diving into the Middle East cauldron.

"I'll be the first one to be assassinated by both the Jews and the Arabs!"[18] he told the Iranian envoy.

Kissinger not only respected the power of the Jewish community in the United States, he and his family were deeply connected to it. They were

Jews who fled Nazi Germany in 1938 when young Heinz—later Henry—was fifteen. As a family, they were committed to the Zionist cause, and that commitment formed the bedrock of Kissinger's view of the Middle East. Moreover, Kissinger's attraction to the shah of Iran was reinforced by the shah's devotion to Israel and by his aversion to Soviet-backed Arab nationalists. In July 1973, Kissinger and the shah, with Nixon's apparent approval, agreed to coordinate on a secret contingency plan to seize control of Saudi Arabia and its massive oil wealth in the event of instability or a radical takeover of the kingdom. Here were Nixon and Kissinger ceding the American security role to a regional autocrat, the shah, whose ambition to dominate the Arabs was growing beyond his competence or capability, as events would later show. But that was the kind of intimate ally the shah had become, on the thinnest record of reliability, except that he was spending billions on American weapons.

"Any contingency planning on Saudi Arabia must be most hush-hush," the shah told Kissinger as the two men met at Blair House, across Pennsylvania Avenue from the White House, on July 24.[19] The shah said he was worried that a coup, whether Soviet-inspired or Arab nationalist–inspired, would invite chaos in Saudi Arabia; steps would have to be taken to protect Western interests. As the shah told Nixon the next day, "The Saudi situation was crucial for the free world" and the kingdom's "oil potential could change for the benefit of the free world."[20]

"As you develop your contingency plans for Saudi Arabia," Kissinger told the shah, "it should be discussed with no one except [Richard] Helms." The former CIA director, whom Nixon had posted to Tehran as ambassador, was designated as the secret conduit for the Iranian design on Saudi Arabia, and though nothing came of this scheme, Kissinger repeatedly warned that "backward" nations like Saudi Arabia were holding the industrialized West hostage by threatening to constrict oil supplies and could continue to do so only at their peril.[21]

Despite these private intrigues, a powerful complacency about the danger building in the Middle East had set in by mid-1973. King Hussein had warned the White House in February and again in May that "a fresh large scale military fiasco is to take place at anytime."[22] The king's generals, after all, were attending the regular war councils in Cairo. In Moscow, Brezhnev felt compelled to try to break the diplomatic logjam because he, more than Nixon, had reason to know that war was coming. The Soviet leader thought that by establishing some principles man-to-man with

Nixon, he could return to the Arabs—Sadat most prominently—and convince them that a negotiation would not be a trap, that Nixon was willing to give a private assurance that Israel was not out to keep Arab lands seized in 1967.

The Arabs had watched the debate in Israel closely after the war. They knew that Dayan, who had twice conquered Sinai, did not want to give it back. Neither did Menachem Begin and his Likud bloc. Further inflaming Arab suspicion, Golda Meir had told the *Sunday Times* of London, "There is no such thing as a Palestinian people," and then added, "It is not as if we came and threw them out and took their country. They didn't exist."[23]

As Israel's commander of the Egyptian front, Ariel Sharon had driven the bedouin population out of northern Sinai to make room for Jewish settlements. The Arabs believed—because there was ample evidence of it—that Israel was seeking to annex Arab lands and that it would adopt a strategy to divide the Arab nations and deal with them one by one to negotiate new boundaries and arrangements for peace and security. The Arabs vowed to stay united.

Brezhnev was concerned that a new war would break out if the superpowers did not do something to prevent it, and that is the likely explanation for his late-night conversation with Nixon at San Clemente in June 1973. Now, seated across from Nixon in the glow of the fireplace, Brezhnev insisted that "we must put this warlike situation" in the Middle East "to an end. The Arabs cannot hold direct talks with Israel without knowing the principles on which to proceed. We must have a discussion on these principles. If there is no clarity about the principle we will have difficulty keeping the military situation from flaring up," he argued. "Everything depends on troop withdrawals and adequate guarantees."[24]

Brezhnev must have thought that he could persuade Nixon with his reference to "adequate guarantees" because it showed that he understood what Israel needed for a permanent peace. But he may not have fully understood the danger such a course posed for Nixon. What if it leaked that the superpowers had colluded at a midnight meeting in San Clemente to establish a principle of total Israeli withdrawal from the occupied territories? The onslaught from the Israel lobby and Congress would cripple Nixon. He was already in the fight of his life with Watergate prosecutors. The scandal had reached the Oval Office. He had been forced to jettison his top aides, H. R. Haldeman and John Ehrlichman. John Dean had told

Watergate investigators that he discussed the cover-up with Nixon dozens of times. The White House taping system had been discovered, and the investigators were aggressively coming after those tapes.

So Nixon was not inclined to enter uncharted territory with Brezhnev. For four years, the Soviets had done little or nothing to help on the diplomatic front, beyond parroting the absolutist Arab positions. They had sent thousands of military advisers into Egypt and Syria to build up the Arab forces with the latest Soviet tanks and modern warplanes. Now, here was Brezhnev, Nixon thought, "trying to browbeat me."[25]

Brezhnev *was* trying to browbeat him, but Nixon and Kissinger misperceived the underlying reason.

"On a subject as difficult as this," Nixon said, "we cannot say anything definitive." Nixon turned to Kissinger for agreement and Kissinger backed him up.

"I am not trying to put you off," Nixon said to Brezhnev. "It is easy to put down principles." But putting down principles could create its own problems, he added.

A frustrated Brezhnev launched into a speech about détente and the superpowers' failure to "find some form of words we can agree on" to win peace in the Middle East. He stated the principles as he saw them: a guarantee for Israel's security, an end to the attacks on Israel from Arab territories, safeguards for Israeli shipping through the Strait of Tiran, and Israeli withdrawal from Arab lands conquered in 1967.

"If we can get agreement on these principles we can then discuss how to use any influence on the contending parties," he said, adding in obvious frustration, "If we don't do that, we have no basis for using our influence." As superpowers, he obviously meant.

More than anyone else in the room, Brezhnev understood that war was coming in the Middle East because the Soviet Politburo had essentially signed up for war when it agreed to rearm Egypt and Syria. Moscow understood in explicit terms—Nasser and Sadat had laid it out—that the Arab states were committed to recovering their lands by force if all attempts at diplomacy failed. No date had been set for such a war, but Brezhnev and the Soviet military leadership could not have missed the many signs of preparation and the joint Arab planning among the general staffs of the Egyptian and Syrian armed forces.

As Brezhnev carried on, Nixon began to lose hope for sleep. He propped his head up with pillows.

"Perhaps I am tiring you out, but we must reach an understanding," Brezhnev said sympathetically. "This is not a demand," he said to Nixon, though his emphasis suggested that it was. "But it is something we should do." He listed the benefits of peace in the Middle East and then said, "We could agree on Vietnam. Why can't we do it here?"

Nixon seemed on the defensive. He told Brezhnev, "We can't settle this tonight."

Nixon went on, "I want you to know I consider the Arab-Israel dispute a matter of highest urgency," but he was sputtering. He started to make a comparison to Vietnam but abandoned the thought. He threw out some stock phrases: "I will say to the General Secretary . . . We disagree only on tactics . . . We must avoid the issue . . ." He couldn't complete a sentence. The president finally said, "We must find words with subtlety that will bring both sides together."

Exactly. Brezhnev said he wanted to try doing so that very night. What was holding back Nixon? Brezhnev wanted to put some of these "principles" into the formal communiqué they would issue as part of their summit: a declaration from the superpowers on the general framework for peace in the Middle East.

"We can't write down everything," Brezhnev said, "but I would like to attach to the communiqué some principles. These would be: withdrawal of Israeli troops, recognition of boundaries, free passage of ships, and guarantees."

Here was Brezhnev, Kissinger thought, springing something at the last moment without any preparation. That may have been how it seemed, but Brezhnev could hardly tell them more explicitly why he feared that war was coming: the Soviet Union was deeply involved in its preparation, Soviet engineers were training the Egyptians on special bridging equipment that could be used to cross the Suez Canal, and Soviet air defense advisers were helping Egyptian forces install a "missile wall" that would stop the Israeli air force. And this was June.

It was well past midnight. Nixon spoke more bluntly. "We are not prepared to go any further. We can't abstractly beat the issue to death. We don't owe anything to the Israelis. That means I'm interested in a settlement. We will work on it." But he admitted that the whole issue of a Middle East settlement was stuck on "dead center."

Brezhnev was tenacious. "I am categorically opposed to a resumption of the war. But without agreed principles that will ultimately help the situation in the area, we cannot do this. We must come to an understanding on this issue," he continued, saying that what he wanted at a minimum was a "gentlemen's agreement" on two or three principles and then they could turn Kissinger and Dobrynin loose to begin the diplomacy to implement them. "We will be loyal to this promise," Brezhnev vowed.

But Nixon said that even an oral agreement was out of the question. "I can go no further," he said.

"Very well," Brezhnev said, how about just one principle: "withdrawal of forces." Was he joking in exasperation? The Soviet leader invoked the spirit of détente; they had worked so hard the previous year to arrange their first summit, despite formidable opposition in the Kremlin and the U.S. bombing in Vietnam.

"Bear in mind this difficulty," Brezhnev warned. "Do not leave me without this assurance."

But Nixon would say only that he would examine the question in the morning. "It's not as simple as all that," he said. "This could be a goal. But it wouldn't lead to a settlement. We have to face the problem in a pragmatic way."

Brezhnev was at his wit's end. "Without a principle, there is nothing I can do. Without a gentlemen's agreement," he added, there would be nothing for Kissinger and Dobrynin to do in the private channel the two leaders had agreed to establish. "We need a friendly agreement, or I will leave empty-handed."

Nixon was tired of being bullied, or just tired. "We have to break up now," he said. "It would be very easy for me to say that Israel should withdraw from all the occupied territories and call it an agreed principle, but that's what the argument is about."[26]

This midnight encounter over the Middle East in June 1973 stands as a tragic failure of American diplomacy, strategic perception, and communication between the superpowers—a failure that did in fact lead to a devastating war. Brezhnev's initiative, born of détente, was a bridge that a weakened Nixon feared to cross. Both Nixon and Kissinger, writing in their memoirs, asserted that the Soviet purpose that night was "to browbeat me into imposing on Israel a settlement based on Arab terms," as Nixon put it. Kissinger, more excitedly, asserted that "twenty-four hours after renouncing the threat of force in the Agreement on the Prevention of Nuclear War, Brezhnev was in effect menacing us with a Middle East war unless we accepted his terms."[27]

But there is scant evidence of this in the official U.S. record, which reveals Brezhnev pressing, cajoling, and almost pleading with Nixon to come to agreement—not on Arab terms but on the "principles" for peace, with equal emphasis on Israel's security needs. Brezhnev made clear that in trying to bring the Arab leaders to the negotiating table with Israel, he needed reassurance from Nixon that Israel would not be allowed to dictate new borders. Kissinger's interpretation that Brezhnev was "menacing" the United States with a Middle Eastern war distorted Brezhnev's mission in the extreme. He was seeking to head off a new round of war through a collaborative diplomatic effort. His plea for a cooperative approach based on shared principles that included "guarantees" for Israel was dismissed by Kissinger as "a blatant attempt to exploit Nixon's presumed embarrassment over Watergate."

In fact, it appears that it was a genuine effort to avert war in the spirit of the agreement on the prevention of war whose terms the two leaders had just blessed. Israeli intelligence, according to Yitzhak Rabin, had confirmed that Brezhnev had been acting with "restraint," admonishing Sadat "not to go to war without coordinating with the Russians."[28] Yet Nixon's stiff and unyielding response to Brezhnev revealed not only the paralysis of Watergate but also a misreading of the Soviet predicament. Most of all, Nixon failed to understand Sadat's determination to change his circumstances even as he built up his army with Soviet weapons and even as warnings came in from other Arab leaders that Sadat was serious.

A week later, as Kissinger was cruising the Potomac River aboard *Sequoia*, he admitted to members of Nixon's Foreign Intelligence Advisory Board that the United States was simply stalling in the Middle East. "Israel is so much stronger that the dilemma is on the Arabs. Right now, Israel is asking for their immediate surrender, and the Arabs are seeking for a miracle. We want to help, but we will not put out a plan for both to shoot at."[29]

Sadat was desperate to break the American complacency. He had invited Arnaud de Borchgrave, *Newsweek*'s senior international editor, to Cairo in March and told him war was the next stage. "If we don't take our case in our own hands, there will be no movement," Sadat said. "Everything is now being mobilized in earnest for the resumption of the battle— which is now inevitable." Sadat added that war "will be the nightmare to end all nightmares—and everybody will be losers."

The Egyptian leader shaped his clipped sentences like artillery rounds of warning. "Everyone has fallen asleep over the Middle East crisis," he said. "But they will soon wake up. The time has come for a shock!"

Sadat said that all of his attempts to offer Israel an opening for negotiations had been rejected by Golda Meir. He would continue to pursue diplomacy, he said, but that would not preclude going to war. "They are occupying territory in three Arab countries. Let's see if they can stay like this," he said. "I say they can't. And you will soon see who is right."[30]

Ashraf Ghorbal, a diminutive diplomat who served as Sadat's spokesman, sat in on the interview, and when he heard those words he blanched. Ghorbal had just returned from a posting as the Egyptian ambassador in Washington. He had been telling American officials, "We want peace. We want peace. We want peace." Now Sadat was talking war.

When the interview ended, Ghorbal spoke up, pointing out to Sadat, in front of the journalist, that the remarks were very strong. "You know what the headlines will be in *Newsweek* and in all the papers? That Sadat wants to go to war."

Sadat flared: "Hell, that's what I just said."[31]

But Washington thought Sadat was bluffing. That was the conclusion the CIA had reached. Israeli intelligence could not imagine that Sadat would try to attack across the canal unless he was sure he could establish air superiority, and Egypt was not even close to that. Thanks to Johnson, and now Nixon, Israel had been able to more than double the combat power of its air force with deliveries of F-4 Phantoms. The Phantom was the top of the line. It could carry seven tons of bombs and missiles and maneuver as tightly as an interceptor. Sadat did not want to go to war, but as Nasser's successor, he had inherited the Arab strategy to remove the "traces of aggression." No Egyptian leader could rest until the Sinai was recovered. Yet the world was not taking Sadat seriously. He had been Nasser's clown, a sycophant known as Major "Yes Sir!" for his obsequious devotion to the boss. Sadat was more religious than most of his corevolutionaries, and his forehead bore the mark of a lifetime of prostration in prayer. But the joke was that his forehead was disfigured because Nasser kept beating Sadat's head against the wall for being thick. Still, Nasser always indulged Sadat, perhaps because Sadat, like Nasser, had come from humble origins.

Sadat's first home was the village of Mit Abu el-Kom, one of a thousand enclaves of mud-brick hovels tucked among the palm and jacaranda trees in the green expanse that stretches from Cairo to Alexandria. Even more intensely than Nasser, Sadat had known the rhythms of agrarian life in the delta, where villagers worked communally at planting and reaping and where only minarets poked above the skyline of vegetation. The air was rich—manure and jasmine—above villages strewn along canals in the dense lushness fostered by the Nile's final run to the sea. As a correspondent for *The Washington Post*, I traveled this country. There, the dawn arrives like fingers through the greenery, illuminating the languid gait of men in cotton galabias as they shuffle toward the fields or guided donkeys to market. Women chatter under their bundles, balancing palm fronds or water jars on their heads, herding children toward the school or mosque. Water buffalo lumber out of the shadows toward the mud paddies for their daily task of muscling the plow while camels sniff regally near brass-pot men who dispensed the *foul*, a starchy bean slurry that is a staple of life.

At the end of each day, dusk softens the brassy hue of the sun and the enveloping desert. The air fills with the haze of homefires so sweet and pungent that it is impossible to be indifferent to the aroma of life. Across these vistas, light fades quickly to blue gauze, then black under the stars. And just before sunrise, the call to prayer starts it all again.

Sadat spent his first six years in the care of a strong grandmother while his father was away in the Sudan working for the British army. He idealized this early period as the one that shaped his identity and formed his connection with the land and people of Egypt. Sadat did so, in part, because the period that followed, when his father moved the family to Cairo and brought two additional wives into the household, was traumatic.

In those Cairo years, Sadat and his mother, the daughter of a slave brought up from black Africa, were marginalized by the other wives in a household of thirteen children. Sadat's mother was relegated to the status of a servant and suffered regular beatings from Sadat's father. As a result, young Anwar, self-conscious and comparatively dark-skinned, spent these years withdrawn. He lived in a state of forced submissiveness to the violence directed against his mother. Mohamed Heikal, the newspaper editor who made the transition from Nasser to Sadat as chief editorialist for the regime, observed that Sadat spent his life searching for "sympathy and understanding." As a leader, Sadat took quite naturally to the sybaritic life in the presidential palace, but he also never tired of speaking about the peasantry or of returning to his village.[32]

As a teenager, he had pursued an acting career, trying to escape the grim reality of family life in Cairo. He loved the theater, and as a statesman, drama, costume, and a sense of timing were the hallmarks of his rule. And because he had experienced violence, he was capable of inflicting it, whether in politics, in warfare, or as a dictator suppressing internal enemies. After Nasser died, few Egyptians and even fewer foreigners believed that Sadat would be anything more than a placeholder until a stronger leader emerged. In Cairo, the betting was that Ali Sabri, who was close to the Soviets, would lead a coup against Sadat, but it took only a year for Sadat to outmaneuver his rivals.

He inherited an Egypt that was virtually bankrupt. The canal was still closed. Instead of providing any revenue to the state, it constituted the front line where Egypt faced the Israeli army that occupied Sinai. The Egyptian cotton crop was mortgaged for Soviet arms. Sadat's ministries begged wheat from Moscow, which had its own shortages. Since 1967, Nasser, and now Sadat, had been living off the generosity of Saudi Arabia and the wealthy sheikhdoms of the Persian Gulf. Nasser had hoped, and so did Sadat, that Nixon would follow in the footsteps of Eisenhower and force Israel to withdraw, but neither the Rogers Plan nor any of the subsequent diplomatic efforts had yielded results.

Moshe Dayan had come up with a suggestion, which Sadat had endorsed, for a pullback by both armies of ten miles or so from the canal, which could then open, but Golda Meir had blocked the initiative, inciting Nixon to seethe about her bullheadedness. Nixon, at times, would tell Rogers to take off the gloves with the Israelis. They had gotten too cocky and the tightening oil markets signaled that America would have to win some Israeli concessions for peace if it was to maintain credibility among the Arabs and the security of oil.

Sadat declared 1971 the "year of decision": either Egypt would get Sinai back through diplomacy, or it would go to war. But the year ended with no decision. Sadat was frustrated. Nixon became obsessed with his reelection campaign, staging a showy visit to Beijing in February 1972 and holding a superpower summit with Leonid Brezhnev in Moscow in May. Sadat had never been close to the Soviets. He suspected that they had backed Ali Sabri during the months of conspiracy following Nasser's death. The Soviets had promised more arms, but they were stretching out the deliveries to keep Egypt on a tight leash. For Sadat, all talk of U.S.-Soviet détente was a betrayal of the Soviet pledge to help the Arabs recover their lands. Détente was a threat to smother the explosion that Sadat desperately needed.

On July 8, 1972, Sadat called in the Soviet ambassador, Vladimir Vinogradov, and told him that Egypt was expelling the Soviet military mission in Egypt, a decision that forced Moscow to evacuate thousands of military advisers in a matter of days, all except those still involved in manning vital air defense systems. Sadat hoped that Nixon would recognize the gesture as an overture to the United States and would respond, but Nixon, and much of America, was preoccupied with the 1972 presidential campaign (Nixon versus Senator George McGovern).

No one was paying attention to the mind of Sadat. He complained to *Newsweek*'s de Borchgrave, "My main difficulty with the U.S. [has been] to get the Administration to take a position in the conflict [with Israel] and put it on paper. To this day, there is no solid position paper on the whole problem. [Secretary of State William] Rogers has said that America's commitment to Israel does not extend to the occupation of our land. But that never became official policy. All we see is retrogression—to the point where [Israeli Foreign Minister Abba] Eban now states policy for the U.S."

It was an overstatement, but true enough; Sadat felt trapped.

"He is cornered on all sides," one of his advisers had told *Newsweek*. "And this, I'm afraid, makes President Sadat a dangerous man."

# 4

## NIXON AND KISSINGER

*Yom Kippur—The October War*

Just after 2:00 p.m. on Saturday, October 6, 1973, Egypt commenced one of the most intense artillery barrages in history along the one-hundred-mile front of the Suez Canal. That near-stagnant ribbon of water choked since Nasser's time with the rusting hulks of ships now rippled under every concussion, and the smoke rising from the surrounding desert soon blotted out the midafternoon sun. Three hundred miles to the northeast, the Golan Heights thundered under Syrian guns, whose echo rumbled ominously through the Jordan Valley.

Almost to the last moment, Israel's military intelligence chiefs believed that the Arabs would not strike. Even when the Soviets flew in special planes to evacuate their embassy personnel in Cairo and Damascus, Israeli intelligence did not think war was imminent, an assessment that was mirrored by U.S. intelligence. It was dawn on the East Coast of the United States when the war broke out. In Nixon's morning briefing, already printed for the president, the CIA said that Egypt was unlikely to launch a war that it could not win. Yet the effects of five years of Soviet resupply, training, and joint Arab planning had changed the calculus of war: the Arab armies were more than double the strength of 1967, and they had integrated new antitank and antiaircraft weapons into their formations. The intelligence analysts had miscalculated how this had magnified their capacity to repel Israeli counterattacks.

Sadat chose Yom Kippur, the Day of Atonement and the holiest day of the Jewish calendar, to stage the most dramatic military performance in Egypt's modern history.

During the first minute of the Egyptian barrage, high-explosive artillery rounds exploded against Israeli defenses at the rate of 175 hits per second. Egyptian armored brigades, arrayed behind an earthen berm on the western side of the canal, laid down fire from more than four thousand artillery pieces, multiple rocket launchers, and heavy mortars, throwing hundreds of tons of ordnance onto the Israeli line. Half of the Egyptian air force, more than two hundred planes, under the command of General Hosni Mubarak, flew bombing sorties against Israeli airfields and command centers behind the vaunted Bar-Lev Line, the system of towers, trenches, and revetments that the Israelis had erected in Sinai. It stood like a Maginot Line in the desert; it was meant to hold back the Egyptians with minimal numbers of Israeli troops, thus sparing Israel the high cost of mobilization and reducing casualties during the war of attrition.

Of the five Egyptian planes shot down in the first wave of attacks, one was piloted by Sadat's youngest brother, Atif, who was killed. Mubarak withheld the news so as not to distract his leader.

The canal was only seventy-five yards wide in some places and, like Washington crossing the Delaware, Egyptian forces were most vulnerable during the frantic opening minutes of assault. They had been spared one terrifying obstacle. During the night, Egyptian commandos had cut the pipelines through which Israeli defenders had planned to pump napalm onto the surface of the canal to create an impassible inferno. The first Egyptian wave comprised eight thousand soldiers in one thousand small boats, which established bridgeheads and set up the water cannon and high-pressure pumps that were used ingeniously to "melt" the forty-foot sand wall the Israelis had erected to thwart an armored advance. The water cannons erased fortifications like waves across sand castles.

The first Israeli position fell within an hour. By the end of the afternoon, the water cannons had sliced eighty holes in Israel's desert ramparts. The Egyptians brought up their bridging equipment as soldiers carrying shoulder-mounted antitank missiles sprinted forward on foot to position themselves against Israeli tanks that were expected to advance rapidly to block the penetrations. But there were few Israeli tanks near the front lines, and the armored vehicles that rushed forward exploded and burned under direct hits from Soviet antitank missiles wielded by well-trained Egyptian soldiers. The Israelis fell back as the Bar-Lev Line was breached over and over along the one hundred-mile front. Israeli warplanes streaking in from bases in eastern Sinai flew straight into the "missile wall" of surface-to-air missile batteries that the Soviets had erected to protect the Egyptian forces. Dozens of Israeli fighters, shredded by antiaircraft missiles, fell the first day, and the front-line Israeli brigades lost half, and in one case three-quarters, of their tanks. The battles raged through the night as tens of thousands of Egyptian troops managed to cross the canal. At daybreak Sunday, they had penetrated the Bar-Lev defenses to a depth of two to three miles and were digging in for the expected Israeli counterattack.

The October War—it was called the Yom Kippur War on the Israeli side—descended on the Nixon White House during the high drama leading up to the resignation of Vice President Spiro Agnew, who was facing corruption charges from his days as governor of Maryland. At the same time, an intense struggle was building between Nixon and the special Watergate prosecutor, Archibald Cox, over the prosecutor's demand for copies of the White House tapes relating to the cover-up of the Watergate break-in. Nixon had fled Washington to spend the weekend at his hideaway home on Key Biscayne in Florida. But when news of war in the Middle East reached him, it had the effect of energizing the embattled president. Nixon told General Alexander Haig, his chief of staff, that they ought to return to Washington immediately. Nixon was stunned that both the CIA and Israeli intelligence had failed to predict the outbreak of hostilities after a massive buildup by the Egyptians.

In Israel, Golda Meir had been lulled by her intelligence chiefs. The day before the attack, an Israeli spy based in Europe had given a specific warning that war would be launched on two fronts against Israel at 6:00 p.m., but the Mossad report did not reach the prime minister until the morning of the attack.[1] When she summoned her ministers, Kissinger's advice lay heavily in the room: Israel should avoid firing the first shot.

Meir's initial message to Washington asked Kissinger to put both Egypt and Syria on notice that Israel had no intention of attacking unless it was attacked. This time Israel would absorb the first blow.

Kissinger was in New York holding court with foreign dignitaries. The annual session of the United Nations General Assembly marked the yearly opening of the diplomatic season. Monarchs and ministers swept through the city by motorcade. They dined and parlayed in the finest salons of the Upper East Side of Manhattan. It was Kissinger's first season as secretary of state. He had devoted his speech at the UN to Latin America, a safe subject but one dear to his early patron, Nelson Rockefeller. A frantic call forwarded from Washington reached Kissinger's attention at 6:15 a.m.—just as Egyptian gunners were preparing to open fire seven time zones away—when Joseph Sisco, assistant secretary of state, burst into the secretary's suite on the thirty-fifth floor of the Waldorf Towers to set off the alarm that the Israelis were bracing for an all-out attack. In fact, it would begin within the hour.

Kissinger waited more than two hours before placing his first call to General Haig, who was with the president at Key Biscayne. Kissinger wanted to demonstrate that he had put diplomacy into action, though his efforts lacked any real substance since war was by then under way. He telephoned Anatoly Dobrynin, the Soviet ambassador, and suggested that the two superpowers "restrain our respective friends." Then Kissinger made a series of calls to Israeli and Egyptian diplomats, urging Israel not to strike preemptively and informing Egypt that Israel had no intention of attacking unless it was attacked.

Finally, at 8:35 a.m., with Egyptian and Syrian artillery booming, Kissinger called Haig and filled him in on the steps he had taken.

"We may have a Middle East war going on today."

"Really?" Haig replied, asking whether Kissinger thought the Soviets were behind it.

"I think it is too insane for them to have started it."

Haig warned him that Nixon was under intense pressure. Agnew's resignation was due at any moment. Watergate was raging.

Kissinger blamed Watergate and the Soviets for the outbreak of war.

"I think our domestic situation has invited this," Kissinger said. "I think what may have happened is the Soviets told the Egyptians . . . that there will not be any progress unless there is stirring in the Middle East and those maniacs have stirred a little too much." The Israelis would cer-

tainly "hit back hard" within a day or two, he continued, and there was little to do but assemble the Sixth Fleet in the Mediterranean to be prepared for any contingency.

When Haig called back around noon, he said Nixon was all revved up
to return to Washington. Kissinger said that would be a "terrible mistake."

"I would urge you to keep any Walter Mitty tendencies under control"
in the president, Kissinger said. "What we don't need now is a war council meeting and getting ourselves into the middle of it. We are not in the
middle of it. To the American people it is a local war. Let them beat them
up for a day or two and that will quiet them down."[2]

Haig assured him that he would restrain Nixon if he could, but he in-
timated that Nixon had to come back because Agnew was on the verge of
resigning and the president couldn't be seen as "sitting here in the sun"
while his administration was collapsing and "there is a war going on."

"If he returns early, it looks like a hysterical move," Kissinger said. "We
should use the president when it will do him some good. He must avoid
looking hysterical."[3]

Both Nixon and Kissinger had assumed that Israel would make quick
work of the Egyptian army; that first weekend, Kissinger assured the Chinese ambassador that "within 72 to 96 hours, the Arabs will be completely defeated."[4] But the closely held Israeli intelligence reports from
the battlefield indicated that its forces were losing aircraft and tanks at a
high rate, and that Israel had suffered hundreds of battle deaths, a catastrophic development for a country of only two million people.

Sadat was so giddy with Egypt's early success that he called the Soviet
ambassador on an open telephone line and exclaimed, "Vinogradov, my
boys are riding on the Bar-Lev line. We've crossed the canal! I want you
to telephone our friends in Moscow and tell them my sons are on the
eastern bank of the canal!"[5]

On Sunday, October 7, Golda Meir sent word to Kissinger, asking that
he delay any cease-fire discussion in the UN Security Council for three
or four days. "I have reason to believe by that time, we will be in a position of attack rather than defense. I am sure you will do all in your power
to enable us to achieve this position."[6] Kissinger told Nixon that he felt
very strongly that if the United States did not "break ranks" with Israel
during the crisis, then Israel would be beholden to Nixon in the future.
But Nixon just admonished Kissinger to stay a little more aloof from the
Israelis.

"One thing that we have to have in the back of our minds is that we don't want to be so pro-Israel that the oil states—the Arabs that are not involved in the fighting—will break ranks," Nixon said, adding, "PR is terribly important, even if we don't do anything."[7]

The Israeli leadership brought Kissinger into its confidence from the beginning. Golda Meir's first private message to Kissinger alluded to his advice that in the event of war, Israel should not be seen as the aggressor.

"You know the reason why we took no pre-emptive action," she told him in a hand-delivered message on October 7. "Our failure to take such action is the reason for our situation now," she said, referring to the heavy losses of Israeli aircraft to surface-to-air-missile batteries. "If I had given the chief of staff the authority to pre-empt, as he had recommended some hours before the attacks began, there is no doubt that our situation would now be different."[8]

By 1973, Israeli leaders considered Kissinger their most important asset in the Nixon administration. And Meir had sought to set the hook that he shared responsibility for Israel's fate in the war. The Israelis were realistic about Kissinger's loyalties. He was an American, ambitious to succeed in the Nixon administration. But he was also a Jew and one not indifferent to Israel. Yitzhak Rabin, the war hero who had served as Israel's ambassador to Washington during Nixon's first term, explained Kissinger to an aide: "First and foremost he's an American, no doubt about it, but deep in his heart, he comes from here"—putting his hand on his heart—"the Holocaust and he's a very warm Jew and for him it is a mission to defend us."[9]

Simcha Dinitz, the new Israeli ambassador to Washington, told Kissinger, "The prime minister wishes to convey to you her profound appreciation not only for your help but for your wise counsel. She says in the cable that you understand exactly the situation that goes on in our minds as if you were sitting with us here."[10]

Nixon was less prone to sentimentality about Israel, and he worried about the political consequences of another Israeli rout. The Arab states dominated OPEC, and there were calls across the Middle East to wield the oil weapon against the West. Nixon told Kissinger that the United States must come out of the war with a permanent settlement to the Arab-Israeli dispute, because he would not tolerate "having this thing hang over for another four years and have us at odds with the Arab world. We're not going to do it anymore."[11] Nixon had missed the military significance of Egypt's crossing of the canal. Nixon assumed the Israelis could not be wrong-footed on the battlefield. "They'll cut the Egyptians off— poor dumb Egyptians getting across the Canal and all the bridges will be blown up. They'll cut them all off—thirty or forty thousand of them." And then, after they had finished "clobbering" the Egyptians and the Syrians, the Israelis "will be even more impossible to deal with than before."

Kissinger agreed. "If this thing ends without a blowup with either the Arabs or the Soviets, it will be a miracle and a triumph."[12]

By the fourth day of the war, Israeli commanders faced the prospect of catastrophic collapse of their forces, even defeat. They had lost five hundred tanks and fifty aircraft. Moshe Dayan was so shaken by the prospect that Egyptian forces could break through and attack Israel's main population centers that he told aides and a small group of senior Israeli journalists that Israel might be destroyed. An editor of a major newspaper burst into tears.[13]

Golda Meir muzzled Dayan thereafter. She also put Israel's nuclear forces on alert. By 1973, these forces comprised a small number of French Mirage warplanes with atomic bombs strapped under their wings, and a small force of nuclear-tipped ballistic missiles. The French-designed missiles were already on their launch erectors and at least one Mirage was ordered to sit on the end of its runway, standing by for an order to execute a nuclear strike against the Syrian or Egyptian front.

On Tuesday morning, October 9, Kissinger convened a special meeting of Nixon's top national security advisers. He told them that he had just met with the Israeli ambassador, Simcha Dinitz, and the ambassador's military aide, General Mordechai Gur, who had painted a bleak picture of Israeli losses. Kissinger, however, withheld even from this small group, which included CIA Director William Colby and Defense Secretary James Schlesinger, the alarming figures that Dinitz had confided. Kissinger argued for urgent American assistance, but Schlesinger challenged him. Why would the United States intervene at a moment when the battle favored the Arabs, who were fighting to retake their lands? A prominent American intervention, he suggested, could have a deep and lasting negative impact on the Arab states and their relations with America. Schlesinger had a powerful intellect. He was a hard-liner on the Soviet Union and a skeptic of détente, and Nixon respected him, but Kissinger mistrusted him and complained to Haig that "Defense wants to turn against the Israelis."[14]

Yet Schlesinger was now positing a critical choice for American national interest, and Kissinger seemed too partisan to take it on board. The United States would go to any length to defend Israel's survival, but it was not bound to defend and protect the conquests of 1967.[15] Colby had pointed out that from the CIA's perspective, Israel was holding its own on the Egyptian and Syrian fronts. The war's development suggested a prudent strategy of restraint and a call for a cease-fire. Such a policy, in and of itself, would suggest to the Israelis that holding on to their conquests was no longer possible.

This milestone of American foreign policy in the Middle East passed without public notice, just as Johnson's decision in 1967 to accept Israel's conquest in the Six-Day War had been lost in the noise and wonderment over Israel's triumph, or diverted by American anger over the attack on the USS *Liberty*. By 1973, the historic flaw in Lyndon Johnson's decision to accept the outcome of the Six-Day War had become apparent: the Arabs were convinced that it was a landgrab. With or without premeditation, Israel's victory (and the ensuing triumphalism) propelled its national politics toward strategies and rationalizations to hold on to its territorial gains.

"We changed our minds" was how Abba Eban explained it, but the fresh Israeli claim to the contested territories had further radicalized the Arab and Muslim world. Kissinger defended Israeli triumphalism, arguing that the defeat of Israel by Arab states using Soviet arms would skew "the political as well as the strategic equilibrium in the Middle East." But the war itself proved that there was no strategic equilibrium; rather, there was inherent instability that could be overcome only by concerted superpower pressure to get a permanent peace settlement since the superpowers supplied the arms and the funding for the contestants. The Arabs in 1973 seized a slight advantage on the battlefield. The question the Nixon administration faced was whether it should stand pat and allow the Israelis to come to terms with the consequences of 1967, or whether America—Nixon—would recognize that the 1967 war results had so polarized the region that only peace negotiations, under the auspices of the superpowers, represented a realistic course toward political settlement and the security that Israel had long sought. Without that, the conflict would just go on.

By all accounts, the Arab leaders were not seeking all-out victory but a credible enough showing against the superior Israeli army to attract sustained superpower diplomacy and the return of Arab lands. The Syrian leader, Hafez al-Assad, had even enraged Sadat by allegedly telling the Soviets after the first day of fighting that he was ready for a cease-fire because he had retaken most of the Golan Heights, which was his goal.

The Arab leaders knew from the Soviets that Israel was now a full-fledged nuclear power. They knew they could not defeat the Jewish state. Israel was a reality. But when Kissinger got to Nixon on the afternoon of October 9, the fourth day of fighting, he seemed bent on undermining American restraint by raising an exaggerated alarm. Diplomatic reports were coming in saying that Soviet ambassadors in the Middle East were urging other Arab states to join in the battle against Israel.[16]

Nixon was with Haig, Ron Ziegler, the press secretary, and General Brent Scowcroft, a thoughtful and soft-spoken air force officer who served as Kissinger's surrogate in the White House. Kissinger's description of the threat they were facing was tinged with panic: "If the Arabs sense that the Israelis have lost more than they have admitted, they might rush in," he told the president.[17] Kissinger had never visited the Arab world, and it is hard to imagine what he meant by this remark, since there was no Arab reserve force that could make a difference in the battle. Yes, the other Arab states could replace marginal losses of Egyptian or Syrian warplanes and tanks, but there was minimal interoperability among the Arab armies. What was clear to any junior military analyst was that Egypt and Syria would win or lose based on their own national forces that were committed in the fight. Kissinger's somewhat discursive account of this critical meeting makes no reference to the debate that turned on the question Schlesinger had raised: Was there a distinction between defending Israel and defending her 1967 conquests? It was a question that Nixon, too, regarded as important. But Kissinger, the diplomatic practitioner who admired subtlety in foreign policy, dismissed this as irrelevant "fine tuning."[18]

Nixon had said, "The Israelis must not be allowed to lose," but that was boilerplate. The question was how to calibrate the American resupply of munitions to limit the war and force the Israelis to reconsider whether the conquest of 1967 had brought them additional security.

Here Nixon's initial decision, had it held, might have changed the course of events: He dictated that there would be no large-scale mobilization to airlift tanks and heavy American weapons to Israel. Nixon said he would replace all the tanks and planes *after* the war, but for the present, he would speed the delivery only of ammunition, missiles, mortars, shells—all those things that could be called the "consumables." They would have to be airlifted discreetly, so as not to provoke the Arab side. Nixon had decided that he would not immediately replace the fifty air-craft that Israel had lost. Instead, he would quietly ship two Phantoms per day, meaning that the bulk of the planes would not be available for the short war that was expected. No tanks would be sent before the end of the fighting (Israel still had more than one thousand tanks), but the United States would replace the losses of Israeli tanks and other heavy equipment after the war.[19]

Nixon had given his tough-minded secretary of defense, Schlesinger, the discretion to adjust the American supply line while the war was going on, but within the boundaries of Nixon's strategic guidance. But Kissinger, from the outset, maneuvered as if he were a partisan for Israel's war aims as they were communicated to him by Meir and her advisers. Kissinger opposed any gain by the Arabs, because, as he had explained to the Chinese ambassador, "Our objective is always, when the Soviet Union appears, to demonstrate that whoever gets help from the Soviet Union cannot achieve his objective, whatever it is."[20] Though Kissinger protested that his concern for Israel was "secondary"—an "emotional problem having to do with our domestic politics here"—his actions throughout the crisis added up to a focused advocacy more for Israel's strategic goals than for those of the United States.

Kissinger came out of the meeting with Nixon and telephoned the Israeli ambassador. The delivery of American war matériel had to be low-key, Kissinger said, insisting "for security reasons" that Israel use unmarked cargo jets to pick it up. He warned the Israeli envoy that Nixon was ready to press for UN Security Council action that might lead to a simple cease-fire resolution. That would lock in the Arab gains. Kissinger said that he did not want to be too explicit on the telephone, "but I think they should be aware in Jerusalem how the tactical situation is develop-ing." His meaning was inescapable: the Israelis had only a few days to erase the Arab gains; otherwise they would be confronted with a cease-fire demand by the superpowers.

"It is very hard for us to resist [the Security Council]," Kissinger said. "Therefore in designing your strategy, you should keep that in mind."[21]

In a foreign policy address that evening, Kissinger could not abide how much he was on the defensive. In the Senate cloakroom, the talk among conservatives was that Moscow was exploiting détente to make gains, that Nixon and Kissinger were getting suckered.

Kissinger countered with a muscular pose before the Washington audience: "Détente cannot survive irresponsibility in any area, including the Middle East. We shall resist aggressive foreign policies."[22]

In Cairo, Sadat was in full-dress uniform, moving between the Tahra Palace and the Egyptian military headquarters, playing the role of commander in chief. His army had paused after crossing the canal, sparing Israel the devastating thrust that Dayan feared. Sadat's army was safe as long as it stayed beneath the umbrella of Soviet air defense missile batteries along the waterway. Any advance of Egyptian forces into Sinai would make them more vulnerable. Mobile antiaircraft missiles would not provide the same protection as the fixed batteries along the canal. But Sadat was under pressure to move. The Israelis had shifted their air power to the Syrian front. In Moscow, Brezhnev and Marshal Grechko were frantic. The Syrians had lost six hundred tanks in the first four days of combat. The Israelis had bombed Damascus and Homs, targeting the civilian population in an attempt to break Syrian morale.[23] Unlike the Egyptians, the Syrians were not equipped with an extensive supply of spare antiaircraft missiles. When the Israelis saw that Syria was husbanding its air defense, they pounced on the weakest segment of the Syrian line and broke through.

In Egypt, on the night of October 9, Mohamed Heikal, the newspaper editor and mouthpiece of the regime, had been with Sadat at the Tahra Palace. The Egyptian leader, dressed in a field marshal's tunic, was pacing up and down and denouncing the loss of momentum, Assad's treachery, and the failure of the Soviets to send weapons. The one bright spot was that word had reached Cairo that Nikolai Podgorny, one of the troika of Soviet leaders, was haranguing the Iraqis and the Algerians to come to the aid of Egypt and Syria.

"What have Iraq and Algeria got all those arms for?" Podgorny had reportedly asked in a series of blunt messages, though Sadat understood that only direct Soviet aid could make a difference.

Heikal drove along the Nile corniche where the lofty palms and high walls protected private mansions and diplomatic residences. Cairo was under blackout, so everything was in shadow and silhouette. Heikal walked into the darkened garden of the Soviet ambassador's home. A secretary met him and led him quietly through the house. In the lightless corridors, Heikal heard strains of Rachmaninoff.

"I went through the door which led into a small reception room on the right and saw by the light of a single candle the Soviet Ambassador seated at the piano," Heikal recalled. Almost all of the embassy staff had been airlifted back to Moscow. Here was the representative of the Soviet empire, alone, a single candle illuminating the keyboard that had transported him away from diplomacy and war.

"In times of tension this is the only way I can really relax," he said, standing to greet Heikal.

Vinogradov was aware of Sadat's foul mood, having been scalded by the president during an afternoon meeting. But now the ambassador was reinforced by his consultations with Moscow. He had received phone calls from Brezhnev and Grechko. "I do not see why your troops are not advancing," Vinogradov said to Heikal. "Why haven't you consolidated your gains and begun to push on to the passes?" he asked, referring to the strategic Mitla and Giddi passes a third of the way across Sinai. Seizing the passes was not only the sensible thing to do, but also would take pressure off the Syrians fighting on the Golan, he argued. What did the Arabs want the Soviet Union to do? he asked. Sadat had told the Soviet leadership that this would be a war of "limited objectives," but he had not spelled out in detail what the objectives would be. In truth, Sadat's relations with Brezhnev and Grechko were terrible. After all, Sadat had expelled thousands of Soviet advisers in 1972 in a futile gesture to attract Nixon's attention. The Soviet leaders suspected (correctly) that Sadat was interested in making a move toward the Americans. Sadat demanded that Moscow make good on its promises to arm him for the battle in which he was now engaged. But where was it going? Vinogradov said a Russian airlift was getting under way to resupply Egyptian forces, but he pleaded for some clarity about the war aims and some understanding for Moscow, which was trying to hold the Arabs together.

"We can do anything," Vinogradov said, "but we must know exactly what it is we are being asked to do."[24]

Nixon favored a cease-fire brokered by the superpowers. He wanted an affirmation of détente, but one that would also set up an imperative for Israeli concessions in the negotiations that would follow.[25] Other pressures were building. The CIA's top oil analyst, James Critchfield, had called the White House to report that the drumbeat for using the oil weapon was intensifying. Saudi Arabia's King Faisal was "very angry at the U.S. position," for it would effectively erase Arab gains. Critchfield reported that Sheikh Zaki Yamani, the Saudi oil minister, had privately provided to American diplomats the outlines of a plan to cut oil production by more than a million barrels per day, and then by an additional 5 percent each month until Israel agreed to withdraw from the Arab lands it had occupied in 1967.

The memo summing up the call concluded with this warning: "Critchfield judges that if Israel begins to score major victories over the Arabs and if the U.S. is actively re-supplying Israel, our oil interests in the Arab world 'have had it.'"[26]


On the morning of October 10, the Soviets made their first big effort to end the war. Yuri Vorontsov, Dobrynin's senior deputy in the Washington embassy, hand-delivered a message to Brent Scowcroft, Kissinger's deputy at the White House, just before noon. Brezhnev's frustration with Sadat and Syria's increasingly desperate situation called for something to be done, but Moscow did not want its fingerprints on any cease-fire, because this might anger some Arabs. The message from the Kremlin said, "The president, of course, understands that in the present situation the Soviet Union cannot vote in the Security Council in favor of a cease-fire resolution, but the main thing is that we will not vote against it; our representative will abstain during the vote." Here was a critical diplomatic opening.

Four days had gone by and Israel had not moved to counterattack in Sinai. From the outset, Kissinger had confidently predicted that the Israelis would achieve a quick breakthrough. As the days passed, he became increasingly blunt with the Israelis, telling them that Nixon was under "unbelievable pressure" at the United Nations and from the oil-producing states to end the war. The "main thing" for Israel to do, Kissinger said, was to push the Arab armies back to their starting lines so the war could end in a stalemate.

There were moments of extraordinary tension. Saudi Arabia informed Jordan that it was sending a major part of its army north across the Jordanian desert to rescue Syria. The Pentagon saw this as a catastrophe, not because the Saudi troops would change the balance of forces against

Israel but because, if Saudi forces were destroyed by the Israelis, the largest oil-producing nation would suddenly be naked, a circumstance that could incite both superpowers to lunge toward the Persian Gulf to protect the "prize" of Saudi oil. Schlesinger called Kissinger at 8:27 a.m. on October 10 to say that "all of our interests in Saudi Arabia are at risk and it might be desirable to examine the fundamentals of our position."[27] By fundamentals Schlesinger explained, "We may be faced with the choice that lies cruelly between support of Israel, loss of Saudi Arabia and if interests in the Middle East are at risk, the choice between occupation or watching them go down the drain."

Kissinger seemed startled, despite the covert planning that the shah of Iran had undertaken with Kissinger's blessing the previous summer.

"Occupation of whom?" he asked.

"That would remain to be seen—it can be partial," Schlesinger replied, still vague in what exactly he was saying.

"But which country are we occupying?" Kissinger insisted.

"That's one of the things we'd like to talk about," Schlesinger replied.

"Who's we?"

"Me," Schlesinger said.[28]

Kissinger later complained to Haig that Schlesinger had "panicked." Kissinger wanted one thing—thirty-six hours for Israel to gain enough ground on the Syrian front so a cease-fire could be orchestrated that would not look like a total disaster for Israel. He told Haig and then Scowcroft that he still had deep misgivings about ending the war in a manner that could look like a victory for Egypt—it would be in possession of both banks of the Suez Canal—on the strength of Soviet arms. The Israelis were making the same case, knowing its effect on Nixon. Détente was giving way to Kissinger's argument that Israel had to win so the Soviets would lose, which seemed a perversion of U.S. national interest given the Soviet overtures to head off the crisis and to work cooperatively for a settlement of the Arab-Israeli conflict.

Kissinger and the White House also were mismanaging the limited resupply of Israeli forces that Nixon had allowed to go forward. The replacement Phantom warplanes were not flying (poor weather had grounded some). Israel could not find unmarked cargo jets to pick up American arms. International air carriers were skittish about leasing to the Jewish state and thereby antagonizing the Arabs. The Israelis asked the Pentagon to arrange the charters, but the airlines still resisted. So for four days, as Soviet cargo jets lumbered across the Middle East with a modest volume of munitions to resupply the Egyptian and Syrian armies, the United States was engaged in a feckless bureaucratic wrangle with airline executives and panicky Israeli quartermasters.

The battlefield situation was increasingly frantic. On the morning of October 12, Israeli forces had advanced to within thirty miles of Damascus, but Israel—and Syria, too—were expending munitions at phenomenal rates. The question was whether Israel would be able to hold its position on the Syrian front and then launch a massive counterattack on the Egyptian front. The Soviets had begun to suspect that Israel would attack the Syrian capital and topple the Assad regime. Moscow put three of its airborne divisions on alert.[29]

Golda Meir sent a personal message to Nixon pleading for immediate assistance. Israeli forces were under enormous pressure on the Syrian front and had been forced by munitions shortages to halt their offensive. Kissinger was embarrassed by Meir's appeal and was almost apoplectic in his phone call to Schlesinger just before midnight.

"They have stopped their offensive. And they are now in deep trouble in the Sinai," Kissinger said. "I am basing this on a message from the prime minister to the president. And you know maybe it's not true, but it is a hell of a responsibility to take."[30]

Schlesinger tried to talk him down. The CIA was reporting that Israel had sufficient munitions for two more weeks of fighting. Schlesinger pointed out that Pentagon officials had been meeting daily with Israeli military attachés and none of them had said anything indicating that ammunition supplies were critically low. Schlesinger urged Kissinger to abandon the unmarked charter concept.

"I think if you really want to do something about it," Schlesinger advised, "you better let U.S. aircraft fly all the way in."[31]

Kissinger said he would have to go to the president; the two men agreed to overcome the problems. They were both now ready for a full-scale airlift to help Israel regain lost ground. But Kissinger showed the pernicious side of his personality, as if he lived by a maxim that no opportunity to denigrate a rival should be ignored. Within a minute of hanging up on Schlesinger, Kissinger called Haig and said he was having "a massive problem with the Israelis because the sons of bitches in Defense have been stalling for four days and not one airplane has moved."[32]

"Oh no," Haig responded.

"Oh yes. After the decision on Tuesday, not one Goddamn shipload—not one has moved. And they are now out of ammunition. They are stopping their Syrian offensive. The Egyptians have transferred artillery to the other side of the canal and may start an offensive tomorrow."

"Oh boy," Haig said.

"So now the question is whether they are going to collapse in the Sinai and you know what this does to the diplomatic scenario I described to you [orchestrate a cease-fire that would lead to negotiations]."

"Yes."

"Which absolutely required an Israeli offensive."

"Yep."

Haig asked what he could do. Kissinger said he should call both Schlesinger and his deputy, William Clements, and "throw the fear of God" into them.

Then, with a tone of grandiosity, Kissinger added, "My orders apparently just aren't carried out over there."

Diplomacy is often a game of who emerges as the least damaged party, which is why laying blame is so critical to the process. Israeli envoys agonized openly to their staunchest friends in the Senate—Javits, Ribicoff, Humphrey, Symington, and Jackson—about the slow pace of the resupply. Dinitz had shared sensitive intelligence: Israel had indeed lost fifty planes. He had also expressed disappointment that Nixon was going to replace them at a glacial pace even as Israel, he claimed, was fighting for its life. Up until that moment, the war had not intruded into American domestic politics, where Nixon, too, was fighting for his life. His approval ratings had plummeted. Watergate investigators had gone to court to force the release of White House tapes. Nixon could not afford to antagonize the Senate. But Scoop Jackson, the tenacious anti-Soviet Democrat from Washington State, was already threatening to hold hearings on whether the Nixon administration had bungled the American commitment to protect Israel, as every president since Truman had pledged to do.

Nixon and Kissinger were all frayed nerves. After a newspaper story questioned the administration's support for Israel, Nixon told Kissinger to warn the Israeli ambassador to get his diplomats under control. "If we hear any more stuff like this I will have no choice domestically except to turn on them," Nixon said, and Kissinger immediately called the Israeli embassy and warned that there would be "hell to pay" if there was any more criticism.

But two days later, Kissinger was back on the phone to Dinitz. "I just again have been called by [Senator] Jackson and threatened with a Congressional investigation," he said, clearly enraged, and suggested that he could bring the airlift to an abrupt halt if the criticism continued. "Our whole foreign policy position depends on our not being represented as having screwed up a crisis and with all affection for Israel, if it turns out that we are going to be under attack for mismanagement in a crisis, we will have to turn on you. I don't care who does it, if that happens, we will defend ourselves."[33] But Nixon knew he couldn't turn on anyone. The president had the weakest hand.


That night, Nixon abandoned all caution and went whole hog with an American airlift to Israel. It turned out to be a sensation, visibly broadcasting to the world that the United States was weighing in heavily on the Israeli side with a bold, extravagant gesture that cut squarely across the course Nixon had earlier set for the United States as a superpower working cooperatively above the fray in the spirit of détente. It made Nixon look strong in what was, truth be told, his weakest hour.

In the White House Situation Room, Kissinger sketched out the lie that the White House would tell the world: "We can now say there was Russian treachery on negotiations. They have made an abortion of our peace move and sent in 200 flights [of arms]."[34] There was laughter in the room when Schlesinger retorted, "We had anticipated that!"

"Russian treachery!" was now the American pretext, invented by a panicky White House, for what followed.

Schlesinger tried to preserve a fig leaf of discretion. The giant C-5A Galaxies and C-141 Starlifters were ordered to make night landings and then get out of Israel before sunrise. But crosswinds over the Azores delayed the chain of deliveries. All of Israel awoke on Sunday morning, October 14, to the scene of flights of U.S. transports stacked up in landing patterns into Tel Aviv's main airport, where they disgorged massive amounts of munitions, M60 tanks, and all manner of battlefield weapons. Nixon's critics in Congress were silenced, American Jews cheered the president's decision, and thousands of residents of Tel Aviv,

including Golda Meir and most of her cabinet, went out to see the spec-
tacle and to express their thanks to America.

After insisting that America keep its hand hidden, Nixon's sharp turnaround proved to be a history-changing decision: The massive airlift
shifted American policy so transparently toward Israel that it undermined
the U.S. image in the region that Eisenhower had established. As a result,
it triggered a major response from the Arab oil producers and prompted
them to enforce an embargo that ravaged Western economies. The dramatic shift pulled the wheels off U.S.-Soviet détente as a realistic vehicle
for joint action; the United States had taken sides with Israel against the
Soviets and their Arab clients, and that had emboldened the militarist instinct in Israel, which was gaining ground with the growth of Israel's nuclear arsenal and its political influence in Washington.

Nixon's actions have to be viewed in light of the sudden threat on the
domestic front. The court decision on the Watergate tapes and, separately, the indignation among pro-Israel senators over what seemed like
the White House's unnecessary delay, or even mismanagement of its support for the Jewish state in time of war, impelled Nixon to abandon the
balance he had been trying to maintain. Over the next weeks, as the war
continued, more than 560 flights of American cargo aircraft delivered to
Israel more than twenty-two thousand tons of military equipment and
munitions along with more than eighty aircraft, including forty Phantoms. Cargo ships, loaded with tanks and heavy weapons, soon followed.
Nixon seemed satisfied. On the morning the first planes landed in Israel,
he got word that Egypt had launched a major offensive in Sinai, striking
out from the canal in an effort to reach the Mitla and Giddi passes, which
had to be taken by any army that wanted to threaten Israel. Kissinger gave
Nixon the first reports from the battlefield, speculating that the Israelis
might be allowing the Egyptians to advance so as to trap them.

"The main thing is who wins this damn battle," Nixon reflected. "It
isn't territory, you know—you can give up gobs of territory, the question is
do you beat the enemy. Now if the Israelis let them—I think they ought
to let them in there and kill them."[35]

"That's right," Kissinger agreed. "Should the Israelis clobber the Egyptians that will turn out to be a pretty good position." Any Egyptian demand that Israel return to the 1967 borders would be "absolutely out of
the question short of a huge defeat as a result of the war. That has to
come as a result of the subsequent negotiations that follow the war."

*The New York Times* had reported that morning that in the Senate there were two views of the war and the opportunity for peace. One group, led by Senator Jackson, asserted that détente with the Soviets was dead and had always rested on quicksand and, therefore, the United States should help Israel win the war convincingly. The second group, led by Senator William Fulbright, the Democrat from Arkansas and chairman of the Senate Foreign Relations Committee, was more pragmatic and was seeking to limit the arms supply to Israel so as to force a cease-fire that would leave the Egyptians in control of their gains on the Western side of the canal. That would lead to a negotiation that would "demilitarize" the Sinai and require the withdrawal of Israeli forces from the peninsula and a return to United Nations supervision.

"The Arabs have gotten some of their honor back, and we don't want the Israelis to take it away. It's time to settle," was how one Pentagon official put it.[36]

Nixon and Kissinger struggled with the same question that morning, with Kissinger seeming to focus on gaining advantage for Israel and Nixon on how to apply pressure to get a settlement. Nixon was thinking back to their encounter with Brezhnev the previous June in San Clemente—that middle-of-the-night session when Brezhnev wanted agreement on a few basic principles, such as withdrawal, and Nixon and Kissinger had simply stiff-armed him.

"Look, we've got to face this," Nixon said. "As far as the Russians are concerned, they have a pretty good beef insofar as everything they have offered on the Mid-East. You know what I mean, that meeting in San Clemente. We were stringing them along and they know it. We've got to come off with something on the diplomatic front, because if we go to the cease fire, they'll figure that . . . the Israelis will dig in and we'll back them, as we always have. That's putting it quite bluntly, but it's quite true Henry, isn't it?"[37]

"There's a lot in that," Kissinger replied, not quite endorsing the president's line.

Nixon said they couldn't put the Russians back in that position. "So we have got to be in a position to offer something," he said. "We've got to squeeze the Israelis when this is over and the Russians have got to know it. We've got to squeeze them goddamn hard. And that's the way it is going to be done." The problem was how to get that message across to Golda Meir because "we told them before we'd squeeze them and we didn't."

Kissinger, however, seemed more determined to perpetuate the status quo. Israel might never part with a portion of Sinai. Therefore, "what we need now" is a UN cease-fire resolution "that doesn't flatly say" that Israel should withdraw to the "'67 borders, but leaves it open—something that invokes the Security Council resolution 242 that speaks of withdrawals and that is something everybody has already agreed to once—plus a [peace] conference or something like that."

Nixon was thinking more grandly. He wanted a victory for his policy of détente, a demonstration that superpower cooperation had worked in the Middle East. That would silence Jackson and the other hard-liners who argued that détente was a mirage. Nixon said the Soviets obviously liked the "condominium" metaphor of superpower collaboration.

"What ought to happen is that even though the Israelis will squeal like stuck pigs, we ought to tell Dobrynin—we ought to say that—Brezhnev and Nixon will settle this damn thing. That ought to be done. You know that."

The problem was that Nixon's vision reached far beyond his political strength to carry it off. He wanted to stand, as Eisenhower had, as the arbiter of war and peace in the Middle East. But because of Watergate he had no stature, and even if he could reach out to Brezhnev for help in imposing a settlement, it was far from certain that Nixon could muster the political authority to overcome what had to be overcome. Most of all, he could not afford to antagonize the Senate, the repository of Israel's most muscular support.

The climactic battle for Sinai was a clash of armor that would echo in history. Sadat had ordered his chief of staff, Lieutenant General Saad el-Shazli, to break out of his defensive lines on the western side of the canal. Shazli resisted, arguing that Israel had massed nine hundred tanks opposite his army. Sadat overruled him. There was a larger political imperative to take the pressure off the Syrian front. Egyptian forces, with six separate attacks, surged forward and engaged the Israelis in savage firefights and aerial combat, but the resupplied Israelis took advantage of their superior firepower, leaving more than 250 Egyptian tanks destroyed on the field at a cost of only 20 Israeli tanks. The Egyptians tried to move forward under the umbrella of mobile air defense teams, but Israeli gunners targeted the Egyptian armored personnel carriers that transported the missile teams. General Shazli also made the fatal mistake of ordering the last of his reserve tank forces across the canal in preparation for the battle: when Israeli intelligence reported this development to Meir, Dayan, and the war cabinet, it tilted the debate toward authorizing Ariel Sharon to cross the canal.

In the boldest stroke of the war, Israeli tanks and infantry charged into a gap between Egypt's Second and Third armies and sent tanks across the canal at Deversoir just north of the Great Bitter Lake on the night of October 15. Egyptian brigades slashed at Sharon's northern flank in a bloody patch of desert known as the Chinese Farm. Sharon described what he said was the most terrible sight he had ever seen in war. All during the night, he listened to the radio reports of the fighting.

"The conflagration of the battle had lit the sky just to the north of us," he wrote. "But as the sky brightened, I looked around and saw hundreds and hundreds of burned and twisted vehicles. Fifty Israeli tanks lay shattered on the field. Around them were the hulks of 150 Egyptian tanks plus hundreds of APCs [armored personnel carriers], jeeps and trucks. Wreckage littered the desert. Here and there Israeli and Egyptian tanks had destroyed each other at a distance of a few meters, barrel to barrel. It was as if a hand-to-hand battle of armor had taken place. And inside those tanks and next to them lay their dead crews. Coming close, you could see Egyptian and Jewish dead lying side by side, soldiers who had jumped from their burning tanks and had died together."[38] More than three hundred Israeli soldiers had died, he said, and the Egyptians had lost even more.

Despite heavy casualties, Sharon had pushed a paratroop brigade under Colonel Danny Matt, plus twenty-eight tanks and a number of APCs across the waterway on rafts, and they began to wreak havoc on Egyptian forces, knocking a gaping hole in the air defense network and allowing the Israeli air force to send its warplanes in to tear up the Egyptian defenses. Careers are made on the battlefield and the canal crossing was the signal achievement of Sharon's military life. Others would follow him into politics, like Colonel Ehud Barak, who led a force into the Chinese Farm inferno to rescue a trapped paratroop brigade. Israel breached the Suez Canal in force, sending elements of three brigades west of the waterway to attack supply lines and to envelop the Egyptian Third Army that was in the southernmost position along the canal. Cairo at that moment lay naked to attack. There was no military force that could stop an Israeli thrust toward the Arab capital.

. . .

The White House was operating with few details beyond what overhead photography from SR-71 Blackbird spy planes could provide and what the Israelis were willing to share. Admiral Thomas Moorer, the chairman of the Joint Chiefs, told a meeting of Nixon's top aides on October 17 that the Israeli crossing was not very significant—"nothing more than a raid on the Egyptian air defense. I don't think they can survive long."[39]

Nixon, now fully invested in his airlift decision, had adopted the mantra that had percolated up from the Israelis, from Senator Jackson, and from Kissinger: "We can't allow a Soviet-supported operation to succeed against an American-supported operation. If it does, our credibility everywhere is severely shaken."[40] Kissinger was preening that morning, certain that he and Nixon, in more than two hours of discussion with a delegation of foreign ministers from Saudi Arabia, Kuwait, and Algeria, had soothed the inflamed sensibilities over the American airlift to Israel.

"We don't expect an oil cut-off now in the light of the discussions with the Arab foreign ministers this morning," Kissinger told the group. But then he wheeled on Bill Clements, the deputy defense secretary and a Texan whose background in the oil industry and whose relations with Arab leaders led Kissinger to suspect that Clements had thrown up obstacles to the airlift.

"Did you see the Saudi Foreign Minister come out like a good little boy and say they had had very fruitful talks with us?—despite what your colleagues have done to screw us up with their messages." Kissinger was referring to American oil executives, who had publicly expressed doubts about U.S. policy.

"They're not my colleagues," Clements shot back. "My colleagues are in this room."

The contradictions in the American strategy were glaring. William Colby, the CIA director, reported that the air- and sealifts to Israel were going far beyond immediate war needs. "You will see the greatest reserve stocks on record in Israel for the next couple years," he said.[41]

Nixon took the point. "We can't get so much to them that they will become arrogant, but we can't be in the position where Israel puts pressure on Congress for us to do more," he said during an Oval Office meeting.[42]

All hope of calibration had gone out the window. Nixon had lost control of events. He could not publicly explain his decision to authorize a huge airlift—beyond Israel's war needs—in the rank political terms that he used in private. Nor could he admit that his own administration had fumbled for the better part of a week trying to get its own airlift under way. So Nixon turned on the Soviets in public, blaming Moscow's "massive" intervention as the tipping point that required drastic American action.[43]

"The Soviet leaders, and I'm not condemning them, felt they should mount a massive airlift," Nixon had told the Arab ministers that morning. "Only after one week had passed, and over 300 planes had gone in, I decided that we must maintain a balance. This is all we're doing."[44]

Up to that point, according to Moorer's briefing on October 17, the Soviets had launched about two hundred flights of war matériel comprising about five thousand tons, far less than the twenty-five thousand tons the Americans were pouring into Israel's pipeline for urgent delivery. But the more relevant point was that the Soviet and the American airlift decisions were made almost at the same moment, near the outset of the war. Both efforts seemed modest in scale. Kissinger, after all, suggested to Moscow the morning the war began that both sides "restrain" their clients. Both sides had been inclined to provide essential items and not massive infusions that would tip the scales. It was the early failure—or mismanagement—of the American resupply effort, especially the refusal to replace Israel's early aircraft losses, that triggered an incipient uprising in Congress just as the U.S. Court of Appeals delivered a devastating personal blow to Nixon: he would have to surrender tapes that he knew would prove his guilt in directing the Watergate cover-up.

By blaming the Soviets ("Russian treachery!") for forcing their hand, Nixon and Kissinger converted the crisis from an exercise in superpower cooperation to a hostile confrontation aimed at producing an Israeli—and an American—victory, one that would leave Israel more heavily armed than at any time in its twenty-five-year history. Nixon pulled back from his talk about a U.S.-Soviet–brokered peace. He told the Arab ministers, "You say a settlement must include Israeli withdrawal [to] the 1967 borders. I could say sure, we accept that, but there is no use making a commitment we can't deliver on."[45]

Kissinger stayed riveted on the war as Nixon prepared for a showdown with the Watergate special prosecutor, Archibald Cox. Nixon asked Haig: "Are we facing the fact that the public attitudes may have hardened to the point that we can't change them?"[46] As Nixon's fortunes declined,

Kissinger's seemed to rise. In Oslo it had been announced that Kissinger was to share the Nobel Peace Prize with Le Duc Tho for their efforts in negotiating an American withdrawal from Vietnam. In meetings of Nixon's top advisers, Kissinger played cheerleader.

"Mr. President, this has been the best-run crisis since you have been in the White House. We have launched a massive airlift yet we have gotten only a small bitch in TASS [the Soviet news agency] and you stand there getting Arab compliments in the Rose Garden."

But downstairs in the Situation Room, a clerk had ripped off the Associated Press wire the bulletin announcing that the Arab states had acted: they were cutting back their oil production by 5 percent and would cut production by an additional 5 percent each month until Israel gave up Arab lands seized in 1967.

The Arabs had reached for the oil weapon, and their act would change the oil markets for decades, undermining stable price regimes, creating new markets for "spot" traders, speculators, and other middlemen who would drive up prices artificially, beyond the normal parameters of supply and demand and to the detriment of nations rich and poor. The West was going to get hit hard. Since 1948, consumption of oil had tripled in the United States, from 5.8 to 16.4 million barrels a day. Between 1950 and the early 1970s, the number of passenger cars registered in the world had increased tenfold, to nearly two hundred million a year, and the United States was up to about ninety million per year. Western Europe's use of coal had plummeted from 75 to 22 percent of its total energy. Crude oil had taken its place, providing 60 percent of total energy use by 1972.[47]

Arab anger over America's open support for Israel emboldened the oil-producing countries. The OPEC ministers voted to raise the price of their crude oil by 70 percent.

On October 18, the Soviets proposed a new cease-fire plan that called for a full Israeli withdrawal to the 1967 borders. Kissinger was not eager to share it with the Israelis. "They are as obnoxious as the Vietnamese," he told Scowcroft, expressing alarm that the Israelis might go too far. "I am afraid it will turn into a turkey shoot," he said. "If they keep going across, somebody is going to get killed, that's for sure."[48]

"The real danger is the Egyptian army is going to panic," Scowcroft said.

Kissinger agreed. "Once they get across in division strength that means the SAM belt is gone." Then the Israelis would start picking apart the

Egyptians from "from top and bottom" and the Egyptians "are going to disintegrate . . . They'll die of starvation." Kissinger wondered aloud whether the war would now force a political collapse in Cairo. "I think this is the end of Sadat," he told Scowcroft.

The U.S. airlift had been followed by a White House message to Congress on October 19 asking for a special $2.2 billion appropriation to pay for the arms being shipped to Israel. That incited an even more intense reaction. The next day, King Faisal of Saudi Arabia announced a total embargo of crude oil exports to the United States. The very consequence that Nixon had sought to avoid was upon him. At the Pentagon, Schlesinger received a telegram from Exxon saying that on the instructions of Sheikh Yamani, the Saudi oil minister, Exxon was cutting off all oil supplies to American military and naval forces in the Middle East and Europe. Meanwhile, the Israeli breakout across the canal had spurred the Soviets into action. The Politburo dispatched Premier Alexei Kosygin to Cairo, where he found Sadat nearly hysterical with recriminations over weapons that had never been delivered and in denial about the reversal that was unfolding on the battlefield. Kosygin's urgent dispatches back to Moscow prompted Brezhnev to send a message to Nixon suggesting that he send Kissinger to Moscow at once to work out a cease-fire.

"I will work for a simple cease fire," Kissinger explained to his colleagues in the Situation Room. "The trouble is that Israel doesn't want anything." The airlift had eliminated any notion of leverage. Israel had gotten what it wanted from the United States—and then some—at no cost in political concessions. Still, Kissinger claimed success. "Everyone knows in the Middle East that if they want a peace they have to go through us. Three times they tried through the Soviet Union and three times they failed."[49] Kissinger also knew a shoe was about to drop in the Watergate affair. He was scheduled to fly to Moscow at 2:00 a.m. Haig called and said that Nixon wanted to announce Kissinger's trip that evening as part of a major statement on Watergate and the Middle East crisis. The president was going to tell the nation that he would not surrender the White House tapes to Cox. He would offer them to Senator John Stennis and Stennis would provide "summaries" for Cox.

Kissinger acted horrified. "Impossible," he told Haig. Why would he join Kissinger's mission to a Watergate announcement?

"There are a couple of reasons," Haig said, implying that it would make the Watergate announcement a little easier.

Kissinger said that would be a disaster. "My honest opinion is that it is a cheap stunt. It looks as if he is using foreign policy to cover a domestic thing."[50]

Haig disagreed. It was not contrived, he said. "I think you have two very important things happening."

"He is not firing Cox?" Kissinger asked.

"As of now, no. Just giving him a desist order which will probably result in his resignation."

"I would not link foreign policy with Watergate. You will regret it for the rest of your life," Kissinger said.

Haig said that Nixon had support from Senators Sam Ervin, Howard Baker, and John Stennis. "We are doing a hell of a thing here. He has to do it."

"It will forever after be said he did this to cover Watergate. I really would plead with you."[51]

Nixon agreed to separate the announcements, but only by a few hours.

Kissinger had ample reason to fear that the firing of Cox would sound the death knell of the Nixon presidency. War, embargo, and constitutional crisis gripped Washington. The moment for a cease-fire in the Middle East was long past, except that Kissinger pushed Schlesinger and Moorer to keep pouring in the arms beyond Israel's requirements and to the detriment of American military forces in Europe. Columnists George Will and Joseph Kraft were criticizing Kissinger as a naïf who had been taken in by Brezhnev while the Soviets were rushing arms to the Arabs. Kissinger's standing as an American statesman was on the line. But the course he pursued reinforced the diplomatic paralysis. It perpetuated Israel's hold on the territories it had occupied in 1967. It led to the transport of an enormous stockpile of military hardware and munitions to Israel, giving its leaders reason to reject the very flexibility that Kissinger had once argued was necessary for compromise, and it intensified the permanent state of grievance and mistrust between America and the Muslim world.

Neither superpower had wanted confrontation, but Kissinger had done more than anyone else to undermine the prospect for a collaborative effort to settle the region's most intractable dispute. Kissinger's strategy was essentially self-centered, the hallmark of his diplomacy. His goal was to protect his own domestic image as the one indispensable foreign policy strategist whose tenure must endure beyond whatever fate was to befall Nixon.

To the Arabs, Kissinger offered palliative phrases: "The humiliation which the Egyptians and, indeed, the Arab world felt after 1967 has been erased," he told them. "A new strategic situation has been established in which reliance by any country on permanent military supremacy has become illusory. Hence, the necessity of a political settlement is becoming much clearer to all parties."[52] But he offered them nothing beyond what had been on the table before they had resorted to war.

Kissinger departed for Moscow in the early hours of October 20. Haig had made clear that the hammer was about to drop on Cox. Kissinger was grateful that he would be six thousand miles away working for peace as Nixon prepared to detonate his most explosive act of defiance in the Watergate drama. But Nixon would not leave the Middle East to Kissinger: after a welcoming banquet in Moscow given by Brezhnev, Kissinger returned to his guesthouse in the Lenin Hills and found a top secret message from Nixon.

"I believe that, beyond a doubt, we are now facing the best opportunity we have had in 15 years to build a lasting peace in the Middle East," Nixon wrote.[53] "The current Israeli successes at Suez must not deflect us from going all out to achieve a just settlement." Israel would win the war, Nixon said, but "in the long run the Israelis will not be able to stand the continuing attrition which, in the absence of a settlement, they will be destined to suffer."

There was a confessional quality to the telegram. "Our greatest foreign policy weakness over the past four and a half years has been our failure to deal decisively with the Middle East crisis." Nixon cited three reasons: Israeli intransigence, Arab rejectionism, and U.S. preoccupation with other parts of the world. "I now consider a permanent Middle East settlement to be the most important final goal to which we must devote ourselves," he said, adding, "I want you to know that I am prepared to pressure the Israelis to the extent required, without regard of the domestic political consequences."

Nixon specifically instructed Kissinger to tell Brezhnev that "I can deliver on commitments" in the Middle East "without the requirement for congressional approval." Nixon told Kissinger to convey that peace in the Middle East could be the crowning achievement of the Nixon-Brezhnev relationship, and that each leader could "keep our commitments in as general terms as possible," understanding that both sides would have to make painful compromises.

Surprisingly, Nixon said he wanted Brezhnev to know "that I realize now that he was right in his concern about the danger of an imminent explosion in the Middle East" when the two men talked through the night at San Clemente the previous June. "One war in the Middle East in 20 years would have been too much," Nixon continued, but "to have had four wars during this period is intolerable, and we must now take decisive action to resolve the problem. Only the U.S. and the Soviet Union have the power and influence to create the permanent conditions necessary to avoid another war."

Finally, he told Kissinger to tell the Soviet leader, "The Israelis and Arabs will never be able to approach this subject by themselves in a rational manner. That is why Nixon and Brezhnev, looking at the problem more dispassionately, must step in, determine the proper course of action to a just settlement and then bring the necessary pressure on our respective friends for a settlement which will at last bring peace to this troubled area."

Kissinger refused to deliver this message to Brezhnev. Instead, he fired back a cable to the White House, telling Scowcroft, "I want you to know that I consider the tone and substance of his instruction to me to be unacceptable." He said he was "shocked" by the "poor judgment" of the president. He said his position was already "insoluble" and that it would be hard enough to get a cease-fire, but that task would be made impossible by going for a "global" settlement. But he did not explain why, especially since he had already secured Israel's private assurance that it would comply with a cease-fire as a condition of Kissinger's agreement to fly to Tel Aviv from Moscow.

Nixon's message did not foist any new terms on Kissinger, but it did bring détente back to the fore, which was the real threat for Kissinger. He was under fire from the conservative establishment in Washington for naïveté with regard to the Soviet Union and was in flight from his own president's policy. At this critical moment, Nixon's interests had diverged significantly from Kissinger's. It is tempting to dismiss Nixon's proposal as the pipe dream of a scandal-weakened president, but the full text of his message demonstrates that Nixon retained a lucid and realistic grasp of the difficult international political crisis that he and Kissinger had helped to create. The American oil industry and the Arab world had lost confidence in the Nixon administration, while Israel, the American Jewish community, and its congressional base expected unerring support for the Israeli position. Nixon was looking for a dramatic, even theatrical, political play to mobilize the country and the international community for a Middle East peace negotiation.

For Kissinger to have withheld this offer from the Soviet leader was a betrayal of American diplomacy, for it denied Brezhnev the gesture of respect that Nixon sought to extend at a crucial moment in U.S.-Soviet relations. Both leaders understood that the conditions they created for ending the war would carry over into the postwar diplomacy, and Nixon, seeking to hoist himself to the highest plane of statesmanship as a defense against the poisonous effects of the Watergate affair, was focused on a constructive superpower partnership that would have strengthened his and Brezhnev's ability to overcome Arab and Israeli resistance to a settlement. Nixon's message threatened to undermine the record Kissinger was seeking to create: that he and Nixon had run the Soviets into the ground and they had protected Israel—these were the critical elements that Kissinger would employ to defend himself in the nasty domestic politics at home.

A big presidential initiative—by Nixon *and* Brezhnev—would have thrust Kissinger into the thankless and perilous role of applying pressure on Israel, and not just on Israel but also on Golda Meir, one of the least flexible Israeli political figures. For that reason, Kissinger surely regarded Nixon's message as dangerous to his own self-interest.[54] His last act that evening was to telephone the White House on an open line from Moscow, one the Soviets were certainly monitoring, to ventilate his rage and anxieties to Haig, who was in the midst of what became known as the Saturday Night Massacre: Nixon's firing of Cox and the resignation of Attorney General Elliot Richardson and his deputy, William Ruckelshaus.

On October 22, 1973, the UN Security Council adopted Resolution 338, calling on the combatants "to cease all firing and terminate all military activity immediately, no later than 12 hours after the moment of the adoption of this decision." The fighting continued as the Israelis and Egyptians struggled for a last-minute advantage: Israel wanted to cut off and destroy the Egyptian Third Army; Egypt wanted to hold its position on the eastern bank of the canal and preserve its supply lines from Cairo and the rear area. Kissinger flew to Tel Aviv to meet Golda Meir and her top aides. But instead of preparing them for difficult compromises in the postwar diplomacy, Kissinger reinforced their most intransigent attitudes, the ones that Nixon had hoped to overcome. In his private meeting with Meir, Kissinger disparaged both Nixon and Brezhnev, telling the Israeli prime minister that Israel had won a great victory, that it had gained more Arab land, and that "my strategy in this crisis, as I explained to Dinitz several times, was to keep the Arabs down and the Russians down."[55] But most destructively, he encouraged the Israelis to violate the cease-fire "even if" the Egyptian side complied.

When Moshe Dayan asked Kissinger directly, "What should we do? I'd not like to stop [fighting]," Kissinger, instead of invoking the cease-fire, replied, "That's in your domestic jurisdiction."

It is difficult to understand Kissinger's motivation, except that the more the Arabs and Soviets lost, the better he would look coming back to Washington with a cease-fire and praise from Tel Aviv. He told Meir that UN Resolution 242 and its call for Israeli withdrawal from occupied territories was "a joke" and that its phrases "mean nothing"; therefore Israel was secure behind the bulwark of its long-standing insistence that it would trade land for peace only in direct negotiations with the Arabs.

Even accounting for diplomatic artifice—identifying with all sides so as to build their confidence—Kissinger here seemed to be encouraging the resistance and triumphalism that had stymied the Nixon administration from the outset.

Washington was a smoldering landscape of impeachment and revolt when Kissinger returned, and within twenty-four hours the Israeli army, operating with the strong sense of impunity that Kissinger had signaled, fought tenaciously to complete its encirclement of the Third Army to the point that Sadat was making desperate telephone calls to the Kremlin imploring Moscow to "save me and the Egyptian capital."[56]

As Israeli tanks and paratroopers under Brigadier General Kalman Magen fought a savage battle to take the city of Suez and Sharon's forces battled for ground south of Ismailia, Sadat petitioned the United States and Soviet Union jointly to insert a military force into the Sinai to police the cease-fire.

By evening on October 24, Nixon, exhausted by the week's events, was drinking heavily. The Soviet leadership suspected, correctly, that Kissinger had given the Israelis a green light to keep fighting. Their proposal to insert forces, American and Soviet, was a test of American sincerity. Dobrynin told Kissinger in the early evening that the Kremlin leaders "have become so angry" over the continued fighting that "they want troops" to get between the opposing armies. Dobrynin was full of recriminations. "You allowed the Israelis to do what they wanted."

"Be that as it may," Kissinger said, "if you want confrontation, we will have to have one. It would be a pity."

"You know we don't want to have a confrontation," Dobrynin replied.[57]

Kissinger told Dobrynin that the United States would veto any resolution calling for superpower intervention. Kissinger made no move to call Nixon, with whom he had spoken fifteen minutes earlier. But Kissinger knew that Nixon was not looking for a confrontation; he considered the cease-fire a "triumph" of détente. But Brezhnev's frustration was boiling over. He and the Politburo drafted a direct appeal to Nixon, urging that the superpowers act together to enforce the cease-fire. Brezhnev had cleared the text with his colleagues, but he apparently appended the toughest sentence himself: "I will say it straight that if you find it impossible to act jointly with us in this matter, we should be faced with the necessity urgently to consider the question of taking appropriate steps unilaterally."

Throughout the day, Kissinger followed with actions that seemed to shape the confrontation instead of trying to avert it. He had not confided in Nixon or Haig the extent to which he had encouraged the Israelis to violate the cease-fire and complete the destruction of the Egyptian army. And he had filibustered in the face of reports that the Israelis had charged into Suez to further encircle the Egyptians. Given the scale of the Israeli violations, it was not surprising that the Egyptians were seeking to fight their way out of an entrapment.

Three hours later, Dinitz telephoned Kissinger. The Israeli attempt to take Suez had not only failed, but a paratroop unit was trapped inside the city and would have to be extracted through further military operations "or they will be slaughtered."[58] Dinitz said an Israeli bombing campaign would soon commence as cover for the rescue. Kissinger again failed to share this critical intelligence with Nixon, Haig, or the Soviets. Instead, he pressed Haig to see Brezhnev's message as a major challenge to a weakened president: "They find a cripple facing impeachment and why shouldn't they [the Soviets] go in there."[59] He asserted to Haig that he didn't believe the Israelis were responsible for the cease-fire violations— "I don't believe that the Israelis started it," he said—and when Haig asked him if he had discussed a course of action with Nixon, Kissinger dismissed the idea as premature: "He would just start charging around."

Haig upbraided Kissinger, rejecting the notion that they should not "bother the president" before they responded to the Soviets. "He has to be part of everything you are doing," Haig admonished. He pressed Kissinger to move the crisis meeting he was organizing from the State Department to the White House, where Haig could monitor it for the president.

As he did in the aftermath of the San Clemente meeting, Kissinger projected the most sinister motives for Brezhnev's actions that night. "It was one of the most serious challenges to an American president by a Soviet leader," he later wrote. Haig, however, seemed willing to give the Soviet leader the benefit of the doubt, given Moscow's constructive behavior in bringing the war to an end.

"It seems to me," Haig told Kissinger, "[that] the Soviets have acted in good faith" and "if this [joint intervention]" would bring "quiet" to the battlefield, perhaps they should consider a joint U.S.-Soviet force. Haig said he worried that if the Soviets went in alone, "there would be some fighting" between "the Soviets and the Israelis" and "then we have a problem." But Kissinger was against a cooperative act. "You cannot be sure how much of this is due to our domestic crisis," he said. "I don't think they would have taken on a functioning president." If the Russians went in, "they [the Russians] would have to attack us to get at them [the Israelis]." Kissinger made a point of mentioning that Senator Jackson had called, "protesting violently" against any concept of a joint U.S.-Soviet force, though a transcript of the call shows that Jackson had only inquired about reports of a joint force.[60]

A joint U.S.-Soviet intervention was undoubtedly a bad idea and might have led to a dangerous confrontation on the ground, but Haig and Kissinger both knew that it grew out of Soviet frustration over the Israeli attempt to cut off and destroy the Egyptian army in the wake of the cease-fire agreement forty-eight hours earlier. (Kissinger admitted as much when Dinitz informed him that night that Israeli forces were engaged in major fighting to extract their paratroopers from Suez.) "If the Soviets have decided to go in, I just think we turned the wheel yesterday one screw too much," Kissinger told the Israeli ambassador, adding that they needed to discuss how to shift the blame for the cease-fire violations onto the Soviets. "Let's look at the tactics of this," Kissinger said. "We have to offer them something which puts them totally in the wrong."[61]

This was the context for the extraordinary meeting of the National Security Council, convened while the president was inebriated and in bed, and run by Kissinger, who was in desperate need of a tactic to shift the onus of violation away from Israel, which was engaged in a harrowing effort to extract its forces at Suez. Colby, the CIA director, delivered a briefing on the agency's latest assessment of Soviet actions and possible intentions. The buildup of Soviet naval forces in the eastern Mediterranean had reached eighty-five ships. Neutron sensors installed for covert surveillance of Soviet naval forces passing through the Bosphorus had triggered alarms on October 15 and 19, indicating that the Soviet fleet was deploying nuclear arms aboard some of its warships. This was not in itself unusual, but it added to the concern about so many Soviet naval combatants intermixed with the U.S. Sixth Fleet.

The big concern, the one that served as the foundation of the decision making that night, was that the Soviet alert of its airborne forces seemed to have broadened somewhat as the Soviet military command ordered its airlift flights to Syria and Egypt to stand down on October 24. The question was: Were those aircraft standing down in preparation to load Soviet airborne troops for insertion into Cairo, or were they standing down because the airlift of war matériel was over? Colby later said that he was most impressed by the fact that the Soviet airborne divisions were "suiting up, putting on packs and were ready to move." In his mind, Brezhnev's letter plus the current intelligence indicated that the Soviets were preparing to make a move into the Middle East on their own.[62]

There was surprising unanimity in the Situation Room: They would draft a response to Brezhnev's letter stating as bluntly and forcibly as possible that the United States could not tolerate a unilateral Soviet deployment to the Middle East. And they would raise the level of alert for U.S. forces to show that Nixon was prepared for a real confrontation. This is the point at which Kissinger's actions are most open to question, for none of the other Nixon aides appeared to be aware that Kissinger was condoning the ongoing Israeli military operations about which he was being informed by Ambassador Dinitz. To the Israelis, this meant they had a green light to keep fighting, both at Suez and against the supply line of the Third Army. Kissinger's messages to the Israelis were not subtle. He went out of his way to inform Dinitz that the United States would veto any United Nations resolutions that called for "military peace keeping forces," that Washington would not itself insert any military forces, and that the Nixon administration would veto any condemnation of Israel for violating the cease-fire.[63] Instead of any demand that Israel cease firing, Kissinger told the Israeli ambassador, "what I must have is your complete circumspection of this military operation." It was a curious choice of words—"circumspection"—because, again, Kissinger conveyed no American demand to obey the cease-fire, merely asking the Israelis to explain what they were doing and how long it would take them to do it. Unwilling to pressure the Israelis, Kissinger had only one alternative: to foment the confrontation with the Soviets to buy additional time for the battlefield finally to settle in Israel's favor.

The other factor was Nixon. He had gone to bed in the middle of the flap over the UN resolution. According to the transcript of their ten-minute telephone conversation just after 7:00 p.m., Kissinger said nothing to bring Nixon up to date on the mounting crisis. Nixon was deeply depressed but focused on détente and how to reward Brezhnev's constructive behavior by convincing the Senate to grant Moscow most-favored-nation trade status.

"Now that you have your cease fire abroad, how are you going about a cease fire at home?" Nixon asked,[64] referring to Senate opposition to détente.

Kissinger said he had been on the phone doing missionary work with Senators Jackson and Humphrey, both Israel supporters whose vote on the Soviet trade concession would be critical. To Nixon, Kissinger again waxed rapturous about the success of détente, saying that the cease-fire and cooperation with the Soviets had been a triumph.

Nixon was morose. Kissinger gently raised the subject of Watergate. Who would have thought, he said, that charges of "criminal activities" in the White House would emerge "at the moment of a diplomatic triumph [and] you would have to fight for your political life?"

Kissinger then asked, "What did you do?"

"Nothing," Nixon lied. "By turning the tapes over there can't be any doubt."

"Your attorney general stabbed you in the back," Kissinger said of Richardson, and then added that he thought the firing of Cox was a tactical mistake.

But here Nixon said something that must have rattled Kissinger, who had not met with the president since returning from Moscow, where he had refused to deliver Nixon's message to Brezhnev.

"The point is that Cox was given an order and he defied it," Nixon said. "If you defied an order when you were negotiating with the Russians, you would go down, too." Kissinger sputtered, "I didn't mean that." He started to say something else, but Nixon cut him off. Had Nixon, even in his beleaguered state, rebuked Kissinger for failing to carry out his instructions in Moscow? Had Haig told Nixon of Kissinger's hysterical call on an open line?

As he always did with Nixon, Kissinger quickly resorted to flattery, crediting Nixon for having made the decision to commit openly to Israel with the American airlift. "It was your decision to push in the chips," Kissinger said.

"I hope you make that point to the [congressional] leaders tomorrow," Nixon replied, reminding Kissinger to tell the senators how tough Nixon had been, that he had said there would be as much blame for launching an airlift of three planes or thirty planes. So Nixon had said to pile it on—and he saw himself as bold for having done so.

Nixon's mood turned dark. He was going to address the nation on Watergate. "I will go on at 9:00. It is really pushing the president to go on and get kicked around by those bastards . . . They are doing it because of their desire to kill the president. And they may succeed. I may physically die," he said.

"You are at your best in adversity," Kissinger soothed him.

"We'll see," Nixon said. "What they care about is destruction. It brings me sometimes to feel like saying the hell with it. I would like to see them run this country and see what they do."

This remark impelled Kissinger to think about his place in the line of succession—fourth after the vice president, the speaker of the House, and the president pro tempore of the Senate.

"Can you see Carl Albert [speaker of the House] in this crisis?" Kissinger asked. "He would be running it from Walter Reed [hospital]. And Gerry Ford, fond as I am of him, just doesn't have it."

Was Kissinger saying that after Nixon, only he could run the country? Perhaps, but it was a heedless point of vanity. What was important on that evening was that at every juncture, critical information about the crisis—a crisis that would build to a dangerous confrontation—was simply not shared with Nixon, who may have been drinking, but who, according to the transcript of this call that emerged many years later, was not incapacitated. And Kissinger's duplicity was so plain as to raise questions of constitutional propriety, not to mention loyalty.

. . .

At 11:25 p.m., Dinitz brought a message from Golda Meir saying that she would refuse to pull back to any cease-fire line. She told her ambassador to explain to Kissinger that *of course* Brezhnev was upset that the Egyptian army was trapped, but the only way the Israelis would agree to release it was if Sadat ordered all his forces back across the canal, and then Israel would do the same. A demilitarized zone could be established between them. The proposal was obviously a diversion. Sadat was not going to give up his canal crossing. His army was on Egyptian soil. How could he withdraw from his own territory? Again, in this conversation with Dinitz, according to the extensive declassified record that has emerged, Kissinger made no effort to press Israel to comply with the cease-fire resolution, though separately Kissinger was assuring both the Russians and the Egyptians that he was vigorously doing so.[65]

At 11:41 p.m., the "rump NSC meeting," as Schlesinger referred to it because it was supposed to be chaired by the president, came to a decision to instruct Admiral Thomas Moorer to raise the worldwide alert of American forces—including nuclear forces—to Defense Condition III, a state of readiness that requires hundreds of thousands of military personnel to cancel their leaves and prepare their air, naval, and ground forces for war. Soviet officials monitoring the American military would have seen communication networks "light up" with signal traffic as bases snapped to higher states of readiness and warships went to sea. Strategic nuclear submarines got orders to disperse and B-52 bombers based in Guam were called back to the continental United States so they could be available for strategic nuclear missions.

At 12:20 a.m., the Kissinger-led National Security Council put the Eighty-second Airborne Division on standby for deployment overseas, the navy was instructed to move a second aircraft carrier to the eastern Mediterranean, and a third carrier was ordered to the Middle East from its station in the Atlantic. Just after two o'clock in the morning, Kissinger had his final conversation of the night with Dinitz, to whom he offered copies of top secret "hotline" communications with Brezhnev, including the one that was about to go out in Nixon's name stating that any unilateral action by the Soviet Union would be regarded by the United States "as a matter of the gravest concern involving incalculable consequences."[66]

Kissinger again made no demand that the Israelis cease military operations but rather warned of the prospect that the United States might have to accept Soviet cease-fire observers who would be dispatched to the war zone in short order. In that case, Kissinger said, he wanted Dinitz to provide him with a private military assessment on "whether you can clean up that pocket quickly" before any Soviet observers "come in."[67]

Dinitz seemed confused by Kissinger's metaphor. "Clean up what Dr. Kissinger?"

Kissinger, still speaking in shorthand, turned brutally concise: he asked how long it would take to "get an Army quickly," meaning presumably the Egyptian Third Army.

This widely overlooked transcript indicates with remarkable clarity how Kissinger had been engaged, far beyond any instructions from Nixon, in undermining the cease-fire in order to allow Israel to destroy or force the surrender of the Egyptian Third Army.[68]

The sustained level of Kissinger's deceit from one conversation to the next is striking. Just twenty minutes after he and Schlesinger and the other members of the NSC agreed to put U.S. forces on a war footing, Kissinger called the British ambassador, George Baring, and read him the threatening sentence from Brezhnev's letter.

"Oh no," Baring said, with obvious concern.

"Our own information is that none of this is supported by [actions] on the ground," said Kissinger, now blatantly misleading America's closest ally. "Things in Israel are quiet, the Security Council meeting this evening was very desultory," Kissinger said, withholding what he knew about Israel's ongoing military operations.

Nonetheless, Baring seemed surprised when Kissinger told him about the worldwide alert of U.S. forces.

"Globally?"

"Globally, yes," Kissinger repeated.

Kissinger told the British envoy that the United States would not provide to its allies copies of the exchange with Brezhnev because "we don't want it to leak," though he was providing copies secretly to the Israelis.

Finally, Baring asked Kissinger what the United States wanted Britain to do.

"Well, don't say the Americans have gone crazy," Kissinger replied.[69]

The Americans had not gone crazy, but their government had been manipulated from within in a manner that raised profound constitutional questions: Hadn't the American secretary of state, throughout the day, arrogated to himself the prerogatives of the president without apparent consultation or instruction? Hadn't Kissinger withheld pertinent intelligence from the president and his National Security Council relating to Israel's deliberate circumvention of the cease-fire and the briefings he was receiving from the Israeli ambassador on the progress of the Israeli plan to deliver a crushing blow to Egypt, a blow that Kissinger apparently believed would topple Sadat? Hadn't Kissinger signaled to Dayan and Meir, without any instruction, that the United States would acquiesce in an Israeli decision to keep fighting? Hadn't Kissinger's actions fomented the confrontation with the Soviet Union, which he and Haig then exploited for domestic political gain in Nixon's dark hour?

The NSC, without the president or vice president in the room, acted in a manner that was outside the scope of the National Security Act. Nixon, Kissinger, and Haig, for some years after, maintained the fiction that the president had been part of the White House deliberations, and they later retreated to a version of events in which Haig said he left the Situation Room and consulted with Nixon in the living quarters. But two key participants in those top secret sessions, Schlesinger and Scowcroft, came to doubt Haig's assertion that he had consulted with Nixon or that he obtained Nixon's approval for the actions that were taken in his name that night.[70]

The next morning, Nixon spent an hour closeted with Haig and Kissinger before they all emerged to astound the world with their account of a middle-of-the-night nuclear confrontation with the Soviet Union. In a news conference that day, dominated by Watergate and impeachment questions, Nixon portrayed his brush with Brezhnev and the nuclear alert as a brutal encounter that prevented the Soviet Union from inserting a "substantial" military force into the Middle East. He invoked the dangers of the nuclear age and suggested that he had backed the Soviets down with language that "left very little to the imagination."

Kissinger feared Nixon's performance had gone too far and telephoned Haig. "The crazy bastard really made a mess with the Russians," Kissinger said. "Brezhnev is known to his Politburo as a man with a special relationship with Nixon and he is being publicly humiliated." But hadn't Kissinger encouraged Nixon? Nixon's critics saw the performance as an attempt to distract the country from Watergate. It was inescapably so. But Brezhnev was a tough and competitive leader who recognized that Nixon and Kissinger had turned on him to score points at home.

"What kind of relationship brings an alert over one letter?" Dobrynin had asked Kissinger. Moscow never got any satisfaction in complaining about Israel's cease-fire violations because Nixon assumed that both sides were guilty. Kissinger had made him no wiser.

War in the Middle East was a matter of marginal territorial adjustments and psychological advantage. In the Arab-Israeli conflict, neither side was sufficiently well armed to vanquish the other. Though Israel had developed into a nuclear-weapons state, its arsenal had failed to deter a devastating Arab attack; for Israel, the atomic bomb could not be hurled against the Arabs without taking a cosmic risk of Soviet retaliation. As the combatants and their patrons moved into the negotiation phase, Kissinger helped to control the context: Just because the Arab armies had acquitted themselves well in the fighting, they could not expect to recover their lands. He advised them to abandon their "romantic" notions of doing so. Kissinger asserted that Israel had learned twin lessons: war was becoming far too costly because the Arabs were getting better at it, and war could be fought only with the enthusiastic participation of the United States. Thus diplomacy—Kissinger's diplomacy—had to be given a greater role.

But the reality was quite different. Israel had learned that a well-targeted campaign in the U.S. Congress could change the mind of an American president, and the implications of this development were profound for Israeli military operations in the future. Moreover, Congress was proving to be an ever more important reservoir of support in resisting American diplomatic initiatives that were not in conformity with Israel's national interest. Nixon's determination to goad the Arabs and Israelis toward a settlement was the most prominent casualty of the war. Watergate soon overwhelmed everything else, except Kissinger, who survived to serve in the Ford administration as the indispensable secretary of state.

Israeli elections in December 1973 brought to power an Israeli government under Yitzhak Rabin that was more conservative and intransigent than its predecessor. The recriminations over mistakes and the high death toll of the war ruined political careers and mortally wounded the Labor Party that David Ben-Gurion, Levi Eshkol, and Golda Meir had built.

The 1973 war inaugurated a sustained and intensified American diplomacy broadly throughout the Middle East. Its immediate goal was to

Henry Kissinger with Anwar Sadat: a basic lack of regard for the Arabs

bring an end to the Arab oil embargo, a crisis that Nixon's and Kissinger's
policies had engendered. Oil politics had arrived and would be the source
of conflict, war, and instability in the Middle East for decades.

Kissinger made his first journey to the Middle East in 1973; its politics, geography, and history all were absent from his intellectual background as a historian devoted to Europe.

"It is a novel experience for the world that 50 million people in a hand-
ful of backward nations can drastically change the style of life of 800 million people in the most advanced nations of the globe," Kissinger later
told a group of journalists, warning that the Arab oil producers had better
find a way of cooperating with the West over energy "if they don't want to
go the way of the Greek city states."[71] His glibness betrayed his basic lack
of regard for the Arabs. Over the next two years, Kissinger's diplomacy
during Gerald Ford's brief presidency would be a study in incremental-
ism, one that protected the status quo and avoided putting forward any
comprehensive proposals for Middle East peace. He would send a secret
envoy, Vernon Walters, to undertake the first clandestine discussions
with senior members of the Palestine Liberation Organization, a recognition that the PLO's campaign of international terror had made the guerrilla organization a force to be reckoned with. But Kissinger shunned any

real dialogue with the Palestinians, perhaps because he remained uncertain whether the Israelis would ever make peace with them, or whether the Palestinians would ever accept the Jewish state or give up their designs on Jordan. But as he had demonstrated time and again in the Nixon years, Kissinger found it impossible to advocate a course in the Middle East that ran counter to the prevailing consensus of Israel's leaders, even to the detriment of U.S. national interest.

# 5

# JIMMY CARTER

*Camp David and the Struggle
with Menachem Begin*

Searchlights raked the skies and swept the tarmac at Ben-Gurion International Airport as if Israel were expecting an extraterrestrial. Anwar Sadat, unbelievably, had set down his presidential plane in the land of the enemy, and when he appeared in the doorway of the Boeing 707 at the top of the stairway that led down to a red carpet, for millions of Jews and Arabs (and the rest of the world) watching on television, it seemed that, for better or worse, he had turned the region's most profound enmity on its head.

Sadat's arrival was an inconvenient miracle for Jimmy Carter, and by stepping onto Israeli soil on November 19, 1977, Sadat had shattered the conventions that had defined the Arab rejection of the Jewish state. Twenty-nine years after the founding of Israel in May 1948, he was granting recognition to the Zionist proposition, though it had been the scourge of the Arabs and, no one could be mistaken, he knew he was tempting the wrath of his brethren by taking this step.

Elected president in 1976 in the aftermath of Watergate, Carter had spent much of his first two years in office trying to convene a Middle East peace summit in Geneva under joint auspices of the United States and the Soviet Union. He had angered Israeli leaders and American Jews by talking up the concept of a Palestinian homeland, and he needed the summit meeting to show that his administration could achieve something significant in foreign policy. But Sadat, the onetime drama student, was exploding all of those carefully laid plans; his critics saw it as a political stunt by the "clown"—that's what some called him—of Arab politics. Yet after all the images of war and carnage emanating from the Middle East, here was a *grand geste* whose wind shear seemed to sweep everyone off their feet.

Sadat descended the stairs and found himself standing nose to nose with Golda Meir, the lioness of Zion, the keeper of the photo albums of the dead, the Jewish mother to all those boys and girls who had fallen in the wars. Now she faced their murderer come to make peace. She just stood there flummoxed by her own emotions, conscious that Sadat was speaking, telling her that he had been looking forward to meeting her for a long time.

"But you never came," she said.

"But now I'm here," he replied.

Sadat's wife, Jehan, had pleaded with him to take special care in greeting Meir, and he had rebuked her: "Do you think I will make less of an effort because she is not a man?"

Now watching a television in Cairo, Jehan could see Meir's face in the greeting line as she listened intently to Sadat.

"You are very well known in our country, Mrs. Meir. Do you know what you are called?"

"No, what?" she asked.

"The strongest man in Israel," Sadat said.

Meir's face crinkled with delight.

"I take that as a compliment, Mr. President," she said, but when Jehan heard it later, she winced at her husband's notion of a compliment.[1]

The sheer proximity of Jewish and Arab nerve endings caused the night air to vibrate as Sadat moved down the line. They were all there, Zion's civilian leaders and generals, staring at this Arab in their midst. The reaction of Israel's intelligence apparatus when it learned that Sadat was coming was to insist—much to the chagrin of the political leaders—that the Egyptian president was creating a diversion so that his army could stage another surprise attack. General Shlomo Gazit, the head of military intelligence, and General Mordechai Gur, the chief of staff, both raised alarms about a repeat of the 1973 Yom Kippur attack. But they had been kept in the dark about the crucial bits of information—that Moshe Dayan and Prime Minister Menachem Begin had been working to encourage Sadat's visit for months and that Dayan had secretly flown to Morocco in September to broach a peace agreement and to discuss the possibility of a meeting between Sadat and Begin.

When Sadat got to General Gur in the line of Israeli dignitaries, he simply said, "I wasn't deceiving you!" and Gur burst out laughing. Facing Ariel Sharon, Sadat again resorted to humor, warning him, if he tried to cross the Suez Canal again, "I will put you in jail!"

"Oh no!" Sharon retorted, his head thrown back in laughter as he pumped Sadat's hand. "I'm minister of culture now!"[2]

David Kimche, the longtime Mossad strategist and diplomat, later said that the joy that welled up in the Israelis, and perhaps Jews everywhere, was the product of a deeply felt sense of recognition, which the idealists of Zion had always believed would come.

"It was, in Sadat's eyes, the greatest possible gift he could bear to Jerusalem, something that Israel needed more than anything else," Kimche observed.[3]

Sadat understood. That was the point—he was looking for reciprocity. He had given the Israelis legitimacy, something that no other Arab leader had been willing to confer on the "Zionist entity." Sadat shook the hands of Israel's leaders and traveled with them up the mountain to Jerusalem, where he paid homage to the victims of the Holocaust at Yad Vashem. He laid a wreath at the country's Tomb of the Unknown Soldier and climbed the stairs (hewn from the honey-colored limestone of the Holy Land) into the Old City and up to the al-Aqsa Mosque. Sadat prayed there, in the Arabs' Noble Sanctuary on the Jewish Temple Mount, where King Solomon had laid the foundations of Hebrew worship in the tenth century B.C., where Christ had preached and suffered, and from where the Prophet Muhammad had ascended to heaven on a winged steed. There, Sadat's prayers commingled at the epicenter of the three monotheistic faiths in the city that has no rival: "None has evoked such awe and wonder or at the same time given her name to peace and to all that is tender in the human soul," wrote Amos Elon.[4]

The Arabs watched in disbelief. O Jerusalem! Even nonbelievers had to stop and bear witness as the Egyptian president walked the land to which Moses had led the Hebrew slaves. Some felt betrayed. Some were hopeful. Some were confused and others seethed. President Hafez al-Assad in Syria was first among those who felt that Sadat had abandoned Arab dignity and humiliated himself by stepping onto the soil of the enemy even as it occupied the Arab homeland. Salah Khalaf, the Black September leader and Arafat's adjutant in the PLO, was watching the scene on television in Beirut. As Sadat came down those stairs, "My throat tightened," he recounted. "He started shaking hands. The butchers of my people filed before our eyes: Begin, Dayan, Sharon, generals in full-dress uniform.

"For the first time, I felt something in me snap. The friendship I'd had for Sadat, despite everything, for over 15 years was irrevocably broken," Khalaf went on. "He claimed to speak in the name of the entire Arab nation, in the name of the Palestinian people, but he abandoned our rights without ever consulting us. He sold a territory that didn't belong to him dirt cheap, at the expense of a people without a country! The friendship—I'm ashamed to admit I even had it—changed to hatred."[5]

Why had he done it? Few people understood how desperate Sadat's position had become. The October War and the disengagement agreements negotiated by Kissinger in 1974 and 1975 had neither won the return of Sinai nor improved the lives of millions of Egyptian peasants. Expectations had been so high. The Suez Canal, closed since the 1967 war, had reopened after the second disengagement agreement, but the Egyptian economy was still barter and penury. Saudi and American handouts were keeping Egypt afloat.

In January 1977, bread riots broke out in Cairo when Sadat had tried to lift the subsidies on essential items. He had been forced to send the army into the streets, and 160 demonstrators were killed. Egypt's domestic scene then turned brutal. Responding to the ever-present challenge from the Muslim Brotherhood, Sadat injected more Islamic piety into government. He tried to pacify student militancy. But it was not just the grinding poverty that was keeping Egypt down; it was *that*, in combination with a high birthrate, a weak agricultural base, and virtually no modern industry. Leadership politics were just as complicated. The army resented Sadat's decision to distance Egypt from the Soviet camp. Sadat also had to contend with the Nasserite orthodoxy—staunch Arab nationalism—that emanated from Egypt's Foreign Ministry, headed by Ismail Fahmy. And then there was the PLO, whose political voice was now as strong as any Arab leader's and whose terrorism was a threat to anyone who was seen as betraying the cause.

Jimmy Carter was fifty-two years old when he defeated Gerald Ford in the 1976 election. Carter, a former governor and a Georgia peanut farmer who had served in the navy's nuclear submarine fleet under Admiral Hyman G. Rickover, was the first American president to come to office strongly committed to working for a comprehensive settlement of the Arab-Israeli dispute in the Middle East. As a Southern Baptist, Carter knew the Middle East from the Bible, and he had been tutored in the modern conflict by advisers such as Zbigniew Brzezinski, Dean Rusk, Averell Harriman, Richard Gardner, and the experts of the Brookings Institution and other think tanks.

The Carter campaign had been founded to a great extent on the moral revulsion against Watergate, the Nixon pardon, and the pervasive cynicism of the Nixon-Kissinger era. In the second presidential debate, Carter had asserted that "as far as foreign policy goes, Mr. Kissinger has been the president of the country" and that he and Ford had "continued on with the policies and failures of Richard Nixon."

Carter wanted a return to American idealism in foreign affairs, respect for human rights, and restraint in arms sales, especially in the Middle East.

"We have become the arms merchant of the world," he said. Though he had waged an insurgent's campaign as an outsider from Plains, Georgia, who would never lie to the American people, Carter had made great use of the eastern foreign policy establishment, asking Cyrus Vance to serve as secretary of state, Harold Brown as secretary of defense, James Schlesinger as secretary of energy, and Brzezinski as national security adviser. All of them had broad experience in government, except Brzezinski, who, like Kissinger a decade earlier, had not served in a major government post but had made a reputation as a leading academic who advised policy makers.

Like Kissinger, Brzezinski was close to the Rockefeller family and had founded the Trilateral Commission with David Rockefeller to strengthen relations among the United States, Western Europe, and Japan. As director, Brzezinski had selected then governor Jimmy Carter to be a member of the commission and thereafter became his tutor in international affairs, a relationship that Carter found both valuable and enjoyable because Zbig—that's what he's called: "Zzz-BIG"—had a lively mind that spun out history, policy, and personal insights with breathtaking clarity. He was clever, humorous, mischievous—fun for Carter, to whom the world was opening up.

In contrast, Vance was dour. He had served under both Kennedy and Johnson in the Defense Department, reversing his initial enthusiastic support for the Vietnam War and then joining the American delegation to the Paris peace talks in 1968 to help Johnson search for a way out. He had great integrity as a public servant and as an international lawyer and was among those stalwarts of cold war diplomacy who believed that the path of negotiation, engagement, and arms control with the Soviet Union—détente, in other words—was the best course for keeping the peace. But Vance had a streak of Yankee rectitude, and his relationship with Carter would never compete with Zbig's. Carter admired Vance and valued his advice, which was often more well-grounded than Brzezinski's intellectual acrobatics. But beyond that, a significant philosophical divide existed between Vance and Brzezinski from the outset of the administration. Where Vance focused on winning Soviet support for a new round of limitations on strategic nuclear arms, Brzezinski argued for doing that *plus* pressing the human rights agenda on behalf of repressed populations behind the Iron Curtain. He was quick to see Soviet adventurism in third world crises and encouraged Carter to confront Moscow more forcefully than the diplomats of the State Department preferred.

Indeed, Vance's allies, chief among them Averell Harriman and his young protégé, Richard Holbrooke, had made an effort during the transition after Carter's election to convince the president-elect that Brzezinski's participation in the new government would not be constructive. Holbrooke, in a telephone call that he would never forget, told Carter that with Vance as secretary of state, Brzezinski would undermine the coherence of his foreign policy team. Their worldviews were too far apart, he said.

Carter hung up frostily and that was the end of Holbrooke's relationship with the president. Brzezinski entered the White House as national security adviser. Vance protected Holbrooke by giving him a job as assistant secretary of state for Asia, but he spent the next four years with a target on his back because Brzezinski understood what the Harriman cabal had tried to do to him.[6]

In the first months of his administration, Carter met the key leaders in the Middle East: Israeli prime minister Yitzhak Rabin, Sadat, King Hussein of Jordan, and Crown Prince Fahd of Saudi Arabia came to Washington. Carter flew to neutral ground in Geneva, Switzerland, to meet Hafez al-Assad of Syria. The new president told them all that what they had been reading about the new administration was true—he was going to go all out for comprehensive peace. The venue for an opening summit would be Geneva. The Soviets would be a partner. The terms would be based on the principles of withdrawal, secure borders for Israel, and justice for the Palestinians. Everyone was going to have to compromise.

Some saw him as naïve. Kissinger, for instance, thought comprehensive peace impossible. He later asserted, in the third volume of his memoirs, that he would have resigned in 1975 had President Ford forced him to formulate terms for an overall peace in the Middle East. He explained: "The disparity between Israel's perception of its margin of survival and ours would become too difficult to bridge. If we prevailed, we would break Israel's back psychologically; if we failed, we would have doomed our role in the Middle East."[7]

This is a bizarre explanation. Kissinger equates the fate of Israel with that of South Vietnam. Having been involved in the settlement that was imposed on Saigon, only to see the country defeated and its government destroyed, Kissinger asserts that his fear of a similar outcome in the Middle East, where a settlement imposed on Israel might lead to its destruction, was too much for him to bear, given his family's fate in the Holocaust.

It is impossible to ridicule any Holocaust survivor's invocation of anxiety over security, but it is also a travesty of logic for Kissinger to maintain that America, in pushing for a comprehensive settlement in the Middle East, would have weakened or endangered Israel's security, or would have tolerated any attempt to do so. Equating American policy toward Israel with the American decision to quit Vietnam was a non sequitur. Kissinger offered an ostensibly profound revelation of psychic angst, but in fact he had set up a straw man so that he could not betray Israel as America had betrayed Vietnam. This straw man distracted attention from the Ford administration's failure of will, a failure that any political realist would understand given the difficult reelection odds Ford was facing. Israel's perception of its margin of survival had undergone manifold improvement. First, Israel was by 1975 a fully armed nuclear power with two delivery systems—aircraft and missiles—for ten or more nuclear weapons.

This comprised a force powerful enough to devastate the armies or the population centers of its main Arab foes. Second, as James Schlesinger had admitted in a meeting with Ford, the United States had "overestimated badly"[8] the quantity of Soviet arms that Egypt had received during the war. Therefore, the massive infusion of arms to Israel had given Israel an even stronger advantage.

Carter saw the imbalance as part of the danger. He later wrote that "it was widely assumed that Israel has atomic weapons or the capability to deploy them quickly and that the Soviets have pledged to protect their client states from such an attack with any means necessary.

"What would the United States do?" he had asked himself. America "could not stand aloof if the Middle East burst into flames," and "it is clear that desperation on either side could precipitate a more serious regional confrontation than has been seen before."[9]

Yet Carter began his diplomacy not as a seasoned or sophisticated statesman, but as a well-intentioned neophyte, who, in the tradition of the civil rights movement, began to speak out about the inequities he believed had to be redressed. "I don't think that there can be any reasonable hope for a settlement of the Middle Eastern question," Carter told a news conference on May 12, "without a homeland for the Palestinians."[10]

The statement rattled the Israelis and American Jews. Carter had said nothing like it during the campaign. Indeed, he had pandered to Israel, as Democratic candidates were wont to do, accusing Ford of overarming Iran and Saudi Arabia at the expense of "our major ally in the Middle East—Israel." Carter had hammered Ford for the so-called reassessment of American policy toward Israel in early 1975, a Kissinger pressure tactic that had backfired.

"We almost brought Israel to their knees," Carter had said in rebuking the Ford record. "And this weakened our relationship with Israel a great deal and put a cloud on the total commitment that our people feel toward the Israelis."[11]

Carter saw the plight of the Palestinians as akin to that of African Americans under segregation. Here was a disenfranchised minority, oppressed, stateless, and living cruelly under Israeli occupation. The comparison with American blacks may not have been exact, but Carter saw a rough symmetry between racial injustice in America and the injustice the Palestinians suffered. In any case, he had decided to act on it.[12]

Yitzhak Rabin was the first to go to Washington to pay a visit to Carter, but he left a grim impression of Israeli resistance to compromise. This was the early Rabin—the warrior who had made an awkward and incompetent transition to politics. This Rabin was not really interested in peace. Peace was something he saw as a distant possibility after a long struggle with the Arabs. This also was an insecure and politically besieged Rabin. The truth was that Rabin did not like Carter from the beginning. "He saw him as a preacher," said Amos Eiran, a Rabin confidant. "He saw him as the kind of preacher who wanted to establish at that time a Palestinian state and Rabin thought it was premature."[13]

The Carter team seemed oblivious to Rabin's troubles at home, where his coalition government was fraying and a scandal over Leah Rabin's American bank account was about to break. Rabin had been pummeled by tough questions during the March 1977 visit. Thomas P. "Tip" O'Neill, the speaker of the House, had asked him at a dinner, "Why don't you negotiate with the PLO?" America had negotiated with the Vietcong, O'Neill pointed out. One had to negotiate with one's enemy if one wanted peace.

Carter "couldn't get him to concentrate on any sort of substance" in their talks. Rabin was inflexible, and asked Carter to tone down his public remarks about the need for a Palestinian homeland. Such remarks were causing Rabin trouble at home while also inciting American Jews, who were even more sensitive than the Israelis. Rabin thought that he had received Carter's pledge to do so and went off to American University to receive an honorary degree. During the ceremony, Rabin's aides got word that Carter had just given a news conference in which he said Israel would have to withdraw from the Palestinian territories in order to make peace.[14] Rabin was incredulous. Carter had just ruined what he had hoped would be a positive visit. After Rabin left, Carter did it again, telling an audience in Clinton, Massachusetts, that "there has to be a homeland provided for the Palestinian refugees who have suffered for many, many years."

Soon thereafter, on May 17, 1977, a political earthquake rearranged the landscape in Israel. Menachem Begin and the Likud bloc won the elections. The Labor Party dynasty that had ruled Israel since its creation had been overthrown by the former commander of the Irgun, a man so reviled for his harsh and rebellious politics that Ben-Gurion had refused to address him by name in the Knesset.

Carter was devastated. The Irgun "terrorist" who was responsible for blowing up the King David Hotel in 1947 had won an election; the militarist of the Israeli right dedicated to expanding Israel's borders by annexing Arab lands, the hard-liner whose political philosophy was indifferent to the suffering of Palestinians living under occupation, was now the prime minister. Carter thought the peace process was over before he had even managed to get it started.[15] White House aides, trying to understand Begin, were scrambling to read *Terror Out of Zion*, the history of the Jewish underground that had been published that year.[16]

No one was more surprised by the victory than Menachem Begin, who had spent a quarter century in political opposition, ranting against Labor Party policies like a populist demagogue filled with Holocaust anger, challenging the pragmatism of the mainstream. In his memoir of the underground, which he flamboyantly called *The Revolt*, Begin had defined the politics of rage: "The Jew whom the world considered dead and buried never to rise again has arisen. We had to hate the humiliating disgrace of the homelessness of our people. We had to hate—as any nation worth the name must always hate—the rule of the foreigner, rule unjust and unjustifiable per se, foreign rule in the land of our ancestors, in our own country."[17]

Thirty years after statehood, Begin's victory was a manifestation of his remarkable perseverance. This frail and balding warrior with thick spectacles, who had suffered a heart attack in the middle of the campaign, had nonetheless prevailed on the strength of irrepressible will and the shifting demographics of the Israeli electorate. An underclass of Sephardic Jews, more hard-line in their view of the Arabs, had come over to Likud to help topple Labor's primacy. Begin had suffered a long purgatory under Ben-Gurion, whom he had admired despite all their differences. But the feeling had never been mutual. Eshkol had shown Begin a modicum of respect by bringing him into the unity government on the eve of the Six-Day War. Begin's mentor had been Ze'ev Jabotinsky, the founder of Revisionist Zionism, which was fearless in its ambition for territory, and its militarist's view of the struggle with the Arabs.

Most of Begin's immediate family had perished in the Holocaust, and he had found his way to Palestine after imprisonment by the Soviets. He had arrived in 1941 with a detachment of the Polish army and promptly defected and began building the Irgun into an instrument of Jewish terror against the British administration in Palestine. But Begin never considered himself a terrorist.

"Our enemies called us terrorists, and yet, we were not terrorists," Begin wrote. "The historical and linguistic origins of the political term 'terror' prove that it cannot be applied to a revolutionary war of liberation. A revolution may give birth to what we call 'terror' as happened in France. Terror may at times be its herald, as happened in Russia. But the revolution itself is not terror, and terror is not the revolution." Begin said he armed the Irgun to overthrow British rule. "The sole aim on the one side is the overthrow of armed tyranny; on the other side is the perpetuation of that tyranny. The underground fighters of the Irgun arose to overthrow and replace a regime. We used physical force because we were faced with physical force."[18]

Years later, Shlomo Gazit, the officer selected by Moshe Dayan to administer the Palestinian territories, observed, "One can only wonder how Menachem Begin, who led the 'rebellion' against the British 'occupier' of Palestine, and who never stopped preaching freedom (and even called his party 'freedom'—*Herut*), could not understand that it was only natural for the Palestinian Arabs under Israeli occupation to have the same feelings."[19]

Since 1967, Begin and his cohorts on the political right had led the campaign to incorporate into Israel much of the land conquered during the Six-Day War, most importantly the West Bank, because the hills and valleys of biblical Judea and Samaria were part of the ancient land of Israel. Begin came into office determined to expand the settler movement significantly in order to populate the West Bank, as well as the Golan Heights, Gaza, and Sinai, with Jewish settlements. This would create facts on the ground and lay the foundation for Jewish sovereignty. Begin had surprised his critics by offering Dayan, a onetime stalwart of the Labor Party and Ben-Gurion ally, a seat in his cabinet. Dayan, too, believed Jews could settle the West Bank, living side by side with Palestinians.

Begin disarmed many of his critics, Jimmy Carter told me in an interview. Carter recalled that "when [Begin] came to the White House, I was really pleasantly surprised because he was much more amenable to taking a bold action, to meeting with Sadat, to working out problems and so forth, than I had ever dreamed. I was very pleased."[20] At the time, Carter wrote in his diary that he hoped Begin would prove to be a "strong leader, quite different than Rabin."[21]

Carter and his aides had seen the huge gap between Begin's position and that of the Arabs, but they convinced themselves that if they could just get all the parties to Geneva, they could get some momentum going and the negotiations would open up opportunities for bridging differences. But Begin's transformation was more of tone than of substance. He came to Washington knowing that Carter was on the defensive with American Jews. Golda Meir, nearly eighty but still a favorite of American audiences, had threatened to take Carter on over his statements about a Palestinian homeland. ("I'm going to have to open up on him," she had warned in an interview.) Jacob Javits, one of the pillars of support for Israel in the Senate, criticized Carter's supposed tilt toward the Palestinians. Carter responded by calling fifty Jewish leaders to the White House and pledging his devotion to the Jewish state.[22] Carter hoped that he could change Jewish attitudes about the Palestinians by persuading the PLO to accept Resolution 242, which implicitly recognized Israel's right to exist. The PLO had refused, saying the Security Council resolution that ended the 1967 war neglected even to mention the Palestinians and their right to a homeland. The PLO's parliament in exile met in Cairo, where Arafat told the forum that he "trusted" Carter and believed that the American president understood the region more profoundly than his predecessors.

"They tell me he mentioned the Palestinian homeland," Arafat said on March 17. "It is a very progressive step because it means he has finally touched the heart of the problem without which there can be no settlement of the Middle East crisis."[23] Arafat had also told Crown Prince Fahd of Saudi Arabia that the PLO would recognize Israel's existence *if* the Americans guaranteed statehood for the Palestinians. At the time, that was a big *if*.

Carter sent Secretary of State Vance to the Middle East in hopes of an early breakthrough that would draw the PLO into talks. "Palestinian leaders have indicated indirectly they might adopt Resolution 242," Carter said from Plains. If they did, "then that would open up a new opportunity for us to start discussions with them, and also open up an avenue that they might participate in the Geneva conference."[24]

Arafat told the Saudis that he would try to convince the PLO leadership. He flew to Damascus but ran into such resistance from "extremists" that he telephoned Prince Saud al-Faisal, the Saudi foreign minister, and told him that he could not muster the votes to change the PLO's stance. "The opportunity has gone," Prince Saud told Vance.[25]

Carter and Vance sent Arafat one more emissary, Rosalynn Carter's Quaker friend Landrum Bolling. But Bolling soon reported that Arafat insisted on a commitment to Palestinian statehood as a precondition. Asked why he wasn't able to accept Resolution 242, Arafat said, "Because the Syrians are against it and the Jordanians are against it. If I started talking to the Americans, then Sadat is out of business. If I accept it, tomorrow the Syrians will shell all of the refugee camps in Lebanon and I will lose 5,000 Palestinians."[26] It may have been an exaggeration, but Arafat had accurately described the pressure points he felt.

On October 10, the State Department formally stated the issues Washington expected to be settled at Geneva. The "status of the Palestinians must be settled" in a comprehensive peace, it said, adding that "this issue cannot be ignored if the others are to be solved."[27] But Syria's foreign minister, Abdul Halim Khaddam, complained that the PLO stood to get nothing from negotiations based on the unacceptable UN resolution.[28]

From Cairo, Anwar Sadat was able to see that the whole concept of an Arab-Israeli peace summit at Geneva had devolved into a power struggle among the Arabs. Comprehensive peace in the Middle East was almost impossibly complex. Geneva meant that the lowest common denominator would form the Arab consensus. That would surely work against compromise. Sadat thought the Arabs would "explode." It would be Assad's hard-liners against Begin's hard-liners. Sadat would have no control. He began to think of how he might short-circuit the Geneva process, how he might put Begin on the defensive and thrust himself back to the fore of the Arab camp.[29]

Begin and Dayan had come to a similar conclusion about Sadat. They, too, wanted to short-circuit the Geneva conference, which threatened to entrap Israel in an extended and unpredictable negotiation over Palestinian national rights, perhaps even statehood. In September, Dayan flew to Morocco in disguise: a wig, fake mustache, and heavy sunglasses instead of the usual eye patch. King Hassan II, who had arranged the meeting, introduced him to Hassan Tuhamy, Sadat's deputy prime minister and a former Nasser confidant.

Sadat was "deadly serious in his quest for peace," Tuhamy said. If Begin was equally serious, he would have to demonstrate that he understood the "questions of sovereignty, of national honor" that were tied to the fate of the Arab territories still under occupation. Israel would also have to come to terms with Palestinian nationalism, for as long as their ambition for "nationhood" was frustrated, the Palestinians would embrace extremism and the Soviet Union would gain more ground in the region. Dayan made it clear that he was there as Begin's messenger, but he observed that withdrawal was "no light matter."

"For 19 years before the Six-Day War our population centers had been attacked from the hills. What guarantee was there that this would not happen again?" Dayan asked. What about the Golan Heights, without which Israelis would be looking up at Syrian gunners once again? What about the Wailing Wall and the Jewish Quarter of the Old City and the Hebrew University on Mount Scopus? These would be wrenching concessions for Israel, but if Israel was to enter such a negotiation, it would have to trust its partners. Dayan was certain that trust could be established with Sadat and the king of Jordan, but Israel did not trust Assad, who still proclaimed that all Palestinians should return to their homes in Israel.

"What would happen if they were indeed to return?" Dayan asked. "They would not be satisfied with living only in the comparatively small enclaves of the West Bank and Gaza Strip. There was not enough room and work for them there. They would stream into Israel and this would be a demographic catastrophe for us."[30]

Ariel Sharon, who had taken the position as minister of agriculture in Begin's cabinet, announced publicly that he had developed a plan to settle two million Jews in a "security belt" extending from the Golan Heights in the north to the tip of the Sinai Peninsula. With characteristic bravado, Sharon told Israeli state radio that he didn't see the move endangering the chances for peace or of triggering condemnation. Israel, he said, did not have to consider world opinion when settling Jews in the biblical land of Israel.[31]

Carter was furious. He had told his top aides just days earlier that he was fed up with a policy in which the United States financed Israeli conquests and got nothing in return but intransigence and defiance that "make a mockery of our advice and our preferences." Carter vented his anger on the first Israeli official he could. That happened to be Dayan, who had arrived in Washington following his secret discussions in Morocco. Carter, Dayan later wrote, "launched charge after charge against Israel" during a meeting in Carter's private study. At one point, the president said, "You are more stubborn than the Arabs, and you put obstacles on the path to peace."

Dayan became angry. "I was disgusted," he said, especially at the way Carter and Vice President Walter Mondale double-teamed him. "Whenever the president showed signs of calming down and holding an even-tempered dialogue, Mondale jumped in with fresh complaints which disrupted the talk."[32] Carter had been on notice that the word was out in the Jewish community "that if they press hard enough the president will yield." He had lost some of his confidence about how hard he could push back.[33] And in private, Carter told Ismail Fahmy, the Egyptian foreign minister, that he needed to clarify an important point: "President Sadat repeatedly asks me to exercise major pressure on Israel, but I want you to know that I simply cannot do it because it would be personal political suicide for me.

"It is important that you do not forget that my influence on Israel is proportionately related to the scope of support which I get from American public opinion, Congress and the Jewish circles in this country," he continued. "I want to be abundantly clear that in the absence of such triangular support, my ability to influence Israel is minimal." Carter said he could not guarantee that the Palestinians would get a national homeland as part of a comprehensive settlement, just as he could not state that Syria would get the Golan Heights back. In addition, Carter had been forced by the backlash in the Jewish community to further restrict contact with the PLO.

"I had the impression that although he was quite familiar with the various issues, he was unsure of himself and he did not feel he could make events unfold according to his plans," Fahmy said.[34] If anything, that was an understatement.

It had become clear that Carter had no negotiating strategy for Geneva. He had rejected Sadat's notion that a substantial part of a comprehensive agreement should be negotiated in advance. That was impossible.

Fahmy returned to Cairo with an extremely negative report for Sadat. "President Carter's weakness loomed large," he said, and the whole Egyptian delegation was affected by Carter's "candid confession of U.S. impotence." The Israelis, it seemed, were correct in their assessment. Carter's many statements about a Palestinian homeland and Israeli withdrawal had inflated hopes and expectations in the Arab world. Disillusionment soon followed.

By the fall of 1977, the Carter administration had invested enormous political capital in the Middle East and had gotten nothing but domestic turmoil and opposition in return. On October 1, the United States and Soviet Union released a joint declaration stating their belief that "a com-

prehensive settlement" in the Middle East could be achieved through negotiations on the withdrawal of Israeli armed forces from territories occupied in the 1967 war and on "ensuring the legitimate rights of the
Palestinian people."[35]

The specter of an "imposed settlement" erupted in Israel and among
American Jews. One was quoted anonymously in *The New York Times*
saying, "This may be the last straw" in the uncomfortable stand-off between Carter and the Jewish community. William Safire, the Nixon
speechwriter turned *New York Times* columnist, accused Carter of "selling out Israel," coddling PLO terrorists, and caving to Soviet pressure.[36]
Rabbi Alexander M. Schindler said the Conference of Presidents of Major American Jewish organizations (of which he was chairman) was "profoundly disturbed" by the declaration "which, on its face, represents an
abandonment of America's historic commitment to the security and survival of Israel."

The reaction was so intense that Carter pulled back. On October 4, he
addressed the United Nations General Assembly. "We do not intend to
impose, from the outside, a settlement on the nations of the Middle
East." For the United States, he had added, "Israel's security is unques-
tionable," and for the Arabs, "the legitimate rights of the Palestinian
people must be recognized." But it was not enough. That evening Carter
met with Dayan. The session was extremely confrontational. Dayan
threatened to incite the Jewish community further against Carter, a step
that Brzezinski considered blackmail.[37]

"We might have a [public] confrontation," Carter told Dayan, "but a
confrontation would be very damaging to Israel and to the support of the
American public for Israel." Carter also knew that Dayan's rivals at home,
Rabin and Peres in particular, were accusing the Begin government of
mismanaging relations with the United States.

The struggle over the Middle East had gotten so intense and complicated that the question for each participant was no longer who was going
to win but who was going to lose the least. The Israelis had become "excessively self-assured" that the president was susceptible to their pressures. Carter had been tough, "but he didn't go far enough to indicate
that if challenged he would go to the country and there would be an all-
out confrontation,"[38] like the one Eisenhower threatened during the Suez
crisis if Israel refused to withdraw from Sinai. What emerged from this
grim and contentious encounter was a new communiqué that paved the

way for Israel's participation in a Geneva peace conference, but with the crucial caveat that "acceptance of the joint U.S.-U.S.S.R. statement of October 1, 1977, by the parties is not a prerequisite for the reconvening and conduct of the Geneva Conference."

Now the Arabs saw Carter as a president who easily lost his nerve. And the peace conference had not even started.[39] On October 21, Carter sent Sadat a handwritten note that stated poignantly, "I need your help." The peace process had reached a critical stage, time was running out, and still there was no agreement on procedures for Geneva.[40] Carter's letter had a profound effect on Sadat. On a visit to Bucharest with Fahmy, Sadat turned to his foreign minister and asked him what he thought about "a trip to Jerusalem to deliver a speech in the Knesset." Fahmy replied that it sounded like a "publicity stunt." He tried to divert Sadat by suggesting they call for a United Nations summit in Jerusalem to launch peace ne-gotiations. The two men wrangled for eight hours over what to do. When Fahmy went back to his guesthouse and told his staff what the president was thinking about, Osama el-Baz, his office director, exclaimed, "This is crazy! This man is not balanced. He should be prevented even by force to go to Jerusalem."[41]

When the White House heard about Sadat's idea, Brzezinski "won-dered whether he was not losing his sense of reality."

"Well, if you don't like my ideas, don't you have any of your own?" Sa-dat asked Herman Eilts, the American ambassador in Cairo.[42]

We have none, Eilts replied.

On November 5, Sadat told his National Security Council, in a ca-sual aside, that he was "ready to go to Jerusalem and to give a speech in the Israeli Knesset if this will save the blood of my sons." After a mo-ment of stunned silence, General Mohamed Gamasy, the minister of de-fense and hero of the 1973 war, said, "No Knesset, no Knesset. This is unnecessary."[43]

Sadat's advisers had come of age under Nasser, and the hallmark of Nasser's rule was uncompromising Arab nationalism. They were shaken by Sadat's flights of fancy. Fahmy, hoping to steady Sadat's nerve, invited Yasser Arafat to Cairo to sit with the Egyptian People's Assembly to hear Sadat's speech on his efforts to reach peace. Hosni Mubarak, the vice president and former air force commander, dispatched a military plane to pick up Arafat. Mubarak explained that Egypt also needed Arafat's help in mediation efforts with Muammar Qaddafi, the Libyan leader, who had been discovered plotting Sadat's overthrow.[44] Sadat took the podium and unwound his theme of peace, and there seemed to be nothing terribly new in the speech until Sadat said, "I am willing to go to Geneva, nay, to the end of the world" for peace. "In fact, I know that Israel will be astounded when I say that I am ready to go to their very home, to the Knesset, to debate with them."

Arafat did not immediately react. He joined in the applause as Sadat came to a conclusion, but the PLO leader quickly rushed to Fahmy and asked him, "What is the meaning of this? Have you invited me to come to Cairo in order to hear such a thing?"

Sadat was like a fox. "It was a slip of the tongue," he protested gaily in the delegates' lounge for all to hear. Then he turned to Fahmy and said, "Please, Ismail, censor it completely." Fahmy was only too happy to do so, but everyone knew that although the remark would be excised from the Egyptian press, it would rocket around the world because correspondents from international news agencies had been present. Begin and Carter would know of it within hours. Mubarak's task was to contain Arafat's anger, and the two men repaired to the vice president's villa. But Arafat refused to stay. He took leave of Mubarak and returned to Beirut. It would be six years before he again set foot in the Egyptian capital.[45]

Jehan Sadat, because she knew the misery of Egypt and the passion of the Arabs, and because she understood her husband's desperation and his vanities, claimed to have suffered a dark premonition: "I knew from the moment my husband announced his willingness to go to Jerusalem to make peace with Israel that he would be killed for it. I did not know when his death would come, where it would occur, or who would kill him. I only knew that my days on earth with my husband were now numbered."[46]

Carter was unhinged by Sadat's announcement. "For the next several weeks, the United States was largely a spectator," Brzezinski later admitted.[47]

The bravest thing Sadat did—braver than landing in Israel—was flying to Damascus for an all-night parley with Assad, trying to convince the Syrian dictator to support the Jerusalem gamble. "I argued with Hafez until four in the morning," Sadat told his wife when he returned to Cairo, his face drained with exhaustion. He told Assad that if his journey failed, "I alone would bear the consequences." As soon as Sadat left Damascus, the chilling reports went out from Radio Damascus: anyone who set foot in occupied Jerusalem was betraying the Arabs.

Sadat took to sleeping with a revolver. Jehan begged him to wear a bulletproof vest to Jerusalem, but he refused. If it were discovered, he would be savaged as a coward.[48] He fended off all efforts at dissuasion. "I will not discuss it with anybody. I don't care for anybody's opinion. I will not do it!" he screamed to his national security advisers.

Fahmy resigned. His deputy, Mohammed Riad, elevated to replace him, also resigned.[49] Yet the news that he was actually going to Jerusalem to speak to the Knesset swept the globe as a sensation. Walter Cronkite, the CBS Evening News anchorman, conducted live interviews with Sadat and Begin to spur them on. Television news now covered Sadat's every utterance, every appearance in public. Begin had no choice but to ride the popular exuberance for Sadat's proposed act of recognition of the Jewish state; he sent Sadat a formal invitation, and Sadat staged a photo opportunity to receive it at the presidential guesthouse on the Nile. The American ambassador arrived and handed Sadat a folded piece of paper, which he accepted with a flourish. It was blank, because the real invitation had been left inadvertently in Cairo, but no one was the wiser.

Once Sadat had landed safely in Israel, everything hung on the speech. The Knesset members were quiet, respectful, and awed. Sadat said he had not come for a separate peace. They could not end the state of belligerency in one day. Peace could come only with justice, and that meant a homeland for the Palestinians and the return of occupied Arab lands. Standing there as an honored guest who had risked all to come, Sadat was imbued with moral authority. Ezer Weizman, numbed by painkillers after an auto accident, scribbled a note and passed it to Begin and Dayan: "We must prepare for war." Both nodded in agreement.

Sadat said he had come to tear down the psychological wall of fear: "You want to live with us in this part of the world. In all sincerity I tell you we welcome you among us with full security and safety. This in itself is a tremendous turning point, one of the landmarks of a decisive historical change. We used to reject you. We had our reasons and our fears, yes. We refused to meet with you, anywhere, yes . . . Yet today I tell you, and I declare it to the whole world, that we accept to live with you in permanent peace based on justice."

Sadat accepted their applause and shook Begin's hand.

Then it was Begin's turn, but his speech offered no concession and made no gesture in recognition of Sadat's journey, a deep disappointment for Sadat. Begin recited the history of Arab aggression. He vowed that Jerusalem would never be divided and that the Palestinians would never have their own state west of the Jordan River. When the two leaders left the building, despair took hold. All that was left to do was to trudge into the King David Hotel for the banquet. Weizman came late, as he had stopped for another injection of painkillers, and when he walked in on the leaders of Egypt and Israel, "They were staring into their soup plates" paralyzed by the distance still between them. Sadat and Begin appeared morose, despondent. Long silences followed perfunctory remarks.

"Your prime minister's speech was disappointing," one of the Egyptian dignitaries said, breaking the silence near Weizman. It was Osman Ahmed Osman, the millionaire contractor who had built the Aswan Dam and rebuilt the cities along the Suez Canal.

"I know the Suez Canal well. One of your snipers shot my son in the head [along the Bar-Lev Line in 1973]," Weizman said.[50]

Begin weighed in. "Two of the ministers seated here with us [Dayan and Yigal Yadin] had brothers killed in the 1948 war." All seemed mired in the past.

Later that evening, Weizman and Yadin settled in one of the King David's rooms with Sadat's new foreign minister, Boutros Boutros-Ghali, and Moustafa Khalil, the head of Egypt's ruling party. Over drinks, the Egyptians were blunt about what was motivating Sadat: Egypt was sinking, despite the gloss Sadat had put on its strength.

"We're like Bangladesh," said Boutros-Ghali, "and Cairo is Calcutta." Someone from the Egyptian side added, "Every year, one million people are added to our population."

The admissions of weakness initially had little effect on the other side. Weizman started talking about Israel's "narrow waist" and how hard it was to defend a state only nine miles wide from Netanya to Tulkarem.

"What are you scared of?" Khalil asked. "We won't defeat you in war. We have no military solution." Later, he repeated it. "Why are you so anxious about your security? After all, you have the atom bomb." They went on like that much of the night.

Sadat went home to Cairo, trying to ignore the anger that was now directed at him from much of the Arab world. Egypt was ostracized, as many had predicted. Begin had given no ground, not an inch; instead, he rushed to Washington that December with his own "autonomy plan" for the occupied West Bank and Gaza. It would put the Palestinians under home rule, except that the Israeli army would really be in charge and Palestinian rule could be suspended at any time if Israel deemed necessary.

Carter was careful not to discourage or offend Begin. He told him that the plan was a "fair basis for negotiations." Begin chose to take that as an endorsement and returned home to meet Sadat, this time in Ismailia, the reconstructed city in the canal zone. There Begin lectured Sadat on international law, which supported, he said, Israel's occupation of the Sinai in 1967. Sadat was so exasperated by Begin's interminable disquisitions on history and law that he turned to an aide and said, "Let's open the window and get some fresh air in."[51]

For all the drama of the first year of Carter's presidency, he had accomplished little or nothing in the Middle East. He had alienated key Jewish leaders. Arab Americans were angry, too. Sadat's journey had broken ranks. Brzezinski even made light of Arafat's inability to join the peace process. ("Bye, bye PLO," Brzezinski said in an interview with *Paris Match*.) It was like giving Arafat the back of his hand.

At the end of January 1978, Sadat told Ambassador Eilts that he was losing confidence in Carter. But Begin's political base was also weakening. In early March, 348 military officers and soldiers signed a "peace" letter calling on the prime minister to avoid taking steps "that might be a cause for lamentation for generations"; many in the army would have "grave doubts," it said, if his government chose war and the pursuit of "Greater Israel" over peace and "friendly neighborly relations." The officers' letter and Sadat's appeal for peace had triggered the formation of the Peace Now movement, the name adapted from the placards of demonstrators outside Begin's residence. A peace rally in Tel Aviv drew forty thousand people.[52]

In the middle of these maneuvers, Arafat, isolated in Lebanon, decided to show that the PLO was still a force that could not be ignored: "If they think they can settle our problem without the PLO, let them try," he told an interviewer.[53]

On March 11, 1978, a PLO terrorist squad of Fatah commandos led by an eighteen-year-old woman, Dalal Mughrabi, landed on a beach south of Haifa. They clambered out of their rubber dinghies and, laden with weapons, ran for the coastal highway. Along the way, they surprised Gail Rubin, a nature photographer and a niece of Senator Abraham Ribicoff. They shot her dead on the beach and kept moving. When they reached the highway, they hijacked a bus full of passengers and raced toward Tel Aviv with their hostages, firing at motorists and pedestrians as they careened southward. Israeli security forces were unable to stop the bus until it reached the outskirts of the city, where a mass of firepower shot out its tires as it slammed into a barricade. The bus burst into flames as hostages and terrorists tried to escape. When the carnage was over, thirty-eight Israelis lay dead and eighty-four wounded. Nine of the Fatah guerrillas were killed. Suddenly, it was as if the war had returned. Begin postponed his trip to Washington. Weizman was called home from New York, and within days, Israel launched a full-scale invasion of southern Lebanon.

Tanks crashed across the border and Israeli artillery unleashed a barrage against PLO positions. Tens of thousands of Lebanese civilians, most of them Shiite Muslims, scrambled in buses and cars or ran on foot in panic.

The death toll in Lebanon stunned the region and angered Western leaders. Carter was furious when he discovered that Israel had dropped American-made cluster bombs on Beirut neighborhoods and other civilian areas, contributing to the more than one thousand noncombatant deaths. Many thousands more Lebanese were wounded and more than one hundred thousand were left homeless by the bombing.

Carter considered the invasion an overreaction to the PLO attack, and with mordant swiftness he sent a private message to Begin threatening that he would go to Congress and make the case that Israel had violated the Arms Export Control Act by using American-supplied arms to go on the offense. Begin read the message, handed to him by an American diplomat. He stood still for a moment and then uttered, "It's over." Israeli troops began to withdraw, but not completely, even after enormous destruction had laid much of Lebanon to waste.[54]

The campaign lasted less than a week and one result was the advent of Israel's long occupation of another swath of Arab territory, this one just north of its border. A surrogate force, the South Lebanon Army, under the command of former Lebanese Army Major Saad Haddad, was financed and equipped by the Israeli army to hold the territory as a "security zone" to prevent PLO guerrillas from staging attacks on Israel from the region.

Since 1975, Lebanon had been wracked by civil war brought on by the destabilizing influence of the PLO ministate located within it. Some of the country's Maronite Christian leaders began to look to Israel as an ally against the PLO. The PLO ministate was there because it had been driven out of Jordan, but more to the point, the PLO was there because the international community had failed to resolve the core conflict. Left to their own devices, the combatants, Arafat and Begin, were turning more aggressive, and Begin was never fainthearted when it came to retaliation against Arabs.

James Reston, the *New York Times* columnist, visited Israel after the fighting and gave voice to "the quiet debate" among young Israelis troubled by the failure of Begin to respond to the expectations for peace that Sadat had raised only months earlier. Many of them found Begin "too rigid and the invasion of Lebanon too extreme," Reston wrote. Television had brought much of the carnage home to the Israelis, and they saw the refugees, the civilian wounded, scenes that "have made thoughtful people here wonder how many more Israeli 'victories' like this the nation can afford." And he asked the more profound question: "One wonders how three million people in this remarkable country can continue to live in a state of tension surrounded by a hundred million Arabs who are outbreeding them every year. Is there no other way?"[55]

There was, but the answer was more complicated. What was lacking was a more robust American diplomacy that could speak convincingly and forthrightly to Jewish and Arab constituencies of the hard requirements for peace. What also was lacking was a strong international response via the United Nations, the instrument created for conflict resolution in the wake of the century's great wars. The United Nations, which had been founded upon so many high principles, chief among them that war was inadmissible as a means to resolve disputes, failed repeatedly to carry out its mandate in Lebanon.

It was easy to blame the parties: Lebanon for its weakness in allowing guerrillas to base on its territory; Israel for its wanton destruction of civilian lives. But Lebanon could not ignore the Arab call to harass "the occupier." And no Israeli government could survive a sustained assault on its security without responding. The ethos of Israeli deterrence was that violence had to be met with violence, preferably disproportionate violence, otherwise deterrence would crumble and Israel would invite attack. The flaw in this logic was not easy for any Israeli to admit and keep his or her credibility as a guardian of Zion, as Moshe Sharett, Ben-Gurion's timid foil, had discovered in the 1950s.

Yet there were many who believed that Israel had proved its military prowess in four wars and could afford to adjust its military strategy. It could employ a more measured response to attacks while actively pursuing a diplomatic path. And it could begin withdrawing from occupied lands if there was an offer of peace from the Arab side. The "activist" instinct, as it was called, a euphemism for militarism, may have been necessary in the years of creation, but Israel faced no existential threat in Lebanon. It was a nuclear power with state-of-the-art conventional forces. Opportunities for peace, still part of the Zionist dream, were beginning to appear, and the proof was Sadat's visit to Jerusalem.

Begin's relationship with Carter spiraled downward. In late March, Carter took Begin into the Oval Office and, face-to-face, listed the "Six No's" that summed up Begin's position: no withdrawal, no halt to settlement building, no dismantlement of Sinai settlements, no recognition that Resolution 242 required withdrawal in the West Bank and Gaza, no grant of real authority to the Palestinians, and no self-rule. Moshe Dayan, who was waiting in the Cabinet Room with Carter's aides for the beginning of the full meeting, described Begin as looking drawn and ashen when he emerged, only to face Carter's glare again as the president bloodlessly summarized what he had said in their private session.

"Though Carter spoke in a dull monotone, there was fury in his cold blue eyes," Dayan recorded, "and his glance was dagger-sharp. His portrayal of our position was basically correct, but it could not have been expressed in a more hostile form."[56]

As a Southern Baptist, Jimmy Carter had a missionary spirit, and his aides said that at times it overtook his political caution and even his common sense. In early 1978, Carter was facing pivotal debates on strategic arms, the Panama Canal Treaty (returning the strategic waterway to Panamanian sovereignty), and a major sale of F-15 fighters to Saudi Arabia. Yet his reserves of political capital were depleted by mistakes.

There were other portents of trouble in the region. In February, Palestinian assassins from the Abu Nidal organization, a splinter group of the PLO, had killed Yusef al-Sibai, Sadat's friend and the editor of the official Egyptian daily newspaper, *Al-Ahram*, during a visit to Cyprus. Al-Sibai had accompanied Sadat to Jerusalem, so the message was clear. Sadat shut down PLO offices in Cairo and frozen relations with the group.

In April, Afghanistan's ruler, Muhammad Daoud, was overthrown in a military coup and his regime was replaced by one much more closely aligned to Moscow. In North Yemen, the president was assassinated in June by a diplomat from the pro-Soviet South Yemen who carried a briefcase bomb into his office.

In Somalia, Mohammed Siad Barre, who had welcomed a Soviet and Cuban presence on the Horn of Africa, turned on Moscow and kicked out its military advisers. In late 1977, the Soviets simply switched sides, backing Ethiopia in the war with Barre's forces over the disputed Ogaden region.

Among those most alarmed were the members of the Saudi royal family. The Saudis felt as if they were the target of a Soviet pincer movement—Soviets in Afghanistan on one side and deploying to the Horn of Africa on the other. Saudi Arabia's King Khalid was nominally in charge in Riyadh, having ascended to the throne upon the assassination of King Faisal, but the real power in the kingdom centered on three senior princes: Crown Prince Fahd, Prince Abdullah, who commanded the National Guard, and Prince Sultan, minister of defense (and Prince Bandar's father). Saudi Arabia pledged $400 million to keep Barre out of the Soviet orbit, and at the same time, the Saudi air force financed the airlift of fifteen hundred Moroccan troops to defend Zaire's southern border from Soviet-backed Angolan forces.

In the late 1970s, the Saudis began to press the Carter administration for tangible military assistance to defend the Arabian Peninsula from Soviet encroachment. Israel opposed such aid, seeing it as a threat that could be turned against the Jewish state.

Crown Prince Fahd and Prince Sultan sent the twenty-nine-year-old Prince Bandar to Washington in the spring of 1978 to help lobby for the sale of ninety-one F-15 fighter-bombers to the Saudi air force. Bandar himself was a jet pilot. He had trained at the Royal Air Force College at Cranwell in Great Britain, and at Lackland Air Force Base outside San Antonio, Texas. A crash landing the previous year had grounded Bandar with a back injury, and his new orders were to ingratiate himself with the Carter White House. He quickly succeeded, beginning one of the longest and most intimate liaisons with a foreign envoy in American history.


Sadat was summering at Fuschl Castle near Salzburg, Austria, and used the European venue to rendezvous with Ezer Weizman, the Israeli minister who had overcome his skepticism and come to believe in Sadat's sincerity about peace. When he found Sadat in a grand suite at the fifteenth-century castle, the Egyptian leader was troubled, threatening to "resign from my position" if "there is no change" in the Israeli position by the fall.

After this initial drama, Sadat fell silent for a moment and then said, "You Israelis must do something for me. No, not for me—for Egypt. When I came to Jerusalem in 1977, if you had only made some gesture in response—if you had only withdrawn to the El Arish–Ras Muhammad line! I was expecting you to do something like that. But you were silent! You thought you were smart and wise. What ever became of Israel's smartness and wisdom?"[57]

The Egyptian and Israeli negotiating teams were due to meet at Leeds Castle in England, but both men knew the effort was going to fail. Armed with some concession from Begin, Sadat could silence his critics. Weizman rushed home to brief Begin on the secret request, but Begin was not enthusiastic. The news then leaked to the Israeli press—it could only have been because Begin wanted it to leak—and when reporters asked Begin about Sadat's request, his retort was both indignant and dismissive: "One doesn't get something for nothing!"[58]

It was a stinging rebuke to Sadat. He was made to look like a supplicant. The conference at Leeds failed, as predicted. (Dayan and the Egyptian foreign minister, Muhammad Kamal, exchanged harsh words on Palestinian rights and Israeli settlements in Sinai.) Sadat called his negotiators home.

This was the state of play when Carter convened the Camp David summit in September 1978. It seemed a risky proposition. Carter, Begin, and Sadat all arrived at the presidential retreat in the Cactocin Mountains near Washington as weakened leaders. For Sadat, it was possibly his last chance to show that his diplomacy in Jerusalem was the act of a visionary and not the publicity stunt that many regarded it as.

Begin departed Tel Aviv physically weakened and with a send-off from one hundred thousand Israelis chanting "Peace now!" There were constant rumors about his health, and rivals in the Likud Party, including Weizman, were waiting for an opportunity to orchestrate his political demise.

Carter went to Camp David after two hard-fought battles in the Senate over the Panama Canal treaties and the sale of F-15s to Saudi Arabia. Pro-Israeli forces were bitter over having lost the F-15 battle and over Saudi Arabia's emergence as an influential player in Washington.

Carter, who had not met an Arab leader or traveled to an Arab country until he became president, was now steeped in the region's conflict, its history and passions. Yet Carter's approach was distinctly American,

Christian, and Southern. Sincerity and doggedness in the face of fierce resistance were the hallmarks of his diplomacy that September. He may not have been the greatest intellect to have captured the White House, but he was among the most disciplined and he had mastered the Middle East's complexity as well as any other president.

As Brzezinski observed, "If in the first year he was occasionally insensitive to the special historical and psychological legacies that so conditioned Israeli attitudes, there is no doubt that by the second year he became increasingly adept even at establishing a better personal relationship with Begin."[59] Even Dayan said, "I enjoyed watching Carter in all his obdurate persistence. He was like a bulldog whose teeth were fastened on his victim."[60]

Where Kissinger had thrived on diplomatic maneuvers and manipulation, on flattery and duplicity, Carter was frank about the difficult problems on the agenda, and he was direct in his appeals to solve them fairly and justly.

Ambassador Hermann Eilts, who came in from Cairo to join the American team at Camp David, was heartened when Carter announced at a luncheon for the negotiating team that he wanted to do something for the Palestinians. It was a risky comment, given all that had passed, but it was sincere and betrayed no rancor for Israel, whose security was paramount in Carter's thinking.

Eilts and Samuel Lewis, the U.S. ambassador to Israel, warned Carter at that lunch that the feelings of bitterness between Begin and Sadat had so intensified during the summer that it would be best to keep them apart as much as possible at Camp David. Begin had arrived carrying a copy of the private letter that President Ford had signed in 1975, containing the pledge that the United States would consult with Israel before putting forward any peace proposals. Carter acknowledged this agreement as binding on his administration, but he also ignored it when he thought it was necessary to do so. Begin suited himself in emotional armor; his admirers and detractors found him inextricably connected to history. Carter's irreverent aides, some of them Jewish, did impressions of how Begin's stock response to any proposal was to start calling the roll of Jews who had perished in the Holocaust.[61]

On Tuesday, September 5, after the helicopters brought Sadat and then Begin across the hardwood forests to the slopes of Camp David, Sadat offered an eleven-page draft, "Framework for the Comprehensive Peace Settlement of the Middle East Problem," a document so overwhelming in its demands that it required Israel, on top of returning Sinai and evacuating the West Bank and Gaza, to give up its nuclear weapons and pay war damages to Egypt and compensation for the oil extracted by the Israelis during their occupation of Sinai. When Carter read it, his "heart sank,"[62] and his first tactical error was to proceed in this straitjacket Sadat had fabricated. The Egyptian leader tried to soften the effect of his document by producing a three-page list of concessions that he would be willing to make. But he wanted these closely held until the right moment.

Carter might have saved several days of recriminations had he simply put the Sadat document in a drawer. Instead, he invited Sadat to read it line by line to Begin, ignoring the ambassadors' advice about keeping them apart. As Sadat began reading, "Begin sat without changing his expression, but I could feel the tension building," Carter recalled. "When it was over, no one spoke for a while, and I tried to break the tension by telling Begin that if he would sign the document as written, it would save us all a lot of time."

Carter's joke, which evinced "gales of laughter," must have also alarmed Begin, since he was inclined to suspect collusion between Carter and Sadat. "Would you advise me to do so?" he asked, perhaps just to let Carter know that he had taken note of the slant. Begin did not explode immediately, but the fuse had been lit. Later in the day, on a walk with Carter, Begin let loose a torrent of indignation. By the next morning, his anger had developed into a full-blown storm. Sadat's document was arrogant and condescending, he said. It "smacked of Versailles" and of Egypt "dictating" terms to Israel. Flanked by Dayan and Weizman, Begin objected to the word "Palestinians" because Jews were also people of Palestine. He objected to the term "conquered territory" because Egypt had "conquered" Gaza in 1948. He objected to the reference to Israeli settlements in Sinai. "There is a national consensus in Israel that the settlements *must* stay." They would never be dismantled, he added.

Carter tried to bring him down from the heights of his anger to the baseline of reality as he saw it. "Are you willing to withdraw from the occupied territories and honor Palestinian rights, in exchange for adequate assurances for your security, including an internationally recognized treaty of peace?" he asked. "If not, Egypt will eventually turn away from the peace process, and the full power of the Arabs, and perhaps world opinion, will be marshaled against you."[63]

They were almost shouting at each other. Dayan demanded to know what withdrawal would mean on the West Bank. "Will I have to get a visa to go to Jericho?" he asked.

Carter said he wanted Israel's views on those very kinds of questions. What did Israel really need for its security? "It is ridiculous to speak of Jordan overrunning Israel!" Carter said. Sadat was primed for compromise. And Carter believed he could get from Sadat what Israel really needed, but he could not do so if Begin was stringing Egypt along with phony home-rule proposals that were a subterfuge for keeping the West Bank.

Begin found the word "subterfuge" insulting.

Instead of separating the two leaders, Carter seemed a glutton for punishment. He took Begin down the leafy pathway to another confrontation with Sadat. In Carter's small office in the Aspen Lodge, Begin started attacking Sadat's paper point by point. The Egyptian leader had tried to be a sphinx, but his blood pressure finally uncorked his temper when Begin disparaged the very notion of reparations or compensation for the oil that was still being pumped out of Egyptian wells by Israeli engineers. Soon they were arguing about conquest, past wars, and Israel's appetite for land, with Sadat reminding Begin that the United Nations had declared itself in Resolution 242 on the "inadmissibility of acquisition of territory by war." He then leaned forward and poked his finger across the distance between them and said, "Premier Begin, you want land!"

Their blood was up. For three hours the two men argued fiercely, accusing each other of bad faith and contesting every imaginable part of the history of their conflict, and of the conflict in Lebanon, too. Carter saw their flushed faces and finally realized that it was completely unproductive to proceed this way. It had been a mistake to take Sadat's proposal as a starting point, but in a way, it had also been useful and cathartic to let each leader touch the depth of his anger, if only to see that anger could solve nothing.

"I did not know where to go from there," Carter recalled in his memoirs.[64] Throughout the third day, Carter let the two leaders clash. In the late afternoon, Begin tried to convince Sadat to allow thirteen Israeli settlements, and their two thousand occupants, to remain in Sinai. Israel also wanted to keep at least two of the three air bases it had built there. Sadat had had enough. He was boiling mad. Carter had to physically get up and bar the door against Sadat's retreat, reminding him how much was at stake.

"I was desperate," Carter later reflected. He pleaded with Begin and Sadat to give him a day to come up with a compromise proposal and, finally, Sadat nodded his head and the two leaders left without speaking to each other.

The entertainment that evening was the marine band. Afterward, Carter, Vice President Mondale, and their aides met again with Sadat and the Egyptian delegation for a strategy session. Carter thought the only chance of success lay in drafting a compromise and taking it to the Israelis to whittle away at the big issues: the settlements and air bases in Sinai, the question of sovereignty in the West Bank, how to devise a "transition" that would keep the prospect of self-rule alive for the Palestinians—all in the hope that whatever they ended with, Sadat might be induced to accept.

"I cannot do the Sinai alone," Sadat had told Carter, making it clear that there had to be some resolution on the West Bank and Gaza. "I am ready to be flexible" on the Palestinian end of the deal, he said, "but not on the Sinai." Sadat said he would give Begin time. "I am willing to give them two years to phase out the Sinai settlements," he said. Carter asked for two to three years, and Sadat immediately said, "Okay."

The next day, Friday, September 8, Carter had to prepare Begin for what was coming. An American proposal would put Carter and Begin directly at odds on critical issues. Begin complained that the Americans had already sided with Egypt over the removal of the Sinai settlements. Israel needed them as a buffer against subversion coming out of Gaza. "I will never personally recommend that the settlements in Sinai be dismantled," Begin told him, adding, "Please, Mr. President, do not make this a United States demand." They circumnavigated the issue once more and Begin repeated, "Mr. President, do not put this in a proposal to us."

Carter finally asked him: Was he opposed to Carter's effort to formulate a compromise?

"Yes," Begin answered emphatically.

An American plan, Begin made clear, would pit the United States against Israel in the eyes of Israelis and American Jews. Carter said he would be willing to take the risk because the alternative was further deterioration and, possibly, a new war.

"We are going to present a comprehensive proposal for peace," the president said, and the meeting ended.

On Sunday, September 10, Carter took both negotiating teams off to

Gettysburg for a tour of the Civil War battlefield. When they returned, Carter presented the American draft proposal to Begin and the Israeli delegation. Begin asked for an adjournment so he and his aides could reflect on it. He asked Carter not to show the proposal to Sadat until the Israeli review was complete and Israel had a chance to make counterproposals. At first blush Begin was angry. Carter had included a prominent reference to negotiations being based on Resolution 242 "including the inadmissibility of the acquisition of territory by war." Begin had spent countless hours trying to convince both Sadat and Carter that since Israel had been defending itself in 1967 from Nasser's aggression—closing the Strait of Tiran—the Six-Day War had been a "war of aggression" and therefore Israel had a right under international law to seize and hold territory. (This concept of law had not been recognized by the UN or any major power.) When the Israelis returned at 9:30 that night, they had developed a point-by-point response, and the first thing Carter saw was they had deleted every reference to Resolution 242 from the draft. Begin's attorney general, Aharon Barak, was reading through the Israeli responses, but Carter interrupted him.

"This is not the time to beat around the bush," he said. "If you had openly disavowed United Nations Resolution 242, I would not have invited you to Camp David nor called this meeting." Everyone knew: Israel *had* accepted the resolution. Dayan raised Israel's deeper concern that acceptance of language would be taken as a precedent by the Arabs for all the territories acquired and that would lock them in to a withdrawal from the Golan Heights, something both Dayan and Begin opposed. The Israelis also whittled down Carter's autonomy proposal for the Palestinians. Begin wanted the right to veto any decision by the new Palestinian self-rule councils. Carter was beside himself. It was proof again, he thought, that Begin really wanted to keep the West Bank.

Secretary of State Cyrus Vance objected too. "The whole idea is to let the people govern themselves. You are retaining a veto!"[65]

Begin protested that Israel would not use the power. "We want to keep the right to do so—but we don't intend to do so."

Carter again said Begin was resorting to subterfuge. "Sadat doesn't give a damn" about niggling changes in the structure of the West Bank government, Carter protested. "What is important is whether these people have an irrevocable right to self-government."

It was well past midnight, and when they had exhausted themselves with argument, Carter asked Dayan to walk back to the presidential cottage. On the way, Carter vented his frustrations about Begin. Dayan asked Carter whether Sadat might allow Israeli settlers to stay in Sinai under Egyptian sovereignty, just as they might if they were living in Cairo or Alexandria. He also hoped Sadat could be convinced to turn one of the Israeli air bases over to the United States and another, at Sharm el-Sheikh, to the United Nations. That was a big step for Dayan, who had once said that he would rather have "Sharm el-Sheikh without peace than peace without Sharm el-Sheikh," because it overlooked the Strait of Tiran.

On Thursday, Sadat told Carter that he would not budge on the settlements in Sinai. They would have to go. He said he could negotiate "when" they had to be withdrawn, but not "if."

Carter realized that the negotiations were up against an immovable obstacle. It looked like Camp David was a failure. The Americans went into damage limitation mode. Carter summoned Walter Mondale to help with a strategy to inform Congress and the Jewish community. They worked through the day on Friday, drafting a joint communiqué that described an amicable breakup and describing the main points of difference. But the Israelis pulled up further: They would not acknowledge agreement on anything at the summit. They would keep their options open.

Sadat exploded. He said he was walking out. How could he acknowledge the concessions he had made, and take the heat at home, if Israel would not? The Egyptian delegation was in turmoil. The foreign minister, Kamal, was threatening to resign: Sadat, he said, had sold out Palestinian rights with the gimmickry of an autonomy agreement that was full of holes. And there was nothing about Arab rights in Jerusalem.

Carter put on a coat and tie and walked into Sadat's cabin to confront his friend. Standing there, projecting all of the authority he could muster, Carter said that U.S.-Egyptian relations would be shattered by a walkout. Carter insisted that they all go down the mountain together, arguing that Sadat's enemies in the Arab world would rejoice at his failure. Only by sticking with Carter for a couple more days was there hope of a last-minute breakthrough, or at least a blameless ending.

On Saturday, Begin moved. He shouted at Carter that he was being forced to commit "political suicide," but he pledged that within two weeks of an agreement, he would submit the question of the Sinai settlements to the Knesset and release its members to vote their conscience.

The breach in Begin's wall of resistance caught Carter by surprise and he wrote "breakthrough!" on the pad in front of him.

Carter was not aware until later that Weizman and others had intervened. They got Sharon to telephone Begin and tell him that if the settlers in Sinai had to be sacrificed for the sake of peace, it could be done. Separately, Harold Brown, Carter's defense secretary, had pledged $3 billion in low-interest loans to build two new Israeli air bases in the Negev Desert to make up for those they would have to give up in Sinai.

Begin played two final cards. He said he would not accept a proposed "side letter" to Sadat restating the American position on Jerusalem—that it is a holy city for three religions and each should control its shrines and religious sites. Begin saw the potential for political blowback from the religious right in Israel. He told Vance that he would not sign any agreement "if we wrote any letter to Egypt about Jerusalem."[66]

Begin's last pirouette at Camp David exceeded Carter's ability to reverse it. The final middle-of-the-night session with Begin haunted Camp David ever after, with Carter asserting that Begin had pledged to suspend settlement building in the West Bank indefinitely so the Palestinians, Israelis, and Jordanians could negotiate self-rule and the future of the territories; Begin asserted that he had agreed only to a three-month moratorium on settlement building. The ambiguity in the record suggests that Carter may have overinterpreted Begin's comments in a late-night session. When Begin qualified his pledge in writing, the summit participants were rushing back for the Sunday night announcement of the Camp David Accords at the White House. Begin's assertion put the lie to any real intent on the part of his government to grant Palestinians self-rule in the West Bank and Gaza. How could conditions for such rule emerge if Begin was also to insist on pressing forward with Jewish settlement building in the same territories where Palestinians were being promised autonomy? Carter and Sadat simply decided to swallow Begin's bitter pill. It was either that or throw away the achievement of restoring the Sinai Peninsula to Egypt. It was one of those moments when waves of desire and exhaustion—the collapse of will—hurled them across a barrier where they had intended to take a stand.

At the White House, Carter summoned Hal Saunders, the Middle East expert on the National Security Council staff, to lay out the finished text before the leaders. After all had examined it, Carter turned back to Saunders and said that the sequence was critical: the framework for peace in the Middle East, the document that dealt with the Palestinian issue, had to be signed first "and removed from the table before the framework for peace between Egypt and Israel is presented for signature." Saunders later reflected that Carter had looked at him "as if he would kill me if his instructions were not followed to the letter."[67] The reason was Sadat. The Egyptian president knew he would be condemned for making what amounted to a separate peace. The Palestinians, the Syrians, and the Jordanians were getting nothing, so Sadat wanted the "framework" accord—with its *promise* of Palestinian autonomy in the future—to come first, to show the Arab world that he had done his best at Camp David.

This was not enough, and it did not take long for everyone to see through it. Yet Sadat had done what he felt he had to do. Camp David broke the cycle of war between Israel and Egypt, though not the cycle of war in the Middle East. The peace was bitter, but it had nonetheless opened a new horizon for Egypt, which was now eligible for a massive infusion of development assistance and American military aid. The accords put Egypt firmly and inalterably in the American orbit in the Middle East, something that Washington had longed for since Nasser's revolution. And this had been done by an Egyptian whom everyone had underestimated.

# 6

# CARTER AND THE SHAH
*Khomeini's Revolution*

In the decades after World War II, the shah of Iran, Mohammed Reza Pahlavi, was among the most exotic of America's allies in the Middle East, a dynastic monarch who sat on the Peacock Throne and whose ambitions for regional power rivaled those of the old Persian Empire. With his empress, Farah, the shah had been something of a superstar of international relations. He had been feted by the Kennedys and the Rockefellers and flattered by Nixon and Kissinger. The shah was smart, handsome, wealthy and, in private, disarmingly shy and engaging. His ambassador in Washington, Ardeshir Zahedi, threw the best parties on Embassy Row and served the finest beluga caviar from the Caspian Sea.

For Richard Nixon, the shah was one of the twin pillars of stability in the Persian Gulf. The withdrawal of British forces from the region in 1971 left a vacuum that the United States sought to fill by promoting arms sales and military training for Iran and for the other pillar in the gulf, Saudi Arabia. The Iranian pillar stood taller because, for America, the shah was the southern flank against the Soviet Union, defending Western interests from a potential Soviet thrust toward the warm-water ports and the oil riches of the Persian Gulf. During the Nixon years, the shah was so sure of his high standing in Washington that he told one of his aides that there was, effectively, no limit to what he could demand. Kissinger, the shah recounted to the aide, had sent a humorous message that reflected official attitudes: "Nixon would have given me every weapon in America if only I'd asked for it."[1]

In October 1971, the shah invited the world's leaders to Persepolis, the ancient Persian capital of Darius and Xerxes, for one of the most lavish displays of pomp ever staged. The occasion was the 2,500th anniversary of the Persian monarchy, an artifice meant to embellish the shah's claim to a royal bloodline, though in reality he had inherited power from his father, Reza Shah, a common cavalryman who overthrew Iran's Qajar Dynasty and established himself on the throne in 1925. Yet the shah owed his position more to the Allies, the United States and Great Britain in particular, than to anyone else. The Allies defeated Nazism, deposed the shah's father for his questionable loyalty in 1941, pushed the Soviets out of Iran in 1946, and installed the shah on the Persian throne. Eisenhower and Churchill protected him as an agent of Western interests, sending their spymasters in Operation Ajax in 1953 to rescue the shah's rule from Iranian nationalists.

Nonetheless, over the years, the shah styled himself as an indigenous ruler and Persian visionary. He launched the White Revolution in 1963 to bring Iran into the ranks of developed countries, though fifteen years later half of Iranians were still illiterate, a quarter of the country's children had no access to primary education, and average life expectancy was fifty-two years, considerably less than the sixty years in neighboring Turkey.[2]

In the shah, Jimmy Carter faced the contradictions of the modern American presidency. The era of Churchill, Eisenhower, and Kermit Roosevelt was past. The adventurism of covert action had given way to a new era of post-Watergate rectitude in foreign policy, with special revulsion for autocrats and their secret police forces. The shah, like Pinochet in Chile, Marcos in the Philippines, and Somoza in Nicaragua, was regarded by much of the public as a throwback to the era of strongmen the United States had propped up to fight communism in the aftermath of World War II but whose dictatorial excesses had discredited them. Carter

Jimmy Carter with the shah of Iran, a strongman of an earlier era

came into office committed to human rights, a movement that gained momentum following the Conference on Security and Cooperation in Europe. No one had foreseen that the 1975 summit meeting in Helsinki, attended by both Gerald Ford and Leonid Brezhnev and designed to reduce cold war tensions, would create an unassailably powerful legal foundation for monitoring human rights in the Soviet bloc. In doing so it gave rise to a new era of political agitation—monitoring led to the exposure of human rights abuses—that would eventually help bring down the Berlin Wall and liberate all of Eastern Europe. The principle of giving greater emphasis to human rights in American foreign policy appealed to Carter. He created a special coordinator for humanitarian affairs in the State Department and appointed Patricia M. Derian, a civil rights activist who had worked on school desegregation in Mississippi, to sit as an advocate in policy debates. One of the first statistics that Carter memorized about

Iran was that the shah's jails were holding two thousand five hundred political prisoners.[3] Carter knew that Iranians who questioned the shah's
policies risked an encounter with the brutal agents of SAVAK, the shah's
dreaded secret police, who wiretapped and shadowed dissidents, and engaged in extrajudicial beatings and killings at secret prisons known for
their torture chambers. Countless Iranians disappeared into this system.
Nonetheless, Carter's pragmatism impelled him to engage the shah—
however warily—because Iran was a leading member of OPEC and still
stood as a pillar of Western security in the volatile Persian Gulf.

Carter invited the shah to Washington for a state visit in late 1977. As
a portent of things to come, thousands of Iranians, most of them students
at American universities, flooded Lafayette Square in front of the White
House and threw themselves against police barricades so forcefully that
police commanders ordered tear-gas volleys. That created the memorable
scene of the president and the shah coughing and choking back tears as the
cloud of gas wafted over the official ceremony on the White House lawn.

Empress Farah later recalled that Carter and his wife, Rosalynn, "begged
us to forget the incident—they were truly embarrassed." But she also
thought "that in Richard Nixon's time the demonstrators would never
have been allowed to come so close to us. Didn't this permissiveness
show a desire on the part of the new administration to embarrass us?"[4]

The empress saw the students carrying aloft the photograph of a stern
cleric with a turban and beard. The students, she said, "were demanding
freedom, which I could understand, but I could not understand how they
could see a mullah as a symbol of liberalization and modernity." She asked
her aides to identify this scowling cleric "who was idolized by our young
demonstrators and whose defiant look meant nothing to me." That was
the Ayatollah Ruhollah Khomeini, they told her. He was a distant memory to upper-class Iranians, a medieval scold who had been sent into exile.

A few weeks later, Carter and his wife stopped in Tehran on their way
to New Delhi, and on New Year's Eve at Niavaran Palace, Carter toasted
Iran under the shah as "an island of stability in one of the most troubled
regions of the world." The president went on: "No other nation of the
globe is as close to us in the military organization of our mutual security.
No other nation is in such close consultation with us on the problems of
the regions which concern us both. There is no other head of state with
whom I feel on friendlier terms and to whom I feel more gratitude."

The shah declared Carter's visit "a most excellent omen" for the com-

ing year, but just a week later, thousands of students in Qom, the center
for Shiite religious study in Iran, clashed with police. The rioting was unexpectedly intense and it turned out that the students had been deeply
offended by the shah's information minister criticizing and demeaning
Khomeini in a leading newspaper. The article accused the ayatollah of
being a "tool" of the British and of other colonial powers; it called him "an
adventurer, without faith," a man with a "dubious past" who wrote "love
poems under the pen name of Hindi,"[5] all of which was intended to denigrate Khomeini in the eyes of Iranian youth.

It had the opposite effect. Khomeini was a cult figure in Qom and in
thousands of mosques across Iran. He was the firebrand ayatollah known
for the ferocity of his attacks on the Pahlavi dynasty and its dependence
on the West. Khomeini was a charismatic populist living in exile in Iraq
and transmitting his sermons against the shah back into the country
via audio cassettes. Few experts in the American government were ac-
quainted with Khomeini since he had dropped off the radar screen of
Iranian politics in 1964.[6] At that time, Khomeini's rebellious oratory had
incited a revolt and a bloody crackdown by the shah's government.
Khomeini was briefly jailed in 1963, but when he was released, he attacked the shah's decision to give American military personnel and their
dependents immunity for any crimes committed in Iran. Khomeini as-
sailed the law, based on a Status of Forces Agreement between the two
countries, as an affront to national dignity: "They have reduced the Iranian people to a level lower than that of an American dog. If someone runs
over a dog belonging to an American, he will be prosecuted. Even if the
shah himself were to run over a dog belonging to an American, he would
be prosecuted. But if an American cook runs over the shah, the head of
state, no one will have the right to interfere with him."

Khomeini's theme had the same broad nationalistic appeal that Prime
Minister Mohammad Mossadegh had trumpeted in 1951 when he seized
British Petroleum's interests in Iran and triggered the wrath of Churchill
and Eisenhower. Khomeini said the immunity bill made President Johnson "the most obnoxious person in the world in the eyes of our people.
Are we to be trampled underfoot by the boots of America simply because
we are a weak nation and have no dollars? America is worse than the
British; the British are worse than the Americans; the Soviet Union is
worse than both of them. Each is worse than the other; they are all despicable. But today our business is not with all these forces of evil. It is
with America."[7]

The students were further inflamed by the mysterious death in October 1977 of Khomeini's eldest son, Mustafa, also a cleric. He died in unexplained circumstances as he slept at his residence in Najaf, Iraq. The students suspected that SAVAK had murdered Mustafa.

On January 9, 1978, for the second day in a row, the students of Qom came streaming out of their mosques fired by the zeal of the end of Muharram, the holy month of the Shiite calendar that commemorates the Battle of Karbala, and the martyrdom of Hussein, the Prophet Muhammad's grandson. The crowd quickly gathered strength on the dusty streets ninety miles south of Tehran. It culminated in a standoff between five thousand young protesters and the shah's security forces. Some of the students reportedly taunted the soldiers, whose muzzles were leveled at them. Suddenly, a volley of shots rang out and dozens of students fell wounded or dead. The shootings went on for more than two hours, according to prayer leaders who later described the event to journalists.

The cry went out from Qom and the violence there became the spark for all that followed. Ayatollah Shariatmadari, the leading cleric of the Qom religious establishment, condemned the shah's government in a public letter. He called the killing "un-Islamic and inhumane," and added that "we are certain that Almighty God shall in time punish those responsible."[8] Khomeini himself, in Najaf, was said to be surprised by the uprising and sent immediate encouragement to the students. "The shah stands on the edge of a precipice," he declared.[9]

The uprising spread over the next several months to Tabriz, Mashhad, Isfahan, Shiraz, and Tehran. At the end of January 1978, the State Department's intelligence bureau postulated that the sudden boldness shown by a "broad range of traditional dissidents" to challenge the shah was linked to Carter's arrival at the White House. Carter's emphasis on human rights was responsible for the shah's decision to "encourage more open political discussion." The new assertiveness of the dissidents "stems from their belief that the shah cannot afford to lose U.S. military supplies" and therefore would be constrained in cracking down on his domestic foes, for doing so might alienate the rights-focused Carter administration. "The greatest potential danger to the shah is that he may lose control over the religious elements and their adherents, leading to the inherently more dangerous confrontation of secular modernizers against fundamentalist religious leaders—a problem that has been avoided for almost 15 years."[10]

Shia Islam calls for a memorial forty days after a death. The Qom killings set up a cycle of mourning, demonstration, and rioting that resulted in more deaths and a new cycle of forty days—an escalating rhythm of dissent through the spring. Rioting broke out in Tabriz in late February and early March; cinemas, whose Western-oriented films offended Islamic piety, were torched, and the chant "Death to the Shah!" rose above the crowd for the first time.[11] The waves continued to build as the shah's police hit back forcefully with truncheons, arrests, and, in some cases, live gunfire directed at demonstrators, who struck back with stones and Molotov cocktails against the symbols of Western and secular influence, especially cinemas, casinos, nightclubs, and hotels.

In May 1978, Nicholas Gage, a correspondent for *The New York Times*, visited Tehran and identified Khomeini as the leader of the "most powerful group opposing the shah." He added that a diverse constituency was coming together in opposition to the shah, with each group harboring different aspirations. The groundswell included merchants and petty tradesmen, commonly referred to as *bazaaris*. It also included secular nationalists, who had supported Mossadegh's government against the shah two decades earlier, as well as students and intellectuals. This diverse coalition was the inevitable convergence of grievance and opposition in the urban population, which had tripled in size since the 1950s. It united a large part of the Iranian political spectrum and, in doing so, it reflected the breadth of the shah's political failure. The shah had so centralized power in Iran that he was the most prominent target for the disaffection. In March 1975, he had banned all political parties and created a single-party system around Rastakhiz, or the Resurrection Party. He said anyone who refused to join was an "outlaw" or a "traitor" who belonged in prison or exile.[12]

Gage noted with a tone of surprise that "even students and intellectuals who once scorned Moslem believers as reactionary, have come to espouse their causes, such as the right of women to wear the chador, a veil covering the whole body, a right that the Shah has tried to discourage."[13]

There were deeper structural problems. By the 1970s, the shah's White Revolution—a program for national development and modernization—had given way to a massive arms-purchasing program; suddenly enriched by oil revenues that had leaped from $1 billion a year in 1970 to more than $20 billion a year less than a decade later, the shah had directed most of this new wealth toward building a modern military that would project Iran's power into the Indian Ocean. Economists had warned of bottlenecks—shortages of skilled labor, port capacity, and raw materials—but the shah, unfazed, pressed on.

Agriculture, too, succumbed to mismanagement and decline, as young Iranians abandoned the rural labor traditions of their fathers to seek jobs, education, and opportunity in the large cities where petrodollars were inflating demand and wages in every sector. Steeped in the pious traditions of the village mosque, many were confronting for the first time the accoutrements of Western culture that had arrived with the forty thousand Americans (and many more Europeans) living in Tehran.

"The West plunders and destroys all our languages, literature, folklore, the identity of all our positive visions, poetic, and artistic rhythms without replacing them with something that can originally be called Eastern," Khomeini preached to them.

Iran's moral decay was attributed to the shah's policies. "A society without moral dimension, which is separate from and beyond material structure, inevitably degenerates into dictatorial and fraudulent practices,"[14] wrote Dr. Ali Shariati, a French-trained academic whose essays were part of the intellectual foundation of revolt.

The sudden and overpowering convergence of volatile social and political forces in Iran was far more visible to analysts looking in retrospect. Ambassador William H. Sullivan recalled in his memoir that the U.S. embassy's efforts to fathom the religious and secular opposition to the shah were constantly frustrated either by the pervasive fear of the shah's secret police, or because "in the minds of the Shiite authorities, Americans not only were directly associated with the shah's policies, but were their inspiration."[15]

John Limbert, a former Peace Corps volunteer who served as a political officer of the American embassy in Tehran, recalled how students in Shiraz reacted to a dance troupe that performed in leotards under an American instructor. A riot in the hall ended the performance as students protested the "immodesty" of the display. Much later, Limbert connected the episode to the American failure to comprehend the passion of the Shiite tradition in Iran.[16]

At the top and in the military, the country had never been so well-off in financial terms, but major components of Iranian society harbored grievances against the long Pahlavi reign, against its suffocating autocratic rule, the failure of education, and the paucity of opportunity for the urban poor. In Iran, as in revolutionary France, the monarch had become the focal point for the hatred of the dispossessed. Alexis de Tocqueville could have been describing the shah: "To see in him as the common enemy was the passionate agreement that grew."

The Pahlavi dynasty was a creation of British colonial power. The shah's father, Reza Khan, served as the commander of a Cossack brigade in Iran and, with British connivance, he overthrew the last shah of the Qajars and declared himself Reza Shah Pahlavi in 1925. His sympathy for the Nazis during World War II—he refused to turn Iran into a land bridge for the Allied resupply of Stalin's army that was defending against German invasion—prompted the Allies to mobilize against him. Stalin's army occupied northern Iran and the British occupied the south, where the British oil concession was concentrated. In 1941, Reza Shah was forced to abdicate, and his twenty-two-year-old son, Mohammed, was allowed to ascend to the throne a year later. At the end of the war, Truman resorted to muscular diplomacy to back the Soviets out of Iran, but the British stayed to develop their large investment in the Anglo-Iranian Oil Company and its Abadan refinery, which comprised Britain's largest foreign asset.

Popular resentment of Britain's exploitation of Iran's oil wealth fanned nationalist fervor, setting the stage in 1951 for Prime Minister Mossadegh to defy the shah and the West by nationalizing the petroleum industry. The Iranian premier stood fast in the face of British sanctions and a naval embargo; in 1953, Eisenhower and Churchill concluded that he was an agent of Soviet subversion. Operation Ajax saved the throne for the young shah. Under Western tutelage, Iran joined the Baghdad Pact alliance with Britain to create a Western-oriented bulwark against Soviet penetration of the Middle East, but also against the growing influence in the Middle East of Egypt's Gamal Abdul Nasser.

In the early 1970s, Iran fit into the Nixon Doctrine, a strategy that called for arming key allies while keeping U.S. troops at home. Nixon had given the Iranian leader what amounted to carte blanche to determine his defense needs and to make multibillion-dollar purchases of American weapons. The CIA had played the leading role in the financing and training of the shah's security service, a fact that was not lost on SAVAK's many victims. The shah became adept at playing off his domestic opponents— secular nationalists, political reformers, and the clergy—but what was extraordinary about the gathering revolution was how these forces merged, led by Khomeini as the most tenacious advocate of rebellion.

A revolutionary in his own faith, Khomeini had come to prominence as an activist in the Shiite clergy in the late 1950s. He had cast himself against the "quietists" of Shiite Islam, those scholars who had attained the status of *marja*—clerics worthy of emulation—but who avoided entanglement in politics and governance. Khomeini was intensely political. He asserted that the tenets of Islam were relevant for every aspect of life, and that included criticizing secular leaders and policies that contravened the faith. That's why, in 1963, he had publicly challenged the Status of Forces Agreement that protected Americans in Iran from Iranian law. The shah responded by unleashing a tough, royalist prime minister, Assadollah Alam, to arrest Khomeini and send him into exile. He took refuge in Najaf in Iraq, the center of Shiite scholarship at the Shrine of Ali, the cousin and son-in-law of the Prophet Muhammad. Ali's failure to win the succession struggle after the death of the Prophet marked the diversion of the Shiite branch from the Sunni majority within Islam.

The gilded dome of the Ali Mosque towers over the low rooftops of the city. Nearby in Karbala, the dome of the Husseini Mosque memorializes the place where the Prophet's grandson, Hussein, and his followers were slaughtered in A.D. 680 as they made their last stand to preserve the rule of the Prophet's household. The domes of these mosques float above the palm groves as glistening orbs of piety and, together, form a Vatican-like magnet for Shiite pilgrims and religious students.

Jimmy Carter accepted the logic of America's long relationship with the shah, but the moralistic spirit he brought to the White House put the Iranian leader on the defensive. In the early months, Carter received a curt message from the shah over the delay in approving Iran's request to purchase AWACS early-warning surveillance aircraft from the United States. Carter was indignant.

"I don't care whether he buys them from us or not," he jotted in his diary.[17]


Khomeini's political comeback seemed accidental, but he exploited the demonstrations in Qom by encouraging the students to escalate. His stature rose with each assault until he became the icon of a movement that was spreading to every major city. By summer, a general strike shuttered Qom. Rioting swept Mashhad; in Isfahan, the violence was so intense that police put the city under curfew. Ramadan, the holy month of fasting that began on August 5, brought the shah out of his shell. In a nationwide address, he promised a fresh start with political reform, elections, and new press freedoms. But his speech was taken as a sign of weakness—throwing "meat to the crocodiles," his critics said—and the demonstrations continued.

On August 19, a fire broke out at a movie theater in the oil-producing center of Abadan. The Rex Cinema was packed that evening when smoke and flames flared within, sending the audience rushing in panic for the exits, but the doors were locked. Some 477 people died as the building was consumed. The government in Tehran claimed that the fire was the work of Islamic extremists who had frightened away audiences and burned dozens of cinemas in other cities in the fury against symbols of Western "toxicity." But the antishah forces accused SAVAK of starting the blaze to discredit the Islamic revolutionary leadership. The truth became whatever people believed it to be. The day after the fire, huge demonstrations spilled across Tehran, and two weeks later the capital stood still as hundreds of thousands of antishah protesters filled the streets.

The rebellion was moving to a new phase. The Iranian monarch responded by changing the government, installing Jafar Sharif-Emami, an aging nationalist reformer, whose first act was to reinstate the Islamic calendar, dropping the imperial Persian variant as a nod to the religious establishment. He closed casinos and pledged to open the political system to opposition parties, but to the masses he was an ineffectual remnant of the elite that had been co-opted by the shah. Events were already beyond the control of the civilian government.

Eid al-Fitr, the festival that marks the end of Ramadan, fell on September 4, two weeks after the Rex Cinema fire, and the largest protest yet against the shah brought Tehran to a halt. Ambassador Sullivan, who had taken a three-month vacation from his post that summer, was shocked, so he claimed, by the tumult that had taken over the country and by the paranoiac delusions of the shah, who told him that he suspected a concert of CIA, KGB, and MI6 forces might be behind what seemed to him a well-financed rebellion against his authority. Jimmy Carter was absorbed with the preparations for the Camp David summit.

The next day, one million people turned out in Tehran, paralyzing the capital again with a spectacular affront to the shah's authority. "It was an awesome display of political power on behalf of the Islamic opposition," Sullivan observed. "The marshals themselves were young men, often moving on Honda motorcycles ahead of the route of [the] march, organizing traffic, blocking cross streets, and preparing the right of way." These marshals were well equipped with "walkie-talkie radios, first aid groups, water and refreshment units, as well as cheerleaders."[18] Photos of Khomeini and other ayatollahs were carried aloft along with banners calling for America to get out of Iran and "Death to the Pahlavis." The drumbeat continued for several days. Massive crowds flooded the center of a dozen major cities. In Tehran a number of public buildings were set afire. The shah's ambassador to Washington, Ardeshir Zahedi, flew in from the United States after receiving a personal appeal from the Empress Farah to help "raise the morale of the shah and the middle class."[19]

Two days after Jimmy Carter welcomed Sadat and Begin to Camp David, the shah declared martial law in Iran and dispatched fresh troops into the streets. The decree was issued late at night and many people did not get the word as they headed out to participate in the demonstrations called for that Friday, the day of prayer. Thousands of protesters had congregated in Jaleh Square, where the army, braced by orders to show an iron fist, opened fire, killing scores and perhaps hundreds of demonstrators. News of the massacre spread quickly. Crowds of angry youths threw stones and gasoline bombs at soldiers and the shootings continued throughout the day. By the end of Black Friday, as it came to be called, hundreds of people had been killed in Tehran and hundreds more wounded.

James A. Bill, an American academic who specialized in Iran, arrived in Tehran just after Black Friday and found a population seething with hatred. He lived, he wrote, "on a small alley behind a gas station" near Jaleh Square. "Here the masses of Iranian people, crowded in line for their kerosene and rationed meat, shouted slogans against the shah. Taxi drivers spit in the direction of the shah's soldiers, and students combed the city for pictures of the royal family to tear down and deface. Luxury hotels, cinemas, and liquor stores stood silent as dark, windowless, bombed-out hulks. Anti-Americanism was intense, and a wild, powerful sentiment pervaded the crowded sidewalks, markets and streets" where "young bearded representatives of 'Aqa' (as they referred to Khomeini) hurried constantly to the key homes and mosques" to organize the opposition and dispense "'Aqa's' latest directives."[20]

Black Friday proved to be the point of no return. A torrent of passion and rage united the country against the shah and his Western backers. The news intruded on Carter, Sadat, and Begin during the tense opening days of their struggle at Camp David. Sadat and Carter both spoke to the shah by phone to express concern and reassure him of their support, but these turned out to be empty gestures. Khomeini began openly directing the opposition from Najaf. He called for a nationwide strike to shift the protest from street to economic pressure. This would deny the shah's martial law forces any visible target. As the strikes developed momentum, the shutdown of oil production and refineries dealt a devastating blow to the regime, creating gasoline shortages and constricting state revenues. Western embassies reported a massive flight of capital, as much as $1 billion a month, as the moneyed class hedged against uncertainty.

In official Washington, there was a strong belief that the shah would survive the crisis, as he had survived the riots of 1963. Americans in 1978, however, were much more alarmed and repulsed by the shah's use of lethal force against unarmed demonstrators than by any prospect that a virulent Islamic extremism was on the rise in Iran. For Americans it was only eight years since the Kent State shootings during the anti–Vietnam War protest era. Carter was flummoxed by the pace and intensity of the revolutionary forces. He had elevated human rights as a prominent feature of American foreign policy and here was the shah hosing down the streets with machine gun fire, killing unarmed students. Yet without tough and resolute action against the mob, the teetering monarchy just might collapse, breaking a critical link in the chain of American security that protected access to Persian Gulf oil and prevented a full Soviet advance into the region.

Carter was a different kind of cold warrior from his predecessors. Suffused with idealism and slow to believe the worst about America's adversaries, Carter looked hesitant standing in the path of a whirlwind. Even the experts on Iran were caught off guard by the swiftness with which revolutionary forces suddenly converged. The CIA was telling him that Iran "is not in a revolutionary or even a pre-revolutionary situation" because the military was loyal to the shah and because the opposition was inept.[21]

Arab nationalism had broken free in the era of Nasser, but Persian nationalism—and the Islamic nationalism that overtook it—had been contained and repressed by the shah. The shah saw *himself* as the revolutionary, but, in reality, his revolution was a house of cards of corrupt and incompetent national management. Khomeinism—nationalism blended with the ferocity of Islamic and Shiite piety—had ignited in Iran the same kind of prairie fire that Mao had lit in China. It mobilized a large and fanatically dedicated cadre of activists who could control the streets and consolidate the power of the clergy.

Moreover, Carter had come into office determined to make progress in the Middle East, where the dominant issue since Truman's presidency had been the Arab-Israeli dispute. Here was Carter buried at Camp David trying to solve the most intractable conflict of modern times, and suddenly the Middle East was exploding with new volcanic forces. The region was simply larger and more complex than Americans had realized.

"Our decision-making circuits were heavily overloaded," Zbigniew Brzezinski, Carter's national security adviser, later acknowledged.[22]

Carter was served by a brilliant array of advisers who, though divided, went straight to the heart of the shah's survival prospects. He could mount a bloody military crackdown, or he could compromise by implementing government reforms, by releasing political prisoners, and with other steps to quench the revolutionary fires. Brzezinski represented the hard line of the American establishment, which included the Rockefellers and their banking interests that were heavily committed to Iran, the U.S. oil industry, and influential advisers like Kissinger. In their view, the shah had to crack down against the chaos wrought by Khomeini's revolutionary incitement, which threatened destruction of a crucial ally against the Soviet Union and a defender of Western interests in the Persian Gulf.

The antishah "compromisers" were centered in the State Department, where a strong consensus developed that the shah was headed for history's dustbin and America should look to the Iranian military to promote a transition in which moderate nationalists, it was hoped with the support of the clergy, would come out on top. As Carter vacillated, those struggling to influence policy leaked the highlights of the internal debate to the media, adding to an aura of indecisiveness.

Caught in the middle, Carter tried to rationalize the contradictions between his human rights commitment and America's support for the shah. He approved a large sale of aircraft and weaponry to Iran during the summer of 1978, along with the sale of tear gas and antiriot equipment. Though the sales were opposed by the State Department's human rights bureau under Patricia Derian, Carter believed he had no choice but to support the shah.

The shah, for his part, seemed unable to find the means to undermine

Khomeini's power. He pressed the Iraqi government, where Saddam Hussein was vice chairman of the Revolutionary Command Council, to do something about the incitement radiating from Najaf. On September 23, Iraqi troops put a cordon around Khomeini's house, but within two weeks Khomeini fled the restrictions aimed at silencing him. He went by plane to Paris and took up residence in the suburb of Neauphle-le-Château, where he achieved instant celebrity and direct communications with the rapidly growing revolutionary network in Iran. The shah told Ambassador Sullivan on October 10 that he "was toying with the notion of inviting Khomeini to return to Iran," but Sullivan dissuaded him, saying he would be out of his mind to do so.[23]

For the Carter administration, Iran became an urgent crisis when Sullivan reported, on November 2, that the shah might abdicate his throne because he saw his options diminishing to a choice between stepping down or turning loose the military for a bloody crackdown. The ambassador asked Washington for official guidance on what to say to him if he solicited American views on the next fateful step.[24] Brzezinski convened a crisis planning meeting at the White House, out of which came a presidential message to the shah saying the United States would support any action he took to restore order, including the establishment of a military government, knowing that such a government would be expected to violently suppress the opposition. Something needed to be done, Brzezinski believed. The wave of strikes in the oil fields had caused Iran's oil output to plummet from almost six million barrels per day to less than two million barrels per day.

But what was most remarkable was that Carter chose not to call the shah in these fateful days of decision. The Iranian leader was obviously suffering a profound loss of confidence and weighing advice that could lead to bloodshed, the end of his long reign, or both. But Carter had stepped back. He gave Brzezinski the task of bucking up the shah as debate raged within the administration. At a time when the shah needed clarity, America was speaking with multiple voices.

The messages from Washington were tentative, convoluted and, at times, contradictory, but most of all, they lacked the precision that Carter's personal intervention might have contributed. Carter's commitment to human rights made it unseemly to speak to the shah about cracking down, since he knew that to do so was in effect to sponsor the shah's violence against his own people with American hardware. And in contrast to Eisenhower, who had taken strong action to keep the shah on the throne, Carter seemed to strike a pose of political correctness, contending it was inappropriate to interfere in Iran's internal convulsion. National self-determination may have been the ethos of the post-Watergate era, but the shah had been placed on his throne by British and American power. Roosevelt, Truman, and Eisenhower had protected him; Kennedy had forced him to undertake reforms to appease his critics following Khomeini's incitement in 1963. The shah had never faced a crisis without the strong advice or intervention of Washington or London. Yet in late 1978, faced with a critical moment as threatening as any that had swept modern Iran, Carter avoided personal contact with the shah as if he were a dead relative.

To Brzezinski, the shah said he had been given to understand from the British and American ambassadors that "extreme measures . . . should be avoided," but Brzezinski tried to disabuse him of this. Brzezinski warned that further concessions might be the path to a "more explosive situation." The shah needed to take specific actions that would "demonstrate effective authority."[25] If that meant a military government, so be it, Brzezinski said. In reversing Ambassador Sullivan, who had apparently advised the shah that a military government probably would have little chance of success, Brzezinski further muddled the American message. After Brzezinski's six-minute telephone call to the shah on November 3, Ardeshir Zahedi appeared in Tehran and reported that Brzezinski had "taken over Iran policy." Zahedi, whom the shah mistrusted, said he had come to deliver the unambiguous message that the shah should "take whatever measures" were necessary to protect his regime. Carter told Zahedi to "stiffen the shah's spine" so as to decisively confront the chaos in the country.[26]

The shah summoned Ambassador Sullivan again and recounted to him the high-level communications he had received from Brzezinski and Zahedi. The shah asked whether Carter had sent a similar message through the embassy. Sullivan replied that he had no new message since Brzezinski's phone call to the shah, but he reread to the shah the cable that had urged the shah to take whatever actions he considered necessary and reassured him of the administration's support. But Sullivan also asserted to the shah that Brzezinski's telephone call "did not mean that the United States favored the military option," only that Washington would go along if the shah saw no other choice.[27] British Ambassador Anthony Parsons chimed in, saying he had no specific instructions from London but that

his "government was firmly in favor of a political solution." The shah
wanted "more explicit instructions." But when Sullivan sought them, a
cable came back "far more reserved than Zahedi's rhetoric." Vance's aides
suspected Brzezinski and the president of overreliance on Ambassador
Zahedi's view of what was going on in Tehran. The administration was
having trouble saying in plain English what it expected him to do.[28] It was
at war with itself.

Former Vice President Nelson Rockefeller called Brzezinski to com-
plain that "a growing body of opinion in America believed that the United
States was doing nothing" and wanted to know "where the United States
stood."[29] Rockefeller was one of Henry Kissinger's principal patrons, and
his call put the White House on notice that the Republicans would soon
attack Carter's management of the crisis. Brzezinski tried and failed to
wrest control of Iran policy from Cyrus Vance as the State Department
focused on bringing Iran's opposition into a coalition government.[30] The
struggle in Washington exacerbated the already poor communications
with Tehran.

On November 5, rioters burst into the British embassy compound and
set fire to the chancery building. Organized arson squads were setting
hundreds of buildings ablaze. Tehran looked like a war zone of smoke,
flame, and rubble.

The shah was astute enough to see that his options were rapidly closing.
The locus of power had moved to Khomeini's sitting room in the Paris
suburb, where it seemed the destiny of the shah, and of Iran, was being
decided. Political and religious figures flew to France to consult with the
ayatollah, including Mehdi Bazargan, the leader of the Iran Freedom
Movement and one of the most respected, and democratic, nationalists in
Iran; Karim Sanjabi, the leader of the National Front, also made a pilgrim-
age. Their decision to throw in with Khomeini dealt a critical blow to the
shah. During Khomeini's four months in France, the seventy-eight-year-
old cleric granted more than 120 interviews to journalists. When asked,
he was vague about what kind of political structure he wanted for Iran.[31]

On November 6, the shah put a military government in power under
General Gholam Reza Azhari with a mandate to restore order in the
country. But General Azhari was no iron fist. The shah's address to the
nation was apologetic. He told Iranians, "I commit myself to make up for
past mistakes, to fight corruption and injustices and to form a national
government to carry out free elections." There was a plaintive quality to

his remarks: "Insecurity and killing have created economic paralysis and the country is in grave danger," he said. "I have asked the religious leaders, the youth and parents to eliminate the present situation. I asked the youth not to drag the country into fire and blood."[32]

But they were already into fire and blood. Ambassador Sullivan told the White House that it was not too early to start "thinking the unthinkable." If the shah and the military "both shy away from the bloodbath," he warned, "it may eventuate that both the shah and the more senior military would abdicate, leaving the armed forces under the leadership of younger officers who would be prepared to reach an accommodation with the religious" leaders under Khomeini.[33] Ali Amini, the respected former prime minister, told the shah that there was no hope of compromise with Khomeini. At a minimum, Amini said, he would have to leave the country so that the opposition forces could decide the future.[34]

Brzezinski was incensed by any course of action other than a bold reassertion of authority by the shah and the military. He was certain that Sullivan and the State Department had fallen victim to "Pollyanna" notions that the fall of the shah "would have benign consequences for American interests." He saw a conspiracy of muddled thinking between Sullivan and the British ambassador, Anthony Parsons. "Sullivan's cables did not give one the impression that the American ambassador was exerting himself to reinforce the shah's willpower," Brzezinski later said.[35] Yet with all the criticism of Sullivan's performance, what was striking was the continued absence of direct contact between the White House and the shah or any sustained presidential engagement of the kind that Carter had exerted at Camp David.

Was Carter overtaxed, or simply lost without the familiar context of Christian values that he had assiduously applied to the dispute in the Holy Land? There was no analogue in Christendom, or Western culture, for that matter, that could help Carter counteract Khomeini's populist Shiite grievances against the shah's secular tyranny, corruption, and the modernizing influence of the West. By November 1978, Carter had no realistic recourse against the power of the religious and social forces that were taking over Iran, though his chief advisers continued to believe America could save the country. But how could Carter know without investigating by communicating directly with the shah? Had the president also canvassed major opposition figures during these months, he might have developed a more finely tuned set of analytical judgments about the shah's weakened state, whether the Iranian military might play a viable role, Khomeini's power, and the convergence of opposition forces. Carter might have better grasped opportunities to mediate a transition that could have given the secular democratic figures a stronger hand in the postrevolutionary government. Carter, who was so guided by his Christian background to search for peace between Begin and Sadat, had very few points of reference—biblical or otherwise—on how to contain the firestorm of Shiite grievance rising in Iran. Valuable time was wasted as the White House lurched in one direction and then another, seeking a unifying intellect that could come up with a formula to rescue Iran. They settled briefly on George W. Ball, the diplomatic troubleshooter from the Kennedy-Johnson era, but his conclusions antagonized hard-liners who still wanted the shah to crack down. Ball found that the shah was "irreparably damaged" and that the United States would be "inviting disaster if we were to continue trying to prop up the shah as a monarch retaining any substantial powers of government."[36]

Carter's ambivalence was recorded during a breakfast meeting with Washington correspondents in December. He was asked whether he thought the shah could survive.

"I don't know. I hope so," he replied. He then cast himself and the United States in the role of spectator to the events. "This is something that is in the hands of the people of Iran. We have never had any intention and don't have any intention of trying to intercede in the internal political affairs of Iran."[37] A noble thought, but America, and Britain, had been doing exactly *that* for most of the century. Carter had thus repudiated the proprietary American role that Roosevelt, Truman, and Eisenhower had established in Iran, and that had fed the populist anger to which Khomeini had given voice.

General Azhari suffered a heart attack on December 20, and if anyone in Washington was hoping for a military crackdown, Sullivan disabused them of the notion when he reported finding Azhari sprawled on a cot in his office with an oxygen bottle nearby. Clad in striped pajamas and covered with blankets, the general anguished about the shah's insistence that his troops fire over the heads of the crowd no matter how violent the provocation. With this, Azhari raised himself on an elbow to draw closer to Sullivan and said, "You must know this and you must tell it to your government. This country is lost because the king cannot make up his mind."[38]

Neither could Carter. He simply was not prepared to "tell another head of state what to do," as he explained to George Ball before Christmas. What he wanted to do was send Brzezinski to Tehran, an idea that Ball successfully opposed.[39] On December 26, the shah again asked Sullivan what the United States wanted him to do: Should he use the iron fist "even if it meant widespread bloodshed and even if it might fail to restore law and order"? Sullivan replied that Washington supported his efforts to restore law and order, but "if the shah was trying to get the United States to take responsibility for his action," Sullivan doubted that he would get a clear answer.[40]

Four days later, the shah persuaded Shahpur Bakhtiar, one of the leaders of the National Front, to form a constitutional government. The shah said he would leave the country indefinitely after swearing in a Regency Council that presumably would preserve the monarchy, even if only in a ceremonial role. Bakhtiar tried to appease critics and colleagues who had joined Khomeini, promising that his government would have the national interest at heart. He disbanded SAVAK, opened the prisons, pledged to prosecute those who had ordered the shooting of demonstrators, and insisted that the shah would soon be leaving.

In the shah's final days, Ambassador Sullivan told Cyrus Vance and the White House that it was time to make contact with Khomeini. The American envoy was worried that if the shah left the country and Bakhtiar's government faltered, a leaderless military would be left to confront the extremist Islamic radicals bent on seizing power. Carter also felt that the Iranian military would be the key to any transition. It was armed with billions of dollars of high-technology American weaponry, and billions more was in the pipeline for delivery. Carter ordered General Alexander Haig, who had been appointed supreme allied commander in Europe, to send one of his deputies, General Robert E. Huyser, to Tehran so the White House could open lines of communication with the shah's generals. Carter and Brzezinski, who did not fully trust Sullivan's reporting, believed a second channel was essential.[41]

Sullivan had come to his own conclusions about the Iranian military. He had received back-channel communications from Henry Precht, the Iran Desk officer at the State Department, indicating that a like-minded group at State agreed it was necessary to work with the Iranian military to find "a graceful exit" for the shah, and then to bring Khomeini's representatives into a "committee of notables" to run the country.[42] On January 3,

Sullivan told Vance that the "moment of truth" had arrived. The shah would not leave unless Carter himself told the shah it was time. Carter convened his top advisers and, the next day, a presidential message went out saying that Carter concurred and supported the shah's plan to leave the country in the hands of a Bakhtiar government and the Regency Council.

Sullivan picked up rumors that a group of officers wanted to block the shah's departure and impose a crackdown. Brzezinski saw the plot as a godsend. Word of it reached Carter and his national security adviser at a summit meeting of the largest industrial nations. The leaders had convened on the Caribbean island of Guadeloupe. While some lounged in bathing suits, Carter rushed to a secure phone in his bungalow to consult with Vance in Washington. Here was Carter speaking into the receiver while Brzezinski frantically passed him notes stating that now was the time to back an army coup that would clean up the streets and prevent a disaster. Carter was concerned about a bloodletting, and Brzezinski, in a tone that could not have cheered the president, said geopolitics was not a "kindergarten class." Carter had to consider the consequences if the military failed to act and the radical Islamists took over Iran.[43]

But the military coup did not materialize. The Iranian army was a shell. General Huyser landed in Tehran the next day only to discover that the shah's military commanders were cowering in their headquarters and making plans to flee with the shah.[44] They would be the first targets of the revolutionaries because of their reputation for enriching themselves through kickbacks and commissions on American defense contracts. Sullivan reported to Washington that a number of key generals wanted the United States to contact Khomeini directly and persuade him to give the Bakhtiar government a chance. For Sullivan, it was perhaps the last opportunity to head off total collapse. Vance had a secret envoy standing by—Theodore Eliot, a retired Farsi-speaking foreign service officer.

But at the last minute, Carter vetoed any approach to Ayatollah Khomeini. He told Vance that that he feared it would look like he was abandoning the shah. He was willing only to send an indirect message to Khomeini through the French president, Valéry Giscard d'Estaing, but it was lost in the noise of events.

Upon getting word of Carter's decision, Sullivan lost his composure. In an "eyes only" cable to Secretary Vance, he said he would carry out his orders, but "you should know the president has made a gross and perhaps irretrievable mistake by failing to send [an] emissary to Paris to see Khomeini." He added that he and General Huyser were in total agreement on this point. Sullivan asked that Vance join with Harold Brown, Huyser's boss, to make a "plea for sanity" to the president to reverse his "incomprehensible" decision.[45]

Carter held firm, and after Brzezinski showed him Sullivan's cable, he wanted to fire the ambassador, but Vance talked him out of it. Sullivan had to break the news to the shah, who was perplexed by it. Sullivan came to believe that until that moment in January 1979 when Carter refused to open a channel to Khomeini, the shah "felt that we had some grand national design that was intended to save his country and perhaps, somehow or other, his dynasty." Sullivan said there must have been a moment of recognition "that we had no design whatsoever and that our government's actions were being guided by some inexplicable whim."[46] The shah was also suffering from cancer that he had successfully kept hidden from his American allies since it was diagnosed five years earlier. An intense awareness of his own mortality and a desire to save the throne for his young son must have weighed in his calculation whether to resort to bloodshed.

The shah and his family left Tehran by plane on January 16, 1979. Iranians honked their horns and raced through the streets rejoicing. Bakhtiar tried to forestall the inevitable by closing Tehran's airport to block Khomeini's return, but he was forced by the threat of massive uprising to relent. On February 1, Khomeini flew from Paris to Tehran on an Air France jumbo jet. A tumultuous street demonstration welcomed him in a capital that had been on fire with anticipation. Khomeini announced that Mehdi Bazargan would head the first revolutionary government.

The ayatollah had won. An appalling period of bloodletting and purges followed. Pro-Khomeini units in the military overthrew their commanders. Every institution of government was overrun, and Komitehs—revolutionary committees—dispensed justice, seized property, and carried out summary executions.

Sullivan witnessed the televised trial of the shah's longtime SAVAK chief, General Nematollah Nassiri. "Nassiri was severely beaten and his windpipe crushed before the trial. I will always remember seeing him in that condition, being interviewed on television, blood oozing down his face from his bandaged head, and aspirating his words with great difficulty through his shattered throat."[47]

The Bakhtiar government's determination to hold its ground soon gave way. This government collapsed when the Imperial Guard lost its first battle with revolting air force cadets. Americans tried to navigate the anarchy. Twenty-six members of the U.S. military assistance command under Major General Philip Gast found themselves trapped at the headquarters of the Iranian armed forces as it came under attack by the revolutionary militia. As Ambassador Sullivan and the embassy worked to rescue them from what seemed a life-threatening situation, Brzezinski telephoned to demand an assessment on whether the Iranian military could be induced to mount an immediate coup and impose military rule in the wake of Bakhtiar's collapse.

Angered by Brzezinski's obsessive hope that a military-based coup might still materialize, Sullivan exploded over the telephone, where David Newsom, the State Department's undersecretary, and Warren Christopher, the deputy secretary, were relaying his comments to Brzezinski.

"General Gast is in the basement of the Supreme Commander's headquarters pinned down by gunfire and he can't save himself, much less this country," Sullivan shouted into the phone. The Iranian military was dissolving. Sullivan made insulting references to the absurdity of Brzezinski's inquiry and his failure to grasp the degree and the rapidity of the breakdown, including within the Iranian military. Newsom appeared shocked by Sullivan's verbal assault on the president's national security adviser, but Sullivan did not relent, and he cast a final aspersion at Brzezinski's heritage. "Do you want me to translate it into Polish?" Sullivan snapped, and hung up.[48]

Bakhtiar's government disappeared that morning. Foreign nationals began to organize their exit and an airlift evacuated thousands of Americans and other expatriate civilians and military personnel in a matter of weeks. Revolutionaries seized the Israeli mission in Tehran and turned it over to associates of the PLO. In Beirut, Yasser Arafat fired his gun in celebration of Khomeini's return to Tehran. Arafat became the first state visitor to the Islamic Republic of Iran. Khomeini declared that Iran's revolution would not be complete until the Palestinians won the Holy Land. Meanwhile, the United States quietly assumed responsibility to exfiltrate thirty-three Israeli diplomats who had gone into hiding in the city.

Americans were devastated. The splendor of Iran that was so accessible to Westerners vanished almost overnight. Thousands of U.S. military advisers and defense contractors supervising billions of dollars in weapons and technology transfers to Iran shut down a thirty-year military-to-military relationship in days. The departing Americans destroyed or took with them inventory lists, repair manuals, and documentation, rendering the American weapons program an incomprehensible mess.

Dozens of U.S. intelligence technicians had to be extricated from their mountain bases in northern Iran, where they had staffed the CIA's listening posts focused on the Soviet missile range at Semipalatinsk. Listening posts in Tehran and other cities continued to function, intercepting all manner of communications.

On February 14, a heavily armed band of revolutionary guerrillas staged a full-scale assault on the American embassy compound. The young Iranians, some of them wearing the checkered kaffiyehs of the PLO, set up firing positions on the rooftops of neighboring buildings that overlooked the compound. At 10:30 a.m., they opened up with thirty-caliber machine guns, raking the embassy from two directions. "Window panes shattered, lead flew everywhere, and we had no recourse but to dive for the desk and slither across the floor to the safest spot we could find," Sullivan recalled.[49] The ambassador organized a staged retreat into a communications vault on the upper floor of the chancery building. The diplomats laid down a billowing fog of tear gas as they fled behind steel doors. The seizure of the embassy lasted only two hours. Revolutionary Guards rushed into the compound and neutralized the attackers. Prime Minister Bazargan dispatched his own troubleshooter, Ibrahim Yazdi, a former Iranian student leader in Houston, Texas, and now foreign minister, to free them. Even Khomeini sent an ayatollah to apologize for the attack. But that was not the end of it.

Days after the shah's departure, Carter undertook an extensive review of American security policy. Carter had dispatched a flight of F-15s to Saudi Arabia during the crisis, only to be embarrassed by an announcement that the warplanes were not carrying weapons; the Pentagon apparently considered the deployment merely symbolic. This episode would reverberate through the region for decades, suggesting to potential foes that America would not vigorously defend its interests in the Middle East.

Carter sent Defense Secretary Harold Brown to the region in early 1979 to clarify the expectations of American allies—Egypt, Saudi Arabia, Jordan, and the other moderates—and to discuss in detail how the United States might project its power into the region to protect them.

Brown told the Arab leaders that the United States was ready to establish its first bases in the Middle East.[50] If the Saudis were not ready for a base on their territory, Brown described how America could pre-position armaments and build up Saudi military facilities so they could accommodate U.S. forces in an emergency. American naval and air forces could establish bases just "over the horizon"—at Diego Garcia in the Indian Ocean, in Bahrain, Oman, and southern Egypt—far enough away to be out of sight but close enough to respond rapidly. Brown's discussions were the precursors to Carter's establishment of a rapid deployment force for the Middle East.

By early 1979, the presidential election season was fast approaching. Brzezinski warned Carter that he either had to bring the Camp David process to a conclusion or abandon the whole enterprise; either they move on to the formal signing of a peace treaty that would return the Sinai Peninsula to Egypt, or the Carter administration would fold its tent on the peace process.

"I am convinced for the good of the Democratic Party we must avoid a situation where we continue agitating the most neuralgic problem with the American Jewish community—the West Bank, the Palestinians, the PLO—without a breakthrough to a solution," he told the president, adding, "I do not believe that in the approaching election year we will be able to convince the Israelis that we have significant leverage over them, particularly on those issues." Most important, Brzezinski said, "We have little time left."[51]

Walter Mondale, too, warned Carter of the high cost of another bruising battle with Begin.

On February 28, Carter summoned his senior aides—Rosalynn sat in as well—to decide whether to cut their losses. Camp David had been a high-water mark—Begin and Sadat had been awarded the 1978 Nobel Peace Prize—but they had to face reality: a peace treaty might be impossible. Brzezinski argued that Carter should take Begin on because the Israeli leader might be playing for time in hope that Carter would be defeated in 1980. Mondale cautioned Carter not to get into the ring with Begin again. Another clash would cost them Jewish support in the election.

When Begin arrived in Washington on March 1, he declared from Andrews Air Force Base, "We cannot be pressed into signing a sham document." At the White House, he was even more pugnacious. He seemed uninterested in the peace treaty that was on the table. Instead, he wanted a formal alliance with the United States that would make the Jewish state an extension of American power in the Middle East. He talked about the superiority of Israeli military forces and how they might be used to defend Saudi Arabia or assist Egypt in humbling Libya, which was fomenting terrorism and subversion across the region with Soviet arms. He even resurrected the idea of basing American warplanes in the Sinai. Begin now found the treaty with Egypt wanting. The fall of the shah raised the question of whether Sadat's successors, with Islamic extremists gaining traction in the region, would feel bound by peace. Begin wanted a prompt exchange of ambassadors and he wanted oil, because Israel's oil trade with Iran had ended. By the terms of the treaty, the Sinai wells would revert to Egypt.

Carter seemed disgusted by Begin's tactics. If Begin had not been his guest, "I would have asked him to get the hell out," he later wrote. He was convinced that the whole peace effort had come to an end. Throughout the official dinner that evening, Carter and Begin put up a front of cordiality, though their relations were bitter below the surface. It was a Friday night. Rosalynn Carter was down with a fever. The president put on a heavy coat and walked into the chill night air on the Truman Balcony to sit alone and consider the disaster of his Middle East policy.

Begin's antics, it turned out, had been a ploy to gain a few more concessions. Over the weekend, Vance came up with new formulations to meet some of Begin's objections, and surprisingly, both Begin and his cabinet responded positively. By Monday, Carter realized they were within range of closing a deal after all, but Sadat would have to make additional concessions. Would Sadat bend one last time? Carter suspected he would, because the peace process was the thing that Sadat was clinging to. Carter went to Egypt. He told the Egyptian National Assembly that while an Egyptian-Israeli peace was an "indispensable" first step, "I also remain personally committed to move on to negotiations concerning the West Bank and Gaza Strip and other issues of concern to the Palestinians and to future negotiations with the other neighbors of Israel."[52]

Sadat gave Carter carte blanche to make what final concessions were necessary. They rode a train together through the Nile Delta to Alexandria. Hundreds of thousands of Egyptians turned out to greet Carter, as

they had Nixon just before his resignation five years earlier. Sadat told reporters that "only a word here, a word there" was standing in the way of a
completed treaty.[53]

When Carter's plane landed in Israel, fewer than one thousand people
turned out in Jerusalem to greet the Jewish state's most important ally.
Some carried signs: "Carter Go Home" or "Welcome Billy's Brother." After dining with Begin, the two leaders went into Begin's study where the
Israeli leader threw cold water on Carter's hope of completing a treaty.
Begin said he could not sign or even initial a document. All the proposed
treaty terms would have to be submitted to the Israeli cabinet for extensive debate.

Carter couldn't believe his ears. He stood up and asked coldly whether
it was necessary for him to stay any longer. The two men began to go at
each other as they had during the worst moments at Camp David. Carter
asked him if he really wanted peace, because it seemed to him that Begin
was doing everything he could to obstruct it. Begin stepped closer. Their
faces were a foot apart. Begin said it should be obvious from the expression
on his face that he wanted peace, "as much as anything else in the world."[54]

The next day, in the formal negotiations, Begin turned combative and
antagonistic, interrupting Carter and rejecting Sadat's proposals. During
the break, Carter took off his shoes and put his stocking feet on the Israeli cabinet table. He grasped his head with his hands, as if he were in
pain, and began to rock back and forth. He cast aspersions at Begin. His
aides seemed startled. Hamilton Jordan and Jody Powell, the press secretary, walked over to Carter and sat on either side. According to Richard
Viets, the consul general in Jerusalem, they spoke to him in "very earthy
Southern lingo": "For God's sake, Mr. President, put something up your
derriere and get on with it. Stop whimpering and feeling sorry for your-
self. You can crack this nut. You can win this but you have to get with it."[55]

Viets passed a note to Ezer Weizman: "You should know that the president has ordered Air Force One ready to take off. This thing is going over
the cliff unless you guys get your act together."[56] Both Weizman and
Dayan worked on Begin, who had been fighting for hours over a key
word—"derogate" versus "contravene"—that would guarantee that the
peace treaty could not be abandoned by Sadat's successor. The United
States offered to guarantee Israel's oil supply. Begin rejected an Egyptian
presence in Gaza to help organize Palestinian self-rule and he made the
thinnest commitment to moving forward with negotiations for self-rule
on the West Bank.

Carter got enough, he thought. He went back to Cairo to sell it to Sadat, to whom he pledged a multibillion-dollar aid program for Egypt and a commitment to sell American arms. Sadat spent little time on the details. He was ready, even if some of his aides were not. At the Cairo airport, under a brilliant desert sky, Sadat and Carter announced that the treaty was done. Two weeks later, Begin and Sadat traveled to Washington, where Carter staged a signing ceremony and a celebration on the South Lawn that resembled an old Southern revival meeting. And Carter, whose voice always floated weakly, without bass tones, quoted Scripture to bless the affirmation of peace.

From the Koran, he summoned the words of the Prophet: "But if the enemy inclines toward peace, do thou also incline toward peace."

Sadat said the American president had prevailed for peace because he had been "armed with the blessing of God."

Begin responded with the 126th Psalm: "They that sow in tears shall reap in joy."[57]

But the festival in Washington did little to lighten the somber mood in the Middle East. The treaty had fallen so short of "comprehensive" that it alienated the Arabs. There was no concrete provision for Palestinian self-rule in the West Bank or in East Jerusalem, or for Syria's return to the Golan. Carter sent Zbigniew Brzezinski out to Saudi Arabia and Jordan to see if he could mobilize support for Sadat, but there were no takers. Saudi Arabia's foreign minister, Saud al-Faisal, said genuine Arab-Israeli peace was not possible without a "comprehensive and total solution" that was acceptable to "the Arab Muslim nations and the Palestinian people."

On Sunday morning, November 4, 1979, in Tehran, Thomas Ahern, the CIA station chief, glanced out the window of his office in the chancery building of the United States embassy and saw a number of Iranian youths running pell-mell through the twenty-seven-acre compound. The three-man CIA station was newly arrived in the country; Ahern ambled over to the political section across the hall and wondered aloud if it might be time to start shredding classified documents.

Barry Rosen, the press attaché, had heard the voices of intruders coming down the hall. He had lived through the brief February takeover of the embassy and was ready for the bearded rabble, no doubt sent by some revolutionary prayer leader angling for power or influence. He was not nearly as frightened as he had been the first time. These were just kids, stirred up by Khomeini's storm. He barred his door with a steel bolt to give himself a few extra minutes to destroy his sensitive files.

Bruce Laingen, the laconic chief of mission—Ambassador Sullivan had resigned during the summer—was out of the building, at a meeting at the Iranian foreign ministry. When the chief of the political section, Ann Swift, tumbled on to what was happening, she asked John Limbert, a political officer, to put an immediate call through to the State Department operations center in Washington, where it was three o'clock in the morning.

Other embassy officers were at their desks; some heard noises in the stairwells, or were just oblivious until the young radicals burst through doorways carrying clubs and other tools. They had climbed walls and rushed in beneath the peripheral vision of an embassy staff that had been living with daily demonstrations, random gunfire, and the knowledge that another takeover was likely. In what seemed an instant, the intruders were swarming the chancery building, rounding up hostages, choking on tear gas as Americans escaped through side gates or retreated upstairs. The upper floor of the embassy was secured by steel doors and, with most of the staff congregated there, Swift stayed on the line with the State Department operations center, reporting that a number of embassy personnel, including the marines who had been hurling tear gas canisters to slow the takeover of the first floor, had been captured. The Iranians were threatening to kill them. It was just a matter of time before the students burned or battered their way to the upper floor.

Two hours into the assault, it was apparent that help was not going to come from Prime Minister Bazargan or Ibrahim Yazdi, his foreign minister. Rick Kupke, a State Department communications officer, had moved into the communications vault just down the hall from where Swift was on the phone to Washington. He was destroying files, encryption equipment, and other sensitive electronics. When he heard that Swift was going to give the order to surrender the building, he just closed the heavy door of the vault and kept working.[58]

"We are going down," Swift said into the phone. The barred steel door was cracked and the mob rushed in.

That summer, Americans had been hit by gasoline shortages, skyrocketing energy prices, high inflation, and growing apprehension about Carter's leadership. And now this, a hostage crisis.

In Washington, the calls went out from the Situation Room and State Department. Cyrus Vance was awakened just after 3:00 a.m. Hamilton Jordan, who was spending the weekend on the Chesapeake Bay with Nathan Landow, a Democratic fund-raiser, at 4:30; Brzezinski, just after 5:00; and Carter, who was at Camp David, at 5:30. No one panicked in the Carter administration. Not yet. There was no reason to believe that the sixty-six diplomats who had been taken hostage would not be free in a few hours. Carter's appointments secretary, Phil Wise, called Jordan and asked him the obvious question: What was this going to do to Carter politically as they prepared for the fight of their lives against Senator Edward Kennedy? Jordan did not see a threat as much as he saw an opportunity. No one had been harmed in the embassy takeover and the likelihood was that all the diplomats would be liberated as soon as cooler heads prevailed.

"Don't forget," Jordan said to Wise that morning, "the press will be looking at this in the context of the campaign. It'll be over in a few hours, but it could provide a nice contrast between Carter and our friend from Massachusetts in how to handle a crisis."[59]

He didn't say Chappaquiddick, but that was what Jordan had been thinking about all weekend. That Sunday night, CBS News was going to air a tough hour-long special on Kennedy's handling of the 1969 accident on Martha's Vineyard, when he left a party with Mary Jo Kopechne and drove off a bridge into Poucha Pond. Ms. Kopechne drowned and Kennedy emerged to face an endless public debate about his actions.

By nightfall Sunday, however, the hostage crisis in Tehran overtook everything else. The perpetrators called themselves Muslim Students Following the Line of the Imam. A huge crowd of supporters descended on the streets surrounding the embassy to protect the "victory" of the students over the "Great Satan," and the cry *"Marg bar Amrika!"*—Death to America—rose as an anthem of defiance.

Carter that summer had come down from a long session of introspection at Camp David over inflation, a weak economy, and domestic turmoil. In an address that would come to be known as the "malaise" speech, he said the fault lay within America. "It is clear that the true problems of our nation are much deeper—deeper than gasoline lines or energy shortages, deeper even than inflation or recession. It is a crisis of confidence. It is a crisis that strikes at the very heart and soul and spirit of our national will."[60]

Ayatollah Khomeini in Tehran, 1979: "Death to America!"

The shah and his family had lingered in Egypt in hopes that Ayatollah Khomeini's revolution might fail. Instead, the shah's health was failing. He and his family went farther west, to Morocco, where they were the guests of King Hassan II. But by April 1979, Hassan was eager for the shah to leave. David Rockefeller (the chairman of Chase Manhattan Bank), Henry Kissinger, and Brzezinski began to press Carter, privately and publicly, to admit the shah to the United States. When Carter resisted, Kissinger scorned him in remarks at a Harvard Business School dinner in New York. The shah, he said, "should not be treated like a Flying Dutchman looking for a port of call."[61]

Carter had been prepared to give the shah asylum. In fact, the Walter Annenberg estate in California was made ready to host the royal entourage in early 1979. But the shah had delayed and conditions had changed. Bazargan's government was struggling to survive against the revolutionary torrent that Khomeini was sanctioning. It gave Khomeini leverage over the secular reformers, who wanted to moderate the revolution. When the Iran Desk at State heard that the White House was seriously considering admitting the shah, Henry Precht wheeled on his superior, "You cannot do that. This is not January. The Iranians will not be happy to see him come [to America]."

Precht then raced to a telephone to call Sullivan in Tehran. The ambassador, who was preparing to leave Iran, was incredulous. "If they let him in, they will bring us out in boxes."[62]

Carter took the warning seriously. He told Rockefeller, Kissinger, and Brzezinski that despite the long-standing alliance with the shah, Carter was not going to risk the U.S. embassy personnel still in Tehran whose offices had been overrun in February. So the shah settled in the Bahamas for a time and, when that did not suit him, he moved to Mexico. In October, when news reached Carter that the shah was suffering from a rare cancer of the lymph system and that an acute blockage in his liver now created an urgent and compelling case to admit him, Rockefeller, Kissinger, and others stepped up their lobbying. Carter was the last holdout, according to Jordan, who argued, "Mr. President, if the shah dies in Mexico, can you imagine the field day Kissinger will have with that? He'll say that first you caused the shah's downfall and now you've killed him."

The remark set Carter off. "To hell with Henry Kissinger," he said. "I am the president of this country!"[63]

Neither Rockefeller nor Kissinger disclosed to Carter the huge financial stake that Chase Manhattan Bank held in the decision the president was about to make. Chase had granted hundreds of millions of dollars in loans to Iran under the shah. Bazargan's government was scrupulously making interest payments on this debt, while at the same time rapidly drawing down its cash deposits in Chase. The shah's borrowing had been contested by the Iranian parliament, and therefore there was a legal question whether the revolutionary government was obliged to pay the shah's debts. One of the last things Carter said in making his decision to admit the shah under duress was, "What are you guys going to advise me to do if they overrun our embassy and take our people hostage?"[64]

The benefit of the embassy takeover was significant for Chase: Carter froze Iranian assets in the United States, including the hundreds of millions of dollars in Chase accounts. The freeze enabled Chase to declare Iran in default on its loans since the Iranian central bank was no longer able to move money between accounts to make interest payments. Chase then seized Iran's cash reserves in the amount of the outstanding loans and walked away clean from the disaster.[65]

Malcolm Kalp, one of the CIA officers who had arrived in Tehran only four days before the embassy seizure, had spoken up at the staff meeting earlier in the morning of November 4, saying that he had actually met David Rockefeller just days before at a function in New York. Kalp said that Rockefeller had told him, "I hope I haven't caused you all too many problems."[66]

Thus began Carter's 444-day agony with the hostages. The assault on the symbols of American power radiated out from Iran. In Saudi Arabia, a band of heavily armed radical Islamists—influenced by an indigenous fundamentalist ideology unconnected to what was occurring in Iran— seized the grand mosque in Mecca, triggering a running gun battle at Islam's holiest site. The siege ended with the death of hundreds of militants and bystanders.[67]

Muslim radicals in Pakistan, inflamed by erroneous reports from Mecca that America had somehow been involved in the assault on the shrine, overran and burned the American embassy in Islamabad. The following month in Libya, another mob burned the American embassy.

Carter went into bunker mode. He sent his wife out to campaign, but he stayed in the White House to work assiduously on freeing the hostages. He sent Ramsey Clark, who had been Lyndon Johnson's attorney general, and William Miller, a Farsi-speaking former diplomat, out to meet with Khomeini, but the ayatollah refused them entry to Iran. They sat on a runway in Turkey, using the communications facilities of the presidential aircraft, to call everyone in the world who might influence Khomeini to relent. Of all people, Yasser Arafat was able to score some success for them, convincing Khomeini to release thirteen of the sixty-six hostages in late November.

Harold Brown, the defense secretary, brought Carter plans for mining or blockading Iran's harbors and seizing or destroying its Kharg Island oil terminal. Brzezinski set up a planning cell at the National Security Council to consider ways to topple Khomeini. "We need to consider military actions which contribute to his downfall, and thus secure the release of the hostages as a consequence."[68]

At the bottom of the memo, Carter wrote in his precise script, "We need to list everything that Khomeini would not want to see occur and which would not incite condemnation of U.S. by other nations." Carter considered all the military options but worried that military intimidation of Iran would draw in the Soviet Union. Anatoly Dobrynin was still the Soviet ambassador in Washington. He told Brzezinski straightforwardly that Moscow could not remain indifferent if the United States took military action in Iran.[69] So Carter waited and mobilized the CIA and the military to recruit everyone they could inside Iran and on the periphery to support a rescue operation if the moment came.

In December, the Soviets sent an invasion force into Afghanistan on what turned out to be a paranoid and futile adventure to discipline a people who tenaciously resisted foreign domination. The seizure of the American embassy in Iran followed by the Soviet invasion had a profound impact on Carter. Much of his diplomacy had failed and the failure hardened him. He put the country on a war footing. In his State of the Union address in January 1980, he set forth a Carter Doctrine: "An attempt by any outside force to gain control of the Persian Gulf region will be regarded as an assault on the vital interests of the United States of America, and such an assault will be repelled by any means necessary, including military force."

The Soviets excoriated Carter for overreacting to the Afghan invasion. They were appalled at the sanctions Carter imposed—suspending the purchase of Iranian oil and freezing billions of dollars of Iranian assets in the United States—and his decision to boycott the Olympic Games set for Moscow in 1980.

In those hectic months, Carter tried every diplomatic channel to win the release of the hostages, but their captivity had become an instrument of Khomeini's consolidation; it was making him more powerful against his internal rivals. Bazargan's government resigned. Abolhassan Bani Sadr, a Khomeini protégé who had returned to Iran with the ayatollah, was elected president.

Blocked diplomatically, Carter dispatched emissaries to the Middle East from the Pentagon and CIA to develop a broad new strategy to secure bases for a rapid deployment force; this mission also provided "cover" for the emissaries to request more immediate cooperation for an attempt to rescue the hostages.

Admiral Stansfield Turner, Carter's CIA director, drafted George Cave, a former CIA station chief in Tehran and one of the agency's foremost experts on Iran, to rebuild an Iranian intelligence network that would be able to support American Special Forces teams if they were ordered into Iran. By the end of 1979, an American network of spies and agents was conducting covert surveillance of the U.S. embassy building in Tehran and of the Iranian Foreign Ministry, where Laingen and two other diplomats were being held. The agents prepared automobiles and buses to transport the hostages, and they rented a warehouse to store their equipment until the operation was ready to launch.[70] They surveilled landing sites for a helicopter assault team.

Brzezinski summoned Prince Bandar, who served as a conduit between the Carter White House and Saudi Arabia's Crown Prince Fahd. The president, Brzezinski said, wanted permission to use Saudi bases to launch aircraft and helicopters into Iran. Bandar asked whether he could guarantee that the Soviets would not "react" and put Saudi Arabia in jeopardy.

"Don't worry about the Soviets," Brzezinski had replied.

"I have to worry about the Soviets," Bandar said. "They are only one thousand miles away from me. You are eight thousand miles, so if you move from Saudi Arabia into Iran and . . . they move, we are in trouble."[71] The Saudis remained wary of Carter, blaming him for the loss of Iran. As a result, Crown Prince Fahd refused to allow America to use the kingdom as a launch point. But the Saudis tried to soften the blow. Fahd sent back a message saying that if the American rescue operation succeeded, the rescue team and the remaining fifty-two hostages could touch down at a Saudi air base to refuel and treat any casualties before flying home.

The rescue never got that far. It failed on April 24 at a place the U.S. military had designated as Desert One, a stretch of hard, salt desert south of Tehran that served as the rendezvous point and staging base for the American commando force under Colonel Charles Beckwith. He and his men had come halfway around the world to mount a daring raid into the center of Tehran. But dust storms and mechanical breakdowns hobbled their helicopters, leaving them one short of the minimum needed to extract the team and the hostages from what would be, by then, a fully alerted Iranian capital. Carter listened to the reports coming in by satellite phone. All he felt he could do was issue the abort order, which he did at 4:57 p.m. Shortly thereafter, word came of a worse calamity: one of the retreating helicopters had crashed into the fuel transport, touching off an inferno that killed eight members of the team. Bad luck, poor planning, and different operating styles among the marines, army, and air force pilots had contributed to the disaster. For Carter, it was one of the worst days of his life. It was as if America, the greatest military power on earth, was itself hostage to the extremist rabble in Tehran.

Had America ever looked weaker?

The shah died a few months later, on July 27, 1980, in Cairo. He was sixty. A decade earlier world leaders had dined with him at Persepolis.

Now, only Sadat and family members stood by the caisson that carried his flag-draped coffin with military escort through the Egyptian capital to the al-Rifai Mosque, where he was buried.

In Libya, Colonel Muammar Qaddafi threatened to attack American ships and planes that entered the two hundred-mile zone of the Gulf of Sidra that he had unilaterally declared closed to international shipping. When a Libyan warplane fired a missile at an American EC-135 reconnaissance flight in the region, the United States took no action and Carter's failure to pull the trigger in the face of aggression became the emblem of his decline.

In Iraq, Saddam Hussein declared his own doctrine in response to the Carter Doctrine. The Arabs, he said, could defend themselves, and he offered an Iraqi-led security alliance for the Middle East. He was no Nasser, and the Arab leaders declined his offer. Still, Saddam stepped up border clashes with Iran, testing Khomeini's strength. The consensus in the intelligence community was that the Iranian army was a shell that could not sustain the pressure and discipline of modern combat operations.[72] America's close allies, Jordan and Saudi Arabia, passed along to Saddam key American intelligence judgments about the state of the Iranian armed forces, most pointedly the view that the young Revolutionary Guard could not mount a disciplined defense, nor could it master the high-technology American weaponry it had inherited.

On September 22, Saddam launched a full-scale invasion of southern Iran, driving toward the oil fields and the heart of Iran's national wealth. He expected that Iraq's military power would overwhelm the Revolutionary Guard and the remnant forces of the shah's army.

Once again, events seemed to spin beyond Carter's control. He didn't know very much about Saddam Hussein. But Khomeini, under the pressure of Iraqi invasion, was going to be even harder to deal with on the hostages, who remained prisoners in the embassy.

"I was deeply resentful [of Saddam]," Carter told me in an interview. "He considered Iran to be so vulnerable." But Carter said he just wanted "to get my hostages out." That would be easier if Iran was at peace.

In October 1980, Libya invaded Chad. Among Qaddafi's armed forces were East German and Cuban advisers. It was another sign that the Soviet Union and its allies were on the march in the Middle East while America seemed paralyzed. In the waning years of Soviet power, with détente discredited by a skeptical American political establishment, there were few incentives for cooperation and more to gain for Moscow, economically, from support for the well-financed radical agenda in the Middle East.

Ronald Reagan's feel-good charm and the Western-state conservatism stole a march on Carter's crumbling administration. Yet Reagan feared an "October surprise," some diplomatic dash that would bring the hostages home before the November 4 election. As much as Carter tried, he couldn't overcome Iran's internal chaos: some Khomeini followers argued for humiliating Carter for as long as possible, and others sought a face-saving compromise that would end the crisis.

The Republican foreign policy establishment savaged Carter as a president whom U.S. foes found so "weak and manageable"[73] that the Ayatollah Khomeini—were he able to vote—would certainly cast his ballot for Carter instead of for a tough cold warrior like Reagan. Henry Kissinger and his former deputy, Brent Scowcroft, both met privately with the Soviet ambassador to sing Reagan's praises, with Scowcroft going so far as suggesting, according to Ambassador Dobrynin, that Reagan was "like Eisenhower"—pragmatic and not nearly as anti-Soviet as his public statements indicated.[74] Scowcroft advised that the fate of the election might rest in Soviet hands: if the Kremlin moved to end the war in Afghanistan, the breakthrough might help Carter get reelected (a different kind of October surprise); or, Scowcroft added, the Kremlin could sit "on the fence." Scowcroft was not subtle about the course he would recommend: Carter, he said to the Soviet ambassador, "had the vehement nature of a missionary, leaning toward exaggerations and overstatements while having no underlying belief in the correctness of his course."

But no stiletto in the ribs delivered in private channels by Kissinger or Scowcroft could do as much harm to Carter as he had done to himself. During Carter's last battle to get the hostages out of Tehran before Inauguration Day, he worked through Algerian lawyers and shadowy Iranian middlemen to trade billions of dollars in frozen Iranian assets for the freedom of the Americans. He was paying ransom to hostage takers (even if it was with Iranian funds), but Carter believed that the American people expected him to do everything he could to end the standoff that had seemed to paralyze the country and shatter all faith in his presidency.

On the morning of January 20, 1980, Carter left the White House for the last time as president. He made the short ride to the Capitol, where Reagan awaited him. Hamilton Jordan stayed behind in the Situation Room, connected by satellite phone with Tehran. The Iranians had bused the fifty-two American captives to Mehrabad Airport, where they boarded a plane, which sat on the runway until Reagan was sworn in.

Before he left, Carter, the Christian engineer, personally checked and double-checked the intricate financial transfers to free Iranian assets. He fought down his bitterness over all of the events that had conspired to bring about his political demise like a convergence of bad luck: Edward Kennedy's challenge in the primaries, the oil crisis triggered by the Iranian revolution, runaway inflation that sapped the economy, and the desertion by American Jews of the political base he had built in 1976. Above all was the loss of presidential inspiration, something Reagan excelled at with his "Morning in America" theme.

"It is impossible for me to put into words how much the hostages had come to mean to me, or how moved I was that morning to know they were coming home," Carter wrote. "At the same time, I was leaving the home I'd known for four years, too soon for all I had hoped to accomplish."[75]

Carter's achievements had all been laced with bitterness. Yet he had done something extraordinary. He had brought Arab and Israeli leaders together and proved that compromise and peace were possible. All of his predecessors, going back to Eisenhower, had come into office with a desire to make peace in the Middle East, but no president in the postwar period had invested as much energy and political capital as Carter. His tactics may have been flawed, he may have bungled the handling of American Jews, whose support he needed, but no other president had ever plunged forward into the details, the drafting, and the hard choices of peacemaking. It was Carter, the obsessive technocrat who wore his idealism like a crucifix and his pragmatism like a slide rule clipped to his waistband, who was most determined to solve the equation and who persevered. He failed to clear the bar on what the Middle East expected of him by way of securing a comprehensive peace. He did not fulfill the expectations of Palestinian nationalism and its demand for a homeland. And he came up short of wresting control of the West Bank and Gaza from Begin. Yet the treaty, so vilified by the Arabs, proved over time that barriers *could* be breached. Carter overcame the rancor and bitterness he felt toward Begin for his bludgeoning tactics and his disdain for the Arabs. For Carter, it was a matter of faith and an act of reconciliation to overcome the psychological divide that separated him from the Israeli leader.

In the end, it did not matter, however. So much of the positive structure of peace that Carter, Begin, and Sadat secured was swamped by violence and militarism. A strong new current of anti-Americanism was coursing through the Middle East. Washington's traditional allies had lost confidence that the United States could protect them. And the Iranian revolution—the Shiite awakening—was spreading a new ideology of fundamentalism and extremism across the region.

# 7

# THE SHAME OF LEBANON

## Reagan's Warriors in the Middle East

Israel's Etzion Air Base is not much more than a runway etched into the desert, but what a desert. From the runway it is possible to behold the mountainous girth of Egypt's Sinai Peninsula, the land in whose valleys Moses and the Hebrew tribes had wandered. Whether or not one has religion, central Sinai, that forbidding protuberance of sharp, crystalline peaks, beckons mystically as hallowed ground. In the middle stands Jebel Musa, or Moses' Mountain, where the Old Testament dramas of the burning bush and Ten Commandments were said to have taken place. Anwar Sadat, a believing Muslim, declared at Camp David that one of his dreams was to build a church, a mosque, and a temple on the summit of Jebel Musa to celebrate a comprehensive peace between Arabs and Jews. It seemed a distant prospect now that the talks for Palestinian autonomy had broken down.

Just over the horizon to the east lies the aquamarine bath of the Gulf of Aqaba, that long narrow embayment that offers a quenching sight to anyone coming down from the anvil of the desert. It was no wonder that since Ben-Gurion's time Israel had wanted a piece of Sinai. It stood there as the biblical vista that conquerors crossed and pharaohs defended. Its vastness offered strategic depth—it protected the Nile Valley from Babylonian encroachment in the same way that Russia's vastness overwhelmed Napoleon's army and, later, Hitler's. Ben-Gurion had wanted strategic depth for Israel, a giant buffer zone on the southern flank that no army could traverse without setting off the clamor of alarm. And Sinai had oil, which, of course, Ben-Gurion also had coveted.

Menachem Begin was said to be in love with Sinai's beauty, and one of the reasons he fought so hard with Sadat to retain the Israeli settlements in Sinai during the Camp David negotiations was that he wanted to retire there. Now, the Egyptians would soon have it back, oil and all.

It was Sunday, June 7, 1981, a workday in Israel and in most of the surrounding Arab countries, but a day off for one hundred or so French, Italian, and Brazilian engineers and technicians working at a sensitive facility at al-Tuwaitha in Iraq, more than six hundred miles to the east and about twenty miles south of Baghdad. They kept to the Christian calendar and so they had paused in their work on the big Osirak research reactor, whose containment building with its distinctive rounded dome was almost invisible where it stood near the Tigris River because it was surrounded by a massive earthen berm that towered above the date palms like a volcano and blocked any view from the nearby roads. Inside the earthworks was a hive of construction. The reactor was being prepared for fueling with enriched uranium pellets in long rods.

Italy had provided a separation plant, or "hot cell," where the Iraqis would, every few months, chemically dissolve the uranium fuel after it had been irradiated in the reactor and recover plutonium from the residue, enough to assemble three atomic bombs a year. Israeli military intelligence figured that Iraq would soon be able to produce three bombs, each with the equivalent power of the bomb dropped on Hiroshima. If dropped on Tel Aviv, Haifa, and West Jerusalem, an Iraqi atomic attack would deliver a genocidal blow to the Jewish state.

Saddam Hussein called the reactor Tammuz after the month in the ancient calendar when the Babylonian destroyer Nebuchadnezzar sacked Jerusalem and pulled down the Hebrew Temple in 586 B.C. There was nothing subtle about his vision of Arab wrath against the Jews.

The French leader, Jacques Chirac, who had wanted to expand French markets in the Middle East, had made a deal in 1975 to sell a nuclear reactor to Saddam Hussein; he had sold French Mirage fighters and other weapons, too. The deal was so large as to make Chirac a hero of French industry. Now, after six years of construction, the reactor was ready. It was just a matter of time and physics before Iraq would become a nuclear power. Menachem Begin, a man for whom the Holocaust was never out of mind, had decided that Israel could not tolerate a hostile Arab state armed with atomic weapons poised within range of Jerusalem and Tel Aviv. The survival of the Jewish state, in his estimation, required nuclear monopoly in the region and he would fight to maintain it for as long as he could.

Israeli leaders could not comprehend that the same France that had helped Israel build its atomic weapons complex to ensure the Jewish state's long-term survival would sell nuclear technology to an Arab radical like Saddam. An assassin and an enforcer for the Baath Party, Saddam had pushed aside his ailing cousin, General Ahmed Hassan al-Bakr, to become president in 1979. Iraq hosted Palestinian terrorist groups that wanted nothing more than to destroy Israel.

The Israelis had done what they could to obstruct Saddam. In April 1979, reports of a large explosion at a French nuclear-component manufacturing plant at La Seyne-sur-Mer, near Toulon, reached Paris. The French authorities clamped a news blackout on the incident. It took days for other Western governments to figure out that a sophisticated infiltration of the plant by saboteurs had taken place. They had packed plastic explosives into the core of the nearly complete Iraqi reactor vessel and detonated it. An anonymous telephone caller told authorities that the "French Ecological Group" was responsible for the blast. No one had ever heard of the group, before or since. British and American intelligence officials were certain that the raid was the work of the Israeli intelligence agency, Mossad.[1]

The damage delayed but did not prevent completion of the Iraqi reactor components. In June 1980, Dr. Yehya al-Meshad, an Egyptian physicist working for the Iraqi Atomic Energy Commission, was in Paris to supervise the shipment of nuclear fuel to Iraq. A prostitute, said to be passing al-Meshad's room, heard a commotion. When hotel security personnel arrived, they found the scientist dead and bloodied with multiple stab wounds. The prostitute was mysteriously killed by a hit-and-run driver a few weeks later. Soon thereafter, bombs went off in Italy, where another company was providing the plutonium separation technology to Iraq.

Even with these setbacks, Saddam was not deterred. Neither was Begin. He pressed Israel's concerns with Washington about the prospect of a nuclear-armed Iraq. If America and the West failed to prevent the nightmare, the implication—the threat—was that Israel might have to act alone. During the last months of the Carter administration, the American ambassador in Israel, Samuel Lewis, used the Cherokee reporting channel, a highly restricted circuit for the most sensitive cable traffic, to inform the secretary of state and the president that "this reactor was something the Israelis could not allow to become critical," meaning operational. Once the fuel rods were inserted and the controlled fission reaction began, the reactor would become highly radioactive.[2] Dropping bombs on a live reactor would spew radioactive fallout across Iraq and neighboring states.

"We were assuring them that we take this very seriously," Ambassador Lewis later said. The message from Washington was, "Don't do anything rash, we are going to do everything we can to stop it diplomatically," but nothing happened.

America was asleep in the Middle East, distracted by presidential politics and the Iran hostage crisis. The threat of war over the Osirak reactor got "lost" in a chaotic transition from the Carter to the Reagan administration and no one in either camp has ever admitted the scale of the blunder. The incoming Reagan team disparaged Carter and his advisers; it was as if, after all of Carter's failures, there were nothing Reagan could learn from him on matters of national security. Carter's advisers were devastated by political defeat. But here was an issue that could trigger war in the Middle East and that would intensify the grievance psychology of the Arabs over American support for Israel. More than at any time since John Kennedy had clashed with Ben-Gurion over the Dimona reactor, here was an issue that deeply affected America's perception of its own security—the spread of nuclear weapons in an unstable region.

And yet the Carter bureaucracy suffered a kind of mass amnesia. The State Department under Edmund Muskie prepared a highly classified report on the Iraqi project and on Israel's determination to stop it. But then Carter and his top aides failed to brief the incoming president or his secretaries of state or defense. Carter was swamped with the last-minute hostage-release drama. Indeed, the entire country was transfixed by it, but that was no excuse for Carter's inaction, since there were legions of national security aides whose job it was to render a change of administrations seamless, especially with regard to passing on any threat of war in a region so critical to American security.

Ambassador Lewis, who was prone to a see-no-evil approach to diplomacy, explained that the Carter team put the Osirak report "in such a high degree of classification that no one in the Reagan team ever saw it."[3] It stayed locked in a safe. But no degree of classification prevented Brzezinski, Muskie, Harold Brown, the defense secretary, or Admiral Stansfield Turner, the CIA director, from raising an alarm to the effect that Israel was considering a major military strike on an Arab state that would have serious consequences for the future of nuclear arms competition in the Middle East.

Alexander Haig, the incoming secretary of state, acknowledged that he only "discovered" after the fact that the Carter administration had received from the Israelis a detailed warning about the Iraqi reactor, about its potential "to make [atomic] bombs," and about the Israeli requests to the U.S. and French governments "to take action to prevent this result."[4] However, from the time he was sworn in as secretary, "it was never discussed with the Reagan administration."[5] Haig did not explain what (if anything) he did to discover how such a critical issue could be "lost" from one administration to the next. Reagan couldn't explain it either. Five months into his administration, he was simply ignorant about the most immediate threat to U.S. security in the Middle East.[6]

After Reagan took office, stories in the Israeli press about progress on and concern about the completion of the Osirak reactor suddenly ceased. "It just disappeared from the dialogue. And they stopped talking to us diplomatically about it also," said Lewis, who has never adequately explained why he, in his many discussions with Haig and other senior officials of the incoming Reagan administration, did not raise the subject that he had so urgently been raising in the last months of the Carter administration.

Just after 4:00 p.m. on June 7 at Etzion Air Base, eight American-made F-16 Falcons and six F-15 Eagles rolled out to the ramp. Each conducted a "hot refueling," getting the tanks topped off with engines running. The F-16s were carrying almost twice their specified payload in bombs and underwing fuel pods for the ninety-minute flight to Baghdad. The twelve hundred-mile round-trip was at the very edge of their range. Ready now, flight leaders Ze'ev Raz, Amir Nachumi, and Amos Yadlin rolled their Falcons down the runway, straining to reach liftoff speed. Their bombs and fuel tanks hung like great pontoons, spoiling the aerodynamic grace of the aircraft. All were soon airborne.

With the sun at their backs, the flight of fourteen warplanes swept low across the Gulf of Aqaba. King Hussein, the Jordanian monarch and a skilled pilot, was flying over southern Jordan that afternoon and spotted the Israeli planes as they streaked through Jordanian airspace and then disappeared over the Saudi desert. Hussein was certain the planes were on a bombing mission and, according to some accounts, he radioed to Jordanian ground controllers that they should raise an alarm with the Iraqi Defense Ministry, though there is no evidence this message actually was sent to the Iraqi air defense command.[7] The warplanes dropped down to as low as one hundred feet over the desert and dashed in silence toward the Iraqi frontier. Near the Iraqi border, the Eagles, which were flying escort, soared to higher altitude to scan the horizon for Iraqi interceptors and to jam Iraqi air defense radars. The blue slash of the Euphrates River appeared on the horizon, signaling the final approach.

"Lock on . . . don't panic . . . Baghdad ahead," the flight leader said calmly, breaking radio silence. Two by two, the Falcons pulled up to four thousand feet to arm their two thousand-pound bombs and then each pilot pushed the stick forward to bring the nose down on the target: the Osirak reactor dome. In little more than a minute, all eight F-16s had released their bombs. All but two of them crashed into the reactor, touching off a cascade of explosions that demolished the concrete containment building and the reactor core. A huge column of black smoke billowed up from Tammuz, an insult to Saddam that towered over Mesopotamia.

The Osirak raid was recognized worldwide as a provocation, one that signaled a new and militant phase of Israel's foreign policy. The condemnations came swiftly. The Soviet news agency called it a "barbarous" act. The British Foreign Office called it a "grave breach of international law which could have the most serious consequences." The French were livid. United Nations Secretary-General, Kurt Waldheim pronounced it a "clear contravention" of international law. Arab leaders said Israel was flaunting its access to American weapons to strike the Arab world, violating Jordanian, Saudi, and Iraqi airspace in a blatant and unprovoked act of war. To them, Washington looked like Israel's patsy.

Israel's defenders hailed the raid as a "nuclear Entebbe," rescuing the world from a nuclear-armed despot. Senator Alan Cranston, a California Democrat, pointed out that nineteen years earlier the United States had faced a similar threat of Soviet nuclear missiles in Cuba. Wasn't Israel's action analogous to Kennedy's finest hour in forcing the Soviets to back down with a blockade and invasion threat? Besides, he argued, there was a very obvious provocation: only nine months earlier Iraq's leading propaganda organ, *Al Thawra*, had declared that "the Iranian people should not fear the Iraqi nuclear reactor, which is not intended to be used against Iran, but against the Zionist entity."[8]

Ronald Reagan was no admirer of Saddam Hussein. In the days after the raid, he called him a "no good nut" in his diary. "Arab indignation on behalf of Iraq is a waste," Reagan wrote. "I think [Saddam] was trying to build a nuclear weapon. He wants to be the leader of the Arab world— that's why he invaded Iran." Nonetheless, Reagan concluded that Israel was wrong to attack. "[Begin] should have told us and the French, we could have done something to remove the threat," he said, adding, "however we are not turning on Israel—that would be an invitation for the Arabs to attack."[9]

Begin was defiant. His rivals said he was trying to improve his reelection fortunes, but he fired back that if the raid had failed—if Israeli pilots had died—it would have devastated his reelection prospects. "Israel has nothing to apologize for," Begin said. "In simple logic, we decided to act now, before it is too late . . . We shall defend our people with all the means at our disposal."[10]

By 1981, Israel was no longer a modest military power equipped with outdated French and British arms.[11] Begin saw Israel's rise as a unique opportunity to shape the strategic landscape in the Middle East, much as Ben-Gurion had wanted to do. And though Israel's national strength was in great measure dependent on American weaponry and economic aid, no American president could easily override the bedrock support for Israel in Congress. Begin had come to believe that Israel could act with near impunity as long as it could make the case that it was removing threats to its long-term security.

"What do you mean we won't get arms?" Begin had once said to Golda Meir. "We'll demand them from the Americans."[12]

Israel's unilateral destruction of the Iraqi reactor burned in Arab and Muslim consciousness, even among those who applauded the disarming of Saddam Hussein. To see Israel act as a unilateral enforcer of nuclear exclusivity in the Middle East was a humiliation that would motivate other states—Iran, Libya and, repeatedly, Iraq—to acquire nuclear technology over the next two decades. But worse, the Osirak episode reiterated the shortcomings of American diplomacy, which had never looked so incompetent in the loss of continuity from one president to the next.

More important, the American-led effort to halt the spread of nuclear weapons through international diplomacy had broken down. The investments that Roosevelt, Truman, and Eisenhower had made in the United Nations as a multilateral institution that nations could rely on to resolve conflicts and disputes and address long-standing grievances had noticeably declined as the cold war polarized the world body and stymied its ability to function in the manner intended by the founders. The cold war also had diminished the capacity for mediation and inspection under the International Atomic Energy Agency, the watchdog organization that Eisenhower had helped to create and whose role had been strengthened by the Nuclear Non-Proliferation Treaty, of which Iraq was a signatory.

Israel had become an extension of American power, yet it was unrestrained, and Arab leaders looked to Washington to restrain it.

Ronald Reagan had been in office just over one hundred days when the Israeli air force attacked Iraq. He was still recovering from the gunshot wound he had suffered at the end of March in an assassination attempt by John W. Hinckley. Though Reagan's overarching goal as president was to confront Soviet power in the world, he had no agenda in the Middle East other than a general ambition to make his own contribution to peace. In fact, the new president showed no signs that he had mastered any of the subtleties of the region. In his diary, he said that he favored peace negotiations between Israel and Saudi Arabia, a line of thinking that suggests that he did not understand the first imperative of Arab politics—a solution to the Palestinian problem above all. After that was settled, and after the Golan Heights returned to Syrian sovereignty, then a general peace could follow, including with the Saudis. Reagan's belief that Saudi Arabia would somehow break ranks with the other Arab nations reflected his personal idealism, but it also revealed how poorly informed or equipped he was for effective statecraft.

Reagan and his team looked out over a changed Middle East. With the Soviet invasion of Afghanistan along with Soviet and Cuban interventions in Africa, the Camp David era of peacemaking had given way to the exigencies of cold war. Reagan was more than ready to roll back Soviet gains and resort to clandestine operations wherever they were needed. Yet for him, the Middle East was terra incognita. Like many Americans, Jew and non-Jew, Reagan admired the idea of Israel. As an actor in Hollywood, he had witnessed the drama of the Jewish experience in the twentieth century: the Holocaust, the exodus of displaced Jews from Europe, and the Zionist transformation of the Holy Land. For Reagan, Israel was heroic—"a small country fighting for the acceptance of neighbors sworn to destroy it" and forced to "live in a perpetual state of war as the constant target of Palestinian terror."[13] Reagan had come into office with considerable respect for Israel's political power in Washington. Though the Jewish vote was not a decisive factor in Reagan's landslide victory, it was well-known that Carter was the first Democratic president in the postwar era to have lost the Jewish vote, as American Jews deserted him for Reagan and John Anderson, the third-party candidate.

The Arab world was even more of a mystery to Reagan. Except for a brief visit to Iran, Reagan had never traveled in the region. He had Alexander Haig as his secretary of state and his tutor, but Haig had so little respect for Reagan's intellect that he could not help but lecture the new president rather than advise him. Haig had almost no experience with the Middle East, either, other than through the lens of Henry Kissinger, whom he had served in the Nixon White House. The new secretary of state convinced Reagan they could build a new kind of anti-Soviet alliance in the Middle East—a "strategic consensus" among like-minded states to break the Soviet occupation of Afghanistan, contain Libya's Qaddafi and Syria's Assad (both Soviet-backed strongmen), and generally roll back Soviet gains.

Reagan selected one of his oldest friends, Caspar Weinberger, as secretary of defense and gave him a mandate to rebuild U.S. military forces in response to the Soviet military expansion under Brezhnev. Another veteran of Nixon's cabinet, Weinberger had returned to government from Bechtel, the private construction conglomerate that had dozens of multibillion-dollar projects in the Arab world. He came with a firm conviction that the United States had broader interests in the Middle East than relations with Israel. His pro-Arab orientation made him an advocate for opening a dialogue with the PLO to help reach a settlement in the Holy Land, a position that would antagonize the pro-Israel Haig.

In the wake of the Israeli strike, Reagan chaired a meeting of his top advisers, his National Security Planning Group. Weinberger expressed indignation that the Israelis had launched American-made F-16s in an offensive strike on an Arab state. "Cap," as everyone called him, saw the attack as a violation of international law.[14] Moreover, it was embarrassing to the United States. U.S. arms export statutes obliged Israel to use American-made weapons "solely to maintain its internal security" for "its legitimate self-defense," not for "any act of aggression against any other state."[15]

Weinberger was ready to send a strong message to Begin by freezing economic and military aide to Israel. But Haig was not. A month before the raid, Haig had secretly sent one of his top aides, Robert McFarlane, to Geneva to meet with David Kimche, the director general of Israel's Foreign Ministry, to discuss "strategic cooperation" between Israel and the United States.[16] Israel's preemptive attack obviously raised the question: How could allies blindside each other like this?

Haig thought that Reagan should do no more than express American disapproval. To turn on Israel would invite the same kind of confrontation that had mobilized the Jewish community—and much of the Senate—against Jimmy Carter. Pro-Israel forces already were up in arms over Reagan's announced intention to sell additional arms to Saudi Arabia, including AWACS (airborne warning, control, and surveillance aircraft), with their sophisticated radar, which would magnify the power of the Saudi air force to see over the horizon.

Reagan decided on a minimal rebuke. He postponed the delivery of four F-16s that were due in Israel that summer.

Reagan had brought one of his most avid cold warriors, William Casey, back to government service as director of central intelligence. Casey, at seventy-one, was spoiling to return to the fight. As a wealthy New York businessman and a stalwart of Republican politics going back to Nixon, he had run Reagan's presidential campaign. Casey's espionage credentials were stamped in World War II, when he served as a covert operator for the Office of Strategic Services, the precursor to the CIA. Now he returned to America's spying establishment in 1981 as an activist in an era of caution. Revelations of CIA assassination plots (against Fidel Castro in Cuba, Patrice Lumumba in the Congo, Ngo Dinh Diem in Vietnam) by the Pike and Church committees of the Senate had hobbled the agency during the 1970s. Casey was determined to reverse the deterioration and re-create a clandestine service that would be the scourge of Soviet communism.

He was not a complicated man. A devout Roman Catholic, Casey understood the world in terms of good and evil, a hallmark of the World War II generation. He looked out at an international system, saw freedom struggling against tyranny, and took sides with the moral conviction informed by his faith. After the war, when there were many OSS men who wanted to take the fight aggressively to Eastern Europe to free the populations trapped behind the Iron Curtain, Casey watched with frustration as Dwight Eisenhower recognized Moscow's "sphere of influence" that cast a shadow over half of Europe. He had witnessed the failed uprisings in Hungary, Poland, and Czechoslovakia with a sense of tragedy. Like the president he served, Casey was convinced that Soviet communism was a sinister force. Moscow, he believed, had accepted Nixon's offer of "détente" to lull the West while seeking to rack up further gains. Casey employed a scorecard approach: How many countries could he and Reagan take off the "Communist" list in eight years?

Casey had a big oval face and wore large-framed glasses, and the first thing anyone observed about him was that he was a man of unsynchronized lips and jowls, which combined to undermine the clarity of his speech, so much so that the dissonance, especially when he lowered his voice, rendered his speech an indecipherable mumble. It became his trademark. The joke at CIA was that he did not need a scrambler on his telephone.

Early exposure to the espionage game had imbued Casey with a sense that the mission was everything and that shaving the law or the rules— and not getting caught at it—was part of playing it smart. Even to those who worked closely with him, he seemed excessively secretive. His deputy, Bobby Ray Inman, called him "the wanderer" because Casey would take off in the director's executive jet for clandestine meetings around the globe that he never reported on. His service under Nixon had made him a bulldog as a bureaucrat and combative with the congressional oversight committees.

A lifetime in business gave Casey a strong sense of strategic priorities. One of the first things he did as director was travel to Saudi Arabia to

Ronald Reagan and King Fahd: a secret Saudi-American alliance

meet Crown Prince Fahd. Fahd's standing was already high among the Reagan team, whose members were aware that Saudi Arabia had increased its oil production by a million barrels a day during the energy crisis that followed the Iranian Revolution. Fahd had done so at the request of Jimmy Carter, who had sent Prince Bandar secretly to his masters in Riyadh to make the case for market stability through increased oil production.[17]

Casey arrived in Riyadh with a proposition: America was looking for partners to challenge the Soviets throughout the region with covert action, military aid, and training—whatever it took—to reverse the sense that America had abandoned or neglected its interests in the Middle East after the fall of the shah. Crown Prince Fahd was surprised. The Saudi royal family had been discouraged by Carter's hesitant steps.

"If you mean what you say," Fahd told him, "you have partners in us."[18]

Fahd also explained to Casey that Saudi Arabia needed a stronger air force: F-15s with full capabilities as well as AWACS, which could see threats far over the horizon. Carter had promised to take another major arms sale package to Congress for the Saudis but failed in the face of resistance during his final year. Fahd saw a quid pro quo, never stated explicitly but nonetheless transparent. The Saudis were willing to finance covert operations against the Soviet Union and intensify a secret Saudi-American alliance. In return they expected Reagan, when the politics were right, to push through Congress arms sales packages that were important to Saudi Arabia's military buildup.

Israel was sure to discover and oppose any secret alliance in the Arab world that might compete with the primacy of Israeli interests in the region, but Casey was the kind of gambler who saw his anti-Soviet agenda as overarching. He almost certainly felt he and Reagan could manage the contradictions between their devotion to Israel and secret U.S. alliances with the wealthy, anticommunist Arabs.

"Let's start with Afghanistan," Casey said. "We will fight the Soviets in Afghanistan and if you are confident, wherever you have threats, we will come and help you." Moreover, if the United States needed help in carrying the fight to other regions, it might ask for Saudi assistance in that regard. Fahd told Casey that he had a deal.

During Carter's last months in office, sixty-eight senators had signed a letter opposing the sale of additional F-15s and AWACS to Saudi Arabia. Reagan, Weinberger, and Casey, however, were ready to go forward with virtually everything the Saudis wanted. They left it to Haig to contend with Israeli demands that the Saudi air force be denied external fuel tanks and bomb racks for their F-15s, thus limiting their range and offensive capability. The Israelis saw this as a prudent hedge in the event that Saudi F-15s were ever turned against Israel, but the Saudis regarded it as an Israeli attempt at humiliation. Weinberger tended to agree with the Saudis.

Yitzhak Shamir, Begin's foreign minister, came to Washington and announced that Israel was strongly opposed to any sale that would materially improve the offensive air power of an Arab state. Begin warned that if the United States sold AWACS to the Saudis, the radar technology would render Israel "naked" militarily.[19]

Haig was worried about a revolt in the Senate that would embarrass the administration in its opening months. Of the sixty-eight senators who had signed the letter the previous year, fifty-five had been reelected. AIPAC, the American Israeli Public Affairs Committee, a pro-Israeli lobbying arm, had put the administration on notice that it was gearing up for a fight. Reagan announced on March 6 that he was going ahead with the sale despite the warnings from Israel and its supporters. The week that Reagan was shot, Haig had tried to split the F-15s and AWACS into two packages—which telegraphed that Reagan might be willing to jettison one system to ensure passage of the other—but Haig was overruled by Vice President George Bush, who was sitting in while the president lay in the hospital.

The AWACS sale was a major issue in Begin's reelection campaign, but while his battle against the White House helped him electorally, Israel would lose the overall struggle to keep the AWACS out of Saudi hands.[20] Begin's reelection—a defeat of the peace camp led by Shimon Peres—set the stage for a grander confrontation. Begin appointed Ariel Sharon minister of defense. It was a fateful decision, as Sharon, and other like-minded activists in the security establishment, had been scheming for a new kind of war in the Middle East. Sharon believed that in one stroke, Israel could destroy the PLO, humiliate and weaken Syria, create a Jewish-Christian alliance with Lebanon, and orchestrate the migration of Palestinian refugees to Jordan, which Sharon considered to be the real Palestinian state, since its population was heavily Palestinian.

Inchoate elements of this plan had existed for years, but the Begin-Sharon partnership and the advent of a strong new Christian leader in Lebanon, Bashir Gemayel, made possible a bolder phase of militarism. The other crucial factor was that Israel no longer had an enemy to the south. The Egyptian front was secured by the peace with Sadat and Israel was thus free to focus its military strength in new directions.

Lebanon lay fragmented by civil war. The PLO ministate had become bolder, importing artillery, rockets, and even some tanks—all the accoutrements of a standing army, not a mobile guerrilla force. And from its increasingly fixed positions and bases, the PLO had stepped up rocket and artillery attacks on Israel's northernmost towns and settlements.

On July 16, the Israeli air force bombed five bridges across the Litani and Zahrani rivers, the major north-south arteries for the civilian population. Bridges had been spared in the past out of consideration for civilians, but Lieutenant General Rafael Eitan, the Israeli chief of staff, said bridges were targets because an "endless stream" of weaponry was flowing across them into South Lebanon. "If others [civilians] suffer, they should press the terrorists to stop their attacks on us," General Eitan said.[21] Eitan's admonition was another milestone on the road to a collective-punishment psychology that was overtaking the upper ranks of the Israeli military with regard to Lebanon. In the absence of international diplomacy to stabilize Lebanon or control its border regions, Israel had begun to take matters into its own hands.

On July 17, Begin and Sharon directed the Israeli air force to bomb the PLO headquarters in Beirut. The late morning attack against the Fakehani district of Muslim West Beirut caused apartment blocks to collapse and touched off a general panic as civilians and Palestinian militants fled for safety. An estimated three hundred people were killed and eight hundred were wounded, most of them civilians. Yasser Arafat's headquarters was not damaged, though other Palestinian offices were.

Reagan had been a tough-talking conservative, but he was a politician in the populist tradition with an affinity for the common man and so he was moved by images of civilian suffering. He pressed Israel for a ceasefire. The F-16s that had been withheld from Israel after the Osirak raid were due to be transferred on the day of these strikes, prompting critics to ask: Was Reagan going to continue supplying Israel the very weapons used for the deplorable bombing attacks in Lebanon?[22]

Israel's militarism deepened Anwar Sadat's isolation. His separate peace had unharnessed Israel in other directions. Sadat went to Washington in August to meet Reagan, but instead of greeting him as a heroic peacemaker, the news media focused on Sadat's increasingly paranoid rule at home. Journalists compared him to the shah. Egypt had lost its leadership role in the Arab world. The Saudi Prince Fahd stepped forward, calling for a new Arab position on peace with Israel because the Camp David Accords had "proved to be a failure," that is, they had delivered nothing for the Palestinians.

"We had hoped, and still hope, that the Administration of President Reagan would concede that the Camp David accords are futile as a framework for a just and comprehensive peace,"[23] Fahd said in a public rebuke. But Sadat would not admit failure, even though his critics were multiplying. In the first week of September, he ordered the broadest security crackdown of his eleven-year rule, and Egyptian security forces arrested 1,536 people who were alleged to be involved in "sectarian sedition." Among those arrested was Mohamed Heikal, the editor of *Al-Ahram* and Nasser's ideological soulmate. Sadat lashed out at Western reporters, who suggested that he might have received approval in Washington for his brutal crackdown.

"You have no right at all to such a question like this," he said. "In other times I would have shot you, but it is democracy I am really suffering from, as much as I am suffering from the opposition."[24] Sadat mocked the Islamic fundamentalists who challenged him. Of one cleric who had criticized his luxurious lifestyle, Sadat remarked, "Now this lousy sheikh finds himself thrown into a prison cell like a dog."[25] The leader seemed at war with his people.

Lieutenant Khaled el-Islambouli was an idealistic son of Egypt, born in 1957 in the village of Mallawi, where his father was a lawyer and where he, his older brother, and two sisters all received sound educations. His devotion to Islam was paramount, and when he joined the Egyptian army's artillery corps, he and some of his comrades had also joined the Gamaat el-Islamiyya, a branch of the fundamentalist underground, but with no apparent intention other than to adhere to the conservative tenets of their faith, like so many young men whose piety impelled them toward the Muslim Brotherhood and its branches.

The crackdown on fundamentalists that September had netted Khaled's older brother, Mohamed. He had been observed tearing down a poster bearing Sadat's image on a wall in the village. Khaled arrived home just after the police took Mohamed away, and he found his mother in tears. Khaled wept, too, because in Egypt one never knew if a relative would return from prison with the scars of torture. Mohamed was the most devout member of the family. He had been in Mecca in November 1979 when a tiny but highly militant cell of Islamic fundamentalists took over the Grand Mosque. When he returned home, he brought Khaled a copy of *Seven Letters*, the pamphlet of Juhayman el-Utaibi, who led the takeover in Mecca.

Khaled and his cohorts had seen the Camp David Accords as a betrayal. Radical clerics had decreed that any good Muslim would be justified in killing Sadat for having made peace with the Jews and for persecuting the Muslim faithful in Egypt. A few weeks later, Khaled's commander asked him to participate in the presidential military parade on October 6 commemorating the 1973 war. At first Khaled resisted, saying he wanted to go home for the Muslim holiday that was to begin two days hence. When his superior insisted, the lieutenant said, "Very well. I accept. Let God's will be done."

That's when the idea had occurred to him. He went back to his comrades and made a pact: they would seize the opportunity. They worked out their plan, and on October 6, Khaled's truck, which was towing an artillery piece in the parade, suddenly lurched to a halt in front of the presidential reviewing stand. Egyptian air force jets were roaring overhead in a salute to Sadat, who was sitting among his generals.

Khaled stepped out of the truck and tossed a grenade. He rushed to the reviewing stand with his comrades and they opened fire on Sadat. The bleachers convulsed with shrieks, explosions, and gunfire. The scream of the jets added to the chaos. One account said that Khaled shouted fiercely at Vice President Mubarak and Minister of Defense Abdel Halim Abu Ghazala: "Get out of my way. I only want this son of a dog!" Then he pumped more bullets into Sadat.

Mohamed Heikal later wrote: "For the first time the people of Egypt had killed their pharaoh."[26]

Reagan and his wife, Nancy, were deeply affected by the assassination of Sadat, if only because Reagan and Pope John Paul II had both narrowly escaped the same fate that year. The Reagans had hosted Sadat at the White House and had looked forward to advancing the peace process with his help. Now he was dead. Reagan did not attend the state funeral: Egypt was judged too dangerous. Instead, former presidents Nixon, Ford, and Carter all traveled to Cairo with Alexander Haig, who raised a furor in private when the Egyptian media paid more attention to the former presidents than to him. Haig ordered the American ambassador in Cairo, Roy Atherton, to threaten the Egyptians with a reduction in financial aid if he didn't get better play in the news media.[27]

Haig was at once brilliant and petty. He had embarrassed himself the day Reagan was shot by charging into the White House press room to announce that he was in charge. (In fact, after the vice president, he was third in line of succession). Nicholas Veliotes, Haig's assistant secretary for the Middle East, had witnessed the contradictions in Haig's character—he was an incisive strategist who foolishly went to war with his rivals in the Reagan White House, alienating the president in the process. In the course of the battle over policy, Haig saw the Israelis as an ally against

Reagan, and, in Veliotes's view, Haig resolved every conflict in favor of Israel's hard-line Likud government.

Haig once opened a meeting with some of Begin's advance men by saying, "Well, we have a problem with President Reagan." All Veliotes could wonder was, "Who is we?"

In October 1981, Haig astounded his Middle East bureau with a proposal to reopen the Camp David treaty in order to get better terms for Israel. Veliotes had insisted on being heard on the subject. "Ronald Reagan will go down in history as the American president that lost the Egyptian-Israeli treaty," Veliotes warned his boss. "You may not care, but I think Ronald Reagan doesn't want to have that stigma—to lose what Carter [had] achieved?"[28]

Haig backed down. Reagan's first year was marked by extensive secret discussions with Israel aimed at striking a strategic cooperation accord that would open the door to new levels of military-to-military coordination against the Soviet Union and other regional threats. Some aides wanted to base American B-52s in Israel, arguing that the Arabs would understand that the bombers were there to deter the Soviets. Yet with all the discussion of coordination, Begin insisted on complete freedom of action without consultation. If he needed to bomb a nuclear reactor in an Arab state, he would do it.

The contradictions in Begin's approach baffled and, at times, infuriated Reagan. Nevertheless, he directed Weinberger to negotiate a strategic cooperation accord with Sharon, the defense minister. But Begin continued to disregard American interests in the Middle East, and Reagan lost enthusiasm for the pact. Weinberger watered it down to insignificance. When Sharon came to Washington to sign it in November 1981, Weinberger would not allow a ceremony at the Pentagon. He met Sharon at the National Geographic Society. No press photographers were allowed.

The strategic pact was supposed to have sensitized Israel to American strategic interests: stable oil supplies, credibility with the Arabs, and continued progress toward peace in the Holy Land. But two weeks later, Begin blindsided Reagan again by announcing his intention to annex the Golan Heights, forcing Syria's leaders to put the country on a war footing. Begin seemed to have made the decision on a whim. He had got up one morning and, while standing in the shower listening to the radio, he heard that the Syrian dictator had said that he would "not make peace in a hundred years with Israel."

Begin got so agitated that he slipped and broke his hip. After the doctors treated him, the Israeli prime minister called a cabinet meeting at his home and, with his leg propped, told his ministers that it was clear that Assad was never going to make peace. "So what's the point?" he asked. If there was no prospect of peace with Syria, Israel might as well incorporate the Golan as a permanent part of Israel. Begin's view was: let the Syrians choke on that.

The news detonated in the White House as it was dealing with the Soviet-backed martial law crackdown on the Solidarity Movement in Poland. Weinberger was indignant. "If there is no real cost to the Israelis," he said, the United States would "never be able to stop any of their actions" that damaged American interests in the region.[29] Reagan suspended the just-signed strategic cooperation agreement.

At a December 17 news conference, Reagan admitted that Begin was making his job harder, but he softened the blow with humor. "Yes, but I've come to the conclusion that there is a worldwide plot to make my job more difficult on almost any day that I go to the office."

Samuel Lewis, the American ambassador, had to formally notify Begin that the strategic alliance was off the table. The prime minister was at home, on crutches. He settled in his chair with a sheaf of papers on his lap that must have been talking points, but he never looked at them. He launched into a tirade that went on for nearly an hour.

"What kind of talk is this—'penalizing Israel'?" he asked. "Are we a vassal state of yours? Are we a banana republic? Are we fourteen-year-olds who, if we misbehave, we get our wrists slapped? You have no right to penalize Israel!"

Lewis could not get a word in, and when Begin was done, the ambassador made a swift exit only to find the entire Israeli cabinet and the senior military and intelligence staff assembled in Begin's living room. He wondered why they were there. In the car, driving down from Jerusalem to Tel Aviv, he heard the Israeli government spokesman reading out Begin's "private" message for Reagan, including the "banana republic" remarks.[30]

Almost anyone who knew Ariel Sharon knew that by the time he became Israel's minister of defense his most deeply seated ambition was to go to war in Lebanon and crush the PLO. Ever since 1970, when the PLO had been expelled violently from Jordan during the Black September crackdown of King Hussein, Arafat had been building up a ministate in Lebanon, and now even the Lebanese referred to the southeast of the country as "Fatah-land." Sharon believed it could be excised.

Ariel Sharon was born in Palestine under the British mandate in 1928. His grandfather Mordechai Scheinerman had been one of the leaders of the Zionist movement in Brest Litovsk (now Brest, Belarus), where he and Ze'ev Dov Begin (Menachem's father) had once broken down the door of the local synagogue to protest the rabbi's refusal to hold a memorial service following the death in 1904 of Theodor Herzl, the Zionist founder.[31] The Scheinerman family's first immigration to Palestine in 1910 ended in despair, forcing a dispirited return to Russia two years later. Sharon's father, Samuel Scheinerman, also was an ardent Zionist and, with his wife, Vera, fled the anti-Zionist purges of the Russian Revolution. They made their way to Palestine in 1922 and settled north of Tel Aviv at Kfar Malal in the central Sharon valley, where they could farm their own land and whence Sharon eventually took his name.

The most important psychological imprint of Sharon's youth was growing up in a village where his parents were ostracized for their refusal to conform to the majority view. Samuel Scheinerman despised socialism, which was the cornerstone of the Zionist collective and the kibbutz movement, and he defied communal decisions on what to grow, how to sell his harvest, and how to divide the land.

"The problem was that the man was by nature unable to compromise," Sharon wrote of his father many years later.[32] The situation was so bad that when Samuel died in 1956, his family discovered that his burial plot had been laid out adjacent to one of his most frequent antagonists in the farming village. Sharon's mother "then and there" directed the groundskeeper to move her husband's grave over by one space, explaining that she would lie, when her time came, between the rivals.

"All of this had its effect on me as I was growing up," Sharon reflected. "I felt isolated, lonely." It became apparent only later how this isolation had hardened him, as Sharon determined to make his own way in life. Sharon's mother, a strong-willed pioneer who had sacrificed a career in medicine to farm, maintained an emotional distance from her children and this only imbued Sharon with a greater instinct for self-reliance. Yet he inherited his mother's dislike for Arabs. He told journalists his mother had kept a baseball bat next to her bed to deal with Arab marauders, and the implication was that Sharon's attitudes had been shaped by the image of that bat.

Sharon was best known as "Arik," the diminutive with which his Russian-speaking mother addressed him as a child. After war broke out in Europe in 1939, Sharon joined a paramilitary youth battalion and then the Jewish underground at fourteen to fight for the cause of independence. The military transformed Sharon, who displayed courage and conviction in carrying out every task. The Jewish militia was a milieu where the burdens of family and isolation were stripped away by the requirements of war: teamwork, leadership, and duty. Sharon was nineteen when Israel's War of Independence was triggered by the United Nations resolution calling for the partition of Palestine into two states. Though wounded in 1948 during the battle around Jerusalem, Sharon's tactical boldness won praise from his commanders. As time went on, civilian leaders were appalled by his habit of interpreting his orders broadly to suit his own purposes, but there was no doubting Sharon's instinctive talent as a fighter.

Begin, for example, was in awe of Sharon's military prowess, but he was also intensely aware of his reputation for intimidation and deceit. Ben-Gurion, who had admired the young Sharon and given him his name, would later fault him for deceiving his superiors. When Sharon became Begin's defense minister, there were jokes that if he did not get his way, Begin might wake up one morning to find the prime minister's residence surrounded by tanks.

But with regard to what needed to be done in Lebanon, Begin and Sharon were as one. A country wracked by civil war, with a government incapable of imposing central authority over rival "confessional" militias—Christian, Druze, and Muslim—could not expect its neighbors to tolerate attacks from its territory. At Sadat's funeral, Begin told Alexander Haig that Israel might send an army into southern Lebanon and destroy the PLO presence that was threatening the northern towns of Israel. "Does that make sense to you, Al?" Begin asked.

Haig responded pointedly: "If you move, you move alone. Unless there is a major, internationally recognized provocation, the United States will not support such an action."[33] But the inverse was also true: if the Israelis made the case that PLO terrorists threatened the security of Israel, the United States could support military operations.

Haig's statement was parsed carefully in Jerusalem. Unlike Jimmy Carter, he had not threatened to cut off Israel's supply of American weapons if they were used offensively in Lebanon. Israel might not win explicit American support, but it would not be opposed or threatened, either. By the end of the year, it was clear that war was coming in Lebanon. In December 1981, Begin called members of his cabinet to his house the day that Ambassador Lewis got his "banana republic" lecture and briefed them on Operation Big Pines, which was the Begin-Sharon vision of how to crush the PLO and make a clean sweep of Lebanon.

Separately, Sharon told a gathering of his generals that "when I speak of destroying the terrorists . . . that includes Beirut." Sharon spoke about "a new political order" in Lebanon—a Christian-Jewish alliance—created by an Israeli military intervention; Israel would then enforce the new order with the presumed backing of the United States.[34] In December, Sharon met with Reagan's Middle East envoy, Philip Habib, a sixty-one-year-old career diplomat and former Kissinger troubleshooter. It had been Habib's job during the first year of the administration to keep the lid on the conflict between Israel and its Arab neighbors.

Sharon was bellicose; he menaced Habib with a warning: if the PLO "terrorists continue to violate the cease fire, we will have no choice but to wipe them out completely in Lebanon, destroy the PLO's infrastructure," and "eradicate the PLO in Lebanon."

"General Sharon," Habib said, "this is the twentieth century and times have changed. You can't go around invading countries just like that, spreading destruction and killing civilians. In the end, your invasion will grow into a war with Syria, and the entire region will be engulfed with flames!"[35]

Sharon pulled back slightly; he emphasized that these were his personal ideas and not yet government policy, but Habib understood that no Israeli defense minister expressed such ideas unless he was testing America's reaction. Habib returned to Washington and briefed Reagan and Haig. But nothing happened. Reagan was absorbed with Poland, where the Soviet-backed government was cracking down on Solidarity. More personally, the CIA had rattled Reagan with reports that Libyan hit teams were in the United States seeking to shoot down the presidential helicopter with a heat-seeking missile. Lebanon had drifted off Reagan's radar; one reason may have been that Reagan believed that he had already tamped down the war talk in the Middle East. After Begin had broached the subject in the fall of 1981, Reagan had sent Haig to meet the Israeli prime minister during a visit to New York. There, Begin conveyed a promise that he would not invade Lebanon "unless some act forced his hand."[36]

Yet what was missing in early 1982 was any concerted effort by Reagan to mobilize the U.S. government and its allies to stop Israel's march toward war. Reagan was too unsure of himself in the Middle East, and the leadership of Israel had changed dramatically. This was not Levi Eshkol, deeply concerned about an American president's approval and support; this was not Golda Meir, hypersensitive to how Washington might react and whether a speedy resupply of weapons would be forthcoming. This was Menachem Begin, the incarnation of Jewish militarism in the modern Middle East. He did not believe in consulting with Washington; he would pursue Israeli security in the manner he saw fit as prime minister and, as he had admonished Meir years earlier, American Jews would force any American president to rearm Israel no matter how controversial the fight.

Haig's sympathies for Israel were another factor, but, more important, Haig failed to perceive the threat posed to American interests if Israel invaded Lebanon when so many revolutionary forces were loose in the region.

Bereft of stable government, wracked by civil war, Lebanon had become more of a battleground than a country. The international community had stood back, leaving it to the Arabs, or even Syria, to stabilize the situation. Lebanese territory, with its easy access to Israel's northern border, had become inextricably connected with the Arab war against the continuing occupation—more than a decade old by this time—of the West Bank, Gaza Strip, and Golan Heights. Without a major intervention by the great powers, the problem of Lebanon was not going to get solved; it could only get worse.

Since 1976, the Israelis had cultivated Lebanon's Christian leadership. The elders of the Christian community, Pierre Gemayel and Camille Chamoun, reached out to their Israeli counterparts to help them in the civil war. To the Israelis, Bashir Gemayel, Shiekh Pierre's youngest son, looked like the best hope to reunify Lebanon: a tough national figure who could share power with the Muslim and Druze communities and who could crush the PLO ministate and expel Arafat's Palestinian government in exile. Bashir had Tony Curtis good looks and an easy smile that radiated charm. He also had a killer's instinct, and he had contested brutally with all the challengers to lead the Maronite Christian community. In 1978, hundreds of his militiamen had surrounded the home of his rival, Tony Franjieh, and slaughtered everyone within, including Franjieh, his wife, his bodyguards, and his servants. Franjieh was the political heir of President Suleiman Franjieh, the clever patriarch who had positioned himself as Syria's chief ally and power broker among Lebanon's warring factions.[37]

Both the CIA and Mossad established lines to Bashir as a new Christian leader. The CIA had recruited him as an "asset" when the young Gemayel interned at a Washington law firm in 1972. Bashir returned home and transformed the Phalange militia (founded by his father) into the most powerful armed force in the country with covert assistance from Israel and the United States, secretly authorized by Reagan.[38] Gemayel saw the PLO presence in Lebanon as a cancer. His dream was to drive all Palestinians out of the country. Another target was the Syrian army, which had deployed to Lebanon in 1976 with the blessing of the Arab League[39] to police a cease-fire in the civil war. But the Syrian army had become its own kind of cancer. The Lebanese came to understand that Hafez al-Assad saw Lebanon as an extension of greater Syria, and it seemed doubtful that the Syrian army would leave unless the Lebanese government was strong enough to force it out.

Assad was at the peak of his power and enjoyed the patronage of the Soviet leadership. In his long and brutal reign, he had become a master of subterfuge, leverage, and control. His family line came from a minority Alawite sect of Islam, one whose very creed was guarded as a secret by its practitioners. The Alawites were strongly represented in the Syrian armed forces, where Assad had learned never to brook a challenge to his authority. He had demonstrated this precept when the Syrian branch of the Muslim Brotherhood protested his rule with a spate of car bombings in Damascus following a June 1980 attempt to assassinate Assad during a state reception. Hundreds of suspected members of the Brotherhood were arrested, then tortured or murdered in Assad's prisons. In February 1982, a full-scale rebellion erupted in Hama, where opposition leaders proclaimed a "liberated" city.

Assad sent his brutish brother, Rifaat al-Assad, with tanks and artillery to unleash a savage and unrelenting barrage against the 350,000 residents, shelling civilian neighborhoods indiscriminately. In three weeks, Assad had killed an estimated twenty-thousand people. Three-quarters of the city was destroyed. The assault on Hama became an emblem of Assad's ferocity—he was called the Butcher of Hama, the Lion of Damascus. But it also symbolized endemic repression in the Middle East. "Hama Rules" became a catchphrase for the tendency of the strong to pummel the weak with disproportionate force over any challenge to clan or legitimacy.[40]

In Bashir Gemayel, Assad saw a threatening new challenger backed by both Israel and the West, whose goal was to smite Syria and humble its pretensions of hegemony over the Levant, the region that frames the eastern Mediterranean shore. Sharon reportedly made the case personally to Casey that young Bashir was the key to a new alignment of American, Israeli, and Lebanese interests. Alliances were fleeting in Lebanon—*The enemy of my enemy is my friend!*—and it was difficult at times to fully understand who was using whom.

In April 1981, Bashir Gemayel's Phalange joined with other Christian militia forces to break a Syrian siege against Zahlé in Lebanon's Bekaa Valley. The Christians were outgunned and outnumbered and they had called on the Israelis to rescue their forces when the Syrians counterattacked with helicopter gunships. Some saw Gemayel's appeal for help as an obvious ploy to goad Israel into the war with Syria. Begin willingly took the bait. His cabinet authorized the Israeli air force to attack the Syrians, and General Eitan, the hard-line chief of staff, was so sure that he would get the green light that all he did was leave the cabinet room for a few minutes before returning to report mission accomplished. He announced that two Syrian helicopters had been shot down.

In response, Syria deployed Soviet antiaircraft batteries in the Bekaa Valley near Zahlé. Israel issued a public warning that the batteries prevented freedom of action for Israeli warplanes over Lebanon and threatened to destroy them. The tensions escalated into a summer of shelling and Israeli bombing around Beirut that Reagan witnessed on television. Moved, he dispatched Philip Habib to get a cease-fire. It held through the fall of 1981.

With Sharon in the Israeli cabinet, 1982 was going to be a year for decisive action. In late May, Sharon flew to Washington to formally brief Haig on a war plan. He laid out big maps in Haig's office. The Israeli army and its Lebanese surrogate force in the south would clear the PLO out of southern Lebanon and then hook up with Gemayel's militia in Beirut to "rewrite the political map of Beirut in favor of the Christian Phalange."

That's how Haig saw it.[41] "It was clear that Sharon was putting the United States on notice: one more provocation by the Palestinians and Israel would deliver a knockout blow to the PLO," Haig later wrote.

It was telling that Haig had excluded his assistant secretary for the Middle East from Sharon's briefing. After it was over, Haig called Nick Veliotes up to the secretary's suite on the seventh floor of the State Department building, where Haig had his own map of Lebanon on an easel. The secretary seemed enthusiastic, enamored of Sharon's plan. Haig replayed the meeting for Veliotes. "You see, if they have to go in, their plan would be to link up the group here in the south with the Christians up here [in Beirut]."[42]

Veliotes had brought his deputy, Morris Draper, a normally circumspect diplomat, who suddenly blurted out, "For Christ's sake, Mr. Secretary, there are a million and a half Muslims between them, and at least a million of them are Shia." A war in Lebanon would ravage Shiite civilian areas, and the destruction would enrage Shiites throughout the Muslim world.

Haig was "really startled; it was as if he'd never known this," Veliotes recounted. The assistant secretary looked at his boss and said they had better send a cable to Sam Lewis pronto, because if the ambassador did not get to Begin and head off an invasion, "that means war with Syria and God knows the carnage. You will have a Middle East policy in tatters— about the only thing we'll have left at that point is trying to make sure the Egyptian-Israeli Treaty survives and Iran doesn't overrun Iraq."[43]

Though Haig had made the case to Sharon that there had to be an internationally recognized provocation, the American secretary of state had conceded to Sharon that only Israel could make a decision about how best to defend its national interest. Just to nail the point, Sharon had replied, "No one has the right to tell Israel what decision it should take in defense of its people."

Haig's words echoed all the way back to Jerusalem, where Sharon told Begin and the Israeli cabinet that Haig had given them a green light.

One of the mysteries of the Reagan administration is why Haig did not raise a powerful alarm with the president, who was preparing for a major trip to Europe, to warn him that war was imminent in the Middle East. Such a war could have catastrophic consequences for the United States if a desperate Syria called on Moscow to help, or Israel triggered a conflagration that required American intervention.

The White House staff had gone through the turmoil of Richard Allen's resignation as national security adviser.[44] William P. Clark, who had been serving under Haig, replaced him. Clark was one of Reagan's oldest friends, having served as his chief of staff in California. Many thought Clark had been initially posted to State to keep an eye on Haig. Now, as national security adviser, he brought little experience to the job.

Did William Casey warn Reagan that a war was coming and describe its possible consequences? It seemed that the Reagan administration had put on blinders as to the broader goals of an Israeli invasion plan: to seize a dominant position in the Middle East based on unconditional U.S. military support. The CIA was providing covert support to Gemayel's Christian forces, while Sharon and Mossad were pressing Gemayel to take an active role with Israeli forces to clear the PLO out of West Beirut.

Reagan's benign neglect was catastrophic. He failed to grasp the complexity of the situation in Lebanon, but he was also ill served by his principal national security aides, who might have warned him that Israel could get bogged down in a quagmire of sectarian warfare that would tear Lebanon apart and force the United States to intervene at substantial risk to its own forces.

Haig certainly offered no plan to head off the war. All Reagan seemed to know was that Lebanon had become a base for PLO terrorism and that Israel had the wherewithal to do something about it. Reagan was sympathetic to Israel, and to the concept as it was presented to him, distorted as this proved to be in retrospect. Reagan viewed Sharon as "a bellicose man who seemed to be chomping at the bit to start a war." Reagan's only act was to parrot Haig's line, appealing "for Israel not to go on the offensive unless it was the victim of a provocation of such magnitude that the world would easily understand its right to retaliate." But Reagan said Israel's response was, "in effect: Mind your own business. It is up to Israel alone to decide what it must do to ensure its survival."[45] Reagan's lack of enough self-confidence to challenge Begin—as Carter had done—may have encouraged Begin's militarism.

By early June 1982, everything had come together for Begin and Sharon, except a provocation. On the night of June 3, London's Hyde Park was a forest of shadows when Shlomo Argov, the Israeli ambassador, slipped out the side door of the Dorchester Hotel, which faces the green expanse of the park at the center of London. Argov had fought in the War of Independence and had worked in Ben-Gurion's office before joining the Foreign Ministry. Educated at Georgetown University and the London School of Economics, Argov had shown wit and tough eloquence during a long career.

At 11:00 p.m., the ambassador was leaving a dinner for the diplomatic corps. A number of cars were idling along Park Lane. Argov moved straight to his sedan with his security man from London's Special Branch. As Argov bent to enter the backseat, a figure stepped out from the shadows and shot him in the head, gravely wounding him. Argov slumped into the arms of a driver who had been standing a few feet away and who held him until the ambulance came.[46] The security agent shot the assailant, a man named Hussein Ghassan Said. Three Arab accomplices fled but were captured by British police. The authorities quickly determined that two of them were members of the Abu Nidal organization—one was Abu Nidal's cousin—and the third was a colonel in Iraqi intelligence, Nawaf al-Rosan.

Abu Nidal was the nom de guerre of a renegade Palestinian terrorist named Sabri al-Banna, a sworn enemy of Yasser Arafat and the mainstream PLO. The hit team had received its weapons from an Iraqi military attaché stationed in London. All the evidence pointed to a joint operation by Iraqi intelligence and Abu Nidal.[47] But what was the motivation?

Saddam Hussein was in deep trouble on the Iran-Iraq War front. Throughout 1981 and into 1982, the Iranian army had been counterattacking, pushing Iraq back and threatening to cut off southern Iraq from Baghdad. Syria had allied itself with Iran. For Assad, Saddam was a dangerous rival, rich in oil and flush with Soviet and French weapons. Saddam could see what the whole world could see: Syria was poised at hair trigger for war with Israel, a war that would divert Syria's energy, and perhaps lead to a devastating military defeat. Iraq would benefit, even if Israel was the instrument—*The enemy of my enemy* . . . Thus, Saddam most likely provided the spark that ignited the Lebanon War.

Begin convened his key ministers the next morning but showed no interest when intelligence officers sought to explain that the Argov shooting was a messy pretext. It was Iraq, not Arafat, throwing gasoline on the fire.

Begin cut off the briefing. "They're all PLO," he said.

General Eitan, the chief of staff, also scoffed at any parsing of terrorists. "Abu Nidal, Abu *Shmeeeee*-dal. We have to strike at the PLO!" he said.

Fatah issued a statement saying it had no part in the Argov shooting. Begin approved an aerial attack on Beirut, and Israeli jets roared into Lebanese airspace less than twenty-four hours later. They bombed PLO camps in Beirut's suburbs and hit a soccer stadium where the bleachers were hiding a PLO ammo dump.

The PLO responded by firing Katyusha rockets and artillery shells into northern Israel; some five hundred of them had landed by Saturday evening.[48]

Reagan was in France for an economic summit with leaders of industrial nations. William Clark, the new national security adviser, convinced him to try to head off the cataclysm. Reagan could have attempted to roll back the invasion by threatening to restrict arms supplies to Israel, as Carter had. But instead, he resorted to writing another letter that was long on admonishment but little else.

War was afoot when Ambassador Lewis, with Reagan's letter in hand, reached Begin at 6:30 a.m. on Sunday, June 6, in Jerusalem. Begin set the letter aside, unmoved. Troops were headed out; the first mechanized brigades of the Israeli invasion force began their push into Lebanon just before noon that day. Some eighty thousand soldiers would follow. Begin wrote to Reagan that Operation Peace for Galilee was going to be of short duration and limited to twenty-five miles from Israel's northern border, just far enough to clean out the PLO artillery and rocket bases.

It was not true. From the outset, the Lebanon War was waged under false pretenses. Not since the Suez crisis had an Israeli government practiced so much deceit in its dealings with Washington. Sharon's commanders already had orders to strike well beyond the twenty-five-mile limit in Lebanon. One commando force was going to land north of Sidon, more than forty miles from the Israeli border, and then head for Beirut, an operation that was so far beyond the twenty-five-mile limit as to make a mockery of Begin's assurances. Other units had orders to strike through the central mountains to cut the Beirut-Damascus highway.[49]

Some of Reagan's advisers were livid.

"Israel takes America for granted and wants to be treated like an ally while acting contemptuously towards us," said Clark.[50] Jimmy Carter, in retirement, couldn't believe that Reagan was standing pat while Israel went on the offensive against an Arab country using American weapons.[51] America's image as the enabler of Israeli aggression was inescapable. Philip Habib was dispatched to Damascus with an unwritten message from Begin to the Syrian president: if the PLO artillery pulled back twenty-five miles and if the Syrians removed their antiaircraft batteries from the Bekaa Valley, there would be no need for Israel and Syria to clash.

But on June 8, with Habib still in the Syrian capital, the Israeli air force staged a massive raid into the Bekaa to knock out the Syrian antiaircraft batteries that had been installed there over the previous year. Syrian MiGs rose to challenge the Israeli F-16s, but the Israelis had planned their attack to draw out the Syrian air force and then pounce on it. By the end of the day, two dozen Syrian planes had been shot down, and over the next two days, the Syrians lost another seventy warplanes without a single Israeli loss. When the air battle was over, Syria's nineteen air defense batteries had been destroyed along with several hundred tanks and armored vehicles. Israel once again owned the skies over Lebanon.

The blow to American credibility was severe. Habib—the United States—had been made to look like Israel's pawn, lulling Assad as Israel struck like a thunderbolt. Habib was left to try to broker a cease-fire between Syrian and Israeli forces in the Bekaa. But Israeli forces would not stand still. They just kept pushing north, and so the Syrians would open fire on them, inciting further combat.

"The Israelis had this strange notion that if you declared a cease fire you could move your troops around," Habib said, adding that he had told Sharon at the time that "I was going to have to get this new definition of a cease fire written up in the annals of the War College."[52] But Habib's humor couldn't mask the damage that had been done to American credibility.

While the opening stages of the Lebanon War were being fought, U.S. intelligence detected a series of Iran Air flights descending on Damascus through Turkish airspace. The Iran Air jets disgorged the first contingents of the Iranian Revolutionary Guard to Syria. The Iranians quickly organized transport and drove their troops into the Bekaa Valley, where they occupied the Sheikh Abdullah Barracks and began turning it into a base. This was the birth of Iranian support for the underground Shiite terror movement in Lebanon, which operated under many names but came to be known broadly as Hezbollah.

Howard Teicher, a young member of the National Security Council staff, observed the Iranian movement with concern, but no one in the White House, CIA, or Pentagon, he said, had any inkling that Iran was preparing to open a new front against America and its allies.

"We had no idea that this action would inevitably lead to the radicalization of large elements of the Lebanese Shiite community, the widespread taking of hostages, a dramatic upsurge in international terrorism and the Iran[-contra] Affair," Teicher wrote.[53]

On June 12, Israeli forces reached Beirut. They linked up with Bashir Gemayel's Phalange, which had stayed out of the fighting. Muslim West Beirut—the PLO headquarters—was now surrounded; Syrian army units in Beirut were cut off from their lines of supply to Damascus. Israel, for the first time in its history, was threatening to enter an Arab capital. Without consulting Reagan, Haig devised a strategy that would "use the shock of the Israeli attack to force the PLO out of Beirut" and thus remove the reason for Israeli and Syrian forces to be there. Haig had effectively joined the Israeli enterprise. He sent instructions to Habib to brief Begin and the Israeli cabinet on his plan and win their assent, again without vetting those instructions with the president. He had locked the White House into a position of aligning itself with the Israeli invasion strategy. Having failed to perceive or warn Reagan of what was coming, he now was arrogating to himself the power, as Kissinger had during Nixon's final days, to commit the administration to an even more dangerous course.

The death of King Khalid of Saudi Arabia gave the White House a chance to repay Haig's abuse of presidential prerogative. Reagan selected Bush and Weinberger to lead the delegation. Haig was left at home to sulk. In Bush's meeting with King Fahd, the Americans and the Saudis agreed that it would be disastrous if the Israeli army entered Beirut, effectively conquering an Arab capital. Bush said the United States would work to prevent it.

Now Haig exploded. Bush's assurance, he asserted, undermined his strategy to keep the pressure on Arafat, who had sent word through the Lebanese on June 16 that he and six thousand fighters were willing to leave West Beirut within forty-eight hours. But after meeting Bush, the Saudis flashed word to the PLO that the Americans might preserve West Beirut as a sanctuary. Arafat suddenly hardened his position about leaving.[54] Haig claimed that he was denied his diplomatic "breakthrough." Blame-laying was rampant.

The siege of Beirut began because Sharon wanted to bomb Arafat out of his sanctuary. Reagan did not yet perceive a danger to American interests. "We're walking a tight rope," he wrote in his diary. With Arafat and part of his army holed up in West Beirut, Reagan seemed to support the Israeli squeeze play. The Lebanese Christian leadership also wanted the PLO to leave Beirut so the country could restore a functional government.

"The world is waiting for us to use our muscle and order Israel out," Reagan wrote. "We can't do this if we want to help" the Lebanese to force the PLO out.[55]

Bush, Weinberger, Clark, and Michael Deaver, the public relations men in the White House, were pressing Reagan to hit Israel hard with a suspension of military aid. That would get Begin's attention. Political voices in Israel had begun to question why Begin and Sharon had dragged the country into an unnecessary war. But Haig, Casey, and Jeane Kirkpatrick, Reagan's ambassador to the United Nations, argued that the invasion was actually benefiting the United States. Syria's Soviet-backed military had taken a devastating blow from American weapons (in Israel's hands). That sent a powerful message to the region, they believed. Moreover, Arafat was part of the Soviet-backed radical Arab front that opposed the Egyptian-Israeli peace treaty. The Soviet-backed Arabs should be the losers. This was the same argument that Kissinger had employed in support of militarism and confrontation during the 1973 war.

Weinberger challenged them. Israeli militarism with American arms, he argued, was hurting America's image in the Middle East, and that would make it harder, not easier, to build a strong anti-Soviet alliance. It was time to open a dialogue with the PLO, Weinberger said. Arafat was a terrorist, but Begin had once been a terrorist, too.

"Cap, you talk about Yasser Arafat as if he's some kind of agrarian reformer," Jeane Kirkpatrick interjected. "Arafat is a Soviet-backed international terrorist. You have lost your sense of perspective."

Reagan said he agreed with Kirkpatrick.

The cold war view of the conflict was always going to prevail, but Reagan was deeply troubled by the carnage being inflicted on civilians by the Israeli bombardment of Beirut. When Begin arrived at the White House on June 21, Reagan spoke to him forcefully in a private session. Haig's talking points had been discarded as "kowtowing" and Clark had prepared a tough set of points and put them on note cards for Reagan. When Begin emerged he looked "rattled," and his voice broke during his own remarks.[56]

Haig was far less troubled than Reagan by images of suffering and bloodshed. Haig had seen combat. He had almost been killed by a terrorist bomb when he was NATO's commander in Europe. In private, Haig fulminated that Reagan "wasn't treating Begin right." He was beating him up. Veliotes believed that Haig was coming unglued by the pressure and by the realization that his relationship with Reagan was irretrievably broken. There was something condescending about the very nature of Haig's approach to the White House.

In his own councils at the State Department, Haig would say things like, "Don't be taken in by the Bush-Baker gang" or "By God, [I'm] going to tell Begin to go into Beirut and finish the job." And word spread among senior aides that he had told Israeli diplomats in advance of Begin's arrival, "We have a problem with President Reagan."

Veliotes looked back on his dealings with Haig at the time and observed, "I figured that I was talking to a man who was disturbed."[57]

On the afternoon of June 25, Haig went to the White House to settle with Reagan once and for all how they were going to run foreign policy. Haig was due at Prince Bandar's home that evening for a diplomatic dinner. Suddenly, the White House announced that Haig had resigned.

Bandar got through to Haig by phone. The shaken secretary of state suggested that Bandar ask the other dinner guests not to come. "Just the four of us . . . ," Haig suggested, meaning the two of them and their wives. It was done.

After dinner, Haig was simply overcome. He began sobbing uncontrollably, so much so that Princess Haifa grabbed Mrs. Haig and fled the room.

"I was set up, and I was so stupid. I let them set me up," Haig said.[58] (Reagan that afternoon had simply told Haig that his resignation letter had been accepted, even though he had not submitted one.) He had been defeated by "them": the White House cabal of James A. Baker III, Michael Deaver, and First Lady Nancy Reagan, all of whom had mistrusted Haig from the moment Reagan had selected him. To Bandar, who was there by accident for Haig's demise, here was the former supreme allied commander, the former battalion commander decorated for valor in Vietnam, the tenacious White House chief of staff who had stood steady at the helm as Nixon unraveled—here he was sobbing because he had failed so spectacularly to dominate the administration for which he seemed to have so little respect.


Cynicism and deception were hallmarks of the Lebanon invasion. There was no question that Israel had a right to defend its border settlements from PLO artillery and rockets. It was true that Lebanon's central government was too weak to control the ambitions of the PLO to use Lebanon as a platform of attack. Syria was encroaching on Lebanon's sovereignty, too. But it also was true that PLO border skirmishes had little to do with the grand design that Ariel Sharon had brought into office—including his determination to remake Lebanon in a new image. His plan depended on his ability to cajole or coerce Bashir Gemayel into signing a separate peace treaty with Israel, as Sadat had. Then, together, they would destroy the PLO. Sharon was unable to understand that it was not possible to destroy the PLO by attacking its bases in West Beirut, and that Lebanon was not going to abandon its ties to the Arab world for the sake of a strategic alliance with Israel.

As for Begin, despite his many protestations to the contrary, it is difficult to believe that an Israeli prime minister with his many informants throughout the Israeli security establishment—the Defense Ministry, Mossad, and the Israeli army—could have been blind to Sharon's scheme, which had significant adherents. Among them was David Kimche, one of the most influential voices in the Foreign Ministry.

The Knesset and the cabinet—the institutions of Israeli democracy—might as well have been locked in a room (as Sharon had wanted to do in 1967) while the IDF did what Sharon thought best for the nation. He did not fight the limited war he had described to his government. Instead he stretched cabinet approvals for military operations beyond recognition, he goaded Syria into a fight he said he was avoiding, he misled his American "allies," and he withheld critical battlefield progress reports from a government that was loath to challenge him. With Begin's full backing, Sharon made a mockery of Israel's democratic government to an extent that neither Begin nor his successors have acknowledged. The idea that Begin was somehow taken for a ride, or outmaneuvered by Sharon, fails to recognize Begin's history as an Irgun leader, as a practitioner of deception and as a student of Sharon.[59] It seems naïve in the extreme to take his statements that he had authorized only a limited operation at face value.

By late summer 1982, Lebanon was literally burning. During July and August, Israel maintained a tight ring around West Beirut, where Arafat was holed up. Columns of smoke rose from abandoned apartment blocks. Sharon drove his armored personnel carrier into Christian East Beirut and upbraided Bashir Gemayel for not sending his forces into Muslim West Beirut to annihilate the PLO.

"On my way here, I thought I would see people digging trenches and filling sandbags," Sharon told the young Lebanese leader. "I expected to see long lines outside your recruiting offices. Instead your people are sitting in cafes, and the only lines I see are outside the movie theaters!"[60]

Syria's Hafez al-Assad went to Saudi Arabia to consult with King Fahd, and suddenly there was a joint Saudi-Syrian proposal that supported the evacuation from Beirut of the six thousand PLO fighters as long as Christian militias guaranteed that Palestinian refugee camps (which PLO gunmen protected) would be safe from Israeli attacks. Habib wrote a long cable back to the White House and State Department making the case for a multinational force that could land in Lebanon and establish some transitional control and protection for the refugees. Habib had been pressing Begin and Sharon to accept a cease-fire, but cease-fire was a threat to Israel's success. Begin wanted a victory. Sharon was running out of time—Gemayel had failed him—to crush the PLO before international pressure forced him to break off the siege. One cease-fire collapsed as Israeli forces took Beirut international airport, bringing them closer to Palestinian camps.

On August 4, the Israeli army unleashed one of the most intense artillery barrages of the war against West Beirut, seeking to flush Arafat from his bunker and kill him. The PLO leader scurried from one hideout to another, as an Israeli intelligence team tried to track him, sometimes calling down bombing strikes where Arafat had been only minutes earlier. Television sent images of the assault out to the world. Reagan was awakened at 6:30 a.m. by William Clark, who described the ferocity of the Israeli assault on the city. An outraged Habib telephoned Reagan from Beirut and described the scene firsthand.

Reagan was as angry as some of his aides had ever seen him. Michael Deaver saw the bombardment of West Beirut as devastating for Reagan's political standing. King Fahd telephoned and pleaded with the president to do something. Clark called George Shultz, the new secretary of state, and said, "The president's friendship for Israel is slipping. Enough is enough."[61] Reagan told his aides during a meeting in the Cabinet Room that he would like to just give Begin hell. Deaver said he had every right to do so. They suggested Reagan call him. The White House operator soon had the Israeli premier on the line.

"You promised me you were pulling the troops out," Reagan said. "I kept the United Nations from condemning you yesterday. You gave me your word."

Begin protested that Israeli forces had pulled back.

"Don't lie to me! I'm sitting here watching it on CNN. What one world leader says to another world leader is his word and you told me yesterday you were pulling out. You're now telling me you did pull out and I'm sitting here watching it." Reagan slammed the phone down.[62]

The scheme to evacuate the PLO fighters from Beirut unfolded as a noisy exodus at dockside as PLO militants fired their weapons in the air and boarded a chartered vessel that would deposit them in Yemen and other distant Arab ports. American marines joined French and Italian troops as a multinational force to supervise the evacuation. Arafat made the best of it, but the PLO had been defeated and was in full retreat under Israel's guns. Syria, too, had been humiliated by Sharon's onslaught. Beirut was quiet for the first time in months. The Lebanese National Assembly met in the basement of a military barracks on August 23 and elected Bashir Gemayel president.

Begin was jubilant. His congratulatory telegram to Gemayel was addressed to "My Dear Friend." It looked as if Israel had suddenly succeeded. Gemayel could be an unruly client, but his interests and Israel's were still congruent. The question for many Lebanese was whether the thirty-four-year-old Gemayel could make the transition from brutish Christian warlord to a unifying national leader, one who could speak to the aspirations of Sunnis, Shiites, Druze, and other communities in the national mosaic.

George Shultz hoped that he could. Like Weinberger, he had come to the Reagan administration from Bechtel, where, as president, he had forged close friendships in the Arab world. Arab leaders were cheered by his appointment, and even more so when he presented the Reagan Plan for Middle East peace on September 1—not because they found it acceptable (they didn't), but because Shultz showed that he understood the heart of the conflict in the region: the Palestinian problem and the continuing occupation.

Shultz was a cautious political operator who had served as labor secretary and secretary of the treasury in the Nixon administration. He had a limited experience in international relations but a strong record as a gifted negotiator and as a mature and seasoned bureaucrat. Almost from the moment he entered office under Reagan, Shultz began searching for a means to shift the focus in the Middle East away from the destruction of Lebanon back to peacemaking. That was certainly what Reagan wanted, too. Shultz had never read the complete Camp David agreement

but, once he had, that became the foundation he decided to build on.[63]
As the last ship of PLO fighters left the pier in West Beirut, Shultz was
ready with what the White House agreed would be called the Reagan
Plan.[64] Shultz had every reason to know that Israel—Begin—might find
an American proposal unacceptable. Sharon had sent a message to Reagan's men via Casey warning that Israel might block a new peace initiative by annexing the West Bank.

Moshe Arens, the Israeli ambassador in Washington, told Shultz's
deputy that a new American peace plan would crash on takeoff. "Look,
we have wiped the PLO from the scene," he said. "Don't you Americans
now pick the PLO up, dust it off, and give it artificial respiration."[65]

But the Reagan Plan did call for Israel's withdrawal from the West
Bank and Gaza and the establishment of Palestinian self-rule under Jordanian sovereignty. It was essentially the same formulation that William
Rogers had floated in 1969. But for the first time since Reagan took office, he was setting forth a strong policy initiative in the Middle East that
spoke to the aspirations of the Palestinians.

Begin saw it as a disaster. Here he was with an army in Lebanon trying to destroy the PLO—at a cost of 340 Israeli dead and 2,200
wounded[66]—and Reagan was trying to give the PLO a state in the very
land that Begin had sworn he would never surrender. Begin suspected
that Reagan was seeking to undermine the Israeli "victory" in Lebanon.
There were still thousands of PLO fighters holding out in northern
Lebanon and an undisturbed mass of Palestinian refugees, most of them
sympathetic to the PLO.

The Reagan Plan landed with a thud. It fell short of Arab demands for
an independent Palestinian state. Its concept of self-rule under Jordan
ignored the PLO's standing since 1974 as the "sole legitimate representative of the Palestinian people." Yet Reagan and Shultz convinced themselves that their effort was proof of their good intentions. In reality their
diplomacy was out of sync with the politics of both Arabs and Israelis.
And neither Reagan nor Shultz was willing to make the kind of all-out effort that Jimmy Carter had made.

As soon as the PLO evacuation ship sailed over the horizon, Weinberger ordered the marines, who had been securing West Beirut, back to
their ships. The specter of Vietnam still hung over the American military
and it had imbued commanders with a strong sense of self-preservation.
No more political wars with impossible military restraints, they pledged.

Weinberger saw no reason for U.S. troops to remain in Beirut when they had no mission. The defense secretary cast himself in the role of protecting the American military from *new* foreign entanglements or fuzzy peacekeeping missions that invited another quagmire.

At the White House, Weinberger and General John W. Vesey Jr., the chairman of the Joint Chiefs, were known as the Never Again Club. They were engaged in rebuilding the military and thus had assigned themselves the task of opposing military deployments that did not have precise military goals, a well-defined enemy, or an exit strategy. Among their protégés were Richard L. Armitage and Colin L. Powell, both Vietnam combat veterans.

Weinberger's decision turned out to be costly for America and Lebanon because Bashir Gemayel was assassinated and then all hell broke loose in Beirut; had the marines stayed, they might have prevented the horror that followed.

On September 14, Gemayel entered the Phalange headquarters located in an apartment building in Christian East Beirut. On the floor above lived a man named Shartouni, who had been recruited, presumably by Syrian intelligence. A large bomb was placed in this apartment by intelligence operatives who were never identified, according to the U.S. ambassador.[67] Just after 4:00 p.m., the bomb detonated and the building collapsed into smoking rubble, sending up a dark cloud signifying to the whole of Beirut that something terrible had occurred.

For six hours, confusion reigned. Was Bashir among the dead, or had he walked away from the devastation in dusty clothes, as one account claimed? Church bells tolled on the strength of rumors that he had escaped alive. But late that evening, as rescuers pulled up slabs of concrete, one of Gemayel's aides spotted a mangled corpse.[68] Its left hand bore a familiar hexagonal wedding ring. Part of the skull was missing, but the aide recognized the Gemayel nose and the dimple on his chin.

"It's Bashir," he said, and anguish and rage rippled across the Christian community. The mood of revenge was apocalyptic. Who had a motive to kill the Christian leader? First, Syria, whose president wanted to dominate Lebanon; second, the PLO, whose chiefs wanted a fragmented state that would give them room to wage guerrilla warfare against Israel.

Sharon, having lost his ally in the blast, sought to capitalize on the chaos. He immediately ordered Israeli tanks into Muslim West Beirut and his troops surrounded the Palestinian refugee camps. Morris Draper, Habib's deputy assigned as the American liaison to the Israeli general, reported back to Washington that Sharon was preparing a killing ground for "terrorists." The Israeli general seemed to be demonizing all Palestinians.

"Let the LAF [Lebanese Armed Forces] go into the camps," Sharon said. "They can kill the terrorists. But if they don't, we will."[69]

The Lebanese Armed Forces commander refused to enter the camps. Instead, the Phalange militia—Gemayel's men—was called up to do the dirty work. Over the next two days, they murdered hundreds of Palestinian civilians in the Sabra and Shatila camps, pulling old men, women, and children from their homes and executing them. Israeli forces stood by as the massacre proceeded. Ryan Crocker, an American political officer under Ambassador Robert S. Dillon, relayed scenes of massacre by walkie-talkie. He counted more than fifty dead bodies, including women and children, during one sweep through the camps. It was his report that reached the White House with its gruesome description of human slaughter. It was read to Shultz at 5:45 a.m. on the second day. Reagan was sickened by it.

"They cried out for vengeance and vengeance they have wrought," William Clark said when top aides gathered at the White House.

Howard Teicher, one of the young Middle East specialists on the NSC staff, openly blamed Weinberger for the massacre. "A key part of the deal with Arafat was for the Multinational Force to protect the Palestinians who stayed behind from Phalangist vengeance. When the U.S. Marines left, and the French and Italians followed suit, who was there to protect the Palestinians? No one," Teicher said.[70]

At the State Department, Shultz told his deputy, Lawrence Eagleburger, "The brutal fact is, we were partially responsible. We took the Israelis and the Lebanese at their word" that the Palestinians in the camps would not be harmed after the PLO pullout.[71]

The outcry in Israel was intense. Abba Eban gave voice to the sense of shame: "a hideous pogrom has been perpetuated with fearful death and torment of innocent people in a place where the Israeli government asserted its responsibility for the maintenance of order and the avoidance of bloodshed."[72]

The Begin-Sharon relationship collapsed in recriminations. More than four hundred thousand Israelis flooded the center of Tel Aviv to express their moral outrage at the government, forcing Begin to appoint an independent commission of inquiry. Yitzhak Kahan, the chief justice of the Israeli Supreme Court, was chosen to head it.

Reagan ordered the marines from their ships back into Beirut over Weinberger's objection. The president felt a moral obligation. But was it guilt or just the desire to avoid blame? Lebanon was Reagan's greatest failure in the Middle East, marked by misperception, poor judgment, and policy failure. This good-natured man of Hollywood could be "unconsciously cruel in his innocence," one of his biographers would later observe.[73] In Lebanon what stood out was his blindness "to the significance of blood" on a sectarian landscape, a significance magnified by regional conflict and the cold war. Reagan was propelled by events as a courtly blunderer who was simply unable to formulate the questions that might lead him to sound judgments and wise policies. And he was too weak to impose order on his own advisers.

Eisenhower had done so; he had created unity behind his decision to dispatch the marines to Lebanon in 1958, saving the country from Nasser's reach and from "international communism." Reagan remembered Eisenhower's boldness in facing down the Egyptian-Syrian threat to overthrow Camille Chamoun's government in Lebanon. The deployment had sobered Nasser and put the region on notice that the United States would guarantee the peace.

To act decisively, as Ike had, Reagan would have to overcome resistance in the Pentagon, where Weinberger and General Vesey opposed any open-ended entanglements; Congress, moreover, feared the morass of Lebanon's sectarian hatreds.

One morning during the crisis, Reagan asked Philip Dur, a navy commander on the NSC staff, to stay behind after a staff meeting to describe in detail how Eisenhower had proceeded in 1958. Dur explained that unlike the current operation in which Reagan had sent eighteen hundred marines ashore, Eisenhower had sent nineteen thousand American troops into Lebanon. He had gone on television and explained his actions to the American people. There were no Lebanese militias then, and no opposing armies (from Syria and Israel) on the ground. It was just an overpowering display of American military might. Reagan looked wistfully at Dur. He turned and walked to the window of the Oval Office. Looking out at the Rose Garden with his back to Dur, Reagan repeated, "nineteen thousand troops."[74]

After a moment, he seemed to come back to the present. "Yeah, but then Ike didn't have to worry about the War Powers Act."[75]

Reagan did not explain his thinking, but it was obvious to Dur that the president was searching for a path that would evoke the same boldness

that Eisenhower had displayed. At the State Department, there was talk
of inserting the Eighty-second Airborne for this purpose, but Reagan
pulled back, again without explaining why. Lebanon was burning, its population held hostage by occupation armies. Reagan lacked the decisiveness to carry it off, or just the will to resolve the ideological clash among
his advisers.

Jeane Kirkpatrick, whom Reagan admired, argued vociferously that the
Israeli "victory" in Lebanon over Soviet-backed Syria and the PLO repre-
sented "the greatest strategic turnaround in the West since the fall of
Vietnam."[76] Her formulation, distorted by the cold war context, appealed
to Reagan's vanity and may well have undermined his instinct to send in
U.S. forces to push the Israelis and the Syrians out.

Looking back, Reagan suggested in his memoirs that he had sought to
avoid another quagmire in Lebanon. "As every president since World War
II has learned, no region of the world presents America with more difficult, more frustrating, or more convoluted problems than the Middle
East," he wrote. "It is a region where hate has roots reaching back to the
dawn of history. It's a place where the senseless spilling of blood in the
name of religious faith has gone on since biblical times, and where modern events are forever being shaped by momentous events of the past,
from Exodus to the Holocaust."[77]

With this flourish, he absolved himself and his administration from
any responsibility for allowing the slaughter of Lebanon to happen.


A small contingent of U.S. marines returned to Lebanon, buttressed
by French and Italian troops. Their mission was no longer clear. The
Lebanese National Assembly elected Amin Gemayel president. Amin
was more cautious than his martyred brother. He immediately looked to
the United States for help in building up central authority, and Washington transferred more arms and training. He went to Washington in October to thank Reagan for the modest steps the United States had taken
rebuild the Lebanese army, but he was worried that America would not
stay the course.

"We have this sense that America sometimes intervenes and gets involved, and then because you lose political support, you pull out and then
you leave those that have sided with you at the mercy of our enemies," he
said.

Reagan looked at the president of Lebanon and told him that America was not going anywhere. "We have no reverse gear in Lebanon," Reagan said, repeating the pledge for emphasis.[78]

The Kahan Commission published its findings on February 8, 1983. Ariel Sharon bore indirect responsibility for the Sabra and Shatila massacres; he was forced to resign as defense minister. Begin escaped condemnation, but his government was so tainted by the bloody episode, and by the failure of the Lebanon invasion to achieve its goals, that it never fully recovered. Begin was slipping into a depression. Those close to him attributed it to the death in November 1982 of his wife, Aliza, a formidable woman who had been his partner since the Irgun days.

Reagan's hope of salvaging something for his peace plan was deflated when King Hussein of Jordan announced that he would not enter negotiations with Israel on behalf of the Palestinians under the so-called Reagan Plan. Hope had been kindled when the king and Yasser Arafat agreed on a concept for a confederation between Jordan and the neighboring West Bank, but the king wanted sovereign authority over both; Arafat insisted that the Palestinians get statehood first and then enter into a confederation with Jordan.

Reagan and George Shultz saw that a major opportunity to build on the Camp David process was slipping away from them. King Hussein told Jimmy Carter, who continued to actively promote a comprehensive settlement, that what was needed was a bipartisan "peace constituency," a group of wise men on the Middle East to help Reagan win over the hard-liners among Arabs and Jews. But the White House was not interested, according to Carter.[79] The presidential reelection season was approaching.

On April 18, 1983, U.S. Ambassador Robert Dillon thought things had settled down enough that he could go jogging on the playing field at the American University of Beirut. The multinational force was patrolling the streets. What was left of the PLO force in the country was encamped around Tripoli in the north. The Israelis had pulled back from Beirut but still controlled all of southern Lebanon. Syrian troops were north and east of Beirut as well as in the Bekaa Valley, where Hezbollah, the "Party of God," was training under the Iranian Revolutionary Guard.

Dillon was a diplomat and veteran. During the Korean War, he had served as a commando, staging raids against the Chinese mainland. He understood the dangers he and his diplomatic staff faced in Lebanon. The French ambassador, Louis Delamare, had been assassinated by gunmen in September 1981. When Dillon arrived to take up his post, he decided he would carry a .357 Magnum in his briefcase: "If we ever got trapped, I wasn't going to sit there and just let things happen without trying to protect myself."[80]

It was the middle of the day and Dillon's office was on the eighth floor of the embassy. A few floors below in a conference room facing the sea, Robert Ames, the CIA national intelligence officer for the Middle East, was in a meeting with six CIA officers, including the station chief, Kenneth Haas, his deputy, and the deputy's wife, who was spending her first day at work for the embassy. Ames was just a couple of years shy of retirement and he had become an influential adviser to George Shultz, who liked his tough professionalism. Ames had been a consultant on the Reagan Plan, and though it had fizzled, it had reestablished a balance in American diplomacy between Israeli and Arab interests that had been missing under Haig.

Most of Dillon's security team was downstairs getting ready to roll. Dillon lingered upstairs, changing into his jogging clothes while trying to return the call of a German banker who had a problem. As he stood in front of the window struggling to get his Marine Corps T-shirt over his head, "All of a sudden the window blew in." There was an instant vision of the world coming at him, and then nothing.

"I was very lucky because I had my arm and the T-shirt in front of my face, which protected me from the flying glass. I ended up on my back. I never heard the explosion," Dillon recounted. The blast set off the embassy's defensive stocks of tear gas, which mixed with dust, causing choking and panic among the survivors, who began to stir, or groan, trying to overcome shock or injury.

At least two vehicles were involved: one scouted the approach to the embassy, then a pickup truck, loaded with explosives, raced down the boulevard toward the embassy's covered entrance. The driver floored the gas pedal and the truck's momentum propelled it up the front steps and through the lobby doors before it detonated. It was just after 1:00 p.m.

The explosion was so powerful that it lifted the center portion of the embassy building into the air, breaking joints and causing it to collapse. Sixty-three people died, seventeen of them Americans. Ames and the six

CIA officers attending the meeting in the conference room directly above the lobby all died. It was the CIA's worst one-day loss ever. Ames's severed hand, bearing his wedding ring, was found floating offshore, where ships at sea had shuddered from the concussion.[81] It was the deadliest terrorist attack ever committed against the United States up until that time.

Shultz chose not to fly to Beirut to bring home the bodies of American diplomats killed in the line of duty. He sent Larry Eagleburger, his deputy, instead. By this time—the spring of 1983—critics in Congress and the press were asking why George Shultz was neglecting the Middle East. He had been in office nearly a year, but the conflict among Reagan's advisers, and Reagan's own ambivalence, made it impossible for Shultz to exercise leadership. Shultz had not come to the Reagan administration as a fountain of experience in international affairs. He was an able economist, a labor negotiator, and a cagey bureaucratic infighter. Up against Weinberger, Casey, or Kirkpatrick, he did not have the intellectual horsepower to become the strongest voice on foreign policy. Yet the White House looked to Shultz the manager to find a solution. Reagan sent him back to the Middle East to bring the nightmare to some conclusion. The Israelis wanted a peace treaty with the new Lebanese government under Amin Gemayel, but with Sharon forced out of the cabinet by the Kahan Commission's findings, Begin had little leverage.

Shultz gathered his regional ambassadors in Cairo and, with little encouragement from them, launched into a round of shuttle diplomacy on the working assumption that a limited agreement—one that called for the withdrawal of foreign forces from Lebanon and the establishment of informal ties between Lebanon and Israel—might be acceptable to the Syrian leader, Hafez al-Assad. Syria had been weakened, its military mauled. The PLO was out of the picture. Shultz thought a limited agreement might work.

Reagan, too, thought American diplomacy could finesse the Syrians. "Let's leave the Syrians on the outside looking in," Reagan had told Yitzhak Shamir, Begin's foreign minister.[82]

But both Reagan and Shultz miscalculated. In the months since Israel devastated Syria's armed forces, the Soviet Union had undertaken a $2 billion airlift and resupply. Assad's military power was restored, and by early 1983 so was his confidence that he could wear down his enemies. He warned Lebanon that there was no need for Amin Gemayel to sign any agreement with Israel. If Gemayel ignored him, he added, the Syrian army would make the Lebanese Christians pay for their act of "surrender." Word of the threat reached Shultz and he decided to fly to Damascus to try to reason with Assad, but his persuasive powers failed him. During a lunch with Assad's foreign minister, Abdul Halim Khaddam, Shultz noticed that Khaddam was on a vegetarian diet. "[If] you stop eating meat, you are supposed to become more peaceful inside," Khaddam explained.

Shultz apparently couldn't resist the irony, given Syria's record of brutality, most notoriously in Hama. He cocked his head and with a deadpan expression he asked, "Oh, really, how's it coming?"

Khaddam's aides twittered, but the foreign minister flushed with anger.

On the way to the airport, Howard Teicher, the NSC aide who was part of Shultz's delegation, exuded American contempt. When a Syrian Foreign Ministry official asked Teicher how he had enjoyed his brief visit to Damascus, Teicher replied, "Things appear fine in Damascus," he replied, "but tell me, how are things in Hama these days?"[83]

The Syrians were spoilers, assassins, and brutes, and Shultz's party was feeling a little like the people of Hama, whose lives had been leveled by Assad's wrath.

The May 17 Accord between Israel and Lebanon was signed in the face of Syrian opposition and Arab rejection. Shultz understood there was no reasonable chance that it would be implemented. The balance of power had shifted back in Syria's favor. The Israeli army was on the defensive, looking for a way to pull back from the mountains above Beirut where it was taking casualties in the gun battles between Christian and Syrian-backed forces.

In Beirut, American, French, and Italian peacekeepers were dug in. Snipers had begun to shoot at them. Soon, incoming artillery rounds were crashing down on their emplacements from Syrian, Druze, or Shiite positions. The Americans just absorbed the blows. The sky over Lebanon was equally dangerous. Soviet air defense crews manned long-range surface-to-air missile batteries so the Syrians could deny Israel—and America—dominance in the air.

When George Shultz was asked whether he would remain in the Middle East to ensure that the foreign armies actually left Lebanon, as the

May 17 Accord required, his aides explained that he was inclined to leave and let the Arabs work on a solution. The signal could not have been clearer. Shultz had tied off the knot and was going to disengage, leaving a rearmed Syria to menace the weak Lebanese state from the east, while the Israeli army occupied the south and the still significant PLO forces were encamped around Tripoli in the north.

Nothing stays still for long in the Middle East. Assad developed a war-of-attrition strategy to wear down both the Israelis and the Americans. He formed the National Salvation Front, which combined the Druze forces of Walid Jumblatt, with Sunni and Shiite militias, and attacked the Christian sectors of Beirut and Christian villages in the mountains above Beirut.

After May 17, Philip Habib was no longer welcome in Damascus as Reagan's Middle East envoy. Assad did not trust him. Habib knew that if he could no longer talk to the Syrians, there was no point in staying in the job. Reagan and William Clark turned to Robert "Bud" McFarlane, the former marine colonel and onetime Kissinger aide. McFarlane was unpretentious in the manner that the Californians respected, a tough soldier who in 1965 had led the first large-scale marine deployment into Vietnam. He was deeply patriotic and astute in strategic analysis but lacked depth of experience in the Middle East. He was smart, but he was no Kissinger, which meant he also lacked those skills of craven flattery and manic competitiveness that had aided his mentor's bureaucratic rise.

Those who worked closely with McFarlane found his stilted briefing style deadly. He droned on in a manner a little too reminiscent of Kissinger's Germanic syntax, always more complex than profound. McFarlane's colleagues found that he appreciated complexity, and sometimes when he briefed Reagan or Clark "he'd try to lay it out in its splendid complication," said one of his colleagues. A quizzical look would come over Reagan's face and those in the room knew that Bud had lost the president.[84]

McFarlane sought out Prince Bandar because the Saudis exercised what little influence anyone had over Hafez al-Assad. But McFarlane and the Reagan White House were slow to understand how deeply the Saudis also opposed the May 17 Accord because they, too, saw it as an affront to the Arabs, a capitulation to Israel, and a violation of Lebanon's sovereignty.[85] King Fahd was offended by the terms of the accord that allowed

Israeli warplanes to use Lebanese airspace and Israel's armed forces to reenter Lebanon in the pursuit of Palestinian militants. The Saudi monarch had told Bandar to find a way to kill it, but to mask this Saudi opposition so as not to offend Reagan. Much of what Bandar did that summer was to help lead McFarlane to the conclusion that Shultz had made a mistake and that the best way out of the conflict was to convince Israel to withdraw. Then the Arabs could resume the diplomacy of putting Lebanon back together and convincing Syria to pull its forces out.

Assad greeted McFarlane warmly. He said he would be happy to resume discussions about the future of Lebanon—as long as it was clear that the May 17 Accord was dead. The Syrian leader also turned up the heat on the American presence. New gun battles erupted. The American ambassador and his wife soon were sleeping in flak jackets at their residence in East Beirut as Druze gunners rained fire down on the Christian domain.

The new CIA station chief in Beirut, William Buckley, pounded the table during a late August briefing with McFarlane, pointing out with maps, intercepts, and other intelligence that Syria wanted a war in the Shouf, the mountainous region overlooking Beirut from which Israel was planning to withdraw. The vacuum would throw the Druze militia backed by Syria against the Lebanese army and the Christian militias.[86] Buckley, a former army colonel and infantry commander in the Korean War, was an experienced Middle East hand, too. He was adamant that the United States had to hit the Syrian artillery positions and hit them hard. That would cause the sectarian forces under Druze leader Walid Jumblatt to back off. Jumblatt was playing the role of Syria's proxy. If the Syrian forces were destroyed, Buckley argued, the Druze would back off.[87]

On September 3, Reagan met with his top Middle East advisers in Washington. McFarlane convinced Clark that they had to do something to prevent the Israelis from pulling back and triggering a war. Shultz squared off against Weinberger in a debate over the use of American power. If the United States did not take on the Syrians, the Soviet-backed forces would win. American credibility in the Middle East would be in tatters. Reagan telephoned Begin to try to convince him to delay his retreat, but Moshe Arens called back saying that the decision had been made. They would get no help from the Israelis. Reagan's reelection campaign was looming. Opening a new war in Lebanon was full of risks. There were just too many scorpions in the sandbox. One of the observers of the debate wrote later, "We did not have the power in place or the will to win, and the Syrians knew it."[88]

The Israelis pulled out of the Shouf and a battle began. Syrian and Druze forces opened up on the decimated Lebanese army. McFarlane and Brigadier General Carl Stiner, the senior military representative in Lebanon, worried that the Lebanese army would collapse at Souk al-Gharb, a crossroads that controlled access to Beirut. U.S. intelligence discovered that McFarlane, staying in a guesthouse, was being personally targeted by Druze gunners. Lebanon was crumbling around him. On September 11, McFarlane sent an urgent, high-priority message to the president from the embassy's radio shack, which had been erected in the backyard of Ambassador Dillon's residence.

The collapse of the Lebanese army was imminent, McFarlane typed. The front lines were just a few miles from the ambassador's house. Michel Aoun, the Lebanese Army commander, was holding off a force of several thousand Druze fighters, supplemented by PLO guerrillas and the Iranian Revolutionary Guard. They were supported by Syrian artillery and Soviet T-34 tanks from Libya. McFarlane emphasized "this is not a civil conflict." He heightened the drama by adding that the previous night's battle had been a "savage" brawl of hand-to-hand combat that included "ax fighting." It was as intense as the worst days of Vietnam, he said.

"I do not say this to be melodramatic, but to make clear that the GOL [Government of Lebanon] is threatened with impending takeover by an uncivilized foreign force." Here was an echo of the Eisenhower era.

McFarlane wanted naval gunfire and air strikes from carrier-based bombers to prevent a military collapse in the Shouf. Reagan met with his aides that evening and approved the request, but the Pentagon, thwarting the White House's intentions, instructed the marine commander on the ground, Colonel Timothy Geraghty, to use his discretion. Geraghty held his fire. He feared that American fusillades directed into the Shouf would further expose his small force of marines, so he did nothing for more than a week.

On September 19, the USS *Virginia*, a guided-missile cruiser with five-inch guns, opened up on the Syrian positions to the great relief of the Lebanese government. The United States had joined the combat; it had taken sides in a civil war. But it had too few forces on the ground to dominate the battlefield. What forces it had were exposed and operating under rules of engagement that kept them from returning fire when attacked. And McFarlane, with the best intentions to save the Lebanese government, had further stampeded the United States into a precarious position with his cable to Reagan that his colleagues in the NSC called his "The sky is falling!" message.

Reagan wanted to do more. After one of his morning briefings he asked, "Well, haven't we got anything bigger than a five-inch gun?" The briefer, Philip Dur, responded, "We've got the [battleship] *New Jersey*. She's back in commission. She has sixteen-inch guns. She can throw a shell as big as a Volkswagen twenty miles."[89] Reagan liked the image. Make it so, he said.

The marines under Colonel Geraghty had entered into a kind of peacekeeping hell, their mission no longer clear. They were sprawled in tents and sandbagged positions in front of snipers and artillery gunners who owned the hills above them. Over time they had garrisoned themselves in a stout concrete hotel that offered the best protection from mortar and artillery rounds. There were days when more than one hundred rounds hit marine positions and Colonel Geraghty was taking casualties. He was under orders to keep his marines out of combat. So they stood watch with empty ammo clips.

At dawn on Sunday, October 23, 1983, the marine sentries outside the main barracks were on alert, but the rapid approach of a big Mercedes water truck still caught them without a defense. A bushy-haired driver wheeled his load over strands of concertina wire, and Lance Corporal Eddie DiFranco remembered looking straight into the cab and seeing the driver looking back. He was smiling.

The big diesel engine was roaring as the truck barreled down on the entrance, where Sergeant Steve Russell turned to face it and recognized, in an instant, what was about to happen. All he could think to do was run. He turned and dashed out the back, yelling, "Hit the deck! Hit the deck!"[90]

The truck crashed into the lobby, and the last thing Russell remembered was the flash. The blast wave picked him up and its hot breath hurled him through air before he ever heard the sound of the massive explosion; its power was equivalent to about twelve thousand pounds of TNT. The force lifted the center of the four-story building, where 350 marines were sleeping, and brought it down into the crater the explosion had gouged through the foundation. The lucky ones were those who had been sleeping on the roof. They had the sensation of "riding the roof down" as support columns snapped and tons of concrete crushed and killed two-thirds of the occupants, 241 people in all.

The cloud rose over the Beirut waterfront like a small nuclear explosion. First there was silence, then, as Colonel Geraghty said later, "The ground was moaning, because there were survivors in there."[91]

Dust and blood, shards of concrete and bodies—often just parts of bodies—filled the crater where the building had stood. Geraghty had never conceived of anything of such magnitude, and the commission that examined the catastrophe later concluded that "the objective and the means of attack were beyond the imagination of those responsible for Marine security."

But after the truck-bomb attack on the United States embassy six months earlier, another strike should not have been beyond anyone's imagination.

Twenty seconds after the marine barracks was hit, a second truck bomber crashed into the French barracks and another powerful concussion sundered the morning, killing fifty-nine French soldiers. Beirut awoke to the awful truth that an assault was under way.

President Reagan was in Augusta, Georgia, for a golfing weekend, which had been interrupted already by his decision to send American forces into Grenada, the Caribbean island that had aligned itself with Cuba. Word of the attack in Lebanon flashed by satellite communications from the Situation Room at 2:00 a.m. McFarlane and Shultz awakened Reagan, who was staying in the cabin that Dwight Eisenhower had used during his golf excursions.

"The president's face turned ashen when I told him the news," McFarlane later wrote. "He looked like a man, a 72-year-old man, who had just received a blow to the chest. All the air seemed to go out of him."

"How could this happen?" he asked in disbelief. "How bad is it? Who did it?"

Not since Vietnam had America suffered such a catastrophic loss in one day. Reagan returned to Washington, and later that day at the White House, he told his aides, "The first thing I want to do is to find out who did it and go after them with everything we've got."[92]

The evidence pointed toward Iran. The attack had been mounted against the two countries that were aiding Iraq in its war against the Ayatollah Khomeini.[93] Also, prior to the attack, U.S. intelligence had intercepted seven messages from Iranian officials urging the Shiite terrorist organizations to attack American and French targets. The "smoking gun" was an intercepted conversation in which the Iranian ambassador in Damascus had instructed Hussein al-Musawi of the Islamic Amal terrorist wing to "undertake an extraordinary attack against the U.S. Marines."[94]

Al-Musawi was the Shiite leader who had put his forces under the command of the Iranian Revolutionary Guard that had set up its headquarters in Lebanon's Bekaa Valley. Hezbollah's terrorism had burst onto the scene as an alarmingly effective network of training, support, and financing for the militant Shiite extremist underground. There were other reports of senior Iranian intelligence officers being present in Damascus and Beirut the week before the bombing; French intelligence had seen an Iranian embassy office evacuated ten minutes after the bombs went off. The suspected mastermind within the Shiite terror network was a shadowy figure named Imad Mughniyah, who had come out of the southern suburbs of Beirut, trained with the PLO, and then migrated into the new Iranian-backed network.

Reagan was determined to strike, and the best target was the Sheikh Abudullah Barracks in the Bekaa Valley, which was terrorist central. The French government conveyed to the White House that it was ready to conduct a joint strike with the United States. Reagan assembled his advisers on November 14. Weinberger opposed military action, but Clark, McFarlane, and Shultz believed that the evidence pointed to Hezbollah and the barracks, where an estimated 250 Hezbollah and Iranian fighters were based. It was a legitimate target in their view.

"Well, I believe we have to do this," Reagan said.[95]

Two days later, the White House was braced for the raid. A strike plan had been developed by Vice Admiral James "Ace" Lyons, the deputy chief of naval operations for plans, and the package was approved for Rear Admiral Jerry Tuttle, commander of the naval task force off Lebanon. At the NSC, McFarlane's aides Teicher and Dur set up an all-night vigil to track the progress of the joint strike force. The aircraft carriers offshore, USS *Eisenhower* and USS *Kennedy*, were primed and on alert, but the hours passed and no launch order arrived. At 6:00 a.m., Weinberger telephoned McFarlane.

"Bud, I had a request [to launch], but I denied it," the secretary of defense said.

McFarlane asked what went wrong.

Weinberger said nothing had gone wrong—he just didn't think it was the right thing to do. It wasn't prudent. There would be repercussions all over the Middle East.

"Cap, the President of the United States approved this," McFarlane said, exasperated. "The President isn't going to be able to understand this, Cap. You were there. You saw how strongly he felt about this."

"I'll be glad to talk to him," Weinberger said, "but I thought it was the wrong thing to do."[96]

For McFarlane and his staff, Weinberger's defiance was almost treasonous. McFarlane went straight in to the president that morning during the intelligence briefing and told him what Weinberger had done. McFarlane was on uncertain ground. He knew that Weinberger was among Reagan's closest friends.

"I don't understand," Reagan said. "Why didn't they do it?"

"There is no excuse for it, Mr. President," McFarlane said. "You approved this operation and Cap decided not to carry it out. The credibility of the United States in Damascus just went to zero. There's no justification. The Secretary of Defense was wrong, and you ought to make clear to him how you feel about it."

But Reagan didn't. He balled up his fist, pounded his desk, and said, "That's terrible. We should have blown the daylights out of them. I just don't understand."[97]

Larry Eagleburger observed the debate and believed it was a mistake to take a big terrorist hit and not strike back. "We constantly tended to think of the problem in terms of who was the perpetrator and where was he located," Eagleburger said, in obvious reference to Weinberger's highly cautious approach to staging retribution attacks to deter further terrorist strikes. To Eagleburger, "It made little difference whom you clobbered so long as you clobbered somebody who had it coming."[98]

Twelve days after the truck bombers struck in Beirut, a third suicide attack was mounted against the Israeli army base near Tyre in southern Lebanon. Again, a truck driver easily crashed through defenses and reached the center of the Israeli headquarters before detonating. More than sixty people were killed, including twenty-nine Israelis.

As Reagan stood idle, flummoxed or just paralyzed by the disagreement among his senior aides, Israeli jets descended on the Bekaa Valley and hit the Sheikh Abdullah Barracks. The following day, French jets followed suit, having lost hope that the Americans were in the game.

This was Reagan's cruel innocence. His failure to retaliate for the marine barracks bombing, the worst terrorist attack on the United States up to that time, probably emboldened the Iranian-Syrian alliance against the United States that would radiate violence for decades. For Assad and the Hezbollah militants, America was risk averse; it had wilted in the face of casualties. It *was* susceptible to terrorism. Reagan's instinct had been to hit back, but he remained unable to dominate his cabinet. He refused to see Weinberger's refusal to strike as insubordination; more important, Reagan lacked the fortitude to unify his national security team or bend it to his will. And so he pounded his desk in private, he temporized and shook his head until the passage of time, or some other event such as Grenada, intervened.

Reagan had burnished the image of a tough ideologue, but as president he had shown a banker's caution, a deacon's humanism—everything but the resolute leadership of a commander. He carried a set of contradictions that seemed uniquely Reaganesque. He could not confront a friend as close as Weinberger. He lacked the intellect to formulate policy options or chart an onward course. Reagan imagined himself as a leader who wanted to "blow the daylights" out of America's enemies, but when his imagination was thwarted, as in a Hollywood script change, he adjusted his presidential role and moved on.

In contrast, Weinberger *was* resolute; he was an ideologue who expressed his loyalty to Reagan by acting on his behalf, notwithstanding that others thought he was disobeying orders. Just as Kissinger had undermined and circumvented Nixon when the power equation shifted between the two men, Weinberger knew the limits of Reagan's character; the president would never turn on so close a friend and so essential a member of the cabinet. Weinberger felt strongly that it was wrong to bomb blindly in retribution for acts of terror, so he had maneuvered, gambling that he could deny his bureaucratic rivals their quest to avenge the death of the marines. (Imad Mughniyah escaped all attempts to bring him to justice during the Reagan years. He was killed on February 12, 2008, by a bomb placed in his car in Damascus, near Syrian intelligence headquarters.)

Strangely, the success of the Grenada operation—the low-risk occupation of a tiny Caribbean island to rescue American medical students and topple a pro-Castro regime—had played well at home and alleviated the urgency for retaliation in Lebanon. A frustrated Shultz, who had been Weinberger's superior at Bechtel, could not understand the Pentagon's excessive caution in the face of catastrophic acts of terror.

"If anyone in this room hears me suggest that the U.S. should send in the Marines to protect U.S. interests, just choke me on the spot," he erupted sarcastically during one of the debates.[99] But he, too, had failed to articulate a set of goals in Lebanon and the broader Middle East that could have rallied Reagan to the cause. He was more the clever bureaucrat than the foreign policy visionary.

Over the next several months, Reagan and senior members of his administration assured the Lebanese and the world that the United States was in Lebanon to secure its vital interests. It was there to thwart Syrian hegemony. It was not going to "cut and run." Vice President Bush put it forcefully: "We're not going to let a bunch of insidious terrorists, cowards, shape the foreign policy of the United States."

But they did. Hezbollah's new network struck again on December 12, this time in Kuwait. Truck bombers drove their loads into the American and French embassies and detonated them to devastating effect, though only six people died. The pattern was the same as in the Beirut attacks: suicide bombers at the wheel of fast-moving trucks. The targets: Iran's enemies in the Iran-Iraq War. The bomb design was also the same: plastic explosives strapped to compressed-gas canisters. The Kuwaitis arrested seventeen people who were part of the plot, all of them members of the Shiite al-Dawa organization, which also was backed by Iran and had branches in Iraq and other Persian Gulf states with large Shiite populations. The Hezbollah link was that three of the bombers were Lebanese, including the brother-in-law of Imad Mughniyah, the mysterious operative who was Hezbollah's middleman between Iran's intelligence arm and Shiite extremist organizations.

The capture and imprisonment of the Kuwait 17 was a milestone in the new era of terror, for it created the conditions for kidnapping, murder, and hostage taking in order to secure their release. Khomeinism was gathering strength among Shiites. In Bahrain, they staged a coup attempt against the ruling Sunni minority of the island state located just off Saudi Arabia's coast. A Jordanian army unit came to the rescue and the coup failed.

At the CIA, Casey confided in friends that he was under increasing pressure to counter the wave of terrorism. He and Weinberger went to Congress seeking funding to equip an elite Jordanian commando unit that could function as the first wave of an American-backed rapid deployment force in the Middle East. It had been given an unobtrusive name, the Joint Logistics Planning Program, but the idea had been a clever melding of military and diplomatic goals: Jordan could serve as an American proxy. The viability of the concept had been demonstrated when King Hussein dispatched his troops to Bahrain to protect the royal family there.

The spread of Khomeinism convinced Reagan of the danger to Western interests from an Iranian victory in the Iran-Iraq War. Reagan brought McFarlane back to the White House as national security adviser, replacing William Clark (who had left to become secretary of the interior). Reagan picked Donald Rumsfeld as his new Middle East negotiator. A business executive and former congressman who had served in the Ford White House and as secretary of defense, Rumsfeld was given the task of seeking U.S. basing rights in the region. But an important part of his assignment was to travel to Baghdad and restore diplomatic relations with Iraq and Saddam Hussein. The United States had come to the conclusion that a reversal of Iraq's fortunes in the war with Iran would be "a strategic defeat for the West."[100]

Rumsfeld reached Baghdad on December 17, 1983. When he was ushered into the presence of the Iraqi dictator, Saddam was cordial. He was ready for better relations with the United States, he said, but Saddam was the epitome of arrogance. His forces were killing Iranians by the tens of thousands that winter; he was gassing them with chemical munitions that Western firms helped him acquire. His troops were acting like exterminators. "Pest control" is how some of his commanders referred to their work.

Philip Dur, who was part of Rumsfeld's party, was sickened (as were his colleagues) at the videos the Iraqis showed them. "They had these bodies stacked like cordwood near Basra, and clearly the bodies were burned" by mustard gas. "We were horrified that they had used chemical weapons to that extent," Dur said.[101]

There was Rumsfeld, sitting with the Iraqi leader who was using chemical weapons—weapons of mass destruction—indiscriminately on the war front, and though Rumsfeld was carrying talking points to raise American concerns about the use of gas, there is no record that he broached the subject with Saddam. The American approach was to have George Shultz and the State Department condemn the use of chemical weapons, but in private channels, there was a recognition that Iraq was in a fight for its national survival. In the White House's view, Saddam was all that stood between the West and a breakout by Khomeini's army into Saudi Arabia and the Levant. American strategic interests clearly required supporting Saddam, chemical weapons and all. That was the private view of many American officials, notwithstanding what was said publicly. Even when the United Nations Security Council condemned the use of chemical weapons in the Iran-Iraq War, Shultz sent a diplomat to tell the Iraqis that the United States did "not want this issue to dominate our bilateral relationship nor to detract from our common interest to see the war brought to [an] early end."[102]

Shultz personally reinforced this message, telling another of Saddam's top diplomats that the American condemnation of chemical weapons use by Iraq was part of a "long standing policy" and not an "anti-Iraqi gesture."[103]

In Lebanon, Syrian forces and their proxies had pushed back into Beirut and surrounded Arafat's last strongholds in the north around Tripoli. The Saudis had become deeply concerned that Arafat would be toppled and that an even more radical PLO leader would emerge. But Arafat, the survivor, escaped with a flourish. He traded six Israeli prisoners of war for four thousand five hundred Palestinian and Lebanese prisoners, and then boarded ships with the last four thousand of his fighters and made his final exit from Lebanon.

Meanwhile, Syria's air defense forces, under Soviet tutelage, menaced the American reconnaissance flights over Lebanon, firing SAM-7 antiaircraft missiles at carrier-based F-14s. Suddenly Weinberger and the military chiefs wanted to teach the Syrians a lesson. Why? Because, for Weinberger, this was a worthy cold war duel of weaponry. The enemy was clear, the retaliation surgical. With Reagan's enthusiastic approval, the fleet launched F-14s to bomb the Syrian antiaircraft sites, but the raid went badly awry. Two planes were shot down, with one pilot killed and a navigator, Lieutenant Robert Goodman Jr., captured. Reagan and his aides were baffled. Every day the Israelis conducted air reconnaissance and bombing missions over Lebanon and never got shot down. The United States conducted one attack mission and lost two planes and one of its pilots. How could that be?

Those in the White House who were charged with winning Reagan's reelection could see that Lebanon was becoming a swamp. Ed Rollins, who had left the White House staff in October to set up the reelection campaign, was one of the voices telling Ed Meese, Reagan's longtime political counselor, and others close to the president that polls showed they were running behind two of the leading Democratic contenders, Walter Mondale and John Glenn, and if they didn't get the troops out of Lebanon, they might not establish any momentum.[104]

On January 18, 1984, Malcolm Kerr, an eminent Arab scholar and president of the American University of Beirut, was murdered in the Lebanese capital just before Rumsfeld was to have lunched with him. In Congress, there were calls demanding that Reagan withdraw the marines, but Reagan fired back that withdrawal was a form of surrender.[105] If the United States left Lebanon, it would send a "signal to terrorists everywhere—they can gain by waging war against innocent people." In his State of the Union address on January 25, Reagan said that America, through its deployment of the marines as part of the multinational peacekeeping force, was helping the Lebanese to "break the cycle of despair."

"There is hope for a free, independent and sovereign Lebanon," Reagan said from the podium in the House of Representatives. "We must have the courage to give peace a chance. And we must not be driven from our objectives for peace in Lebanon by state-sponsored terrorism."

Yet Reagan decided to pull out. The political realities of the reelection campaign had overtaken any instinct to take more risks in Lebanon. On February 7, the White House issued a presidential statement: "The bloodshed we have witnessed in Lebanon over the last several days only demonstrates once again the length to which the forces of violence and intimidation are prepared to go to prevent a peaceful reconciliation process from taking place . . . Yielding to violence and terrorism today may seem to provide temporary relief, but such a course is sure to lead to a more dangerous and less manageable future crisis . . . Recent events only confirm the importance of the decisive new steps I want to outline for you now."

Buried in the penultimate paragraph was the news: "I have asked Secretary of Defense Weinberger to present me a plan for redeployment of the Marines from Beirut airport to their ships offshore." Reagan promised future aid and the protection of "naval gunfire," and he tried to put the best face on withdrawal by concluding, "These measures, I believe, will strengthen our ability to do the job we set out to do and to sustain our efforts over the long term."

What measures? The United States had just abandoned Amin Gemayel's government and any hope for the unity of Lebanon. Reagan turned his back on the vital interests of which he had just days before spoken, and he left his onetime ally alone to face the tender mercies of Syria and its vengeful leader, Hafez al-Assad.

Donald Rumsfeld had been in Beirut on the eve of this statement and called the White House on a satellite phone asking that the president make a declaration in support of the Lebanese government. He asked for any action that might save the disintegrating Lebanese army. But it was too late. Since the bombing of the marine barracks, Congress was on to the chaos inside the administration over what course to take in Lebanon. Reagan could not imagine himself getting more deeply committed to an unpopular course that might threaten his reelection chances. The marines began their redeployment (the French and Italians followed), and by February 26, the last of the multinational forces was out, leaving the Syrian army and its proxies rampant while Israeli forces hunkered down in the south. During the American withdrawal, the USS *New Jersey* laid down fire with its sixteen-inch guns to cover the retreat. American warships wantonly and needlessly fired more than eight hundred rounds into the hills above Beirut, as a final, pointless statement of American anger.

On March 5, Amin Gemayel formally abrogated the May 17 Accord with Israel. Hafez al-Assad had won. The grand strategic gambit of Begin and Sharon to make Lebanon a Christian-Arab ally against the Muslim world had turned to ashes. America's intervention, unlike Eisenhower's a generation earlier, had ended as a bloody humiliation at the hands of Soviet-equipped Syrians and Iran-backed terrorists. The PLO had been purged from Lebanon, but its political power still pulsed throughout the region. Its former base in Lebanon was a shambles, seething with renewed hatreds directed not at the PLO but at the Jewish state and at America. Tens of thousands of Lebanese and Palestinian civilians had died. And Israel had lost hundreds of soldiers on the battlefield, prompting many Israelis to ask what had been the purpose of their sacrifice.

King Hussein chose that moment to assail U.S. policy in the Middle East. "We see things this way," the Jordanian king told *The New York Times*. "Israel is on our land. It is there by virtue of American military assistance and economic aid that translates into aid for Israeli settlements. Israel is there by virtue of American moral and political support to the point where the United States is succumbing to Israeli dictates."[106]

Reagan was wounded by the king's rebuke. George Shultz, always astute when it came to the politics of blame, faulted the American ambassador for not warning Washington that the king was in a foul mood. The American plan to build a Jordanian rapid deployment force was dropped, along with a plan to sell hundreds of Stinger antiaircraft missiles to Jordan and Saudi Arabia for their defense. It was an election year. The pro-Israeli forces in Congress would use King Hussein's blast against Reagan to defeat any arms sale that came to Capitol Hill.

Reagan knew that he had cut and run. "We're going to pay a price for this downstream," he told McFarlane. It didn't take long.

On February 10, Frank Reiger, an electrical engineering professor at the American University of Beirut, was on his way to meet a friend when a husky Arab came up to him and put his arm around his shoulder. As Reiger tried to pull away, he felt the barrel of a gun pressed to his head. His captor shoved him into a car with three men. They wrapped him in packing tape, bundled him into a trunk, and took him to a hideout where he was chained to a radiator.[107]

On March 7, Jeremy Levin, the CNN bureau chief in Beirut, was seized in a similar manner.

On March 16, a carload of gunmen seized William Buckley, the CIA station chief, the second highest ranking American official in Lebanon.

On May 8, another American, a sixty-year-old Presbyterian minister, Reverend Benjamin T. Weir, left his home for a morning walk with his wife when three armed men grabbed him in front of his apartment.

The image of America's fate in the Middle East was now a blindfolded captive.

# 8

# THE IRAN-CONTRA AFFAIR

*The Clash of Saudi and
Israeli Influence*

Lebanon was Reagan's nightmare. Americans were held hostage. The president who had run hard against Jimmy Carter by vowing to play a tougher hand in foreign policy now looked powerless. Reagan and William Casey, the CIA director, were frantic: the agency's station chief was in chains in some basement, and all they could do was to try to figure out how to rescue him—and all of the hostages—before the Beirut kidnapping spree turned into the hostage crisis of 1979–80 all over again and made Reagan look as powerless and as weak as Carter.

The American captivity in Lebanon helped to lay the foundations of what became known as the Iran-contra affair, which would divide the intelligence community and Reagan's foreign policy team into two camps who saw the Iran-Iraq War in starkly different terms. For most of Reagan's advisers, the Ayatollah Khomeini was *the* enemy, and Iraq—Saddam Hussein—was the best hope to contain the virulence coursing out of

Hezbollah hijackers in Lebanon: Reagan's nightmare

Iran. The other Arab leaders supported this view. But to a crucial minority of presidential advisers, whose views were heavily influenced by Israel's leadership and by a hard-line assessment of Soviet intentions, Iran was the prize and was ripe for plucking if Khomeini could be pushed aside. Reagan never really mastered the debate but was driven by his sympathy for the American captives to veer toward the side that advocated a secret opening to Iran.

Here, over a two-year period from 1984 to 1986, Reagan reached the nadir of muddled thinking that was the hallmark of his approach to the Middle East. In his diary, he worried about the onset of "Armageddon"—the climactic battle between good and evil—as if that justified any head fake or suspension of principle that was necessary, in his view, to save innocent lives—and help to defeat communism. In opening a secret channel to Iran, that country's desperate need for weapons and spare parts in the war with Iraq was never going to be separated from Iran's sponsorship of the hostage takers in Lebanon. Reagan seemed to walk into this trap with eyes open and hearing only what he wanted to hear—that trading weapons (he convinced himself this was not ransom) would lead to the release of hostages.

Since the collapse of the shah, Israeli political operatives and middle-men had been opening discreet lines of communication to Tehran, where Israelis had once been welcome during the long Pahlavi reign. The loss of Iran as an ally was a serious blow to Israel, not just for the lost oil trade but also for the strategic relationship Iran represented in conjunction with American and Western interests. Israel's strategy in the era of Khomeini was to open clandestine trade lines through middlemen in the shadowy weapons trade and thereby make contact with moderate members of the Shiite clergy who were disenchanted with the ayatollah's revolution. After Iraq's invasion of Iran in 1980, the Israeli military also secretly shipped spare parts to Iran for use in the country's American-made warplanes, tanks, and other weapons—in violation of American sanctions banning any kind of trade with Iran.

The Ayatollah Khomeini could be overthrown—that was the premise in Israel's security establishment. Tehran was a nest of internecine war-fare, and hundreds of political rivals had blown each other up; thousands had been executed or imprisoned as revolutionary cells struggled for dominance and Khomeini's approval.

In the play for Iran, the contras—the American-backed counterrevolu-tionaries who were fighting the Sandinista regime in Nicaragua—were a passing beneficiary but an important one, too, for the administration. William Casey had done such a poor job of winning support for this fight against Soviet-backed revolutionaries in Latin America that Congress passed what was known as the Boland Amendment to cut off funding for the contras. Reagan and Casey were determined to sustain their "freedom fighters," a paramilitary force that had been outfitted by the CIA from bases in Honduras to harass the Marxist Sandinistas across the border.

In early 1984, McFarlane was tasked by the president to find a secret source of funding. He went straight to the Israelis, using a young aide as his messenger. Howard Teicher, the NSC assistant who was traveling with Rumsfeld, had been summoned to the U.S. embassy in Tel Aviv to take a secure phone call from Washington. When Teicher picked up, McFarlane and Lieutenant Colonel Oliver North were on the other end. North was a new NSC staff member devoted to intelligence operations. McFarlane laid it out: Go to David Kimche, the former Mossad official in the Israeli Foreign Ministry. Don't tell the U.S. ambassador, Sam Lewis. Ask Kimche if Israel would be willing to channel several million dollars to the contras while Reagan worked on lifting the funding ban in Congress.

After a few days, Kimche called Teicher in Washington and told him that Yitzhak Shamir, the new prime minister (after Begin's resignation in September 1983), had concluded that Israel could not help with the contras. McFarlane frowned, but he did not tell Teicher that he had another option: Prince Bandar.

Bandar was already a favorite in the Reagan White House. After he was appointed Saudi ambassador in 1983, Bandar went to the Oval Office to present his credentials. Reagan reached out for Bandar's hand and held it for a long time, reminding Bandar of their first meeting on Reagan's porch in Pacific Palisades in 1978 talking about Jimmy Carter's difficulty in getting the F-15 sale through Congress. Carter had sent Bandar to ask for Reagan's support as a prominent Republican, and Bandar had delivered by telling Reagan that Saudi Arabia was staunchly anticommunist and would stand with America.

"Well, young man, you came a long way. When I first met you, you were a young major and a fighter pilot. Today, you are your country's ambassador to the United States. I am proud of you."

Bandar answered in kind. "Well, Mr. President, you didn't do too shabby either. When I first met you, you were an unemployed governor, and today you are the president of the most powerful country in the world."[1]

Bandar's access to the Reagan White House was such that Moshe Arens, the Israeli ambassador, complained. When told that Chief of Staff James Baker did not see ambassadors, he fired back on the telephone, "Well, he sees Prince Bandar!"[2]

Now that he had been named Saudi ambassador, Bandar's goal was to become the indispensable envoy. He would work with Nizar Hamdoon, Saddam's ambassador, to solidify an Arab alliance with Washington against Iran, which would mean big arms sales to key states like Saudi Arabia. Bandar was everywhere in Washington in the first Reagan years. He worked Capitol Hill, he worked the press, but most important, he worked the White House, where James Baker, George H. W. Bush, and Reagan himself all accepted his friendship. They relied on him as a secret channel to King Fahd but also as a political operative who could invoke Saudi Arabia's financial clout to sway business and political leaders.

Bandar saw his success in becoming a lobbyist not just for the kingdom, but also for the American president in domestic politics. He knew this would make him competitive with the "Jewish lobby" in Washington, and he seemed to relish the competition. After all, he would say, he was the Arab diplomat who had beat AIPAC not once, but twice, first on the F-15 vote in the Carter years, then on AWACS under Reagan.

This was the period when I first met Bandar. He was standing on the lawn at Ben Bradlee's and Sally Quinn's enormous Georgetown home, carrying on as if he were some Arabian Gatsby, drawing laughter from Katharine Graham, the matriarch of the American press, showing off an astute knowledge of sports and politics to Washington's power brokers and media stars and, most compellingly for me, offering himself as an access point to the secretive kingdom. This was no small thing, as Saudi Arabia had been dominated by inaccessible bedouin princes for nearly a century, and I was a correspondent for *The Washington Post* preparing for a tour as Middle East bureau chief.[3]

Whereas I wanted access to Saudi Arabia for journalistic pursuits, William Casey and the CIA wanted something more tangible. The CIA director was careful not to discuss contra funding directly with King Fahd, Bandar, or any other Saudi official, but he concurred wholeheartedly with McFarlane's efforts. In the space of a few weeks in early 1984, Bandar was approached first by the CIA's division chief for the Middle East, Chuck Cogan, and then by McFarlane. Bandar wasn't even sure the conversation with Cogan amounted to a request.

"As a friend, he was sort of telling me—giving me a hint on how we can beat the Israelis" in Washington and "get into the American system by being involved [in covert affairs] and winning [over] the agency," Bandar said.[4]

Bandar sent a private note back to King Fahd informing him of the conversation, and Fahd sent an immediate reply: if the Americans ask for help, tell them Saudi Arabia is willing to help them. A few days later, McFarlane called Bandar at the Saudi ambassador's residence, perched on the high bluff over the Potomac River just west of Washington. McFarlane said he needed to have a "no-conversation conversation" and proceeded to make the case that the president badly needed to find a way to sustain the contras until the vote in Congress could be turned around. He said Reagan would be grateful to whoever helped.

"What do you want?" Bandar asked.

One million a month for six months, said McFarlane.

Fine, you've got it, Bandar replied. Just tell us where and when you want the money.


It was the Saudi way of investing in America, according to Bandar. Of course, he was putting a gloss on a sophisticated brand of checkbook diplomacy, but it was more than that. Fahd was after Saudi-American alignment, a relationship competitive with Israel despite the intensity with which Israeli leaders jealously guarded their special status as America's most intimate ally in the Middle East. Fahd stood as the most pro-Western of Saudi monarchs in a half century. As the ruler of a fabulously wealthy but vulnerable kingdom that was sitting on the largest oil reserves in the world, he took the view of his father, King Abdul Aziz, who had built the first partnership of common interest with Franklin Roosevelt at the close of World War II.[5] For King Abdul Aziz, the bargain had been simple: World war had proved that control of oil was essential to victory. The old king detested the British; America was a more idealistic power and the king wanted the American oil industry, whose four largest companies banded together as Aramco, the Arabian American Oil Company, to develop the kingdom's Promethean potential in energy. With it would come a superpower's protection for the kingdom from the Soviet empire and from the inherent instability of the Middle East. Three decades on, after Aramco had been nationalized and Saudi Arabia was much more fully in charge of its destiny, King Fahd saw the need to redefine the terms of the relationship. It was necessary to do more than just pump oil to grease the seams of alliance.

The Saudis felt increasingly vulnerable. The Iran-Iraq War had moved into the Persian Gulf, where Iraqi jets armed with French Exocet missiles were striking at Iranian shipping. Saudi Arabia's main oil-loading terminal at Ras Tanura seemed naked to attack. What if Iran retaliated against the Saudis? Khomeini had threatened to close the Straits of Hormuz, through which 20 percent of the world's oil supply passed every day.

In 1983, when Bandar was named ambassador to the United States, he was tutored by his sovereign to assist American presidents in quiet ways that would build up a viscous layer of trust over time. "The United States is the most dangerous thing to us," Fahd had admonished Bandar. "We have no cultural connection with them . . . no ethnic connection to them . . . no religious connection . . . no language connection . . . no political connection. We are a monarchy, they are democratic."

America is "too big to be hurt," he told Bandar. Saudi diplomacy had to deliver a premium that would keep America at its side, even when the public mood was sour, even when competing demands pulled America's attention elsewhere, and even when the powerful Israeli lobby stood in opposition. Fahd, who had witnessed the blowback from Western societies over the massive run-up in oil prices during the 1970s and early 1980s, knew the risks. It was King Faisal, a Saudi monarch, after all, who had led the Arab oil embargo against the West in 1973. Saudi monarchs had backed and financed the Palestine Liberation Organization during its years of terror and assassination against American and Israeli targets. Americans had little knowledge of or sympathy for bedouin oil sheikhs who rejected the modern world, who practiced a fundamentalist version of Islam.

Yet both countries stood in opposition to Soviet expansion into the Middle East. Both also sought to contain Iran's Islamic revolution, whose radicalism threatened to incite the Shiite minority in the Arab world, not least in Saudi Arabia. Without strong ties, America could just run roughshod, exploiting Saudi weaknesses and intimidating its rulers. Fahd did not want Saudi Arabia to be among those states that feared that when America appeared over the horizon, "They will come and they will ride us. And they will never get off until our backs are broken."

Fahd sent Bandar to the West to be an enabler, an envoy of alignment, a fixer and financier, someone who could bind the two worlds. His charge was to "invest, invest, and invest." Fahd said, "I want you to keep your eyes and ears open for policies and issues that are important to them so I can voluntarily offer to do it instead of them asking me because I want to maximize my investment—and there will come a time when I will cash it in."

Saudi-American coordination in covert operations blossomed under Reagan: Saudi Arabia and the U.S. Congress wrote the checks, CIA officers purchased weapons (from Egypt, China, and other states) and funneled them through Pakistan's intelligence service to Afghan rebel commanders fighting the Soviet army. It was proving a signal success. Casey boasted in one briefing that for the price of $200 million to the American treasury, the Afghan rebels had inflicted an estimated $12 billion in costs on

Moscow.[6] By the mid-1980s, Saudi Arabia was a substantial partner, not only in matching dollar-for-dollar the funding the CIA was putting into the anti-Soviet war in South Asia; the Saudis were now the principal funding source for the contras fighting in Nicaragua. They were spending millions of dollars to assist Jonas Savimbi's "freedom fighters" in Angola against a Soviet- and Cuban-backed government.

The United States tilted heavily toward Iraq, reestablishing formal diplomatic ties in early 1984 and upgrading its mission in Baghdad. The American contribution to the Iraq war effort was the regular delivery of high-resolution satellite images of the battlefield and Iran's rear area, which helped Saddam's generals to spot any weak points.[7]

American forces stood prepared to fire on marauding Iranian gunboats in the Persian Gulf. Somehow, in the Persian Gulf, America looked more resolute when oil was at stake than it had in Lebanon, where terrorism and hostage taking were rampant.[8] The dilemma caused George Shultz to warn publicly that the United States could not afford to become the "Hamlet of nations, worrying endlessly over whether and how to respond" to violence against American diplomats overseas.

Ronald Reagan retained the White House with a landslide victory over Walter Mondale in November 1984. Like Eisenhower's victory in 1956, or Nixon's in 1972, Reagan's triumph gave him a great reservoir of political capital.

Eisenhower, facing the Suez Crisis, had used his electoral mandate to force Ben-Gurion to give up his conquest of the Sinai. Nixon, flush with victory, had used his strength to extract America from Vietnam, as Charles de Gaulle had abandoned Algeria. In 1984, Reagan stood powerfully poised over the American agenda, but he had so squandered U.S. credibility in the Middle East that no dramatic move on the diplomatic board was open to him. Syria and Hezbollah had chased America out of Lebanon. Israel was so divided politically that Begin's successor was a two-headed government—neither Likud nor Labor had polled a majority—and a power-sharing arrangement was in place between Yitzhak Shamir and Shimon Peres. They alternated in the prime minister's chair, each working to undo the other's policies.

Since Eisenhower's time, the Arabs had been waiting for an American leader who possessed the political strength necessary to make peace in the Middle East. Reagan's dismal record left him powerless to act without some miracle of statecraft, which the dowdy George Shultz was unable to muster. The Middle East's conflicts and challenges had expanded far beyond the problems of refugees and borders that Eisenhower had faced in the Holy Land. Lebanon stood as a failed state. Iran was pulsing with revolution. Iraq, at war against Iran, was in danger of collapsing. Libya was destabilizing North Africa and running schools for international terrorism. And the Soviet army still occupied Afghanistan.

Reagan had, if anything, become a reactive president. He rationalized the Middle East's passions by scribbling those references to "Armageddon" in his diary. He showed no ability to organize the American government or its allies to stanch the cold war rivalry in the region, choke off the flow of dangerous weapons, or set an agenda for mediating the growing number of conflicts there. Yet Reagan seemed supremely confident that his administration was on the right course.

It was during this period of postelection celebration that King Fahd made his first official visit to the United States. No Saudi monarch had been to Washington since 1971, when King Faisal had come to tell Nixon that Israel must give up its conquests from the Six-Day War. In those days, oil was cheap, the Arabs were weak, and the Persian Gulf was stable.

Now King Fahd arrived in the American capital to highlight Saudi Arabia's value as an ally against the Soviets. Fahd's mission was complex: He wanted billions of dollars' worth of new weapons systems, planes and missiles most of all. He was willing to up the ante in Afghanistan with an even larger contribution to the covert war. He had extra funds for the contras and for anti-Marxist rebels in Angola. And he came bearing extravagant private gifts for the president and first lady.

The contras were critical to Reagan's anticommunist strategy, and Casey had cleverly moved the funding mechanism into the White House so he could say the CIA's skirts were clean. No CIA funds were going south. McFarlane signaled Bandar that $1 million per month was not enough to sustain the contras and the White House was hoping for an increase to $2 million per month. Bandar replied that it was no problem.

Fahd wanted another forty F-15s for the Saudi air force. And he wanted surface-to-surface missiles to counter the Soviet-made Scud missiles that were beginning to appear in South Yemen, Iraq, and Iran. Saddam had fired dozens of Scuds at Iranian cities near the border in 1984, and Iran was purchasing Scuds from Libya to return the favor. Fahd was not an expert on missiles, but his military advisers had told him that the United States had the Lance missile, which had been developed in the early 1970s to carry nuclear, chemical, or conventional high-explosive warheads up to seventy-five miles. The Lance was famous as the planned delivery system for the ill-fated neutron bomb. (President Carter had decided against deploying the Lance with neutron bomb warheads in Western Europe after a groundswell of public opinion opposed it.)

The Pentagon told Bandar that Congress would oppose selling the Lance, even fitted with conventional warheads, to Saudi Arabia just as Carter had refused Israel's request for the Lance. It was associated with nuclear warfare. Soundings on Capitol Hill also indicated that AIPAC and the pro-Israeli camp would vigorously oppose another F-15 sale to Saudi Arabia. The Israelis were upset that the restrictions placed on the first squadrons—no bomb racks or range-extending fuel tanks—had simply been dropped by the Pentagon.

Amid these complexities, Fahd swept into Washington with a huge retinue in early 1985, welcomed by a twenty-one-gun salute on the South Lawn of the White House. In their private meeting at the White House, Reagan explained that he did not think he could prevail in Congress if he took the F-15 package forward, but he would be willing to try if Fahd wanted him to do so. This was where Fahd ingratiated himself with Reagan, telling him that Saudi Arabia didn't want Reagan to lose in Congress. If it was a choice between Reagan's losing and Saudi Arabia's forgoing more F-15s, it was better that Reagan stay strong.

A friend indeed, Reagan must have thought.

Fahd then returned to *his* problem. He needed to build up the defenses of the kingdom. What should he do? Reagan knew that both the British and French governments were champing at the bit to sell weapons to Saudi Arabia. He told Fahd that he had America's blessing to buy what he needed from Britain or France.

When they appeared in public, Fahd put on the mantle of Arab leadership, telling Reagan that he should use his strength to pursue a peace settlement in the Holy Land. Standing in his traditional robes on the South Lawn, Fahd said that the Palestinian question "is the single problem that is of paramount concern to the whole Arab nation and affects the relations of its peoples and countries with the outside world.

"It is the one problem that is the root cause of instability and turmoil in the region," he said, adding, "I hope, Mr. President, that your administration will support the just cause of the Palestinian people."[9]

Reagan had very little to offer on that score, however. The Reagan Plan was long dead, effectively discredited. But Reagan still wanted to cast an image as a peacemaker. King Fahd, ever wary of his image in the Arab world, wanted to know what Reagan planned to say at the state dinner set as the climax of his visit. All during the day, Bandar had not been able to get a copy of Reagan's dinner speech from McFarlane or from the State Department. By the time King Fahd sat down at the head table, his suspicions were up.

Yogi Berra, the manager of the New York Yankees, was implausibly seated next to the king, along with Nellie Connolly, the wife of the former Texas governor. Fahd turned to the State Department interpreter and asked him if he could see Reagan's remarks, but the interpreter said he had strict instructions to keep them confidential.

The king turned to Reagan. "Mr. President, have you seen my speech?"

Reagan replied he had not.

"Give the president my speech," Fahd said to the interpreter. "I haven't seen your speech. May I look at it?" Fahd asked.

Reagan said of course he could see it.

Fahd scanned the text and quickly spotted the reason for the secrecy. The president was planning to wrap up his tribute to U.S.-Saudi relations with a flourish in which he would extend his hand to King Fahd, invoking the spirit of Camp David, and invite the King to extend his hand to Israeli Prime Minister Shimon Peres. With hands thus joined among Reagan, Fahd and, symbolically at least, Peres, they would promise to complete the peace that Carter, Begin, and Sadat had begun.

Reagan's idealism and the White House's cluelessness about the realities of Arab politics had overtaken reason. Here the president was attempting to stage a dramatic stunt that would generate headlines and portray him as a peacemaker, but with absolutely no constructive result except more Arab rage. Fahd could imagine how such remarks would play in every Arab capital. He would be denounced and condemned as Reagan's "Lassie," being led to another separate peace with Israel. If he challenged Reagan's words or refused to take his outstretched hand, it would ruin the entire visit—and possibly the budding Saudi-American alliance.

Fahd suddenly was making hand motions across the room to Bandar, who was seated at Vice President George Bush's table. Bandar slipped to Fahd's side. The king's face betrayed his anger.

"Go out right now and call McFarlane. The whole speech of the president must be canceled except the welcoming and ending statements or else tonight might be the end of U.S.-Saudi relations."

Bandar was shaking. "Your Majesty, how do you know?"

"Never mind. Go," the king said.

Bandar left the room and sent a butler back to retrieve McFarlane.

"Bud, what the hell do you have in the president's speech?"

"How do you know?" McFarlane asked.

"I don't know, but His Majesty knows," Bandar said emphatically.

McFarlane took a menu and scribbled a note inside and sent it to the president. He said he would go back inside, and if he gave Bandar a signal across the room, it meant that the president agreed to cut the remarks. If not, they would step out and discuss it further.

It was a tribute to Reagan's skill as an actor, Bandar thought, that the president got up at the end of dinner and gave a warm, witty, but highly truncated speech in honor of Saudi-American friendship. He had seamlessly dropped the whole "handshake" passage.

Fahd was grateful, and it was all the more satisfying when the next morning, before Fahd had breakfast with Reagan, Bandar was able to affirm to McFarlane that Saudi Arabia would start paying $2 million a month in aid to the contras into the bank account that was being managed by Oliver North and one of the contra leaders, Adolfo Calero.

But that wasn't the final gift from King Fahd. For the president, Fahd had arranged to have two of the kingdom's finest Arabian horses flown to California, where they were billeted at Bill Clark's ranch for the president's use until he was out of office. Then they could be transferred to the Reagan ranch. The king had wanted to present the horses directly to the president, but Bandar had warned him that if he did so, the horses would end up in the stables of the National Park Service because the president could not legally accept them.

"Leave it to me," Bandar had said to the king.[10]

For Nancy Reagan, the king sent a briefcase containing $2 million in diamonds. They would be held and mounted in a tiara by the jewelry designer Harry Winston in New York and would be available to the first lady whenever she summoned them. The obfuscations to cover the transfer of the Saudi gifts were worked out by a very small circle of aides in the

White House.[11] Some loyal Reagan aides felt that both the president and his wife were "receptive" to such lavish gifts in the atmosphere of entitlement that pervaded their household. Of course, the American tradition is that presidents accept gifts on behalf of the American people, not for themselves. Reagan showed no ability to parse the issue. He simply considered it an invasion of his privacy for the government to interfere in the process of gift giving by people he considered friends. Some of his staff members, however, worried that they would all be caught in a violation of the law; it had the appearance of official bribery.[12]

There *was* a sense of entitlement about the Reagans that grew clearer as the years passed. According to Bandar, Nancy Reagan asked that he hire Michael Deaver, who was leaving the White House broke, facing legal problems, and drinking heavily. Deaver had come to Bandar's office and told him that he could help Bandar a lot. He could, for instance, introduce the prince to many of the world leaders Deaver had met in the White House. Bandar asked him to look around the office at the photos of Bandar with kings, presidents, and prime ministers.

"Which world leaders do you think I am having trouble meeting?" he asked.

Yet because Nancy Reagan had asked him, Bandar hired Deaver as a "consultant" for $50,000 a month. The two men never spoke again during the year that Bandar kept him on the payroll.

At the end of his state visit, King Fahd was due to fly to Cannes in southern France, one of his favorite haunts as a young prince, when he was well-known in the casinos of Monte Carlo.

"Is your airplane here?" Fahd asked Bandar.

"Yes sir," the prince replied.

"Well, tell them to fly to Nice with your clothes because you're coming with me."

As they headed across the Atlantic, Fahd vented his anger and frustration with the Reagan administration. He felt that he had been used and manipulated by the White House. It was hard to look at Reagan's aborted dinner remarks and not see a biased American outlook or an Israeli-inspired effort to embarrass him. Saudi influence was rising in Washington and the pro-Israeli forces were alarmed by it. Reagan had been oblivious to Arab politics and the Arab context, but Fahd felt that he had discharged his duty to America. The kingdom needed state-of-the-art weaponry for its air force and air defenses. Fahd's brother, Prince Sultan—Bandar's father and the defense minister since 1962—had engendered a vibrant competition between Britain and France to sell the kingdom the high-performance fighter-bombers that would fill the Saudi air force's requirements.

It would come down to the French Mirage or the British Tornado, but it was soon apparent that the deal was tilting toward the British, raising immediate suspicions of behind-the-scenes influence or corruption. King Fahd made the first overture by dispatching Bandar to Prime Minister Margaret Thatcher to propose what would become the largest arms purchase in British history, comprising more than 130 aircraft and other weapons worth more than $70 billion over the course of the contract. The high price of the aircraft also raised questions of official bribery, which was widely believed to be endemic to Saudi arms transactions. Since Bandar's family, most prominently his father, Prince Sultan, and his older brother, Khalid bin Sultan, had supervised the kingdom's weapons purchases for decades, rumors and allegations of corruption swirled around them, though no Western government had ever presented irrefutable evidence or successfully mounted a prosecution that directly linked them to bribery. Still, as Bandar said in a 2001 interview, "If you tell me that building this whole country and spending $350 billion out of $400 billion, that we had . . . misused or got corrupted with $50 billion, I'll tell you, 'Yes.' But I'll take that any time. What I'm trying to tell you is, so what? We did not invent corruption . . ."[13] The al-Yamamah deal—the dove in Arabic—would eventually draw Bandar into the allegations of corruption arising from Britain's Serious Fraud Office.

Ian Gilmour, a Conservative minister in Margaret Thatcher's government, later said, "You either got the business and bribed, or you didn't bribe and didn't get the business."[14]

As part of the deal, Fahd also asked where the kingdom could acquire missiles sufficient to deter Iran or any other rival. Bandar told him only Russia and China (apart from the United States) produced ballistic missiles whose range and payload would make them effective as a deterrent. Fahd said that buying missiles from Moscow, whose army occupied Afghanistan, might be too much for the Americans to bear. So it would have to be China. Thus Bandar was dispatched on a double mission: he was to inform Margaret Thatcher that the kingdom was ready to enter serious talks for the largest foreign arms purchase in Great Britain's history, and he was to travel secretly to China to negotiate the purchase of surface-to-surface ballistic missiles.[15]

Fahd's visit to the United States in 1985 demonstrated the complexity of America's relationship with Saudi Arabia. What bound the two countries were covert struggles against Soviet adventurism and Iran's revolution. Yet Fahd appreciated that the Arabs were engaged in a strategic competition with Israel for influence in Washington. It would be a long struggle. Israel's bonds to America were more strongly rooted in a European intellectual tradition and a democratic system, which were plainly lacking in the kingdom. Yet because Saudi Arabia and Israel pursued congruent strategies to oppose Soviet gains in the Middle East, they both were pillars of American policy in the region, as the shah had been. It was a triangle that Machiavelli would have appreciated. The Saudis stood for oil, price stability, and anticommunism, but their culture was deeply mysterious, and their fundamentalist Islamic traditions stood in fierce opposition to many facets of Western civil society. Israel's insecurity about America's relations with the Arabs triggered competition in the American bureaucracy between advocates for an Israeli-centric policy versus an Arab-centric policy.

Shultz, the great friend of the Arabs during his Bechtel days, turned his back on his longtime Arab friends, reportedly telling them not to call him anymore, to protect his neutrality.[16]

Among Reagan's aides, William Casey was the most successful in bridging the two worlds. Both Arabs and Israelis saw him as a warrior against communism. He had no jurisdiction over the Palestinian problem and thus could not be blamed for Shultz's disinterest or fecklessness.

"Casey was an old fox," according to Prince Bandar, who admired his bureaucratic skills. "Let's say he has authorized $6 million for a legitimate operation that has been approved by the committee in Congress. He will ask us for $6 million to do the same thing. Now, we don't know that Congress has authorized [in secret] the same money. He can finance two operations and nobody can figure it out."

Casey had wanted to avenge the deaths of U.S. marines and diplomats in Lebanon and was the first among Reagan's advisers to think of Hezbollah as a target for American covert action. Hezbollah was still holding Casey's station chief, William Buckley, and this prompted U.S. and Israeli intelligence officials to focus on Sheikh Mohammed Hussein Fadlallah, who was considered to be Hezbollah's spiritual leader. A charismatic Shiite cleric, Fadlallah tended to the poor in South Beirut, and though he claimed no formal connection with the shadowy Hezbollah, he championed its cause.

On the morning of March 8, 1985, a pickup truck loaded with vegetables to conceal 750 pounds of explosives was parked in the busy market street outside Fadlallah's headquarters. The street, in the urban canyon of the Bir al Abed district, was crowded with pious Shiites, who lived in the apartment blocks that rose on either side above the shops. In late afternoon, about 250 girls streamed out of the Imam Rida Mosque after Friday prayers. The pavement was thronged with shoppers, most of them women, when the air split with the deafening roar. Fire, hot shrapnel, glass, and masonry shredded the crowd. Smoke and fire billowed, and when it cleared, bodies lay strewn grotesquely on the ground, many of them burning.

"When I woke up I found myself on fire," Hana Doughan Awali recalled. "My hair was in flames, my clothes were ablaze. I used a red wool sweater I had to put out the flames. I tried to get up, but I couldn't so I stayed on the ground, face down, with thick black smoke billowing from behind me."[17]

The blast incinerated a seven-month-old baby in its crib. In Sobhi Turmos's lingerie shop, his daughter Zeinab had been helping a bride with her trousseau. The explosion pinned them under burning debris, along with Zeinab's brother, Ahmed.

"He saw his children burning alive and he could not get to them," Fatimah Turmos said of her traumatized husband.

On the street outside, the inferno killed three children from one family who were walking home together. They were among the 80 people who died. Some 256 were injured, including nine-year-old Zeinab Darwish, who lost two of her sisters. She was left severely handicapped by shrapnel lodged in her brain. Sheikh Fadlallah was uninjured.

In the anarchy of Beirut, an elite Lebanese Christian commando unit that had been trained by the CIA, but was no longer under the direct control of any government or intelligence agency, was suspected of carrying out the bombing, perhaps with Saudi encouragement.[18] Had the Americans or their allies suborned the attack? The CIA denied it. Bandar asserted that the Lebanese unit had no sponsor but was hoping to garner American support. "The Americans didn't ask them to go and do this,"

Bandar said. "Those people [in the unit] thought if they do it, then they can buy a favor with the Americans and get them reengaged."

Many years on, it is impossible to discern the truth about the episode. But for the Americans, there would have been significant risks in striking Fadlallah while William Buckley was still captive. Any hint of CIA involvement in an attempt on Fadlallah's life could have led to Buckley's immediate execution. For the Saudis to be involved in an assassination of a revered Shiite figure would have been a high-risk venture for the Sunni kingdom at a time when King Fahd had taken a leading role to put Lebanon back together.

In the Middle East, the Saudis were better known for paying their way out of trouble, for buying protection, than for involvement in murder or assassination. Indeed, after Fadlallah survived the bombing, King Fahd sent a personal envoy, Rafik Hariri, the Lebanese billionaire, with a message that Fahd wanted to strengthen Sunni-Shiite ties.[19] The Saudis offered Fadlallah several million dollars in compensation, which he accepted in the form of medical supplies, food, and other essentials for his followers.

In the destroyed neighborhood of Bir al Abed, a banner was draped across the wreckage: "Made in U.S.A." Hezbollah grew stronger.

In the wake of the Fadlallah bombing, Hezbollah went on a kidnapping spree in Beirut. In March, they seized Terry Anderson, the Middle East correspondent of the Associated Press, two French diplomats, and a British journalist, Alec Collett. And in May and June, after *The Washington Post* published Bob Woodward's account of CIA involvement with the Lebanese commando unit, five more hostages were seized, including David Jacobsen, the director of the American University Hospital, and Terry Sutherland, the acting dean of the university's school of agriculture.

Anonymous phone callers to news organizations demanded that the United States and France end their support for Saddam Hussein's war on Iran and warned of "catastrophic consequences" if the Kuwait 17 terrorists were not released. Sometime in June, Buckley, who had been beaten and tortured, died in captivity.

Terrorism was rampant across the region. A Royal Jordanian jet with sixty-five passengers was hijacked in Beirut on June 11 and blown up the same day after the passengers were released. Three days later, TWA's Flight 847 from Athens to Rome was hijacked, leading to seventeen days of tense negotiations over Israel's release of Shiite prisoners taken during the Lebanon

War. One American passenger, Navy diver Robert Stethem, was murdered and his body dumped out of the plane in front of television cameras.

In October 1985, Palestinian terrorists under the command of Muhammad Abbas, also known as Abu Abbas, seized the Italian cruise liner *Achille Lauro* in the Mediterranean, killing a disabled American passenger, Leon Klinghoffer, and dumping his body in the sea. Reagan authorized an assault on the ship by U.S. Special Forces, but the Palestinian gunmen stayed one step ahead of them, disembarking in Egypt and fleeing Cairo on an Egyptian airliner. American warplanes intercepted the plane, bringing it down in Sigonella, Italy. But the U.S. commandos soon found themselves, and their prey, surrounded on the tarmac by Italian police. Italian Prime Minister Benito Craxi, outraged that U.S. officials were taking Italian sovereignty for granted, allowed the terrorists to leave by another plane to Belgrade. From there, Abbas made his way back to Baghdad.

In early 1986, Duane R. Clarridge, one of the CIA's top covert officers and the one who had supervised the early contra war for Casey, flew into Baghdad on a mission that experienced Middle East experts told him was insane and sure to fail.

Clarridge had requested that Jordan's intelligence agency, one of the CIA's closest allies in the Middle East, provide him with an introduction to Saddam Hussein, or someone close to the Iraqi dictator who could make a decision to bring Iraq into the fight against terrorism, the one that Clarridge hoped to manage.

Clarridge was educated at Brown and Columbia universities and was a born adventurer. Among his heroes were Lawrence of Arabia and Frederick Townsend Ward, the nineteenth-century mercenary who helped the Chinese emperor put down the Taiping Rebellion. He knew more about Nepal and India, his first postings as a clandestine officer, than about the Middle East. But he had served in Turkey and Rome, where he had helped run plots to overthrow Colonel Qaddafi.

Casey liked his spirit. Dewey, as everyone called him, was an innovator who worked around obstacles and took chances because he hated to fail. His critics worried that he always flew a little too close to the sun. Now he was chief of the CIA's counterterrorism center, an organization that many believed was doomed from the outset because the CIA's culture was organized geographically. There was a Near East Division, a European Division, etc. Without "turf," the new center had no claim to CIA officers and agents in the field. They reported to station chiefs and regional division chiefs, all of whom jealously guarded their domain.

But Casey, with Clarridge's help, was out to change the culture because it was failing in the battle against Islamic extremism. In December 1985, Clarridge went up to the seventh floor at CIA headquarters to tell Casey what the director already knew: The agency was on the back of its heels. They had to go on the offensive or the terrorists would win, Clarridge said. The word was out in Iran, Lebanon, and across the region that America was susceptible to terrorism. Casey agreed. He said he was under pressure from Reagan to do something and asked Clarridge to drop everything and put his thoughts on paper. A month later, Casey established the counterterrorism center with Clarridge as its director.[20]

Right off the bat, Clarridge looked for something spectacular to put the new center and its mission on the map. The *Achille Lauro* disappointment was still fresh in the public's mind. What if he could capture Abu Abbas? Clarridge asked his senior staff whether Saddam Hussein might be induced to give up Abbas if Iraq's role could be hidden. The agency had been supplying so much satellite intelligence to improve Saddam's fortunes in his war with Iran that Clarridge believed the CIA was entitled to some payback. He decided he would personally go for it. During his final approach into Baghdad across the Euphrates River and then the Tigris, which meanders through the center of the Iraqi capital, Clarridge was glued to the plane's window. When the door of the executive jet opened, the blast of an oven rushed in mixed with sand and grit.

Dr. Fadil Barak, Saddam's director of general intelligence, greeted Clarridge unsmilingly in Baath Party dress: green khaki and a sidearm. They drove to a guesthouse in a convoy of black Mercedes Benzes. Clarridge was under the mistaken impression that Iraq, in order to receive American satellite imagery, had promised to cease all support for terrorism and to "provide the U.S. government with information about terrorists and their activities."[21]

Perhaps someone at CIA headquarters believed this pledge to be sincere, if it was ever really made, but the overwhelming evidence was that it had been repeatedly violated and the CIA knew it. The agency had blithely ignored this condition of its assistance in the same manner that it had effectively ignored Saddam's use of chemical weapons. So there was Clarridge telling Dr. Barak that he had come from Washington for the express purpose of asking Saddam to turn over Abu Abbas so he could be tried for the murder of Leon Klinghoffer. Iraq, as Clarridge knew very well, was an ardent supporter of the Palestinian cause. Abbas was something of a hero there, a Palestinian freedom fighter who sat with Arafat on the PLO's executive committee.

Dr. Barak's eyes widened as Clarridge explained his plan: the CIA and Iraqi intelligence could work together to induce Abbas to fly to Yemen, one of the few countries that would receive him, and while the plane was in flight, U.S. air force jets would force it down in a friendly Persian Gulf country, Bahrain or Saudi Arabia, and arrest him.

"By the time I finished, his demeanor clearly signaled that he, too, thought I was insane," Clarridge later recalled. "In a bizarre way, Barak took it almost personally. He seemed insulted that we would dare ask such a thing."[22]

Clarridge pressed to see Saddam personally, but his host stalled. There was lunch, then a meeting with Tariq Aziz, Saddam's foreign minister, who told Clarridge that he was asking the impossible. After a frustrating day, Dr. Barak treated Clarridge to a wild ride to the airport at speeds over 120 miles per hour. As the car careened down the airport highway, Clarridge's blood boiled.

"I felt the Iraqis had acted in bad faith, they had suckered the U.S. government into a deal with no intention of fulfilling their end of the bargain," Clarridge wrote. "I felt frustrated that the American government was helping them at all and enraged that Iraq was getting away with harboring criminals who murdered innocent people in acts of terror. I suspected that my government, and this was what really pissed me off, would uphold our part of the agreement."

And he was mad that he had failed. Dewey did not like to fail. So he turned in his seat to face Barak, who had taken the wheel of the Mercedes for the Nascar-like run to the airport.

"Tell Abu Abbas I am coming after him, and when I find him, and I will, I am going to kill him," Clarridge said. He repeated the threat. Barak was silent.[23]

Within weeks of Clarridge's secret mission to Baghdad, President Reagan dispatched American warplanes to bomb Libya to punish Muammar

Qaddafi for his extensive involvement in the training and financing of terrorism. Suddenly, Weinberger's objections to using military force melted away. Qaddafi's support for terrorism was blatant and had been well documented by intelligence monitoring of Libyan communications.

The triggering event for the bombing raid was a terrorist attack on April 5 in West Berlin at the LaBelle Disco, a hangout for American servicemen. A bomb went off, killing one American and mortally wounding a second. Dozens were injured. U.S. intelligence intercepted two messages from the Libyan Peoples Bureau in East Berlin. One, just before the bomb went off, said that a "joyous event" was imminent. A second message, just after the explosion, reported that the operation had been executed successfully. It was enough of a smoking gun for Reagan to act.

François Mitterrand, the French president, and Felipe González, the Spanish premier, both refused permission for American F-111 bombers, flying from bases in Great Britain, to cross their territory. The bombers had to fly a long dogleg over the Atlantic to the Straits of Gibraltar and then turn eastward into the Mediterranean. One bomber was lost on the Libyan coast, but the others hit an array of targets in the middle of the night on April 15, destroying bases and barracks, including Qaddafi's headquarters in Tripoli, where one of his adopted daughters was among those killed.

Though Qaddafi was defiant in his condemnations of American militarism, the Libyan leader went into seclusion and Libyan support for terrorism seemed to decline for a time, but that would prove an illusion.


In May, a secret American mission landed in Tehran, led by McFarlane and Oliver North. McFarlane had left the White House to work as a consultant to the NSC. Rear Admiral John Poindexter had taken over as national security adviser. McFarlane's journey to Tehran would go down as one of the most bizarre episodes of American diplomacy, one that was rich in rationalizations of its import but devoid of any practical result beyond a craven offering of sophisticated American weapons in exchange for American hostages being held in Beirut.

For McFarlane, the secret mission represented a strategic opening to Iran, much like the opening to China that Nixon and Kissinger staged in 1971. McFarlane had joined the camp of muddled thinkers who, like the Israeli operatives working directly under Prime Minister Shimon Peres,

had convinced themselves that Ayatollah Khomeini's revolution was teetering: it was vulnerable to submission by the Communist Tudeh Party, or
it might be shoved aside by a Soviet invasion force or toppled by Iraq, a
Soviet client. By reaching out to "moderate" forces in Iran, America could
win back Iran as the West's natural ally in the Persian Gulf.

This line of thinking cut the Arabs completely out of the equation. Indeed, it required a betrayal of the Arab agenda, which was to support Iraq
as the bulwark against Khomeini's rising power in the region.

Aboard the plane with McFarlane were Howard Teicher of the NSC
staff, George Cave, the former CIA station chief in Tehran during the
time of the shah, and Amiram Nir, a counterterrorism adviser to Peres,
who kept senior intelligence officials in the dark.

Philip Dur, the NSC aide who left his White House job as the enterprise got under way, said he believed that the Iran initiative was driven by
Israeli diplomacy that also appealed—because it was perceived as a
strategic play—to the vanities of some of the American participants. But
more important, it grew out of the pressure that Reagan was applying to
the NSC to win the release of the American hostages in Lebanon.[24]

Two influential voices in the intelligence community, Graham Fuller,
the CIA's national intelligence officer for the Middle East, and Winfred
Joshua, the Pentagon's intelligence officer for the Soviet Union, argued
that Iran was surrounded by Soviet threats and so it was in America's interest to seek an immediate rapprochement.[25]

Fuller had made his case in a draft Special National Intelligence Estimate that was debated in the spring and summer of 1985. The most controversial aspect of Fuller's argument was that by providing selected arms
and military spare parts to Iran, the United States could demonstrate the
seriousness of its intentions to improve relations.

Weinberger and his aides said the idea was "absurd." Shultz at that
time was carrying out a policy called Operation Staunch, aimed at shut-
ting off the flow of arms to Iran to force it to accept a cease-fire in the
war. American policy, always of two minds, had developed full-blown
schizophrenia.

Israel's leaders fanned the notion that Iran's revolution was teetering
because their own national interests were at stake. There were still thousands of Iranian Jews in Iran, many of whom wanted to leave and others
who had been imprisoned. McFarlane had sent Michael Ledeen, an
NSC consultant who was also a right-wing activist, to Israel to discuss

what to do about Iran with Prime Minister Peres. And Peres, always the one to spot an opening, went into action, sending David Kimche, the former Mossad official, to Washington with an astounding message.

"A year or so ago," Kimche told McFarlane on July 3, 1985, "we began talking with Iranians who are disaffected by all the turmoil in their country. We believe we have made contact with people who are both willing and able over time and with support to change the government."[26] Not only that, he added, they were willing to establish their bona fides by arranging for the release of all the American hostages in Lebanon.

McFarlane said he would take the offer straight to the president. Kimche pushed hard. The Israelis were aware—because Bob Woodward had disclosed it in an article—that the CIA and the Saudis had been engaged in covert antiterrorist operations against the Iranian-backed Shiite underground in Lebanon. Ever jealous of Saudi access, the Israelis were now making their own powerful play for Reagan's attention—the release of all American hostages.

Before he left, Kimche pressed McFarlane on how far America was willing to go to change the regime in Tehran. "You know, Bud, things could get violent at some point."

"Well, yes, they often do in the Middle East," McFarlane replied.

"I mean, what if Khomeini should die?"

McFarlane was now staring intently at his guest. "Are we talking about old age, or some less natural cause?" he asked.

Kimche, the Oxford-educated sophisticate who as a senior Mossad official had undoubtedly sanctioned assassinations, replied, "Well, accelerated perhaps by one means or another."[27]

McFarlane rebuffed the assassination talk, but he and Kimche shared an exaggerated fear that the Soviet Union threatened imminently to overrun Iran. McFarlane could recite the ominous statistics of Soviet forces in the region: one hundred thousand troops in Afghanistan, twenty-six divisions stationed on Iran's northern border "conducting daily exercises that involve the same tactics that would be used in a thrust toward the Persian Gulf," where the Soviet navy had coveted a warm-water port since the days of the czars.[28]

The flaw in McFarlane's "strategic" justification from the beginning was that he was never forthright about how remote such a threat was in fact. Soviet troops in Afghanistan were bogged down fighting the CIA-backed insurgency. For Moscow to contemplate yet another invasion, this time of revolutionary Iran, was virtually unthinkable. Yet without this "strategic" rationale, any Iran opening looked more like a blatant arms-for-hostages transaction.

The day before Kimche came to the White House, McFarlane had accompanied Reagan and the first lady to Arlington National Cemetery to the grave of Robert Stethem, the navy diver killed in the TWA hijacking. Later they met with the returning hostages from the flight. Reagan had been overcome, and McFarlane realized that this tough-minded and ideological president was quick to surrender to his emotions.

A president should stand aloof, McFarlane thought. Displays of emotion, in McFarlane's view, were a "serious flaw" that made Reagan vulnerable "to foreign exploitation of human suffering." He had tried to warn the president of the "consequences of such a weakness." But Reagan said he couldn't help it.

"I just can't ignore their suffering."[29]

Despite his public resolve not to reward terror, Reagan was eager to pursue any opening that might free the hostages. He was far less interested in strategic dialogue with Iran's mullahs.

On July 13, 1985, Reagan went into the Bethesda Naval Hospital for surgery to remove several polyps from his colon. Five days later, as Reagan sat in pajamas still recovering from the surgery, McFarlane asked for permission to open a channel to Iran through the Israelis and, in the presence of Chief of Staff Donald Regan, Reagan replied, "Yes, go ahead. Open it up."[30]

After Reagan returned to the White House, McFarlane presented a more detailed proposal to approve a secret Israeli sale of American anti-tank missiles and other weapons to Iran. This time McFarlane spelled out the transaction in front of the National Security Planning Group—Reagan, Bush, Shultz, Weinberger, Casey, and Regan. Shultz and Weinberger led the opposition, but Bush and Casey were in favor of playing out the string with the Iranians. Reagan deferred his decision, but only for a matter of days.

According to McFarlane, the president summoned him to the Oval Office and said, "Well, I've thought about it and I want to go ahead with it. I think it's the right thing to do."[31]

In the wake of this decision, the Israelis covertly shipped more than five hundred TOW antitank missiles to Iran on August 30 and September 13. The next day, Hezbollah released the Reverend Benjamin Weir, who had been held captive in Lebanon for more than a year. McFarlane had wanted the CIA's missing station chief, Buckley, to be the first hostage released, but he could not explain his disappointment without tipping the kidnappers as to his identity. Nor did he know that Buckley was already dead.[32] Israel was back in Washington's graces and the Arabs were being deceived like the rest of the world.

The arms had flowed, increasing Iran's potency on the battlefield. The shadowy middlemen the Israelis had introduced to the Reagan White House promised that Iran's powerful parliament speaker, Hashemi Rafsanjani, the leader of the so-called moderate faction that hoped to take power after Khomeini's death, was ready to open a dialogue.

In early 1986, McFarlane got Reagan's permission to fly to Tehran. But after three frustrating days in the Iranian capital, McFarlane was repulsed by the chaotic and undignified reception he was getting. He ordered the mission home on May 28, leaving behind another load of weapons.

The secret unraveled in the fall of 1986, when a Lebanese newspaper disclosed that the Reagan administration had been selling arms to Iran to obtain the release of the hostages in Lebanon and that McFarlane had secretly traveled to Tehran. Within the U.S. government, it was soon discovered that McFarlane, North, and their cohorts had provided Iran with detailed intelligence about the Iraqi military. In other words, after years of sharing intelligence with Iraq aimed at preventing an Iranian victory, the covert operatives of the White House had delivered to Iran a complete profile of Iraq's military deployments, strategic assessments, and plans for upcoming campaigns.

Documents later emerged showing that the CIA's deputy director, John McMahon, had pleaded with Casey to stop the White House from turning over sensitive intelligence to Iran.

"Everyone here at headquarters advises against this operation," he wrote. "We would be aiding and abetting the wrong people," and it would put the United States in the position of "tilting in a direction which could cause the Iranians to have a successful offensive against the Iraqis with cataclysmic results." It was one thing to provide the Iranians with some defensive antitank missiles, "but when we provide intelligence on the order of battle, we are giving the Iranians the wherewithal for offensive action."[33]

The White House stalled and prevaricated. Reagan complained about the damage that was being done to his presidency. "We must say something, but not much. I'm being held out to dry."[34] Washington was awash with news media leaks and exclusives on the secret opening to Iran. The revelations, startling enough as they were, were followed by a report on November 25 from Attorney General Edwin Meese that money generated from the sale of arms to the Iranians had been diverted to the contras in Nicaragua, all without notification to Congress.

The Iran-contra scandal shook the foundations of government in Washington. The White House had gone operational as a spy agency to circumvent the Boland Amendment ban on such funding. Constitutional prerogatives had been trampled by a rogue operation implanted in the offices of the National Security Council with the approval of the president and the vice president and the cabinet-level officials charged with overseeing U.S. national security, most prominently Weinberger and Shultz.

Reagan, in effect, paid ransom for hostages, something that he had said was anathema to his administration. The revelations weakened Reagan's stature, which had grown with the prospect of more frequent summit meetings with the new Soviet leader, Mikhail Gorbachev.

Three months later, when the Tower Commission laid before the Congress and the public the evidence of Swiss bank accounts, secret White House meetings, and backdated presidential approvals for covert weapons transfers to Iran and covert funding for the contras, Reagan seemed confused, uncertain of his memory. But more damning was the incompetence of the whole affair. The "strategic" opening to Iran was based on faulty or exaggerated assessments of the threat posed to Iran from the Soviet Union and an equally exaggerated confidence in the ability of Iran's so-called moderates to topple the Ayatollah Khomeini. In any case, Reagan was forced to clean house. In February 1987, Don Regan resigned as chief of staff to make way for former senator Howard Baker. Frank Carlucci, a careful technocrat, had already taken the post of national security adviser, and he brought General Colin Powell, one of Weinberger's favorites, to the White House as his deputy.

America's Arab allies were outraged to discover that Washington had been arming Iran so as to bring about the very breakthrough by Khomeini's fanatical Shiite army that they had all been working to prevent.

By early 1987, the administration was under pressure from those allies to demonstrate that it was still committed to stopping an Iranian breakthrough in the Persian Gulf. Weinberger argued in January that it was time for the United States to drop any pretense of evenhandedness and give visible support to Iraq. If that meant providing arms to Iraq, so be it, he said, knowing such a proposal would raise a storm in Congress. The real problem was not that Iraq lacked weapons. What the Iraqis needed, Weinberger admonished Carlucci and Powell, was strong leadership and a boost in morale.

"We need to stiffen them up some way," he said.

The man that the Defense Intelligence Agency chose to save Iraq from military defeat was army Colonel W. Patrick Lang, the DIO (defense intelligence officer) for the Middle East. Pat Lang, as he was known, was a beefy former Special Forces officer who was fluent in Arabic and French. The son of an army officer, Lang had been president of his high school class in Maine and married his high school sweetheart. He attended VMI, the University of Utah, and the U.S. Army War college, then served two years as an infantry officer in Vietnam. In late 1968 and early 1969, he had defended a firebase at Song Be northeast of Saigon against withering attacks by North Vietnamese divisions trying to clear the route to the capital.

Vietnam had left its mark on him. After one horrific night at Song Be, Lang had noticed that "there was one NVA [North Vietnamese army] soldier hanging on the wire with a strand supporting his chin so that his open, dead, black eyes mutely examined the Americans," asking a question that for Lang would never be answered.

"The question was, Why? Why had this been allowed to happen? Why were Americans condemned to fight these brave men so far from home? What 'threatened' American interest was worth this?"[35]

The DIA had been studying Iraq's military failures for some time. After Iran seized the Faw Peninsula in 1986, cutting off Iraq's access to the Persian Gulf, the agency's director, Lieutenant General Leonard Perroots, had come to Lang with a question. "Let's say we are asked to redirect Iraqi air power to make sure they don't lose the war. Could you do that?"

Lang said it could be done. The exercise was code-named Elephant Grass and Lang took the detailed contingency plans, laid out on maps and charts, over to the White House Situation Room, where he briefed a group of senior Reagan aides and senior military advisers. The contingency plan was on the shelf, but the Iran-contra affair had brought it back to life. As Iraqi forces faced withering attacks from Iran throughout the first half of 1987, Perroots ordered Colonel Lang to implement it.

Within the government, Lang had been the designated DIA briefer on the Iran-Iraq War. Often, Richard Armitage, Weinberger's enforcer, would dispatch Lang to brief Prince Bandar or the Kuwaitis, and at times, Lang got orders to go out to Jordan to brief King Hussein, who passed everything on to Saddam Hussein in Baghdad. The Ayatollah Khomeini had promised that 1987 would bring a crushing final offensive to topple Saddam, but the Iranians had not been able to break the Iraqi lines. They had taken the war out into the Persian Gulf, where Iranian gunboats attacked the shipping lanes on the Arab side, setting oil tankers alight and terrorizing their crews. Iran used its forward position on Faw to fire Chinese-made Silkworm missiles out into the shipping lanes, where they scored a direct hit on a Texaco supertanker. Iranian commandos laid mines in the shipping channels and it seemed the oil commerce of the Persian Gulf might come to a halt.

Reagan responded by dispatching a naval force to escort oil tankers that were placed under the American flag. Called Operation Earnest Will, this was the largest naval escort operation since World War II.

The Iraqis had their own anti-shipping weapons. The most effective was the French-made Exocet missile, which skimmed eight feet above the waves at nearly the speed of sound. On May 17, a marauding Iraqi pilot flying a Mirage F-1 with Exocets slung under the wings had loosed two of his missiles at a radar image. The target turned out to be an American frigate, the USS Stark, whose captain, Glenn Brindel, realized the danger too late.

The missiles streaked across the sea and tore through the thin aluminum hull of the warship just after 9:00 p.m. Twenty-nine sailors died immediately, and another eight died later from burns and other injuries. Among the survivors were five men who were blown through the gaping hole in the ship. They treaded water through the night, fending off poisonous sea snakes that slithered among them as they watched their ship burning in the distance.

The Iraqis said the attack was a case of mistaken identity, but the halls of the Pentagon burned with speculation that the Iraqis had been engaged in payback for the betrayal that the Iran-contra investigation had revealed.

Pat Lang was assigned to the U.S. investigating team that traveled to the Persian Gulf to interview the crew of the Stark. In Baghdad, they sought answers from Iraq's military and intelligence chiefs. They never found any evidence that the Iraqis had deliberately launched the attack, but Lang used his time in Baghdad to introduce himself as broadly as he could to the Iraqi high command. Over a period of months, the DIA sent a variety of signals to Baghdad that if they were unhappy with the CIA for betraying them, the DIA was ready to open a new intelligence-sharing relationship.

The Iraqis bit, but Lang wondered if he was getting out on a limb. There was so much paranoia in the bureaucracy about conducting covert operations in the wake of the Iran-contra affair that Lang insisted his team be given written authorization for what it was about to do. The authorization arrived on a plain piece of paper bearing Frank Carlucci's signature. The new operation was called Druid Leader, an updated version of Elephant Grass, and when Lang and his deputy, Lieutenant Colonel Rick Francona, reached Baghdad, they unfurled a huge map of the war front in a conference room of the military intelligence headquarters. The Iraqis could see that the Americans had prepared the plans for an air war against Iran comprising more than twenty major targets behind the Iranian lines that were critical to sustaining the Iranian war effort.

For each target, Lang had brought a large pouch containing "beautiful drawings" made from satellite images. They showed Iranian air defense emplacements, structural details of buildings and fortifications. A sixty-member team from across the intelligence community had prepared a road map for destroying Iran's war-fighting capability.[36]

With this secret American assistance, the Iraqi military campaign in the spring of 1988 broke the back of the Iranian armed forces. The Ayatollah Khomeini's final offensive never materialized. The Iraqi army unleashed a series of counteroffensives that relied heavily on chemical weapons to kill Iranians in larger numbers and to break Iranian morale. Lang, Francona, and the team supporting them at DIA headquarters were intimately familiar with Saddam Hussein's reliance on chemical weapons. For Lang and for many senior officers in the Pentagon, Iraq's use of poison gas in a war of national survival was not a matter of deep concern. In April, the Iraqi army retook the Faw Peninsula, reclaiming Iraq's outlet to the Persian Gulf. Francona had flown down to Faw with an Iraqi escort to take a look at the scene of the battle, and he reported back that there were spent atropine injectors all over the battlefield. Atropine was the antidote for nerve gas and its presence indicated that the Iraqis had used gas and that it had drifted back over their own lines, forcing soldiers to stab themselves in the thigh with the injectors.

As a correspondent for *The Washington Post*, I visited the Faw battlefield on May 2, 1988, shortly after Colonel Francona, and also took note of the signs of chemical weapons use during the battle two weeks earlier. I wondered how the Reagan administration could appear so passive in the face of so much evidence that Iraq was, with explicit U.S. knowledge and complicity, violating all of the international conventions against the use of poison gas.

All along the southern front, the Iraqis punched through Iranian lines and, as they did, they launched lethal gas shells and blistering agents onto the Iranian troops. Lang and Francona commuted back and forth to Baghdad, bringing the Iraqis bomb damage assessment reports on the effectiveness of their air strikes behind the lines and offering new target packages for the Iraqi air force.

The level of American participation in the battles that made Iraq's victory in the war more certain has never been fully reported to the public. As American officials stood watch, Saddam's commanders added chemical weapons to their attack plans.

In the north, Saddam turned his poison gas arsenal against the Kurds. The mostly deadly attack took place in March 1988, at Halabja, a city framed by snowy peaks and sweeping meadows that run down to a pristine lake surrounded by fields of sunflowers. Saddam's forces turned Halabja into a gas chamber where as many as five thousand Kurdish civilians perished. I visited the town after the attack, flying in an Iranian helicopter (an American-made Huey left over from the shah's rule) because the Iranian government wanted American correspondents to see what had happened.

Iraqi jets were searching for us, hoping to block our access to the city. We flew through gorges and perilously close to the mountains as our pilot, an Iranian air force officer, violated Iraqi airspace to get to the scene of the massacre. We landed just outside Halabja on a field pocked by shell bursts.

The town was silent, seemingly empty at first. Then we saw hundreds of bodies in all manner of everyday poses. Some corpses may have been rearranged by the Iranians to maximize the impact of the image they wanted the journalists to broadcast to the world. One powerful image was a grandfather clutching an infant on a doorstep. Another family lay on the ground in a courtyard with the lunch table still set and food rotting. But no rearranging of corpses by Iranian propagandists was needed to amplify the crime that Saddam's forces had committed.

My most lasting memory of that day was of crossing a small bridge over a creek. I just happened to look down from the truck bed in which we were riding to see the bodies of a dozen or so small girls who had been playing the day of the attack. They lay like dolls splayed randomly on the gravel bed, eyes open in some cases, staring skyward. The faces seemed to beckon, as if impatient for the living to gather them in. The Iranian driver, oblivious to the scene, kept the truck moving.

The American DIA officers neither condoned nor condemned the chemical weapons attacks, though some were appalled at the civilian deaths. They were aware, as some of them explained to me later, that Saddam was adding chemical "fires" to the plans they either reviewed or discussed. Their reporting to Washington on the Iraqi chemical weapons program amplified what the Reagan administration had known since 1983—that Iraq was making extensive use of poison gas to catastrophic effect on Iranian front-line troops.

Iran may have countered with a limited number of chemical attacks with cyanide, phosgene, or chlorine, but these were random and ineffective attempts to deter the Iraqi chemical onslaught. In chemical warfare, it was a one-sided contest.

The outcry rose in Congress after those images of women and children came to light, but Republican leaders—among them Dick Cheney, who was his party's Whip in the House of Representatives—were able to block the calls for sanctions against Saddam. At the time, the Reagan strategy was regarded as realpolitik, but as time passed, it was apparent that Reagan and his top aides had rationalized their involvement with a client state that was blatantly employing weapons of mass destruction against its own people and against Iran.[37]

Of all the policy makers who were involved in the effort to shore up Iraq in its long war with Iran, only Prince Bandar has publicly expressed, in interviews with me and his biographer, any regret about the complicity of Saddam's allies in his use of gas.[38] Bandar said the simple rationale in dealing with Saddam and chemical weapons was, "This man is evil, but Khomeini is more evil. Iraq is bad. Iran is worse." Looking back, Bandar said simply, "This was not my proudest moment . . . We let humanity down."

Iran had become the enemy for America, too. On April 14, 1988, a month after Halabja, one of the U.S. warships on escort duty in the Persian Gulf hit an Iranian mine, with catastrophic results.

The USS *Samuel B. Roberts* was a light frigate and was pulling escort duty at the southern end of the Persian Gulf when one of its lookouts spotted mines in the water off the starboard bow.

Commander Paul X. Brinn, captain of the 4,000-ton vessel, ordered full stop. The ship's turbine quickly reversed thrust, sending shudders through the hull. Brinn's only choice was to retrace his course, and he nudged the vessel into reverse. The ship was gently backing through the light chop just before 5:00 p.m. when it suddenly lurched up and bowed. The sea erupted. A thunderous blast enveloped the stern, sending a hundred-foot shaft of flame up through one of the exhaust vents from the engine room four decks below. A mine had detonated directly under the ship, snapping the keel and ripping a twenty-five-foot hole in the hull. The ship's engine was blown off its mounts. Seawater flooded into the vessel, but miraculously no one was killed and the frigate did not sink. The crew fought a raging fire and flood belowdecks until the ship was stabilized.

The mine attack, which could be traced by U.S. intelligence directly to an Iranian mine-laying vessel seized the previous year, was an act of war. The mood among Reagan's senior advisers was overwhelming for retaliation. Reagan had no inhibitions. It was time to teach the Iranians a lesson. Cap Weinberger was no longer there to block the initiative.

Yet this was not the Reagan of the first term. Frank Carlucci and Colin Powell would brief the president on developments in the Middle East or Soviet Union and, afterward, walking down the hall, one of them would ask, "Do you think that was an approval?"

Reagan may not yet have been afflicted overtly by the onset of Alzheimer's disease, whose symptoms emerged definitively in 1992. But there was so much anecdotal evidence of Reagan's forgetfulness from 1987 onward that it is impossible to know to what extent he remembered, from one day to the next, the threads of American foreign policy. Nevertheless, the president authorized a frontal attack on the Iranian naval forces in the Persian Gulf. The Joint Chiefs under Admiral William J. Crowe Jr. came up with a plan to destroy two Iranian naval bases on oil platforms. The third element of what was called Operation Praying Mantis was to attack and sink the Iranian warship *Sabalan,* a 310-foot frigate with a crew of five hundred that had been harassing and firing on commercial ships passing through the Strait of Hormuz.[39]

Reagan was increasingly absent as commander in chief. He met with his aides in the Oval Office or Situation Room and he listened to the intelligence briefings and made comments that sounded like assent when a consensus formed around a recommendation. But Reagan didn't probe, and that was unsettling because it raised the question in the minds of his aides of what he really understood. As one of his top national security aides told me in an interview years later, Reagan's advisers were genuinely nervous about whether the president could comprehend the fast-moving and complex military challenge in the Persian Gulf. And if that was the case in the Middle East, what did it imply for the larger questions of the superpower standoff?

Four days after the *Roberts* was crippled by the mine blast, Frank Carlucci, the technocratic defense secretary, stepped into the briefing room at the Pentagon to say that retaliatory strikes were under way. He called it a "measured response" and withheld any information about the plans to sink Iranian warships. American vessels supported by A-6 Intruders from the carrier USS *Enterprise* moved in on the two oil platforms, surprising a large contingent of Iranian Revolutionary Guards, some of whom returned fire while others heeded a warning and boarded their boats to evacuate unmolested.

Just after 9:00 a.m., marines landed by helicopter on the Sassan oil platform, cleared it of weapons, and then set charges that detonated after they departed. To the east, another naval group destroyed the Nasr platform on Sirri Island, near the Strait of Hormuz.

The American action triggered a rash of gunboat attacks. A half dozen Iranian speedboats were blown out of the water, along with a larger Iranian fast attack vessel, *Joshan*, which fired an American-made Harpoon missile that barely missed striking the USS *Wainwright*, a destroyer.

All during the day, U.S. ships and warplanes searched for the *Sabalan*. Finally it was spotted "hiding" at anchor between two oil tankers at Bandar Abbas, the Iranian port. Carlucci and Crowe would not give permission to attack the ship out of fear that the commercial vessels would be damaged. The Iranian frigate *Sahand*, the sister vessel of the *Sabalan*, came out from its base at Bandar Abbas to challenge U.S. warships. Carlucci, who was with Admiral Crowe in the Pentagon's underground command center, authorized a navy task force to sink the *Sahand*. Just after 4:00 p.m., a news media pool on a command ship heard the radio message come in from the commander of the Middle East Force: "*Sahand* is in your vicinity, take him."

Within minutes, A-6 Intruders raced in, launching a dozen Harpoon missiles and laser-guided bombs at the frigate. The USS *Joseph Strauss* joined the melee. *Sahand* took devastating hits. Smoke engulfed the vessel. A helicopter scout reported that bodies were "everywhere" on deck and in the water. Then the ship's magazine exploded and the vessel went down within minutes. The American warships did not move in to rescue survivors.

It looked as if the battle was over. Then, just as the sun was dropping behind the peaks of Oman that loom over the Strait of Hormuz, the *Sabalan* slipped out of its hiding place and ran for open water. It was blocked by three American warships that arrayed themselves across the channel. A lone A-6 swooped down on the trapped frigate and dropped a five-hundred-pound bomb down its smokestack, triggering a massive engine room explosion. Crippled and dead in the water with numerous casualties belowdecks, the *Sabalan* was burning. In the Pentagon command center, Crowe turned to Carlucci and said, "I think we've shed enough blood."

"I think you're right," Carlucci replied.[40]

*Sabalan* was left for the Iranians to recover. Operation *Praying Mantis* was over.

Carlucci felt that he and Crowe had shown some restraint. He said the military "didn't like that decision" to spare the *Sabalan* once she was crippled and on fire, an easy trophy for the fleet. But to Iran, whose leaders had sacrificed hundreds of thousands of young men at the front and who had seen America and its Arab allies lend support to the Iraqi war machine, Operation Praying Mantis was a disproportionate act of bloodletting.

There is little evidence that Reagan understood the battle plan and its results well enough to appreciate the impact of one of the largest U.S. naval engagements since Vietnam.


Iran was now suffering as never before in the twentieth century, and its leaders worked to keep the country's anger focused outward. Iraq had unleashed new long-range ballistic missiles that could reach Tehran in a new round of what was being called the "war of the cities." (In earlier missile exchanges, Baghdad had been hit, but Tehran was beyond the range of early Scud variants.) Suddenly hundreds of thousands of Iranians fled the capital. On a visit to Tehran, I caught a glimpse of an incoming Iraqi Scud. It arched across western Iran, coming down from the stratosphere at seventeen thousand miles per hour and sending out a sonic boom that meant to all who could hear it that it was about to obliterate an apartment block or incinerate a neighborhood.

There was a new sense in the Middle East that America was on the offensive, but as a clumsy giant. On July 3, the USS *Vincennes*, an Aegis-class guided-missile cruiser stationed off the Iranian port of Bandar Abbas, challenged a commercial airliner that had just taken off from the port city for its regular flight to Dubai across the Strait of Hormuz. The airliner did not respond to repeated radio warnings to change course, and the captain of the *Vincennes*, Will C. Rogers III, became convinced that he was facing a hostile Iranian F-14 fighter.

Rogers and his highly trained crew simply misread all the signals that should have indicated to them that the approaching plane was a civilian commercial flight. In one of the most tragic mishaps of the American deployment in the Persian Gulf, *Vincennes* fired one of its antiaircraft missiles and destroyed the airliner as it was still climbing through twelve thousand feet for its twenty-minute flight to Dubai. The Airbus disintegrated in midair. All 290 passengers and crew, including 66 children, fell into the sea. For months, Iranian television replayed video from the rescue boats that journeyed out in the eerily calm waters to retrieve bodies.

With America so prominently engaged, and with Saddam rampant on the battlefield, Khomeini took the "bitter poison," as he called it, and ended the war.

The conclusion of the eight-year contest brought no peace to the Middle East. Iran, like a defeated Germany at Versailles, was nursing a towering set of grievances against Saddam, the Arabs, Ronald Reagan, and the West. And Iraq ended the war as a regional superpower armed to the teeth with boundless ambition. But it would take some time for America to understand.

Reagan had effectively given up on achieving anything in the Holy Land, and since December 1987 the region had convulsed in a new spasm of violence—called the intifada—but this one was unlike anything the region had witnessed in a century of conflict.

Yitzhak Rabin was in Washington that December when an inexplicable uprising erupted in the Gaza Strip, the twenty-five-mile stretch of sand dunes along the Mediterranean.

It came from nowhere: a traffic accident in which an Israeli truck crashed into a line of cars, killing four Palestinians. The young men of Gaza turned the funerals of their comrades into a mass demonstration that spilled out of the Jabaliya refugee camp to the rest of the strip and then to the West Bank, where it ignited day after day of stone throwing, rioting, and strikes.

Clearly something had snapped in the Palestinian community. Its children were no longer passive. What was striking was that they were so young. Palestinian boys raised under occupation had tapped some vein of courage to face Israeli tanks. They threw rocks at armored Israeli vehicles with slings, as David had against Goliath. They blocked intersections and set tires alight. They wrapped their checkered kaffiyehs tightly around their faces so the Israeli undercover police could not identify them.

Rabin had been in a meeting with Colin Powell, Reagan's national security adviser, and Powell's Middle East aides on the NSC staff, Robert Oakley and Dennis Ross. Powell wanted to know how Rabin was going to deal with the phenomenal violence that was unfolding in the occupied territories.

Rabin was not a man to mince words. He looked at them and said he had given orders for the uprising to be crushed in two weeks' time.[41]

The Americans were surprised that Rabin could not see what the world could see: children with stones fighting the Israeli army. They had stolen the David-and-Goliath paradigm from Israel, which had always seen itself as the underdog against one hundred million Arabs. The rebellion had no name, until the young men began to refer to it as their "intifada"—a word that connotes the physical throwing off of oppression.

Yasser Arafat, the chairman of the PLO, and his top lieutenants, all living in Tunis since their exile from Beirut, were astounded by the television images. "Nobody had been calculating on such an *intifada* with its force and power," Salah Khalaf observed, and Arafat immediately embraced the uprising, speaking out about the heroic youth—"children of the stones"—fighting for their freedom in the territories.[42]

At the same time, Arafat frantically opened lines of communication through Fatah agents in Gaza and the West Bank to assert some leadership over the rebellion. It was already being said that the rebellion had started because there was no Palestinian leadership. And it was true. There was no government to do anything for the young generation of Palestinians who had little prospect for jobs or hope in the squalid confines of the camps.

True to his word, Rabin returned home and tried to crush the uprising, ordering Israeli security forces to shoot rock-throwing youths, which they did. But the shooting of young Palestinians drew international condemnation. Rabin's longtime aide, Eitan Haber, said that, faced with this dilemma, Rabin and his chief of staff, General Dan Shomron, came up with the idea to break the bones of the young men through a policy of "might, power, and beatings."

During this period, I visited Gaza and went straight to Shifa Hospital to see these young fighters. There I encountered, in bed after bed, young boys with their arms suspended in the air in plaster casts. Their bones had been broken systematically by Israeli Shin Bet officers of the internal security service. Soon, news photographers caught some of the beatings on film, setting off new waves of condemnation.

Rabin became frustrated. "What can we do now, go back to killing?"[43]

Many people close to Rabin say that it was during the early intifada that he began to realize that there was no military solution to the struggle with the Palestinians, a native population that was so intensely opposed to occupation that its youth were spontaneously rebelling, fighting tanks with stones twenty years after Israel had seized their grandfathers' lands during the Six-Day War. Powerful voices urged Rabin to take a harder line, including Henry Kissinger, who told a group of American Jewish leaders over breakfast in February that the intifada should be "brutally and rapidly" suppressed.

"The first step should be to throw out television, a la South Africa," Kissinger told them, referring to the apartheid government's attempt to block the release of images of beatings and killings by security forces. "To be sure, there will be criticism," he said, "but it will dissipate in short order. There are no rewards for losing with moderation."[44]

Arafat had put his top military commander, Khalil al-Wazir, known as Abu Jihad, in charge of binding the PLO to the intifada, and by early 1988 he had established lines of communication with the intifada's leaders, working out of his villa in Sidi Bou Said, a village outside the capital of Tunisia. It was a traditional streetscape of high whitewashed walls and terraces, where bougainvillea accented lush gardens that were decorated with hand-painted tiles.

It was there, against Arafat's military commander, that Rabin decided to strike. A force of Mossad officers and commandos landed from the sea. Others had flown in on Lebanese passports and rented minivans for transport. Outside Abu Jihad's villa, they cut the phone lines and killed a driver and two bodyguards, using guns with silencers. About twenty commandos maintained a perimeter while the hit team moved into the villa. One of them was a tall, blond woman with a video camera recording the assault. Abu Jihad heard the disturbance in the house. He grabbed a pistol and rushed into a corridor, but he was cut down in a hail of gunfire. When he hit the floor, there were more than sixty bullet wounds all over his body.[45]

Israel's leaders were veterans of such operations. Dan Shomron had planned the rescue raid at Entebbe that saved one hundred passengers of a hijacked Air France flight in 1976. His deputy chief of staff, Ehud Barak, had led a raid into Beirut in 1973, in which a team assassinated two of the planners of the Munich massacre. The chief of military intelligence, Amnon Shahak, had also been on the Beirut raid with Barak.

The next day, they radiated a celebratory mood. Shimon Peres fended off a question by saying, conspiratorially, "I am not here." Prime Minister Yitzhak Shamir, who had hunted and killed ex-Nazis for the Mossad after World War II, told the cabinet that he had heard the news on the radio, "just like you."

The assassination of Abu Jihad was in all likelihood a warning to the PLO not to exploit the intifada, which posed a new kind of threat to Israeli society—the radicalization of the internal Arab population. The assassination had followed a PLO raid into the Negev, also planned by Abu Jihad, in which three Israelis had been killed near the Dimona reactor; the Palestinians had been trampling across Israeli "red lines" more brazenly.

For the Reagan administration, the Palestinian uprising was a painful reminder of how much the president had hoped to accomplish in the Middle East and how little he had to show for his electoral mandate and his two terms in office. George Shultz, the Bechtel man who might have been expected to develop a strong rapport with Arab and Israeli leaders, had instead spend most of his long tenure dealing reactively, and often churlishly, with Middle Eastern events. Now he was poorly positioned to influence them.

Reagan was more and more detached—whether it was Alzheimer's-related dementia, fatigue, or an incurious nature about the region that had disappointed him—and so for Shultz there was little time left. Israel's democracy was dysfunctional. Neither Likud nor Labor could muster a majority; its leaders shared power in a paralyzing coalition. Shultz went to the Middle East in early 1988 to push for new talks on Palestinian autonomy, an issue that had been stuck since the Camp David Accords in 1979. When it became clear that the American secretary might table a peace plan that would go beyond Camp David in conferring self-rule on the Palestinians, Shamir and the Likud side of the divided Israeli government worked assiduously to undermine him. Shamir sent Ehud Olmert, then a rising Likud parliamentarian, to tell Shultz, "If the secretary expects us to accept the principle of territory for peace, I don't think anything will start."[46] Other warnings came in from Likud channels to Washington: Shultz would be inviting a confrontation if he pressed a proposal with tight deadlines for negotiations that could lead to Palestinian self-rule. Menachem Begin even roused himself from his isolation to denounce the plan.

Yet Arafat saw Shultz's diplomacy as an opportunity. He was eager to turn the power of the intifada into political gain. The PLO leader worked behind the scenes to stage a meeting in East Jerusalem between Shultz and Palestinian notables who were loyal to the PLO. But Arafat was embarrassed by the young leaders of the intifada. They saw Shultz's mission as a ploy to tame their rebellion with a false promise of peace. Their opposition caused Arafat to back off.

There was Shultz in the lobby of the American Colony Hotel in East Jerusalem, where the news media was encamped, but no Palestinians showed up to meet him. Yet perhaps because he was near the end of his tenure, Shultz spoke with a new clarity about the region that had defeated his modest statecraft. In Cairo, he told the Egyptians that the Arab-Israeli conflict was a "competition between two national movements for sovereignty on one land." It was the first time a secretary of state had returned to the language of the United Nations partition of Palestine, when sovereignty had been a concept the world embraced for the Palestinian Arabs, just as it embraced it for the Palestinian Jews. From Cairo, Shultz spoke with a wisdom that went beyond the circumscribed Middle East diplomacy of the Reagan years. The fate of Zionism, he said, was intertwined with the fate of Palestinian nationalism. His very presence also made the point that the fate of both was dependent on American leadership.

The Shultz peace initiative collapsed, but his efforts were not for naught. A Palestinian aide to Arafat, Bassam Abu Sharif, wrote an authoritative essay that showed that former radicals within the PLO movement were ready for peace. Abu Sharif had come out of the Popular Front for the Liberation of Palestine, the hard-line faction dedicated to terrorism, and the scars he bore—his four missing fingers and pockmarked face— were the traces of an Israeli letter bomb that had nearly killed him in Beirut.

"We believe that all peoples—the Jewish and the Palestinians included—have the right to run their own affairs, expecting from their neighbors not only non-belligerence but the kind of political and economic cooperation without which no state can be truly secure." Abu Sharif said that the Palestinians were ready to search for a political model to end the conflict "because no one can build his own future on the ruins of another's."[47]

In Algiers that summer of 1988, Arab heads of state endorsed the "heroic" Palestinian uprising as an expression of national will. King Hussein failed again to best Arafat in the rivalry over who should speak for the West Bank Palestinians. It was the last time he would try. On July 31, the king went on television to declare that "Jordan is not Palestine," and therefore he was renouncing Jordan's long effort to reclaim the Palestinian West Bank or ever speak for the Palestinians again. He cut all legal and administrative ties, including the payment of salaries to municipal employees in West Bank towns.

Arafat saw only treachery in King Hussein's act, which created a power vacuum. How could the PLO administer the occupied territories? How was Arafat to deliver salaries in the West Bank? The king seemed engaged in an effort to demonstrate that the PLO could not deliver peace or stability. Indeed, the king passed a message to Shimon Peres indicating that Jordan's decision to remove itself from the West Bank was taken in hopes that the PLO would "see the light and come to terms with reality."[48]

"The king was betting that the PLO would not be capable of making an initiative [for peace]. The bet was that either there would be a failure to make a decision, or a failure to implement, and that in either case the PLO would have to go back to him," Salah Khalaf told an interviewer.[49]

Arafat and his colleagues repaired to Baghdad to debate how to respond. Out of those sessions came the conclusion that it was time the PLO entered the diplomatic arena in earnest. If they ever hoped to see a state in Palestine, they would have to accept the UN resolutions that created Israel as part of a two-state solution to the conflict.

The 1988 U.S. presidential elections were approaching and Reagan would take no step—no risk—that would endanger the candidacy of Vice President Bush.

One of Arafat's intermediaries was Mohammed Rabieh, a Palestinian American who approached William Quandt, the former Carter NSC aide, and asked him to take a query to the White House. Would the United States government establish a dialogue with the PLO if it recognized UN Resolution 242 and renounced terrorism?

Shultz responded, "If the PLO meet the three U.S. conditions, we will start talks with them."[50]

Saudi Arabia's King Fahd also intervened, sending Prince Bandar to the White House to tell Reagan that it was time to open a dialogue with the PLO. Bandar's aide, Rihab Massoud, said that Shultz's "eyes popped out" when Bandar suggested recognizing the PLO, calling it a "major shift" in U.S. policy.

"Why the hell are we doing this?" Shultz asked.[51]

It is impossible to discern why Reagan approved a message back to King Fahd that in his final days he would work to open the dialogue that was so important to the Arab leaders. Since coming into office, Reagan had seen "Armageddon" building in the Middle East, but he had refused to make any sustained investment of time and attention to act on his deeply felt conviction. Now, Fahd's message seemed to motivate him, perhaps because the Saudi monarch had helped him over eight years to fight the Communists in Afghanistan, Angola, and Nicaragua, or because the king had lavished Reagan with friendship and gifts. It is certainly possible that Reagan's sense of gratitude was reason enough to explain his willingness to take a risk near the end. Fahd's message arrived as Reagan and his wife were thinking about his legacy. The success side of his ledger in the Middle East was virtually empty.

Reagan's political aides cited polling by Dick Wirthlin, which showed that 59 percent of Americans favored opening a dialogue with the PLO, versus 19 percent opposed, and so Reagan did not have to worry about detonating a surprise in the midst of Vice President Bush's campaign for the presidency.

Still, Shamir had made it abundantly clear that Israel opposed the American dialogue.

Shultz, knowing how much Reagan wanted it, told Howard Baker, the chief of staff, "We really have no choice. If the PLO meets our conditions, we have to honor our commitment to start a dialogue."[52]

Bandar went to Tunis in October 1988, and it soon became apparent to him that the PLO leadership was working on a schedule that would bring them to the point of a new political declaration after the U.S. presidential election in November and thus Shultz's admonition that politics would not play a role was somewhat disingenuous.

A week after the election of George H. W. Bush as president, the Palestinian National Council, the PLO's parliament in exile, met and declared a state in Palestine in the name of the Palestinian people and of the "glorious and blessed *intifada*." Yasser Arafat tapped the pride of Arabs in an indigenous revolt of Palestinian youth that had done more to change the political architecture in the Middle East than any act of war or political posturing by Arab nationalists. Speaking past the lame-duck Shultz to the new administration, Arafat said, "I appeal to President Bush to adopt a new policy, not one simply aligned with Israel. We are not asking for the impossible."[53]

It took a month of complex negotiations to agree on the words that Yasser Arafat would have to say that would satisfy an irritable secretary of state who was being forced to take all the risks in succumbing to the wishes of allies.

The PLO was still an organization of factions that included Habash, Hawatmeh, and Abu Abbas of *Achille Lauro* fame, as well as other unreconstructed radicals who still dreamed of destroying the Jewish state. Shultz, with Reagan's support, infuriated all those who were working to support Arafat's declaration by denying the PLO chairman a visa to make his statement before the United Nations in New York. In a rebuke to Shultz, the UN moved its debate on Palestine to Geneva, where Arafat formally extended the "hand of peace" to Israel. He called for negotiations under the sponsorship of the UN. Arafat had not read the text that was provided to the Americans, drafted in Stockholm and approved by the PLO executive committee. That text said the PLO, speaking as the

"Provisional Government of the State of Palestine," condemned "individual, group and state terrorism in all its forms and will not resort to it."

When the State Department said Arafat had not gone far enough, he read out a second statement, saying "we totally and absolutely renounce all forms of terrorism," and then told his aides that that should be enough.

"Do you want me to striptease?" he asked.[54]

It was enough. The barrier had been broken. Shultz asked the White House for permission to declare the opening of a dialogue and Colin Powell called back in ninety minutes and said that Reagan approved. The United States was talking to the PLO. The Israelis were wounded by what they saw as a betrayal of their efforts to develop an alternative Palestinian leadership in the occupied territories. A new era of negotiation seemed possible for the first time in forty years.

As Reagan's presidency drew to a close, the shame of Lebanon weighed heavily on his record and there was a strong sense that he had left the Middle East far worse off than he found it. He had wanted to advance the peace process but was not a sufficient master of his own administration to direct the effort. He had been constrained by Congress and political currents, but also by inexorable forces over which any president has little control. An Islamic revival, secular radicalism, and unchecked militarism continued to plague a region over which no great power had been able to assert hegemony. America was only one of the players, albeit a superpower, but Reagan had discovered that, despite all of its battleships, carriers, and bombers, America was nonetheless hampered by the sheer complexity and relentlessness of the region's problems.

Reagan had been an amiable spectator who had lurched first one way and then the other under the shifting influence of his advisers. Only a crippled administration could have secretly joined both sides of the Iran-Iraq War, rationalized the use of chemical weapons, or abandoned Lebanon for blatantly political reasons.

The final anonymous attack on Reagan was delivered by Muammar Qaddafi, though it would take years for the link to Libya to be established,[55] leaving Reagan absolutely powerless, in his final days, to strike back.

On December 21, 1988, the sky erupted over the small town of Lockerbie, Scotland. With no warning, debris from a Boeing 747 jumbo jet—Pan American World Airways Flight 103—crashed to earth, killing a total of 270 people, including 11 residents of Lockerbie. Someone had smuggled a bomb into the forward cargo hold, and the explosion was triggered by an altimeter fuse after the plane climbed to thirty-one thousand feet bound for New York.

Following the attack on the marine barracks in Beirut in October 1983 (241 dead), the downing of Pan Am 103 was the most deadly terrorist strike on an American target.

Was there any limit to what the terrorist mind could imagine and what could be executed?

# 9

# NEBUCHADNEZZAR-LAND

*Saddam Hussein and*
*the Persian Gulf War*

The president of the United States was strapped into a small Gulfstream jet, flying three-quarters of the way across the country at a moment of international crisis with few of the modern accoutrements of presidential power. The reason was that Air Force One, a lumbering Boeing 707 packed with electronics, could not set down on the relatively short runway that had been carved out of the shoulder of the Rocky Mountains at Aspen, Colorado.

It was August 2, 1990, and George H. W. Bush was on his way to deliver a speech about how the end of the cold war was going to confer a peace dividend on America. It was supposed to be a time of retrenchment, with the country looking forward to bringing home U.S. troops from Germany, Japan, and elsewhere around the world. And though America had to stay strong, the defense budget was supposed to shrink as a percentage of the overall economy, and as a result it was expected that a new prosperity would envelop America.

In the cramped cabin of the Gulfstream, Bush was knee to knee with Brent Scowcroft, his diminutive national security adviser and close friend since the days when they had both navigated the egos of the Nixon and Ford administrations. They were both furiously rewriting and reworking the speech. It was going to be difficult to get too enthusiastic about a peace dividend when *The Washington Post* was calling Saddam's lightning invasion of Kuwait the "first major crisis of the post–Cold War era."[1]

An epoch had ended in the first year of George Bush's presidency and he and his political advisers had come to the conclusion that they had better start demonstrating to voters that there would be a peace dividend or there might not be a second term for the Bush administration. Now Saddam had thrown a monkey wrench in the works.

Aspen was dressed in verdant foliage under the brown peaks of the Rockies. Bush ducked and crab-walked to dismount the jet and then rushed to the Aspen home of Henry Catto, the American ambassador to Great Britain. Margaret Thatcher, just in from London, was waiting for him. The British prime minister had been invited especially to endorse the big speech that, because of Saddam, was now a hash of contradictions.

Soon they were ensconced in Catto's comfortable retreat overlooking the end of summer.

Bush brought Thatcher up to date on what he had said on the telephone to President Hosni Mubarak of Egypt and Jordan's King Hussein. Thatcher, too, had spoken with the Jordanian king, and she was disgusted with the line he was taking.

"He told me the Kuwaitis had it coming," she related to Bush. The king had added that the Kuwaitis "are not well liked" in the Arab world. Her tone indicated that she believed the cheeky little Jordanian monarch had thrown in with Saddam. No help there, in other words.

Thatcher told Bush that the Saudis were going to be the critical link in turning the situation around—"We can't do anything without them." Both leaders understood the geography of the Gulf. If Saddam's army decided to rush south along the Saudi coast, he could overrun the ports that American or British forces needed to land troops and war matériel in the region. They would have to use the Red Sea ports five hundred miles across the desert to land an army and then move it into fighting position.

"If Iraq wins, no small state is safe," Thatcher said. "They won't stop here. They see a chance to take a major share of oil. It's got to be stopped."

That made Saudi Arabia doubly crucial. "Losing Saudi oil is a blow we could not take," she added.

George Bush realized that he probably had already waited too long. He gave instructions to get King Fahd on the telephone. He and Scowcroft repaired to Henry Catto's bedroom, where the president sat on the edge of the bed and took the call. The king spoke in Arabic, but Bush could tell from the tone of his voice that he was agitated. Fahd said Saddam had lied to him. He had lied to everyone and now the Arabs faced a disaster.

"He doesn't realize that the implications of his actions are upsetting the world order. He seems to think only of himself. He is following Hitler in creating world problems—with a difference: one was conceited and one is both conceited and crazy."

The king added: "I believe nothing will work with Saddam but the use of force."[2]

Fahd said that he had already spoken to Saddam by telephone. The Iraqis had announced that the Kuwaiti ruling family would never return to power. In effect, Saddam had decapitated Kuwait's royal family. The House of Saud had shuddered. At that moment, whatever rage the Saudi royal family had directed at the greedy Kuwaitis was replaced by common cause: it was the monarchs against the destroyer.

The Saudis also suspected that Jordan was in league with Saddam for nefarious reasons. Was King Hussein hoping that his alliance with Saddam might restore the Hashemite dynasty in Saudi Arabia?[3]

"My conversation with him was strict and strong," Fahd said. "I asked him to withdraw from Kuwait now, and [said] that we would not consider any [imposed] regime" as legitimate.

"Mr. President," Fahd continued, "this is a matter that is extremely serious and grave. It involves a principle that can't be approved or condoned by any reasonable [nation]." If Iraq refused the world's demand to withdraw, "Saddam must be taught a lesson he will not forget for the rest of his life—if he remains alive."[4]

Not since King Faisal's time had a Saudi monarch spoken so forcefully. Yet in the face of this Saudi militancy—exactly what America needed at that instant—Bush fumbled. He offered King Fahd a squadron of F-15 fighters. That was it. That is what popped into the president's head. It must have been a shocking moment for Fahd. There he stood seven thousand miles away facing an army of one hundred thousand Iraqis with tanks, artillery, and armored cavalry poised on his northern border, and the president of the United States was offering a couple dozen airplanes?

The echoes of Jimmy Carter's deployment of unarmed F-15s must have been clanging in Fahd's head. Was this another pusillanimous act by a wimp in the White House? Even Bush noticed a sudden change in tone. The king did not accept his offer but said hesitantly that he thought they should discuss the options further. The phone call was over. The president wondered whether he had blown it.

Saddam's invasion of Kuwait had blindsided Washington. On August 2, hundreds of Iraqi tanks crashed across the border and soon were rolling through the fashionable shopping districts of Kuwait City. In the blink of an eye, Iraq had a stranglehold on its fabulously rich neighbor and no one could do anything about it. The emir of Kuwait and the crown prince fled by car to Saudi Arabia. The Kuwaiti army, such as it was, surrendered, and Saddam Hussein was in charge with one hundred thousand mechanized troops to enforce his will.

All the warning signs had been there, and the Bush administration had misread them. The CIA had said that Iraq was exhausted and nearly bankrupt after eight years of war with Iran and could be expected to more or less cooperate with the West as a member of the moderate Arab camp. Iraq owed more than $30 billion, principally to Kuwait and Saudi Arabia, and Iraq had also borrowed heavily in Europe and from the Soviet Union to purchase arms.

But the CIA assessment proved wrong. The war had strengthened Saddam and enlarged his ambition. The size of his army had more than doubled. By 1990, it comprised sixty-three divisions and more than fifty-five hundred tanks supported by a large Soviet- and French-equipped air force. Saddam's forces had inevitably improved because combat skills grow with experience.

Saddam had vanquished the Iranian army. In the final battle, which Saddam had named "In God We Trust"—perhaps as a tribute to America and to the assistance he had been receiving from Colonel Lang's team in Operation Druid Leader—the Iraqi army had penetrated more than sixty miles into Iran and had seized or destroyed most of the Iranian army's tanks, artillery, and war matériel, according to intelligence estimates. Khomeini had had no choice but to accept the United Nations cease-fire resolution.

In the aftermath, Iraq stood as a regional powerhouse, whose ferocity was magnified by the chemical weapons that the generals had used with devastating effect. Saddam had multiple grievances against Kuwait, whose ruling family had demanded prompt repayment of the massive debt Iraq had run up during the war. Kuwait, moreover, was cheating on its OPEC quota; its overproduction was driving down the price of Iraq's oil, along with everyone else's. There was also the Rumaila oil field dispute. Rumaila bore a rich strata of oil-bearing rock beneath the Iraq-Kuwait border zone; Saddam believed he deserved a greater share of Rumaila's bounty, since for the last eight years Iraq had been defending the Arab nation from Khomeini's assault. In payment for defending the eastern flank of the Arab nation, Saddam also wanted two Kuwaiti islands—Warbah and Būbīyā—that would improve Iraq's access to the Persian Gulf. Kuwait was having none of these demands.

The decline of Soviet power and the end of the cold war had enlarged the power vacuum in the region and Saddam was busy preparing to fill it. His view was that Iraq was entitled to leadership, notwithstanding American power.

George Herbert Walker Bush would have been willing to cede Saddam Hussein a great deal, if only the dictator had joined the ranks of the moderate Arab leaders like Egypt's Hosni Mubarak, Saudi Arabia's King Fahd, and King Hussein of Jordan. The difference between Bush and Ronald Reagan was that Bush (more than Reagan, at least) had an understanding of the world that was rooted in study, experience, and travel, all of which were missing from Reagan's background. Reagan was an attractive Hollywood icon, a conservative humorist in the vein of Will Rogers, but his mind treated history cinematically—as a jumble of fact and fiction. As a leader, Reagan had failed to overcome the rivalries of those around him. Bush was more comfortable with the push and pull of foreign policy. He had no qualms about asking dumb questions. He was able to marshal his experience and absorb the views of advisers in order to formulate a set of pragmatic options or to evaluate, realistically, their chances for success. He consulted broadly with other world leaders because of the strong relationships that he had built and invested in over time. He could commit to and stick with a decision because, while no intellectual, he had a settled understanding of political and economic forces.

Throughout his career, Bush had operated on the basis of friendship, trust, and instinct about finding the right thing to do in the world and working with allies to accomplish it, even if his worldview was that of the son of Yankee privilege. Bush had gone to Yale, made his money in the oil industry, and exuded the chamber-of-commerce goodwill that sees the world through the lens of industry and capital. There were no charity workers or squishy civil-rights liberals in the Bush dynasty.

Bush had a strong sentimental streak, but even so, he did not radiate that sense of the common man that had extended Reagan's appeal across party lines. Bush was not an actor; he was a good-natured Republican, and though tainted with a country club sense of privilege, he nonetheless had brought a raft of skills to the presidency that had been missing in Reagan (though Bush had contributed to some of Reagan's greatest mis-judgments, Iran-contra most prominently). Among those skills was how to pick key advisers and cabinet members who would not be constantly at each other's throats.

The cold war had ended, an epochal change, during Bush's first year in office. That had been the story of Bush's life. He had come of age in the last world war. He had seen the birth of the United Nations, served as U.S. ambassador to the world body, and witnessed its descent into cold war paralysis. He had joined the Nixon administration and witnessed the diplomacy that ended the Vietnam War. He had been there for the open-ing to China and served as Nixon's first envoy to Beijing. And he had run the CIA during the years Washington was tearing itself apart over Soviet intentions and détente.

Now Bush was on the cusp of a new era that he could not describe, but his experience had imbued him with a subtle—if inarticulate—perceptive power; it made him cautious but also restless in searching for the right answer, and his sometimes outwardly ponderous but always in-stinctive approach was often defamed as a lack of vision. Bush was no glib Kissinger, but he was far more grounded in the pursuit of the national interest than Reagan had been.

Bush and Brent Scowcroft were an effective team, and in Cheney, Powell, and Baker, Bush was fortunate to have gathered what he believed to be the most pragmatic and experienced of the Reagan-era bureaucrats; they all had seen the destructiveness of an anarchic foreign policy in the Middle East. Even the sharks of the Reagan years were tamed by the Bush approach, among them Bush's closest friend, James Baker, the Texas lawyer who, like Bobby Kennedy, had carried the stiletto as con-sigliere for the older-brother figure Bush represented in Baker's life.

Bush had just gotten through one of the most challenging years of his career. Germany had reunited after the Berlin Wall had come down, and a wave of largely bloodless revolutions swept Eastern Europe. Mikhail Gorbachev was keeping the Soviet army on the sidelines, just barely at times.

In the Middle East, the end of the Iran-Iraq War led to an abrupt cancellation of American military cooperation with Iraq. Colonel Lang of the Defense Intelligence Agency, who had worked so closely with the Iraqi military command, found Saddam's generals incredulous that America would simply turn its back on the relationship.

"They believed they should be our surrogates," Lang said. They believed that they were the logical partner for America to re-create the "twin pillars" alliance of the 1970s, only this time there would be only one pillar, Iraq. Who else was there? The Israelis could never fulfill such a role in the Arab world. The shah of Iran was gone. There was only Iraq and, to a lesser extent, Saudi Arabia, but everyone knew the Saudis, pampered by their oil wealth and bedouin traditions, could not be relied on to fight.

"I couldn't tell [the Iraqis], 'You're crazy, it's never going to happen,'" Lang said. Instead, he just left Baghdad and his team closed up Druid Leader and sixteen other military-to-military programs.[5] The realization that America had rejected him poisoned Saddam against the great powers. In 1989 he formed the Arab Cooperation Council with allies Jordan, Yemen, and Egypt.[6] "There is no place among the ranks of good Arabs for the faint-hearted who would argue that, as a superpower, the United States will be the decisive factor and others have no choice but to submit," Saddam told his allies gathered in Amman. Unless the Arab world was vigilant, "this area will be ruled by the United States."[7]

A new assertive belligerency was emanating from Baghdad. In February 1990, Iraqi intelligence arrested a British journalist of Iranian origin, Farzad Bazoft, and accused him of espionage. The fate of Bazoft, who was not a spy, quickly became a test of Saddam's willingness to work constructively with the West. King Hussein flew to Baghdad and urged Saddam to spare Bazoft, but as the king was returning to Amman, the journalist was hanged.

Saddam accelerated his efforts to acquire new unconventional weapons. Iraqi scientists perfected a binary nerve-gas shell just as Saddam was trying to purchase a "supergun" that could throw conventional or chemical artillery shells up to fifty miles with great accuracy.[8] Separately, U.S. Customs agents seized a shipment bound for Iraq of high-speed electronic triggers that could be used in nuclear weapons development.

In early April 1990, Saddam shocked Arab leaders by boasting about Iraq's chemical weapons' arsenal in a speech to army officers that went out over Baghdad Radio. In the middle of the speech, he warned that if Israel ever attacked Iraq again, as it had in the 1981 Osirak reactor raid, "I swear to God that we will let our fire eat half of Israel if it tries to wage anything against Iraq."

The chilling words ricocheted around the world, triggering expressions of concern and condemnation. Suddenly Iraq was an even greater menace to peace in the Middle East, and Arab neighbors rushed to Baghdad to urge caution on Saddam. Prince Bandar flew in to the Iraqi capital with instructions from King Fahd to find out whether Saddam had come unglued. Bandar's report ran to eighteen pages, a verbatim record of Saddam seething with discontent and murderous resolve.

Saddam explained that his tough words in public were intended for his domestic political audience. He was trying to "mobilize the people in part to distract them from their [economic] problems." Bandar nonetheless was nervous, because while discussing the execution of the journalist Bazoft and the assassination of a former Iraqi premier in London, Saddam said, "When I am suspicious of a guy, I kill him."

"How do you know if he is guilty?" Bandar asked.

"I look into his eyes and if I see it in his eyes, I kill him," Saddam replied, terrifying Bandar with a cold-blooded gaze as the prince wrote down the dictator's words.

Saddam walked Bandar to his car. There, under the canopy of greenery on the banks of the Tigris River, Saddam came close to the prince and told him to write down one more message for King Fahd: "Be careful of Zionist plotters and Westerners who want to split us by putting rumors of plots by us against our brothers in the Gulf. We have to be careful of these rumors." He repeated his words, saying this message was "vital" and calling Bandar "Abu Khalid," a term of endearment that means "Father of Khalid," referring to Bandar's eldest son.[9]

In May 1990, Saddam called an Arab summit meeting in Baghdad, where he projected himself as the leader of the Arab world. With Iran defeated, he said that the enemy of the Arab camp was now "Greater Israel" and its ambition to dominate the Middle East from the Nile to the Euphrates. Arafat was sitting among the leaders, and Saddam lavished praise on the intifada, committing another $25 million to sustain the Palestinian uprising. He also promised to endow the family of each Palestinian "martyr" with a generous grant.

Saddam was no Nasser, but he stood before the Arab world as a brute force, more fearsome than Nasser in what he had demonstrated in battle. He turned to the emir of Kuwait, Sheikh Jaber al-Sabah, and told him in front of the heads of state that Kuwait's actions since the end of the war—the demands for debt repayment and Kuwait's oil sales outside its OPEC quota—were punishing Iraq. The declining price of crude oil was cutting deeply into Iraq's revenues. For Kuwait to continue to violate the price discipline of OPEC amounted to a kind of economic warfare, Saddam said.

"War doesn't mean just tanks, artillery or ships," he told the Kuwaiti leader. "It can take more subtle and insidious forms, such as the overproduction of oil, economic damage, and pressures to enslave a nation."[10]

Some Arab leaders thought Saddam exaggerated his grievances to force concessions from Kuwait over the Rumaila oil field and the islands he was after. One thing was sure, Saddam was making his case. If the superpowers were no longer competing for influence in the Middle East, the role of regional powers would expand, and this realization impelled Saddam to take a harder and harder line.

At the end of the summit, Saddam, with help from Libya, unleashed a terrorist operation that sent six boatloads of Palestinian commandos against the beaches of Tel Aviv. The raid—intended to win the release of Palestinian prisoners—failed, but the effort was nonetheless celebrated in the Arab capitals. Saddam's fingerprints were everywhere. The Arab commandos were Abu Abbas's men, whose Palestine Liberation Front was still based in Baghdad and financed by Iraqi intelligence. It was the same group that had attacked the *Achille Lauro* in 1985.[11]

With this stroke, Saddam had made all of the Arab leaders complicit in his act of terror. Arafat, who had just received Saddam's grant of $25 million, could not disassociate himself from Abu Abbas's "heroic" strike against the "Zionist entity."

The Israelis raised the immediate question of whether Arafat's renunciation of terror in 1988 had meant anything. "The United States holds talks with the PLO on the assumption that the PLO has ceased terrorism," said Moshe Arens, the foreign minister of Shamir's Likud Party government. "Now we have additional proof that the PLO in fact continues terrorism," he said, adding "you can't fool all the people all the time."[12]

Bush had no choice but to suspend the dialogue with the PLO. Saddam had undermined moderation. And it was just the beginning.

As vice president and then as president, Bush had carefully avoided any condemnation of Saddam's baser instincts. He had accepted the view of King Fahd, President Mubarak, and others that Saddam was a tough customer but that he was on his way to becoming a constructive actor over time. As president, Bush had issued a secret National Security Directive that had effectively elevated Iraq's status to that of a regional force for stability: "Normal relations between the United States and Iraq would serve our longer-term interest and promote stability in both the Gulf and the Middle East," the directive said. It instructed the bureaucracy to "propose economic and political incentives for Iraq to moderate its behavior and to increase our influence with Iraq."

It was too late. Scowcroft wrote afterward that, "In early 1990, it gradually became apparent to me that Saddam had made an abrupt change in his policy toward the United States."[13] But neither Scowcroft nor any other senior Bush adviser had grasped the full meaning of Saddam's new belligerence, and they certainly took no action to deter the Iraqi dictator.

On July 17, 1990, Saddam sent Tariq Aziz to the Arab League headquarters in Cairo with a letter accusing Kuwait and the United Arab Emirates of overproducing oil and driving down prices in a manner that had cost Iraq more than $14 billion in lost revenue. He also said that Kuwait's refusal to settle the border dispute constituted "theft" of oil from the Rumaila field and that Kuwait's unwillingness to cancel Iraq's war debts constituted "military aggression."

On the same day, Saddam dispatched the first Republican Guard division to the Kuwait border. Two more would follow over the next several days.

At DIA, Patrick Lang saw the satellite imagery of Iraqi artillery and T-72 tanks coiled in new deployments near the Kuwaiti frontier and didn't know what to think. He put a call through to the American defense attaché in Baghdad, Colonel Jim Ritchie, and asked him to get in his car and drive as far south as he could and report what he saw. What Colonel Ritchie and other Western defense attachés observed confirmed the satellite imagery. The highways to the border were choked with Iraqi troop convoys.

George Bush had never met Saddam Hussein. Neither had James Baker, the secretary of state, who was off in Mongolia and Siberia preparing for talks with Eduard Shevardnadze, the Soviet foreign minister. They were busy dismantling the ramparts of the cold war. It fell to Ambassador April Glaspie, a career diplomat whose relationship with Saddam was nonexistent—she had never met with him one on one—to try to discover his intentions.

On July 24, Pentagon officials announced that the United States was going to conduct joint military maneuvers with the United Arab Emirates. Pentagon spokesman Pete Williams read a statement saying the United States remained "strongly committed" to the "self-defense of our friends in the gulf, with whom we have deep and longstanding ties."

Soon Glaspie was seated before Saddam for the first time.

"So what can it mean when America says it will now protect its friends? It can only mean prejudice against Iraq," Saddam pointed out, sounding aggrieved. "This stance, plus maneuvers and statements which have been made has encouraged the UAE and Kuwait to disregard Iraqi rights."[14] Were it not for Iraq's sacrifice of "rivers of blood" during the long war with Iran, he told her, Khomeini would have "overrun the region" and "American troops would not have stopped them except by use of nuclear weapons." But now, Saddam said, just as Iraq was engaged in trying to win some satisfaction from Kuwait through debt forgiveness and border concessions, America had intervened with warnings and joint military exercises.

He disparaged American resolve. "Yours is a society which cannot accept 10,000 dead," Saddam told Glaspie, touching a nerve that had frayed in the American psyche since Vietnam. "We know that you can harm us although we do not threaten you. But we too can harm you. Everyone can cause harm according to their ability and their size. We cannot come all the way to you in the United States, but individual Arabs may reach you."

His words, none too subtly, conjured a threat of terror attacks.

Glaspie told Saddam that she was under instructions to express American concern over his military buildup and to determine Saddam's intentions, but she added that Washington was not trying to interfere excessively. "We have no opinion on the Arab-Arab conflicts, like your border disagreement with Kuwait," she said, restating the boilerplate of American policy over nettlesome local problems over which Washington avoided taking sides.[15]

Saddam said his intentions were to keep meeting with the Kuwaitis as long as there was some promise of reaching a solution favorable to Iraq. "When we meet and when we see that there is hope, then nothing will happen," he said, "but if we are unable to find a solution, then it will be natural that Iraq will not accept death, even though wisdom is above everything else."

Glaspie seemed to hear what she wanted to hear, that Arab diplomacy was active and working to defuse the crisis. She was due to leave the country for a vacation. She told Saddam that he had given her enough reassurance for her to leave. (She later said she was "foolish" to do so.) But it is also clear that Glaspie ignored the larger reality: a rapid military buildup was under way while Kuwait's leaders were adamant that they would not cave in to Saddam's demands. They believed that Saddam was engaged in naked coercion.[16]

Saddam continued to soothe the Jordanian, Egyptian, and Saudi leaders about his military build-up, which by July 31 had reached nearly one hundred thousand Iraqi troops near the Kuwaiti border. April Glaspie's message to the president said, "I believe we would be well-advised to ease off on public criticism of Iraq until we see how the negotiations develop."[17]

Bush and his wife, Barbara, were still in bed reading the newspapers when Scowcroft appeared in the living quarters of the White House at 5:00 a.m. with the news that Kuwait belonged to Saddam. The emir of Kuwait, Sheikh Jaber, and his brother, Sheikh Sa'ad, had fled their seafront palaces. The Saudis were furious at the Kuwaitis: from the Saudi point of view, the Kuwaiti rulers had been too greedy in the oil markets and had needlessly provoked Saddam. The Saudis understood they might have to choose between Kuwait and Iraq. Saddam's major oil export pipeline lay across the Saudi desert to the Red Sea, where it disgorged 1.5 million barrels of oil per day into tankers headed for world markets. If King Fahd shut down the pipeline, Saddam would have a pretext to invade Saudi Arabia, which stood defenseless against the Iraqi army now deployed on its northern border.

Prince Saud al-Faisal, the Princeton-educated foreign minister, took a telephone call from a journalist the day of the invasion. Saud was exasperated. "I am afraid that we may have to sacrifice Kuwait as we knew it to get out of this one," he said.[18]

In the weeks leading up to the invasion, Bush had got nothing but assurances from King Fahd, King Hussein, and Hosni Mubarak—and from April Glaspie—that Saddam was engaged in coercive diplomacy but was not going to do anything rash. The United States should stand back and let the Arabs sort it out, they had advised.

Before Bush had left for Aspen, he met with his National Security Council. Journalists were allowed briefly into the Cabinet Room, where Bush surprised some by saying he would not be "discussing" or contemplating "intervention." The whole meeting lacked focus.

Dick Cheney, the defense secretary, and Nicholas Brady, the treasury secretary, debated the relative merits of blocking oil exports from Iraq and from occupied Kuwait. John Sununu, the chief of staff, pressed for economic sanctions against Iraq. General Colin Powell, chairman of the Joint Chiefs of Staff, had brought General Norman Schwarzkopf, head of the U.S. Central Command, for the military brief. The Central Command had been established to protect the Middle East from a Soviet invasion and so had been slated to be dismantled. Now Saddam had given it a new mission.

General Schwarzkopf explained how the United States could defend Saudi Arabia with air strikes against the Iraqi tank divisions. To do more, he said, would take time. It would take weeks or months to move a big ground force to the Middle East to protect the Saudi oil fields. Saudi Arabia would have to agree to let a couple hundred thousand American troops into the country. His tone implied that this would require moving mountains.

Cheney responded rather sharply, "Saudi Arabia and others will cut and run if we are weak."[19] Cheney didn't explain what he meant, but it was one of those moments when the question of "appeasement" hung over the room. Powell jumped in to ask whether they should draw a red line by declaring Saudi Arabia a vital interest of the United States. Bush agreed that they should, but that left the question begging of what to do about Saddam's army in Kuwait.

Powell's emphasis on deterring an Iraqi attack on Saudi Arabia was deliberate. He didn't think there was a national consensus to send American boys to die for some fabulously rich oil sheikhs in Kuwait, but Saudi

UNITED ST

George H. W. Bush with Brent Scowcroft: surprised by Saddam

Arabia had been America's ally since Roosevelt's time. He and Cheney had already argued the point. Powell had predicted that Saddam would install a puppet regime in Kuwait and then withdraw after a few days and the Arab world would accept it.

"We can't make a case for losing lives for Kuwait, but Saudi Arabia is different," Powell had told Cheney, adding that he was "opposed to dramatic action without the president having popular support."[20]

Cheney did not say he disagreed. He just wanted Powell to drop the post-Vietnam angst and give the president the broadest possible advice. "I want some options, general," Cheney said.

Powell had chilled. The meeting ended. "Yes, Mr. Secretary," was all he said.

At the White House, Bush didn't say what he thought about the military options. When Richard Darman, the budget director, questioned the efficacy of an oil blockade on Iraq and Kuwait, Bush interjected, "But we can't just accept what's happened in Kuwait just because it's too hard to do anything about it."[21]

That's when Powell asked the president whether they should draw a line at Saudi Arabia. Tom Pickering, the ambassador to the United Nations, pointed out the obvious—that doing so would leave Kuwait in the hands of Saddam.[22]

When Bush left the White House that morning for Aspen, he had already come to the conclusion that the United States could not accept Iraq's conquest, but what was he going to do to enforce that kind of decision? He had phoned King Hussein, who implored him to let the Arabs work out a solution. Bush found himself telling the Jordanian monarch that the world would not accept the status quo and that the invasion was unacceptable to the United States. Once the plane to Aspen was airborne, Bush heard the baritone Arabic of Hosni Mubarak on his handset. Mubarak had sworn that Saddam would not invade. He was still reeling. Bush knew that Mubarak and Saddam talked frequently on the telephone.

"Please tell Saddam Hussein that the United States is very concerned about this action. We are very concerned that other forces will be released—you know what that means, my friend. Tell Saddam *that* if you like."[23]

Did the president mean that American military forces would be released? His comment was anything but clear. In fact, it *was* a little wimp-

ish and it is hard to imagine that this tentative presidential warning rattled Saddam, who was sitting in the catbird seat with Kuwait in his hands
and no one even remotely in a position to take it away from him.

Yet by the time Bush landed in Aspen, whatever moment existed in
which the world considered it too difficult or too costly to dislodge Saddam Hussein from Kuwait was rapidly dissipating, not out of any affection for the Kuwaitis, but because the consequences had begun to sink in
of what it would mean to allow control of Persian Gulf oil to fall into the
hands of one of the most brutal and violent despots in history.

Bush's first words to Thatcher summed up what he had said spontaneously to King Hussein: "I said we couldn't accept the status quo. It had
to be withdrawal and the restoration of the Kuwaiti government."[24]

But Bush soon realized that he had gotten way out in front of himself
when Thatcher pointed out how critical the Saudis were going to be, and
all Bush could do when he got the highly agitated Saudi monarch on the
telephone line was promise him some planes.

"King Fahd's hesitation rang alarm bells in my head," Bush later wrote.
"I began to worry that the Saudis might be considering a compromise."

No wonder. If the Americans were not willing to act, the Saudis would be
forced to cut the best deal they could with Saddam. Bush had missed the
whole point of Fahd's militant tone: to encourage the United States to lead.
The United States was the only power capable of rolling back the Iraqi invasion. But it couldn't do that with words, sanctions, or joint statements.

On the morning of August 3, the National Security Council reconvened. Bush agreed that Scowcroft should set an uncompromising tone.
"My personal judgment is that the stakes in this for the United States
are such that to accommodate Iraq should not be a policy option," Scowcroft said.[25] Now the cabinet understood that Bush was establishing a
direction.

Cheney followed up. "You can't separate Kuwait from Saudi Arabia,"
he told the group. "When the Iraqis hit the Saudi border, they're only 40
kilometers from the Saudi oil fields. We have the potential here for a major conflict."[26]

CIA director William Webster had driven home the point with statistics. After taking Kuwait, Saddam possessed 20 percent of the planet's oil
reserves. If he took Saudi Arabia, he would control 40 percent. Iraq's

army was the fourth largest in the world, but with the bounty of Kuwait's oil and banking resources, his military power would mushroom. Even if he didn't take Saudi Arabia, he would be the thousand-pound gorilla next door. The dimensions of the threat came into sharper focus.

Scowcroft said the administration should pursue two tracks to defeat Saddam: one required overt military force to stop him, and the second required robust covert action to undermine and topple his regime.[27]

Powell decided it was his task to sober the civilians. An invasion of Iraq was a huge military undertaking, he told them, much bigger than the Panama incursion, where U.S. forces had driven General Manuel Noriega from power in December 1989.

"This would be the NFL, not a scrimmage." The Iraqi army was battle hardened and experienced. Saddam, he said, "is a professional and a megalomaniac. But the ratio [of forces] is weighted in his favor." Saddam had a million-man army on the ground in the Persian Gulf and the United States had virtually nothing.[28]

Powell recommended planting the American flag visibly in Saudi Arabia, assuming the Saudis would let them in with a large force to deter Saddam from moving south. But then he cut hard against the grain of Scowcroft's presentation by posing the question of whether it was worth going to war to liberate Kuwait.[29] He detected a chill in the room. The president and Scowcroft looked annoyed, though neither confronted the question. Bush was keeping his own counsel until his advisers were unified on the critical question of using force to dislodge Iraq's army from Kuwait.[30]

Bush had reason to believe that Powell would come around. Powell was no bull-headed Weinberger, though he had been influenced by Weinberger about the need to resist sending the U.S. military on ill-considered foreign adventures. Powell was a soldier who insisted that it was his prerogative as the president's senior military adviser to present his fully considered view, but Powell was not going to dig a trench and fight the civilian leadership he served. They all knew that about him. There was a strong consensus to deploy American forces in large numbers to Saudi Arabia and then to apply diplomatic and economic pressure to force Iraq to give up Kuwait. But everything seemed to hang on King Fahd.

Prince Bandar was in London when the news of the invasion came and he raced back to Washington on his private jet. The Saudis were facing a catastrophic choice. King Fahd had signed a nonaggression pact with Saddam in 1989. If the king made a move toward the Americans, if he cut off Iraq's oil pipeline that crossed the Saudi desert, he might provoke an invasion.

Bandar was shown into Brent Scowcroft's office in the West Wing of the White House just after 11:00 a.m. Bandar's close relationship with Bush and Baker during the Reagan years didn't intimidate Scowcroft, who understood that behind Bandar's irrepressible good humor was a direct line to King Fahd. Scowcroft briefed Bandar on the intelligence showing that at least one of the Iraqi divisions in Kuwait was dug in right up against the Saudi border. Its patrols already had made minor incursions into Saudi territory. Then Scowcroft got to the conclusion: the United States was considering making an offer of American military forces to help with the defense of Saudi Arabia.

Bandar interjected sharply. "Why would we want to be defended by you?" he asked.

"What on earth do you mean?" Scowcroft replied, as if he had been punched.[31]

Bandar explained the complexity of the Saudi position and the prevailing perception of American weakness in the region. When the shah was toppled, the United States had sent a few F-15s, and then (while they were in midair) the Pentagon had leaked that they were not carrying any weapons. In 1982, the United States had put marines into Lebanon only to pull them out after a terrorist attack killed 241 of them, leaving the Lebanese at the mercy of Syria. Frankly, Bandar said, his masters did not want to invite the United States to defend Saudi Arabia because there was so much uncertainty about American staying power. If the American military came and then pulled out, leaving Saddam in power and full of vengeance, Saudi Arabia would be in dire straits.

Scowcroft tried to reassure him that America would do what was necessary. But President Bush needed to know whether the Saudis would accept the American offer of forces. Bandar replied that he needed to know in detail what America was prepared to do before he could accept anything. Just then Bush walked into the office. Bandar was on his feet. He knew it was never an accident when the president broke in on a meeting. This was a "drop by" because Bush had a message.

The president's arms were folded. Bush reminded Bandar how he and the Saudi royal family had defended Saddam. The prince had characterized the Iraqi dictator as a stalwart of the Arab camp, someone who deserved American support.

"Water over the dam, Mr. President," was the only thing Bandar could think to say.

Bush said they now needed to trust each other.

"Mr. President, we trust you," Bandar replied, but "the survival of my country probably depends on this. We need to know how far you are willing to go."[32]

King Fahd would not make a commitment until he understood in detail what the United States was willing to do to defend Saudi Arabia—how many planes, tanks, troops. How long would they stay?

George Bush extended his hand to Bandar, who took it.

"If you ask for help from the United States, we will go all the way with you," the president said. He had framed his words carefully, recognizing that the decision affected Saudi sovereignty and, with the kingdom in peril, recognizing also that the king needed a solemn pledge that if America came to the rescue, it would not do so halfheartedly.

They shook hands. Bandar was at a loss for words. He knew that Bush's words implied that other wheels were turning in the bureaucracy. But the handshake and the pledge meant more because, above all else, Bush respected personal relationships.

Bush left Scowcroft and the prince to take a call from Turgut Özal, the president of Turkey, a member of the NATO alliance. Bush wanted to ascertain whether Özal was willing to shut down Iraq's other crude oil pipeline, the one that ran across Turkish territory to the Mediterranean Sea. Özal was vague. The Turkish leader expressed his anger at Saddam, but he reported that he also had been on the telephone to King Fahd, who gave him cause to worry. Saudi Arabia might not be willing to confront Iraq.

Leaders were sitting on the fence, waiting to see who, if anyone, would oppose Saddam. François Mitterrand, the French president, told Bush in one call, "If Saudi Arabia takes a courageous stand against the annexation of Kuwait, this would bring along others."[33]

Bush was beginning to understand that Bandar needed something dramatic to assuage King Fahd's anxiety. Scowcroft called Cheney and told him what was at stake and what was needed. The president wanted to make an explicit commitment of American forces. The Pentagon now needed to give Bandar a full-dress briefing on what the United States could do to defend the kingdom, so Fahd would get the message.

Bandar was soon called to the Pentagon. He had every reason to believe that the National Security Agency had monitored his calls back to

Saudi Arabia. The Americans were either going to lay out a dramatic proposal or they were going to filibuster and punt. Bandar was seated with
Dick Cheney and Colin Powell in the secretary's office. Cheney liked to
do business at a small round conference table away from his massive
desk. Powell's relationship with Bandar was more intimate than Cheney's
(Cheney had never served in the military). Powell and Bandar had met
when they were both protégés to power. They related to each other in the
jocular and profane parlance of the military barracks. Powell liked to call
the prince "Bandar the Magnificent," and Bandar liked to cut through
Powell's careful military pose by calling him a "bullshitter" because "it
takes one to know one."[34]

Bandar was biting down on an unlit Cuban cigar. Powell laid out high-
resolution satellite images showing the disposition of Iraqi forces, including the strike forces deployed on the Saudi frontier.

"We're prepared to help you defend yourselves from Saddam," Powell
told him.

"Like Jimmy Carter did?" Bandar asked. The comment dripped with
skepticism.

Cheney ignored it. If the United States was invited in to defend the
kingdom, Cheney now assured Bandar, it would come in massively,
meaning with large-scale forces on the ground and air forces to support
them. This would not be a onetime movement of an aircraft carrier whose
planes might bomb a few Iraqi positions.

"Tell Prince Bandar what we are prepared to do," Cheney said to Powell, who then unfurled the Joint Chiefs' plan to defend the oil fields of
Saudi Arabia in the event of a Soviet thrust into the region. It was old
school, boots-on-the-ground American intervention. First an entire tactical fighter wing would fly in along with the Eighty-second Airborne Division, followed by heavy divisions in ships carrying tanks, artillery, and
other mechanized armor. The plan called for an initial aircraft carrier
to move into the Gulf, followed by others that would get under way to
the Middle East. The transport command would start an airlift of war
matériel to support an initial force of one hundred thousand troops. That
was "for starters," Powell said.

"I see," Bandar replied. "This shows you *are* serious."[35] Bandar was
elated. His mind was racing when he left the Pentagon because now it
was a matter of how to convey the extraordinary offer to King Fahd. What
would Fahd need to consolidate support in the royal family? Bandar was

trying to anticipate. He wanted Fahd to see the satellite images of Saddam's army hard up against the Saudi border.

When Fahd heard Bandar's report about the satellite photos, he wanted them brought to Riyadh, and Bandar understood that the king needed documentation so the senior princes could see for themselves.

Colonel Lang was feeding analysis and data on Iraq's moves to Cheney and Powell, and when Lang saw how the Iraqi divisions had lined themselves up to hold Kuwait, but also to threaten Saudi Arabia, he asked himself, Would they invade? Lang's view was that Saddam would not risk an invasion of Saudi Arabia, but as an experienced intelligence officer, Lang looked at capabilities, not intentions.

Saddam had the capability to drive south and take the Saudi ports and oil fields. What if this was an invasion in phases? The first phase was the buildup on the Kuwaiti border. The second was the invasion of Kuwait with deployments near the Saudi border. The third phase had the potential to take the invasion deeper into the Arabian Peninsula if the order came.[36]

On Saturday, August 4, Bush went by helicopter to Camp David and chaired a large National Security Council meeting. Cheney and Powell had resolved their differences. Powell believed that the hard questions he had asked about whether it was worth going to war to defend some oil sheikhs in Kuwait were raised on behalf of soldiers who had fought and died in Vietnam and Lebanon. If he was the skunk at the picnic, so be it.

In truth, the post-Vietnam "never again" attitude that so dominated Pentagon thinking in the Weinberger years (when Powell had come of age as a policy adviser) had temporarily blinded Powell to the larger threat from Saddam. If Saddam were allowed to seize the oil assets of the Persian Gulf, he could build a fearsome war machine. It had taken a couple of days, but Powell had recovered his realism. Cheney's focus had been sharper, perhaps because his first thoughts were never chastened by the risks of taking young men into battle, for he had never commanded soldiers on a battlefield.

That morning, Bush sat in the log-hewn lodge where Eisenhower had pondered Suez and where Carter had wrestled with Begin and Sadat. Under the late-summer canopy, he listened as General Schwarzkopf worked through how long it would take to build up a massive force in the desert to defend Saudi Arabia—four months—and then to prepare for an invasion of Kuwait—twelve months. The one bonus seemed to be that even though the military chiefs wanted a big ground army, they also believed that air power could be decisive against Iraq because there was nowhere to hide in the desert. The Iraqi army had never had to fight an adversary with air superiority and precision weapons. It might be possible to substantially pick Saddam's forces apart from the air.

But the president was beset with anxiety. "My worry is the lack of Saudi will and that they might bug out. We need to ask them," the president said. What if they decided to accept an Iraqi puppet regime in Kuwait?[37]

Powell didn't respond. He focused on how to protect Saudi Arabia. He said he did not think that Saddam wanted to mess with the U.S. military.

But the President was obsessively fixated on the worst case. "We have a problem if Saddam does not invade Saudi Arabia but holds on to Kuwait."

Bush seemed still on the fence about Kuwait and whether Saddam could get away with it. "Lot's of people are calling him Hitler," he said.

It would not be easy, Cheney agreed. The American people might have a "short tolerance for war." And it would cost "one hell of a lot of money" to send the American military halfway round the world to fight. We'll be seen as helping royal families," Cheney said, referring to the problem of selling the war to the public. "You must be prepared to defend Saudi Arabia and put the [Kuwaiti] royal family back [on the throne]."

The meeting broke up on a note of strong doubt about King Fahd and the Arabs in general. Bush decided to call the king from Camp David. It was always awkward with an interpreter on the line, but Bush emphasized the gravity of the military situation. It was important that the king make a decision on accepting American forces. The king evaded the question. Something was not right.

"First, the only solution must involve the return of the Emir to Kuwait," the king said. "Second, there are no Iraqi troops near the Saudi border, but Saddam is not to be trusted. That is why it is important for the team to come as soon as possible to coordinate matters to prevent that from happening."

The king kept referring to "the team" and Bush didn't know what he was talking about, but it was suddenly clear that the king was signaling that this would help the Saudis make the momentous decision with which they were struggling.

Before signing off, Bush gave his word of honor to King Fahd that the United States took responsibility for the security of Saudi Arabia. "I am determined that Saddam will not get away with all this infamy," Bush said (weakly parroting Roosevelt's reference to Pearl Harbor as a "day of infamy"), and if American troops came to the kingdom, they would "stay until we are asked to leave. You have my solemn word on this."[38] His clumsiness notwithstanding, Bush seemed to have come to the conclusion that he stood at the front of a line of presidents committed to the protection of the commodity that was essential to American power.

The only question left was the team. Bandar was soon at the White House and proposed that he and Scowcroft fly together to Saudi Arabia with the military briefers from the Pentagon. However, Cheney wanted to lead the team, and since Scowcroft was never one to fight over turf (which is why Bush's administration functioned so much better than Reagan's), Scowcroft stayed in Washington.

As Cheney and a large military contingent flew off to Jeddah, Bush heard that Saddam had sent an emissary to the Turks to say that Iraq would annex Kuwait and had no intention of giving up its military gains.

"The West is bluffing," the Iraqi dictator had said.


It had been four days since the invasion. The United Nations had voted its condemnation. Not since Nasser had stretched his hand across the region had a military dictator made such a bold bid for hegemonic power. Bush had shown caution. He had let the crisis develop. It was time to speak to the country and to lay the groundwork for what was to come.

After he landed on the South Lawn of the White House Sunday afternoon, Bush walked over to the news media pool and said, "I view very seriously our determination to reverse this awful aggression." He said some countries might not agree, but that he would be working for collective action.

"This will not stand, this will not stand, this aggression against Kuwait," Bush said.

Given all that Bush had just heard, and the uncertainty about King Fahd and the Arabs, he had no idea whether he could back the muscular statement he had just made, but he had settled on the notion that it was the right thing to do.


Bandar was the first to leave for Saudi Arabia so he could fill in King Fahd on what to expect from the Americans. Cheney flew with Robert Gates of the NSC staff, Paul Wolfowitz, Cheney's undersecretary for policy, and Pete Williams, the press spokesman. Cheney spent much of the sixteen hours rehearsing the briefing they would give the king and his entourage. Also on the plane was Chas. W. Freeman Jr., the American ambassador to Saudi Arabia, who was a shrewd judge of King Fahd and the Oriental style of the Saudi royal court. After seeing a dry run of the intelligence briefing on the plane, Freeman warned Cheney that King Fahd would likely be confused. The vocabulary of assigning percentages to possibilities, of hedging intelligence judgments, would not be as helpful as a straightforward military assessment on the threat. Cheney agreed and assigned the intelligence briefing to General Schwarzkopf.[39]

When they assembled in Fahd's palace in Jeddah, the king quickly invited Cheney to get down to business, and Cheney was to the point. "Saudi Arabia faces what may be the greatest threat in its history," he said.[40] The whole international system had a stake in stopping Saddam, and Bush was organizing the great powers to put pressure on Iraq. The plan that they would lay out, Cheney said, would emphasize first the defense of the kingdom and then a campaign of economic, diplomatic, and military pressure to squeeze Iraq until it gave up Kuwait.

He then introduced Schwarzkopf, a bear of a man who went down on bended knee so he could lay out the satellite imagery in front of the king and show him the line of the Kuwaiti-Saudi border because, he said, it was important to understand that there were hundreds of tanks, artillery pieces, and even Scud missiles arrayed near the Saudi frontier. Armed Iraqi reconnaissance patrols had made incursions into Saudi territory. The king and his advisers were aware that the Iraqis were no longer answering the hotline that had long been established between the Saudi and Iraqi militaries. This had driven the Saudi royal family into a state of "controlled panic," as Bandar described it.

Crown Prince Abdullah, the king's half brother and commander of the Saudi national guard, was hovering over the king's shoulder to get a look at the photographs. Prince Saud, the foreign minister, was next to the king, as was Bandar, who was translating Schwarzkopf's military staccato into Arabic. The chief of staff of the Saudi military listened intently, as did the deputy Saudi defense minister.

With every hour that had passed since Cheney left Washington, the Iraqi buildup in Kuwait had intensified. As they spoke, it comprised eleven divisions, including two divisions that were newly dug in on either side of the highway into Saudi Arabia.

"Is the threat to Saudi Arabia as grave as I believe it to be?" the King asked.[41]

Schwarzkopf said that Saddam's intentions were unclear, but the Saudis faced a perilous military situation with a seasoned and battle-tested army pointed at the heart of their oil-producing region.

King Fahd betrayed no skepticism when Schwarzkopf concluded that Saddam had many more forces in Kuwait than he needed and no longer could be trusted.

Cheney pressed to close the deal. Further delay could tempt Saddam to move against Saudi Arabia. American forces were far away.

Fahd turned to his advisers and asked if anyone had a comment.

Crown Prince Abdullah spoke up. "Don't you think we ought to take some more time to consider this before we make this decision?"

They were speaking in Arabic and Bandar stopped interpreting for the Americans, but Freeman's Arabic was good enough to catch the gist of it.

"No," Fahd replied. "We don't have any time. We have to make the de-cision now, or what happened to Kuwait will happen to us. There is no more Kuwait."

"Yes, there is still a Kuwait," Abdullah insisted.

"And its territory consists solely of hotel rooms in London, Cairo, and [Saudi Arabia]," Fahd retorted.

Abdullah had to agree. There were no other dissenters. Fahd turned to Cheney and said Saudi Arabia consented to the principle of an American deployment to the kingdom. They should now move to working out a de-tailed military mobilization, including the question of who else might be invited—he mentioned Egypt and Morocco—to join in the defense of the kingdom. The Americans were a little dizzy. No one had imagined that King Fahd would make the decision on the spot. Cheney telephoned the president from Jeddah. He asked for permission to order the Eighty-second Airborne, a tactical fighter wing, and an aircraft carrier to Saudi Arabia. These forces would be the first line of defense until a massive air- and sealift could bring the rest.

"Go," Bush said, worried they might be too late.

On the morning of August 8, Bush was at his desk in the Oval Office, cer-tain that he had done the right thing, but he still was restless, full of doubt and anxiety. So many things could go wrong. He was all the more nervous because he was about the address the nation.

Technicians and aides moved about the room. Bush was a solitary figure before the camera. During the night, Saddam had sent a warning. It had arrived via Joseph Wilson, the ranking American diplomat in Baghdad. The Iraqi dictator had summoned Wilson to the presidential palace. Saddam had told him that Iraq would never give up Kuwait and that Bush should consider the emir and crown prince as relics of history. They would never be coming home.

If America attacked, "you will never bring us to our knees," Saddam had admonished Wilson, and "we will not remain idle in the region."

Bush took that as a threat. He had been hearing through the grapevine that Saddam was offering billions of dollars to Mubarak, to King Hussein, and to Yemen's Ali Abdullah Saleh to keep them in the Iraqi camp. With Kuwait's billions, Saddam might think he could buy enough Arab allegiance to defeat America. There were indications that King Hussein and the Yemeni leader had been swayed by Saddam's offer of financial inducements, and Mubarak asserted that he had turned down a $20 billion offer to purchase Egypt's loyalty.[42]

These were the factors that preyed on Bush's mind that morning, as the minutes counted down to 9:00 a.m. Bush read through his text one more time. He was not as polished as Ronald Reagan at these moments. Reagan had stage presence and a sense of timing honed in Hollywood. When Bush thought no one was looking, he stuck his hand out in front of him to see if it was shaking. Despite the flutters he felt, it was steady. He was pleased.[43]

Then the red light went on. He was live.

"In the life of a nation," he began, "we're called upon to define who we are and what we believe . . ."

The engines of American military mobilization stirred, and over the next six months, the United States deployed more than a half million troops to the Middle East. Bush and Baker built a coalition for war that included not only Britain and France but also Egypt and Syria, although Assad had never imagined himself fighting alongside America against an Arab enemy. Bush won a hard-fought battle for a United Nations Security Council resolution authorizing the use of force if Iraq did not withdraw from Kuwait by January 15, 1991. Congress, on January 12, narrowly voted its approval to wage war under the United Nations mandate.

Americans and the Saudis seemed frantic that Saddam would preempt their strategy and attack the Saudi ports and airfields that the Americans were using to land tanks and artillery, but Saddam held his fire. The Pentagon encouraged journalists to report on the daily arrival of C-5A Galaxy transports and C-141 Starlifters as if to telegraph to Saddam that he had missed his chance to attack, but in fact the vulnerability extended into October 1990.

Meanwhile, a great chasm opened in the Arab world. Images of Yasser Arafat hugging Saddam two days after the invasion and calling him an "Arab patriot" inflamed the Gulf Arabs who were Saddam's victims. Arafat shuttled around the Middle East in an Iraqi executive jet trying to broker a settlement—mostly on Saddam's terms—but this only repulsed a broad audience in the region and the West. King Hussein proved to be Saddam's most enduring ally. Since the 1980s and the war with Iran, he gave over Jordan's port of Aqaba to the Iraqi military. He once explained himself to Efraim Halevy, the Mossad envoy, by saying that in Arab eyes, Saddam was a hero who had saved the Arab world and its Sunni majority from the Shiite hordes of Ayatollah Khomeini. To the Arab street, Saddam was the reincarnation of Nebuchadnezzar, the fearsome Babylonian conqueror.[44]

King Hussein, the PLO, and Libya joined in voting against the Arab League condemnation of Iraq's invasion. Then, as the American buildup was beginning to secure Saudi Arabia, the Jordanian monarch called for all foreign forces to leave Saudi Arabia, asserting that they were desecrating the holy places of Islam. He even seemed to endorse Saddam's claim to Kuwait, stating that the Iraqi-Kuwaiti border had been imposed by colonial powers.

Prince Bandar could not abide King Hussein's hypocrisy. From Washington, he penned a letter to the Jordanian king and released it to the news media. Bandar pointed out that Jordan was now allied not only with Saddam but also with "that unholy crowd" of Palestinian terrorists that he was harboring in Baghdad, including Abu Nidal and Abu Abbas. Bandar wrote that it was strange for King Hussein to justify Saddam's erasure of borders that were created by the colonial British, since "your whole country was created by the colonial British."[45]

The Israelis also detected Jordanian treachery during this period. Shortly after the invasion, Iraqi warplanes bearing the insignia of the Royal Jordanian Air Force began flying reconnaissance patrols in Jordanian airspace south of the Dead Sea. That could mean they were planning an attack against Saudi Arabia, or against Israel. Israeli military chiefs were outraged that the king, with whom they had excellent clandestine relations, would allow Saddam's air forces to penetrate under false pretenses so near to Israeli's Dimona nuclear reactor.

Some of the hard-liners in Prime Minister Shamir's cabinet called for an attack on the Jordanian military and on Iraq, hoping that they could kick the legs out from under King Hussein's regime and pave the way for a Palestinian takeover. Then Jordan could become Palestine and the Palestinians would give up their quest for statehood on the West Bank. Cooler heads prevailed. In late September, the Israelis delivered an "uncompromising warning that the Iraqi flights must stop," and they did.[46]

The Israelis were a wild card whose actions could bust the coalition; no one understood this as well as Saddam.

"Oh, Arabs, Oh Muslims and the faithful everywhere," he called out to the Arab leaders gathered in Cairo on August 10, two days after Bush's speech from the Oval Office. "This is your duty to rise and defend Mecca which is captured by the spears of the Americans and Zionists. Revolt against oppression, corruption, treachery and backstabbing . . . revolt against the oil emirs who accept to push the Arab women into whoredom."[47]

For some Saudis, the sight of American military forces flooding into the kingdom was profoundly unsettling. King Fahd was known to his people as the "Custodian of the Two Holy Mosques"—meaning the shrines of Mecca and Medina—and no righteous custodian of the faith could easily invite an army of nonbelievers into the sacred land. Conservative Islamic clerics feared the taint of the infidel—uncovered women, sex, and alcohol. They saw the West as a source of moral corruption. The kingdom had spent billions on modern weapons. Why did it have to invite foreigners for protection?

Osama bin Laden was among those concerned. A scion of the kingdom's largest construction empire, the Binladen Group, he was well known and well regarded for his support of jihad against the Soviets in Afghanistan. Prince Turki al-Faisal, the chief of Saudi intelligence, had found bin Laden a useful ally, and in the fall of 1990, bin Laden approached the royal family, offering his services to drive Saddam out of Kuwait.

Some members of the royal family took him seriously, but most considered him eccentric or even deluded. How could the unruly mujahideen take on the Iraqi army?[48]

Bin Laden could not get an audience with King Fahd, but Prince Sultan, the defense minister and Bandar's father, welcomed the young sheikh and listened to his proposal. Sultan was not a complicated man. He had been running the kingdom's military affairs since John Kennedy was in the White House. He understood both guerrilla tactics and terrain warfare. So he pointed out to bin Laden that Kuwait was a desert, completely different topography from Afghanistan.

"You cannot fight them from the mountains and caves," he said. "What will you do when he lobs the missiles at you with chemical and biological weapons?"

"We will fight them with faith," bin Laden replied.[49]

The royal family's rejection of bin Laden's offer marked the beginning of an estrangement that would lead him, ultimately, to violent opposition against the House of Saud.


In the United States, Congress was deeply divided about war with Iraq as the best way to end its occupation of Kuwait. Democrats controlled both houses, so Bush would have to make a powerful bipartisan appeal.

Senator Daniel Patrick Moynihan, one of the stalwarts of the cold war, questioned whether what had occurred in the Persian Gulf was even an international crisis. He disparaged the fabulously wealthy Kuwaiti royal family "who have taken over the Sheraton Hotel in Taif [Saudi Arabia] and they're sitting there in their white robes and drinking coffee and urging us on to war."[50]

Moynihan had visited Taif with a Senate delegation and could not even get an audience with the emir of Kuwait, who had hired the American public relations firm Hill & Knowlton to improve Kuwait's image. In the January debate over the war resolution, Moynihan said, "All that's happened is that one nasty little country invaded a littler but just as nasty country." Senator Sam Nunn, chairman of the powerful Armed Services Committee, said, "I don't think a war at this time is wise and I think there are alternatives." Nunn urged Bush to let the sanctions and a maritime blockade grind down Saddam's defiance.

Bush, with the concurrence of British Prime Minister Margaret Thatcher—and her successor, John Major—believed that the coalition against Iraq would not hold indefinitely. Sanctions were no guarantor of success.

Senator Edward Kennedy called on Congress to save Bush from himself "and save thousands of American soldiers in the Persian Gulf from dying in the desert in a war whose cruelty will be exceeded only by the lack of any rational necessity for waging it."

Senator John Kerry asked, "Are we supposed to go to war simply because one man—the president—makes a series of unilateral decisions that put us in a box—a box that makes that war, to a greater degree, inevitable?"

It was a remarkable moment at the end of the cold war, the passing of which had engendered strong expectations of peace. As in the Eisenhower era after World War II, many Americans saw no crying need to dash into battle again. But Bush saw plenty of reasons. Saddam stood athwart the industrial world's petroleum lifeline. He was holding hundreds of Westerners hostage and using them as human shields at factories and other military targets. His occupation army was torturing, raping, and killing Kuwaitis; erasing their national history; and looting their banks, factories, and cities of anything of value. His troops were laying siege to Western embassies in Kuwait, seeking to starve them out so their diplomats would flee to Baghdad and renounce any recognition of Kuwait as a separate sovereign entity. If there ever was an argument for a defensive war that was both just and necessary, Saddam's invasion had provided one.


On January 12, the House passed a resolution authorizing the use of force by a vote of 250–183. The vote was much closer in the Senate: 52–47.

The Persian Gulf War began on January 18, 1991, as Operation Desert Storm and proceeded as a forty-day campaign of aerial bombardment against the entrenched Iraqi divisions in Kuwait and against many other military, economic, and leadership targets across Iraq. Then, in the early morning hours of February 24, General Schwarzkopf released his ground forces for the large-scale invasion of fast-moving armored formations with close air support. The Marines drove straight into Kuwait near the coast and a phalanx of army divisions swept in a "left hook" maneuver from the west to hit the Iraqis on their unprotected flank, crashing into the rear area of Iraq's front-line forces.

Though there were pockets of intense fighting, the Iraqis could not mount a defense while under constant air attack. The ground war lasted only one hundred hours as the front-line Iraqi divisions collapsed. Tens of thousands of Iraqi soldiers surrendered or started walking north toward home. Many of them died as American fighters swooped down to bomb and strafe their retreating columns along what became known as the "highway of death." Meanwhile, Saddam's reserve of elite Republican Guard divisions evaded, for the most part, the onslaught and pulled back into Iraq.

George Bush declared a cease-fire on February 28.

At the outset of the air campaign, George and Barbara Bush, along with the Reverend Billy Graham, sat in front of a television in the residence quarters of the White House and, like much of the rest of the world, watched as the lights of Baghdad flickered just before the sky erupted into a latticework of antiaircraft tracers and the flashes of explosions. Bernard Shaw and Peter Arnett of CNN provided a nightlong commentary from the Al-Rasheed Hotel.

Bush had been to war as a young man. He had flown fifty-eight combat missions as a naval aviator in World War II and survived being shot down by antiaircraft fire. He still remembered the day in August 1942 when his father, Prescott Bush, who served in the Senate from Connecticut, sent him off to war. Bush had hugged his father on the platform at New York's Penn Station. The eighteen-year-old Bush had cried on the train because he was headed off "into the unknown."[51]

On the second night of the bombardment, Saddam began firing Scud missiles at Israel, triggering panic as well as demands that Israel be allowed to enter the conflict. Moshe Arens, the defense minister, wanted to send a sizable commando force into western Iraq to hunt down the mobile Scud launchers.[52]

Surprisingly, after all Bush's efforts to convince the Israelis to stay on the sidelines, as soon as the first Scuds hit, Cheney proposed that Israel be allowed to join the coalition fight. He argued that there was little Washington could do to stop Israel's military leaders and that Bush might make a bad situation worse by attempting to do so.[53]

But this was where Cheney's judgment faltered. His assessment proved wrong. The United States was in control of the war zone. Israeli planes and commandos could not enter without coordination lest they be targeted as hostile forces by American gunners. The military men, if not Cheney, understood this instinctively.

Bush called Shamir and offered a compromise. He encouraged Shamir to consider firing Israeli ballistic missiles at Iraqi air bases. That would keep Israeli troops out of the war zone but give Israel a measure of retaliatory satisfaction. The Israelis, however, declined the offer. Moshe Arens's view was that the military effect of a missile attack would be zero; it might not even be noticed by the Iraqis.[54]

Shamir was reluctant to risk sending Israeli forces through Jordan's air defense network. Though the Israeli prime minister was under intense pressure to strike back, the failure of the Iraqi Scuds to inflict any significant damage gave him enough room to maneuver. Washington shipped Patriot missile batteries to beef up Israel's air defense. Schwarzkopf escalated the Scud-hunting tempo of American forces in western Iraq. Larry Eagleburger, James Baker's deputy at State, was dispatched to Tel Aviv to buck up Shamir's resistance to the hard-liners of his party. As it turned out, the greatest Scud fatalities were inflicted on American forces in Saudi Arabia. A Scud fired on February 25 crashed into an American military barracks in Dhahran, killing twenty-eight soldiers and wounding nearly a hundred.

The morning after the war ended, Bob Gates, the deputy national security adviser, told Bush that history would look kindly on Bush's war because America did not pile on—it crushed Saddam's divisions in Kuwait but then "we stopped" the killing and let Saddam's forces limp home. That was not entirely true. To see Iraq, as I did soon thereafter, was to understand the scale of devastation that America had inflicted on its civilian population. I toured the country to view the result of the forty-day bombing campaign on Iraq's infrastructure. Powell and Schwarzkopf had set out to demonstrate that modern warfare could defeat an enemy simply by rendering a country dysfunctional. U.S. warplanes had knocked out the national electrical power grid, flattened water purification plants, and destroyed telephone exchanges, highways, and bridges.

A senior United Nations official who toured the country at about the same time said, "The recent conflict has wrought near apocalyptic results . . . Iraq has, for some time to come, been relegated to a pre-industrial age."[55] This was an overstatement but an understandable first reaction to the scale of destruction.

A rapid degradation of general health and nutrition occurred that would become a permanent feature of Saddam's Iraq. The Iraqis would not starve, they would merely go hungry, and the time would come when America would be blamed for the wretched state in which millions lived after the war.

Bush had told the Iraqis there was another way for the bloodshed to end: "The Iraqi military and the Iraqi people" should "take matters into their own hands and force Saddam Hussein, the dictator, to step aside, and then comply with the United Nations resolutions and then rejoin the family of peace-loving nations."[56]

Bush's call for a general rebellion contributed to the messy ending of the war. Saddam ordered his military commanders to blow up Kuwait's oil industry. Hundreds of wells were set alight and Kuwait became a vision of environmental apocalypse. There were voices within the Bush administration that urged Cheney, Powell, and the president to take the war into Iraq, to support the Shiite rebellion. But the coalition's stated goal was the recovery of Kuwait. The conquest of Baghdad would have shattered the consensus binding the coalition under a United Nations mandate.

General Schwarzkopf had little to guide him when the Iraqi army collapsed. Bush had not thought through the endgame. Without waiting for instructions from Washington, Schwarzkopf arranged a meeting with the Iraqi military chiefs in a tent erected on an airfield in Safwan, the highway town just inside Iraqi territory, and there he arranged for a cease-fire, the first exchange of prisoner information, and guidelines for withdrawal of the remaining Iraqi forces.

Lieutenant General Sultan Ahmed, the chief of Saddam's defense ministry staff, requested that Iraqi commanders be allowed to continue flying their helicopters because so many bridges were out. Schwarzkopf said he would allow it, though flying fixed-wing aircraft was forbidden (because they could treaten U.S. forces in Kuwait or be used to bomb Iraqi civilians). The Iraqis turned this good deed to evil purpose. They used their attack helicopters over the next several weeks to slaughter Shiites and put down the rebellion in southern Iraq. Many Shiites fled for the borders in desperation, where American troops turned them back to face the machine gunners of Saddam's Republican Guard.

In the north, the Kurds, fearing similar treatment, fled across the border with Turkey by the tens of thousands, perching perilously on hillsides until the coalition organized Operation Provide Comfort and pushed the Iraqi army out of northern Iraq. Much of the north was declared a safe haven against the Iraqi army and no-fly zone for the Iraqi air force, all to protect the Kurdish minority.

"Still no feeling of euphoria," Bush wrote in his diary early on February 28. What was wrong with this American leader who had fought in the great war of 1941–45? "It hasn't been a clean end," Bush continued, "there is no battleship *Missouri* surrender. This is what's missing to make this akin to WWII, to separate Kuwait from Korea and Vietnam . . ." Bush could see that much of the Arab world was still aligned with Saddam. This was the moment when Bush's vision and his leadership weakened. He didn't know what to do about the enemy whose army he had defeated. No security alliance existed in the Persian Gulf to secure the American "victory" in the long run. Cheney had told Congress that whatever security structures the United States had relied on in the past— British colonial power, Iran under the shah, American naval forces during the cold war—had failed to prevent Saddam's emergence as a regional strongman, now more dangerous than ever. All Bush could do was write in his journal, "He's got to go."[57] But Bush lacked the means, and also perhaps the will, to make it so; he let Robert Gates soothe him by saying that history would look kindly on the decision to end the war and stop the killing before Saddam's elite divisions were captured or destroyed. And Bush seemed not to be aware that Saddam's generals had won the right to use their helicopters to slaughter Shiites in the weeks that followed.

Nevertheless, Bush had said, "When all this is over, we want to be the healers," and he kept his word; it was the only way to prevent Saddam from stealing the victory.

On March 6, 1991, Bush told a cheering Congress, "Aggression is defeated. The war is over." That moment may have been the pinnacle of George Bush's political career.

"Our commitment to peace in the Middle East does not end with the liberation of Kuwait," he said. It was time to do something about the depth of bitterness between the Arabs and Israelis and their intractable conflict in the Holy Land. "By now it should be plain to all parties that peacemaking in the Middle East requires compromise," he continued. "We must do all that we can to close the gap between Israel and the Arab states and between Israelis and Palestinians."

It was the first time since Jimmy Carter had been in the White House that a president had spoken so directly of the requirements for justice in the Holy Land: peace and security for Israel in exchange for returning Arab territories and recognizing the legitimate political rights of Palestinians. "Anything else," Bush told Congress, "would fail the twin tests of fairness and security. The time has come to put an end to Arab-Israeli conflict."[58]

In early April, the UN Security Council passed Resolution 687, requiring Saddam Hussein to make a full accounting of his nuclear, chemical, and biological weapons programs. Until he did, heavy economic sanctions, including a ban on Iraqi oil exports, would stay in place. Saddam tried to conceal his weapons programs from the inspectors of the International Atomic Energy Agency. At a factory near Tarmiyah, north of Baghdad, his security men fired warning shots over the heads of UN inspectors. Nonetheless, the IAEA teams were able to seize documents and other evidence establishing that Iraq had a highly developed nuclear weapons program. It had secretly employed the same method of uranium enrichment—electromagnetic separation with devices called calutrons— that the United States had used in the Manhattan Project. In September 1991, an inspection team headed by David Kay captured the full archive of Iraq's nuclear program. The discovery startled the American intelligence community. Iraq had been much closer to producing its first atomic weapon than either the CIA or the DIA had estimated.[59]

In the aftermath of the war, Robert Gates, on behalf of the president, declared a new policy of "regime change" in Iraq. Bush had named Gates CIA director, responsible for the covert action programs aimed at building an opposition force capable of toppling Saddam. Laying out the policy in a speech to American publishers meeting in Vancouver, Canada, in May 1991, Gates said, "Iraqis will pay the price while he is in power . . . All possible sanctions will be maintained until he is gone." The Iraqis "will not participate in post-crisis political, economic and security arrangements until there is a change in regime."[60]

But that was not enough. Saddam was still the hero and the patron of the Palestinian people, whose plight was the touchstone of politics in the Middle East. Bush would have to show them that America offered hope where Saddam offered hate.

The threat of postwar disillusionment impelled Bush. The American victory was far more precarious in the Middle East than most Americans perceived, and the perception of victory was critical to Bush's bid for re-election. With the economy weak, his management of foreign policy was all he had to run on. That was the calculus from which the idea for an international conference on Middle East peace emerged. It fell to James Baker to make it happen.

All during the war, Bush and Baker had fended off attempts by Mikhail Gorbachev to link an Iraqi withdrawal from Kuwait to a resolution of the

Palestinian problem. That had been a clever device that the Soviet foreign ministry and its chief Arab-world envoy, Yevgeny Primakov, had devised as a face-saving exit strategy for Saddam. But in beating back the effort, Bush and Baker had given their word that when the shooting stopped, the United States would lead a new peace initiative. Baker had no reason to be optimistic. Dennis Ross, a senior Baker aide, told him that the region had been hit by an earthquake and that the interval for diplomacy would be very short before the earth settled. In other words, the window of opportunity would soon close. Harvey Sicherman, a former adviser to Al Haig with strong pro-Israeli sympathies, told Baker that all the United States could hope to do was "rearrange some of the furniture in the bawdy house" of the Middle East.[61] Both of these assessments proved wrong.

The other problem was that Baker already had a terrible relationship with Israel's leaders and with American Jews in general. They saw him as a Texas oil lawyer more interested in Saudi Arabia and the Arab world than partnership with Israel. Prince Bandar was closer to Baker than any Israeli diplomat could claim to be. Baker had not even visited Israel during his first two years in office, and he felt that he had wasted the first year butting heads with Shamir.

Bush had wanted to build on the Camp David process, but Shamir was a boulder of opposition. Baker had riled American Jews by delivering blunt remarks to the annual meeting of AIPAC in May 1989. He had called on Israel to "lay aside, once and for all, the unrealistic vision of a greater Israel," to end settlement building in the occupied Palestinian territories, and to recognize Palestinian political rights.[62] He had prodded and poked Shamir, and worked behind Shamir's back with Yitzhak Rabin and Shimon Peres—the Labor Party leaders—to undermine Shamir's resistance. Shamir saw Baker's actions as a plot to bring down his government, and he was not far from the truth.

Just a few months before Saddam's invasion, and after Shamir had won re-election, Baker had rebuked the new Likud government for its paltry offerings to the Palestinians. He told a hearing of the House Foreign Affairs Committee that he did not think Shamir's government was serious about peace, and he addressed Shamir from Capitol Hill, stating, "When you're serious about peace, call us," and then he read out the telephone number of the White House switchboard.[63]

During the first week of the war, Israel's finance minister, Yitzhak

Modai, announced that the Israeli government was preparing a request for $13 billion in additional aid from the United States, including $10 billion in loan guarantees to settle hundreds of thousands of Soviet Jews who were streaming into the country. Ariel Sharon, as housing minister, sketched plans for massive new settlement construction in the occupied territories. A month later, after the United States had dispatched Patriot missiles to Israel, Baker publicly rebuked the Israeli ambassador, Zalman Shoval—and seriously considered expelling him—for complaining that Israel "has not received one cent in aid" to compensate it for the losses incurred from Scud missile attacks. Shoval accused the administration of giving Israel the "runaround."

Baker, ever the infighter, made it clear that no Israeli ambassador could bully the secretary of state. "Were times not so tense and critical as they are now, I would not accept that he continue as your representative in Washington," Baker told Shamir in a letter. "However," he added, "should there be a repetition" of the ambassador's performance, "I would have no choice but to ask him to leave."[64]

Thus, the prospects for a breakthrough were slim. Israel and the Palestinians could not have been farther apart. Arafat had sided with Saddam in the war and the PLO dialogue with Washington stood suspended. Shamir was the least interested in compromise. By faith and ideology, he was determined to keep the West Bank, Gaza, and the Golan Heights.

Yet America's standing in the world had never been higher, and that gave Bush leverage. The fact that he was willing to employ that leverage distinguished him from Ronald Reagan, who had been far less self-assured about taking risks in a Middle East he considered treacherous, and where the downside was an antagonistic Congress or Israeli lobby. Bush and Baker were different. Their Texas oil industry associations put them in touch with the Arab point of view; they were far more astute at reading internal Israeli politics, where the Labor Party and the Peace Now camp had become frustrated with Yitzhak Shamir's obstreperous opposition to negotiation. Bush's worldview was that high principle trumped politics. He felt a deep commitment to the Arab states that had participated in the Gulf War coalition and to those Israelis who wanted peace.

The Iraqi defeat had left Yasser Arafat and the PLO leadership isolated. For his part, Shamir could not ignore the fact that the American-led coalition had reduced to rubble the only army in the region that posed an existential threat to the Jewish state. Even Syria's Assad had joined the coalition in hopes that the peace might win him the return of the Golan Heights.

Baker formulated a plan that on one track would open a dialogue directly between Palestinians and Israelis, and on another would bring Arab leaders together to sit with Israel at an international peace conference. Some of the region's most reluctant players encouraged Baker. In March 1991, King Fahd told the American secretary that if a Palestinian homeland could be established, Saudi Arabia was ready for full economic and diplomatic relations with Israel.

"We know there is a state called Israel," the king said. "No one is denying it and no one should deny it."[65] Fahd said he wanted once and for all to reach a settlement of the Arab-Israeli dispute. "The Palestinian-Israeli problem is the main headache in the region, the crux of all our problems," he continued. "It gives Saddam and others, like Qaddafi, material on which to promote themselves. It should no longer linger on. It must be solved."[66]

In the run-up to Madrid, the venue set for a Middle East peace conference, Baker fought another bruising battle in Congress with AIPAC and with Shamir over loan guarantees to finance immigration and housing for newly arriving Soviet Jews. It was the worst time to link America, even indirectly, with financing Israeli settlements on occupied lands. AIPAC sought to force the issue in advance of the conference, perhaps to help Israel exert its own leverage, but Bush laid down a veto threat and, with the help of Senator Patrick Leahy of Vermont, chairman of the Appropriations Subcommittee on Foreign Operations, the White House was able to delay consideration for 120 days.[67]

The fight Bush waged over the loan guarantees was not economic but psychological. He understood that immigration of Soviet Jews was crucial for ensuring the Jewish character of the state against a fast-growing Arab minority. He was willing to quietly assist Israel through loan guarantees that lowered the interest rates when Israel borrowed funds for new housing. But Bush and Baker insisted that it was not in America's interest—at the very moment they were bringing the Arab leaders to the first peace conference of its kind—to prominently embrace the loan guarantee program, which for Shamir and Sharon was integral to their plan to expand settlements in the occupied territories.

The issue of land was critical to peace. Every new settlement the Israelis declared inflamed Arab sensibilities and undermined the peace initiative that Bush and Baker had undertaken. On the Palestinian street and in the Arab world more broadly—indeed, throughout the world— nothing symbolized Israeli bad faith as much as the settler movement that was seizing land, uprooting olive groves, and destroying Palestinian homes to make room for new Jewish communities in the very place where Palestinians hoped to establish their state.

In April, Shamir rejected the American proposal that Israel curtail settlement building as a goodwill gesture that would bring more Arab leaders to the peace conference. Instead, Israel announced a new settlement, Revava, in the West Bank. When Washington protested, the Israeli housing ministry under Sharon declared that it would build twenty-four thousand new housing units in the occupied territories for eighty-eight thousand settlers.[68] Bush said he felt like "one lonely guy" fighting "powerful political forces" amounting to "something like a thousand lobbyists."[69]

It took eight months of wrangling, but a Middle East peace conference convened at the royal palace in Madrid in the fall of 1991.

Arab and Israeli leaders, wary and nervous before a worldwide audience, gathered under the crystal chandeliers of the Spanish monarchy that hosted them in corridors girded by marble pilasters and Renaissance tapestries. Their assembly was to be the antidote to Saddam. An army of Spanish security agents protected them in presidential suites and grand salons from which they looked out on lush gardens.

The delegates met under the sponsorship of the two superpowers in the last season when two superpowers ordered the world. The international system of diplomacy was on the cusp of something new, and that notion lay as heavily on the assembly as the giant tapestries on the walls. Bush and Gorbachev were eloquent conveners, but the display of U.S.-Soviet cooperation was a finale. Gorbachev had survived a coup attempt in August by desperate and besotted colleagues seeking a return to Soviet orthodoxy. The coup had collapsed in the face of popular opposition symbolized by Boris Yeltsin shouting defiance from atop a tank. The Soviet Union would not survive the year.

Cynics saw the Madrid peace conference as nothing more than meaningless political payback by Bush to the Arab states for joining the coalition. But despite the cynicism, Bush had captured the spirit of changing times. His life had been lived on the seams of great changes. Real peace might seem impossible, he said, but who would have predicted that France and Germany—bitter rivals for a century in Europe—would become close allies after World War II?

"And who, two years ago, would have predicted that the Berlin Wall would come down? And who in the early 1960s would have believed that the cold war would come to a peaceful end?"[70] Peace was possible, he said, and it was, but no one who was a realist believed it would come soon. The question was whether the Madrid process could put it within reach, say, within a decade. Or would it take another fifty years and additional bloodshed for the right convergence of personality and politics to make it possible?

Madrid was remarkable because Shamir and the Arab leaders were forced to acknowledge their innate desire for peace in front of their peoples. Neither side—Arab or Israeli—wanted to be blamed for failure once a peace process got started. The tension could not have been greater when Shamir, the man of secrets and few words who had come to politics from the shadows of Jewish extremism, voiced the historic claim of his people.

"Jews have been persecuted throughout the ages in almost every continent. Some countries barely tolerated us, others oppressed, tortured, slaughtered and exiled us. This century saw the Nazi regime set out to exterminate us. The Shoah, the Holocaust, the catastrophic genocide of unprecedented proportions which destroyed a third of our people, became possible because no one defended us. Being homeless, we were also defenseless.

"But it was not the Holocaust that made the world community recognize our rightful claim to the Land of Israel. In fact, the rebirth of the state of Israel so soon after the Holocaust has made the world forget that our claim is immemorial. We are the only people who have lived in the Land of Israel without interruption for nearly 4,000 years. We are the only people, except for a short crusader kingdom, who have had an independent sovereignty in this land. We are the only people for whom Jerusalem has been a capital. We are the only people whose sacred places are only in the land of Israel."

Shamir's metallic and defiant oratory carried no trace of a compromising spirit and seemed lacking in any compassion for the plight of the Palestinians. It incited the Arab speakers to rise to the challenge. The Palestinian representative, Haidar Abdel Shafi, a soft-spoken doctor known for courtly manners in his native Gaza, replied, "We, the people of Palestine, stand before you in the fullness of our pain, our pride, and our anticipation for we have long harbored a yearning for peace and a dream of justice and freedom. For too long, the Palestinian people have gone unheeded, silenced and denied, our identity negated by political expediency, our rightful struggle against injustice maligned, and our present existence subsumed by the past tragedy of another people." He didn't even speak their name.

Instead, he raised his voice against the brutality of the occupation and the imprisonment of "thousands of our brothers and sisters," and he called across the table to Shamir to "set them free!"

It was an awkward affair, especially during the intermissions. The news media focused on the question of which Arabs would shake hands with Shamir and other members of the Israeli delegation. At the T-shaped table, Shamir was forced to look across at Saeb Erekat, a Palestinian whom the Israelis had tried and failed to exclude from the delegation and who publicly stated that he would be speaking for the PLO at the conference. Saudi Arabia and the other five Arab states that comprised the Gulf Cooperation Council attended as observers, a feat that Baker had engineered with the assistance of King Fahd.

Prince Bandar sat as the representative of the Saudi monarch, and in contrast to the pinstripes, he wore his traditional Saudi robes and red-and-white-checkered kaffiyeh. During the proceedings, he and Shamir shot glances at each other.

All of the Arab leaders warned that Israel's continued settlement building in the occupied territories would undermine the credibility of any peace process, but the Arabs also offered nothing that suggested they were ready to accept the legitimacy of the Jewish state or the Zionist enterprise as a permanent proposition in the Middle East. Instead there were low moments. Not least was the decision of Farouk al-Sharaa, the Syrian foreign minister, to hold up a wanted poster of Shamir at the age of thirty-two, when he was part of the underground Stern Gang waging a terrorist campaign against the British occupation of Palestine.

"I shall just show you if I may a photograph, an old photograph of Mr. Shamir," he said, addressing his colleagues in front of Shamir. "It was distributed because he was wanted. He himself recognized that he was a terrorist, that he practices terrorism and that he helped in the assassination of Count Bernadotte, the UN mediator in Palestine."[71]

After three days, the conference adjourned. Over the next year, Arab and Israeli delegates met for a half dozen negotiating sessions that reconfirmed how far apart they remained after forty years of conflict. No architecture for agreement emerged or even took shape in the broadest sense, but the Madrid meeting was a success because it served to regularize a diplomatic process from which all of the sides gained important insights about the leaders involved and about the national politics that shaped positions.

In the end, Hanan Ashrawi, the Palestinian spokeswoman, said the major problem with the Israelis under Shamir was that the Likud government simply would not accept the principle of exchanging land for peace, and therefore no Israeli proposal, no matter how artful in offering elections or limited local autonomy under Israeli suzerainty, could substitute for the minimum Palestinian demand for statehood.

Farouk al-Sharaa, who had started off so disparaging of Shamir, told journalists in September 1992 that Syria was ready for "total peace" with Israel if Israel was ready to withdraw from all the Arab territories it had occupied in June 1967. But Syria had yet to define total peace. Was it simply a return to the old lines and the old enmities? Or was it an offer of trade, tourism and diplomatic relations?[72]

Madrid was just the first step in a series of hopeful developments. In June 1992, Israeli voters rejected Shamir's reluctant approach to the Arabs and returned the Labor Party to power after fifteen years in opposition. Yitzhak Rabin, the general of few words who personified Israel's quest for security, headed the Labor ticket.

"We must overcome the sense of isolation that has held us in its thrall for almost half a century," he told the Knesset in his inaugural address. "We must join the international movement toward peace, reconciliation and cooperation that is spreading over the entire globe these days, lest we be the last to remain, all alone, in the station."[73]

Rabin declared that a new period of negotiation had dawned for Israel, and to prove it, he announced that he was reversing Israel's policy on the Golan Heights. Where Begin had annexed the promontory, saying it was exempt from the land-for-peace formulation of Resolution 242, Rabin indicated that Israel could give it up in the right circumstances.

"We are not starting from the assumption that in return for peace, we can give only peace when it comes to Syria," Rabin told the Knesset. In the face of catcalls from hard-liners, Rabin went on record arguing that Syria would never make peace without the return of Golan.

Rabin's thinking was changing. Syria and the Palestinians no longer posed existential threats to Israel. The future threats would come from Iran or from a resurgent Iraq. Rabin thought it was time to make peace on the immediate borders to gird for the more complex threats in the future. That meant he must confront the settler movement and the Israeli right wing to end the national obsession with expanding Israel into the West Bank and Gaza. He told the Bush White House that he was going to cancel seven thousand contracts for housing units planned by Shamir and Sharon in the West Bank.

He would give Bush the assurances he needed to approve the loan guarantees. The financing would not be used to expand settlements. At the end of Shamir's term, there were 110,000 settlers in the West Bank and Gaza, and Shamir, sulking after his defeat, pronounced Rabin's new broom a "nightmare." He confided in one interview that he would have dragged out any negotiation with the Palestinians for ten years while using the time to populate the occupied territories with Jewish settlers.[74]

When Bush and Baker did not immediately respond to Rabin's peace agenda, Rabin turned to Dennis Ross during an elevator ride at the King David Hotel and said, "Dennis, tell the secretary he is dealing with a different Yitzhak now."[75]

Arafat, who narrowly survived a plane crash in April 1992, certainly saw the shifting balance of power in the region and began to distance himself from Saddam. In a radio interview, he asserted that Saddam had misled the Palestinians "under the illusion that his missiles were to liberate them from Israeli occupation."[76]


Rabin's warning about the threat from Iran proved to be prescient. The legacy of the previous decade—the Iran-Iraq War and Israel's war in Lebanon that had devastated the Shiite community—had awakened a new militancy; it laid the foundations of a terrorist network—Hezbollah was the center—that connected Shiite extremists in Lebanon, Kuwait, Bahrain, and Saudi Arabia with Iran's Revolutionary Guard.

As in Khomeini's revolution, the emergent radicals of Shiite extremism espoused nationalistic ideology as well as Islamic fundamentalism. Many of them accepted arms, training, and support from Iran, whose leaders sought to export revolutionary extremism throughout the Middle East to blunt the unwelcome advance of America and its Western allies.

. . .

Argentina was as far from the Middle East conflict as one might imagine, yet the vibrant capital of Buenos Aires was home to large minorities of Arab and Jewish immigrants. The country sheltered a Jewish population of 250,000 and more than one million Arabs, including the family of President Carlos Saúl Menem, who was of Syrian extraction. The ethnic mixture made it possible for agents of Islamic extremism to move freely in a Latin American metropolis.

In March 1992, one such agent guided a truck loaded with explosives through the traffic to the front entrance of the Israeli embassy at the corner of Arroyo and Suipacha streets in a gentrified district of the city. The driver detonated his load, creating a dreadful fireball and shock wave that destroyed the five-story building, where eighty diplomats, guests, and Argentine nationals were working.

All that was left standing was the smoldering shell of the collapsed structure. Virtually every window in the district was shattered, and as the air filled with smoke, dust and the cries of victims, there was also, strangely, the smell of a fresh-cut lawn because the canopy of trees that shaded the boulevard had been shredded by the bomb.[77] The greenery rained down to mix with blood and dust. The explosion destroyed not just the well-secured Israeli compound but also three other nearby buildings, including a retirement home and a Roman Catholic school, where forty students miraculously escaped with light injuries. When the rubble was cleared, the toll was twenty-nine dead with more than two hundred wounded.

Buenos Aires was at the other end of the world from the jihadist currents that were coursing through the Middle East. But no target was too distant. The investigation, assisted by the CIA and Mossad, determined that the attack had been carried out by Hezbollah with assistance from Iranian diplomats. Islamic Jihad Organization, a Hezbollah front, claimed responsibility.[78] They said the attack was retaliation for Israel's assassination on February 16 of Sheikh Abbas Musawi, Hezbollah's leader in Lebanon. Musawi, his wife, Siham, and six-year-old son, Hussein, were killed when two Israeli helicopters struck Musawi's convoy after the Shiite leader had left a rally in the southern Lebanese town of Jibchit. The deaths occurred on the landscape of low-intensity warfare that Israel continued to face a decade after its invasion of Lebanon.

Hezbollah guerrillas mounted ambushes and rocket attacks in the bor-

der region against Israeli targets, civilian and military. Hezbollah had celebrated its capture, in February 1988, of a former military aide to Caspar
Weinberger. Lieutenant Colonel William R. Higgins was part of the
United Nations peacekeeping force in southern Lebanon. As Hezbollah's
power grew, Israel lashed out again at its leadership, launching a commando raid in July 1989 to kidnap Hezbollah spiritual leader Sheikh
Abdel Karim Obeid. With Obeid in custody, Israel offered to trade him
for all missing Israeli servicemen and Western hostages, including Colonel Higgins. But Israel's counterhostage strategy failed. Instead of engaging the Israelis in the swap, Hezbollah executed Higgins and released
a videotape of the act. Hezbollah vowed to drive Israel out of Lebanon,
including from the southern "security zone" patrolled by the South
Lebanon Army, the surrogate Lebanese force that Israel directed. Then
came the explosion in Buenos Aires.

Israeli officials initially cast doubt on Hezbollah's claim of responsibility for the Buenos Aires attack, but then the group released a surveillance
tape of the Israeli embassy before it had been blown up. It was not ironclad proof, but was chilling enough.[79]

The phenomenon of religion as the engine of extremist violence and
warfare was growing, not receding, at the end of the cold war. As Gamal
Abdel Nasser had discovered, Islamic fundamentalism pulled on the
masses as much as Arab nationalism, communism, or democracy. Given
an opportunity, the fundamentalists—whether the Muslim Brotherhood
in Egypt or Hezbollah in Lebanon or Hamas in Gaza—moved into any
vacuum and created an organizing structure that offered health and welfare to the poor and dispossessed. In parallel, they also supported terrorism against their enemies, Israel and America. Islamic fundamentalism
was gathering momentum across the Middle East, South Asia, and beyond, to Malaysia, the Philippines, and Indonesia. And extremist ideologies had taken firm hold—for different reasons and through different
pathways—on the fringe of the predominant Sunni population and among
Shiites.

The most traditional Islamic societies were among the most vulnerable
to fundamentalist revival. Saudi Arabia's royal family cohabited with a
fundamentalist religious establishment, effectively an arm of the Saudi
government, whose history was intertwined with the House of Saud. For
decades, Western expatriates living in the kingdom had learned the rules:
no consumption of alcohol; women have to be well covered in public,

women are not allowed to drive. Many had marveled at "chop Thursday" in Riyadh, when towtrucks sweep into the central market to remove cars and make way for the executioners—state-employed grim reapers who behead criminals convicted of murder, rape, or blasphemy.

Despite these puritanical traditions, the monarchy had also sent its sons, and some of its daughters, for secular education in the West, and few had imagined that embedded within this system was a latent, virulent power that could turn against the modernizing forces of the West.

During the 1980s, the Saudi royal family fatefully pandered to the jihadist movement when it appealed to the religious "patriotism" of Saudi youth, sending many off to Afghanistan to fight "godless" communism and the Soviet army. In the wild landscape of the Hindu Kush, thousands of young Saudis, along with Jordanians, Yemenis, Moroccans, and Egyptians, felt a deeper call to jihad against infidels and invaders.

Militant Islam had declared a great victory over the Soviets in Afghanistan. News of that victory rang out in official channels. Saudi embassies abroad used their offices of religious affairs to spread the word and a fundamentalist reading of the Koran. In the central Asian republics of the former Soviet Union, Saudi officials distributed one million copies of the Koran to awaken a new population. Embassies served as a network for distributing funds that often found their way to radical mosques and to groups like Hamas, the fundamentalist Islamic social organization—with a terrorist wing—that had taken hold in the Gaza Strip. Like Hezbollah in Lebanon, Hamas distributed food and provided medical care. It organized schools and religious training, gaining a dedicated, grassroots following among dispossessed Palestinians in Gaza.

Just as America had ignored the welling discontent in Egypt during Anwar Sadat's final days, the Bush administration—the entire West, really—was largely blind to the diffusion of an inchoate jihadist movement that had been trained in the mujahideen camps of Afghanistan and indoctrinated by the charismatic preachers in the mosques of Peshawar, Islamabad, Karachi, Riyadh, and Cairo. In the 1980s, many of these preachers, persecuted at home, migrated to the West to run storefront Islamic centers in Hamburg, Brussels, London, and New York. They heeded the call to oppose the great secular powers that had shaped the modern world against Islamic rule. These idealists longed to restore the caliphate of Islam and create a modern Islamic empire to contain the West, or at least cauterize its influence.

Efraim Halevy, the former Mossad chief, looked back later to say, "It was not only the United States that ignored the potential of Muslim radicalism. In truth, it must be admitted that even in Israel, which was so close to the Arab world and was monitoring every change and trend in its neighboring countries, the precise implication of what was going on did not register."[80]

The end of the anti-Soviet campaign in Afghanistan had left a devastated country. America declined to step into the vacuum and the CIA program to fund and arm the mujahideen rebels came to an abrupt end. In September 1991, the United States and the Soviet Union agreed to stop shipping arms to the residual armies that were gearing up for civil war. For the Soviets that meant cutting off their former client in Kabul, President Najibullah; for the United States it meant cutting off the warlords of Islamic insurgency. By April 1992, Kabul had fallen to indigenous forces. The regional warlords who had built an army of jihadists from all over the Muslim world prepared for a new battle. In the north was Ahmad Shah Masood, whose troops were the first to enter Kabul and topple Najibullah. And in the south was Gulbuddin Hekmatyar, head of the Hezb-i-Islami, or Party of Islam.

These Islamic warriors could no longer rely on their Saudi patron, Osama bin Laden. He, too, had turned his back on Afghanistan. His onetime ally, Prince Turki, the chief of Saudi intelligence, had broken off relations. So bin Laden accepted the invitation of the Islamic party leaders in Sudan and established an al-Qaeda base near Khartoum. As he did, a major terrorist plot against the United States was already in the planning stages.

In seeking his party's renomination in 1992, Bush hoped he could trump the negative politics of Patrick Buchanan's conservative challenge by reminding the country—constantly, it seemed—of the Persian Gulf victory. With the connivance of Scowcroft, Cheney, and Powell, the administration orchestrated a plan to bomb Baghdad, yet again, as the backdrop for his acceptance speech at the August convention. Live television would have enabled Bush, in Houston, to stand before giant TV screens showing the pyrotechnics from the Iraqi capital. But the plan was aborted when it became public through a leak to *The New York Times*. The United Nations, whose inspectors were scheduled to force the confrontation by demanding access to Saddam's Ministry of Defense headquarters, pulled back so as not to be tainted by political manipulation from Washington.[81]

Bush won his party's nomination, but his very strength, his leadership in foreign policy, had become his weakness. Domestic discontent, an anemic economy at home, accentuated the perception that Bush, unlike Reagan, had no inkling of the problems of average Americans.

But Bill Clinton did. A provincial Southern governor, educated at Georgetown, Yale, and Oxford universities, he mounted a campaign based on empathy for working and middle-class Americans caught in the economic downdraft of 1992. The Clinton campaign line that signified Bush's shortcoming was, "It's the economy, stupid."

Yet while Bush busied himself with electioneering, a profound migration—and transformation—was under way in the Middle East as jihadists made their way home from Afghanistan. Their movement had become transnational and America was no longer its patron. Hadn't America supported autocrats whose regimes repressed Islamic parties of every stripe? American foreign policy stood largely mute in the face of the growing power of Islamic extremism that was racing across national boundaries and spawning an intensified jihadist ideology that targeted Israel and the West.

It wasn't that Bush was too culture-bound to grasp the significance of what was occurring. Nor was he lacking in good intelligence from abroad. Many analysts were warning of these new developments. The reality was that Bush had been burned by every attempt to engage Islamic fundamentalists, most prominently when he supported Reagan's attempt to trade arms for hostages in the Iran-contra affair. Six years on, Bush was still being pursued by an independent prosecutor, Lawrence Walsh, who was determined to fathom the depth of Bush's knowledge of the affair.[82] And so Bush, who during his term in the White House had celebrated great openings—the Berlin Wall, the Soviet collapse—had reached a limit in the Middle East.

On September 1, 1992, just after Bush returned to Washington from the Republican convention in Houston, a young Kuwaiti of Pakistani origin named Ramzi Yousef arrived at New York's John F. Kennedy airport on an Iraqi passport that contained no visa to enter the United States. In the wake of the Persian Gulf War, anyone escaping from Saddam's Iraq and arriving in America had a good shot at asylum, and Yousef was only briefly detained before he was released pending a hearing. Yousef, who was in

his early twenties, was the nephew of Khalid Sheikh Mohammed, a
Kuwaiti radical (also of Pakistani origin) who was a member of the Muslim Brotherhood underground. (Khalid Sheikh Mohammed would become a senior operative for bin Laden's al-Qaeda network and the
mastermind of the September 11 attacks.)

Once in New York, Yousef quickly disappeared into the radical Islamist
circle of young men who followed Sheikh Omar Abdel Rahman, known
as the Blind Sheikh, who had fled persecution in Egypt for his Muslim
Brotherhood activities and for his fiery speeches against Mubarak.
Within a few months, Yousef and his fellow conspirators had constructed
a crude but powerful bomb to strike a blow for their version of jihad.

On February 26, 1993, scarcely a month after Bill Clinton had been
sworn in as president, they rented a truck and transported the bomb to
the underground parking garage beneath the World Trade Center. It was
the second anniversary of the coalition victory over Saddam Hussein.
They successfully detonated the device, hoping the massive explosion
would destabilize the foundation and bring down at least one of the towers, perhaps both. Yousef then fled the country.

Law enforcement and intelligence officials were not able to establish
whether Saddam's intelligence service was behind the plot, which killed
six people. The circumstantial evidence suggested there could be a connection. When Yousef arrived in the United States, he went straight to
the apartment of an Iraqi, Musab Yasin, and he enlisted Musab's brother,
Abdul Rahman Yasin, to help carry out the attack. Abdul Rahman Yasin,
after being questioned by the FBI, flew home to Baghdad, where he was
imprisoned in 1994.

In an interview from prison, Yasin said that Yousef had talked him into
joining the bomber squad by appealing to his Arab dignity, telling him
"how Arabs suffered a great deal and that we have to send a message that
this is not right" and "to [seek] revenge for my Palestinian brothers and
my brothers in Saudi Arabia." But also, importantly, Yousef had appealed
to Yasin's national pride as an Iraqi, arguing that he should help avenge
Iraq's defeat at the hands of America. If they knocked down the twin towers, Yousef told him, they might kill 250,000 people—many of them
Jews—and this would rival the destruction wrought by the Hiroshima
and Nagasaki bombings of World War II.[83]

In the end, the question that lingered over the first World Trade Center bombing was whether Ramzi Yousef had acted alone. Was he simply a

freelance jihadist who had come home from Pakistan, where he had trained in the mujahideen camps on the Afghan frontier, so soaked in hatred of America that he was compelled to go to New York and organize taxicab-driving militants to commit a monumental act of terror? Or had he tapped the jihadist network that his uncle Khalid Sheikh Mohammed had entered, where the outlines of grand terrorist acts—blowing up airliners with liquid explosives and knocking down skyscrapers with crude truck bombs—were circulating among men who had engineering backgrounds, knowledge of explosives, and the extremist zeal of the West-hating Islamic idealists who had come home from the Afghan war in search of another mission of faith?[84]

George H. W. Bush had not seen it coming, and Bill Clinton was not prepared for it.

# 10

## BILL CLINTON

*Tilting at Peace, Flailing at Saddam*

Bill Clinton was beside himself, obsessing over the prospect that Yasser Arafat, who was due at the White House the next morning, September 13, 1993, for the signing of the Oslo Accords, was going to kiss the president of the United States with those big, stubble-framed terrorist lips. Clinton was seized with anxiety that White House photographers were going to record the moment and that the photo, or the video, would go out to the world with an image that would become the bane of Clinton's political career from that moment on.

Clinton had to find a way to head it off.

Not yet a year in the White House, he was desperate to have his first big foreign policy success, and he was trying to figure out who could handle the delicate task of conveying to Arafat the message that he should not even think about planting those smackers on the leader of the free world. Clinton knew he had to do this in a manner that did not set off a volcanic reaction in the Palestinian camp, now settled in at the Ritz-Carlton Hotel, because Arafat's first White House visit was already set to be a big piece of symbolism if it came off. The whole event was going to elevate Clinton to the stature of international statesman, a peacemaker, though his administration had scarcely been involved in the breakthrough.

Clinton, heretofore the governor of Arkansas, was prone to shouting and swearing, and he was somewhat worked up when he told his secretary to get Prince Bandar on the telephone. Bandar had been Saudi Arabia's ambassador for a decade and the new White House team, which had scant experience with the Arab world, looked to him for help with Arafat and the Palestinians. There was a crisis a minute over how the ceremony on the South Lawn would unfold. It was going to bring Arabs and Israelis together, belly to belly, on live television.

Shimon Peres, the Israeli foreign minister, had been opposed to Clinton's inviting Arafat to the White House. Arafat had so much Israeli blood on his hands. He had been the face of Palestinian terror since Munich. He had invented Black September's blood-soaked campaign, including the assassination of the U.S. ambassador in Khartoum in 1973. But Clinton had insisted that only Arafat could represent the Palestinian people and Clinton's aides had looked at each other and said, "Arafat is coming!"—as in, *Yikes!*

The Israelis had insisted that Arafat not show up wearing his trademark revolver and the uniform of a militant—that olive-colored ensemble with the checkered kaffiyeh. But Israel was in no position to play chicken with last-minute demands. This was the World Series of peace. You either showed up to play, or stayed at home.

Arafat, too, had induced a panic in his delegation when he realized that the words "Palestine Liberation Organization" did not actually appear anywhere in the text of the Declaration of Principles—the Oslo Accords—that the two sides were about to sign. He wanted those words in the document. The PLO was the sole representative of the Palestinian people. Israel's recognition of the PLO's legitimacy as a negotiating partner was what the forty years of struggle had been all about.

But these were small problems compared with Clinton's, at least in the president's mind. He had his principal Middle East aides, Dennis Ross and Martin Indyk, both scions of the Jewish political establishment in Washington, working on the loose ends, along with Warren Christopher,

Clinton's reliable secretary of state, who fussed over details like a hen over chicks.

Bandar also had been faced with a dilemma about the ceremony. Was the ambassador from Saudi Arabia going to shake hands with Yitzhak Rabin? The prince had spoken with King Fahd to make sure he realized that his envoy was about to be the first member of the royal family to shake the hand of the prime minister of the "Zionist entity." He was pretty sure what Fahd would say—that there was no other choice—but Bandar wanted to cover his flanks in case he was criticized at home by the conservative religious authorities who were a power in their own right.

To the White House, Bandar had made only one request of the protocol chiefs: that Arafat stand on the left of the president during the ceremony, because that meant when they came down off the stage to shake hands with the invited guests, Arafat would reach Bandar first and the live video going out to the world would show this Arab-to-Arab embrace—a symbol of their victory—before Bandar had to confront Rabin, who for so long had been the enemy. It was Rabin who had taken Jerusalem from the Arabs in 1967.

"Bandar?"

It was Clinton on the telephone line with that Huck Finn voice that made the president from Arkansas so instantly likable. But there was also a note of alarm.

"Bandar, you are the only person who can save me."[1] Clinton explained the problem and the politics of the Arafat kiss. It would be the kiss of death if it went out on the wires, Clinton said.

Bandar was not an intimate of the new president. The Saudis, especially Bandar, had been devastated by Bush's loss in the 1992 election. The prince had come of age during the elder Bush's presidency, and building the Persian Gulf War coalition had been the finest hour of his service to king and country. Bandar had demonstrated that Saudi Arabia could be the indispensable ally, like Israel—even more so since the cold war had ended. Bandar had bonded so closely with the Bush team that friends called him "Bandar Bush." Now, his job as ambassador required him to adapt. He was trying to master the Clinton crowd.

The prince had met Clinton when he was governor of Arkansas. Clinton had pursued an appointment with Bandar seeking $17 million in funding for a Middle Eastern studies program at the University of Arkansas. Bandar had thought Clinton, and his request, a little quaint, even silly. Why would the kingdom invest in a farm-state university as opposed to Harvard or Stanford? Still, he passed the request to Riyadh and was surprised when someone at home approved a $3 million grant.

After Clinton's victory, King Fahd had called Bandar to ask whether there was anything the Saudis could do to ingratiate themselves with the president-elect. They worked out a simple scheme to increase the amount of the grant from $3 million, which they called a down payment, to the full $17 million. When the grant became public, the Saudis simply explained that the whole transaction had predated Clinton's victory. It had, but only in part.

Now with the president on the telephone, Bandar explained to Clinton that Yasser Arafat was not exactly under his control and it was not going to be easy to restrain the man from leaping up to plant a big kiss on the president to show his gratitude and affection for the American leader. "I'll do everything I can, Mr. President."

"No," said Clinton. That was not good enough. He wanted an unconditional promise—100 percent—that Yasser Arafat was not going to kiss him in front of one hundred million million people. He would not let Bandar off the telephone until he got an absolute assurance that it was not going to happen. Bandar gave it, ever wanting to please the president. He just hoped he could deliver.

Before he signed off, Clinton changed the subject. He was working on his speech for the ceremony. "Do you guys have something about peace in your book?" Clinton asked. He was referring to the Koran. Bandar said he would get back to him.

The prince rushed to Arafat's suite at the Ritz-Carlton and shooed all of the Palestinian aides out of the room. Bandar told the PLO chairman that King Fahd was hoping for a display of dignity and poise at the White House ceremony because the whole Arab world would be looking on. Arafat, therefore, should extend his hand prominently and powerfully to Rabin; to Clinton, he must do the same.

Arafat protested. He said he wanted to show the affection of the Palestinian people for the American president.

No, Bandar said. So open a display of affection to Clinton would be undignified since Arafat just two years earlier had been seen kissing and hugging Saddam. It was too soon after the "earthquake"—that's what

Bill Clinton with Yasser Arafat: A handshake, or a kiss?

Bandar called the rift in the Arab world caused by the Persian Gulf War; it would hurt Saudi Arabia's relations with the Palestinians. The argument barely made sense, and Bandar knew it, but it was plausible enough if Arafat believed it was coming from King Fahd.

Better to be dignified, Bandar said. The Arabs would understand that.

The next morning, Arafat arrived at the White House in his uniform—but without a gun. Rabin and Peres knew it was too late to do anything about the militant garb. Arafat was accompanied by Nabil Fahmy, the Egyptian ambassador. Fahmy had gone straight to Shimon Peres and told him that it would be a disaster for Arafat if the PLO's name was not in the document. After some wrangling, the words "PLO Team" and "for the PLO" were written in with a pen.[2] After all the last-minute disputes had been settled, they stepped out into the sunshine of a late summer morning in Washington and Arafat extended his hand firmly and prominently to Rabin and then to the American president.

The speeches soared with the rhetoric of peacemaking.

When the leaders stepped down from the stage, Arafat greeted the dignitaries and diplomats. When he came to Prince Bandar, he hugged him like a son, kissing him five times, including on the mouth. Clinton was standing behind Arafat, smiling at Bandar.

Clinton's remarks had been full of hope, and he basked in the radiant goodwill that the White House ceremony had engendered around the world.

For a president who had virtually no experience as an international statesman, Clinton was suddenly standing like a prodigy of foreign policy. He may have had few strong relationships with world leaders, many of whom had been looking forward to another four years of Bush, but there he stood before the world as full of rapture as Moses come down from the mount and with Rabin and Arafat in his arms.

With this come-from-nowhere breakthrough of Middle East diplomacy, Clinton had overcome all of the unfavorable comparisons. He silenced those who said that he simply did not project the weight that Bush, Baker, and Scowcroft had accumulated as helmsmen in the currents between changing epochs. Clinton may have been a domestic policy wonk who slept late and kept his CIA briefers cooling their heels in the West Wing hallway, but here it was exam day and Clinton had aced Middle East peace.

The 1993 Oslo Accords gave Clinton an enormous boost and an entrée into the Middle East peace process that he had never imagined possible. Here was a set of issues and an intractable conflict on which Clinton could display his greatest attributes—empathy for those afflicted by pain and suffering and a charismatic laying on of hands to persuade old enemies to compromise. He was among the smartest men to have won the presidency in this century, and here was a chance to use his laser intellect to formulate the comprehensive peace that had eluded every president since Truman, a chance for this small-state governor to catapult himself beyond the Bush foreign policy legacy with an enviable grandiosity. The risk was that Clinton's weaknesses—a prodigious lack of discipline, endless empathy that hobbled decisiveness, and principles that shifted like the winds—would undermine him.

He had come to office at a time of rare convergence for the forces of peace in the Holy Land, but also at a time of threat from the nascent jihadist movement, whose adherents saw peace with Israel—saw even Israel's existence—as a threat to the revival of a pan-Islamic empire. And then there was Saddam Hussein, still caged but relentlessly trying to break the sanctions that contained him.

President-elect Clinton immediately tried to distinguish himself from

George Bush. He declared that he would not be "obsessed" by Saddam, that he believed in "deathbed conversions" even among tyrants, and that if Saddam wanted a relationship with the United States "all he has to do is change his behavior."[3] Clinton's remarks triggered a storm of criticism and he was forced, even before he took the oath of office, to adopt a tougher line against Saddam, one that precluded rehabilitation. Yet it was an early signal that Clinton's inclination was to see Saddam as Bush's obsession and that he would resist entanglement in Iraq if he could.[4]

The new paradigm of conflict in the Middle East was not the old Nasserite struggle—Arab nationalism against colonial writ and Zionism. The cold war had ended; Moscow's clients were exposed and on their own. America was a lone superpower: Arab holdouts against peace would have to beat a path to Washington—Syria first and then the Palestinians. Saddam could be contained as a brute, along with Iran—"dual containment" was the term invented by the Clinton team to describe what, in reality, was a perpetuation of the status quo.

Yet there was a new source of conflict rising: the Islamic fringe against modernity. Radical clerics, and there were many of them, capitalized on the piety of youth; their audience was the burgeoning population of young Muslims born into repressive societies, bereft of opportunity and dependent on the West. Peace with Israel was not on their agenda.

What became known as the Oslo Accords had emerged from months of secret negotiations between the PLO and an Israeli foreign ministry team headed by Uri Savir, a quiet and cerebral diplomat. If any other government deserved credit, it was that of Norway, whose foreign minister, Terje Larsen, served as a go-between and provided a series of secret venues in the Norwegian countryside where Israeli and PLO negotiators erected a framework that would lead, they believed, to Palestinian statehood and peace.

Savir had plump Santa Claus cheeks and an easy smile. He came from a diplomatic family. His father, Leo Savir, was one of the founders of the Israeli foreign service and believed strongly that Israel had to talk to its enemies. To him, the Zionist dream was to break the psychology of the ghetto—the notion that Jews were a people apart—and instead engage the world as a nation with robust diplomacy and cultural interchange. Leo Savir also believed, and his son followed him in this, that the occupation of the West Bank and Gaza was a disaster for the Jewish state and that over time the occupation would erode Israel's moral fiber and its humanity.[5]

The PLO team was headed by Ahmed Qurei, known to most Palestinians as Abu Ala. Along with Mahmoud Abbas, Abu Mazen to his colleagues, Qurei was among the old guard of PLO chiefs representing the most respectable face of the organization. He and Abbas came from prominent Palestinian families. Qurei, born in 1937 in Abu Dis on the edge of Jerusalem, had joined the PLO in 1968 and had supervised the economic department of the executive committee. Qurei believed, as many Palestinian leaders did—though not all of them—that the Palestinians would never find peace until they accepted Israel and constructed a modus vivendi that gave both sides what they needed: for Israel, security; for the Palestinians, statehood on the land of Palestine that remained for them in the West Bank and Gaza.

Rabin wanted to make a deal with the Palestinians and had told Israelis that his goal was to do so within nine months of his election. After Clinton's election, Rabin went to Washington and laid out his plans to the president-elect.

The Madrid process that Bush had started had reached a dead end. And though Israeli contact with the PLO was still forbidden by law, Rabin saw that the Palestinian delegation that was established in Madrid was taking its instructions from PLO headquarters in Tunis. In essence, Israel already was negotiating with Arafat by fax. So Rabin had begun thinking seriously about talking to Israel's nemesis face-to-face.[6]

The other factor shaping Rabin's outlook was change in Israel. The pioneer spirit was fading, and so was the spartan instinct to fight. On a helicopter flight up to the Golan, Rabin had told his friend Shlomo Ben-Ami that the dreams of the younger generation in Israel were about business and the technological revolution. Israelis were looking for personal fulfillment. That required peace.[7]

Rabin had brought Shimon Peres into his government, an old rival but also a big thinker. Peres came with an idea, formulated by his protégé, Yossi Beilin, about creating a vehicle for secret negotiations. It called for using a pair of academics, Yair Hirschfeld and Ron Pundak. They were in contact with the PLO in London. Soon, Peres had Rabin's assent to open private talks in which both the Israeli and Palestinian participants could put things on the table they did not dare propose in Washington.

Peres justified the risk. "The peace process is in danger of collapsing, even though the ground is fertile for progress,"[8] he told Savir, and dispatched him to Norway with a warning that the government would disavow the talks if anything leaked to the press.

The secret channel, which took the negotiators into the Norwegian wood, was successful in part because Savir and Qurei were like-minded humanists. Both believed that it was possible to end the conflict. They debated history ferociously and struggled over new concepts of transition and of what a dignified coexistence would look like. By the end of summer, they had drafted a declaration of principles that laid out the steps for Palestinian self-rule. It would extend over five years and end with a full and final settlement between the two peoples. The terms of that settlement were left open, but the process was predicated on bringing the occupation to an end and on the withdrawal of Israeli military forces in stages to make way for an independent Palestinian Authority. Both understood it would eventually be a state.

Israel recognized the PLO on September 9, 1993, and Arafat, for the PLO, recognized Israel in an exchange of letters with Rabin. Arafat also pledged to bring the intifada, now six years old, to an end. The PLO renounced terrorism and took responsibility for "all PLO elements and personnel" to end the use of violence in resolving differences.[9] Israel agreed to negotiate so-called interim and final status arrangements that could lead to a sovereign Palestinian state on Israel's border.

The Oslo Accords represented the greatest diplomatic achievement in the Middle East since Sadat and Begin had signed the peace between Egypt and Israel. For Israel, the Palestinians were an intimate enemy. They were claimants for the same land and their history was intertwined with the Jewish narrative. The accords crossed a new threshold, but they were not without critics. PLO hard-liners resigned from the executive committee and denounced Arafat. To the Israeli right wing, the accords were anathema. Benjamin Netanyahu, a rising figure in the Likud Party who was establishing himself as Rabin's paramount challenger in the opposition, accused the prime minister of "allowing the PLO to carry out its plan to destroy Israel." Here was the fundamental difference in perception. The young "princes" of the Likud didn't trust Arafat's peace overture. Sure, Arafat might make a temporary peace to lull his neighbor, they believed, but this was just a strategy to build a PLO state on Israel's border and then, at the time of Arafat's choosing, to attack and destroy the Jewish homeland.

Netanyahu went before the Knesset on August 30 and savaged Rabin: "Mr. Prime Minister, there have been examples, in this century, when heads of state have gone crazy." He compared Rabin to Neville Chamberlain, who, he said, acted "with blatant stupidity when he believed the liar Hitler and that is exactly what you are doing." Rabin, he said, "was far worse than Chamberlain. You are endangering the security and freedom of your own people. In this case, you are giving credence to the liar Arafat, as if his promises, his words, his agreements have some value." Netanyahu vowed to "use all legitimate means at the disposal of a democratic opposition to stop this foolish process, which endangers the very future of the country."[10]

Even a Rabin protégé, General Ehud Barak, the chief of staff of the Israeli Defense Forces, found fault, saying the accords were "riddled with holes."

Nonetheless, the Oslo Accords opened a new era of peacemaking with a sense of hope and confidence that had been absent since Jimmy Carter's presidency. The accords also had a domino effect, for as soon as King Hussein of Jordan heard about them, he saw an opportunity to join in and by doing so rehabilitate his relations with the United States, which had frayed following his alliance with Iraq during the Persian Gulf War.[11] In Syria, Hafez al-Assad was thrown into a profound reassessment of his long stalemate with Israel. Had the political winds shifted so dramatically that he might win the return of the Golan Heights?[12]

Over the next eight months, the Oslo process produced an initial agreement that established a Palestinian Authority in Gaza and Jericho. This began the five-year interim period of Palestinian self-rule. By the end of this transition, "final status" negotiations were to fix the final boundaries, powers, and security arrangements for a Palestinian state. Ahead of them lay tough negotiations on the "right of return" for hundreds of thousands of Palestinian refugees still living in camps. Negotiators would have to settle the status of Jerusalem as a capital that both peoples claimed.

Assad, too, was thinking about making peace. In January 1994, Clinton met with him in Geneva, and after a marathon discussion about what peace would mean, Assad appeared with Clinton at a press conference and listened intently—without contradicting him—as the president explained that peace between Syria and Israel would mean embassies and trade across borders. Assad had met three previous American leaders—Nixon, Carter, and Bush—but Clinton had the greatest personal effect on him, because Clinton said right up front that he understood the significance of the Golan Heights to Syria and how crucial it was for Assad to recover it with dignity.[13]

"Clinton is a real person," Assad said to Clinton's Middle East specialist Dennis Ross after the meeting, using flattery that he knew would get back to Clinton. "He speaks to you with awareness and understanding. He knows our problems better and he is committed to solving them. I haven't felt this from an American president before."[14]

To the Israelis, the mechanics of peace were everything. If peace with Syria had no content beyond withdrawal, the two sides would simply revert to the days of hatred and mistrust, when the Jewish farmers and villagers of Galilee lived in fear of Syrian artillerymen. Peace had to mean the end of belligerence and the beginning of normal relations among neighbors—who talked to each other, worked out disputes, sold goods to each other, and visited each other's cities, monuments, and antiquities.

Assad, whose long-term health was uncertain because of a history of heart trouble, was engaging the idea of real peace with his enemy for the first time. Assad had always said that the Jews were not a nation but rather a people, and that Syrian hegemony was the natural order of things in Palestine and the broader Levant, including Lebanon, because Damascus had been the seat of Arab power since the Umayyad caliphate (established A.D. 660). Indeed, to understand Syrian radicalism it was necessary also to perceive that the historic chip on Syria's shoulder stood for all that it had lost since the days when Damascus was the glory of the Islamic empire.

To recognize Israel permanently would be a momentous step for Assad, for he would have to accept the legitimacy of Zionism, which had always been an alien concept in Arab nationalist orthodoxy. And yet change and opportunity were in the air. Rabin was the strongest figure in the Israeli security establishment since Dayan, and as Assad observed him taking on the deeply entrenched settler movement, he calculated that if Rabin succeeded, the Golan would come back to Syria and, if Rabin failed, the benchmark for peace would have been set for the future.

This awakening was still under way in Damascus when on January 21, 1994, just days after Assad had met Clinton, Assad's eldest son, Basil, was killed in a car crash on the Beirut–Damascus highway. General Hikmat Shihabi, the chief of staff of the Syrian military, and Adnan Makhluf, the head of the Republican Guard, brought the news to Assad. When he saw them, he asked, "What is it, a coup?"[15] Assad was crushed by the news. He had been grooming Basil to succeed him and he had only one other son, Bashar, who was neither as strong nor as clever.

Rabin had his own problems and Clinton was scarcely paying attention to them.[16] The right wing was working to undermine peace. In February 1994, an American émigré to Israel, Dr. Baruch Goldstein, a religious settler from a Jewish enclave in Hebron called Kiryat Arba, walked into the Cave of the Patriarchs, leveled an automatic weapon at the Arabs gathered for Friday prayers, and opened fire. He kept firing until 29 of the Arab worshippers lay dead and more than 150 wounded. The remaining worshippers themselves rushed to overcome Goldstein, using a fire extinguisher to subdue him, then they beat him to death.

It was Ramadan. The cave is an ancient excavation in the Judean Hills containing the tomb of Abraham. The site is revered in Judaism, Christianity, and Islam. For centuries, the Arabs have worshipped at the Ibrahimi Mosque—the Mosque of Abraham—and no figure from the Old Testament so aptly symbolizes the common root of the three monotheistic faiths. Like Mecca and Jerusalem, Hebron is an ancient nexus of the faithful, and the arc of history radiates out from Abraham's life, from his recorded communion with God and, in modern times, from the rocky vault that holds his dust. Naturally, Hebron is a tinderbox for religious conflict. Some 450 militant Jewish settlers had seized outposts in and around the Arab city of 150,000, requiring thousands of Israeli soldiers to protect their beachhead.

Goldstein's religious zeal overpowered every other instinct in his life. A member of the Jewish Defense League, the militant organization founded by Rabbi Meir Kahane, Goldstein was repulsed by Rabin's peacemaking and his reconciliation with the PLO. To him it was an unforgivable surrender. As a doctor, he had treated the victims of Palestinian violence. The prospect of turning over biblical lands to the Palestinians was sacrilege. He had decided to make a statement through violence that he knew might lead to his own death. His passion didn't quite make him a suicide bomber, but the instinct was the same.

Palestinians came out of their mosques and homes and rioted in the wake of the massacre. Stone-throwing youths confronted Israeli armor. Dozens of Arabs died and hundreds were wounded in the weeks after the attack. From Tunis, Arafat demanded a strong response from Rabin. The PLO leader refused to return to the Gaza-Jericho talks until the Hebron settlers were removed and a Palestinian police force established in the city under the supervision of an international security force. Clinton called on both parties to come to Washington so he could mediate, but Arafat would not budge.

The Hebron crisis reflected the deep flaw in the Oslo process. The breakthrough had promised an almost revolutionary change for two societies that had been at each other's throats for much of the century. The handshakes on the South Lawn and the coming together of old foes denoted a new era, a new attitude. Yet the problem that Rabin and the entire Israeli security establishment did not foresee was that nothing had really changed for the Palestinians still living under occupation. As the rioting spread across the West Bank in mid-March, Peres sent two of his aides to Tunis to try to persuade Arafat to return to the talks, but Arafat wanted Israel's leaders to address the psychology of the occupation.

"I don't understand your logic," Arafat told them. "Thirty-nine Palestinians have been killed since February 25. Four hundred have been wounded, and you place the West Bank under curfew? You punish the victims?"

The Israelis, most pointedly the Israeli Defense Forces, were not accustomed to treating the Palestinians as human beings of equal standing. Yes, the Palestinians were a people, and the Israeli courts were full of Palestinian petitions to enforce their rights, but underneath the façade, Palestinian humanity had been horribly degraded by occupation. Prominent analysts, including Shlomo Gazit, a former chief of Israeli military intelligence, warned that occupation was dehumanizing the Arab population. They saw how difficult it was for the occupier to remove the protective mantle of superiority and accept the occupied as equals. And when violence intervened, from either side, the obstacles to reestablishing trust were formidable.

The settler movement had created a new incentive to keep the Palestinians down because the Israeli military was responsible for protecting the settlers, their children, and their homes. Thus the physical movement of Palestinians from village to village, from home to the fields, was subjected to greater and greater levels of control by the Israeli military, which seemed unaccountable to any international legal authority in the administration of Palestinian lives.[17]

In the aftermath of the Hebron massacre, Arafat was also playing the politics of leverage. He stood on the shoulders of his people to do it. "In Jordan, Lebanon and Syria, I'm accused of being a traitor. A traitor, gentlemen. A traitor. My people are living in dread of yet another massacre. You must take steps to rebuild our trust, otherwise the peace process will die. But instead, your army fires on my people."[18]

Arafat had hit the nerve that had been deadened by nearly three decades of domination. Israeli prime ministers, one after the other, had surrendered to, indulged, or coddled the settler movement. Goldstein's act was broadly condemned in Israel; steps were taken to ensure that his burial place did not become a shrine.[19] But in Kiryat Arba, where he had lived, the wife of the mayor said publicly that while she would not teach her children to emulate Goldstein, his act had important implications.[20] The message, reinforced among extremists, was that murder was an individual choice and that murder, even mass murder, could have important consequences for Jewish nationalism and the Zionist cause.

Of course, appeals to Israeli humanism from Arafat, the former terrorist leader, did not register as profoundly as they might have from another authority of unimpeachable moral stature—a Mandela, for instance—but Arafat *was* the Palestinian leader, the one whom Rabin had decided to engage as a partner. Arafat needed to know whether the Israelis understood the poison that Goldstein's shooting spree had injected into the Palestinian psyche. But Rabin—and the Americans—treated Arafat's demands as if they were a negotiating gambit. They believed he was using Goldstein's act to gain advantage in a zero-sum game between the occupier and the occupied. And, of course, the cynical political calculation was always present with Arafat. He was playing grievance politics, but that didn't make it any less true that Palestinians were being killed and many were turning against peace because Oslo had changed nothing on the ground.

Rabin had sent a message to Arafat through Dennis Ross saying that Goldstein had brought dishonor on the Israeli military by his act. Rabin and General Amnon Lipkin-Shahak, the chief of staff, apologized to Arafat, and their contrition appeared to register. Arafat was trying to lead Rabin to the conclusion that the settlers of Hebron were the destroyers of peace and that he had to remove them. Rabin was leaning in that direction.

The Americans were far less sensitive to the Palestinian turmoil that had been caused by Goldstein's assault; they were more attuned to the Israeli political clock. The Americans could engage Arafat's dilemma, but not to the point of pushing Rabin into dangerous political waters, which was where he would be if he were to expel the settlers from Hebron or to accept an international force in Hebron that would reaffirm to the Palestinians that the international community regarded their protection as essential.

Instead, on the evening after their discussion, Ross undermined whatever goodwill Rabin's apology had created by threatening Arafat: unless he returned to the negotiating table, the United States would veto the United Nations Security Council resolution that expressed the international community's shock at the "appalling massacre committed against Palestinian worshippers in the Mosque of Ibrahim in Hebron" and underlined "the need to provide protection and security for the Palestinian people."

Arafat blew up at the American threat. Ross had adopted a patronizing tone, dictating an ultimatum after Rabin's respectful apology. Clinton's fabled empathy was absent because he was absorbed with domestic scandals (Whitewater, Paula Jones), and the Americans seemed oblivious to what the Palestinians desperately needed—reaffirmation that the period of dehumanization was going to end. They needed a tangible sign that the Israelis, especially the army and the security services, were going to change the rules that had made life on the Palestinian street subject to arbitrary power and to random acts like Goldstein's. When the Israelis suffered an act of Palestinian rage or terror, they constantly received reaffirmation from the institutions of the Jewish state and from Washington. But the Palestinians were still waiting.

Ross's tactic revealed the shortcoming of the White House's approach to Middle East diplomacy. Clinton's team accepted all too quickly the "red lines" that Israeli political authorities laid down, while assigning themselves the task of crafting formulas that the Palestinians might be induced or cudgeled into accepting.

Clinton, notwithstanding his capacity for empathy, seemed unable during this early crisis over Hebron to engage the plight of the Palestinians living under occupation. It was as if he could not perceive that the morning after he presided over the signing of the Oslo Accords on the South Lawn, the roadblocks and checkpoints that constricted Palestinians' movement, smothered their commerce, and robbed them of their dignity were still there, as was the contempt radiating from young Israeli soldiers who, when polled, evinced hostility for the population they controlled.[21]

Israeli society was deeply conflicted by the occupation. A large segment of the population had over the years come to believe that the West Bank and Gaza would never be returned to the Arabs because these lands—Judea and Samaria especially—were part of historic Israel. Yet, at the same time, another large segment supported Oslo and was prepared psychologically to retreat from the territories to make way for a Palestinian state as long as peace meant security.

At its essence, this was the old debate between idealism and militarism in conflict within the Zionist code. The former sought a Jewish state whose diplomacy and peacemaking could stand as a moral example in the world, and the latter accepted the Hobbesian notion that conflict with the Arabs was a never-ending reality, that combat was brutal and, therefore, there was no sense lamenting the harsh requirements of military domination.

Oslo had done nothing to begin the necessary psychological transformation. Instead of confidence-building measures, "both sides [descended] into an ugly and demagogic battle of declarations, while attempting to establish new facts to strengthen their hands towards the final settlement talks," as Shlomo Gazit has observed.

For all of their determination to make peace, Rabin and Peres did not anticipate the strategic consequences of business as usual.

Nothing moved Arafat until Rabin took the first step toward evacuating the Jewish settlers from Hebron, a move that was violently opposed in the Knesset. Arafat saw that Rabin was trying—though failing—to respond to the Palestinian demands. From Tunis, Arafat sent the message: "Tell Rabin that I understand his difficulties and that I expect he'll do what's necessary when the time is right."[22]

The first milestone of the Oslo peace process was the Gaza-Jericho Agreement, signed in Cairo in early May 1994. It established a Palestinian Authority and began the clock ticking on five years of interim Palestinian self-rule and a permanent settlement—meaning statehood—by May 1999. During that time, the size of the Palestinian Authority area was to expand out beyond Jericho to include the other cities of the West Bank and, at the end of the period, the two sides were slated to conclude a "final status" agreement.

The ceremony in Cairo was a near disaster. At the last moment, Arafat insisted that the agreement provide for a Palestinian policeman to stand on the Allenby Bridge, the new border crossing between Jordan and the Palestinian Authority at Jericho. The Americans were furious. The Israelis smelled treachery. The Egyptians were exasperated. Arafat was throwing a tantrum over a single policeman?

But that was Arafat. He was on television fighting for his people as if he had a rifle and this was the Battle of Karameh. To the other leaders it seemed a display of childish antics, but Arafat wanted a symbol that the Palestinians were going to get a state with borders that Palestinians would control and, therefore, that single policeman symbolized statehood and control, as Israeli soldiers manning checkpoints symbolized occupation. Arafat angered everyone that day, but he displayed to his own people how tenaciously he was fighting for dignity—and for inches of additional territory. It diverted attention from how small a slice of the pie the Palestinians had actually received.

On July 1, Arafat made his entrance to Gaza. Ever the showman, he knelt at the Rafah border crossing, and with tears in his eyes he kissed the ground. By the time he got to Gaza City, a crowd of one hundred thousand Palestinians flooded the central square to welcome him and the promise of Palestinian independence. He signaled his seriousness about quickly expanding the boundaries of his territory and vowed that the Palestinians would never end their struggle until they reached Jerusalem to pray.

The crowd responded in an emotional chorus: "To Jerusalem . . . To Jerusalem . . . To Jerusalem."

Standing there dressed for battle below the dusty rooftops of Gaza looking out over the chanting mass of Palestinians near the shore of the Mediterranean, Arafat warned the Israelis that signing the "peace of the courageous" was not enough. "The peace needs more courage from all of us in order to hold up, and we must uphold this peace."[23]

A few days later, he flew to Jericho, swore in a cabinet, and took control of the Palestinian Authority. The immediate question was whether Arafat could quell the terrorist violence that emanated from Palestinian extremists, notably Hamas, the Islamist party that supported a terrorist underground. Israelis were still reeling from a car bomb attack that had killed eight people on a bus in Afula and wounded scores of others. A week later a suicide bomber had struck in Hadera, detonating his explosives on a bus, killing five passengers and wounding thirty. Rabin had ordered the army to undertake a prolonged closure of the West Bank and Gaza Strip, preventing thousands of Palestinians from commuting to jobs in Israeli towns and cities. Even when Rabin reopened the territories, there was more bloodshed when rioting broke out at the main crossing out of Gaza to Israel over the intrusive searches that were instituted to root out terrorists.

For Rabin, Arafat's arrival and the setting up of a PLO-led Palestinian Authority was the direct and inevitable consequence of the decision he had made to pursue peace. The right-wing opposition, however, was on fire with dissent over the path he had chosen. They called Rabin a traitor and tested the boundaries of political opposition with their threats.

Two days after Arafat landed in Gaza, Rabin told a Labor Party gathering that "the extreme right in Israel celebrates the bloodshed by the terrorist murderers of extremist Islam, trying to use the Israeli victims as a lever against the agreement." He complained that the suicide bombers of Hamas had become "the tool of the extreme right in Israel."[24]

As the new Palestinian entity began to take shape, King Hussein became more desperate to reconcile with the United States and turn his back on Iraq. Jordan was struggling financially. The king could no longer depend on Saddam for oil or economic support. Rabin wanted to help. He introduced Efraim Halevy, his deputy Mossad chief, to Clinton's Middle East aides Ross and Indyk in late April, telling them that Halevy had just returned from secret consultations in Amman and that King Hussein was ready to enter negotiations for comprehensive peace.

Ross and Indyk showed no enthusiasm. They told the Mossad official that the Jordanian monarch had a credibility problem, having earlier flirted with making peace only to withdraw at the last moment. They were wary about urging Clinton to climb out on a limb, though Clinton desperately needed to change the subject from his domestic travails (Hillary's $100,000 windfall on a cattle futures trade now among them). But Halevy's view was that circumstances had changed. The old dangers for an Arab leader going it alone had been overtaken by the momentum toward peace after the cold war. Plus, King Hussein could see what anyone could: Jordan was the gateway to Baghdad and to bringing greater pressure on Saddam, and the CIA was interested in rebuilding America's ties to Jordan.[25]

King Hussein arrived in Washington in June and engaged in a shrewd round of bargaining at the White House. What was extraordinary about the visit was that Rabin had sent his Mossad man, Halevy, to try to convince Washington to sell weaponry to its old enemy with whom it still shared a fortified border. It was surreal. The Israelis lobbied for the sale of a squadron of F-16s to Jordan's air force, something Clinton thought might be possible after Jordan signed a full peace treaty with Israel. The arguments over the F-16s were heated. At one point, Ross had snapped at Halevy, "Tell me, Efraim, who are you representing here? Israel or Jordan?"

"Both," Halevy snapped back.[26]

Clinton's bargaining approach—seeking dramatic and visible concessions from King Hussein—reflected the skeptical mood in Washington toward a president who had let a murderous warlord run U.S. troops out of Somalia and who had done nothing when genocide leveled the Tutsi population of Rwanda. Midterm congressional elections loomed, and the White House feared being attacked by Republicans for rewarding Saddam's little friend, the king of Jordan. Clinton suggested that if King Hussein met publicly with Rabin, it would be easier for the White House to go to Congress with a big aid package and to consider canceling $700 million in Jordanian debt to the United States, which was also prominent on the king's wish list. In the privacy of the White House, Clinton spent nearly an hour trying, without success, to persuade the king to purchase American-made Boeing jetliners for Royal Jordanian Airlines.

King Hussein returned home and declared before the Jordanian parliament that if it would serve the cause of peace, he would meet publicly with the prime minister of Israel. Rabin was listening. He sent Halevy secretly to the king. Before the end of July, Halevy emerged from Amman with the text of a joint declaration for Jordanian-Israeli peace.

Success had a thousand fathers, and the breakthrough with Jordan aroused the political vanities of almost everyone associated with it. Clinton wanted credit because it would help in the midterm elections. Peres claimed credit for his role, which had been incidental to the Mossad channel. Rabin withheld the draft declaration from Peres and from the Americans. The Clinton team sought to insert text stating that Israel and Jordan were committed to reducing threats from "conventional and nonconventional weapons" in the Middle East. Rabin killed the American language as it seemed to challenge Israel's secret nuclear weapons program.[27]

Rabin and King Hussein agreed to stage their joint declaration for peace on the border between Israel and Jordan, but the White House got indignant. It was "paying" for the peace with debt relief and weapons for Jordan. Clinton believed he had every reason to expect the parties to stage their Middle East peace pageant in Washington, where he would get some credit.

So Rabin and the king traveled to Washington. Clinton pushed the ceremony beyond the previous year's cinematic benchmarks, arranging for both leaders to address a joint meeting of Congress, where the oratory soared.[28] Abba Eban, writing from retirement in Herzliya, tried to put the Jordanian monarch's life in perspective.

"As an ardent Arab nationalist, King Hussein would probably have preferred a Middle East without Israel, but he was quicker than any other Arab leader to understand that Israel had passed the threshold of destructibility.

"As the years went by," Eban continued, "he must have been painfully aware that nothing protected Jordan's survival more effectively than Israel's interest in preserving it."[29]

That was certainly true, but Eban's tribute distorted history. Hadn't Ben-Gurion contemplated pushing the young king off his throne? Hadn't Sharon revived the idea of toppling the king and turning Jordan into a Palestinian state?

On October 7, 1994, Prince Bandar was in Oxfordshire, England, when his secure CIA phone started going off. Bandar had purchased an estate called Glympton Park from a British tycoon who had gone belly up. Bandar and his wife, Princess Haifa, were in the midst of rebuilding and refurbishing the manor house, which sat regally by a stream surrounded by two thousand acres of pheasant-hunting meadows in the English countryside, just down the road from the Duke of Marlborough's Blenheim Palace. As much as Bandar loved America, he was equally at home in England, the country to which his father, Prince Sultan, had sent him as a lad to learn how to fly with the Royal Air Force.

Whenever the CIA phone rang, Bandar knew that the president or a senior aide would be on the other end. The voice that day was Sandy Berger's, the stout international lawyer who served as Clinton's deputy national security adviser. Berger had garnered a reputation as a foreign policy troubleshooter with a nose for how foreign policy developments affected domestic politics, a subject for which his boss, Anthony Lake, expressed a lack of interest.

It was Columbus Day in Washington. Berger was calling to report that Saddam's army was on the move. There had been no warning. It looked like the Hammurabi Division of the Republican Guard had deployed in a menacing formation on the Kuwaiti border; another guard division was headed south. It was anyone's guess what Saddam was up to, but the CIA believed he was making some kind of play to break free from the United Nations sanctions. Clinton was prepared, he said, to take military action to deter Saddam from a new invasion of Kuwait.

As it happened, General John Shalikashvili, the chairman of the Joint Chiefs of Staff, was visiting Saudi Arabia. Berger wanted to get Shali (that's what everyone called the general) in to see King Fahd on an urgent basis so he could brief the king on U.S. military plans.

Bandar was apprehensive. The Americans were a month away from Election Day. Domestic politics was going to be a big motivating factor in any presidential response.

"Sandy, could you give me a heads-up?" Bandar asked. "What is the general going to propose, so I can prepare His Majesty?"

Berger said the president was prepared to take military action if Saddam did not back down. Clinton had decided to launch cruise missile attacks on two radar stations in northern Iraq.

Bandar paused. He wondered if he had heard correctly. "Saddam is moving divisions in the south and you are going to hit some missile batteries up north?" Bandar asked.[30]

Berger explained that the cruise missile attacks would show Saddam that the United States was serious, and they would stand as a warning to withdraw his army from the south.

In Washington, Clinton warned during a news conference that "it would be a grave mistake for Saddam Hussein to believe for any reason that the United States would have weakened its resolve on the same issues that involved us in that conflict just a few years ago."[31] He said nothing of plans to launch cruise missile strikes in northern Iraq. He simply said he had taken precautionary steps, which included, according to Pentagon officials, the deployment of an aircraft carrier and an Aegis-class cruiser equipped with cruise missiles.

Bandar thought quickly. He knew King Fahd was deeply troubled by the circumstances that had left Saddam Hussein in power at the end of the Persian Gulf War. There was talk in the royal family about reconciling with Saddam, but that was a terrible option for Saudi-American relations.

"Sandy," Bandar said, "I am going to prove to you right now that I am your best friend. Not only am I *not* going to talk to His Majesty about the general's request to see him, I'm going to talk to His Majesty and insist that he does not see the general." Bandar had reason to believe he was on safe ground. Berger was proposing a flyswatter assault on a rogue elephant. It was the kind of response that King Fahd would ridicule. Did he have to mention Jimmy Carter and unarmed F-15s again?

"Hit the radar stations in the north if you want to," Bandar continued. "We won't stop you and in any case you don't need our assistance or approval to do that."[32]

Berger asked Bandar what he thought was the appropriate response.

"If Saddam moved three divisions, the president should be talking about bombing the shit out of those three divisions," Bandar said. "Demolish them totally so we can tell Saddam Hussein that you cannot do this again. Then send the general to ask us to join."

"Bandar, that means war," Berger protested.

"Of course it does. What do you think Saddam is trying to do?"

Instead of mounting a warning strike with cruise missiles, Clinton over the next forty-eight hours ordered 36,000 American troops to the Persian Gulf along with more than 350 additional warplanes. The deployment cost hundreds of millions of dollars.

On October 10, Iraq announced that it was pulling its forces back from the Kuwaiti border. But the seventy-two-hour crisis and costly deployment had raised a new dilemma for the Clinton administration: What if Saddam did the same thing a month or six months hence? The Saudis saw the same problem. King Fahd wondered whether the kingdom should adjust its policy toward Saddam—not reconciliation, but a step in that direction, because it seemed implausible that America could fully contain a wounded and angry predator.

In the final two weeks of the midterm election campaign, Clinton traveled to the Holy Land so that he could stand with Yitzhak Rabin and King Hussein as they signed a formal peace between Israel and Jordan. The trip was marred by violence and dissonance. A week before Air Force One bearing Clinton and a large entourage touched down, a Hamas suicide bomber blew up a bus in Tel Aviv's Dizengoff Square, killing twenty-two people and wounding forty.

The Oslo peace process had triggered a horrific new tactic among Palestinian extremists—recruiting pious youths willing to die in the war on Israel and packing plastic explosives into vests or belts to be detonated on a bus or in a crowded street. For Israelis, the death toll from terrorism

following the creation of the Palestinian Authority was becoming a volatile political issue. Rabin, responding to public opinion, once again closed
Gaza's crossings into Israel.

But peace with Jordan went forward. The Jordanian-Israeli treaty was
signed at a ceremony in the Negev's Arava Valley. Clinton shared the
stage with King Hussein, Rabin, Peres, and Ezer Weizman. Arafat was
not invited. The advent of suicide bombing had sidelined the Israeli-
Palestinian peace process.

Clinton journeyed to Damascus, where Assad told him that Israel
could not have five years to vacate the Golan, as Rabin was proposing.
Sixteen months at the most, Assad said, but he was willing to allow an
Israeli diplomatic mission in Damascus four months prior to the completion of the withdrawal.[33]

Clinton went to Kuwait to pay tribute to the U.S. troops whose deployment had forced Saddam Hussein to back down. But there was another
item on the agenda, a short diversion across the Kuwaiti desert to Saudi
Arabia, where Clinton touched down at an air base just inside the border
at Hafr al-Batin. King Fahd and Prince Bandar were waiting for him.

For Clinton and King Fahd, it was a first meeting. The endless desert
surrounding them accentuated the intimacy of the rendezvous. Bandar
was ecstatic at the reaffirmation of the Saudi-American alliance that
Franklin Roosevelt had sealed with Bandar's grandfather. Fahd was a student of American presidents. He had grown up watching and studying
and he had high hopes for Clinton, because the new president had shown
compassion for the Muslims being slaughtered by Serbs in Bosnia.

The sectarian killing in the former Yugoslavia, where Muslims had
come as conquerors in the heyday of empire, had been a sore point between the Saudis and George H. W. Bush in the final days of the first
Bush administration. Fahd could not believe that in the twentieth century, Muslim minorities in the heart of Europe could be singled out for
annihilation. Fahd had sent Bandar to offer Saudi troops to intervene
with American and other forces, but Bush had disappointed the king.

"I am not willing to risk one American soldier's life in Bosnia, because
there is no national interest for America there," he said. Bush feared that
if he humiliated Gorbachev by intervening militarily in Eastern Europe,
the heart of what the Soviets saw as their sphere of influence, "the [So-
viet] military might take over" in Moscow and there would be an even
bigger crisis.[34]

Clinton had come in with a completely different attitude.[35] When Bandar met the new president in Tony Lake's office for an initial discussion, Clinton was interested in creating a coalition to rescue the Bosnian Muslims in the same way that the Desert Storm coalition had rescued Kuwait. "The Europeans see Bosnia as a problem," Clinton said. "I see it as an opportunity."

Imagine, Clinton continued, if Americans and Europeans sent a predominantly Western and Christian army into Bosnia to save the Bosnian Muslims. Such an act would confer great moral authority on the West to then ask Muslims to protect minorities throughout the Muslim world. Clinton had deeply impressed the Saudis with empathy for the plight of Muslims, greater empathy than their friend Bush had shown. The only problem was that Clinton didn't have the discipline to follow through. He couldn't bring the Europeans together. When British Prime Minister John Major resisted committing ground forces, saying intervention was a hard sell for British public opinion, Clinton and his secretary of state, Warren Christopher, wilted. Bandar came to believe that Clinton lacked strength of will. He had so much empathy for each side's arguments that he veered from one course to another. Empathy without principle or resolute action was empty emotionalism; it could only disappoint.

During Clinton's first year, when the "Black Hawk Down" clash in the Somali capital of Mogadishu resulted in the deaths of eighteen American soldiers, Clinton had rationalized withdrawing U.S. troops after the Somali warlord, Mohamed Farrah Aidid, pulled off a bloody ambush.

"We are not running away with our tail between our legs," Clinton told his aides. But in fact, he did. He brought control of the peacekeeping deployment into the White House until the United Nations was ready to take over.

From that moment on, "No more U.S. troops get killed. None," he instructed them.[36]

"We're also not going to flatten Mogadishu to prove we are the big badass superpower. Everybody in the world knows we could do that. We don't have to prove that to anybody."

The message radiated out to the bureaucracy. Clinton's presidency would be marked by risk avoidance in foreign policy. Rwanda would be the worst example, with a quarter million slaughtered in a genocide that America and the great powers watched from a distance.

At Hafr al-Batin, King Fahd greeted Clinton in a royal pavilion. Fahd had grown rotund. It was as if opulence itself were consuming him. Still, he had the bearing of a Saudi king, with that enormous noggin and the great Abdul Aziz nose. His still lively dark eyes hung like watery orbs under the fine fabric draped over his head. Fahd could be blunt. "We should not allow Saddam to dictate to us how to play the game. We should be the ones in the driver's seat," Fahd said.

Clinton agreed. He was also frustrated and told the king that they had to find a way to prevent the Iraqi dictator from "jerking us around."

Fahd said Saudi Arabia, too, simply couldn't afford to mobilize every time Saddam moved a division. The question was whether they could craft an effective counterstrategy.

Clinton had inherited the CIA's effort to build an anti-Saddam network that would be capable of overthrowing the Iraqi dictator. This was the work that Bush, Scowcroft, and Gates had begun. But, in fact, after all of their public allusions to the effort, the covert network barely existed except as a concept.[37]

King Fahd surprised Clinton by proposing that the two countries commit to overthrowing Saddam by rebuilding the alliance that had driven the Soviets out of Afghanistan. "We could repeat what we did in Afghanistan," Fahd said. "We will put one billion dollars and you will put one billion dollars and we will not rest until we get rid of this guy because he cannot divide us."[38]

To the Saudis, Clinton seemed to have enthusiastically accepted the king's proposal. In any case, he extended his hand to the king and they shook on it. Clinton said he would send his director of Central Intelligence to follow up.

A senior CIA official did travel to the kingdom, according to the Saudis. He was ushered into the king's presence and he said he was traveling under instructions from the president to follow up on the conversation at Hafr al-Batin. He did not brief the Saudis on what kind of covert operation the United States had in mind. The king asked what kind of commitment Clinton wanted from his friend King Fahd.

The CIA official said he wanted $50 million.[39]

After the CIA official departed, the king turned to Bandar and said, "The Americans are not serious. Give them the money. Get them off our back."

That was the beginning of the Saudi disillusionment with Bill Clinton. The Persian Gulf War had left a powerful rogue on the doorstep of Saudi

Arabia and Fahd looked to Washington to finish the job. For Bandar, Clinton's failure to pull the trigger after the famous handshake at Hafr al-Batin—famous to the Saudis, that is—was emblematic of his most profound flaw as a leader: he lacked a resolute and disciplined will that Carter, Reagan, and Bush, for instance, had shown in Afghanistan and that Bush had shown in Desert Storm.[40]

"The center was always fluid," Bandar would say.

Yet Clinton was not the only president prone to risk avoidance. His caution was rooted in the same prudence that his predecessor had exercised at the end of the war that liberated Kuwait. The U.S. military and the CIA had strong institutional reservations about a major intervention in Iraq. James Baker, writing in his memoir, disclosed how "senior officials" in the Desert Storm coalition had urged the United States to mount such an insurgency. He quoted one of them saying, "You must treat the Iraqi opposition as you did the *mujjahedin* in Afghanistan. This is the only way to separate the Iraqi military from Saddam." Another unidentified Arab leader argued to Baker that the United States and its allies needed to convince the Iraqi military "that as long as Saddam is in power, the army will have to fight a long and costly internal war. When that realization sinks in, the military will be more willing to act against Saddam."

Fahd was thus repeating in 1994 what he and others had argued in 1991.

And Baker provided the rebuttal to this line of thinking. "We did not assist the insurrections militarily primarily out of fear of hastening the fragmentation of Iraq and plunging the region into a new cycle of instability." With words that seem prophetic in retrospect, he added that such an insurrection created the risk "of having the U.S. military bogged down or sucked into an Iraqi civil war."[41]

Thus Bush had adjusted his covert strategy in hopes that the Iraqis themselves would remove Saddam. In the spring of 1991, he had signed a secret presidential finding authorizing the CIA to work toward undermining Saddam gradually through economic sanctions, intrusive inspections by United Nations teams looking for weapons of mass destruction, and diplomatic isolation. As Baker had said, "We would shed no tears if Saddam were overthrown." But the hoped-for outcome was a lightning coup by some collection of Iraqi military or Baath Party leaders. Saddam would be out and Iraq, the Bush White House had hoped, would become more moderate, or at least less militant.

But a coup had not materialized. Instead, Saddam had grown more repressive. Clinton inherited a weak hand, which explained his postelection remarks that he would not "obsess" over Saddam. But the Iraqi leader was not one to remain quiet.

In early 1993, months after Bush had left office, the Kuwaitis uncovered a plot by Saddam's agents to assassinate the former president using a car bomb during Bush's visit to Kuwait in April of that year to commemorate the victory in the Persian Gulf War. Two months later, Clinton ordered a cruise missile attack on the Iraqi intelligence headquarters. The missiles were fired in the middle of the night, when the headquarters was empty, rendering the retaliation more symbolic than lethal. In the Middle East, America looked weak again.

It wasn't until the Iraqi mobilization of October 1994 that Clinton cautiously upped the ante, pressing the CIA to come up with a solution to keep Saddam in his box.


Warren Marik, a fifty-year-old veteran of the CIA's Afghan campaign, and Robert Baer, a six-foot downhill skier with a wry wit and restless manner, were among the CIA officers who rumbled into northern Iraq from Turkey in late 1994 and early 1995. They came in teams, one replacing the other in six-week shifts. They came in trucks along snow- and ice-encrusted roads to the Khabur River crossing near Zakho, where the stream cuts through the foothills of the Zagros Mountains, whose snowy peaks are central to the topography of the Kurdish region. Kurdistan spans a broad swath of Asia Minor and includes much of eastern Turkey, Syria, Iran, and northern Iraq.

Baer was a born adventurer. He had traveled Europe in his youth, most of the time in the company of an academic mother who exhibited a bent for the leftist politics of the 1960s. At the CIA, Baer had been a charter member of Dewey Clarridge's counterterrorism center under William Casey. Baer spoke French and Arabic and, by 1995, he had been in the field for more than a decade, most of the time in the Middle East. He had chased terrorists in Lebanon and Syria and had helped to pick up the pieces from the 1983 truck bomb attacks in Beirut. He had seen the Soviet collapse from the vantage point of Dushanbe when Tajikistan convulsed with civil conflict after Moscow lost control of its Islamic republics.

Marik and Baer had lobbied their superiors to establish a base in the Kurdish safe haven of northern Iraq. Baer took two staff members of the Senate Intelligence Oversight Committee to northern Iraq in September 1994 to convince them that conditions were ripe.[42] The agency already had an operation running out of Jordan to recruit defectors and gather intelligence from the refugees streaming out of the country. After the showdown with Saddam on the Kuwaiti border, anyone could see that Iraq was where the action was for clandestine officers.

The Clinton administration was calling its policy "dual containment" of Iran and Iraq, but the policy was devoid of any real content, more a holding strategy. The Kurds, the Shiites, and the exiled Iraqi opposition were the only potential sources of leverage against the Baghdad regime.

In the summer of 1994, Baer had been introduced to Ahmad Chalabi, the president of the Iraqi National Congress and an affable and energetic figure in the Iraqi exile community centered in London, where the CIA had recruited him, and dozens of other Iraqis, to conduct propaganda and paramilitary operations against Saddam.

Baer and Chalabi met twice. Chalabi shared a copy of his takeover scheme, called Operation End Game—a plan to foment an uprising in Iraq with Kurdish forces in the north and Iranian-backed Shiite forces in the south. The idea was to gradually seize territory and foment defections until Saddam was reduced to being the mayor of Baghdad.

Chalabi incited strong reactions among people. Like many upper-class Arabs, he was at home in two worlds and understood the contradictions inherent in both. He had studied mathematics at the Massachusetts Institute of Technology and had received a Ph.D. in numbers theory from the University of Chicago. He had a round face and a wizardly smile that betrayed a teeming sense of mischief. He gossiped incessantly and could be disarmingly candid and, when called upon, he could deliver a trenchant analysis of prevailing political currents inside Iraq. He could also dissect the power balance of Washington.

Chalabi had grown up in postcolonial Baghdad, where Great Britain was still the protective power over the monarchy of King Faisal II. In the Iraq of his youth, the Iraqis were in charge of their destiny and the Chalabis, a secular Shiite clan, were among the political elite. Chalabi's father was a prominent member of parliament, and Ahmad was thirteen years old during the coup of 1958, when the young Faisal was murdered along with most of the royal family. Nuri as-Said, the prime minister, was dragged through the streets by Arab nationalists inspired by Nasser's call to overthrow the corrupt monarchies that were in thrall to the West.

Chalabi's family fled, and Ahmad grew up in Beirut and London, in households where the topic at the dinner table every day was the politics of Iraq—and how the Chalabis might help reclaim the country from the tribal gangs and thugs who had stolen it.[43]

The family eventually settled in Lebanon, where Chalabi taught mathematics at the American University of Beirut. But by the 1980s, he had invested family money in the Petra Bank of Jordan and moved to Amman. When I first met Chalabi in 1987, I was a traveling foreign correspondent based in Cairo and he was a Shiite businessman in the capital of Saddam's closest Sunni ally during the Iran-Iraq War. Yet Chalabi had managed to ingratiate himself at King Hussein's court.

The king's 1988 decree separating Jordan from the West Bank triggered economic turmoil and a run on the Jordanian currency. Petra Bank developed a liquidity crisis. Chalabi was unable to extract himself from the run on the bank. He and his family fled to London after diverting millions of dollars in Petra Bank assets to banks in Europe. He blamed Jordanian politics, Iraqi pressure, and a hostile Jordanian central bank for his actions. A military court in Amman found him guilty of bank fraud in absentia and sentenced him to seventeen years in prison, though he remained free, living in London more as a political exile than an accused fraudster.

The unresolved issue of Petra's diverted assets, and the losses suffered by Jordanian account holders, would cast a permanent pall over Chalabi's reputation, one that seemed to ebb and flow depending on Chalabi's support in the U.S. government and among influential members of Congress and the news media. The CIA and British intelligence certainly had shown no scruples about bank fraud when they recruited him to help build the Iraqi National Congress.

Chalabi had beaten a path to the CIA's door when word of President Bush's May 1991 decision to work for the removal of Saddam circulated in the exile community. By June 1992, he and a large group of exiles, most of them vetted by or on the payroll of the CIA and Britain's MI6, convened the Iraqi National Congress in Vienna, an umbrella organization encompassing the dominant elements of the opposition community.

The congress included the two main Kurdish parties, Shiite factions from the south and Sunni tribal leaders.

Yet this collection of exiles and Kurdish chieftains was not so much a creature of Western intelligence agencies as it was an enterprise of common cause. No one could credibly assert that the Shiite parties from Najaf were CIA "assets," or that the Kurdish leaders took their orders from Langley. Rather, the congress was a unique attempt to build a national institution in exile, whose legitimacy would radiate into Iraq, creating opportunities to rid the country of Saddam.

Ahmad Chalabi was elected INC president. In late 1994, he too lobbied the CIA to establish a presence in northern Iraq. In early December, Saddam's chief of military intelligence, General Wafiq al-Samarrai, fled his headquarters in Baghdad and defected, alerting Western intelligence networks that Saddam's inner circle was fracturing. Marik and Baer gained approval to deploy a team of CIA officers to northern Iraq. A parallel CIA operation was taking shape in Jordan based around a different group of former Iraqi army officers. The two cells were instructed to work independently, but they saw each other as rivals from the outset.

The CIA's code name for the overall anti-Saddam operation was DB/Achilles. DB was a CIA digraph for Iraq; Achilles was the "compartment" into which a restricted set of officials were cleared for access.[44]

When Bob Baer and his team reached Zakho in January 1995, two people were eagerly awaiting his arrival. One of them was General Samarrai and the other was Chalabi. Baer would later assert that he had no idea that anyone was planning a move against Saddam, but over the next six weeks, he did everything he could to start a war—not just a war but a frontal military assault on the Iraqi army—and he later acknowledged that he was operating "on the edge of my orders."[45]

In Baer's first meeting with Samarrai, the general said that he represented a group of Iraqi officers who were poised to strike at Saddam. The conspirators were all related. Each commanded a sizable combat formation. Samarrai said everyone involved knew the risks. If the plot was detected, their families would be tortured and murdered. But they knew what they were doing. All they wanted from Baer was some indication from Washington about its intentions.

In 1988, General Samarrai had worked with Colonel Pat Lang and the DIA team planning the final battles of the Iran-Iraq War. In the years since, Samarrai had come to fear Saddam's sons, Uday and Qusai, who were as brutal as their father. The general had slipped out of Baghdad the previous November and, with the help of the Kurds, made his way to Kirkuk. He then walked for thirty hours to the safety of the Kurdish zone.

What Samarrai wanted from Baer was a signal. Was the United States willing to countenance a coup? Or did it want to keep Saddam in power? It was a strange question, but a common one among the Iraqis. Many believed that the reason the coalition forces had not sent their army to Baghdad in 1991 to remove Saddam was that the West saw Saddam as the glue that held Iraq together, preventing Shiite rule or Kurdish independence.

"We need to know whether your country will stand in our way or not," Samarrai told Baer.[46]

None of this information reached the president or his national security adviser.[47]

When Clinton returned from his meeting with King Fahd, he issued new presidential directives authorizing the CIA to increase the pressure on Saddam Hussein in the hope that this would induce a coup or at least deter Saddam from massing his army again. The CIA got permission to move into Jordan and northern Iraq to look for some combination of opposition forces that could turn up the heat on Saddam. It was the most aggressive covert mobilization against Saddam since the Persian Gulf War.

Tony Lake, however, was agitated from the outset. By 1995, he knew that he was working for a president who was neuralgic about using force, who didn't trust and seldom met with his CIA director, James Woolsey, and who was not very attentive to foreign policy overall. Those around Lake thought the national security adviser smelled disaster in Iraq, but they also observed that he jealously guarded all pathways to the president. No one got through.

Lake was a quiet and driven intellectual. Seven years older than the president, Lake had been an aide to Ambassador Henry Cabot Lodge in Vietnam when Clinton was still in college at Georgetown. Lake studied at Harvard, spent two years at Cambridge University in England, and took his Ph.D. at Princeton. After he returned from Vietnam, Americans had turned against the war and so had he. Lake was best known for resigning from Henry Kissinger's staff over Nixon's secret decision to expand the war into Cambodia, a course of action that led to the destruction of that country and the deaths of more than one million people.

For most of his professional life, Lake had been trying to reconcile moral principle with the conduct of foreign policy and, of course, Iraq already was a test case. Millions of Iraqis were suffering under Saddam's rule and under sanctions; Bush had exhorted them to revolt, then abandoned them. Brent Scowcroft, on the eve of Clinton's inauguration, had imprudently revealed that Bush had authorized the CIA to go after Saddam, putting the political onus on Clinton to carry on an effort that had little chance of success.

Clinton's secret Iraq policy got off to a shaky start. After Clinton agreed to expand covert operations in Iraq, Woolsey, deeply dissatisfied over his lack of access to the president, resigned as CIA director. During this period, Clinton's national security advisers spent very little time with the president. That was Clinton's style; he would keep his daily CIA briefer waiting in the hall for hours and then cancel the briefing.

Les Aspin, the president's first defense secretary, had once called Woolsey and said, "Woolz, didn't you think that when we got these jobs, we would actually meet with the president and talk about policy?"[48]

Nonetheless, Lake insisted that he wanted intensive White House supervision of the Iraq program. From the outset, he saw the potential for a nightmare scenario in which overly exuberant CIA cowboys might induce the Kurds to attack Saddam's army, only to have Saddam unleash hell in retaliation. Then what would Clinton do? All he could think about was the Bay of Pigs, in which anti-Castro CIA commandos were wiped out because of lack of promised American air support. Clinton would be savaged by Congress, where Newt Gingrich was leading a Republican rebellion.

American policy in northern Iraq prohibited any action that would provoke a full-scale Iraqi attack on the Kurdish safe haven. Of course, nothing was spelled out, but the United States was poorly positioned to project military force into northern Iraq without Turkey's or Saudi Arabia's permission, and both were disinclined to grant it.

The CIA team's mandate was to work with the Kurds and to keep Langley apprised of any promising possibilities to orchestrate a pressure campaign against Saddam, or a coup strategy that might have some chance of success. Those who read the text of Clinton's authorization said it conveyed ambivalence about whether the goal was pressure on Saddam or all-out regime change. Lake lived with the contradiction. He had to contend with British government lawyers who were always arguing that the moment the United States said its goal was to overthrow Saddam, they would be in violation of the United Nations resolution that empowered the coalition only to establish a safe haven for the Kurds in a "no-fly" zone. In any case, the president's authorization to the CIA did not include a frontal assault on the Iraqi army, but that became Baer's plan.

For years, Washington had been hoping that a senior military officer of General Samarrai's stature would defect. And there he stood in front of Baer, a barrel-chested Sunni warrior with a big mustache just like Saddam's and nerves of steel.

And there stood Baer, an ambitious CIA officer who had just arrived with a covert action team. Samarrai had a plan. All they needed was a signal; maybe an American warplane could blaze through the sky over Baghdad at a prearranged moment, as a herald of American support for an uprising. Baer cabled a lengthy report to Washington and waited.

Chalabi was in a hurry, too. Some Kurdish leaders thought he was a little desperate, unable either to unify the opposition or convince Washington that Saddam was vulnerable. Chalabi had formulated a "two cities" plan that called for mounting coordinated attacks against weak Iraqi garrisons at Mosul and Kirkuk, both on the edge of the Kurdish zone. He hoped the attacks would trigger defections and a "rolling rebellion" that would move south, picking up more army units along the way and turning them against Baghdad.

Chalabi's militia consisted of a few hundred men mainly drawn from Iraqi defectors and exiles, but they would be buttressed—or so he hoped—by the much larger and better-armed Kurdish militias under the command of Massoud Barzani and Jalal Talabani. The CIA had set up its base in Salahaldin, a small town perched on the promontory above Erbil, the capital of the Kurdish region. Chalabi's headquarters was in a hotel just down the street. Barzani's headquarters stood on an adjoining hilltop.

Baer had arrived in Iraq at a time of great dissension. The Kurdish factions were nearly at war. Barzani's Kurdish Democratic Party (KDP) controlled the main smuggling route into Turkey. For Saddam to sell oil, it had to pass through Barzani's domain, which was protected by American F-16s patrolling the no-fly zone. Barzani was collecting millions of dollars a month in tolls on thousands of tanker trucks that were delivering Saddam's crude to the Turkish market. On many days, the line of trucks was backed up for twenty miles on the oil-soaked highway.

Jalal Talabani's Patriotic Union of Kurdistan (PUK), was not so fortu-

nate. The PUK was cut off from this lucrative revenue stream, and Talabani was demanding a cut. Barzani refused. It was a tawdry economy, but
Barzani controlled it.

It took the CIA a week to respond to Baer's message about Samarrai's
plot. What came back was a five-word message from a midlevel officer on
the Iraq desk: "This is not a plan." There is no evidence that Baer's startling report of coup plotting reached Clinton or senior White House
aides, but the president's passivity and lack of focus on foreign policy was
now legend to administration insiders, and it led ambitious aides and
field operatives, like Baer, to rush into the vacuum, more so than in previous administrations.

If Washington didn't see a plan, Baer would produce one. Samarrai
unfurled the details of his scheme, which would organize key units of
mutinous troops to trap Saddam's motorcade on a visit to Samarra or
Tikrit and kill him there, perhaps as he was crossing a bridge. Samarrai
claimed that he and his conspirators, all of them relatives, commanded
four major military units. At his signal, they would make a move designed
to flush out Saddam and drive him into their trap.

Chalabi's plan was more elaborate and called for infiltration of Mosul
and Kirkuk. As they discussed how to synchronize their plans, out of the
blue on February 12 an Iranian-backed Shiite militia in southern Iraq
called the Badr Brigade attacked an Iraqi army unit at al-Qurnah in the
southern marshes near Basra. Here were Iraqis taking on Saddam's army
and winning a skirmish. Baer was excited by the opportunity this presented. The sudden activation of the southern front was a signal that Iran
had its own interests in toppling Saddam.

The Badr Brigade, trained and equipped in Iran, had been formed by
an Iraqi cleric, Ayatollah Mohammed Baqr al-Hakim, during the Iran-
Iraq War. Hakim was a Shiite leader who had lost dozens of family members to Saddam's executioners and, with support from Iran, Hakim had
unified the religious opposition under the Supreme Council of the Islamic Republic of Iraq. Baer was transfixed by the Badr Brigade's success.
The question that hung over the CIA enterprise was whether Baer could
somehow telegraph his moves to the Iranians, in the hope that Iran would
send the Badr Brigade back into action.

"Let's do the plan from the north and the south," he told Chalabi. Baer
could see a squeeze play, if only the stars would line up.

That was the moment when Baer decided to communicate with the

Iranians through Chalabi. A number of sources describe a meeting at Chalabi's headquarters in Salahaldin between Chalabi and two Iranian intelligence officers. Baer made a cameo appearance in the lobby to help Chalabi establish his bona fides as a messenger of the U.S. government.[49]

"The United States would not object to Iran joining in the fight against Saddam Hussein provided it is committed to the territorial integrity of Iraq," Chalabi told the Iranians.[50]

Clearly, Tehran was intrigued, but it was impossible to know what the Iranians would do. Through Baer, Chalabi relayed a direct message to Washington from the Iranians: Would the United States accept greater Iranian military pressure on Saddam?[51]

"The clock is running out," Chalabi told Baer over dinner a few days later. Unless the CIA endorsed an attack on Saddam's forces from the north, Talabani and his Kurdish militia would probably go to war against the Barzani Kurds over money.

"Only a preemptive strike can save the situation," Chalabi said, and then he suddenly asked, "What will Washington do if I organize an uprising? It's the only way to stop Talabani from attacking [Barzani]."

"Schedule one and then ask," Baer replied.[52]

The CIA operative believed that no one in Washington would put any credence in Chalabi's uprising plan, just as he believed that no one cared if the Kurds started shelling each other. As Baer saw it, Washington's only interest was to keep the Kurds and the delicate situation in northern Iraq off the front pages. Baer thought, "Why not let Chalabi propose his uprising?" At least it might force Washington to decide whether to back it along with Samarrai's plan to trap Saddam.

Ahmad Chalabi's war on Saddam Hussein was launched on March 3, 1995.

The first sign of trouble arose before the first shot. At the White House, Bruce Riedel, a CIA specialist on Middle Eastern affairs seconded to the NSC staff, walked into Martin Indyk's office with an intelligence report that lifted Indyk's eyebrows. Soon they were hoofing it over to Lake's office in the West Wing to explain that Saddam's army was mobilizing to strike the Kurds because Saddam had detected the CIA plot.

Lake's reaction was volcanic. He flew out of his chair, arms gesturing. Here was his nightmare—a Bay of Pigs disaster! Lake and the president had been kept in the dark. Who the hell was General Samarrai? Lake wanted to know. He slashed the air as if he were wielding a Japanese samurai sword, mocking his predicament. He telephoned the acting CIA director, Admiral William O. Studeman, who claimed total ignorance of the imminent hostilities fomented by the CIA's officer in the field. Indyk, who had known the most and who had encouraged Baer and the CIA to move boldly, was frozen by Lake's rage and gave answers in a kind of monotone, according to one person present.

Lake dictated a priority message to Baer, but also to the Kurdish leaders, using the CIA's satellite channel: "The action you have planned for this weekend has been totally compromised. We believe there is a high risk of failure. Any decision to proceed will be on your own."

The message landed like a thunderbolt. Baer and Chalabi could not figure out exactly what had occurred. Of course their action was "compromised." They were openly plotting with the Kurds and were soliciting Iranian coordination. Baer briefly considered telephoning Indyk to explain, but then realized how ludicrous it would seem for a covert field officer to call the White House for clarification. Chalabi defiantly decided the operation would go ahead and loaded his Iraqi National Congress recruits into trucks and Toyota Land Cruisers and headed for the front.

But Chalabi's forces never reached the front lines, nor did they fire a shot. The battle went forward only because Talabani's *peshmerga* fighters[53] struck the Iraqi V Corps on the Kirkuk axis of what was to have been the battle for Mosul and Kirkuk.

Chalabi's troops were blocked by Barzani's Kurdish militia at the Great Zab River, miles from the Iraqi front lines.

General Samarrai meanwhile put on his Iraqi military uniform and drove his Mercedes toward Tikrit, Saddam's hometown, where his arrival was to be the signal for the divisions commanded by his relatives to move against the Iraqi leader. Saddam's location would be pinpointed by a spy in the presidential palace.

But Samarrai, Baer, and Chalabi had not counted on one tenacious obstacle in their path: Massoud Barzani, the strong-willed Kurdish leader who was against starting a war that might trigger a devastating attack on Kurdistan. Who would save the Kurds? Not Robert Baer. Not Ahmad Chalabi. Barzani wanted to preserve the status quo. To Barzani, it appeared that the White House wanted the same thing and he suspected that Baer was operating beyond his orders. Barzani had used his own channels back to Washington and determined that Chalabi's war had not been sanctioned. Moreover, given the lucrative oil trade that was financing Kurdish prosperity, Barzani did not want to risk a war.

Barzani was the son of Mullah Mustafa Barzani, the icon of the Kurdish rebellion for half a century until his death in March 1979. The Barzanis had a long history with the United States and the CIA. In the early 1970s, the shah of Iran, with help from the CIA and Mossad, had armed the Kurds to bring military pressure to bear on Saddam to settle a festering border dispute along the Shatt al-Arab waterway, where Iran's oil industry was concentrated and where Iraqi harassment of Iranian vessels was a threat to trade. Saddam had relented in 1975, giving the shah the border agreement he wanted, and the CIA, under orders from Henry Kissinger and President Nixon, had turned its back on Barzani. No one could save him.

The Iraqi army routed the Kurdish forces in the north and Mullah Mustafa fled to the United States, where he died in exile.

His son, Massoud, was conspicuously short of stature, baby faced, and somewhat self-conscious in manner. The impression was that Massoud was not entirely comfortable living in the shadow of his charismatic father, who had been a loquacious rebel commander. Massoud was anything but loquacious, yet he was a clear-headed realist, especially when it came to navigating great power interests in Iraq.

From the day Baer had entered Kurdistan, Barzani saw him as a rogue and a pawn of the Chalabi-Talabani camp. Barzani was a Kurdish patriot, but these were the years when he and Talabani had daggers drawn for each other. Barzani once remarked to a friend that if he were seated with a gun on the table between Saddam Hussein and Jalal Talabani, he "would shoot Jalal."

Baer had made the mistake of telling Barzani that the United States was fed up with Kurdish brawling and might pull out of northern Iraq. Barzani had come off his chair and walked up to Baer, pointing his finger directly at him to say, "Don't threaten me."

For Barzani to join the plot, he would have to know whether the Americans would provide air support. If the Kurds attacked Mosul and Kirkuk, how would the Americans distinguish between Kurdish and Iraqi forces? Who would block the Iraqi reinforcements? According to several witnesses to these conversations, Baer had an answer for every contingency, including his implicit pledge of air support, as if he were speaking for the president of the United States.[54]

Clinton was oblivious, uninformed, and diverted. He spent the first months of 1995 trying to regain the initiative after the Republican landslide in Congress and to counter the political momentum of the Republicans' Contract with America.

In Iraq, Barzani took matters into his own hands; he sent his men to physically stop Chalabi from starting a war. General Samarrai was similarly blocked from reaching Tikrit, his black Mercedes turned back by Barzani's men. In the wake of the failed uprising, Saddam's intelligence services arrested Samarrai's network. The general fled to Syria with his family.

Talabani's forces, having entered the fighting unassisted, reportedly did well against Iraqi garrisons, but Talabani had to abort the operation when Turkey suddenly sent its army into Kurdistan, ostensibly to attack the bases of the Kurdish Workers Party, whose members were Kurds from the Turkish mountains who used the Iraqi border region as a safe haven from which to stage ambushes against the Turkish army. Talabani could see that he was fighting alone. He had to fall back in any case to protect the Kurdish capital, Erbil, in case the Turks advanced farther.

The little war was over. It had scarcely been noticed in Washington.

Baer and his team were pulled out of northern Iraq, and Baer was subjected to an FBI investigation for allegedly plotting the assassination of a foreign leader.[55]

John M. Deutch, an arrogant and vain MIT scientist who had been deputy defense secretary, was selected by Clinton to be the new CIA director. In the wake of Chalabi's aborted war, Deutch promised the White House that he would personally get the agency's covert action directorate under control and would take out Saddam, no problem. Here was a professional chemist, weapons scientist, and MIT professor promising the White House that he would succeed in removing one of the most heavily protected dictators in the Middle East, that he would master the black arts of clandestine warfare in a matter of months, and that he would prevail in a region about which he knew very little.

Chalabi was now out of favor because he and Baer had made the agency's once-vaunted clandestine service look foolish. The action shifted to Amman.


Amman is a city chiseled from the warm golden limestone of the Jordanian rift valley. With King Hussein back in the Western camp following the peace treaty with Israel, the Jordanian capital became the locus of anti-Saddam plotting.

On August 7, 1995, General Hussein Kamel and a motorcade that included his brothers and their wives and children drove boldly across the Iraqi desert and into Jordan, where they asked for and received political asylum. Among the wives were two of Saddam's daughters, Raghad and Rina. But Hussein Kamel was the prize. A member of Saddam's clan, he had risen to become the top Iraqi official for military industries and weapons procurement. Kamel had overseen the secret programs to produce unconventional weapons. His defection not only allowed the United Nations inspection team under Rolf Ekéus to confirm Iraqi advances in chemical and biological warfare, but it also led to the discovery, at a chicken ranch, of an archive of documentation on all of Iraq's secret weapons programs. Kamel's betrayal of the regime triggered a burst of unexpected cooperation from Baghdad, where officials asserted that it was Kamel who had been responsible for the years of obstruction and concealment.

Saddam sent his son Uday and his defense minister, Ali Hassan al-Majid (known as Chemical Ali for his role in chemical weapons attacks), Kamel's uncle, to demand from King Hussein the extradition of the wayward weapons chief and the return of Saddam's daughters, but the king held fast, saying that he would watch over the girls. The defection represented another crack in the regime. Kamel had been a rival for power with Uday Hussein, whose violence and instability had raised questions about whether Saddam could control him.

Much to Washington's satisfaction, King Hussein used the defection to demonstrate the clean break he had made with the Iraqi dictator. In an interview with the Israeli newspaper *Yedioth Aharonoth*, the Jordanian monarch said it was "the right time for change" in the Baghdad regime and "if a change occurs it will only be a change for the better."[56] President Clinton telephoned him with congratulations and a promise to defend Jordan against any vengeful move by Saddam.

Hussein Kamel's defection lasted for only six months. He had wanted America to raise an army that he would lead to Baghdad and topple Saddam;[57] he was ready to be Washington's new strongman, but it was a pipe dream. Disillusioned by the lack of Western enthusiasm, Kamel actually thought he could return to Baghdad as if nothing had happened. He was induced by promises from Saddam that all could be forgiven. But as soon as Kamel's motorcade crossed the border in February 1996, Uday was there to take control of Saddam's daughters. They were forced to divorce their husbands. Kamel and his brother were cornered at their sister's home, where they engaged in a gun battle with forty members of Saddam's presidential guard, in which they had once served. Kamel, his brother, father, and sister and her children all died in the shootout.

The plotting against Saddam would soon resume under the direction of John Deutch, the MIT chemist in the CIA director's chair.

In Israel on the night of November 4, 1995, Prime Minister Yitzhak Rabin was trying to sing, but he couldn't carry a tune.

The Kings of Israel Square in central Tel Aviv is not a dramatic landscape, surrounded by 1960s-era apartment blocks and storefronts, but on that evening, it pulsed with amplified music and the rhythm of more than one hundred thousand Israelis whose voices had unified in song.

There on a platform above them, Rabin was singing, if you could call it singing. Indeed, he had confided to aides that he could never remember the words to the "Song of Peace" and requested that the lyrics be typed up so he would have something to rely on that evening. He put on his glasses and followed the words for a few lines and then folded the paper into quarters and slipped it into his pocket as he muddled through the chorus.

Rabin looked stiff and uncomfortable, as ever, standing in the lineup of dignitaries under the lights, holding hands in the chain with Peres, his colleague and rival, because the two of them were joined in a fight for their political lives against the Israeli right wing and the settler movement. Extremist rabbis had brazenly petitioned the higher rabbinical authorities to ratify a death sentence on Rabin for betraying the Jewish state. Of course they were rejected, but there were still rabbis out there condemning Rabin for the "crime" of turning over a significant part of the historic Land of Israel—Judea and Samaria—to the Palestinians.

A kind of Armageddon fever had settled over the Israeli polity. Carmi Gillon, the director of Israel's internal security service, Shin Bet, for months had been admonishing opposition political figures, including Benjamin Netanyahu, and members of the Israeli news media to tone down the rhetoric because, he feared, there was a real danger that it could incite extremist elements to violence against the democratically elected government. But Gillon's caution was hooted down as an attempt to interfere in the political process and, of course, police admonition to tone down a political debate is a slippery slope in any democratic society.

Tens of thousands of Israelis had come out that Saturday evening to sing for peace and to support the dramatic new interim accord that was dubbed Oslo II. It called for Israel to further roll back the occupation of Palestinian cities. At a White House ceremony in September, Rabin had warned about the culture of violence.

"We who have killed and have been killed"—those were the words he chose to address the Jews and Arabs assembled in Washington. "If the partners in the peace process do not unite against the angel of death that is terrorism, all that will be left of this ceremony is a souvenir photo, and soon rivers of hatred will flood the Middle East."[58]

It had been a tough negotiation, but under Oslo II, the Israeli military was set to pull back from seven Palestinian cities—Ramallah, Nablus, Bethlehem, part of Hebron, Jenin, Qalqilya, and Tulkarm—which would join the Palestinian Authority. The Palestinians would then hold elections for an assembly and an executive. The Israeli military was reluctant to relinquish that much control, but Peres chastised its leaders.

"I'm fed up with your fear of what the settlers will say," he told them during a session in Taba. "You want 150,000 [Palestinian] Hebronites to remain under our control because of 400 Jews? There is a limit to arrogance and a limit to timidity. I'm telling you that we can break Arafat, if that's what you want. But then we'll be left with Hamas, an intifada and terror."[59]

Rabin had told Arafat that there was no way he was going to turn over the West Bank just like that, and Arafat shrieked that he could not face his people if Israel offered a few cantons—"Bantustans," he called them—dotting the landscape and surrounded by Israeli tanks, checkpoints, and bypass roads used only by Israelis.

But both sides compromised. "Arafat was his partner," Amos Eiran, a longtime Rabin confidant, said of the prime minister.[60] When Rabin and Arafat met in Casablanca in late 1994, Arafat pleaded for the release of Hamas's spiritual leader, Sheikh Ahmed Yassin, who had been imprisoned since 1989 on charges of incitement.

"I know him, he will call for an end to the violence," Arafat said, and then listened to Rabin's assessment: "We've checked. He's not prepared to do that."

Both men knew that public opinion in Israel was nothing less than "rebellious," as Rabin described it. "There are calls among the Jews to kill me," he said.

Arafat had looked at him with those wide eyes and rejoined, "Me too."[61]

They had rapidly developed a deeper understanding of each other's political problems, and with that came forbearance and a measure of respect that neither had thought possible. Rabin confided in aides that Arafat was working assiduously to crack down on militants and bring terrorism to an end. Why? Because Palestinian statehood was taking shape. Dennis Ross, Clinton's Middle East negotiator, observed that by the summer of 1995, Rabin "had come to appreciate Arafat," once the implacable foe. In the year since those handshakes on the South Lawn, Rabin, Peres, and Arafat had crossed into a new era, and Rabin understood that Arafat "was taking steps that were hard for him."[62] The distance both men had traveled was recognized by the Nobel committee, which awarded Rabin, Arafat, and Peres the Peace Prize in December 1994.

In the month before the peace rally, right-wing groups had handed out photographs of Rabin in a Nazi SS uniform. Settlers brought their children to rallies wearing a yellow Star of David on their arms, as if Rabin was running a Nazi state. The Kach organization (a far-right political party, an offshoot of Meir Kahane's JDL) sent a group to Rabin's home in Tel Aviv to call down "avenging angels" on the prime minister. A mob attacked Rabin's car, ripping off the hood ornament and spitting on the windshield.

"If we managed to get Rabin's Cadillac emblem, we can get Rabin," one of the youths told a newspaper reporter.[63]

At the end of October, Dennis Ross had met with Rabin in Jerusalem to plot strategy on how to break the stalemate with Assad on the "Syrian track" of negotiations. Rabin was all business. A few days earlier, Mossad had carried out the assassination of the founder of Islamic Jihad, Fathi Shikaki, on the island of Malta. The Mossad team had laid an ambush as Shikaki was in transit back to Damascus from Libya. Rabin the soldier had struck a blow, now he seemed determined to move forward on the peace front. His oft-quoted slogan was, "We shall fight terrorism as if there is no peace process, and pursue the peace process as if there is no terrorism."

As Ross was leaving that day, Rabin said, "Dennis, expect anything."

The peace rally broke up at 9:30 p.m. and Rabin had just walked down the stairs to his car when Yigal Amir, a twenty-five-year-old right-wing extremist, walked through the cordon of security men, pointed his pistol at Rabin's back, and fired three times. Rabin went down hard. He was helped into his car, complaining of the pain. His driver rushed him to Ichilov Hospital in Tel Aviv, but Rabin died during surgery. Police arrested Amir, who said that he had no regrets in murdering the prime minister because he was acting on God's orders.

The assassination of Yitzhak Rabin was the first such political murder in the history of the Jewish state.[64] The news beamed out to a world that seemed to freeze in numbed reflection of the enormity of the loss. Many had seen Rabin's premiership as a convergence of political and historical forces that would make an Arab-Israeli peace possible. Just as Nixon had gone to China, Rabin, the hard-line warrior who had fought for Jerusalem in 1948 and liberated the Old City and the Western Wall in 1967, could make peace with the Arabs. And the Arabs were interested in making peace.

Now he was dead.

Shimon Peres, who had spent a lifetime as Rabin's rival in the Labor Party, suddenly was alone. Peres had vision, he had helped develop Israel's nuclear weapons complex, but next to Rabin, he was a lesser figure, lacking that essential element of military leadership and combat experience.

"I am on my own," he told Savir the day after the shooting. "He is irreplaceable."

Savir understood that despite the years of competitiveness and mistrust, Rabin and Peres, as old men, had come to depend on each other. Trust may not have been complete, but in old age, each had come to accept the other's strengths and was more willing to indulge them without resorting to the zero-sum mania that had marked their competitive years.

Just a few steps from where Rabin fell that night, I met Savir at a coffee shop during the tenth anniversary of the assassination. "You could see in these two men, both just about seventy, a tendency to close themselves together in a tête-à-tête"—whispered discussions not shared with aides—"where they made all the decisions," he told me.[65] It was recognition between them, he said, that they were the last of the founding generation of Ben-Gurion's party and they arrogated unto themselves the shared responsibility for the welfare of the state, to the exclusion of their foes on the right, just as Ben-Gurion had done.

The state funeral on Mount Herzl, named for the founder of Zionism, brought together eighty heads of state. Eitan Haber, who had announced

Rabin's death to a stunned nation, described how the doctors and nurses wept, and how they found in Rabin's pocket the bloodstained copy of the "Song of Peace."

King Hussein, who that day had gazed at the golden Dome of the Rock for the first time since 1967 when Jordan lost Jerusalem, recalled how his grandfather, King Abdullah, had been gunned down on the steps of the al-Aqsa Mosque. He called Rabin a "soldier of peace."

Clinton, always at his best in delivering a eulogy, simply quoted what Rabin had said six weeks earlier in Washington.

Rabin had begun with humor: "First, the good news. I am the last speaker." Then he had summoned the people to consider the distance they had traveled in a short period of time.

"Take a look at this stage. The king of Jordan, the president of Egypt, Chairman Arafat, and we, the prime minister and foreign minister of Israel, on one platform. Please, take a good hard look. The sight you see before you was impossible, was unthinkable, just three years ago. Only poets dreamt of it, and, to our great pain, soldiers and civilians went to their deaths to make this moment possible."

The irony was that Arafat was not at the funeral. Peres had decided that his presence would be divisive for the Israeli political establishment and a security nightmare for everyone else. Abu Mazen represented the Palestinians.[66]

Clinton ended it with simple words that lingered in Israel for years: "*Shalom, chaver.*"

"Farewell, friend."

Before he left Israel, Clinton had another delicate task to perform, telling Peres that Rabin had made a secret commitment to the United States that Israel would withdraw completely from the Golan Heights in exchange for full peace with Syria. Peres seemed startled when Clinton explained what Rabin had confided only to the Americans, but Peres said he would stand by any commitment that "Yitzhak ha[d] made."

The hopes of the peace camp now rested on Peres's shoulders. As acting prime minister, he announced that the planned Israeli troop withdrawal from the seven Palestinian cities would proceed on schedule. But the real focus was Syria, where leaders in the Israeli, Arab, and American camps saw a new opportunity. Clinton's aides, Indyk and Ross, believed that Rabin's death could help consolidate Arab-Israeli peace more momentously than just moving forward on the Palestinian track. Syria was the last remaining military threat on Israel's frontiers. Assad was in declining health and, given that the threats of the future would come from Iran or Iraq—as Rabin believed they would—a stable peace on Israel's borders was a prerequisite to security.

King Fahd, who did not attend Rabin's funeral, also thought that a great opportunity had opened with Syria. No sooner had Clinton and his aides returned to Washington than Dennis Ross received a call from Prince Bandar, who conveyed the king's belief that "if [they missed] this moment, it [might] not come again for a very long time."

On November 10, Ross drove to Bandar's residence to discuss the new landscape in the Middle East. But he surprised Bandar by boldly stating that the Saudis should establish full diplomatic relations with Israel. The prince was taken aback. Here was the American Middle East envoy speaking as if he were Peres's campaign manager. From an Israeli perspective, it made perfect sense. A Saudi breakthrough would be extremely helpful to Peres's political standing. But from an Arab political perspective, it would be a disaster. Why would Saudi Arabia establish relations with Israel in advance of any peace with Syria? That would only antagonize and isolate Assad, something neither America nor Israel wanted to do.

Ross's failure to analyze Arab politics as faithfully as he did Israeli politics was the reason he was not accepted in the Arab camp with the same trust and confidence that he inspired in Israel. Bandar respected Ross because he had seen him maneuver in the interests of peace through two administrations. He could see what Ross was after and so he told him that Saudi Arabia was ready to make peace with the Israelis when the time was right. The Jewish state was a fact. King Fahd had come to that conclusion long ago. But overall peace, in the Saudi view, was not possible before Israel satisfied the demands of Palestinian independence and reached an accord with Hafez al-Assad on the return of the Golan Heights.

From Damascus, Assad signaled that he was amenable to a new round of negotiations. The government-controlled press, analyzing Rabin's death, said "something good" might come of "something bad." The Syrians had refused to send anyone to the funeral; Assad had not expressed condolences to Leah Rabin as had other Arab leaders. He was the last holdout, but it seemed possible that he would make peace if he could get back the territory he had lost in 1967.

Peres was not sure he was strong enough politically to make peace with Syria. He would have to face down twenty thousand angry Israeli settlers who had cleared fields of stone and built the farms of the Golan kibbutz community, whom Rabin had promised not to abandon. The first effort—comprising three negotiating sessions between Syrian and Israeli delegations at the Wye River Plantation on the eastern shore of the Chesapeake Bay near Washington—failed. The timing was bad.

Peres, in November, had told the Americans that he was going to "go for it." He was willing to lose the Golan or the elections, but not both. What he needed, he explained, was some drama. Couldn't they stage a summit with Assad, or couldn't he, Peres, fly to Damascus unannounced, as Sadat had done?

"Why not, Dennis?" Peres had asked Ross. "I don't mind the risk [of getting shot down]. It may be safer than here."[67]

A lot was riding on whether Assad would make peace, and for the Arabs, there could be no Arab-Israeli peace without Syria. Assad may have also feared how Iran might react to a Syrian peace with Israel. As Savir observed, "Only when you made peace with Syria, and only when Hafez al-Assad announces to the Arab League that he has decided to allow Israel to open an embassy in Damascus, will the rest of the Arab states follow suit." But what about Iran and its Shiite ally, Hezbollah, in Lebanon? No one knew.

Peres's calculation was that he could fly high and go fast—make peace quickly with maximum drama—or fly low and go slow. Yet by the time Ross returned to Israel in early December 1995, Peres had grown cautious. The addition of the ambitious Ehud Barak as foreign minister in Peres's Cabinet was the reason.

Barak did not want Peres to stage an early summit with Assad lest he look desperate to make a deal. This was the reverse of the reasoning of just weeks earlier when there had been a consensus that Rabin's death made drama and risk possible.

Peres arrived in Washington in December to consult Clinton. The Israelis focused on what the Americans might do to help Peres politically, and Peres always thought in sweeping terms. The Israeli prime minister proposed that the United States enter into a formal U.S.-Israeli defense alliance. That would provide Peres with a dramatic boost at home. But an alliance was not going to fly. Ever since Ben-Gurion first proposed such an alliance to Eisenhower, American leaders had regarded the step as unwise; it would antagonize the Arabs just as they were thinking about peace. Peres had run out of gimmicks and was unwilling to take a bold risk on the Syrian front, and after three rounds of bruising negotiations, the public mood in Israel had turned against the whole Syrian gambit. This led Peres to conclude that he needed an electoral mandate to make peace. If Assad would not agree to a series of high-profile summit meetings that would enhance Peres's image as a statesman and protect the peace process in Israel, Peres would advance the election timetable from November to May to get a fresh mandate.

Assad was not going to help. He told Ross in early December that he thought they were at "a turning point," but he was not going to grant favors to Peres while Israeli troops still occupied the Golan.

In the midst of these diplomatic maneuvers, Israel was carrying out a muscular campaign against terrorist attacks. Shin Bet, the internal security service, had been searching in Gaza for a particular Palestinian known as "the engineer" because he was believed to be responsible for planning at least seven suicide bomb attacks in which sixty-seven Israelis had died and nearly four hundred had been wounded.

His real name was Yehiya Ayyash, a leading militant of the Hamas organization and an expert designer of explosive suicide vests. Peres had personally urged Arafat to find him and arrest him. Shin Bet's chief, Carmi Gillon, had done the same.

At first Arafat temporized, saying Ayyash had fled to the Sudan, but Mohammed Dahlan, Arafat's security chief for Gaza, acknowledged he was hiding someplace in Gaza, though Arafat's men had not been able to locate him. In early January 1996, Shin Bet found him and, through an agent, managed to infiltrate a portable telephone to replace the one that Ayyash was using at his uncle's home in Gaza's Beit Lahiya district. At the chosen moment on January 5, a Shin Bet officer placed a call to Ayyash's phone, and when he answered, the explosives in the handset detonated, nearly blowing off his head.

The Americans and Israelis who had been concentrating on the peace process underestimated the intensity of the terror war that was under way. The bloodshed was inciting passions in Arab and Jewish communities. The assassination of Ayyash propelled young Palestinians into the streets, praising him as a hero who had struck a blow against occupation. More than one hundred thousand Palestinians attended his funeral the following day, with leaders of Hamas and Fatah joining the march from the Gaza City mosque to the cemetery.

The peace camp was on the defensive.

On February 11, Peres announced the decision to call early elections, and on February 25, Israeli and Syrian negotiators returned to the Wye Plantation to keep their efforts going on a low-key basis.

No sooner had they arrived at the Chesapeake resort than word came that a pair of Hamas suicide bombers had struck in Israel: one on a No. 18 bus in Jerusalem and another at a busy hitchhiker junction at Ashkelon, killing a total of twenty-seven Israelis and wounding eighty. The young Hamas militants who carried out the Sunday attack identified themselves as part of the New Generation Yehiya Ayyash Brigade. Uri Savir was leading the Israeli delegation and he soon learned that the son of one his close friends was among the dead. The Syrians expressed their condolences in private but refused to make any public statement. That blackened the mood.

Savir wrote later, "We were reacting just as the terrorists wanted us to, as they drove a wedge between us and our peace partners."

The next day, a Palestinian rammed his car into a group of Israeli pedestrians, killing an Israeli woman and injuring twenty-three people. The Israelis responded with a total closure of the West Bank and Gaza Strip.

On Sunday, March 3, a Hamas suicide bomber selected a bus on the same route as the previous Sunday's bomber in Jerusalem with the same horrific effect: eighteen passengers died in the blast and seventy were wounded. The following day another Hamas bomber, smuggled into Israel by an Israeli Arab, struck in the heart of Tel Aviv. He made his way to Dizengoff Center, the city's largest shopping mall, where crowds of children were out in costumes for the Purim holiday. When he saw police at the mall entrance, the bomber moved to a crowded intersection, where he detonated himself. The explosive vest was laced with nails and screws to magnify its lethality. The blast killed 14 people and wounded 130. Many children were among the dead and wounded.

In nine days, four suicide bombers had killed nearly sixty Israelis, most of them civilians, including many women and children. Israeli and American intelligence had information that Iran was encouraging and supporting the wave of terror, hoping to disrupt peace negotiations that held the potential to leave Tehran further isolated in the region. But a Mossad official said that Hamas did not need Iran's encouragement or assistance to carry out these assaults.[68]

Clinton was on an election-year fund-raising trip to Michigan when he got the news. He telephoned Peres to express condolences, but the subtext of their conversation was that the suicide-bombing wave was devastating to Peres's political fortunes. In Taylor, Michigan, Clinton addressed reporters, saying, "Once again, the enemies of peace have murdered completely innocent Israeli citizens, including children, in their hysterical, determined, fanatic attempt to kill all hope for peace between Israel and the Palestinians and others in the Middle East."[69]

Peres's government fell into crisis. Palestinians, who had just witnessed the end of the Israeli occupation in their communities, now saw the tanks and soldiers come rushing back. Palestinians who supported peace and opposed the terrorist actions of Hamas and Islamic Jihad were bitter at how quickly the occupation resumed. Clinton hurried back to Washington, vowing to provide Israel with new intelligence resources to fight terrorism and to call a summit meeting of "peacemakers" to buck up Peres.

One Israeli cabinet minister emerged from frenetic discussions to say, "The Oslo agreement is in critical condition. Either we operate and we save it, or the operation will fail and the agreement is dead."[70]

Benjamin Netanyahu proclaimed that Israel had made a fatal mistake in subcontracting its security to the likes of Yasser Arafat. "We have to say honestly and courageously that this policy has failed," he told a news conference.

Stan Moskowitz, a newly appointed CIA station chief, arrived in Israel just as the first of the four bombers struck. He observed that the Israeli security services saw a strategic threat from these bombers—an asymmetrical weapon against which the Israeli arsenal was useless. Its delivery vehicle was the young Palestinian indistinguishable in the crowd and so radicalized that he was willing to give up living to strike a blow for lost parents, brothers, or sisters.[71]

Israel's failure to cope with suicide bombers mirrored America's failure against Saddam. In June 1996, all of the CIA's carefully laid plans, the best chance the agency felt it had in a decade to overthrow Saddam Hussein, reached that crucial point. The Amman-based clandestine network had infiltrated a large number of agents who were awaiting a signal to seize control of barracks and headquarters in a struggle for power.

Instead, the first signs appeared that Iraqi intelligence was arresting hundreds of infiltrators suspected of being trained and equipped by the

CIA. As more reports came in, CIA handlers and their allies in Jordanian intelligence were paralyzed. Communications with agents went dead. Family members of agents who were in Iraq were stricken with fear about the fate of sons, brothers, husbands. Hundreds of Iraqis simply disappeared, most probably into Baghdad's Abu Ghraib prison.

"I'm sure they died horrendous deaths," said Rick Francona, a member of the CIA team.

Francona was a Defense Intelligence Agency officer who had cut his teeth in Iraq with Patrick Lang when the DIA was helping Iraq win its war with Iran. A fluent Arabic speaker, Francona had come full circle. He had been part of the covert effort to help Saddam win the war against Khomeini. Then he had witnessed the American disillusionment. He had seen the evidence of Saddam's use of chemical weapons and observed the cynicism of American leaders who had rationalized Saddam's horrors and then reversed themselves when public revulsion mounted to chemical attacks on the Kurds.

Francona had gone on to other assignments in the Middle East, and then the CIA had recruited him to return to covert operations, this time to overthrow Saddam. His career kept pulling him back to Iraq and the fate of its people.

Now Francona wished he had never accepted the summons because in that summer of 1996, he observed the terror of the telephone calls that he has never forgotten. The calls came in to the home of General Mohammed Abdullah al-Shahwani, the former commander of Saddam's special forces. The general was a big man, with the bearing of an Iraqi warrior, proud and stoic. His defection, like the earlier defection of General Samarrai, had been an exciting development, even more so because General al-Shahwani had a broader base of support among Iraq's military chiefs. Three of his sons still held commands in the Republican Guard and all three of those sons had agreed to join the CIA plot to rise up against Saddam. Each conspirator was to carry out his mission when the signal came. The concept had been to employ key military units to control the Iraqi army, turning it against Saddam. But one by one, the conspirators had been arrested. Days of terror about their fate had run together. Then the phone rang in the Shahwani home. An Iraqi intelligence officer informed al-Shahwani that his sons were about to be executed.

Francona just sat there feeling the horror, absorbing the look on the face of the general, and then on the face of his wife. The mother of these soldiers took the phone, anguish in her eyes, and between sobs offered Arabic expressions of love and grief. Then there was silence. They had all died. Not just al-Shahwani's three sons, but all of those who had joined the feckless and ill-fated American effort to overthrow Saddam, all of the infiltrators the CIA had sent in, and probably many others who had fallen under suspicion.

As the death toll mounted, blame laying followed. The officers in the field focused on reports and rumors from Washington that Tony Lake, the national security adviser, had pulled the plug on the operation because the White House did not want to risk a foreign policy failure during an election year.

Clinton and Lake were blamed by agents in the field for sending mixed signals. "We should never have sent them in unless we had a full go," said one of the officers. "The Clinton team caused the death of about three hundred Iraqis who agreed to work with us. We sent them in. Then Tony Lake called off the operation. They all died."[72]

It was, perhaps, the worst disaster since the Bay of Pigs operation that foundered on the shore of Cuba in 1961, but Clinton and his principal advisers concealed as much of the failure as they could. The American public never received a full accounting.

The operation was made possible by King Hussein's return to the American camp, paving the way for the CIA's return in force to Jordan, where it set up a base for plotting against the Iraqi regime.

Al-Shahwani had been recruited at roughly the same time as Ayad Alawi, a powerfully built physician who had risen through the ranks of the Baath Party before defecting to the West with the help Britain's MI6. The CIA and British intelligence had found Alawi in the Iraqi exile community in London, where they had also found Chalabi—or he had found them. Alawi and Chalabi were distant cousins and would become prominent rivals because both were secular Shiites and, as such, they would be important if the West succeeded in replacing Saddam with someone who could unite Iraq's ethnic and religious communities.

Alawi had defected in London and nearly paid with his life for his "betrayal" when Saddam sent an ax-wielding assassin to kill him one night in 1978. Slipping into Alawi's bedroom at 3:00 a.m., the killer came at Alawi in the dark, landing three blows with the ax—to Alawi's head, chest, and leg, and leaving him for dead. Miraculously, Alawi survived the attack, spending a year in recovery, and emerged from the hospital more determined than ever to work for Saddam's overthrow.

. . .

With Robert Baer out of Iraq and under investigation, the CIA's Northern Iraq Liaison Element, the name assigned to the Kurdish front, had effectively been shut down. The Amman operation, known as the West Iraq Liaison Element, was centered on the Iraqi National Accord, which Alawi had formed with a group of former Iraqi army generals. The CIA was financing the group to the tune of hundreds of thousands of dollars per month. The agency hoped to recruit and equip as many as three hundred Iraqi agents who would infiltrate Iraq, each creating cells of opposition that would then multiply, drawing in disaffected military men and tribal leaders who could consolidate control quickly after a military coup.

"We hoped to leverage five into five hundred," said one of the CIA officers.[73] President Clinton had signed a top-secret order in January 1996 authorizing an intensified effort to foment a rebellion to oust Saddam.[74]

The CIA's deputy director for operations, David Cohen, and his Near East division chief, Steve Richter, went to Saudi Arabia for an extraordinary conclave of spymasters that also included Britain's MI6 and Jordanian and Kuwaiti intelligence. Prince Turki al-Faisal, Saudi Arabia's intelligence chief and veteran of the Afghan campaign, played host for a detailed discussion about strategy and tactics in the anti-Saddam campaign. Prince Turki handed over a large computer database of tribal names and families that would assist the recruitment effort. If King Fahd or Clinton was monitoring the operation, it was not apparent to senior aides.

Since Iraq's creation after World War I, Britain's intelligence chiefs had held the view that only a Sunni strongman from central Iraq could hold the country together, and the CIA plotting raised the question of whether a broad-based insurrection would turn forces loose that could not be controlled.[75] This was the very issue that James Baker had raised at the end of the first Bush administration.

Soon after the meeting in Saudi Arabia, the CIA team in Amman got authorization from Washington to launch a large-scale infiltration. Over the next weeks and months, CIA officers and Iraqis activated infiltration routes of more than one hundred agents. With some, they sent sophisticated communications gear; other agents pre-positioned weapons caches for when they would be needed. But, as one member of the team described later, the agents were traveling under "light cover," meaning their cover stories were simple: a family visit or a business deal. The longer they stayed in Iraq, the more vulnerable they were to detection.

In February, the Iraqi National Accord leaders were so confidant of their prospects for success that they called a news conference in Amman to announce the opening of an official representation office. Alawi emerged as a public opposition figure. He condemned Saddam and told reporters that the Iraqi National Accord had undertaken secret activities, implying they were working to bring down Saddam's regime. The activities, he said, "must remain secret if we are to succeed in our work and ensure that lives are not unnecessarily put at risk."

With this bugle call, Alawi alerted Saddam that clandestine operations were under way.

In the United States, Clinton was running for reelection against Bob Dole. By launching a new covert operation against Saddam he had silenced some of his critics in Congress that he wasn't doing enough to bring down the dictator. Republican leaders, including Dole, who was entitled to briefings on clandestine activities, were constrained from attacking Clinton for wimpishness. Whatever Clinton's motivation for launching this coup plot, the CIA team in the field soon began to detect a wavering level of commitment from the White House. After the bulk of the infiltrators were in place, instructions came from CIA headquarters to put the operation "on the back burner," as one member described it. That was difficult to do, he explained, with agents already in the country.[76] One White House aide responsible for Iraq said, "This was an administration that from the beginning was schizophrenic on Saddam and Iraq. It didn't like the issue, didn't want to have to deal with the issue. It had other priorities and would have allowed Saddam to get off the hook had he given them the minimum rationale for doing so."

In March, Ahmad Chalabi showed up in Washington with an alarming assertion: The infiltration operation had been infiltrated. Saddam's intelligence service was on to the whole thing. How did Chalabi know? He was not supposed to be aware of the Amman-based operation, but with Alawi holding press conferences, it was no surprise. If Chalabi could detect it, couldn't Saddam's agents? The CIA regarded Chalabi's intervention with suspicion. A terrorist bomb had devastated the Iraqi National Congress headquarters in Salahaldin the previous October, killing twenty-eight people including the INC's chief of security. Chalabi suspected that Alawi's group was behind the bombing at a time when their rivalry was rampant.

Chalabi asked to meet the CIA director. With an introduction from

Richard Perle, a conservative activist who had served in the Pentagon,[77] Chalabi went to a rendezvous set at the Ritz Carlton Hotel near the Pentagon. There, in a suite on the thirteenth floor, he met John Deutch and Steve Richter. Chalabi's conversation with Deutch was affable. They chattered about their shared connection to MIT, but Chalabi soon spelled out his warning: Saddam had penetrated the Amman-based operation to stage a coup.

"You are a great power, you can do what you want," Chalabi said, "but when we hear something that is dangerous to you, we tell you and I am here to tell you [that the operation has been blown]. Chalabi said he warned Deutch that the CIA was using an Egyptian courier to bring communications gear into Iraq for the U.S.-backed infiltrators. But the Egyptian was a spy, Chalabi asserted, a spy who had been identified to Chalabi by a defector from Saddam's intelligence service. The Egyptian had been on Baghdad's payroll for years.[78]

Deutch may have viewed Chalabi's presentation as a transparent attempt to undermine a rival—Alawai—but it was too risky to disregard a danger as great as the one Chalabi says he described, affecting operational security. What happened next is still somewhat murky. Deutch neither recalled the infiltrators nor activated their uprising. President Clinton, perhaps relying on faulty or incomplete information, took no steps in early 1996 to disband or recall the largest covert operation that had ever been mounted against the Iraqi dictator. Iraqi intelligence appears to have detected many of the infiltrators as they entered the country. Soon Saddam's secret services had other plotters under surveillance or in custody. Saddam apparently did not act immediately to roll up the network. He waited as more infiltrators made their way into the country each week. Some reports said Iraqi intelligence was able to use the CIA communications gear to query the agency's officers in Amman by pretending to be part of the infiltration team, even using the agent's code words extracted under torture.

On June 17, Saddam ordered the arrests. According to Ahmad Chalabi, Iraqi intelligence files show that sixty-eight military officers were arrested during the third week of June and, after trials in August, thirty-seven of them were exected on September 5. The total number of arrests and executions exceeded these numbers, however, according to one member of the CIA team in Amman.

It is difficult to assess whether the operation ever had a chance to succeed. If it was penetrated from the outset, it would have failed whether or not the White House lost its nerve. Still, if the White House sent an army of Iraqi agents into Saddam's lair and then abandoned them without seriously evaluating Chalabi's warning, America was guilty of an act of betrayal as devastating as Kissinger's abandonment of the Kurds in 1975, or Kennedy's loss of nerve at the Bay of Pigs.[79]

In the aftermath, and for the balance of his eight years in office, Bill Clinton did not speak of the extent to which he took personal responsibility for the fiasco. The White House, in its internal damage assessment, deflected the blame to Deutch, who would lose his job by year's end. But Deutch was not the commander in chief. The authorization of covert action is a war power uniquely reserved for the president, and there is little evidence that Clinton exhibited the requisite discipline to supervise the largest, the most risk-filled and, in human terms, costly covert action of his presidency.

# 11

# CLINTON

*Flight from Terror; Lost Peace*

In the Persian Gulf, the sandy rim of the Arabian Peninsula looks across a shallow and pale blue sea to the mountainous profile of Iran. Throughout history it has marked the boundary of two worlds and, in modern times, the place where the languid and unruly bedouin civilization of the Arabs ended, and where Persia, with all that its civilization entailed for industry, politics, and passion, began.

The Saudi Arabian coastline is a sauna in June. Crude oil–gathering terminals fed by a sprawling spaghetti of pipelines reflect the glint of sunlight that soaks the desert. Sunset brings little relief from the cloak of humidity that weighs heavily on the land. The Saudi side of the gulf is flat and featureless, and Dhahran, the city that Aramco built in the heyday of America's lock on oil resources, wraps around a commercial port and a military complex.

During the cold war, President Truman had secured permission from

King Abdul Aziz to base B-52 bombers loaded with nuclear payloads at Dhahran air base. Their mission, in the era that preceded ICBMs, was to strike targets in the Soviet Union and "Red" China in the event of World War III.

By 1996, the Soviet Union no longer existed, yet the Americans were back protecting the region from Saddam Hussein. One of those Americans was Alfredo R. Guerrero, an air force staff sergeant from Modesto, California. Trained for security, Sergeant Guerrero was standing at his post the night of June 25 atop the eight-story building 131 at the Khobar Towers housing complex in Dhahran, where hundreds of American airmen and soldiers were watching television, writing letters, or otherwise relaxing. They were part of the American, French, and British contingents that were engaged in Operation Southern Watch in Iraq.

A terrorist warning had circulated that Americans might be targeted for an unspecified strike. It was Guerrero's job as chief of the watch to keep an eye on everything that moved in the vicinity of the compound. Terrorism against American military targets was no longer an abstraction in Saudi Arabia. The previous fall, a car bomber had struck in Riyadh at the residence compound for American contractors who were training the Saudi National Guard, killing five Americans.[1] In May, the Saudis had executed several men they said were responsible for the Riyadh blast without giving American investigators a chance to interview them.

Just before 10:00 p.m., Guerrero heard an engine roar. A big olive-colored tanker truck came down the street toward the barracks. It was following a white Chevy Caprice. Both pulled into the parking lot outside the perimeter fence that surrounded the building. Guerrero stood transfixed as the truck slowly backed up to the fence on the north side. Was it carrying water, gasoline, or . . . ? Suddenly the driver leaped from the cab of the truck and dove into the waiting Chevy. It sped away, followed by a Datsun sedan. There sat the truck. Its very stillness induced an electrifying jolt of terror-induced adrenaline that hit Guerrero in an instant.

*Oh, shit,* was all anyone had time to think before Guerrero radioed an emergency evacuation alarm and then clambered down the stairwell, pounding on doors and yelling for people to get out. This act of bravery undoubtedly saved lives during the three minutes that passed before a thunderous explosion sheared off the face of the building and dug a crater thirty-five feet deep and eighty-five feet across.[2]

A few seconds later, all that was left of building 131 was a smoking and sundered hulk enveloped in dust like a grotesque dollhouse suddenly pried open to expose splintered furniture, mattresses, and plumbing fixtures hanging precariously in the wreckage and from which rose the groans and the cries of the wounded. Stunned and dust-covered airmen blinked open their eyes to see Dhahran's lighted skyline where the walls had been. When they pulled all the bodies out, 19 servicemen were dead and 372 were injured. Many more would have been killed except for the fact that the bombers had parked the truck perpendicular to the building. They had also added a layer of water over the explosives to hide them. The effect was to force the blast downward and to the sides.

In Washington, President Clinton expressed outrage. "The cowards who committed this murderous act must not go unpunished." He vowed that the FBI would pursue the investigation relentlessly, adding, "America takes care of its own."

Prince Bandar flew to Dhahran, where he caught up with Warren Christopher, who had diverted from his Middle East diplomatic rounds to tour the scene of the bombing. With Prince Saud al-Faisal, the Saudi foreign minister, as guide, they visited the survivors at King Abdul Aziz Military Hospital. Sergeant Guerrero was among them.

Prince Bandar told one of the wounded airmen, "We'll catch the guys who did this, and I promise you it won't be an O. J. Simpson trial," meaning that those responsible would be punished. Bandar announced a reward of 10 million Saudi rials—about $3 million—for information leading to the arrest of the bombers.

The Khobar Towers attack was the first action in a renewed terrorist war against the United States and its allies in the Middle East. The preeminent terror base was in Iran, where the Revolutionary Guard that Khomeini had created saw itself in a long-term struggle against American power in the Middle East. Its Shiite networks—Hezbollah being the most prominent—extended throughout the region. Separately, a new nexus of terrorist planning had taken root. Al-Qaeda was the most recent terrorist manifestation in the Sunni Muslim world and traceable to the jihadist alliance that had driven out the Soviet occupation of Afghanistan.

Al-Qaeda's network trained in weaponry and explosives and was rapidly taking on a global character. Its cells were linked by cell phone message drops and Internet pathways. Its early operations had been modest. Al-Qaeda trained or financed extremists in Yemen and Somalia. In June 1995, one branch of the Egyptian underground allied with al-Qaeda had attempted to assassinate President Hosni Mubarak as he arrived in Addis Ababa for an Organization of African Unity summit meeting.

The threat was growing.

A month before the Khobar Towers bombing, the Sudanese government expelled bin Laden in an effort to dispel criticism that the country was becoming a haven for terrorists. Bin Laden returned to Afghanistan, and soon thereafter, a top secret State Department analysis expressed concern that bin Laden's "prolonged stay in Afghanistan—where hundreds of 'Arab *mujahedin'* receive terrorist training and key extremist leaders often congregate—could prove more dangerous to U.S. interests in the long run than his three-year liaison with Khartoum."[3]

The evidence from the Khobar Towers bombing pointed toward Iran, particularly the Qods Force of the Revolutionary Guard. Its agents, by some accounts including Imad Mughniyah, trained the Saudi Hezbollah team that carried out the bombing.[4] A critical piece of evidence was that two months prior to the bombing, Saudi security forces had intercepted a carload of plastic explosives en route from a camp in Lebanon's Bekaa Valley to the kingdom. The camp was in the Syrian sector of the Bekaa and under the control of the Iranian Revolutionary Guard, which was training Saudi terrorists. The intercepted explosives, discovered in a search by a bomb-sniffing dog on the Jordanian-Saudi border, were intended for an attack against an unspecified U.S. military facility in Saudi Arabia, and so the Saudis had every reason to suspect that they had only interrupted a plot that might still be in progress. But they failed to share this critical development with the Americans.[5]

Tony Lake, Bill Clinton's national security adviser, concluded that Saudi Hezbollah was the likely culprit, but the CIA was far less certain. It was the FBI's job, under Director Louis J. Freeh, to prove who was responsible—and when they did, it led to bitter disillusionment over his president's unwillingness to confront the culprit: Iran.

In the Holy Land, Clinton faced a new challenge.

On May 29, 1996, Benjamin Netanyahu, known universally as "Bibi," defeated Shimon Peres in national elections and brought the Likud Party, a coalition of nationalist and religious forces, back to power in Israel.

Netanyahu had become the most attractive political figure on the Israeli right. He had youth, a muscular frame, and granitelike self-assurance.

Bibi was a scion of Ze'ev Jabotinsky's revisionist movement (his father had been an aide to Jabotinsky). He was fortified by a strong military background in the same elite commando unit as his older brother, Yonatan, who was killed while leading the 1976 Entebbe raid. Bibi had bested Benny Begin, the former prime minister's son, for leadership of the Likud. Ariel Sharon had withdrawn from the contest as soon as he discovered that his popularity was still in the dungeon because of Lebanon. Besides, Sharon was no match for Bibi's charm and his glib Western style, which convinced the Israeli electorate that he was the man to deliver security and peace.

For Americans following Middle East developments, Bibi was a familiar face. He had served in the Washington embassy under Ambassador Moshe Arens and had then moved to New York as Israel's ambassador to the United Nations. He was the most Americanized of Israeli prime ministers since Golda Meir, having attended high school in Philadelphia, taken degrees in architecture and management from MIT, and worked briefly at the Boston Consulting Group.

The more Netanyahu attacked Peres for compromise and weakness in the face of terror, the more Clinton and his Middle East team tried to rescue their sagging ally and the peace process. After the wave of suicide bombings, Ross had convinced the president to organize a "summit of peacemakers"—an attempt to make Peres look like he was still in control of events. It was held in March 1996 at Sharm el-Sheikh in Egypt, just as the CIA was launching its infiltration to topple Saddam.

Peres assumed the role of statesman, but that didn't mask the palpable sense of desperation about the terrorist wave, fomented in no small measure by Iraq, from where Saddam was sending a cash reward to every "martyred" suicide bomber's family. Iran also cheered from the sidelines. Clinton could do nothing but ask the French and Germans to pass Iran a warning: "If you want to have contacts with the outside world, terrorism in Israel must cease immediately."[6]

It was not exactly a muscular bit of diplomacy. What had Clinton ever done to demonstrate that he would back up such a threat?

Among the Palestinians, where the suicide bombers made a mockery of Arafat's authority, the PLO leader claimed that he had too few tools with which to fight terrorism. Clinton offered the CIA's assistance, signing a directive authorizing the agency to train a Palestinian security force. It was treated as a covert operation though it was an open secret in Israel.[7] Soon the CIA was flying Palestinians to remote training camps to help create a professional cadre of security officers. Israeli and Palestinian intelligence officials met for a joint review of how to control terrorism. It was the first meeting of its kind.[8]

With Peres and the peace camp so weakened, the Israeli government was hypersensitive to Netanyahu's taunts that it could not provide security. Of course, that was the moment when Hezbollah militants along Israel's northern border provided a new provocation with rocket and mortar attacks. After a series of border clashes that killed one Israeli soldier (and several Lebanese), Peres ordered the army into action against Lebanon on April 11. Operation Grapes of Wrath was a large-scale assault that included eleven hundred air raids, the bombing of Beirut neighborhoods, Lebanese power plants, and dozens of villages in southern Lebanon. In a matter of days, four hundred thousand Lebanese civilians were put to flight, hundreds wounded, and more than thirty killed. The operation was broadly perceived in the Muslim world as a cynical exercise of power designed to enhance Peres's election fortunes. In Germany, Mohammed Atta, who would become the leader of the 9/11 hijacking team, was a twenty-seven-year-old student. On the day of the Israeli attack he pledged his life, in a testament filed at a local mosque, to avenge the innocent victims.[9]

The Clinton administration stood virtually mute in the face of the destruction. U.S. policy and Clinton's hopes for peace hinged on Peres's political survival, and if he needed to do some muscle flexing in Lebanon—that tragic sideshow—to help his election prospects, what was Washington to do? Condemn its partner? That was the attitude that pervaded the Clinton team, setting a precedent that would be repeated.

The distraught and exasperated Lebanese prime minister, Rafik Hariri, flew to Paris seeking help from the French. Hariri refused to blame either Hezbollah or the Syrians, who still had a thirty-five-thousand-man army in Lebanon, because Israel continued to occupy southern Lebanon.

"If there were no occupation, there would be no reason for Hezbollah to exist," he said, adding that Israel's demand that Hezbollah be disarmed was unreasonable. "What they want us to do is make the occupation easy. We cannot do this."[10]

The French, too, seemed powerless.

On April 18, Israeli artillery gunners unleashed a barrage of 155-millimeter shells aimed at what turned out to be the United Nations refugee center at Kana in southern Lebanon. The shelter, packed with women and children, became a fiery death trap as the projectiles exploded among the mass of people, shredding limbs and torsos. The Israeli army had known the location of the UN camp, but Israeli commanders said they fired in error, seeking to silence nearby Katyusha rockets.

The scenes of the carnage were overpowering. When the body parts were assembled, more than 102 Lebanese civilians lay dead in the sanctuary of the United Nations. Arabs, and many Israelis, were in shock. Peres had been in a press conference with Arafat when he got word and immediately returned to Jerusalem. Uri Savir, flying across central Israel with the army chief of staff, General Amnon Lipkin-Shahak, uttered a grim assessment. "The peace camp just lost the elections," he told the general.[11]

Savir proved to be correct. The month of bloodletting incited a bitter reaction among Israeli Arabs, who tended to vote the Labor Party ticket. Their leaders called for a boycott of the balloting.

Israel's 1996 assault on Lebanon—not just on Hezbollah bases but also on the country's power plants, infrastructure, and Beirut neighborhoods where Hezbollah offices were located—reflected poorly on American leadership and the spirit, almost forgotten, it seemed, of the United Nations Charter, whose preamble had motivated Eisenhower to act in 1958. The charter had imposed a responsibility on the great powers "to save succeeding generations from the scourge of war, which twice in our lifetime has brought untold sorrow to mankind." The international system was at a loss to function in the Middle East as it dispatched peacekeeping troops in Europe to prevent genocidal killing and ethnic cleansing in the former Yugoslavia. Now Lebanon again was the battleground of a broader Middle East conflict. The United Nations— and its five permanent members who dominate the Security Council— did precious little to protect Lebanon's civilian population; that failure was compounded by the inability of the Lebanese state to control its territory and to prevent its being used as a staging area for attacks on Israeli civilians, but the greater blame could be attributed to the long failure of international diplomacy.

The obligation that Eisenhower had felt to ensure that foreign forces—whether Nasser's or the Soviet Union's—not be allowed to destabilize Lebanon had been forgotten in the Clinton White House, as it had been in the Reagan White House. The United States could not be the

world's policeman, but how was Lebanon's sectarian struggle and humanitarian pain less important than Bosnia's or Rwanda's?

The failure of American diplomacy tempted Syria and Iran to fill the
vacuum and spurred Israeli leaders to act unilaterally, with devastating
results for the civilian population. Here was a state that had been destabilized repeatedly by the Arab-Israeli conflict; the advance of so many
armies across its territory contributed to the radicalization of politics.
Sunni and Shiite extremism tapped this wellspring of pain and disillusionment to spread a new ideology of antimodernism and anti-Americanism.

Israel was not to blame for defending its population, though Israel's excessively destructive military policy in Lebanon was conducted wantonly
and with the aim of punishing a civilian population, as General Eitan had
acknowledged during the 1978 incursion.

Rather, the destruction of Lebanon was the sanguinary consequence
of failure by the great powers to orchestrate a comprehensive settlement
in the Middle East. Such a settlement might have been possible in
Nixon's time, when Brezhnev was eager to head off the 1973 war. It
might have been possible if Carter had won a second term, or in the wake
of Reagan's 1984 landslide if only he had had the foresight to block the
ill-conceived Israeli invasion of 1982.

Instead, what stands out today in Lebanon is the anguishing toll inflicted on a small nation that had lived in peace until Black September,
when the PLO—ejected from Jordan— rebuilt its ministate in Lebanon,
destabilized the sectarian balance, and triggered civil war. Syrian intervention and occupation were followed by Israeli invasion and occupation.
The radicalization of Lebanon's Shiite community has been one of the
most fateful developments of transnational extremism, spreading Iranian-
based militancy to new territories.

Peres's military campaign in Lebanon was short and disastrous and
conducted just in advance of the Israeli elections. Clinton virtually endorsed him over Netanyahu by stating that Peres's reelection was essential for the peace process. Dennis Ross and the Middle East team of the
State Department tried to go even farther. They recommended that Clinton reverse long-standing American policy and move the United States
embassy from Tel Aviv to Jerusalem, an act that would have deeply antagonized the Arab world and much of the international community.[12] Sandy
Berger managed to fend off the attempt.

Peres lost the election by thirty thousand votes. Netanyahu had run an
American-style campaign of attack ads and sound bites.

"There is no peace; there is no security; there is no reason to vote for Peres," was Bibi's mantra. But the election was less about the two men than about colliding national instincts and impulses. A majority of Israelis had believed in peace with the Arabs. They had cheered Rabin and suffered stoically through his death and the onslaught of terror. But another significant number "saw the same [peace] process as a nightmare," as Savir later wrote. To them, it left "the nation defenseless against violence. This was the 'Jewish condition,' and had been for centuries. We were [the] 'people that dwells alone.' Trusting others meant delivering ourselves into their hands."[13]

All of Israel understood the hard-line political current that Netanyahu represented. The question was, could he ignore Rabin's agenda of peace by paying mere lip service to it, while bringing back the militant agenda of the "activists" and reversing the Oslo process?

As Netanyahu went through the ritual of negotiating with Israel's political parties to form a new government and parliamentary majority, Saddam Hussein seized the lull in attention to make another move. The Iraqi leader had shown a poor understanding of American politics over the years, but he correctly assessed Clinton's reactive approach in the Middle East. Like a late summer storm, Saddam's army broke across the rolling plain of northern Iraq and enveloped the Kurdish capital of Erbil, firing artillery and heavy machine guns at Kurdish *peshmerga* defenders, who were forced to retreat into the hills north and east of the city.

Saddam announced on August 31 that he had dispatched his army at the request of Massoud Barzani and his Kurdish Democratic Party. How could anyone object? Talabani had been in control of the Kurdish capital ever since he seized it to gain some political leverage over the oil-smuggling trade that Barzani controlled. Now Talabani had to abandon the city. Baghdad's troops moved in along with a phalanx of intelligence officers, rounding up suspected "traitors," especially anyone who had been involved with the CIA or with Chalabi's Iraqi National Congress. About fifty Kurds from Talabani's garrison, which had been holding Erbil for two years, died defending the city. Iraqi troops executed forty more and killed nearly one hundred at nearby Qushtapa.

Another bloodbath was under way in Iraq. America stood still. Thousands of Kurds rushed north with bundles of clothing and few possessions to the Turkish border, seeking protection.

Clinton was campaigning in Tennessee. "I have placed our forces in the region on high alert and they are now being reinforced," Clinton said. "It is premature at this time—and I want to emphasize that—it is entirely premature to speculate on any response we might have. But we are prepared to deal with these developments."[14]

It seemed a strange comment from a president who had received numerous warnings through intelligence channels that Saddam was preparing an attack on the Kurdish safe haven. The conflict between the Kurdish factions in the north over revenue and dominance had been building for two years. In the weeks before Saddam made his move, skirmishes had erupted between Barzani's KDP and Talabani's PUK.

Talabani's side had reached out to Iran for arms. It was inevitable that Barzani's side would reach out to Baghdad, its partner in the oil-smuggling trade.

Clinton had been receiving intelligence reports that Saddam was preparing to make a move. The State Department summoned Kurdish representatives to London, but diplomacy gave little promise of relieving the pressure. American credibility was at an all-time low after the CIA's catastrophic failure in Operation Achilles. Clinton had the option of launching air force fighters from the NATO base in Turkey to blunt the Iraqi attack. But he refused, wary of taking sides in the internecine Kurdish conflict.[15] He simply let it happen.

Saddam's forces stormed north and took Erbil in a matter of hours, just as they had mopped up the CIA coup plot and just as they had defeated the halfhearted uprising of March 1995 incited by Bob Baer and Ahmad Chalabi. Clinton was batting zero-for-three against Saddam, and the president's reticence, just three months before Election Day, seemed more political than strategic. There was no easy way to defeat Saddam Hussein short of a full-scale invasion. He had learned that lesson at the cost of hundreds of Iraqi lives. But surely one of his options was to bomb the Iraqi forces as they crossed the boundary into the protected zone.

Instead, Clinton authorized cruise missile attacks against Iraq—in *southern* Iraq. As Kurds were dying in Erbil, American warships fired cruise missiles and B-52 bombers flew all the way from the United States to strike a series of air defense installations that were completely unrelated to what was going on in Kurdistan.

It led one journalist to observe, "Aside from standing up to Mr. Hussein—an obvious political plus in an election year—it is hard to discern concrete American goals in today's military operation or what would constitute an acceptable change in his behavior."[16] Of course, Clinton had not stood up to Saddam; he had just created the appearance of doing so.

Nearly four years into his presidency, Clinton was still fighting the war against Saddam that Bush had started. The consequence of Clinton's inaction was that over the next month, some sixty-five hundred members of Chalabi's Iraqi National Congress, their families, and other Iraqis who had cooperated with the CIA effort in northern Iraq were evacuated across the border to Turkey and flown by U.S. military transports to Guam. There, they were meticulously—sometimes cruelly—screened for political asylum. This mini-Dunkirk cost $100 million, according to an administration official who was involved.

The perception that America was weak and could be driven out of the Middle East by feats of defiance and large-scale terror was becoming widespread. Few Americans had heard of Tora Bora in 1996, but from that epicenter of anti-Soviet glory achieved by the mujahideen of the 1980s, Osama bin Laden, on August 23, issued a declaration of war against the United States, Israel, and the Saudi royal family.

There was no press conference. America's network anchors probably would not have been able to pick bin Laden out of a lineup or find Tora Bora on a map. The words came down from bin Laden's cave in the Hindu Kush as if from another century.

"It should not be hidden from you that the people of Islam had suffered from aggression, iniquity and injustice imposed on them by the Zionist-Crusader alliance and their collaborators," he wrote in his manifesto. He decried the "massacre at Kana," referring to the Israeli artillery strike on the United Nations compound. He blamed America for the deaths of more than six hundred thousand Iraqi children who had suffered during the long United Nations sanctions regime imposed on Iraq.

In the Islamic world, bin Laden's words registered. That autumn, Abdel Bari Atwan, a respected Arab commentator and editor of *Al-Quds al-Arabi* newspaper in London, made the journey to bin Laden's hideout high above Jalalabad to conduct the first interview with this strange son of Saudi wealth who had turned on his family, his country, and America. They met in a two-room cave. One room was full of crates containing antiaircraft guns and rockets.

Osama bin Laden: not the obvious arch-terrorist

"He was extremely natural, very simple, very humble and soft spoken," Atwan said. "You feel he is shy. He doesn't look at you eye to eye. Usually when he talks to you he talks by looking down. His clothes are very, very humble, very simple."[17]

"To be honest, the man is likable. He is really nice," Atwan continued. "You don't see him as somebody who will be the arch-terrorist, who will be the most dangerous man in the world. He doesn't strike you as charismatic."

It was that same soft-spokenness that impressed Peter Bergen, the journalist who arranged bin Laden's first interview with an American correspondent, Peter Arnett of CNN. Later, Bergen remarked, "If you didn't know what he was saying, you would have thought he was talking about the weather, but when you read the transcript of his remarks [translated from Arabic] they were full of rage and of fury against the United States."

Bergen had found him a seething Islamic nationalist in the broadest sense: one who believed that the record of Arab humiliation began in 1919, when the colonial powers carved up the Middle East, apportioning its oil resources among themselves and trampling on Arab aspirations. The humiliation had continued through the century. Whether it was in Palestine or Kashmir, Muslims had been victimized.

"As far as he is concerned, this war is about humiliation and reclaiming Muslim pride," Bergen observed.

A war was coming, but nothing bin Laden had said gave it any form or described the venue of battle.

In Israel, Bibi Netanyahu enjoyed a few months of political honeymoon before it became apparent that he possessed no magic formula for providing peace or security.

On July 28, he gave an interview on national television marking the one-year anniversary of his premiership. He took credit for the improvement in security, saying that the Palestinians understood "very well that the game of tipping the wink to Hamas and to Islamic Jihad and telling them that they may go ahead and blow up buses in Israeli cities [is over and they] will not get off scot free. That is why the Palestinians have taken measures to restrain them."[18]

Two days later, Hamas unleashed a series of suicide bomb attacks. Twin bombers struck at the Mahane Yehuda market in Jerusalem, killing

16 people and wounding 150. On September 4, another Hamas bomber blew himself up on the Ben-Yehuda pedestrian mall in Jerusalem, killing 5 and wounding 181.

Netanyahu was both incensed and embarrassed. Politically, he knew he needed to strike a spectacular blow against Islamic extremism. He chose Amman, where the residents of the Jordanian capital build their houses behind walls with iron gates for security. The Mossad team that was sent to assassinate Khaled Meshal, one of the founders of Hamas, decided to move on him during the brief interval in which he walked from his car to the door of his office in a quiet neighborhood near the center of the city.

It was Thursday, September 25, 1997, and Israel was doing what it viewed as occasionally necessary: assassinating its enemies.

After the first suicide bombing, Netanyahu had called together his inner cabinet to authorize Mossad to target senior Hamas leaders. Danny Yatom, the retired general who had served as Rabin's military assistant, was the chief of the spy agency, and within weeks he presented a plan to the prime minister to hit Hamas leaders in Damascus or Amman. Netanyahu ruled out hitting anyone in Damascus. The risk was too great. If anything went wrong, Hafez al-Assad would not hesitate to execute any spy he captured, as his predecessors had hanged Eli Cohen, the Mossad officer, after he had penetrated the Syrian high command in the 1950s.

Jordan was a different story. Israel now had diplomatic relations with Amman. The border was open. An Israeli embassy stood in the Jordanian capital as a refuge of last resort if anything went wrong. The question was, How to do it?

"We ruled out in advance any proposal for a noisy operation because in the wake of an operation that involves shooting, there is a body with a hole in the head and then it's obvious that it was a hit and an investigation is launched and all kinds of unnecessary questions are asked," Yatom said later.[19] In a previous assassination abroad, Rabin had ordered the killing of the founder of Islamic Jihad in Malta and the hit team had cut him down in a hail of bullets. The episode triggered intense diplomatic protests.

Instead of bullets, a powerful neurotoxin was selected for injection— a "quiet" assassination. The team was composed of six Mossad officers. The two who would carry out the hit checked into the Intercontinental Hotel as tourists with forged Canadian passports identifying them as

Shawn Kendall and Barry Beads. They had done their surveillance work in advance while others rented a car to stand nearby for a getaway.

Meshal arrived on time. His driver and bodyguard, Mohammed Abu Saif, did not notice the two men lingering on the sidewalk. Meshal stepped out of the car. The men rushed forward. One of them clamped an injector, wrapped in cloth, on Meshal's neck from behind.

"At that moment, I realized there was an assassination attempt without resorting to gunshots," Meshal said later. Soon, "I felt ringing in my left ear. I had shivers, and something that felt like an electric shock running through my body."[20]

The Mossad men turned and ran as Abu Saif took off after them. Within moments, the Mossad officers jumped into their getaway car. Abu Saif flagged down a passing vehicle and gave chase. Both soon were screeching around corners at breakneck speeds. After a short chase, the Mossad car halted and the Israeli officers took flight again on foot, but Abu Saif leaped from his car and overtook them. He grabbed one of the Israelis by the back of the shirt.

Eyewitnesses said that the Israeli wheeled and hit Abu Saif in the head with a blunt object, opening a wound that later required eighteen stitches, but the bodyguard knocked the Mossad man to the ground and turned on the second officer, pummeling him severely before throwing him down an embankment. At that moment the police arrived and arrested all three men.[21] There was a lot of shouting at the police station as the Mossad men said they did not want help from the Canadian embassy and asked that their names not be released. The police initially did not know what to make of Abu Saif's tale of an assassination attempt.

Meshal did not immediately fall ill. He was driven to a safe house. But two hours later he began vomiting. He lost his sense of balance and was feverish. By Friday morning, he was in a coma. That's when King Hussein got involved. And that's when Efraim Halevy got the call.

After Israel's peace treaty with Jordan, Halevy, the Mossad deputy director, had been rewarded by Rabin with an ambassadorship to the European Union. Halevy had hoped to become the first Israeli ambassador to Jordan, but Peres, who was then the foreign minister, blocked his appointment—out of pettiness, Halevy thought. And so when Netanyahu hit the panic button, he called for Halevy to get back to Jerusalem ASAP to help calm down the Jordanian royal court.

The two Mossad officers in custody admitted on videotape who they were and what their mission had been. The Canadian government confirmed that their passports were forged. The four other Mossad officers from the team took refuge in the Israeli embassy.

For King Hussein and his brother, Crown Prince Hassan, the realization that Israel had sent assassins to the heart of their kingdom was an outrage that put national honor on the line. But more, it confirmed the king's deepest reservations about the character of Netanyahu. After all the king had done for peace, and after his strong partnership with Rabin, Netanyahu seemed out to humiliate him. The king had not forgotten an incident the previous March, when he had invited Arafat to fly with him on a royal jetliner from Amman to the new Palestinian Authority landing strip that had been completed at Rafah at the southern end of the Gaza Strip. While they were in the air, Netanyahu had ordered air traffic controllers to forbid the king's plane from flying over Israeli airspace. The king had been forced to decide whether to defy the ban and risk being shot down by Israeli air force jets, or return to Amman. He turned his plane around, but when he landed, he sent a bitter message to Netanyahu.

"You are piling up tragic actions" and broken promises, Hussein told him. "You are pushing all the Arabs and Israelis toward an abyss of disasters and a bloodbath." Personal communication between the two leaders all but ceased.[22]

Now the king was on the telephone. A few days before the assassination attempt, he had sent a diplomatic message to Netanyahu that Hamas's leadership was offering a thirty-year truce with Israel. Who could tell if it was sincere, or a Hamas trick, but the king thought it was worth pursuing since Hamas was the fastest-growing Islamic resistance movement in Gaza. But the king heard nothing back from the Israelis. He was perplexed about Israel's lack of interest in a potential breakthrough.[23]

With Meshal close to death, this no longer mattered.

The tension on the phone between Bibi and the king was electric. If Meshal died, the king said with controlled fury, the two captured Mossad men would be subjected to trial and execution. Further, Jordan would renounce the peace treaty with Israel and would withdraw its embassy. He demanded that Netanyahu immediately provide the antidote to the poison injected into Meshal.

Netanyahu tried to negotiate. He wanted a guarantee that all of his Mossad officers would be liberated. But the king would not tolerate any conditions.

The king gave him an ultimatum: either he produce the antidote or the king would break relations and mete out the most extreme punishment for the Mossad team. The antidote was dispatched with Yatom, but the Israelis refused to identify the poison.

Netanyahu began to zigzag chaotically over what to do next. King Hussein was holding all the cards. On Friday afternoon, Halevy arrived at Mossad headquarters. He had a strange feeling when he reentered the building where he had built a career in espionage. "It was like returning to the scene of the crime," he later wrote.

Yatom and his senior staff were trying to figure out what broader concession Israel could make to defuse the king's anger. Would new night-vision sights for Jordanian tanks salve the wound? How about an upgrade for his F-16s that Israel might obtain for him in Washington? Halevy was thinking about the king's embarrassment. He was also aware, because he had been briefed, that Hamas had made an offer of a truce that Netanyahu had fumbled. The Mossad men were arranged around a conference table and all eyes were on Halevy. He told them they had no choice but to release the spiritual leader of Hamas, Sheikh Ahmed Yassin, who had been in prison since 1989 for "incitement."

The room went silent, deafeningly silent, Halevy thought. A rigorous debate followed. It would certainly look like a cave-in. It might strengthen Hamas in the long run. It might weaken Israel's deterrent. But in freeing the crippled holy man, they would also be giving the king something that would garner great credit for him in the Arab world. The Mossad chiefs asked Halevy to try the idea out on Netanyahu. When the prime minister came on the line, he rejected the idea out of hand as "unthinkable."

Yet Netanyahu was stuck. He had dispatched the antidote to Amman, but King Hussein had summoned an American medical specialist on toxins who said he could not assure the king that Meshal would recover unless he knew the exact chemistry of the poison. Netanyahu had refused to reveal it, so the king called the White House. When Clinton came on the line, the king vented his rage over Netanyahu's mendacity.

Netanyahu was aware that Clinton disliked him. So he called the one person who would feel obliged to get him out of a jam. He used a secure phone to call Dennis Ross. Netanyahu explained that he had been withholding information on the poison until he got a promise from King Hussein that the Mossad officers trapped in Amman would be released.

"Prime Minister, you have embarrassed the king, you have taken advantage of your special relationship in security, and you are going to have to make amends," Ross told him.

But Ross did not advocate a gesture of any magnitude. "Make an apology and promise you won't do anything like this again and these agents will never again set foot in Jordan," Ross suggested.[24] That would never have been enough, as Ross should have known.

Meshal's condition began to improve, but Yatom, the Mossad chief, had gotten nowhere in trying to extricate his officers. The king had set a deadline of midnight Saturday for a full disclosure on the nature of the toxin that Mossad had injected in Meshal's neck.

Saturday morning, Netanyahu called Halevy and told him cryptically that he was authorized to proceed with his plan. But Halevy did not trust Netanyahu. He demanded that the prime minister explicitly state what he was authorizing. After all, the day before he had said it was "unthinkable."

Bibi laid it out: They would release Sheikh Yassin, and perhaps others, to get their Mossad team back. He wanted Halevy to come up to Jerusalem to try to finalize a swap.

Before he left for the hour's drive up to Jerusalem, Halevy sent a message to Amman through Mossad channels laying out for the king the outlines of an offer to release Sheikh Yassin. The Jordanians responded that Halevy should come to Amman the next day.

When Halevy reached Jerusalem, he learned of King Hussein's demand for details about the neurotoxin. The king was threatening to call a news conference that evening to expose the aborted operation to the media and to suspend the peace treaty with Israel.

"He is not bluffing," Halevy told Netanyahu.

After a time, the prime minister folded. The Clinton White House was not going to rescue him. How could Clinton in any way defend an assassination attempt? Netanyahu agreed to all of the king's demands in order to get his Mossad officers back. Halevy drove alone to Amman the next day. He found the king angry and bitter. These two warriors, one a monarch and one a former Israeli spymaster, had more in common with each other than either had with Netanyahu. They had worked together to make the Jordanian-Israeli peace, and they shared a disdain for Arafat, who had spoiled their plans to create a Palestinian entity under Jordanian sovereignty. They both were dedicated to peace, real peace.

The king accepted the proposal for the release of Sheikh Yassin, but he demanded and got the release of other prisoners as well. Halevy won the freedom of the four Mossad officers hiding in the Israeli embassy. The two in Jordanian custody were released after weeks of further negotiations. The Israelis made sure that Sheikh Yassin, who was blind and disabled, was put on a helicopter and flown to Amman so that the king—not Arafat—would get the credit from cheering Hamas supporters. But that didn't stop Arafat. He flew to Amman and rushed to Yassin's bedside, where he kissed him excessively before television cameras. Soon thereafter, the sheikh returned to Gaza, where he was greeted by tens of thousands of supporters. He was carried aloft on the shoulders of Hamas faithful and his power continued to grow at the expense of Arafat's.[25]

Strangely, Hamas had come out ahead. Its suicide bombers had killed and wounded hundreds of Israelis. Yet Netanyahu's decision to strike back so ineptly and so exotically turned the tables against Israel. Had Yatom really believed that Israel would call less attention to itself by injecting Meshal with poison on a public street in front of witnesses than by shooting him in the head? Further, Israel's culture of using assassination as a state weapon recalled the blowguns and poisons of an earlier era of CIA "wet work" that had repulsed Americans and much of the world. It led to a presidential executive order against assassination and it distinguished, uncomfortably for many hard-liners, America's outlook from Israel's.

The *Economist* put Bibi's picture on its cover under the headline, "Serial Bungler." Had Netanyahu been waging peace as if there were no terror—in the Rabin mode—some of the criticism might have been muted. He might even have been able to call on King Hussein to arrest Meshal and extradite him for trial. But Netanyahu's tenure was marked by so little goodwill that he limited his options.

Bibi had appointed Ariel Sharon as minister of infrastructure, and in August 1996 the cabinet lifted all restraints on settlement building; it granted $500 million for economic development within existing settlements. Three thousand West Bank housing units, frozen by Rabin because they were on occupied land, were put on the market for Israelis.

When Arafat asked Netanyahu at their first meeting to limit new construction in the territories, Netanyahu had boomed, "Out of the question! First of all, nothing in the Oslo accords prevents us from building." He reminded Arafat that, "Ideologically, we're different from the Labor Party."

His words had stunned Arafat, and one of his colleagues, Yasser Abed

Rabbo, showed his contempt by replying, "We haven't come here to listen to your thoughts about differences between you and Labor."

The next day, the Palestinians learned that Netanyahu, at an internal Likud meeting, pledged that "there will never be a Palestinian state between the Mediterranean and the Jordan [River]."[26]

What point was there in working with him? Palestinians asked themselves.

Netanyahu also was not willing to reaffirm Rabin's commitment to give up the Golan Heights. He told Clinton as much. He sent an assistant, Dore Gold, to Washington to secure a signed statement that Rabin's commitment was not binding. Netanyahu also demanded that Clinton reaffirm the secret pledge that Kissinger had made in 1975 that the United States would "give great weight to Israel's position that any peace agreement with Syria must be predicated on Israel remaining on the Golan Heights." Even though these new promises were not binding, it was humiliating for Clinton to allow his secretary of state, Warren Christopher, to renounce Rabin's policies in writing.[27] Gold later bragged that he had "saved the Golan."[28]

The years of Netanyahu's government marked a significant backtracking on the progress that had been made toward peace. And while it is understandable that the ebb and flow of Israeli politics made this inevitable, it was not inevitable that America, too, would retreat from the benchmarks Rabin had set. American constancy suffered as Clinton allowed his administration to cave to Netanyahu's demands to wipe clean the slate on which Rabin had charted a path to comprehensive peace and reconciliation.

After his first meeting with Netanyahu, Clinton complained, "He thinks he is the superpower and we are here to do whatever he requires." More often than not, however, Clinton indulged Netanyahu's demands because Netanyahu swept through Washington like a bodybuilder, flexing the political muscle of the pro-Israeli bloc in Congress.

Rabin had played the game differently. Rabin saw himself as the chief lobbyist for Israel in Washington and had little patience for AIPAC or Jewish community leaders who sought to speak for Israel in policy debates. Moreover, Rabin's positions on peace were so revolutionary after a decade of stasis under Begin and Shamir that the Israeli lobby, AIPAC and its allies in Congress, was flummoxed by its own right-wing tilt. Rabin had silenced them, but under Netanyahu they were back.

The Oslo breakthrough, which was built on trust and confidence between Palestinians and Israelis, was breaking down, and as it did, the Clinton team was pulled in as mediator, albeit one inclined to be more responsive to Netanyahu's requirements than to Arafat's.[29] And in its mediation role, Clinton's team under Ross allowed itself to be hobbled by the twenty-year-old Kissinger pledge to preview American negotiating initiatives with Israel, keeping the Palestinians in the dark until any proposal had been vetted by the Israeli side.[30] This built-in bias, which easily could have been dropped by a new president given the bonds of trust forged in the Oslo Accords, gave Israel not only a negotiating advantage but also an opportunity to alter or block unwanted measures. The practice was frequently discovered and resented by the Palestinians and it contributed to negative Arab perceptions of Ross, though Arafat and his colleagues continued to place great faith in Clinton's personal empathy for their cause.

So much of the Oslo process had been linked to the symbolism of trust: Rabin's handshake with Arafat, their willingness to sit at the same table. But the new symbolism, under Netanyahu, was about tearing down what had been erected. Snubbed by Netanyahu for months, Arafat had told a rally in Gaza that the Palestinians were indebted to the legacy of all "the martyrs who died for Jerusalem" down to "the last martyr—Yehya Ayyash," a reference to the Hamas bomb maker who had the blood of dozens of Israelis on his hands.

Netanyahu sank even deeper in the mire of mistrust. On September 24, 1996, he opened an ancient tunnel in the Old City of Jerusalem, between the Western Wall and the Muslim Quarter, ostensibly to improve the movement of tourists, but the tunnel's proximity to the foundations of the mosques standing atop the Temple Mount incited Muslim suspicion and anger. Netanyahu's intelligence chiefs had warned—just as they had warned previous prime ministers—that opening the tunnel could lead to widespread violence. The plan had come from the municipality of Jerusalem, then headed by Mayor Ehud Olmert, and the Israeli Ministry of Religious Affairs. It is impossible to underestimate the capacity for suspicion among believers who claim the holy ground of Jerusalem. Any archaeological activity in the vicinity of the Temple Mount or Noble Sanctuary triggered religious paranoia, in this case Muslim fear that Jewish authorities were preparing to destroy their shrines—the Dome of the Rock and the al-Aqsa Mosque—and rebuild the Jewish Temple as an affirmation of Hebrew nationalism.

As Amos Elon had written, "The city attracts the pious as well as the mentally disturbed, and innocent pilgrims as well as the cranks." Even among the high priests of faith, however, where one might expect tolerance and restraint, there were "rich deposits of malevolent superstitions, of which Jerusalem seems to have an almost inexhaustible supply."[31]

The fact that Netanyahu had acted in the dead of night, using workers guarded by armed soldiers, had added to the pall of suspicion. By morning, the alarm had gone out from the Old City. Palestinian rioting broke out in Jerusalem and quickly spread to other West Bank cities. Arafat denounced the tunnel opening as a "big crime against our religion and our holy places."[32]

The scenes of violence were terrifying for some Israeli commanders: young Palestinians charging heavily armed clusters of Israeli soldiers behind fortified checkpoints, from which they fired rubber bullets at close range, often with fatal results. Israel Hasson, the deputy director of Shin Bet, described the scene outside Ramallah on the road to Jerusalem: "A wave of young people is coming forward, throwing stones. The soldiers open fire, like shooting ducks. Young people are falling, are carried over to the ambulances. A new wave comes on, and it begins all over again. I can see the faces of the Palestinian police, and I turn to the general, I tell him this has to be stopped right away, because we are attacking the honor of the Palestinian Authority. They are not going to stand there, and they might return fire with real bullets."[33]

Soon, they did. The Palestinian police turned their guns on the Israelis and all pretense that the Israeli and Palestinian police were on the same side disappeared. In Nablus, a mob attacked the Israeli army detachment that guarded Joseph's Tomb, revered as resting place of the Hebrew patriarch whose bones were carried out of Egypt by Moses. Palestinian policemen joined in the assault. By the time the Israelis were extracted by a rescue force, six soldiers had been killed.

The CIA station chief, Stan Moskowitz, who had been training and arming Palestinian security forces, now wondered whether trust could be recovered. When he saw Arafat, the Palestinian leader was livid—hyperventilating—because, he said, the Israelis had used tanks and heavy weapons (including fifty-caliber machine guns) against the Palestinian police.

He raged about the "slaughter" of his men. Eighty Palestinians were killed and more than twelve hundred wounded, while Israel lost only fifteen soldiers in the violent exchanges.

"This will not happen again!" the PLO leader shouted.

That may have been the moment, Moskowitz reflected later, when Arafat decided to start smuggling heavier weapons with which to arm his security forces.[34]

Clinton was in the middle of his reelection campaign. Bob Dole had mocked him as a scandal-ridden "Bozo."[35] But Clinton decided the best course for renewal of the peace process was to summon Arafat, Netanyahu, and King Hussein to Washington. The problem was that the peace agenda was so threadbare that Arafat threatened to boycott. What was the point in dealing with Netanyahu? How could America remain silent as he rolled up Oslo? Arafat believed that Ross was using the Washington summit to protect Netanyahu politically against a challenge from the Labor Party. But Clinton just wanted calm in the region.

In the capital, Netanyahu refused to make any concessions, triggering at least one presidential tantrum staged while the Israeli prime minister was in earshot in an adjoining room. On the second day of the summit, King Hussein, frail and fighting cancer, confronted Netanyahu over lunch, decrying his immaturity and poor judgment.

"I have never been so worried for the region," the king told him.[36]

Just as the summit seemed a failure, Netanyahu turned to Arafat and said, "Believe me, I am a man of peace; I want to make peace."

Up to that point, six of the seven major Palestinian cities had been turned over to the Palestinian Authority. The transfer of Hebron had been delayed, first by Peres, who had been paralyzed by the suicide attacks on Jerusalem buses and Tel Aviv's shopping district in February and March, then by Netanyahu. For him, Hebron was a hard case because the settler movement regarded Hebron as a shrine. They wanted it as part of Israel.

Martin Peretz, the editor in chief of the *New Republic*, pointed out that for some Jews it was as difficult to leave Hebron as it would be to leave Jerusalem. "It is true, of course, that only several hundred Jews now live within Hebron proper. But that is only because the Jews of an immemorial community were driven out by massacre in 1929," he wrote. "Hebron is the literal birthplace of the Jewish people and where the matriarchs and patriarchs of Israel are buried."[37]

Clinton managed to prevent a breakdown by persuading Netanyahu and Arafat to shake hands in front of the cameras at the summit. This photo op was taken as a sign that the peace process was back on track, but that was an illusion. On the way home, Arafat stopped in Morocco to brief King Hassan II, who heard Arafat's report on Netanyahu and pronounced: "This man is definitely dangerous."

By virtue of his ideology, Netanyahu was in fact a danger to peace as it had been envisioned by Rabin. Arafat understood this, but he stayed in the game because there was still a chance to resuscitate Oslo and the promise of statehood under a future Israeli prime minister. Arafat was building credibility with an American president while Netanyahu's stock was declining.

It took three more months after the summit to actually get an agreement on Hebron, the last major Palestinian city from which Israeli forces were due to withdraw, in Hebron's case from 80 percent of the city. Though the 400 Jewish settlers were allowed to remain, the city of 150,000 was effectively returned to Palestinian control. Netanyahu's hardline coalition could barely stand the strain of conceding land in the West Bank. Worse, he was accused of trading a government appointment for support of the Hebron deal in the Knesset.[38] Benny Begin, the son of the former prime minister, resigned from the cabinet after the contentious vote on Hebron.[39] The agreed text set mid-1998 as the deadline for three "further redeployments" the Israelis were to make from the rural lands of the West Bank so the Palestinian Authority would begin taking shape as a state. Most important, the two sides agreed to complete a permanent status agreement by May 4, 1999. That was the new target for statehood.

Instead of capitalizing on the Hebron agreement, Netanyahu destroyed any sense of momentum by announcing a major new settlement on a hilltop south of Jerusalem at a place called Har Homa. If built, it would cut off the Arab neighborhoods of Jerusalem from Bethlehem. At the White House, Clinton stormed and cursed. He couldn't believe that Netanyahu would be so destructive to peace. Netanyahu responded that he had no choice but to placate his coalition after the Hebron agreement. Sharon and other hard-liners in the cabinet wanted Har Homa badly. The National Religious Party and a smaller faction called the Third Way were threatening to bring down Netanyahu's government if construction work did not begin right away. Clinton's top foreign policy aides, Sandy Berger and Madeleine Albright, regarded Bibi as a man out to deliberately destroy the peace process, and the British ambassador in Tel Aviv likened Netanyahu to "a drunk who lurches from lamppost to lamppost."[40]

Mahmoud Abbas, the Palestinian leader known as Abu Mazen, tried to explain to a group of Israeli officials the disaster that Netanyahu's policies were creating.

"You are turning a diminishing dispute, an Israeli-Palestinian dispute that was about to be resolved, into a hopeless Jewish-Muslim dispute. Do you have any idea of the effect of the television images on millions of Muslims who view Har Homa as a provocation? Have you any idea how many of them will decide to do something about it? The tension and the strained atmosphere are liable to lead a few lunatics to carry out terrorist actions, against the wishes of Arafat's government!"[41]

Here was a warning that no one in the Clinton administration, or in Israel, was heeding. The images of humiliation and confiscation were going out to the Middle East and the Muslim world; radical ideologies were gaining ground, invoking the glory days of Islam and—however freighted with distortion and mythology—they appealed for the support of the moderate Muslim majority. It was a powerful call to alienated youth yearning for a noble cause or feeling injured by the West. Shiite and Sunni insurgencies such as Hezbollah and al-Qaeda were crossing boundaries and communicating in real time with satellite phones and Internet links.

And lunatics were at large. In March 1997, a deranged Jordanian soldier opened fire on a group of Israeli schoolgirls touring the southern border region, killing seven girls from the town of Bet Shemesh.

Three days after Netanyahu sent the bulldozers to break ground at Har Homa, a suicide bomber walked into the Apropos Café in Tel Aviv and detonated an explosive, killing three women and wounding dozens of others. Netanyahu blamed Arafat directly, saying he had given the green light to terror, but Netanyahu's military intelligence chiefs contradicted him, pointing out that Arafat was working to prevent terrorism. Still, it was clear that the Palestinian leadership was under enormous pressure as the peace horizon receded. Arafat warned Israelis and Americans that he could not contain the "explosion" that was coming from young Palestinians who saw no results from the peace process. The Americans and Israelis knew that Arafat had his finger on the terror button and he could push it at any time to show his radicals that he could still fight.

Netanyahu was listening only to his coalition. On March 7, he offered only 2 percent of the West Bank as the first of the redeployments required by the Hebron accord. The Palestinians had been hoping for 30 percent; Netanyahu's offer confirmed to them that he was not serious about the Oslo process.

.        .  .  .

Clinton seemed powerless to move events constructively. In the early hours of Sunday, January 18, 1998, the Drudge Report, an Internet news site, posted an item saying that *Newsweek* magazine, just hours earlier, had killed a major story alleging that President Clinton had been carrying on an affair with a White House intern, who was described as twenty-three years old and a "frequent visitor to a small study just off the Oval Office where she claims to have indulged the president's sexual preference."

The American capital was vibrating with an air of intense anticipation. There were times in the history of the city that work seemed to stop as the denizens of the country's three branches of government and the unofficial fourth branch, the news media, awaited word of a significant presidential moment, as they had when Lyndon Johnson announced he would not run for reelection, or when Nixon resigned, or when the Iran-contra scandal broke.

By Monday, January 19, the White House was a fire brigade trying to contain the story before it exploded in the establishment news media. But there were other items on the presidential agenda. Netanyahu and Arafat were due to arrive in Washington the next day. Clinton had arranged to meet with them sequentially in an attempt to break the impasse over the turnover of additional land.

Israel's Mossad station had undoubtedly informed Netanyahu that Clinton would soon be facing a firestorm. Allegations of Clinton's sexual misconduct while governor of Arkansas already had been the grist of diplomatic and intelligence dispatches from the American capital. Russia's intelligence service had informed President Boris Yeltsin in late 1996 that Clinton's political enemies in the Republican Party were planning to capitalize on his "predilection for beautiful young women" by planting "a young provocateur in his entourage who would spark a major scandal capable of ruining the president's reputation."[42]

With Clinton weakened, Netanyahu had come prepared to offer the Palestinians nothing. The prime minister believed, though he did not say it at the time, that by turning over Gaza to Arafat along with seven West Bank cities, Israel had done enough to fulfill the self-rule aspirations of the Palestinians. If he hung tough, he calculated, he might induce Arafat to accept a Palestinian self-rule entity on about 40 percent of the West Bank. This formula, he later acknowledged, represented a return to the Begin and Shamir approach. It would lead to the creation of an autonomous Palestinian polity that would not become a state but rather a series of well-guarded cantons on the West Bank, surrounded by layers of Israeli settlements and bypass roads that only Israelis could use.

As the White House prepared for his arrival, Netanyahu flexed his political sinews by scheduling meetings with Jerry Falwell and Pat Robertson, Republican evangelical leaders whose followers believed, as "Christian Zionists," that the return of Jews to the Holy Land was an essential precursor to the Second Coming of Christ. The Israeli prime minister also brought relatives of Israelis who had died in suicide bombings. By the time he got to the White House he had demonstrated that he commanded as much political strength in Congress—perhaps more—as Clinton. The intern scandal just tilted the balance further in Netanyahu's favor.

The formal U.S.-Israeli meetings at the White House got nowhere on that Tuesday. Late in the day, it became clear that *The Washington Post*, the *Los Angeles Times*, and other mainstream media outlets were going to publish their first accounts of the allegations about Clinton's relationship with Monica Lewinsky. Clinton asked Netanyahu to come back to the White House for further discussion that night.

The first editions of the newspapers rolled onto the street at 10:30 p.m., and the story was on the wires a half hour later. Dennis Ross was at the White House, standing by because Clinton was trying for a breakthrough. The president and Netanyahu were in the residence as the storm burst. Political aides and spokesmen were drafting statements full of denials. Lawyers were working on a strategy to meet whatever demands for information came from the special prosecutor, Kenneth Starr, who had been appointed in 1994 to continue the Whitewater probe. According to Ross's account, the president and Netanyahu carried on their meeting "until after midnight" while the Monica Lewinsky story was beaming on the twenty-four-hour news channels.

Thus perched precariously behind defensive ramparts, Clinton that night offered Netanyahu something that no president since Harry Truman had offered to an Israeli prime minister: a formal alliance with the United States through a defense treaty.[43]

What Clinton had rejected when Shimon Peres raised the issue of a treaty he now offered to the prime minister who had destroyed much of the Rabin-Peres legacy. What concession did Clinton ask in return? Merely that Netanyahu increase by a few percentage points the minimal

offer on land he had made to the Palestinian Authority. Clinton's offer, if
accurately described by Ross,[44] is difficult to understand as a rational advance of American foreign policy, and more as an attempt, if it had succeeded, to divert public attention from the sex scandal that was about to
burst. It harked back to Nixon's hyping his nuclear confrontation with
Moscow at the height of the Watergate investigation. In Clinton's case, it
seemed a craven offer thrown up in panic by a president who feared that
the newspapers at dawn might irrevocably tarnish his presidency and, because of that, it reflected poorly on American diplomacy in the Middle
East.

If Netanyahu had in any way indicated that he was ready for an end-
of-conflict peace with the Arabs, then a defense treaty would make
sense—with Israel and key Arab states—in a regional security pact. But
to elevate U.S.-Israeli relations at a time when the effects of Netanyahu's
policies were radiating so negatively throughout the world could be
viewed only as a desperate act of a president whose personal behavior
had triggered an embarrassing fit of scrutiny.


Within a very few months, in May and June 1998, Clinton got his first
opportunity to strike a blow against the terror network that had publicly
declared war on the United States. The CIA had begun seriously tracking Osama bin Laden in 1996, after it established a special unit at Langley to interdict terrorist financing. The agency wasn't prescient. Bin
Laden's profile, after his declaration of war, as a rich Saudi willing to provide funding and weapons for others made him a prominent target, because the CIA believed one way to attack terrorism was to go after the
funding sources.

That same year, in May, a few months after the Khobar Towers bombing, a "walk-in" informer to an American embassy in Africa had presented
the CIA with a detailed profile of al-Qaeda, its goals and planning. The
informer, Jamal al-Fadl, was deemed to be genuine when another informer confirmed his account of bin Laden's was building a worldwide
network to strike American targets. Al-Qaeda had formed a military committee; bin Laden operatives were scouring the globe for access to nuclear material.[45]

The telltale signs of grand terrorism were there: Ramzi Yousef, the man
who had conceived the first World Trade Center bombing in February

1993, had been tried and convicted by early 1998. Part of the case against him was that he had in mind an even more diabolical plot to hijack and blow up as many as twelve jumbo jets flying from Asia to the United States. Yousef may not have been directly associated with al-Qaeda, but his uncle, Khalid Sheikh Mohammed, would become a major al-Qaeda figure and mastermind of the September 11 attacks. Al-Qaeda was both a network and a source of inspiration.

The CIA developed a plan to capture bin Laden at Tarnak Farms, a compound near Kandahar airport in Afghanistan that bin Laden had developed as a base. He often stayed there with one of his wives (at the time, he had three) and a large number of retainers. The assault was to be conducted by Afghan fighters who had worked with the CIA during the anti-Soviet war. More important, they had demonstrated their reliability during the 1997 capture in Pakistan of Mir Aimal Kansi, the young Muslim who had gone on a shooting spree outside the CIA headquarters in Langley in January 1993. He killed two CIA employees and wounded three others before fleeing the country.[46]

The Tarnak Farms assault figured to be a classic paramilitary action: well-trained Afghan agents working under the guidance of experienced CIA case officers in Islamabad. The Afghans were to infiltrate bin Laden's compound of eighty buildings from one side by crawling through a drainage ditch that passed under the ten-foot-high perimeter wall. Another team would storm the front gate. But the plan set off a debate in Washington over collateral damage. Would women and children be killed? Would bin Laden be taken alive? The answer to both questions was maybe. Satellite imagery showed that women and children lived in some of the buildings.

The CIA was under new management.

George J. Tenet had taken over the agency the year before after serving under John Deutch as deputy director. Tenet never lost his up-from-the-neighborhood character; he seemed tough, but his manner conveyed his belief that only fools take themselves completely seriously. He carried out his duties in the style of a fraternity scrum, where the first rule was to play the game hard and smart, and where friendship and loyalty counted almost as much as winning.

Tenet signed off on the bin Laden operation on May 18 and sent a Memorandum of Notification to the White House for review and approval. The Pentagon's Special Forces commanders saw nothing wrong with the concept for the operation, although there were doubts in the agency's chain of command and in the White House among the NSC staff.

On May 20, Tenet was called to the White House for a meeting in which he briefed Sandy Berger on the risks of collateral deaths and the possibility that bin Laden might be killed. A meeting of Clinton's top national security advisers was scheduled for May 29, and Tenet was on notice that the agency would have to defend the operation before a potentially skeptical audience. But the meeting was canceled. Had Clinton pulled the plug?

Six years later, the exhaustive investigation of the 9/11 Commission under Thomas H. Kean and Lee H. Hamilton was unable to report on any discussion involving the president on this unique opportunity to capture bin Laden.

"Impressions vary as to who actually decided not to proceed with the operation," the commission stated. Some in the CIA thought it was Berger's doing, others thought Tenet had reconsidered. One authoritative reconstruction said, "Tenet never formally presented the Tarnak Farms plan for President Clinton's approval." But how had the president reacted *informally* to a major covert action proposal that spent more than a week on his desk?[47]

Neither of these accounts mentioned that in May 1998, the president was fighting for his political survival against the tenacious Kenneth Starr, who was waging a battle in federal court to dismiss the executive privilege claims that Clinton had asserted to protect key White House witnesses from being called to testify before a grand jury in the Monica Lewinsky matter.

The message that went out to the CIA officers in the field was that cabinet-level officials thought the risk of civilian deaths was too high and that "the purpose and nature of the operation would be subject to unavoidable misinterpretations and misrepresentation—and probably recriminations—in the event that bin Laden, despite our best intentions and efforts, did not survive."[48]

Clinton had punted. There were no official fingerprints and Clinton has remained silent on the matter, but the conclusion is inescapable among those who know how covert operation plans circulate in the West Wing. The president is the first, not the last, to hear about them. It was not Berger's or Tenet's call. The plan did not go forward because in all likelihood Clinton, somehow at the last minute, did not want it to.[49]

Clinton had taken concrete steps to strengthen the country's defenses against terrorism. He had signed presidential directives, sat through hours of detailed discussions with Nobel Prize–winning scientists on how to defend against biological and chemical weapons. He had read prodigiously about the "coming ability to sequence and recon-figure genes" and how this had "profound implications for our national security."[50]

But with bin Laden in his sights at Tarnak Farms, a bin Laden who had not yet launched al-Qaeda's most infamous acts, but a bin Laden who had financed and trained terrorists who had carried out attacks, a bin Laden who had declared war on America and who was understood to be seeking nuclear material and chemical weapons with which to strike more devastatingly at American targets, Clinton wilted.[51]

Clinton believed that Kenneth Starr was trying to criminalize his personal life with the aim of driving him from office.[52] It seems unavoidable to conclude that Clinton also feared that any misstep in the wilds of Afghanistan by a CIA-backed team would redound against him in the domestic political battle that (it was already clear) would consume his final years as president.

As it turned out, bin Laden made good on his promise to strike. On August 7, truck bombers rolled through the teeming midmorning streets of Nairobi and Dar es Salaam, the capitals of Kenya and Tanzania, in East Africa. The al-Qaeda bombers emulated the coordinated strikes by Hezbollah in Lebanon and Kuwait more than a decade earlier, and with devastating effect. Here were Sunni terrorists borrowing tradecraft from Shiite terrorists, both acting as agents of free-form transnational movements encouraged by some states and sheltered by others.

In Nairobi, the big Toyota cargo truck, heavy on its springs, had turned off the palm-lined Haile Selassie Avenue into the U.S. embassy parking compound. One of the al-Qaeda suicide bombers, Mohammed al-Owhali, jumped from the cab with a pistol and a stun grenade, tossing the latter onto the pavement with a bang as he pointed his gun at a guard and de-manded that he raise the drop-down gate that would give the truck access to the inner courtyard. When the guard refused, Owhali couldn't decide what to do, so he turned and ran. The explosion of two thousand pounds of TNT blew him down. The concussion, fireball, and shock wave turned every window of the embassy into lethal shrapnel that shredded the bod-ies of those who had been drawn to look outside by the grenade's noise.

The truck's detonation stripped concrete like cardboard from the faces of buildings. Most tragically, it brought down an all-girls secretarial school next door at Ufundi Cooperative House. Many of the 240 dead were innocent Kenyans who perished in the rubble of this building. Twelve Americans died, but the toll did not reflect the overall trauma of nearly 5,000 people injured by flying glass—150 of them blinded—in the densely populated city center.

In Tanzania, a converted gasoline truck carried its load of explosives interlaced with gas canisters to magnify the power of the bomb and add to the deadly splay of shrapnel. About ten minutes after the Nairobi bombers struck, Ahmed Abdullah, an Egyptian, gunned his truck down the American embassy driveway. There he discovered a water tanker blocking his path, but he hit the electronic trigger anyway. The blast threw the water tanker into the air and shattered the embassy, even though the bomb's concussive power was absorbed in part by the water tanker. The second blast failed to kill any Americans, but eleven Africans perished and eighty-five were injured.

The attack on the American embassies in Africa was the beginning of Clinton's final chapter in the Middle East, played out against the drama of impeachment in the House of Representatives and trial by the Senate. While the effort to drive him from office eventually failed, it left him diminished as a leader, ever more eager to resuscitate his presidency.

Clinton was losing his battle against becoming the first sitting president to be questioned by a grand jury examining his conduct in office. The day before the attacks in Africa, Monica Lewinsky was called to testify. It was thus impossible to separate Clinton's domestic crisis from his conduct of foreign policy. And so he invested himself with almost religious devotion to the redemptive powers of any foreign policy success while avoiding risks that (he thought) could only make matters worse.

Tenet felt that Clinton was hemorrhaging political capital by the hour, and so he was especially alert for intelligence that the president would regard as "actionable," the new watchword for a generation of intelligence officers less interested in comprehensive understanding than in the pursuit of data to support covert strikes and other "action" that put the CIA at the top of the president's agenda.

In the days after the Africa bombings, the CIA developed information that bin Laden had summoned a number of senior al-Qaeda figures back to Afghanistan to plan the next attacks on America. Suddenly Clinton's caution evaporated with the calls in Congress for America to strike back at the terrorists.

"As we were searching for ways to respond, we received a godsend," Tenet later wrote, saying that "signals intelligence" revealed that bin Laden would preside over an al-Qaeda summit on August 20 in the mountain redoubt of Khost.[53] During a Cabinet Room session with Clinton a week after the attacks, Richard Clarke, the White House antiterrorism coordinator, passed a note to Tenet saying, "You thinking what I'm thinking?"

"You better believe I am," Tenet wrote back.[54]

Clinton and his senior aides thought that here was an opportunity to retaliate against a group of al-Qaeda leaders, but that they also might hit the jackpot and kill bin Laden. They broadened the target set to include two facilities in Sudan they thought were still associated with bin Laden: a tannery and a pharmaceutical plant. The tannery was dropped by Clinton at the last minute because he feared too many civilians might be killed there.

The mood in Washington at summer's end was called "Wag the Dog" fever, characterized by intense public cynicism. Many Americans wondered whether Clinton, like a fictional leader in the movie *Wag the Dog*, had invented a war to deflect the public's attention from a domestic scandal. The question was whether Clinton would overcome the fever and take a bold step, like the one he had failed to take at Tarnak Farms.

Tenet told him that there was no question that the bombings in Africa were the work of al-Qaeda. "This one is a slam dunk, Mr. President," Tenet said,[55] using the phrase that he would later make famous in the run-up to the war in Iraq.

On August 17, 1998, Clinton went on national television and admitted that he had had a sexual relationship with Lewinsky. Three days later, Clinton ordered the cruise missile attack against al-Qaeda camps in Afghanistan and against the pharmaceutical plant in Khartoum, where the CIA believed al-Qaeda might be running a chemical weapons factory based on a soil sample scooped up by an agent that tested positive for a chemical component of VX nerve gas.

Much of the "actionable" intelligence that Clinton had relied on in these strikes proved to be faulty. The CIA was not able to establish that a high-level al-Qaeda meeting had in fact taken place at Khost. And the Al-Shifa Pharmaceutical factory proved to have no connection to either al-Qaeda or VX. It had been, however, a vital facility for producing desperately needed drugs for Sudan's civilian population and its destruction resulted in further deprivation for the Sudanese.[56]

Clinton was embarrassed by the "Wag the Dog" outcry. It seemed that he had gone for the hair trigger, expending hundreds of millions of dollars to kill a few unaffiliated jihadists while failing to diminish in any material way al-Qaeda's operational structure. He had further impoverished Sudan and lionized bin Laden, whose stature grew as the Islamic warrior who had pulled America's tail. To a generation of Muslim youth exposed to the imagery of Israel's seizure of Arab lands, of its repression of Palestinians, and of America's moral decline—represented by the president chasing a young woman in the White House—bin Laden was becoming a mythic figure who spoke eloquently about the quest for the Islamic ideal based on piety and justice.

In the parlors of Cairo, Amman, and Beirut, Osama bin Laden may have been regarded as another beard from the fringe, but his message pulsed with an undercurrent of Islamic rectitude and grievance against the injustice visited from the West. As the White House was pelted by its critics, Clinton literally pounded the table the day after Labor Day in meetings with Sandy Berger and Madeleine Albright, who had replaced Warren Christopher as secretary of state. He wanted progress in the Middle East peace process and he wanted it in a hurry. He demanded that they bring Arafat and Netanyahu to Washington to complete the turnover of additional land to the Palestinian Authority and pave the way for a final peace and Palestinian statehood.

Albright complained that dealing with Netanyahu had become like "negotiating in hell."[57]

Ross observed that Netanyahu had transformed America's role. "He wanted to negotiate with us and then have us sell it to—or more likely impose it on—the Palestinians, letting us do the dirty work and keeping a safe distance for himself."[58] Yet while Ross recognized the trap into which Netanyahu had maneuvered the American negotiating team, instead of rebelling, he accepted the role and spent much of the next two years trying to persuade Arafat, with each incrementally larger offer, that it was the last and best offer the Palestinians were likely to receive. It was never true.

The Palestinians, too, saw that Ross had become Bibi's negotiator. They understood he had no choice—other than resignation. What impelled Ross was a personal conviction that forward motion, however constricted or perverted, was better than a declaration of failure, which invited the explosion of frustration and violence. Yet the strategy bound him to Netanyahu.

The Palestinians knew that, ultimately, America would be the arbiter of peace. Clinton's empathy extended to both sides. He *got* the Jewish and Palestinian narratives. This was his greatest strength, but also his greatest weakness, since he found it extremely difficult to shift from empathy to political realism. What seemed to be missing always was the follow-through on an agreed formula, or the application of necessary pressure to close the deal.

Clinton was driven more by domestic requirements and less by the real exigencies of Middle East peace. The only pressure he applied was an unfocused—and untimely—push to get any kind of progress when he needed it for domestic purposes. Ross was under "daily assault" from Berger and Albright as Netanyahu and Arafat watched the Lewinsky scandal unfold in Washington.

"The president doesn't have the authority or clout with them now that he had previously—and they won't make concessions just because he needs them to do a deal," Ross told the White House.

After weeks of intense negotiations, the Israelis and Palestinians agreed to come to the United States for another summit, this one with Clinton at the Wye River Plantation. Sharon was making his debut as Netanyahu's foreign minister. The two delegations squared off over how much land Netanyahu would cede to the Palestinian Authority. But Netanyahu was holding back by demanding that Arafat present a security plan pledging to arrest known Hamas and Islamic Jihad terrorists on a specific schedule. That would show Israelis he was cracking down on extremists and suicide bombers.

The Wye summit of October 1998 marked the final breakdown in trust between Clinton and Netanyahu, for it had become clear that Netanyahu's strategy was to orchestrate a settlement that would leave the Palestinian Authority with less than half of the West Bank, a collection of Palestinian "islands" or cantons surrounded by the Israeli army that could not function as a viable state. Netanyahu may have figured that Clinton needed tangible signs of progress on the peace front so badly that he might be induced to accept Netanyahu's terms for a truncated Palestinian entity and, separately, that Clinton might agree to one spectacular demand.

On the first day of the summit, Netanyahu pressed for the release of Jonathan Pollard, the former U.S. navy analyst who had been convicted of spying for Israel. Pollard, using a top-secret clearance, had given thousands of classified documents to his Israeli intelligence handlers. And according to Tenet, he had "offered to spy for other countries as well."[59]

The summit was contentious enough and so the Pollard gambit, which Clinton deflected by saying he would consider it, hung over the weeklong deliberations like a dark cloud.

Arafat insisted that Israel transfer more land as a matter of good faith. He also wanted Netanyahu to release Palestinian prisoners. Netanyahu wanted Arafat to arrest thirty proven or suspected terrorists, some of whom were serving as Palestinian police officers. Netanyahu had added a demand that the Palestinian National Council, the longtime parliament in exile for the PLO, formally abrogate that portion of its charter that called for the destruction of Israel.

During one negotiating session, Netanyahu asked to see Clinton and Arafat alone and told them that he was willing to release five hundred prisoners if Arafat would "take care of" some of the most wanted Palestinian terror suspects serving as police. They included the Gaza police chief, Ghazi Jabali.

"What am I supposed to do with Jabali, execute him?" Arafat asked in astonishment.

"I won't ask, you won't tell," Netanyahu responded.

At that point, Clinton exploded and stormed out. Here was the prime minister of Israel presuming to involve the president of the United States in an assassination conspiracy.

"This is outrageous, this is despicable," Clinton shouted. "This is just chickenshit, I'm not going to put up with this kind of bullshit!"

Netanyahu immediately went into victim mode. "Why is Israel treated this way? Why am I treated this way? What have I done to deserve this?"[60]

Clinton was calling Netanyahu an SOB and Sandy Berger was trying to keep the president's anger stoked so he would stay focused on pushing Netanyahu to close the deal.

Soon, he had. They got a deal. The Wye River agreement included Palestinian commitments to fight terrorism. Arafat and his security chief, Mohammed Dahlan, put a detailed work plan on paper that had Tenet's blessing.[61] The Palestinian Authority would get control over 13 percent of the remaining land, still a pittance, but it was one step with more to come.

The agreement took final shape at dawn on October 23. Tenet had bet Dahlan that Netanyahu would sign. As the sun rose over the Chesapeake's tidal marshes, Tenet, bleary for lack of sleep, told Dahlan that it was over.

"You lost. He's going to sign!" Tenet exclaimed.

"Hold on. It's not a done deal yet," Dahlan replied.

As a final pressure tactic, Netanyahu leaked word to the Israeli press that he would be coming home with Jonathan Pollard. He was going to squeeze it out of Clinton. The Israelis, aware that Tenet was threatening to resign if Pollard was freed, sent Yitzhak Mordecai, the defense minister, to say to him, "You know, we really must have Pollard."

Tenet refused. He believed that Pollard's release would signal that major breaches in discipline—even treason—were somehow pardonable. How could they be if he was to continue to ask CIA officers to risk their lives to protect national secrets?

But the drumbeat continued. John Podesta, Clinton's chief of staff, called Tenet. "The vice president asked me to phone you," he said, but it was obvious that Clinton, having already pressed Tenet, was invoking Al Gore's name to take another run at him. Also, since Gore might be the next president and determine whether Tenet stayed as CIA director, it was a clever tactic.

"Do you know how important this agreement is?" Podesta asked. The House of Representatives had authorized an impeachment proceeding against the president. They were days away from midterm elections that could further weaken Clinton's support in Congress.

"Yes, I know it's very important," Tenet replied.

"Well, the Israelis won't sign unless they get Pollard," Podesta said.

"John, this agreement is in their interest. They will sign it. Don't give them Pollard," Tenet pleaded. "If you give them Pollard, I'm done . . . Just hold fast."[62]

Clinton did hold fast, but the pressure he brought to bear on Tenet suggests that Clinton was perfectly willing to give up Pollard to an Israeli prime minister who had demonstrated that he would not fulfill the promises of the Oslo Accords and would instead pursue robust Israeli settlement building on confiscated land, the only land left for a Palestinian state.

Netanyahu went home without Pollard. He faced an immediate revolt from extreme right-wing parties. For weeks he refused to bring the Wye River agreement before the Knesset for approval. Clinton could not wait. The impeachment storm in Washington was upon him.

On December 11, the House Judiciary Committee approved three articles of impeachment, alleging perjury and obstruction of justice.

Clinton fled the capital for a stage in the Middle East, where he appeared before the assembled Palestinian leadership in Gaza and told them, "For the first time in the history of the Palestinian movement, the Palestinian people and their elected representatives now have a chance to determine their own destiny on their own land."

Clinton's presidential helicopter had landed at Gaza's new international airport. The scene was decked out in the Palestinians' national tricolor, and virtually all of Gaza had turned out to greet the first American leader to step down on Palestinian soil and in so doing recognize that their parallel national struggle had been overwhelmed by the rise of the Jewish state.

"I am proud to be the first American president here, standing side by side with the Palestinian people as you forge your future," Clinton said.[63] The president looked on, and so did Netanyahu and Sharon, as the Palestinian parliament, whose members had assembled, made a show of hands to endorse Arafat's pledge to excise the offensive text from the Palestinian charter.

"You did a good thing today in raising your hands," Clinton told them. "You know why? It has nothing to do with the government in Israel. You will touch the people of Israel."[64]

Clinton's visit to Gaza, a consecration of the embryonic state of Palestine, was the high-water mark of nascent Palestinian independence under the Oslo Accords. Netanyahu thought he would be the winner, having the president of the United States preside over the renunciation of the PLO Charter. Instead, the image was of a grand validation for Palestinian statehood. Netanyahu's coalition cringed.

With the help of the CIA, Arafat and the Palestinian security organizations began a serious and sustained crackdown on Hamas and other terrorist organizations. Arafat placed the disabled Sheikh Yassin, released two years earlier, under house arrest. Netanyahu treated every new terrorist incident as a sign that Arafat was cheating or not doing enough, but the Israeli military establishment did not support most of the prime minister's assertions.

By the end of December 1998, Netanyahu's government could no longer sustain the loss of confidence emanating from all parts of the Israeli political spectrum. Bibi, the youthful and Americanized prime minister, proved remarkably incompetent as a political leader. Elections were called for May, which meant a six-month suspension of the peace process while a new government was formed, a delay that begged the question, How could the Palestinians be expected to fulfill their commitments when Netanyahu had frozen the Oslo, Hebron, and Wye River agreements?

America's attention soon shifted elsewhere, to Iraq, where Clinton decided to launch air strikes against military and industrial targets as punishment for Saddam's decision to cease cooperation with United Nations inspectors. Saddam had been escalating his interference with the UN monitoring program over eighteen months. In November 1998, Clinton had pulled back from one strike at the last minute when the Iraqi leader allowed inspectors to resume their work.

Clinton, in facing his domestic trials, thus reached for questionable military options in Iraq. He struck the pose of a president showing resolve, yet there was strong argument within the intelligence community that any attack, however satisfying politically, would lead to the permanent withdrawal of the United Nations monitoring program in Iraq. The bombing would mean the end not just of intrusive inspections that had kept Saddam in check since 1991, but also the dismantling of cameras, recording devices, heat sensors, and other instruments that helped the United Nations keep close tabs on Iraq's arsenal, including factories and laboratories that could be converted to chemical or biological weapons production. American intelligence would be blinded.

In an address to the nation on December 17, Clinton said, "If Saddam defies the world and we fail to respond, we will face a far greater threat in the future. Saddam will strike again at his neighbors. He will make war on his own people. And mark my words, he will develop weapons of mass destruction. He will deploy them and he will use them."

Clinton said his national security team and the military chiefs had unanimously backed the decision to strike and, in a reference to the impeachment proceedings, he added that if Saddam thought "that the serious debate currently before the House of Representatives would distract Americans or weaken our resolve to face him down," he was mistaken.

The cruise missile attacks commenced. UN inspectors had gotten just enough notice to flee across the desert. With seventy hours of bombing (December 16–19, 1998) against an array of targets, Clinton sought to demonstrate that he was still commander in chief. In truth, he was distracted and somewhat frantic. In Gaza, Ross had observed the president

Saddam Hussein: unfinished business from Bush's war

writing compulsively on a legal pad, "Focus on your job, focus on your job . . ."[65] But the Desert Fox campaign, as it was dubbed by the Pentagon, seemed another hermetically contained strike from over the horizon that entailed minimal risk and accomplished little in the way of reducing the potency of Saddam's military.

Clinton was still fighting Bush's war. His opponents in Congress and his political enemies harped on the failure of American will to topple Saddam. A bipartisan groundswell appeared in support of "regime change" in Iraq, creating a consensus that was enshrined in the Iraqi Liberation Act. Passed by Congress and signed by Clinton that fall, it required the president by law to work for the removal of the Iraqi leader and to support the establishment of democratic government in Iraq.

"So long as Saddam remains in power," Clinton told the country on December 19 at the end of the bombing campaign, "he will remain a threat to his people, his region and the world." The best way to eliminate the long-term threat, he said, "is for Iraq to have a different government. We will intensify our engagement with the Iraqi opposition groups, prudently and effectively," and "we will stand ready to help a new leadership in Baghdad."

But Clinton was dead in the water in the Middle East. He had no option for regime change. He had no CIA network. His agents had all been executed.


All of the hopes of the peace camp rested on Ehud Barak's shoulders. He was a man of compact dimensions and a chipmunk grin that was his only concession to mirth. A protégé of Yitzhak Rabin's, he was one of Israel's brightest and most daring commanders, who had risen to become chief of staff of the Israeli Defense Forces; he had protected Sharon's flank in Sinai during the 1973 crossing of the Suez Canal, and he had led commandos into Beirut to kill PLO leaders connected to the Munich Massacre. Yet as prime minister, all that military discipline and strategic vision served him poorly, or at least it translated poorly to politics. Barak quickly developed the reputation as a prime minister who was so arrogant, so secretive, and so dismissive of anyone else's views that his coalition soon turned against him.

Stan Moskowitz, the CIA station chief, said of Barak that "he had absolute faith that he was the smartest person around," and he treated both friends and adversaries as if they were extraneous appendages in the heroic drama at whose center he stood. He called meetings for 9:00 a.m. and would show up at noon; he rang up the president of the United States, sometimes more than once a day. Clinton's aides complained that this manic Israeli prime minister was treating the leader of the free world like his clerk.

Barak's election brought such relief from the wasteland of the Netanyahu years that many Israelis, as well as Western leaders, projected onto the new prime minister the image they wanted to see. They forgot that he had opposed the Oslo Accords when he was Yitzhak Rabin's chief of staff, and that he had rejected Rabin's notion that peace with Syria meant withdrawing to the 1967 borders. They forgot that he believed in separation from the Palestinians more than peace or engagement. And Barak was no different from Labor prime ministers since 1967: he was incapable of controlling the settlement juggernaut as thousands of Israelis continued to seize Palestinian land, orchards, and hilltops throughout the West Bank, in an openly avowed strategy to deny the viability of any Palestinian state that emerged.

At the Dan Hotel in Tel Aviv, the night of his election, Barak warmly invoked his mentor, Yitzhak Rabin, when he laid out a vision for peace. But when he addressed the crowd in Rabin Square at 2:00 a.m., he shocked some supporters by speaking of "red lines" protecting "a united Jerusalem under our sovereignty as the capital of Israel for eternity, period." Israel "under no conditions" would "return to the 1967 borders," and "most of the settlers in Judea and Samaria will be in settlement blocs under our sovereignty."

There was a duality in Barak's nature from the beginning. He had none of Rabin's desire for an intimate partnership with Arafat and other Palestinian leaders. Yet he set out to make peace in all directions almost at once. His ideas lacked a basic political soundness, yet his aides and friends in Washington were loath to challenge him. It was quickly apparent that while Barak talked the language of peace, of Palestinian statehood and compromise with Syria, when it came down to it he was too constrained by his coalition to make any "preemptive concessions," as he called them.

To secure a majority in the Knesset, he had loaded his government as a right-leaning vessel that was taking on water from the outset. He told his colleagues what they wanted to hear; he indulged the settlers and generally hewed to a hard line. When the moment was ripe, he told the Americans, he would dazzle the Middle East with new peace agreements and present them to his cabinet as a fait accompli. If the cabinet objected, he would call a plebiscite and defeat his rivals by running as a proven peacemaker.

Barak laid down precise time lines for peace; the problem was he had the wrong skill set to achieve it. For the Palestinians, who had watched Netanyahu undermine the Oslo timetable and its commitments for transferring land, Barak was not a breath of fresh air. He shocked Arafat by insisting that he needed to stretch out the Oslo process. His coalition needed time.

With Clinton, Ross, and Indyk doing much of his staff work, Barak finally reached an interim agreement with the Palestinians to transfer another small increment of land to the Palestinian Authority. But the reality was that the five-year clock of Oslo had run out. There was no final status negotiation under way, the occupation had grown more oppressive, terrorism had escalated, and trust had broken down.

Instead of throwing his energy into a final settlement with the Palestinians, Barak veered off toward Syria. He felt that Hafez al-Assad was the key to removing the last existential threat Israel faced on its borders. If Assad could be induced to make peace, then Israeli troops could finally come home from Lebanon—Barak had promised voters to bring them home—and all that would be left would be a final settlement with Arafat, who would pretty much have to accept what Barak dictated. Then there would be peace, real peace.

In December 1999, Assad signaled that he was ready to sign a peace treaty quickly. He would give full peace in return for a full withdrawal. That had been the deal discussed with Rabin and, secretly, with Netanyahu, though Netanyahu tried to deny it.

Farouk al-Sharaa, the Syrian foreign minister, flew to Washington to test Barak's sincerity. Clinton was prepared to announce that the two sides were going to resume peace negotiations near Washington in early January. But when Barak's plane landed, the Israeli prime minister was seized with panic. The El Al jet was standing there on the tarmac at Andrews Air Force Base. Martin Indyk, who had been named assistant secretary of state, was leading the official greeting party at the bottom of the stairs.

Barak would not come out. He summoned Indyk onto the plane.

"I can't do it," he said.

"What? What do you mean?" Indyk asked incredulously. "You were ready to do it, you were ready to have us convene the Syrians!"[66]

Barak was plagued with second thoughts, his mind ricocheting off the latest polling data showing that while Israelis in large numbers supported peace with Syria, only 13 percent believed in total withdrawal from the Golan Heights. Barak suddenly feared that he could not sell it. Prominent Israelis, like the novelist Amos Oz, had mocked Syrian sincerity, saying that in exchange for the Golan, Israel might get a receipt from Damascus "by fax." In other words, there was no sign that the Syrians were ready for a real relationship. They just wanted Israel to surrender territory taken in the wars that Syria had provoked. What was to be said for all that Jewish blood?

All Indyk could do, when Barak eventually disembarked, was run to Dennis Ross and Madeleine Albright in a panic, parroting the famous call to Earth from stricken astronauts: "Houston, we have a problem."

It came down to whether Barak would honor Rabin's pledge. And would he say that to the Syrian leaders.

"While my government has made no commitment on territory, we don't erase history," Barak told al-Sharaa at the White House.[67] But that is exactly what Barak was doing, erasing history because he had come to the conclusion that he could not face down the twenty thousand settlers of the Golan and all of their supporters.

When Clinton assembled the Israeli and Syrian negotiating teams at Shepherdstown, West Virginia, on January 3, 2000, it took only a few hours for the Syrian foreign minister to realize, as Ross put it, "that he had been had." Clinton had drafted a treaty with bracketed language showing the final areas of disagreement on borders, security, and the exchange of diplomatic embassies, but at dinner al-Sharaa confronted Barak on the central question: Would he reaffirm Rabin's pledge to withdraw to the 1967 lines?

Barak just smiled.

Clinton stared at him, baffled by his tactics. For al-Sharaa, the meeting was a disaster. He went home and told Assad, whose health was failing, that Syria was the victim of an Israeli ruse, despite Clinton's protestations to the contrary. Barak's zigzagging inflamed every conspiratorial instinct with which Assad had regarded the Jewish state.

Crown Prince Abdullah of Saudi Arabia, with Clinton's blessing, sent Prince Bandar to Geneva to meet Assad and find out if a deal might be salvaged. Bandar reported back at the end of January that Assad was angry and no longer sure that Barak was a peace partner. Yet Assad, for his own reasons, was willing to try again. He told Bandar that the Americans should organize one final round to finish everything. Assad's priority was to demarcate the border, to define the 1967 cease-fire line precisely, because there were still areas of dispute, some of them going all the way back to 1949. It could be done in secret to protect Barak—and Assad—from political blowback. But it must be done, Assad said.

Barak waffled. He shifted again. During his election campaign against Netanyahu, he had pledged to bring Israel's troops home from Lebanon after eighteen years. Now he asked for Assad's cooperation in paving the way for a withdrawal. Would Syria restrain Hezbollah while Israeli soldiers packed up and came home? Could he count on Syria to keep Israel's northern border peaceful in return for a full withdrawal? But Assad said the price of resuming negotiations on Lebanon was demarcation of the border with Syria. Give back the Golan Heights first, in other words.

Barak was isolated. The Knesset enacted a law requiring that any vote to give up land (such as the Golan Heights) had to pass by a supermajority. It was a shot across Barak's bow. The Palestinians were infuriated that he was spending all his time on Syria—"the other woman," they called it—while he delayed appointing a negotiator for final-status talks with the Palestinians.

Barak turned to the Americans. He insisted that Clinton go to Geneva to try again to sell Assad on a peace treaty, but Barak then hobbled the president by insisting on a border scheme that was such an obvious gerrymandering of the lines that it would push the Syrians far back from the water sources that had once been part of the boundary system.

When Clinton arrived in Geneva that March, Assad was curt and dismissive despite the president's attempt at charm.

"They don't want peace," Assad said, interrupting Clinton. Assad looked at the maps. He saw the Israeli lines; he saw that Barak wanted years to withdraw Israeli settlers from the Golan. Assad thought it should take months. It wasn't going to work. Clinton was crestfallen at the Syrian leader's unwillingness even to negotiate.

The Geneva summit was another disappointment for Clinton. In the long reach of history, Assad had arrived at the threshold of decision at a moment of exceptional weakness by an Israeli prime minister, whose vacillation under the glare of rivals prevented him from acting. Rabin's pledge to return the Golan was now a casualty—Barak's casualty.[68]

Assad died three months later, on June 10, 2000. Perhaps the Syrian leader saw that it was too late, that there was not enough time and, therefore, he wanted to avoid inflicting so much uncertainty on his son and heir, Bashar al-Assad, for whom the status quo was secure.

In late May, Barak decided to cut the knot and withdraw Israeli forces from Lebanon unilaterally and rapidly, abandoning the security belt the army had defended for two decades. The abrupt pullout triggered panic in the surrogate Lebanese militia that Israel had built and relied upon, the South Lebanon Army. Faced with the prospect of retribution from Hezbollah and other extremists, more than six thousand Lebanese militia members and their families abandoned homes, cars, and possessions and raced to the Israeli border to seek asylum.

Israel's flight from Lebanon engendered even more troubling consequences for peace. Barak did not foresee that, as the tanks rumbled home, Hezbollah would declare victory. Years of guerrilla attacks and armed struggle against Israeli occupation forces had driven the "occupier" off Arab land. Palestinians, Arafat especially, looked weak in comparison. What had *he* done to push the Israelis off the occupied West

Bank and Gaza? On the Lebanese front, Israel was forced to withdraw to the 1967 borders. Yet, on the Palestinian front, it still refused to do so.

Abu Ala, the PLO negotiator and Arafat aide who had framed the Oslo Accords, rushed to his old partner, Uri Savir, and warned him of the implications. "What will the Palestinians say?" he asked. They had been asked to fight terrorism alongside Israel and they had killed and jailed Hamas and Islamic Jihad extremists, but all they had received in return was a very modest transfer of land while Barak's government continued building settlements in the occupied territories at the same furious pace as had Netanyahu and Sharon.

Hezbollah rained rockets and mortars on Israeli towns; its militants ambushed, killed, and kidnapped Israeli soldiers. And what was Israel's response? Withdrawal! It looked like surrender.

"The message for every Palestinian will be clear: kill Israelis and you'll get the land," Abu Ala said.[69]

Sooner or later there was going to be an explosion, he warned. Palestinians could see that the Oslo process had become a travesty of peacemaking. Edward Said, the Palestinian firebrand at Columbia University in New York, stated what was becoming shockingly obvious.

"It is worth noting that there are 13,000 settlement units now under construction [in the West Bank], and that no less than 42 hilltop settlements have been established in the West Bank since last year (1998–99).

"Along with the already existing 144 settlements and, including the population of annexed Jerusalem, there are about 350,000 Israeli Jewish settlers on Palestinian land," he wrote.[70]

The Oslo period had brought about a doubling of the number of Jewish settlers and a steep decline in Palestinian living standards as the seven small islands of Palestinian autonomy were further constricted by checkpoints and economic controls.

"For the first time in the twentieth century, an anti-colonial liberation movement [the PLO] has not only discarded its own considerable achievements but has made an agreement to cooperate with a military occupation before that occupation has ended," wrote Said. It was criticism pointed directly at Arafat and the Palestinian leadership.[71]

By mid-2000, Barak's tenure was proving as disastrous as Netanyahu's, and after a tumultuous first year, Clinton and Barak came up with the idea of a summit meeting at Camp David as a way to save Barak's government from falling apart, perhaps rescue Clinton's presidency from a legacy of scandal, and achieve statehood for the Palestinians.

The Camp David summit was convened with enormous fanfare and high expectations internationally; it was the first such gathering focused on forging a comprehensive settlement since Jimmy Carter had welcomed Sadat and Begin in September 1978.

Clinton's summit came at a time of maximum political instability. A weakened American president, increasingly eclipsed by the campaign that would elect his successor, reached out to Israeli and Palestinian leaders to embrace each other, but he offered them no formula to succeed. Barak and Arafat were under enormous pressure. They had lost trust in each other; in the weeks before they met, Barak reneged on his promise to add several Arab villages around Jerusalem to the autonomous Palestinian Authority.

Sharon, seeking to emerge as the main opposition voice from the right, taunted Barak as a weakling: "When you've given them Abu Dis [one of the villages], they'll be able to shoot from their rooftops at Jerusalem. Is that what you call separation from the Palestinians?"[72]

Sharon was busy reestablishing his reputation as a tough leader who could stop suicide terrorism and prevent a "terrorist" state next door to Israel.

Arafat didn't want to come. He feared that at Camp David, he would be facing the combined pressure of Clinton and Barak to make peace on Israeli terms. They would try to force him to accept a deal that would not give him what Palestinians needed on borders, on the right of return for refugees, or on Jerusalem as an Arab capital. Barak had not lived up to the Oslo pledges. He could not even keep a promise about a few villages.

Yet Clinton promised the Palestinian leader that he would not blame him if the Camp David summit failed. Thus Arafat arrived in the United States in a deep sulk and his mood never really improved. He told Clinton at the outset that Palestinians demanded that the right of return, as a *principle*, be acknowledged. Then they could negotiate the practical details.

"It is impossible for all the refugees to come back, since some of them are settled in the countries they live in," Arafat said.[73]

Clinton discouraged this line of thinking. He wanted to know whether Arafat could compromise on Jerusalem.

"It's simple," Arafat said. "East Jerusalem for us, West Jerusalem for Israelis. It will be the capital of the two states, and there will be a joint commission for water, roads, electricity . . ."

But Clinton was closer to Barak's position. "Israel will never give up sovereignty over East Jerusalem," he told Arafat.

Arafat shot back, "Nothing can be substituted for Palestinian sovereignty over East Jerusalem."

Clinton had underestimated how profoundly Jerusalem called out to both camps. He and Barak were cracking open a cave so ancient that the rush of escaping air swept them chaotically toward a negotiation for which they were little prepared. The fate of Jerusalem seized the attention of the world and awakened all the old enmities. The emotive president and the supremely self-confident prime minister took the first steps of discovery, as if by torchlight, into the realm of mythology about Jerusalem, and Clinton's enthusiasm for the task dulled the sense of danger. He began with no realistic notion of how he might reconcile the irreconcilable assertions of sovereign attachment.

By the end of the two weeks at Camp David, Clinton was exasperated. Yet because Barak had moved the most, offering the Palestinians sovereignty over the Muslim and Christian quarters of the Old City in East Jerusalem—but not over the Noble Sanctuary where the mosques stood— and because Barak had made other concessions on territory, Clinton tilted again toward Barak.

Arafat was defiant. "I'd rather die than agree to Israeli sovereignty over the Haram al-Sharif [Noble Sanctuary] . . . I won't go down in Arab history as a traitor," he told Clinton, triggering a presidential eruption in the final night of wrangling.

"Barak has made so many concessions. And you've made none!"

Clinton continued, "You could have gotten sovereignty over the Christian and Muslim districts of the Old City and full jurisdiction over the Haram al-Sharif . . . You missed an opportunity in 1948 and let another one go by in 1978, at [the Carter summit in] Camp David . . . And now here you go again! You won't have a state, and relations between America and the Palestinians will be over. Congress will vote to stop the aid you've been allocated, and you'll be treated as a terrorist organization. No one in the Middle East will look you in the eye."

When they came down from Camp David on July 25, Clinton told reporters that Barak had made brave decisions, especially on Jerusalem, and "moved forward more from his initial position than Chairman Arafat."[74] Recriminations flew from the Palestinian side over this assignment of blame because it represented a betrayal of Clinton's pledge.

What seemed clear was that the Israelis and the Americans had expected Arafat to accept the best that they were able to muster at that moment. They expected Arafat to regard the hourglass with the same anxiety that drove their frantic efforts. But to the Arabs, what Clinton was offering the Palestinians was less than what Israel had offered Egypt, Syria, Jordan, and Lebanon—a full return of the occupied land in exchange for peace. To the Palestinians, the "land" in "land for peace" included East Jerusalem.

Saeb Erekat, the American-Palestinian who had become the lead negotiator for Arafat, made the Palestinian case in the face of Clinton's explosion at Arafat.

"Mr. President. It doesn't cost you anything to blame and threaten us," he said. "The Palestinian people . . . have accepted and recognized the State of Israel." Israel, he pointed out, comprised 78 percent of historic Palestine. But no Palestinian leader until Arafat, he said, had agreed to base a Palestinian state on the 22 percent that was left in the West Bank and Gaza.

"Now you are saying that Arafat did not come a long way! . . . He agreed to the 22 percent because the preceding American administration, and the one before that, and Europe along with them, said they would support those who worked for peace. Well, that's exactly what I expect of you, Mr. President."

In truth, Barak and his negotiators had come face-to-face with the Israeli myth of Jerusalem. It had never been a united city. The western portion was Jewish and the eastern portion Arab. The Old City had Christian and Armenian quarters as well as Jewish and Muslim quarters. Barak and his principal aides knew that once his concessions were exposed, there would be a massive political reaction from the right wing to refortify the myth of an undivided Jerusalem. But that was not the core of the problem. The searing center of it all was the Temple Mount at the heart of the Old City.

Many Jews believe that it is forbidden to ascend the Temple Mount until the Messiah comes; thus they pray behind a foundation wall on a plaza where they scribble their prayers and address them to God by slipping them into the cracks of the stones. Those foundation stones, many archaeologists believe, frame the ruins of the ancient Jewish temples that date to King Solomon's time (971–931 B.C.). The mosques that stand on the thirty-five-acre plaza were constructed in A.D. 690 (Dome of the Rock) and A.D. 710 (al-Aqsa) and are under the management of a Muslim council called the *waqf*.

Astoundingly, though, on September 28, 2000, Ariel Sharon climbed up to the plaza of the Temple Mount and stood there, in front of whirring and clicking cameras, radiating Jewish defiance and demonstrating that "Arik" was back, ready to save the country from the new scourge of terrorism.

Surrounded by one thousand armed policemen, some of them in riot gear carrying batons and shields, Sharon strode across the Noble Sanctuary, marking his territory in the company of an Israeli archaeologist. He stopped here and there, smiling impishly and referring to himself as a man of peace in the shadow of the two mosques.

Hundreds of Palestinians rushed in to defend their holy places, some hysterical with anger that Sharon, the villain of the Sabra and Shatila massacres in Lebanon, the man who stood for the most brutal anti-Arab policies of the last half century, had come to defame Muslim history with a show of force.

No city in the world conjures as much love, hope, and hatred as Jerusalem, the heavenly polity where religion and politics fuse under the intense heat of history and memory. The city imposes memory; one poet said it was the place "where all remember they have forgotten something," and Sharon was reaching back to Jewish glory to put down another stake affirming Jewish sovereignty on the Temple Mount that had been in Arab hands since the Islamic warrior Saladin dashed Christian hopes in the Third Crusade.

The poet Yehuda Amichai has observed that "The air over Jerusalem is saturated with prayers and dreams / like the air over industrial cities. / It's hard to breathe." Religious nationalism was born in Jerusalem as the landscape most intimately connected with the God of Abraham and Isaac, with Christ and the Crucifixion, and the ascent of the Prophet Muhammad, the messenger of Allah.

The ancient metropolis stands as the fulcrum on which three monotheistic faiths tilt for the advantage of God's favor and where the struggle for territory is in itself a form of worship. No one understood that as well as Ariel Sharon, the soldier of Hebrew nationalism, when he made his well-planned advance onto the Temple Mount that September to show that Jews, who had reclaimed the hallowed ground during the Six-Day

War, did not intend *ever* to give it up; it was *their* eternal capital. This was Sharon's response to Camp David, an attempt to galvanize the Israeli political establishment to close the door of Jerusalem that Barak, Arafat, and Clinton had pried open.

After a long political exile following the Lebanon War, Sharon was back, had taken the Likud Party away from Netanyahu, and was battling like a tank commander to destroy the framework that Barak had erected, which would lead to imminent Palestinian statehood on nearly all of the land of the West Bank and Gaza. The talk of such far-reaching compromise had given Sharon his opening, and he pounced on every concession Barak had proposed as an endangerment of the Jewish state. Jerusalem was the crux of the matter.

Modern Israel's capture of the Old City during the Six-Day War was an electrifying moment. It marked the return of the Jews to the temporal foundations of their faith, to the altar of the ancient nation, and to the still hidden vault where the Ark of the Covenant once encased the tablets that God delivered to Moses in Sinai. In 1967, Israeli soldiers gasped and wept standing before the Wailing Wall, that stretch of mammoth foundation stones that mark the cradle of Hebrew civilization. Its return to Jewish hands seemed a religious fulfillment, not just to Jews, but to many fundamentalist Christians, too, who saw it as a precursor to the Second Coming.

Moshe Dayan, the architect and hero of the 1967 victory, walked into the Old City with Yitzhak Rabin, his chief of staff, and up to the Temple Mount to see for himself. Dayan ordered Israeli soldiers to take down the Star of David they had hoisted over the mosques as a sign of respect for the edifices of common heritage Israel now possessed and over which no nation could claim full spiritual sovereignty. During the decades of Israeli occupation, successive Israeli governments had allowed Muslims to supervise the mosques, from which beacons of Arab prayer rose against the occupation.

But Sharon was not Dayan.

No Israeli had ever done what Sharon did that day, staging a muscular reoccupation of the Temple Mount to protest what had transpired at Camp David—talk of sharing Jerusalem with the Palestinians. That was what Arafat had demanded and what Barak had conceded in obeisance to the fact that Jerusalem had for more than twelve hundred years been an Arab capital, too.

Police erected barricades to hold back the Palestinians as Sharon, wearing sunglasses and a striped tie, moved in unison within a tight cordon of security men and jostling photographers. His warrior brow and unmistakable profile were barely visible in the sea of moving legs and torsos, bulging weapons, battery packs, and ammo clips.

From behind the barriers, the young Palestinians began to shout *"Allahu akhbar!"*—God is great!—and "Murderer, get out!"

Cries of protest filled the air that pulsated with the noise of a police helicopter hovering over the scene. "With our souls, with our blood, we will defend you al-Aqsa!" they chanted.

Soon stones and other objects began to fly. Police opened fire with rubber bullets. The sounds of gunfire, screams, and more chants rose from the plaza and echoed in the alleyways.

Sharon made his retreat to a news conference in which he denied that he was committing historic mischief. "It was no provocation whatsoever," he said of his armed promenade. "It is our right. Arabs have the right to visit everywhere in the Land of Israel, and Jews have the right to visit every place in the Land of Israel."[75] But there was no escaping the symbolism. Sharon had been out to make a provocative territorial point. The consequences were disastrous.[76]

The lid came off in the Palestinian territories the next day. Some Israelis blamed Arafat for planning the violent eruption, but Mossad and military intelligence chiefs eventually came to the conclusion that it had been spontaneous. The rioting went on for days, then weeks and months, as Palestinians rampaged through the towns and cities of the West Bank, hurling abuse and stones at Israeli soldiers who came in force to block their advances and opened fire in the familiar cadence that sent a new death toll soaring from a new intifada.

On the second day, a Palestinian cameraman for French television filmed the death of a twelve-year-old Palestinian boy, Mohammed al-Dura, who was caught in crossfire at Gaza's Netzarim junction, a dusty crossroads just south of Gaza City. The fifty-five-second video clip went out to the world on global networks and aired repeatedly on Arab satellite networks. It showed the boy cowering with his father behind a concrete barrel; then suddenly the boy was hit by a bullet and died in his anguished father's arms. Even though there was a long and recriminatory debate over whether an Israeli bullet or an Arab bullet had killed the boy—or whether the boy's death had been staged—it did not matter for much of the world. The Israelis were to blame. Sharon was to blame. Not since the First Intifada, when Israeli soldiers were captured on tape brutally beating Palestinian boys with clubs, had Israel's image declined so precipitously.

Days later, two Israeli reservists, Vadim Nurzhitz and Yossi Avrahami, made a wrong turn and were set upon by a mob in Ramallah. Palestinian police took them to a police station, but it was quickly overrun by the angry mob. Young Arabs beat and clubbed the soldiers to death and mutilated their corpses. One young Palestinian appeared at a window and waved his bloody hands to a cheering crowd. The barbaric episode was captured by Italian television and was greeted by revulsion around the world.

Mayhem was back, too. It played into Sharon's hands. Fear, instability, and terrorism are the adrenaline of right-wing politics in Israel, triggering the deeply ingrained instinct for self-protection in the Israeli psyche. Sharon, as well as anyone, exploited that instinct—it was where he came from.

Yossi Beilin had tried to understand the complexity of bringing Jerusalem into the negotiations. As a protégé of Shimon Peres and one of the architects of the Oslo Accords of 1993, Beilin sought out Faisal Husseini, a prominent Palestinian leader in Jerusalem, and asked him to explain the significance of Arafat's position on the Noble Sanctuary.

"Let us suppose," Husseini responded, "that in seven or eight years' time there is an earthquake, and the two mosques collapse. If sovereignty remains with you, you will be able to build the [Jewish] temple there!"

Beilin protested that a secular Israeli government would never allow it and no religious authority would be capable of doing it.

Nevertheless, Husseini articulated the underlying Arab fear. "An Israeli government would not allow the mosques to be rebuilt. Only if it was in Palestinian hands could they be rebuilt."

Beilin had reported this conversation to Barak, and Barak had consulted rabbinical authorities, who told him that possession—sovereignty—over the Temple Mount was the best insurance to prevent the Arabs from destroying the Hebrew heritage underneath it.

"If the Palestinians have sovereignty over the Temple Mount," Rabbi Eliyahu Bakshi-Doron, a leading religious figure, told Barak, "they will do everything they can to wipe out the remnants of the temple. They will dig, destroy, and erase the remnants of our roots."

Suspicion throttled both communities.

The common view of Palestinian leaders was that the archaeological record of the Jewish Temple was thin. "They have dug up tunnel after tunnel, with no results," Yasser Abed Rabbo told *Le Monde*. "Even if we suppose there was a temple there, can somebody today use three-thousand-year-old history to claim sovereignty?"[77]

Jews across the spectrum answered yes.

Sharon's act was the magnification of that affirmation, and that was why his march onto the mount was like gasoline to a house fire.

At first it seemed that Camp David had been Clinton's last chance. He had presided over so much Middle East diplomacy, yet there was no single breakthrough or milestone that constituted a Clinton legacy in peacemaking. At times, he felt like the wooden Indian on which others nailed their achievements. But a Palestinian state, a final settlement in Jerusalem, the West Bank, and Gaza, a peace treaty that secured Israel for a new era of peace in the Holy Land—*that* was a prize worth shooting for even if he had to work right up through Inauguration Day to close the deal. Clinton could probably taste it after all he had been through.

Hillary Clinton was on her way to winning a Senate seat from New York. Al Gore was in a close contest with George W. Bush. But on the streets of the Holy Land, a daily battle of stones and bullets continued. Satellite television had shrunk the region dramatically and all sides competed to control the imagery of violence and the politics of blame.

Osama bin Laden also wanted a broader reach for the new ideology of jihad against America. On the morning of October 12, a small boat that rode heavy in the water motored across Aden Harbor. The USS *Cole* had arrived in Yemen to take on fuel. Commander Kirk Lippold, a 1981 Annapolis graduate, was taking the 505-foot destroyer on a mission to join the naval task force in the Persian Gulf enforcing United Nations sanctions against Iraq.

The *Cole* had passed through the Suez Canal two days earlier and then knifed southward through the Red Sea before steaming east through the Bab al-Mandab Strait at the tip of the Arabian Peninsula. Aden's historic harbor took shape from the contours of a dormant volcano whose basin captured the sea to form a deep-water bay.

The wooden hulks of small trading dhows bobbed on the late morning tide. It was one of those moments when the warship's crew was more in tourist mode than combat readiness mode. Many were lined up for a hot meal in the crew's mess belowdecks. Terrorist alerts had been broadcast to American facilities all over the Middle East, but what was about to happen to the *Cole* had never happened in U.S. maritime history. The fiberglass boat pulled close to the warship's portside hull plates, so close that some sailors leaned over the rail so see what the visitors were doing, or to shoo them away.

The men on the boat waved and stood suddenly erect as if at attention. A whiteout of sound and light followed, then a thunderous and blinding burst of fire and concussion convulsed the ship. The hull opened in the crew's mess with a sheet of fire rushing in. The shaped charge had focused the energy of the blast into the hull, which easily gave way. The explosion ripped a hole forty feet in diameter. The sea followed the fireball into the ship, forcing the crew to fight to keep it from sinking. The shock wave knocked out windows and moved cars on shore. Ships at anchor heaved and shuddered under the power of the eruption.

It should have been on television. That's the way al-Qaeda planned it. But the operative in charge of setting up the camera overslept that morning and so the triumph that bin Laden had hoped to show the world was seen only in the aftermath—a vessel sundered and blackened but still afloat and flying its colors. Seventeen sailors perished and dozens were wounded.

Hard up against a crucial election, Clinton did not strike back at al-Qaeda though the CIA reported a strong circumstantial case that al-Qaeda was behind the bombing. Bin Laden even dispersed his leadership, thinking that a retaliatory strike would come.

The attack on the *Cole* was devastating to American military prestige in the Middle East. It was an expert and successful demonstration of asymmetrical warfare, in which cheap or incongruous delivery platforms could be rigged to deliver a catastrophic blow to a billion-dollar warship, a military barracks, or an embassy.

The CIA had been tracking bin Laden with renewed intensity. On September 28, just two weeks before the *Cole* was hit, the CIA had conducted a trial flight of its Predator surveillance drone. Amazingly, it streamed video that bounced off a satellite and down to the Predator control room directing its flight from computer screens.

"We observed a tall man in flowing white robes walking around surrounded by a security detail," Tenet recorded after the first operational flight over Afghanistan. "While the resolution was not sufficient to make out the man's face, I don't know of any analyst who didn't subsequently conclude that we were looking at UBL [bin Laden]."[78] After the attack on the *Cole*, the CIA once again tracked bin Laden to Tarnak Farms near Kandahar, but Clinton declined to take the shot.

At the end of his presidency, Clinton did not see himself as a warrior against terrorism or Osama bin Laden. After the feckless cruise missile raids in response to the African embassy bombings of 1998 brought nothing but scorn, Clinton had soured on the military or the CIA's ability to perform with precision. For Clinton the fear of political blowback weighed more heavily in his decision making than the need for brutal retribution to deter further attacks.

There was a part of Clinton that seemed not to want to know who was responsible. Louis Freeh, the FBI director, had built a strong case showing that Iranian intelligence was behind the Khobar Towers bombing in 1996, but Clinton and his national security adviser, Sandy Berger, backpedaled and delayed any declarative finding of Iranian complicity, because it might lead, Freeh thought, to calls for military retaliation.

Freeh, who wrote that "a blind pig couldn't have missed the outlines" of the Iranian hand behind the operation that had killed nineteen servicemen, was bitter that Clinton seemed more interested in encouraging a moderate regime in Tehran under Mohammed Khatami than in taking revenge for those who died at Khobar Towers.

When Clinton reflected on these choices later, his reticence was apparent but not well explained. He wrote that getting to the bottom of major terrorist acts that had state sponsorship "could raise difficult and dangerous questions.

"Even if we had a good defense against attacks, would law enforcement be a sufficient offensive strategy against terrorists? If not, would greater reliance on military options work?"[79] Clinton admitted that he didn't have the answer, not in 1996 after Khobar, not in 1998 after the embassy attacks, and not in 2000 after the *Cole*.

Two days before Christmas, ten days after Al Gore had conceded the presidential election to George W. Bush, Clinton called the Palestinian and Israeli negotiators to the White House, where he presented them with his "parameters" for a final negotiation that could lead to a peace settlement and the creation of a Palestinian state.

That state, Clinton said, would comprise between 94 and 96 percent of the West Bank and, in compensation for the land they would give up to Israel for the large settlement blocs near Jerusalem, the Palestinians would get from Israel the equivalent of 1 to 3 percent of additional land; there would be no recognized right of return for Palestinian refugees, who would be getting their own new state. Palestine would have sovereignty over the Arab neighborhoods of East Jerusalem, as well as over the Arab and Christian quarters of the Old City. Clinton proposed Palestinian sovereignty over the Noble Sanctuary and Israeli sovereignty over the Western Wall and some unspecified holy spaces connected to it, which was a euphemism for the foundations of the Jewish Temple.

Clinton told the two sides they had five days to accept the parameters as the basis for a final crash negotiation. Prince Bandar, who was in Aspen with his family for a skiing vacation, had spoken to President-elect Bush, who had conveyed that he would honor an agreement if one were concluded in the final days of the Clinton administration. But conversely, if Arafat and Barak could not come to terms, the incoming administration would not be obligated. Any deal on the table would expire and the slate be wiped clean.

Five days went by. Barak had fallen behind Ariel Sharon in the polls. He swung between cracking down on Palestinian violence and trying to pull the peace rabbit out of the hat. Barak convened a "peace cabinet" because most of the right-wing parties had deserted his government. The cabinet voted on December 27 to accept Clinton's proposals with reservations.

Clinton was hopeful that he could pull it off. He passed up flying to North Korea to close a deal to shut down Pyongyang's missile program because Middle East peace seemed within his grasp. Dennis Ross was talking to Arafat's negotiators, who were in Washington trying to close the distance between them and the Israelis. Two of Arafat's aides, Mohammed Dahlan and Mohammed Rashid, were the most forward leaning in their belief that Arafat was ready to sign a deal. He would split the remaining differences.

For his part, Arafat had been flying around the Middle East consulting Arab heads of state. On New Year's Day, Ross reported to the Israelis that Arafat had responded positively to Clinton's parameters but had requested clarification on percentages of territory, the Western Wall, and refugees. Clinton was going to call him to Washington and pin him down. Late that night, Arafat took Clinton's call and promised to come to Washington the next day to explain his reservations.

Clinton then called Barak. Witnesses to the call heard an angry prime minister who no longer wanted a deal, at least not before Clinton left office.

"Arafat is fueling the violence. It's being carried out by his security people. He wants . . . maximum internationalization . . . and new concessions from the two of us, and he is dragging his feet. I cannot carry out any type of negotiations without a dramatic decrease in violence on the ground [and] cooperation on preventing terror attacks. It is for Arafat to prove that he is actively combating terrorism."

Barak was in extremis. "I am being asked to jump into an empty pool, with the hope that in mid-air Arafat will fill it with water!" Barak complained. Arafat would have to put an end to the violence immediately and "then, and only then, could I accept your invitation to participate in another round of talks.

"I have to tell my public the truth. I have no intention of concluding any accord before the elections."[80]

It was true that Arafat was back on top in the Arab world. The intifada had unified the Arab street behind the Palestinian cause once again. Sharon was the face of the enemy, and many Palestinians did not believe, despite the polling data to the contrary, that Sharon could win. But even if he did win, Arafat and most Arab leaders saw there would soon be another Bush in the White House and, notwithstanding their affection for Clinton, they believed the Bush family was good for the Arabs. Just as Bush the father had been, Bush the son was expected to be a friend of big oil, the Saudis, and the Arab cause in general. A Bush administration would be more willing to bring the necessary pressure to bear on Israel to make peace on better terms. At least that was the expectation.

Moreover, Colin Powell, another friend to the Arabs, was going to be secretary of state. Prince Bandar felt the same way. His expectations for a new Bush administration were soaring. Yet Bandar was under instructions from Crown Prince Abdullah to do everything he could to midwife an eleventh-hour peace if Clinton, Arafat, and Barak could pull it off.

Arafat landed at Andrews Air Force Base at 8:00 a.m. on January 2. Bandar drove to the air base with Hassan Abdul Rahman, Arafat's unofficial ambassador in Washington. They had arrived an hour early so they would be there when his plane pulled up to the gate.

Bandar was ebullient. All of the Arabs, he said, stood with the Palestinians. When Arafat climbed down from his jet, Bandar told him, "I am one of your soldiers. I consider myself a member of Fatah." The Saudi government and Crown Prince Abdullah, he added, supported the Palestinian cause without condition.

Referring to the agreement that Clinton had laid out, Bandar explained the Saudi position. "This is up to you," he said. "If you take it, the Saudi government will support you. If you don't take it, the Saudi government will support you, but I am telling you that I am for it and I think you should take it."[81]

When they reached the Ritz-Carlton Hotel a few blocks from the White House, they were met by Nabil Fahmy, the Egyptian ambassador, who explained that he too was under instructions to support Arafat in any way he could. What did he need?

Arafat said that if he accepted the deal, he wanted the Saudi Arabian and Egyptian leaders to stand up and endorse it so Arafat would have some heavyweight political cover. That would give him time to get back to the West Bank to explain the difficult parts of the agreement, especially the loss of the right of return, and the drawn-out Israeli withdrawal that would take place—tens of thousands of settlers moving into newly consolidated blocs around Jerusalem.

Bandar and Fahmy said that not only would their leaders support the deal, but they would work to have other Arab leaders make similar statements. Bandar suggested that if Arafat closed the deal in the meeting with Clinton that morning, he could come directly to Bandar's house on the Potomac, where they could huddle and notify the Arab governments. That would make the Saudis—and Bandar—stand out as sponsors of the peace. Arafat said okay and then left the hotel for the White House.

Once he was on his way, Bandar called the White House and reported that the chairman was in an upbeat mood, that he was asking for support and political cover to accept the deal. That could only mean he was close to accepting it. Clinton was heartened.

The morning session between Arafat and Clinton, however, was all over the map. Clinton thought the PLO chairman was unfocused, even confused. Arafat had real concerns and lots of questions. He didn't think the Jews should get the whole Western Wall, only the Wailing Wall portion that was visible on the plaza where Jews prayed. He wanted part of the Armenian Quarter under Palestinian sovereignty in the Old City because some Christian churches were there. Arafat was effusive in his praise of Clinton and said he wanted to reach a deal, or the outline of one, before Clinton left office.

Then Clinton brought Ross in and the meeting went south. Arafat's disdain for Ross had grown in the last weeks because Ross had staked out "final" positions, saying they were the best the Palestinians could ever get, but the next day saying that the Israelis would concede more ground, indicating there was more to give. Ross ended up looking like a patsy for Barak. But Clinton was also using Ross to push Barak farther than he wanted to go, so Ross was under suspicion from both sides.

The meeting ended without any clarity. Clinton said he wanted Arafat to come back to the White House that evening.

Across town, Bandar was getting restless. It had been hours since Arafat had left for the White House, and he still had not returned to Bandar's residence as planned. The prince was watching television for any sign that the White House talks had adjourned. What the hell had happened? Finally, he asked his security men to call the White House.

They learned that Arafat had returned to the Ritz-Carlton. Bandar got through on the phone to Arafat's suite. He received a garbled report that Clinton was sending Tenet to the hotel to work on some of the issues Arafat had raised at the White House. Bandar hung up wondering what he should do. The phone rang again. Arafat wanted him to come to the hotel immediately.

Bandar and Fahmy jumped into a car and raced for the city. When they walked into Arafat's suite, they both thought that Arafat looked dreadful. He was pale, the skin hung from his face, and his eyes showed a despondent mood. Everyone else in the room looked the same.

"How was the meeting?" Bandar ventured.

"Well," Arafat said. Clinton had responded to his questions. There was a rough patch when Ross came in and began "interfering," but overall, it had been a good meeting and Arafat said he had agreed to the parameters with some questions and reservations.

"Great! Congratulations," Bandar said. "So it's just a matter of fine tuning."

But there was no euphoria in the room.

Bandar suggested that maybe he and Fahmy should call their bosses, the crown prince and President Mubarak, and advise them to prepare other Arab leaders for an announcement.

"No, wait until I come back," Arafat said, "then I will talk to them and explain everything."

Just then one of Bandar's security men came in with a slip of paper. It said Clinton urgently wanted Bandar to call the White House. Bandar was uneasy. He told Arafat he had to go make a call.

"Who's calling?" Arafat asked.

"My father, Prince Sultan," Bandar lied.

"Oh, I want to talk to him," Arafat said.

But Bandar said it was a private family matter and hurried out of the room, where he picked up a phone and got a White House operator to patch him through to Sandy Berger.

Berger started in on Bandar. Arafat was out of bounds. Bandar had better get Arafat's attention because "this is really it—Arafat got everything we can give him. He is not going to get anything more. If he comes back here with no answer, then there is no deal."

"Sandy, I'm surprised, because Arafat just briefed us that he had a good meeting and there is an agreement, but with just a few things on security that the president offered him, and Tenet is to come talk to him, then there will be another meeting and the announcement made."

Berger said no way *that* was true.

Then Clinton came on the line. "Listen, Arafat got more than we think Barak can cope with, but I'm holding Barak's feet to the fire and I insisted there are no more changes on the Israeli side." Clinton went on about how it was the greatest deal the Palestinians would ever get and that the president-elect, Bush, would support it.

Bandar said he knew that Bush would support it.

"Well then," Clinton said, "it is time for him to say yes for God's sake."

Bandar repeated what Arafat had said about his questions and reservations and that Tenet was supposed to come work out some of the problems. "That's absolutely not true," Clinton said.

"Now look, you tell him if he comes back with a negative answer, not only will we not have an agreement, but I will withdraw my proposal. Let him start fresh with the other guy. If he thinks he can get a better deal with Sharon, he's welcome to it."[82]

Bandar just listened to Clinton let loose and wondered why the president himself had not made those points to Arafat. Clinton wanted Bandar to be the heavy. He expected Bandar to deliver Arafat, just as he had that day seven years earlier when Arafat wanted to kiss Clinton on the White

House lawn. The prince said he would try, but Bandar now saw he was being played by both sides and seemed to suffer a profound loss of faith.

He returned to Arafat and questioned him about the meeting with
Clinton. Arafat insisted, once again, that he thought Clinton was in the
process of addressing the Palestinian concerns. A final negotiation with
the Israelis was still possible. That being the case, Bandar begged the
chairman's indulgence to be allowed to return to Aspen. It he left at that
moment, he might be able to fly into the small Aspen airport before it
closed for the night and rejoin his family.

Arafat would hear none of it. He wanted Bandar to stay.

But the agreement was essentially done, Bandar pleaded. Fahmy, the
Egyptian ambassador, one of the most experienced Arab diplomats, could
easily hold the fort. Bandar would be a phone call away.

"I'm telling you, I am leaving," Bandar said, and as he made for the
door, Arafat was up tugging him back into the room. Bandar pulled away,
good-naturedly but insistently. Arafat followed him out into the hall and
all the way to the elevator, trying to drag him back, but Bandar excused
himself over and over.

"You don't need me here," he protested and finally made his farewell.

Bandar was upset. Arafat had lied to him about what had happened at
the White House. Clinton was posturing, expecting Bandar to produce a
miracle. People were setting up blame strategies. It was time to head for
the exit.[83]

Arafat returned to the White House that evening for a private dinner
with Clinton in the living quarters. They thrashed out all of Arafat's reservations, with Clinton going through every point to reassure Arafat that
with good faith and American partnership, the deal would work; Palestinians would decide to live with it. Arafat was not happy about giving up
the right of return, and Clinton had patiently gone through the politics of
the issue. Israel could not absorb another large Arab population without
putting in jeopardy the Jewish character of the state. The Palestinians had
agreed to a two-state solution in 1993. The Israelis might be willing to accept a token number of humanitarian reunions for families that were divided, but that would be a sovereign Israeli decision. The rest of the
refugees should go to the Palestinian state, or emigrate to Europe, Canada,
or the United States. There would be generous compensation for their
losses, too.

But Arafat was deeply vexed about how his decisions would play on the street. And his advisers were divided about whether he should accept the parameters as Clinton had framed them. Everyone in the Palestinian leadership circle called Arafat the "old man," in part out of affection, but in part out of recognition of his patriarchy and a sense that one never knew what he was going to do. His zigzags were legendary, as were his stubbornness and duplicity. He would say things for effect and, the next day, deny that he had ever done so.

All of his adult life, Arafat had been a practitioner of Arab politics and the art of leverage, and he knew when the leverage had tilted in his direction. With Clinton and Barak both desperate, with a Bush inbound to the Oval Office, the momentum was in Arafat's favor and he was less likely to be impressed by histrionics from Ross, Berger, or Clinton saying that this was his last chance, whether it was or not.

It was 10:30 p.m. when Arafat returned to the hotel. All of his aides and negotiators were waiting in his suite. Someone asked if he had accepted Clinton's parameters.

"Half accepted," Arafat said.

Arafat's longtime secretary, Nabil Abu Rudeina, had been at the dinner with him to help with translation. "I think it went okay," he told everyone in the room.

"Did you accept?" asked Saeb Erekat.

Arafat nodded. Some of his aides applauded. Erekat said it was a disaster if he had really accepted the deal as it was.

The next morning, CNN correspondent Andrea Koppel called Hassan Abdul Rahman and asked what had happened at the White House.

Abdul Rahman asked Arafat what he should tell the news media. "Did you accept?"

"Yes, in principle, with my own interpretations," Arafat replied.

"Can I tell the media that?" his envoy asked.[84]

Arafat said yes. The story went out on January 3 via CNN to the world that Arafat had accepted. Clinton and Ross, too, reported to the Israelis that they both thought Arafat could work within the parameters, though that was a stretch of what they had been told.[85]

The PLO chairman flew to Cairo, where Tenet had convened the security chiefs of Israel, Egypt, and the Palestinian Authority to get the violence of the intifada under control so negotiations could resume.

As Clinton counted down the days to the end of his term, Barak steadily lost ground in his election battle with Sharon. Neither Clinton nor Barak made an all-out push to convene the two sides at Camp David or anywhere else. Barak was waiting for Arafat to quell the violence and was infuriated at his predicament. Arafat stood fast, waiting for Clinton to make a move, or to let the time run down before Bush's inauguration.

Clinton was busy mixing up the tawdry with the profound.

In his final months as president, Clinton allowed himself to be duped and bribed—there is no other reasonable description for it—by a group of people who were closely connected to the Israeli intelligence agency, Mossad, to grant a presidential pardon to the fugitive financier Marc Rich.

Rich and his partner, Pincus "Pinky" Green, were oil traders who had rapaciously violated the Nixon-era price controls on crude oil and had reaped millions in illegal profits. When federal prosecutors were closing in on the illegal operation, Rich and Green fled the country and attempted to renounce their U.S. citizenship, causing Rich's defense attorney, the famed Edward Bennett Williams, to accuse him of spitting "on the American flag" and the "jury system."[86]

In a tight circle of White House lawyers and Rich allies, Clinton kept his pardon considerations secret from prosecutors and law enforcement and intelligence officials who would have vigorously opposed any reprieve for a man who had mocked and evaded the U.S. justice system with impunity.

Clinton relied on the recommendations of a small circle of advocates for the pardon that included Barak; Avner Azulay, a former Mossad official; Denise Rich; and her close friend Beth Dozoretz, the Democratic Party fund-raising chief. Rich and Dozoretz had directly contributed or raised millions of dollars for Clinton's campaigns, and Rich had, in addition, made a reported $450,000 pledge to the Clinton Library in Little Rock. Though she and her husband had divorced in 1993, Denise Rich had become a tenacious advocate for a pardon. There was a strong presumption among some Clinton friends that Rich was willing to pay almost anything for presidential clemency.[87]

One could only imagine the scene in the Oval Office during the last days. On the one hand, the president was trying to find a formula for Middle East peace and was closer than any other president had come. He held himself out as empathizer in chief, the ultimate honest broker, but at the same time, he was running a covert operation, haranguing White House lawyers and other senior staffers, at the behest of the agents of a foreign-based initiative, to wipe clean the slate of one of the most brazen white-collar fugitives of the era.

The pardon of Marc Rich triggered congressional investigations that established that Clinton had essentially been duped by a tapestry of false statements from Denise Rich and the team of lawyers working for her ex-husband. The team was coordinating its efforts with Avner Azulay, a former Mossad official who was running the (Marc) Rich Foundation in Israel.

The excerpt of Clinton's telephone conversations with Barak relating to the Marc Rich pardon were released to Congres by the Bush White House, and featured the Prime Minister of Israel stating, "I believe it [the pardon] could be important [gap] not just financially, but he helped Mossad on more than one case."[88] This reference to the possible financial impact of the pardon has never been addressed or explained by either leader, nor has the gap in the transcript that was released by the White House. The Rich team had gamed the White House on behalf of the fugitive and they organized themselves as if they had been engaged in an intelligence operation. Denise Rich and Beth Dozoretz both refused to testify before Congress, invoking their Fifth Amendment rights against self-incrimination.*

Clinton was never called to account for his actions. He later told *Newsweek* magazine that the pardon "wasn't worth the damage to my reputation."

He was right.

Three hundred Palestinians had died in the new intifada and the Arab world was seething because Clinton had failed. One of Arafat's negotiators, Yasser Abed Rabbo, called Barak a "war criminal" in public. The momentum that both sides had developed for peace was dissipating rapidly. Arafat and Barak, like tribal leaders, reverted to combat mode.

Barak's advisers pleaded with the prime minister to meet with Arafat,

---

*Denise Rich, through her attorney, declined numerous requests for an interview. President Clinton declined an interview request and, separately, declined to respond to questions, submitted to his counsel, about the Rich pardon. Barak also delined an interview request.

but Barak seemed paralyzed by the violence and by Sharon's formidable traction with the Israeli electorate.

Clinton had run out of proposals. Neither the Israelis nor the Palestinians felt they could live within the president's parameters. Barak told his negotiators privately that he needed a minimum of 8 percent of Palestinian territory to annex if he was to accommodate all of the settler blocs in the West Bank. That put him outside the 94–96 percent range, though not by much.

On January 11, 2001, Saeb Erekat briefed the Israelis on the reservations that Arafat had laid out to Clinton. Arafat wanted some recognition of the right of return even if it was not implemented; he wanted one-for-one land swaps for any land he had to give up around Jerusalem. The outline of a deal was still there, and the negotiators reconvened at Taba in one desperate last effort, but neither side came with leaders who were fully on board. Meanwhile, Clinton's presidency expired with a fusillade of recriminations.

On the day before the Bush inauguration, Arafat called Clinton to thank him and to tell him he was a great man. The Clinton proposal would live on, Arafat said, even if the time was not yet ripe. His negotiators were going to keep working with the Israelis.

Clinton responded, "Mr. Chairman, I am not a great man. I am a failure, and you have made me one."[89]

It was a harsh judgment, and it raised a critical question about Clinton's presidency: With all of the high-mindedness of his peacemaking efforts in the Middle East, what had really undermined Bill Clinton in the end?

It may take years to answer the question satisfactorily, but the dominant threads were visible all along: Clinton's lack of discipline, his unwillingness to table his own proposals early in the process, his reliance on Barak to frame the tactics and terms for compromise, his prodigious capacity for empathy that mired him in sentimentalism and undermined the resolute pressure that is the hallmark of leadership.

The truth was that Clinton had been the beneficiary of a great convergence: the end of the cold war, the advent of Yitzhak Rabin's premiership, and the PLO's decision to recognize the Jewish state and make peace. Clinton performed admirably in the fat years when the White House was needed as a backdrop for handshakes and signing ceremonies. But after Rabin's death, Clinton did little to oppose Netanyahu's willful disman-

tling of a peace process that had broad support among Jews in Israel and
the United States.

Clinton's style was to stage tantrums in adjoining rooms so Netanyahu
could hear; he disparaged the Israeli prime minister to other people, but
in the main he allowed Netanyahu to intimidate official Washington by
shows of force in Congress and verbal bullying supplied by members of
his coalition, most prominently Ariel Sharon. As Netanyahu did so, the
deadlines and milestones of the Oslo peace succumbed to cynical delays
and robust expansions of settlements. That was the old Shamir strategy.
The continuous building enraged Arabs, inciting a terrorist response and
the steady strengthening of Hamas, which rejected Arafat's engagement
with the Zionist "enemy."

Arafat was a controversial figure, too, a skilled liar and a political survivor, and when he saw that Netanyahu was gaming him and that Fatah's
support was eroding, he played the terror card to show he still led a po-
tent liberation movement. But no objective analysis of Arafat's leadership
from the mid-1980s onward could fail to conclude that he personally had
pulled and tugged the PLO into the political process that he hoped
would lead to peace. How else to explain his behavior over fifteen years?

Arafat's concept of Palestinian statehood rested on manifold assurances for Israeli's security even as he secretly smuggled in larger weapons
for his security forces so they could face the fifty-caliber machine guns
that Israel had turned on them. Arafat's reticence in January 2001 was
not an indication that he opposed the agreement that had taken shape.
Indeed, he was on the knife's edge, as his pleas for Saudi and Egyptian
support indicated. Rather, it showed that the Palestinians were reading
the incoming Bush administration—incorrectly, it turned out—as a reincarnation of the first Bush administration. Arafat gambled that the political environment for a peace settlement would improve with George W.
Bush and that Sharon, if he were elected, would be disciplined by an
American president who, like his father, was believed to be capable of
taking a tough stand with an Israeli prime minister.

After he survived impeachment, Clinton had taken an approach to the
Middle East peace process that had too firmly put the United States in
the thrall of Barak's frenetic tactics. Barak's strategy, churlish in its lack of
regard for Arafat as a partner, failed to recapture the trust and confidence
of the Palestinians, which was the most constructive achievement of Rabin's tenure. Even the Israelis lost confidence in Barak.

Clinton also failed to hold the trust he had built with Hafez al-Assad of Syria, who was ready for a compromise based on the Rabin formula of full withdrawal in exchange for full peace. Clinton's aides complained that Barak had turned the American president into a clerk, and there was some truth to the charge.

Clinton exuded remarkable characteristics of empathy and understanding, but his approach was missing the most essential ingredients: trust that he would do what was necessary, unwavering principle, and political discipline.

# 12

# GEORGE W. BUSH
*A World of Trouble*

On January 19, 2001, the White House operator telephoned Colin Powell, the incoming secretary of state. It was around four o'clock in the afternoon on the eve of the inauguration of the new president when Bill Clinton came on the line. Powell had a mental image of the outgoing president, surrounded by packing boxes in the Oval Office, cleaning out his desk yet still obsessed about how his presidency was ending.

Clinton's manner was easy and familiar. Powell had been chairman of the Joint Chiefs of Staff when Clinton entered the White House eight years earlier. It was Powell who, in 1993, had come up with the plan to offer U.S. soldiers to serve as a buffer force on the Golan Heights in the event Israel decided to withdraw, as Yitzhak Rabin had said it would in a peace with Syria.[1]

Clinton admired Powell. He congratulated him on being named secretary of state, but Powell was caught off guard by the sudden turn in Clinton's voice and the vehemence with which he expressed himself. The president began to unload on Yasser Arafat, the person who had robbed him of the one achievement—namely, Middle East peace—he had hoped to salvage from the wreckage of Lewinsky, impeachment, pardons, the whole tawdry mess.

Arafat was a "goddamned liar," an unreliable and no-good so-and-so, a deceiver, a dissembler, a phony. The president used barnyard epithets that Powell hadn't heard since he was an infantryman in the army.

Powell didn't defend Arafat. He had no illusions about the PLO leader as a dissembler; that was a given of Middle East politics. But Arafat had been both Clinton's and Rabin's partner in the peace process; the Palestinian leader was now hoping for a new partner in the White House to close the deal that Clinton had formulated with his December parameters.

Now, strangely, Clinton was trying to poison the well.

Powell was not an expert on the Middle East, but with Dick Cheney, Powell, and Donald Rumsfeld, the new defense secretary, who had been Ronald Reagan's Middle East envoy, the incoming Bush administration was brimming with experience, much of it painful, gained during the Reagan and first Bush administrations. The new Bush team understood that the region was complex and treacherous and its tentacles intruded into domestic politics—big oil and the Jewish community for starters. Powell didn't need Bill Clinton's farewell rant to instill a certain caution. He already had come to the conclusion that he could not recommend that a new president jump immediately into the Middle East peace process.[2]

The region was in crisis. A new president would have to be active, but it seemed to Powell that there was not much to work with. The new secretary of state believed that Clinton and Madeleine Albright had been too desperate and too naïve; they had attempted to overcome huge impediments to peace in ridiculously short time frames, such things as sovereignty in Jerusalem, the Palestinian right of return, water rights, and settlements. Arafat's caution had been understandable, and so had Barak's. The time had not been ripe, Powell believed, to solve complex issues with bumper-sticker formulations from Dennis Ross's overnight memos.

Powell was not at all sure that Ehud Barak could have made a deal even if Arafat had agreed to all of Clinton's parameters. Barak's parliamentary majority had collapsed, violence was out of control, and elections were only weeks away. Clinton's telephone call reinforced Powell's instinct that it was best to avoid the Middle East peace process, at least until the parties got the violence under control and showed some interest in returning to negotiations.[3]

The next day it rained as Bush stood before the gleaming white dome of the Capitol to take the oath of office. In his inaugural address, he told Americans that his presidency would radiate idealism to the world as a continuation of the American "story."

"It is the story of a new world that became a friend and liberator of the old, a story of a slave-holding society that became a servant of freedom, the story of a power that went into the world to protect but not possess, to defend but not to conquer."

The son had also risen and the presumption of a Bush dynasty lay expectantly on the country. Undoubtedly there would be differences between Bush 43 and Bush 41, but many Americans thought there would also be visible dynastic threads—an inclination in American foreign policy for collaborative diplomacy and principled leadership. Despite the wrenching postelection struggle over whether Bush had actually defeated Al Gore, much of the nation seemed willing to engage a president who talked about compassionate conservatism, in part because it reminded them of Bush the father. And for those Americans concerned about the Middle East, it seemed that a new Bush in the White House might be just what the region needed: a steady hand with Israel and the Jewish community, a resolute approach to Iraq, and a self-confident vision for comprehensive peace that might finally end the Israeli occupation in the West Bank and Gaza and establish a Palestinian state that could live in peace with Israel.

Yet Bush entered the White House at a time of dangers he did not recognize and of opportunities he could not discern. Two of the 9/11 terrorists already were in the United States, preparing for flight training and the horrific task that lay just eight months ahead of them. The Second Intifada was raging in the Holy Land. And the last-ditch peace talks between Israelis and Palestinians at the Egyptian resort of Taba were failing. Neither Barak nor Arafat seemed inclined to compromise in the midst of an Israeli election campaign or while a new American president was getting on his feet. The strategic environment for peace was unstable, and strong leadership was in demand.

Two weeks after Bush's inauguration, Ariel Sharon, riding a wave of fear and insecurity, soundly defeated Ehud Barak, and that was that for peace talks. The spirit of Yitzhak Rabin was suddenly a distant memory. The Labor Party and the peace camp had lost their footing in a population traumatized by suicide bombers and firefights between Israeli army soldiers and Palestinian police. The intifada no longer involved young Palestinian Davids taking on Goliath with slings and stones; instead, it was a battle of automatic rifles and high explosives.

On February 7, Sharon appeared before his cheering supporters and surprised them by extending the best wishes of the new American president. Bush had telephoned him just as the Israeli leader entered the victory hall in Jerusalem. Sharon explained to the cheering crowd that Bush offered America's unwavering support for his government. The president, he said, had reminded him of the day in 1998 when Bush visited Israel as the governor of Texas. Sharon had given him "the tour," that rite of passage in which Israeli leaders seek to indoctrinate American political figures about Israel's geographic vulnerabilities. The retired general dazzled Bush with a helicopter ride north of Tel Aviv to see firsthand the delicate nine-mile-wide "waste" of Israel where the Arab West Bank looms above the plain that runs down to Jewish Netanya on the Mediterranean.

"We have driveways in Texas longer than that," Bush had remarked.[4]

They flew on, northeast to Galilee, where the earth heaves upward to create a massive wall on whose crest the farms and villages of the Golan Heights stand. Sharon showed Bush how Syrian gunners had used the promontory to rain fire on Israeli farming towns around the Sea of Galilee. He might have pointed out the place where, in 1966, the Syrian leader Hafez al-Assad, addressing his soldiers, vowed to drive the Jews into the sea.

In short, Sharon had imprinted on Bush the visual justification for the "activist" or militarist instinct in Israeli policy. Sharon told the crowd in Jerusalem that Bush, in harking back to their time together, said, "No one believed then that I would be president and you would be prime minister. But as things turned out, despite the fact that no one believed us, I have been elected president and you have been elected prime minister."[5]

Bush was impressed by Sharon, the general so vilified as a rogue during the Reagan era. Where a younger Powell, as Weinberger's aide, had seen Sharon as a destroyer, Bush saw a rugged iconoclast fighting for the survival of his people. To Powell, Sharon was a unique figure who personified the Israeli right wing. Even more than Begin or Shamir, he was the architect of the Israeli settler movement, which America officially, if fitfully, opposed and which inflamed the Palestinians hoping for statehood. Powell saw Sharon as a bull elephant, a battalion commander, now prime minister, who hated Arafat and, more broadly, probably hated the Palestinians and the Arabs. Who from the Reagan era could look at Sharon without hearing those carping lectures to Ronald Reagan, delivered by a table-pounding general, about Israeli strategic superiority? Sharon was the epitome of military excess in the Lebanon War and of the brutality that had led to the massacres at Sabra and Shatila.

Now Sharon was promising to become a different kind of leader. With leadership, perhaps, would come a certain pragmatism. Some of his American supporters, such as the columnist William Safire, believed that just as it took a Nixon to open China, it would take a Sharon to make peace with the Arabs.[6]

In any case, the new Sharon styled himself as a prime minister who was interested in peace through security, and most Israelis understood, though it was not certain that Bush did, that Sharon meant there could be no genuine Palestinian state, the kind envisioned by the Oslo Accords. Sharon had come to power to fight terror, and many Israelis and Arabs believed that he also was determined to destroy his old nemesis, Arafat, who had eluded him in Lebanon and who was using the intifada to discredit him, if he could, before the world.

If there was one lesson Sharon had learned from Lebanon it was that American support was essential to any Israeli prime minister. Thus, Sharon must have been pleasantly surprised to find that Bush the son was more an admirer than a critic. When the two leaders sat down for tea at the White House in March, Bush spoke with a ferocious enthusiasm for the Jewish state: he said he would use force to protect Israel.

Some of Bush's aides in the room were thinking, "Whoa, where did that come from?"[7] It almost sounded like a defense pact. Was there a Christian dimension to Bush's feeling for Israel? It was difficult to say because there was so much about Bush that he himself found difficult to articulate.

After Sharon returned home, there were cursory attempts by Bush to engage the Arab camp, desultory meetings between Bush and the Egyptian and Jordanian leaders that accomplished nothing except to confirm that Bush did not connect with them as his father had. And why should he? He had no experience in diplomacy, the clandestine service, or international relations, three roles that led his father to form strong ties with the Arab world.

Arafat, conspicuously, was not invited to the White House, though Bush had said at the first meeting of his National Security Council on January 30 that he wanted to make personal assessments of Sharon and Arafat before he would commit himself to getting involved.[8] Both Cheney and Donald Rumsfeld, the defense secretary, told the president that dealing with Arafat was a waste of time and of political capital.

It was left to Powell to establish the new administration's relationship with Arafat during the secretary's first swing through the region, but Powell, having caught the tone emanating from the Oval Office, was not going to get out in front of his president. From the outset of the administration, Bush expressed a near total disdain for the Middle East peace process.

"I only have so much political capital and I'm going to use it carefully and I'm not going to do what my predecessors have done; I've seen several of them squander their political capital," Bush explained to one of his national security advisers.

Bush had arrived with no discernible Middle East policy goals. Clinton had warned him personally that al-Qaeda and Osama bin Laden were serious threats to American security. Richard Clarke, Clinton's antiterrorism adviser who stayed on to work for Condoleezza Rice, the new national security adviser, also harped on al-Qaeda as the number one priority, but the Bush White House—and it was not the first to do so— did not want to define itself by its predecessor's objectives. Instead, Bush was out to project a decidedly *un*-Clintonian approach to foreign and domestic policy. If Bush had any interest in the Middle East, it was an inchoate desire to finish off Saddam Hussein, but the politics were complicated; he had no mandate to go after the Iraqi dictator. There would have to be a clear and broadly recognized provocation.

In foreign policy, Bush's overarching theme was to enhance American security by erecting a national missile defense system, a step that required abrogating the Anti-ballistic Missile Treaty with Russia. This was Rice's project, one that showed her expertise on the Soviet-era military balance. It also showed her narrow range as a policy adviser. She didn't grasp the Middle East.

Prince Bandar had returned to Washington from Aspen for the inauguration. He had never been closer to an incoming American president. He knew the younger Bush from the Reagan years, when George W. was known only as the eldest of the vice president's four sons. The prince was a favorite of the Bush circle and had entertained the Bush family at the Saudi ambassador's mansion overlooking the Potomac. Bandar and the younger Bush had hit it off as hard-drinking and fun-loving ex-fighter pilots and, at least from Bandar's side, there was always the intimation that they had sowed some wild oats together in the Reagan years. That would certainly explain the relaxed manner when they were together, the profane repartee of a couple of flyboys. To Bandar, Bush could refer to Steven Hadley as "my national fuckin' security adviser," and Bandar indulged himself in pronouncing some presidential opinions "bullshit."

Bandar had lived in Texas for a time, training at Lackland Air Force Base outside San Antonio. He loved the rowdy spirit of the place. Thirty years later, the wallpaper on his laptop computer screen said "TOP GUN" over a Dallas Cowboys football helmet. The same infectious charm that had made Bandar a phenomenon of the royal family served him in politics and diplomacy. He was the incandescent pal, the fighter jock who loved Texas football, the political junkie who watched a dozen television screens at once, and the generous and affable patron, the giver of extravagant gifts. But another face was always turned east to the Oriental court of the House of Saud, with its internecine politics and its distinctive agenda in the Middle East.

Bandar was the first foreign envoy to be invited to the White House after Bush was sworn in. He and the new president sat on the Truman porch, overlooking the Washington Monument, and, with great expectation, Bandar listened to Bush talk about his goals.

"We all were riding high on expectations and I really thought this is going to be my best four years in Washington, and the sky is the limit," Bandar said later. The feeling was, "We will just conquer the world and do the right thing—solve most of these problems that have been hanging."[9]

Bush exuded that same sense of confident expectation in their private conversations. No one should look at the narrow margin of his victory and think that he would be a cautious leader, he would say. The world was going to see what he could do. Many had thought it was an accident when George W. won the governorship in Texas, and they were even more surprised when he was reelected. He had been underestimated all of his life.

When Bandar brought up the Middle East, Bush showed a hard edge. "I told you what my position was going to be," he said. He wasn't going to be spending weeks at a time at Camp David breaking his head against Middle East intransigence. The White House was not going to be a Motel 6 for Arafat, either. The fiasco of Florida had showed that the Jewish vote in one state might determine whether Bush was reelected four years hence. Bush said he was a politician; he had to face political reality.

Bandar argued that America could not afford to disengage from the Middle East peace.

Bush replied that that was well and good, but he was not interested in committing political suicide by squandering political capital on a problem that had shipwrecked Clinton.[10]

Despite the grim assessment, the message that Bandar sent home to Crown Prince Abdullah was upbeat. Bush needed some time to get his administration up and running; Powell would conduct reconnaissance, and that would surely lead to the formulation of a strategy.

Instead, Bush ignored the Middle East even as it convulsed with daily violence. In late March, Bush dodged a reporter's question about why he had not met with Arafat, while his senior aides picked up the themes that Clinton, Ross, and others were propagating in the news media: Arafat was to blame, especially for the violence; the Second Intifada was a historic blunder.[11]

"The signal I'm sending to the Palestinians is stop the violence. And I can't make it any more clear," Bush said. "And I hope that Chairman Arafat hears it loud and clear."[12]

At the same time, Sharon had shown Washington that he did not need any advice on how to attack the infrastructure of terror. He sent tanks into the West Bank and Gaza after suicide bombers attacked Israeli buses and after an Israeli infant was shot in Hebron. Israeli gunships destroyed Arafat's home in Gaza, and Arafat, from Amman, denounced Sharon, alleging that Israel had a one-hundred-day military plan "against our people, against our institutions, against our houses—everything." Arafat warned Sharon that he should remember the lesson of Beirut, where Sharon's excesses in 1982 led to his political downfall.

But Arafat miscalculated. Sharon's war in Lebanon had appalled Ronald Reagan, who had looked at the human suffering and demanded that Israel desist. But in 2001, there was very little sympathy in the White House for the plight of Palestinians. Bush was going to support Sharon. And Clinton had so poisoned Arafat's well that recriminations echoed broadly in Congress and the news media. There was no restraining force emanating from America.

Powell was suddenly under siege. Arab leaders were beating him up on the telephone. What was he going to do? they demanded. American inaction and Bush's open tilt toward Sharon triggered indignation. The violence was falling disproportionately on Palestinians. Powell was frantic and vented his frustrations during evening bull sessions with Bandar.

By the summer of 2001, Powell frequently stopped at the Saudi ambassador's mansion on the way home from the State Department. The two men commiserated over a drink. They had known each other since the Reagan years. They saw America's leadership role—the need for a strong military posture—in similar terms and they shared a love for gossip and intelligence about the power currents of Washington and the Middle East. Each had learned from the other.

Powell urged Bandar to use his influence. Why was Bush taking so long to respond to the explosive situation in the Middle East? When was Bush going to have a heart-to-heart talk with Sharon and explain America's interest in returning to the peace agenda? Did Sharon really think there was a military solution?

Bandar was in a vise: Bush was his friend. He believed in the new president. But Crown Prince Abdullah was his boss. They were headed for a collision over Sharon and the escalating violence. Bush sent messages through Condoleezza Rice that the administration needed more time to get organized, to formulate a response. In May, the elder Bush, apparently with his son's assent, telephoned the Saudi ruler and reassured him that the younger Bush was going to do the right thing.

But things just got worse.

On June 1, a suicide bomber mingled with a large crowd of young Israelis, many of them Russian immigrants, outside the Dolphinarium disco in trendy Tel Aviv. When the bomber pushed the button around midnight, the blast, its shredding power magnified by metal screws and ball bearings, tore through the youthful crowd, killing 21 and wounding 120.

Israelis were devastated. It was the worst attack since the intifada had begun. Surprisingly, Sharon initially held back, allowing the outrage to build in Israel, but also in Washington. Arafat was on the defensive. He angered Sharon's intelligence chief by saying the attack was the work of the Mossad, as if Sharon would kill young Israelis to make the Arabs look bad.[13]

First George Tenet and then Powell were dispatched to the region to get a cease-fire. Sharon demanded a complete cessation of terror before he would even consider negotiations. And though Arafat had the power to tone down some of the violence, he had little incentive to do so; at best, Sharon's idea of peace was, in his view, "imprisoning" Palestinians in "Bantustans" surrounded by Jewish settlements and army checkpoints. Besides, Arafat did not control Hamas and other extremists who wanted to destroy the Jewish state.

On a sultry morning in August, Prince Bandar was awakened at his home in Aspen, Colorado, at six o'clock by the crown prince. The Saudi ruler's anger crackled over the telephone line. He had been watching Arab satellite television and suddenly there was—so he said—an Israeli soldier hitting an old woman. She fell and the soldier put his boot on her head, and that had sent Abdullah into a rage. George W. Bush was doing nothing to stop it.

"Now I understand," said Abdullah. "It's my fault. I was stupid. He [Bush] was just diddling us. The president is not only *not* trying to help us, or to be an honest broker—he is one hundred percent with Sharon!" It was all the worse that Bush 41 had called Abdullah and reassured him about Bush 43, because now Abdullah believed that both men had deceived him.

"You tell him right now that I don't want to have anything to do with him or with America."[14]

Bandar was floored. He told his sovereign that he would immediately convey Abdullah's anger and discuss it with the president, but Abdullah upbraided him.

"I am not asking you to pass a message so you can get me a reply. I am telling you to give a one-way message and after you give it, come back here [to Saudi Arabia]."

Bandar worried that Abdullah had lost all confidence in his judgment. He flew to Washington and met Condoleezza Rice, delivering Abdullah's message. Bandar summarized Abdullah's long tirade: Bush did not care about Palestinian blood, only Israeli blood; America had completely surrendered to Sharon's agenda.

Bandar's version, handwritten in Arabic, had run to twenty-something pages on a legal pad. He had decided to deliver it to Rice because it was such a stern rebuke. He feared that if he delivered it directly to Bush, things would get personal and lead to an irrevocable rupture.

Bush was at his ranch in Crawford, Texas. He conferred hurriedly with Cheney and Powell and they decided to draft a letter that Bandar might give to Abdullah. In it, Bush told the Saudi leader that he *did* care about Palestinian blood and that his goal in the Middle East was the creation of a state for the Palestinians.

Bandar was hopeful. Bush's letter used language that was simple and declarative about a Palestinian state, more specific than even Clinton had been. The letter seemed to advance American policy on statehood. Bandar flew through the night to Riyadh. When he reached the palm-lined boulevards of the Saudi capital, he found that Abdullah was not alone. He had convened a group that included Prince Sultan, Bandar's father, Prince Saud, the foreign minister, and Ghazi Gosaibi, a longtime diplomat and adviser to the royal family.

Abdullah's blood was still up. He disparaged Bush's letter. "I wish you didn't bring this letter. It is even more insulting. He gave me nothing in it. He explained nothing. He is confirming my worst suspicions."

Abdullah said he wanted to call an Islamic summit in Mecca so he could tell the world about Bush's perfidy.

When his aides winced with alarm and pushed back, Abdullah said, "Are you all cowards? Are you all scared of America? Man is not worth a thing if you lose your dignity, and honor and dignity have been lost here."

Abdullah picked up the phone and told his chief of protocol to start preparing the invitations to the summit. He issued orders for a speech to be drafted.

"I am going to tell the Muslim world exactly what I think. This is no more my responsibility. I'll tell them everything and we'll make a common position vis-à-vis the U.S.A.

"Forget Israel," he said, "Israel is no longer the enemy. The enemy is America!"[15]


Prince Sultan, one of the most seasoned—and cagey—operators in the royal family, looked at the stunned faces in the room and said, "You have all heard what His Royal Highness has said. I want everyone to go and do their duty exactly as instructed, whatever time it takes."

Bandar returned to his palace and threw himself despondently on his bed. Prince Saud telephoned. Should they meet? The last thing Bandar wanted to do was have a meeting. "Let's just take a deep breath and see what happens tomorrow," he said.

In the middle of the night, Abdullah summoned Bandar back to the royal palace. His mood had calmed. He asked Bandar to read to him Bush's letter one more time. He asked him to explain again why it was an improvement over previous positions. Then he asked him to read it again, and they discussed it sentence by sentence, with Bandar explaining where Bush had gone farther than previous statements about his support for a Palestinian state.

Abdullah's rage had subsided. But he did not trust Bush. He said he would write to Bush, telling him candidly that Saudi Arabia asked for nothing more than for Bush to say in public what he had said in the letter.

They drafted the reply through the night, arguing finally over whether Abdullah should sign it "your friend." That was the tradition.

But Abdullah had said reproachfully to Bandar, "He's your friend, not my friend."

Bandar was stung by the remark. But before he departed, Abdullah handed him a personal note to Bush, a traditional Arab greeting to his family that would accompany the rather dry and impersonal letter.

Bandar carried the two messages back to Washington, where Bush, Cheney, Powell, and Rice were waiting for him. At the White House, Bandar rode up to the residence with Powell in the private elevator.

"What the fuck are you guys doing?" Powell said once the doors were closed. "You scared the shit out of us."

"Fuck you, we scared the shit out of ourselves," Bandar replied. He knew that Powell was secretly delighted. The Abdullah explosion was just what was needed to prod Bush into action.

After the president read the letters from the king, he said to Bandar, "Well, I guess the crisis is over."

"Mr. President," Bandar quickly interjected, "does that mean you are going to give a speech?"

"Yes, in the United Nations," Bush replied. Powell and Bandar were pleased.

At that moment, however, Dick Cheney intervened. He suggested that Powell give the speech and then the president could endorse it. Bandar's face showed that he considered this a step back.

"You don't seem very hot about this," Bush said.

Bandar trod carefully, not wanting to antagonize Cheney. He said that in Saudi Arabia, the king makes policy speeches and the foreign minister then explains the details.

"I make the fucking policy in this government," Bush said.[16]

Over the next week, the draft of the speech emerged as Powell and Rice collaborated with others. On September 10, a meeting to present the final draft to Bush had to be delayed because of Powell's trip to Peru. Bandar had decided to stay at home and rest that Tuesday. It was September 11.

The attacks against the World Trade Center and the Pentagon and the deaths of nearly three thousand people changed America profoundly. A decade of warning had failed to rouse the country. The Middle East had come ashore with weapons of grand terror whose dimensions should have been imagined, but were not. Bush—like Clinton—had absorbed the briefings about the threat from al-Qaeda but failed to recognize that the impulse for suicidal terrorism was now rampant on the extremist fringe of Islam, that it had been activated by the Afghan campaign, and that some of its most prominent advocates, Osama bin Laden and Ayman al-Zawahiri among them, were inculcating a large group of young radicals, many of them well educated, with the notion that America was the source of injustice in the world.

The roots of Islamic anger that bin Laden and al-Qaeda harnessed tapped a century of grievances across the same landscape that Eisenhower had tried to tame in Nasser's time. The danger of these new cave-dwelling clerics was not that they were intrinsically heroic figures—they were not—but that they were able to channel diverse currents of dissent and rage across a broad hinterland. America was a target because it could be credibly defamed as the aggregation of all the wrongs that came from contact with the West, as a symbol of humiliations (for which America was not really responsible), and as an offender of pious Muslims struggling against the intrusion of modernity. The vast majority of Muslims may have been shocked by bin Laden's act; they may have understood that it would reflect unfavorably on all Muslims. But the blow that was struck was also cheered by Muslim brothers persecuted in Egypt, by embittered Palestinians who had lost homes or sons to Israeli tanks, by Iraqis who suffered under United Nations sanctions, and by Iranians aggrieved by America's support for Saddam.

Osama bin Laden may have been just another beard from the fringe, but his success in striking a blow against the world's greatest power touched a deep chord of satisfaction in that part of the Muslim world that gave way more easily to passion than to reason.

A half century earlier, Eisenhower had looked out across the Middle East and seen that America's war in the postcolonial era would be for the hearts and minds of populations roiling with anger. It was striking how little had changed. America's five decades of international leadership had established Washington as an unrivaled center of power, but because of the failure to secure a comprehensive settlement of the Arab-Israeli dispute, the scars of Lebanon, and the revolutionary anger of Iran, America was the target of blame and, at the same time, the source of hope, the instrument of deliverance.

In the wake of 9/11, however, Americans wanted, most of all, reassurance against attack. Headlines suggested that more suicide bombers might be coming, that the anthrax attacks might be just the beginning, that Chicago's skyscrapers also were a target, and that the detonation of a "dirty" bomb or a small nuclear device in Manhattan was within the realm of possibility.

Shopping malls, football stadiums, mass transit hubs—all of them loomed as targets before a government that was not equipped to protect them from jihadists determined to keep testing the entry portals to the United States or from domestic terrorists whose motives remained a mystery.

Tens of millions of Americans welcomed the appearance of strong and resolute leadership that Bush radiated in those early days. The country seemed willing to accept more invasive security measures at home and demanded a firm response to bring bin Laden and al-Qaeda to justice. Americans looked to Bush to mobilize like-minded nations against the new threat because, as the French paper *Le Monde* had said, "We are all Americans."

George W. Bush may have been the first to understand that out of this catastrophic attack could come the organizing principle of his presidency, because the global terror threat had gone local; it had brought a firestorm, and anthrax, to the streets of New York and Washington. When he started thinking that big—that strategically—it was inevitable that the campaign against the Taliban in Afghanistan would not be enough. That was pounding rocks. Here was an American mission—fighting terror and the states that supported it—that pulled everything together, including Bush's inchoate desire to finish off Saddam Hussein. Phase one against the Taliban, phase two against Iraq, and phase three wherever the war led America, perhaps to Syria or Iran; it would all depend on whether they fell in line.

George W. Bush in the War on Terror: the appearance of strong leadership

Bush briefly called the mission a "crusade"; he seemed oblivious to Muslim sensibilities about armies arriving from the Christian West to rampage through the land of the Prophet. Still, Bush knew what every leader knows: crisis creates opportunity. Statesmanship, decisiveness, and steady nerves carry their own reward. It was not cynical to assert that the massive loss of life impelled Bush to realize that the modest political ambitions with which he had entered the White House—tax cutting and missile defense—could be overwritten in far bolder type. In the wreckage of September 11 lay the opportunity to channel the nation's energy, its fear and anger, into a global campaign of high purpose.

Bush had garnered a mandate like nothing an election could confer. He could finish the job his father had started in Iraq as a necessity for long-term security and, by mobilizing the country for war, he would reap unmistakable political benefits that might more easily propel him into a second term, a goal his father had failed to reach.

. . .

The victory over the Taliban in the fall of 2001 and the routing of al-Qaeda forces at Tora Bora—notwithstanding the escape made by Osama bin Laden—begged the question of where the global war on terrorism would go next.

By early 2002, Bush realized that he needed to start laying the foundation for the broader campaign. In his State of the Union address, he defined the "axis of evil" as Iraq, Iran, and North Korea and accused them of "arming to threaten the peace of the world."

"I will not wait on events while dangers gather," Bush said. Secretly, he had put war planning for an Iraqi campaign in motion and had signed a presidential order that the administration was seeking "regime change" in Iraq.

And Bush did not wait. Through the summer and fall of 2002, Bush, along with Tony Blair, his principal ally, unveiled new concepts of preemptive war that each said was necessary in a new age of terror, and they issued intelligence estimates that warned of imminent dangers of Saddam Hussein and his arsenal of unconventional weapons.

In the White House and Justice Department, Bush, Cheney, and their legal advisers secretly promulgated new presidential powers to seize suspected terrorists, to hold and interrogate them (using means that many would later call torture) in secret prisons, and to intercept communications suspected as terror related, without the long-established judicial reviews that had been set for just such national security requirements. They exempted themselves from political accountability by arguing that the president's authority as commander in chief demanded broad latitude in suspending legislative or judicial review in wartime.

The Palestinian project was jettisoned, despite Saudi anger. Arafat's headquarters in Ramallah was surrounded by Sharon's tanks. In the face of further acts of horrific suicide bombing, Israel's security establishment debated whether to expel Arafat and destroy what was left of the Palestinian Authority. In June 2002, Bush suspended any American consideration of returning to the negotiating table or of putting pressure on Sharon.

Sharon, Bush said, was a man of peace.

Instead, the president said the Palestinians needed new leaders. Arafat would have to go, terrorism would have to end, and democracy would have to prevail. If the Palestinians did all that, he could see them getting a state in three years.[17] Sharon was silent, because he knew it would never happen. Privately, Bush told Jordan's King Abdullah (King Hussein had died in 1999) that Arafat was "a loser" and added, "I'm not going to spend my political capital on losers, only winners. I'm still in a war mode, and the war is terrorism. If people don't fight terrorism, I'm not going to deal with them."[18]

Bush then turned to resolving the dilemma over how to take the country to war against Iraq. The role of the United Nations was going to be a critical factor in determining how the world regarded any American action. Blair and Powell argued that if Bush wanted allies in a military campaign to invade Iraq and topple Saddam Hussein, the allies would need a covering UN resolution.

Bush accepted Powell's argument—over Cheney's, which was to go it alone. America, Powell argued, should challenge the United Nations to live up to the expectations of its founders by declaring Saddam Hussein in violation of UN resolutions and by giving him one more chance to give a full and final accounting of his weapons of mass destruction.

"We have been more than patient," Bush told the General Assembly on September 12, 2002. "The conduct of the Iraqi regime is a threat to the authority of the United Nations, and a threat to peace."

Bush's tone was lecturing. He made unflattering allusions to the League of Nations and implied that if the United Nations did not move quickly and resolutely to enforce its authority in the world, America would fill the vacuum. "The purposes of the United States should not be doubted. The Security Council resolutions will be enforced . . . and the regime that has lost its legitimacy will also lose its power."

Bush seemed to relish hectoring the institution that his father had served and that had sanctioned his father's coalition to remove Saddam Hussein from Kuwait. There was a tone of scorn for for those who counseled patient diplomacy. To anyone watching the speech, it was a marvel that Bush considered his performance as a unifying act, or as a contribution to the work of winning hearts and minds. His condescension engendered wooden expressions and muted applause among the General Assembly delegates. But Bush called his speechwriter, Michael Gerson, afterward and said, "I *really* liked giving that speech."[19] He felt he had done the international body a favor.

For Powell, too, the speech was a victory. America had assumed its leadership role at the United Nations. Powell led the diplomatic negotiations to produce the strongest possible resolution, believing that if Saddam *did* open all doors to satisfy UN inspectors—and if no weapons were found—then Bush would take the last "off-ramp" and avoid war.

The unanimous vote of the Security Council on November 8, 2002, was a milestone of unity that papered over the French and German resistance—they wanted no "automaticity" about going to war without a second, authorizing resolution. Over the next sixty days, however, Bush abandoned the consensual approach. Military planning required that an invasion get under way in March or await the return of cool weather in the autumn. The watchword in the White House was "marketing," how to package the decision to go to war for the public. That's where Tenet had weighed in with his flawed intelligence estimate—as flawed as the one Blair had foisted on the British public—and with talk of a "slam dunk" presentation that Powell, to his everlasting regret, delivered before the UN Security Council on February 5, 2003. Hans Blix, the Swedish diplomat in charge of the UN inspection team, had found no stockpiles of weapons; he needed a few months, he said, to complete his mission. But the military schedule took precedence, despite the opposition of Europe's major powers.

The American invasion of Iraq in March 2003 was a model of military efficiency that forced Saddam to go into hiding by early April. The gratitude of the Iraqis was apparent in many parts of the country. The idealism of the officers and soldiers conducting the American and British enterprise gave the world a remarkable vision of hope following decades of brutal dictatorship under Saddam Hussein.

But the telltale signs of catastrophe were also soon apparent. The American army had not planned on meeting an army of looters. A terrible lawlessness unfolded before American and British forces that were massively underequipped and understaffed to reestablish law and order or the functions of government. Saddam had opened his prisons six months before the invasion to free tens of thousands of criminals, and they were soon busy destroying the institutions of government and stripping them bare.

The travesty of the Bush approach to the Iraq war was his failure to make any commitment to a postwar model. His administration became a debating society among rivals. Some wanted to turn power over immediately to a provisional government headed by Kurdish leaders, Shiite religious officials, and secular figures such as Ahmad Chalabi and Iyad

Allawi. Others wanted to give command to an American occupation czar, a MacArthur who could control, or at least shape, the destiny of the new Iraq with White House supervision.

One model required a minimal commitment of managing refugees and relief supplies before turning the country over to provisional leaders. The other model required extensive planning, expertise, and a force at least twice the size of the 130,000 troops that raced from Kuwait to Baghdad.

Bush could blame no one but himself for the breakdown of order, the failure of planning, and the incompetence of American postwar management. He had not asked tough questions, he had hoarded the decision to go to war, and he had failed to settle on a single concept for the occupation: short duration with rapid turnover to the Iraqis, or long duration with heavy American intervention. He sent an army equipped for the first and then overrode his generals and opted for the second.

In surrendering to an instinct to control Iraq after it was shorn of its strongman, Bush did not see that he was setting America up to lose the postwar struggle for security and order, and that stripping away Saddam's totalitarian control would lead eventually to the delamination of Iraqi society, the very thing that James Baker had warned of a decade earlier.[20] America had not come equipped for a long and intensive occupation. Retired general Jay Garner, the first administrator of postwar Iraq, arrived with a few dozen interpreters, borrowed diplomats, and virtually no budget to run a country. He believed he would be turning things over to a provisional Iraqi government and said so. Instead, Garner himself was replaced.

In May 2003, Iraq was turned over to L. Paul Bremer III, an excessively self-confident Washington bureaucrat and a longtime protégé of Henry Kissinger. During an interview that summer, Bremer told me that the extent of his knowledge about Iraq, its history, and Saddam's long rule had been gathered in ten days of reading after accepting the presidential assignment. Bremer's first and most ill-considered act was to insist that Bush withdraw Zalmay Khalilzad, the only envoy the president had in Iraq with long experience in working with the Iraqi opposition.

As a correspondent for *The New York Times*, I was sitting in the hall when Bremer mounted the stage at the Baghdad convention center and, with a flourish, disbanded the Iraqi army, the one national institution that blended Iraq's sectarian diversity into a disciplined and patriotic corps. Bremer also issued a de-Baathification decree that was so broad as to disqualify tens of thousands of teachers, police officers, engineers, and

other vital civil servants. Bremer to this day defends these initial decisions,[21] even the cashiering of army men with no means to feed their
families and who possessed the kind of martial skills—bomb making and
ambush—that could wreak havoc in postwar Iraq.

Hubris clung to Bremer like vicuña to a vamp. His appointment just
compounded all of the errors that Bush had made. I remember thinking
that his triumphalism was out of sync with reality outside the Green
Zone, where Bremer lived in isolation from the latent power of Iraqi nationalism. Bremer's Green Zone was attached to Washington, not to Iraq.
He exuded political ambition in his approach to every event and public
statement. Bush had given him a job where success could easily catapult
Bremer to a cabinet-level post. In those press conferences, he spoke like
a man who was running for office.

John Limbert, the American ambassador to Mauritania, a Farsi speaker
who had been among the American hostages held in Tehran during
the Carter years, was pulled from his post in Africa to join the team
in Baghdad and saw what many of his colleagues saw at the outset.
"We knew it was going to be a disaster," he said. "We were simply not
prepared."[22]

Rulers had been toppled in Iraq in the past without triggering general
mayhem. Bush's failure to accomplish the task in 2003–08 stemmed
from the conceptual failure at the top, an unwillingness or incapacity to
impose a single vision among his national security advisers, and then to
galvanize the bureaucratic resources of the government to work the problem in detail. Bush prides himself on management skill as a graduate of
Harvard Business School. Yet he failed to imagine that he would need a
strategic concept—provisional government or lengthy occupation—and
a requisite business plan to support it.

He is not a detail man, and it is this weakness that was most observ-
able in other facets of foreign and domestic policy, from his handling of
the Darfur crisis in Sudan to Hurricane Katrina at home.

Bush, Defense Secretary Donald Rumsfeld, who was Bremer's immediate supervisor, and Bremer himself failed to see the wave of rebellion
that rose out of the Iraqi populace and was soon magnified by the ingath-
ering of Muslim jihadists from across the region. This was where Bush's
naïveté about the Middle East failed him most profoundly. The depth
and power of the Sunni insurgency shocked and paralyzed an administration that spent a year listening to Bremer and to military commanders

who had compromised themselves by buying into recommendations calling for a minimum force to secure the country.

The American public had never imagined a war whose price tag would climb into the hundreds of billions and leave thousands of American soldiers dead and thousands more maimed or seriously injured. In the end, the war could not meet any realistic standard as just or necessary. And who would take responsibility for how the war had deepened the American predicament in the Middle East?

It still seemed possible that the end of Saddam's blood-soaked reign in Mesopotamia could lead to a positive outcome. The war may have been a babel of mismanagement, but, for the Iraqis, the gradual return of security and a functioning government could still lead to a new stability. That would be an accomplishment, though at the cost of great suffering. For the first time in the modern era, a moderate regime dominated by Arab Shiites in a new and fragile national bargain with Sunnis and Kurds was struggling to emerge and to dedicate itself to the pursuit of tolerant rule and economic prosperity for a battered but still robust population.

The strong democratic impulse among the Iraqis to rebuild their state was evident in the 2005 election, where images of long lines at polling stations and purple fingers raised in national pride had a deep impact in the West. Americans played a part in this—some of them died for it and many remained dedicated to honoring the incalculable investment made by a new generation of young and idealistic Americans, and many more Iraqis.

The war may have been an unnecessary catastrophe enabled by incompetent intelligence analysis, cynical politics, and prodigious blundering, but history would not mourn the passing of one of its most brutal tyrants. Since the end of the Persian Gulf War in 1991, a strong bipartisan consensus had developed that if there was an opportunity to finish Saddam off, America and its allies should take it. But the Iraq war of 2003 was a forced and fraudulent act of militarism that weakened America's moral profile.

But admitting error is not a Bush family trait.

George H. W. Bush had sent thousands of Shiites to their death, by encouraging the uprisings at the end of the 1991 war and he never had the decency—and he is a decent man—to acknowledge his error. He had had no intention of backing their rebellion, but he should have apologized for the devastating consequences of his incitement.

America sent its sons and daughters to Iraq on a pretext, but the vast

majority of them acquitted themselves honorably. Many showed great in-
genuity in the face of adversity: generals saw the need for gasoline, so
they trucked it in from Kuwait; civil affairs officers from National Guard
units repaired roads and bridges, got water plants up and running, helped
find generators for hospitals, and cleared rubble to get schools, streets,
and markets open.

For anyone who had lived through the Vietnam experience, it is heart-
ening to witness how intensely Americans support the highly motivated
American soldiers—thousands of whom left professional careers as part
of the National Guard call-ups—who tried to make a difference in Iraq.
Their sacrifice is selfless and sincere, and the inherent desire to honor
their service moderates opposition to and frustration over the war.

In his final two years in office, as Bush struggled with Iraq and considered whether to strike at Iran, influential voices were framing a new paradigm of global conflict that threatened to extend Bush's militarism into
a new administration.

One of them was Professor Bernard Lewis of Princeton University,
who warned in early 2007 that there were "signs of a return among Muslims to what they perceive as the cosmic struggle for world domination
between the two main faiths—Christianity and Islam.

"There are many religions in the world," Lewis told an American Enterprise Institute audience that included Dick Cheney, "but as far as I
know there are only two that have claimed that their truths are not only
universal—all religions claim that—but also exclusive; that they—the
Christians in the one case, the Muslims in the other—are the fortunate
recipients of God's final message to humanity, which it is their duty not
to keep selfishly to themselves—like the Jews or the Hindus—but to bring
to the rest of humanity, removing whatever obstacles there may be on
the way.

"This self-perception, shared between Christendom and Islam, led to
the long struggle that has been going on for more than fourteen centuries
and which is now entering a new phase."[23]

Lewis was certainly the most prominent academic to suggest that Islamic revivalism held the potential to threaten the West in a manner that
might be compared to the rise of fascism or communism during the last
century. Many Muslims were offended by the assertion that militant extremism represents a mainstream trend in the Islamic world. It clearly
does not, even though the five-year American and British campaign in
Iraq has fueled an intense reaction from Islamic militants worldwide.

Nevertheless, many mainstream Muslim leaders, even the royalists and autocrats, were searching for a progressive way forward, one that emphasized stability, security, and economic fulfillment, one that created space for Islamic revival without rejecting modernity or secularism. And some were experimenting with democratic institutions as they imprisoned or persecuted internal opponents to their rule.

Both Bush and Rice, who became his secretary of state in 2005, presented themselves as ardent and well-intentioned advocates for democracy in the Middle East, setting for themselves a task for which neither was well prepared, well educated, or well served by ideologically driven aides. In 2006, Douglas Hurd, the foreign secretary to Prime Minister Margaret Thatcher, acidly rebuked the Bush-Rice approach, lecturing them that the path to democracy "must grow from the roots of its own society and that the killing of thousands of people, many of them innocent, is unacceptable whether committed by a domestic tyrant, or for a good cause."[24]

Nothing seemed more indicative of the know-nothing approach of the Bush years than to see Rice careering around the region puffing herself up with high-sounding rhetoric—"It is time to abandon the excuses that are made to avoid the hard work of democracy"—when the administration had avoided hard work across the board.

In Lebanon, after the February 2005 assassination of Prime Minister Rafik Hariri, a window had opened for the United States to join with France, Lebanon's historical patron, to put the country back on a stable footing. The Cedar Revolution forced Syria to withdraw its occupation army and put Bashar al-Assad on the defensive. But Bush was powerless to galvanize America's natural allies for a larger task in Lebanon.[25] Instead, when Hezbollah stepped up as spoiler, ambushing and kidnapping Israeli soldiers on the border in 2006, Bush again lost control of events. In another great tragedy, Israel devastated Lebanon that summer with airpower and ground invasion, killing more than one thousand Lebanese civilians and destroying bridges, airports, hospitals—all manner of civilian infrastructure—in what could be viewed only as a war of collective punishment.[26]

Hezbollah fought back with surprising ferocity, firing thousands of rockets into Israel, killing 160 people and setting off an exodus of civilians from the border region. In the face of it, American leadership stood mute; Bush lacked a humanistic response to the suffering or the will to insist on a cease-fire. There is no evidence that Bush and Ehud Olmert, who had become prime minister after a stroke felled Sharon, even spoke to each other as Israeli forces ravaged Lebanon. America had forfeited its role as the indispensable and trusted broker of Middle East peace.

It wasn't that Israel acted without justification in defending itself from Hezbollah's attacks; no state can tolerate incessant violence directed across borders uncontrolled by a neighboring government. But what state of international relations had come to pass in which anarchic Hobbesian forces ruled? The United States—and the United Nations it had helped to create—had slid back down the slippery slope to the tolerance of brute force, even collective punishment. What had happened to the spirit of the Tripartite Declaration that enjoined the great powers to act in concert to prevent conflict and protect vulnerable populations, Israeli or Arab?

As Douglas Hurd had said just a few months earlier, in hopes that Rice would take the message home, the world works only if the great powers, including the superpowers and regional powers, are bound by the same rules as everyone else. Was Israel's only recourse following the kidnapping of two Israeli soldiers a full-scale invasion that killed so many and devastated Lebanon?[27] Was the international system erected after World War II completely bankrupt in the Middle East?

By late 2006, Bush's misjudgments in Iraq, and the growing insurgency that was lacerating the American occupation army, brought to a head a political debate that led to the chastening of his leadership. Democrats reclaimed Congress in the midterm elections and Bush faced the uncomfortable reality that his final two years would require a battle for history.

Senator Harry Reid, the Senate Democratic leader, declared the war "lost," and Bush, on the recommendation of General Daniel Petraeus, responded by dispatching a "surge" force of thirty thousand troops to employ counterinsurgency techniques—to "clear, hold and build" security street by street—to restore stability in Baghdad and then perhaps in the rest of the country. The question that consumed the White House was whether Iraq had been saved, or whether a staged withdrawal would allow—or force—the Iraqis to implement the compromises they had reached for a unified national government.

Though Americans had tired of the war, many still hoped for some measure of success, if only to validate the sacrifice so many had made. It was no longer a question of Bush only. The flaws in his leadership and the weaknesses of his administration were manifest. It was a question of America's mission in the Middle East and the world.

. . .

In September 2006, Tony Blair and Prince Bandar urged Bush to dedicate the last two years of his presidency to achieving Palestinian statehood on a specific timetable.[28] Blair would help convince Europe to back the proposal and Saudi Arabia would mobilize the Arabs. A paragraph setting out a specific timetable for Palestinian statehood was drafted for Bush's speech to the United Nations. Bandar, who made a series of clandestine visits to the White House that summer, made a personal appeal to Bush using a mixture of humor and realism. Bush would still be a young man when he left the White House. The war in Iraq had made him one of the least popular chief executives in a generation.

"Do you ever want to leave that ranch?" Bandar had asked him in jest, but it was not a joke. Bush could end up a pariah of American politics, much like Johnson after Vietnam, or Richard Nixon after Watergate. But if he fulfilled the promise of Palestinian statehood—peace between the Arabs and the Israelis—such a prize could bolster Bush's unenviable legacy. Bush must have recognized how much this formulation echoed Bill Clinton's final days. Moreover, Bandar argued, if Bush was seriously considering a military option to destroy Iran's nuclear industry before it could produce atomic weapons, as Bandar believed he was, the only way to prepare international public opinion was to get heavily engaged in the Middle East peace process. (One of the most sensitive projects Bandar was pursuing at that time was to try to convince George W. Bush to extend a Western nuclear umbrella over Saudi Arabia and other moderate Arab states that feared the advent of a nuclear-armed Iran. Russian president Vladimir Putin made a sensitive and secret proposal to King Abdullah in 2006, offering nuclear cooperation with Saudi Arabia, "including in the military field," according to one of his aides.

Two weeks before the United Nations speech, Bandar slipped into Washington one more time to see Bush, and he was disappointed to hear that the answer was no. Bush would make no commitment to a specific timetable for Palestinian statehood. He would merely reiterate his position: "I'm committed to two democratic states—Israel and Palestine—living side-by-side in peace and security." Without a plan or a timetable, what did it mean?[29]

Just as when he stood before the General Assembly that September in 2006, Bush seemed unable to grasp the contradictions of history, in which a democratic current in the Palestinian territories had brought Hamas, the Islamic extremist party, to power on a platform of ending corruption and improving the lives of the Palestinians while militantly confronting the Israeli occupation.

"Some have argued that the democratic changes we're seeing in the Middle East are destabilizing the region," Bush had told the UN delegates. "This argument rests on a false assumption: that the Middle East was stable to begin with. The reality is that the stability we thought we saw in the Middle East was a mirage. For decades, millions of men and women in the region have been trapped in oppression and hopelessness. And these conditions left a generation disillusioned and made this region a breeding ground for extremism."

Speaking to those "extremists in [their] midst" who "spread propaganda claiming that the West is engaged in a war against Islam," Bush added, "This propaganda is false, and its purpose is to confuse you and justify acts of terror. We respect Islam, but we will protect our people from those who pervert Islam to sow death and destruction."

With this jumbled view of history, Bush suggested that his interventions in the Middle East, though they had calamitous consequences and had intensified Islamic extremism, had left things no worse than if he had taken no action at all.

By the end of his presidency, Bush's tenure appeared as a cynical opting out of the labor-intensive Middle East peace process. He had done so little to act on the principles he espoused from the outset of his administration. He had said in 2002 that a Palestinian state could be established in three years, but what had he done, what risk had he taken, as his predecessors had, to try to make it happen? Certainly, the desultory peace conference staged five years later in Annapolis could not stand as a credible American initiative, since Bush avoided tabling any framework for statehood, or setting the mechanism for sustained negotiation under a schedule that would bring pressure to bear on all parties.

Had Bush set the goal of Palestinian statehood on the fixed timeline that Tony Blair and others had urged, the momentum toward peace might have been strong enough to sweep Hamas onto the same path of negotiations promoted by Arafat's successor, Mahmoud Abbas. Instead, without a political horizon, and with encouragement and funding from Iran, Hamas responded by letting loose a fusillade of rocket attacks on Israeli towns adjoining the Gaza Strip. And Israel retaliated with more targeted killings and helicopter assaults that raised the death toll in the pressure cooker of the refugee camps cordoned off by Ariel Sharon. He then pulled the Israeli army out of Gaza under his disengagement plan.

The path of negotiation is still where the majority of Palestinians want to be, despite their attraction to the Islamic party, because they see negotiation as the best chance to secure their Palestinian state, end the long occupation, and build a new sovereign entity in the Middle East, capable of living side by side, in peace, with Israel. But the human impulse to compromise, to talk with one's enemy, is quickly perverted in a cycle of violence and in the absence of strong and principled intervention by a trusted mediator.

Bush seemed destined to leave the matter in violent stasis. His legacy in the Middle East would be defined as much by the forsaken mantle as by the blunder of an unnecessary war. Why Bush declined to take risks for peace in the Middle East would be the subject of lengthy reexaminations, unaffected by his own self-justifications—as a fighter against terror and a champion of freedom—for that was the Bush solipsism. From his lame-duck pulpit, Bush advocated a two-state solution in the Holy Land; he allowed Rice to practice the same Flying Dutchman diplomacy that had been practiced by Colin Powell while Bush, unceasingly, escalated American rhetoric to define Iran as an overarching American enemy in the region and began preparing American allies, with new weapons sales, for war.

A new military confrontation was building in the Middle East, one concealed by the global economic crisis of 2008. Bush had laid the groundwork for military action against Iran if diplomacy failed. The next president was left little room to maneuver.

In September 2007, Israeli warplanes bombed a nuclear reactor under construction at a clandestine site in the Syrian desert, opening a new chapter in the nonproliferation struggle in the Middle East over the control of nuclear weapons technology, and it seemed possible that the White House had not abandoned a determination to orchestrate a follow-on confrontation with Iran.

In April 2008, seven months after the Israeli raid, the White House gave a detailed briefing to Congress, using an impressive CIA-produced video released to the public, to lay out the intelligence case against Syria. The briefing included damning photos from the interior of the North Korean-designed reactor building, showing unmistakably that it was near completion, all to support the attack as a justified intervention to prevent Syria from producing a nuclear weapon.

I was in Israel at the time of this briefing and observed how the news of it swept across the Middle East. During an interview, a senior Israeli intelligence official pointed out to me that there was very little outcry in the international community over the raid. He suggested that this could be taken as a form of approval, since the moderate Arab states would fear a nuclear-armed Syria almost as much as they feared a nuclear-armed Iran, Syria's ally. This official suggested that the Israeli attack had established a precedent for action, and for how the world might react if Israel or the United States, or both countries together, mounted a similar attack on Iran to destroy its nuclear facilities that are enriching uranium, which could be used to fabricate an Iranian nuclear weapon (despite Iran's assurances that it is not pursuing a nuclear weapons capability).

He said that for Israel, such an attack faced "insurmountable obstacles" unless it was conducted with American participation. When Bush visited Israel the following month, many analysts took note of an authoritative news report stating that a senior member of Bush's party had told the Israeli prime minister, Ehud Olmert, that Bush intended to destroy Iran's nuclear complex before he left office. The White House denied the report, but Bush, in his speech to the Israeli Knesset on the sixtieth anniversary of the Jewish state's founding, signaled a muscular resolve that seemed telling.

"America stands with you in firmly opposing Iran's nuclear-weapons ambitions. Permitting the world's leading sponsor of terror to possess the world's deadliest weapon would be an unforgivable betrayal of future generations. For the sake of peace, the world must not allow Iran to have a nuclear weapon." This was the legacy that seemed more compelling to Bush—striking a blow to prevent a nuclear Iran. (In July 2008, Israel conducted a military exercise to simulate an attack on Iran's nuclear complex. Iran responded by test firing ballistic missiles capable of striking Israel.)

Bush's comments and the bombing raid on Syria's nuclear reactor made me think of Eisenhower, and I said as much to several Israeli officials. The covert Syrian reactor was an example of nuclear proliferation that cried out for an international response. The intelligence case was powerful and seemingly irrefutable. Why had the White House, which reviewed the intelligence before Israel struck, failed to present the evidence to the United Nations Security Council and set a tight deadline for Syria to dismantle the reactor or face military action? The United States and Israel, faced with Syria's illicit act, could have constructively presented a declaration of their findings in a manner that would have contributed to the rebuilding of the multilateral institutions that enforce the Nuclear Non-Proliferation Treaty. If the UN failed to respond in a timely and vigorous manner, the military option could still have been exercised. As events unfolded, Bush asserted he was still committed to diplomatic options in dealing with Iran while condoning an abrupt military attack on Syria.

Both Israel and the United States have become strong critics of the United Nations as a mediator, peacekeeper, nuclear watchdog, and enforcer of its charter in the Middle East, but it is easy to forget that the United States—under Roosevelt, Truman, and Eisenhower—was at the forefront of creating and building the UN as an instrument of war prevention, joint action, and international law. To undermine the international system—now a strong impulse in American politics—is to revert to the Hobbesian model of unilateral force driven inevitably at times by domestic politics or narrow national interests. Of course Israel has a right to defend itself, and America stands committed to reinforce that defense, but for America and Israel to act, or appear to act, in concert to enforce an unstated policy of nuclear exclusivity in the Middle East will do little over time to deter continuing efforts by Arab and Muslim states (Pakistan was the first) to obtain their own nuclear deterrent. This was the nightmare that Eisenhower and Kennedy foresaw.

It would take an American president more perceptive than Bush to complete the peace agenda and to begin the arduous task of rebuilding American leadership.

America's destiny in international relations is to play the role of a just, magnanimous, and stabilizing power. Its failure to live up to these standards in the war of perceptions among the peoples of the Middle East may well determine the level of global stability for much of the century that stands before us. And within this struggle, it will also be America's destiny to take powerful and intrusive positions—both diplomatic and military—not only because oil resources of the Middle East remain critical to the energy future of industrial economies, but also because Islamic extremism has staked out an ideological challenge whose momentum cannot be ignored.

Islamic extremism beckons young Muslims to a triumphal past and a separation from the West and much of modernity. Imagine China, in the midst of its juggernaut to global economic leadership, swooning to the siren's call of its imperial past. The call of history is a powerful tool of demagoguery. Any self-interested foreign policy could not neglect this danger. Thus prudence, the constant gardener of diplomacy, must set an example of tolerance and accommodation while opposing violence and repression. The West must make greater accommodation as Islamic revivalism seeks a level of assimilation while holding on to traditions.

On the night in June 1989 that Ayatollah Khomeini died, I had an encounter with an Iranian Revolutionary Guard. I was the only Western correspondent in Tehran, and this fierce young man used the barrel of his AK-47 to tap on my car window at a roadblock. I slowly rolled down the window to face the muzzle and to gaze up into his serious and bearded face. He stooped to draw close and asked in halting English, "Excuse me, sir, but if you were going to select the best American university to study electrical engineering, which one would you choose?"

It is easy to forget the struggle for hearts and minds and the relentless shifts of generations that follow the great turns of history. One thing is certain: Muslim youth yearns for the same personal fulfillment and opportunity as youth everywhere. They seek the same advancement in culture, science, and technology that market capitalism can deliver to peoples who have been held back by dictators and the orthodoxies of the old world.

Ideally, for generations of young Muslims, it will not take long to see the fallacy of Islamic imperialism. But for better or worse, we live in the world as it is, and our best hope to avoid war, expand liberty, and enable prosperity is to project, from the highest political authority, our ideals, our tolerance, and our willingness for taking risks.

# NOTES

# ACKNOWLEDGMENTS

# INDEX

# NOTES

## Prologue: America in the Middle East

1. Tenet, in an interview, emphatically denied making the comment.
2. Saddam was captured in December 2003 and reportedly made this statement to FBI interrogator George Piro. See George Tenet with Bill Harlow, *At the Center of the Storm: My Years at the CIA* (New York: Harper, 2007), p. 332. In an interview, Tenet said that Charles Duelfer, who succeeded David Kay as head of the Iraq Survey Group, was the source of this report about Saddam's interrogation.
3. Tenet made the remark during a meeting in December 2002 when the CIA briefed Bush, Cheney, Rice, and Powell on the evidence they could lay before the public to help with "marketing" a decision to go to war. The context in which Tenet used the term "slam dunk" was contested after it appeared in Bob Woodward's 2004 (*Plan of Attack*) reconstruction of Bush's decision to go to war. In 2007, Tenet argued that he made the remark in passing when discussing how to prepare the public by presenting the best intelligence. Woodward later suggested, in a review of Tenet's memoir, that by December 2002 the president had not made up his mind to go to war and therefore Tenet's "slam dunk" assertion was highly influential. Tenet argued that the decision to go to war had effectively been made by Bush and Cheney months earlier and, therefore, the "case" for war was a matter of marketing. In the end, Tenet admitted to a flawed intelligence process but sought to excuse himself and the CIA by pointing to evidence that Bush was hell-bent on going to war in any case.
4. L. Paul Bremer III with Malcolm McConnell, *My Year in Iraq: The Struggle to Build a Future of Hope* (New York: Simon & Schuster, 2006), p. 209.
5. On February 5, 2008, CIA director Michael Hayden stated publicly before the Senate Intelligence Committee that the agency had employed waterboarding during the interrogation of three al-Qaeda detainees in 2002–2003: Khalid Sheikh Mohammed, Abu Zubaida, and Abd al-Rahim al-Nashiri. "There was the belief that additional catastrophic attacks against the homeland were inevitable," Hayden said in defending the use of this technique, which many regarded as torture.
6. Author interview with an official who was present when Bush made the remarks. A written request to President Bush to comment on these conversations and on his point of view with regard to the secret interrogation program was presented to his spokesman, Tony Snow, and to White House counsel Fred Fielding in August 2007. Neither official responded.
7. The question of torture, and of America's role in practicing and condoning it, became a polarizing issue in the 2008 presidential election campaign from the moment that John McCain stood up, alone, among Republican candidates at a May 2007 debate in South Carolina and opposed it. Speaking with the

moral authority of a former prisoner of war in Vietnam, McCain said, "We could never gain as much from that torture as we lose in world opinion." He spoke after Tenet had published a memoir defending the interrogation program, asserting that it had saved lives. Rudy Giuliani, the former mayor of New York, endorsed the techniques, saying he would tell interrogators to use "every method they could think of" to extract information from suspects believed to harbor knowledge of impending attacks. "It's not about the terrorists, it's about us," McCain said softly. "It's about what kind of country we are."

8. For Powell's view of Middle East peace, see his speech on November 19, 2001, at the University of Louisville: "The United States Position on Terrorists and Peace in the Middle East"; also Karen DeYoung, *Soldier: The Life of Colin Powell* (New York: Knopf, 2006), pp. 354–57. For Tenet's view, see Tenet, *At the Center of the Storm*, pp. 491–92.

9. Nixon, in his first months in office, created a small group of senior aides to examine the intelligence on the Israeli nuclear weapons program and to develop a U.S. response. Henry Kissinger reported to Nixon in July 1969 that Israel would have a force of at least ten nuclear-tipped ballistic missiles by 1970. The group, he said, was divided both on tactics in dealing with Israel and on what assurances to seek. Some aides wanted to hold up delivery of F-4 Phantoms, due for delivery in September 1969. Nixon, however, abandoned any attempt to use the available leverage to prevent the expected deployment of the first Israeli nuclear warheads on missiles that Israel had purchased from France. See Memorandum for the President from Henry A. Kissinger, "Israeli Nuclear Program," National Archives, National Security Council (NSC) Files, Country Files, Middle East. This memorandum was not declassified until November 2007.

## 1. The Arab Awakening: Eisenhower, Nasser, and Suez

1. Memorandum of Conversation, October 28, 1956, Foreign Relations of the United States (FRUS), 1955–1957—Suez Crisis, July 26–December 31, 1956, vol. XVI, pp. 808–10.

2. Abba Eban, *An Autobiography* (New York: Random House, 1977), p. 126.

3. Britain had also promised, in the Sykes-Picot Agreement of 1916, to divide up the crumbling Ottoman Empire by granting French influence over modern Lebanon and Syria and British influence over Mesopotamia, the Jordan Valley, and the Holy Land in the Ottoman Province of Palestine. The following year, Britain also promised Zionist leaders in the Balfour Declaration that it would work for the "establishment in Palestine of a national home for the Jewish people."

4. King Abdullah was assassinated on the steps of the al-Aqsa mosque in 1951, an event that his horrified sixteen-year-old grandson and successor, King Hussein, witnessed.

5. FRUS, 1955–1957, vol. XVI, p. 289.

6. Dulles told Eisenhower on October 15 that the Israelis might be considering such a move due to the "concatenation of several circumstances": (1) the virtual collapse of Jordan; (2) distraction of Egypt in the confrontation with Britain and France over the canal; and (3) the presidential election in the United States. Ibid., pp. 722–23.

7. Abba Eban, *Personal Witness* (New York: Putnam, 1992), p. 256.

8.   Steven L. Spiegel, *The Other Arab-Israeli Conflict: Making America's Middle East Policy from Truman to Reagan* (Chicago: University of Chicago Press, l985), p. 51; Abraham Ben-Zvi, *Decade of Transition: Eisenhower, Kennedy, and the Origins of the American-Israeli Alliance* (New York: Columbia University Press, 1998), p. 63.

9.   Dean Acheson, Truman's secretary of state and close friend of Supreme Court justices Louis Brandeis and Felix Frankfurter, both ardent Zionist leaders in the United States, expressed the intellectual opposition to the creation of a Jewish state in a manner that has echoed through the foreign policy establishment ever since. He argued that "to transform the country into a Jewish state capable of receiving a million or more immigrants would vastly exacerbate the political problem and imperil not only American but all Western interests in the Near East." From Brandeis and Frankfurter, Acheson said, he had learned to understand, "but not to share, the mystical emotion of the Jews to return to Palestine and end the Diaspora. In urging Zionism as an American government policy they had allowed, so I thought, their emotion to obscure the totality of American interests." Dean Acheson, *Present at the Creation: My Years in the State Department* (New York: Norton, 1969), p. 169.

10.   Eban, *Autobiography*, p. 186.

11.   Stephen E. Ambrose, *Eisenhower* (New York: Simon & Schuster, 1990), pp. 421, 424.

12.   FRUS, 1955–1957, vol. XVI, pp. 835–36.

13.   In a stirring precursor to the era of human rights monitoring, the British historian Arnold Toynbee in 1961 engaged Yaacov Herzog, the Israeli diplomat and adviser to prime ministers, in a debate on the question of the morality of war and occupation, particularly Israel's treatment of Palestinian Arabs. Toynbee approached the subject by recalling the British bombing of civilian targets in Egypt during the aborted Suez campaign as a morally reprehensible act. Because Britons had been mercilessly bombed by Germany in World War II, Toynbee argued that "what is really tragic is that people who have suffered a thing and had experience of it should inflict that suffering on other people." He drew a parallel with Jewish suffering in Europe and what the Jewish state had then inflicted on Palestinians. See Yaacov Herzog, *A People That Dwells Alone: Speeches & Writing* (London: Weidenfeld and Nicolson, 1975), p. 26.

14.   The declaration was the first major postwar statement on a common Middle East policy. On May 25, 1950, the United States, Britain, and France agreed that they would work to prevent aggression and arms sales in the Middle East. The powers opposed "the use of force or threat of force between any of the states in that area." Most important, "The three governments, should they find that any of these states was preparing to violate frontiers or armistice lines, would, consistent with their obligations as members of the United Nations, immediately take action, both within and outside the United Nations, to prevent such violation."

15.   Michael Bar-Zohar, *Ben-Gurion: A Biography* (New York: Delacorte, 1977), p. 274.

16.   Moshe Sharett, *Personal Diaries*, ed. Yaacov Sharett [Hebrew] (Tel Aviv: Maariv, 1978); interview with Yaacov Sharett, October 17, 2006 (conducted by Omri Sender, research assistant).

17.  Bar-Zohar, *Ben-Gurion*, p. 236.

18.  Moshe Dayan, *Moshe Dayan: Story of My Life* (New York: Morrow, 1976), pp. 174–76.

19.  Herzog, *A People That Dwells Alone*, p. 177.

20.  Speech to the House of Lords, Lords' *Hansard*, vol. 54, col. 669, cited in Harold Wilson, *The Chariot of Israel: Britain, America and the State of Israel* (New York: Norton, 1981), p. 65.

21.  Wilson, *Chariot of Israel*, p. 51.

22.  Estimates of the death toll ranged from 100 to 254. See Benny Morris, *Righteous Victims: A History of the Zionist-Arab Conflict, 1881–2001* (New York: Vintage Books, 2001), p. 208.

23.  Benny Morris, *Israel's Border Wars, 1949–1956* (New York: Oxford University Press, 1993), pp. 379–80.

24.  Richard B. Parker, ed., *The Six Day War: A Retrospective* (Gainesville: University Press of Florida, 1996), p. 275.

25.  Jean Lacouture, *Nasser: A Biography*, trans. Daniel Hofstadter (New York: Knopf, 1973), p. 86.

26.  Anthony Nutting, *Nasser* (New York: Dutton, 1972), p. 7.

27.  Nigel John Ashton, *Eisenhower, Macmillan, and the Problem of Nasser: Anglo-American Relations and Arab Nationalism, 1955–59* (New York: Macmillan, 1996), p. 13; Chester L. Cooper, *The Lion's Last Roar: Suez, 1956* (New York: Harper, 1978), p. 279.

28.  Lacouture, *Nasser*, pp. 183–84.

29.  Gamal Abdel Nasser, *The Philosophy of the Revolution* (Buffalo, NY: Economica Books, 1959), pp. 32–33.

30.  The "Turkish clause" was shorthand for the agreement reached in 1887 between Britain and the Ottoman sultan to withdraw British troops from Egypt, with the stipulation that they could return "if there are reasons to fear an invasion from without, or if order and security in the interior were disturbed." See Kennett Love, *Suez: The Twice-Fought War* (New York: McGraw-Hill, 1969), p. 179.

31.  Wilbur Crane Eveland, *Ropes of Sand* (New York: Norton, 1980), p. 98; Cooper, *The Lion's Last Roar*, p. 67; Miles Copeland, *The Game of Nations: The Amorality of Power Politics* (New York: Simon & Schuster, 1970), pp. 175–77.

32.  Kennett Love, "U.S. Envoy Lauds Egyptian Regime," *The New York Times*, December 6, 1954.

33.  The British were skeptical of Nasser from the outset. They saw the Hashemite kingdoms of Iraq and Jordan as a potential hub of leadership in the region under the Baghdad Pact, a regional defense alliance that would link Turkey, Pakistan, and Iran along the southern flank of the Soviet Union. Eisenhower and Dulles had initially supported the Baghdad Pact as part of the containment activities of the cold war. But as time went on, America refused to join the pact, because Dulles was loath to provoke Nasser, who saw the pact as a British attempt to undermine Egypt's regional leadership.

34.  Eveland, *Ropes of Sand*, pp. 99–102; Copeland, *The Game of Nations*, pp. 146–51.

35.  Copeland, *The Game of Nations*, pp. 146–47.

36. Ibid., p. 153.

37. Known as the Lavon Affair, the incident roiled Israeli politics for almost a decade. It was sensitive not only because it involved acts of terror against Americans but also because of the dispute over who ordered the sabotage. Moshe Sharett, the prime minister, was said to have been kept in the dark. Pinhas Lavon, the defense minister, claimed that military intelligence acted without his order. The chief of military intelligence claimed that Lavon personally authorized it. There was evidence that Lavon had sanctioned the attacks; there also was evidence that military intelligence officials had doctored records and suborned perjury in order to "backdate" approvals. See Dan Raviv and Yossi Melman, *Every Spy a Prince: The Complete History of Israel's Intelligence Community* (Boston: Houghton Mifflin, 1990), pp. 54–62; also Bar-Zohar, *Ben-Gurion*, pp. 208–15.

38. Eisenhower also promoted the Atoms for Peace program, to spread the promise of civilian nuclear power for a coming era of cheap energy that could also be employed for agriculture, industry, and desalinating water in arid regions. Israel was a recipient of a research reactor under this program, but Israeli leaders withheld from Eisenhower their plans to build a large reactor at Dimona in the Negev Desert, where Israel produced its first nuclear weapons a decade later.

39. See Avner Cohen, *Israel and the Bomb* (New York: Columbia University Press, 1998), pp. 65–66; Seymour M. Hersh, *The Samson Option: Israel's Nuclear Arsenal and American Foreign Policy* (New York: Random House, 1991), p. 23; Michael Karpin, *The Bomb in the Basement: How Israel Went Nuclear and What It Means for the World* (New York: Simon & Schuster, 2006), p. 51.

40. Copeland, *The Game of Nations*, p. 188.

41. Ibid., p. 111.

42. For a discussion of the "activist" or "militarist" strain in Israeli policy, see Shlomo Ben-Ami, *Scars of War, Wounds of Peace: The Israeli-Arab Tragedy* (New York: Oxford University Press, 2006), pp. 53–54; Morris, *Righteous Victims*, pp. 272–88; Yoram Peri, *Generals in the Cabinet Room: How the Military Shapes Israeli Policy* (Washington D.C.: United States Institute of Peace Press, 2006), pp. 17–32.

43. "Nasser Criticizes West," *The New York Times*, September 28, 1955.

44. Evelyn Shuckburgh, *Descent to Suez: Foreign Office Diaries 1951–1956* (New York: Norton, 1986), p. 346.

45. Love, *Suez*, p. 215.

46. Cooper, *The Lion's Last Roar*, p. 79.

47. Dwight D. Eisenhower Presidential Papers, Document No. 1773, Diary, March 8, 1956.

48. Nasser may have received intelligence reports from a Baghdad Pact meeting in Tehran where Egypt was discussed, and he may have had other sources who were keeping him apprised of American attitudes. See Mohamed Heikal, *The Cairo Documents* (New York: Doubleday, 1973), p. 64.

49. "Egypt Nationalizes Suez Canal Company; Will Use Revenues to Build Aswan Dam," *The New York Times*, July 27, 1956.

50. Cooper, *The Lion's Last Roar*, pp. 105–06.

51. Douglas Little, "Mission Impossible: The CIA and the Cult of Covert Action

in the Middle East," *Diplomatic History*, 28, issue 5 (November 2004): 663–701; Archie Roosevelt, *For Lust of Knowing: Memoirs of an Intelligence Officer* (Boston: Little, Brown, 1988), pp. 444–45.

52. Memorandum of Conversation Between Prime Minister Eden and Secretary of State Dulles, London, September 20, 1956, FRUS, 1955–1957, vol. XVI, pp. 545–46; Memorandum of Conversation, British Foreign Office, London, September 21, 1956, FRUS, 1955–1957, vol. XVI, pp. 548–49.

53. International communism may well have been stoking the crisis in Lebanon, as the KGB was perceived to be working hand in glove with Egyptian agents. This was the period when Kim Philby, the notorious Soviet agent who had risen to the heights of British intelligence before falling under suspicion, was a fixture in Beirut, still working secretly against the West, dining out with CIA and MI6 colleagues, and carrying on an affair with Eleanor Brewer, the wife of *The New York Times*'s Middle East correspondent. (Philby and Brewer ultimately married.)

54. James Reston, "Capital Softens Mideast Position," *The New York Times*, November 4, 1956.

55. FRUS, 1955–1957, vol. XVI, p. 835.

56. Ibid., p. 850.

57. Ibid., p. 908.

58. Dulles was days away from being diagnosed with cancer and entering the hospital. His excessively rigid argumentation may have been attributable to ill health.

59. Eisenhower Presidential Papers, Document No. 2064, Letter to Alfred M. Gruenther, November 2, 1956.

60. Bar-Zohar, *Ben-Gurion*, p. 253.

61. Eban, *Personal Witness*, pp. 275–76.

62. Memorandum of Conversation, December 28, 1956, FRUS, 1955–1957, vol. XVI, pp. 1341–44.

63. William S. White, "Dulles Faces Fire on Mideast Plan; House Unit for It," *The New York Times*, January 25, 1957.

64. Copeland, *The Game of Nations*, p. 216.

65. Text of Statement of Harry S. Truman to the Senate Foreign Relations Committee, January 24, 1957, *The New York Times*, January 25, 1957.

66. Eban, *Personal Witness*, p. 280.

67. Cohen, *Israel and the Bomb*, pp. 88, 92.

## 2. The Six-Day War: Johnson and Israel

1. Presidential Diary, June 5, 1967, Lyndon Baines Johnson Library (LBJL), Austin, Texas.

2. Johnson's infatuation with the Krims was so intense that he insisted they purchase an adjoining ranch, which they did, maintaining their tie to Texas, and to the Johnson family, long after LBJ's death. Author interview with Mathilde Krim, January 18, 2006.

3. After U.S. marines occupied Lebanon in 1958, the Eisenhower administration sold Israel one thousand recoilless guns. See Bar-Zohar, *Ben-Gurion*, p. 265.

4. Arthur B. Krim, Oral History, June 29 and November 9, 1982. LBJL. See also

Memorandum for the President from Walt W. Rostow, re: Meeting with Abe Feinberg and David Ginsberg, May 15, 1967, National Security Files (NSF), Country File: Israel, LBJL. Feinberg was a major contributor to Democratic candidates going back to Truman, and he was also a major fund-raiser for Israel. Kennedy, though a grateful recipient of campaign funding that Feinberg organized, was said to have resented Feinberg's attempt to demand substantial control over Middle East policy as a quid pro quo. See Hersh, *The Samson Option*, pp. 96–98.

5. Johnson explained his attitude toward the Jewish state and the war in his memoir: "I have always had a deep feeling of sympathy for Israel and its people, gallantly building and defending a modern nation against great odds and against the tragic background of Jewish experience. I can understand that men might decide to act on their own when hostile forces gather on their frontiers and cut off a major port . . . Nonetheless, I have never concealed my regret that Israel decided to move when it did. I always made it equally clear, however, to the Russians and to every other nation, that I did not accept the oversimplified charge of Israeli aggression." Lyndon Baines Johnson, *The Vantage Point: Perspectives of the Presidency 1963–1969* (New York: Holt, 1971), p. 297.

6. Presidential Recording, February 20, 1965, LBJL.

7. Author interview with Harry C. McPherson, Jr., January 26, 2006.

8. Interview with Mathilde Krim.

9. The shah of Iran maintained discreet relations with the Jewish state and shared Israel's view that Nasser was the scourge of the Middle East: his war in Yemen, his use of chemical weapons supplied by the Soviets, his plots to overthrow the region's "feudal" monarchies. All of these rendered him exceedingly dangerous, in the shah's view, and the Iranian leader would support any policy that would end Nasser's power in the region. The shah's antipathy toward Nasser is documented extensively in Asadollah Alam, *The Shah and I: The Confidential Diary of Iran's Royal Court, 1969–1977* (New York: St. Martin's Press, 1991). On the first day of the 1967 war, Averell Harriman, then undersecretary of state, cabled Johnson and Rusk from Tehran, saying the shah was eager to support a policy that destroyed Nasser, though he still supported the Muslim cause in Palestine. The Iranian leader chided the United States for assisting Nasser with food aid and for not opposing his aggressive policies. He said there had been missed opportunities to stop Nasser over other issues, such as his invasion of Yemen and his "outrageous actions" in using poison gas there. The main objective for long-term stability in the region was to find a way to destroy Nasser, "otherwise there could be no peace in the Middle East." NSF, History, vol. IV, LBJL.

10. Author interview with Miriam Eshkol, December 1, 2005.

11. Ami Gluska, *Eshkol Give the Order! Israel's Army Command and Political Leadership on the Road to the Six-Day War, 1963–67* [Hebrew] (Tel Aviv, MOD, Ma'arachot, 2005), pp. 322–65; Zeev Schiff, "1967—The Generals in the Eyes of the Government" [Hebrew], *Haaretz*, June 6, 1997.

12. Memorandum of Conversation, FRUS, vol. XIX, pp. 140–46.

13. Michael B. Oren, *Six Days of War* (New York: Oxford University Press, 2002), p. 125.

14. Arthur B. Krim, Oral History, May 17, 1982, LBJL.

15. Harry McPherson, Oral History, January 16, 1969, LBJL.

16. Memorandum for the President from Walt W. Rostow, NSF, History, vol. III, LBJL.

17. Lucius D. Battle, Oral History, July 10, 1991, Association for Diplomatic Studies and Training (ADST), Parker, *The Six-Day War*, pp. 263–64.

18. Lucius D. Battle, Oral History, Parker, *The Six-Day War*, p. 219.

19. Ben-Gurion had used almost the same words with Eisenhower in March 1960. "Israel has only two alternatives: either Israel remains free and independent or Israel will be exterminated just as Hitler exterminated the Jews in Germany. It was not possible to believe that Israel could simply be defeated. If Nasser won he would feel compelled to cut every throat in Israel, which is our last stand after fighting for survival for the last 4,000 years." Memorandum of Conversation, Eisenhower–Ben-Gurion, March 10, 1960, NSF, History, vol. XII, LBJL.

20. Parker, *The Six-Day War*, p. 127.

21. The United Arab Republic was established February 1958 as part of the pan-Arab ferment in the region. Syria withdrew from the UAR in 1961 when its government changed, but Egypt remained the United Arab Republic during Nasser's years.

22. The origins of the Soviet intelligence reports of Israeli mobilization were an enduring mystery after the war. Given that both the Soviet foreign ministry and the KGB dispatched their representatives to formally warn Egyptian officials, it suggests a coordinated decision, perhaps at the Politburo level, to spread reports that were soon proved to be disinformation. Some senior Soviet officials were interested in goading Nasser to declare solidarity with Syria in the face of perceived Israeli threats to attack Syria and topple the Soviet client regime.

23. President's Daily Briefing, May 16, 1967, NSF, History, vol. VI, LBJL.

24. Memorandum to the President, Walt W. Rostow, May 15, 1967, NSF, Country File: Israel, LBJL.

25. Eban, *Personal Witness*, p. 357.

26. State Department Telegram: Johnson to Eshkol, National Archives, Central Files 1967–69.

27. Wilson, *The Chariot of Israel*, p. 331; Oren, *Six Days of War*, p. 84.

28. Yitzhak Rabin, *The Rabin Memoirs* (Boston: Little, Brown, 1979), p. 77.

29. Dayan had lost his left eye in June 1941 when he raised a pair of binoculars to peer across a battlefield while fighting with British and Australian forces against Vichy-French allies in Lebanon. A bullet fired from a Vichy bunker smashed into Dayan's binoculars, sending glass fragments into his eye. The damage was such that he could not be fitted with a prosthesis; hence the patch.

30. Presidential Statement, May 23, 1967, NSF, History, vol. I, LBJL.

31. Memorandum for the Record, NSC meeting, May 24, 1967, NSF, History, vol. I, LBJL.

32. Rabin, *Rabin Memoirs*, p. 81.

33. Raviv and Melman, *Every Spy a Prince*, pp. 157–59.

34. Dayan, *Moshe Dayan*, pp. 257, 263.

35. Notes of Meeting, May 25, 1967. I am indebted to Dr. Ronen Bergman for providing a copy of Efraim Halevy's notes of the meeting. Bergman first published the details of the encounter in the Israeli daily *Yedioth Ahronoth*. Reference to the meeting was made by Walt Rostow in a note to Johnson at 6:00 p.m. on May 25. It states that Amit requested that his alarming views be transmitted to Helms. Rostow also noted that CIA headquarters had issued its own appraisal, "which throws a great deal of cold water on the Israeli estimate." Memorandum for the President, Walt W. Rostow, May 25, 1967, NSF, History, vol. II, LBJL; author interview with John Hadden, April 5, 2006.

36. "Arab Israeli Crisis," CIA Memorandum addressed to "White House Situation Room," portions redacted, May 25, 1967, NSF, History, vol. II, LBJL.

37. Interview with Miriam Eshkol.

38. Marshal Abdul Hakim Amer, Nasser's overall military chief, may have issued orders on May 25 for an Egyptian air attack on May 26, but Egyptian officials who were involved at the time, including General Mohamed Fawzi, the chief of staff, and Mohamed Heikal, Nasser's confidant and propagandist, reported in their memoirs that Nasser canceled the order.

39. Memorandum for the Record, FRUS, vol. XIX, pp. 127–36.

40. Memorandum for the Record, "Meeting on the Arab-Israeli Crisis," May 26, 1967, NSF, History, vol. II, LBJL.

41. Memorandum of Conversation, FRUS, vol. XIX, pp. 140–46.

42. Presidential Diary, May 26, 1967, LBJL.

43. In early 2001, General Yaakov, then living in New York with American citizenship, drafted a memoir documenting his role as Israel's first nuclear-weapons commander. He showed it to an Israeli journalist, whose report about it was censored by the Israeli military. Yaakov, then seventy-five, was lured home, arrested, charged, and convicted for breaching Israel's security.

44. Miriam Eshkol blamed her husband's poor performance on the fact that there had been handwritten changes to the text of the government statement he read out on the radio. He stopped, whispered to an aide, and then continued reading haltingly. Miriam Eshkol said his recent cataract surgery plus the messy text caused his alarming performance. (It also seems clear that Eshkol may have suffered a failure of leadership. He was mouthing the words of a legalistic government text instead of reassuring a nation frightened by speculative reports indicating that tens of thousands of Israelis might be killed or wounded in a war with Egypt.) Interview with Miriam Eshkol; see also Tom Segev, *1967: Israel, the War, and the Year That Transformed the Middle East* (New York: Metropolitan Books, 2007), pp. 290–91.

    Golda Meir penned a moving tribute to Eshkol in her memoir, saying he was "most unfairly" abused for his hesitancy about sending Israel's army into battle in 1967. She said he was weighed down by the staggering responsibility. "Only a fool would have felt differently, and if he stuttered a little when he spoke about sending his people to war, it was only to his eternal credit." Golda Meir, *My Life*, (New York: Putnam, 1975), pp. 122, 362.

45. Gluska, *Eshkol Give the Order!*, p. 333; Segev, *1967*, p. 293.

46. Gluska, *Eshkol Give the Order!*, p. 334.

47. Ibid., p. 336.

48. In July 2007, Efraim Halevy, a former Mossad director, told me that Amit's ac-

count of his visit to Washington in June 1967 was quite possibly tailored to give the Israeli public reassurance that Israel had had no choice but to attack.

49. A draft declaration was being circulated by American embassies around the world: "Our Governments reaffirm the view that the Gulf is an international waterway into and through which the vessels of all nations have a right of passage. The views we express in this Declaration formed the basis on which a settlement of the Near East conflict was achieved in early 1957—a settlement that has governed the actions of nations for more than ten years. These views will guide our policies and action in seeking to assure peace and security in the Near East." NSF, History, vol. III, LBJL.

50. Richard Helms's memorandum is not part of the declassified record of the Six-Day War; it was obtained from a private collection.

51. Amit was accompanied home by Avraham Harman, Israel's ambassador to Washington for a decade. Harman believed that Israel should give Johnson more time. Amit laid out his doubts about the American plans for a declaration of maritime nations and a naval challenge to the blockade. Rabin's record of the meeting says that Amit recommended giving Johnson one more week (seven to nine days). Other accounts say that Amit suggested that Israel send one of its own flag vessels through the Strait of Tiran, and if Egypt fired on it, that would provide a clean pretext as Egypt would be seen firing the first shot. Ambassador Harman's deputy, Ephraim "Eppie" Evron, possibly in collusion with the Mossad chief, raised the same idea at the White House to Johnson's national security adviser, who sent it immediately to the president with a recommendation that he "should most urgently consider" it. David Ginsburg, the Washington lawyer who served as a White House intermediary to Eshkol, also promoted the idea of sending a ship through the strait in a phone call and letter to Rostow. But Dayan, now in charge of war planning, rejected these proposals. Setting a trap with an Israeli ship as bait would send a transparent signal to Nasser that Israel was going to attack. Nasser could ignore the bait and launch Egyptian forces. Israel would lose the element of surprise. Dayan said they had to start the war immediately with a massive air attack followed by an armored thrust into Sinai to destroy Nasser's ground forces.

52. Gluska, *Eshkol Give the Order!*, p. 347.

53. Memorandum: Saunders to Rostow, NSF, History, vol. III, LBJL.

54. Memorandum: Walt Rostow to Johnson, NSF, History, vol. VIII, LBJL.

55. Richard Witkin, "Johnson, in City, Vows to Maintain Peace in Mideast," *The New York Times*, June 4, 1967.

56. Notes of Meeting, NSC, FRUS, vol. XIX, pp. 236–40.

57. Interview with Harry C. McPherson, Jr.; Memorandum from the President's Special Counsel, FRUS, vol. XIX, pp. 433–36.

58. The most authoritative study is A. Jay Cristol, *The Liberty Incident* (Washington, D.C.: Brassey's, 2002). Cristol, a federal judge and former naval aviator, spent a decade reconstructing the attack.

59. FRUS, vol. XIX, p. 424.

60. Presidential Diary, June 10, 1967, LBJL.

61. Memorandum for the Record, Re: Hot Line Meeting June 10, 1967; NSF, History, vol. VII, LBJL. This document is dated October 22, 1968, and represents a reconstruction of the crisis under the direction of Harold H. Saunders of the National Security Council staff.

62. President's Daily Brief, June 9, 1967, NSF, History, vol. VI, Appendices A–D, LBJL.

63. CIA Situation Reports, 1400, 1630, and 1930 hours, June 9, 1967, NSF, History, vol. XI, LBJL.

64. Israeli leaders decided that in order to avoid international condemnation they would obscure who fired the first shot. Abba Eban was designated to inform foreign governments that Israeli forces had come under attack and then launched a counterattack. The ruse worked. Rostow and McNamara engaged in speculation on June 5 that Egypt had agreed to send its vice president to Washington on June 7 as a means to "cover" an Egyptian surprise attack. The Israeli lie was soon overtaken by a lie on the Arab side, when King Hussein and then Nasser announced that American bombers had joined the Israelis in the attack.

65. FRUS, vol. XIX, p. 295.

66. Department of State telegram: Barbour to Rusk, NSF, History, vol. IV, LBJL.

67. Memorandum for Walt Rostow from Mathilde Krim, June 7, 1967, Presidential Diary, Appointment File, LBJL.

68. CIA Situation Report, 0800 hours, June, 12, 1967, NSF, History, vol. XI, LBJL.

69. Mohamed Heikal, *Road to Ramadan* (New York: Times Books, 1975), p. 55.

70. Ibid., p. 64.

71. See excerpt of interview with King Hussein in Avi Shlaim, *The Iron Wall: Israel and the Arab World* (New York: Norton, 2001), pp. 258–59.

72. Israeli leaders would thereafter argue that the wording of Resolution 242, which called for Israel's withdrawal "from territories" occupied during the war instead of "from *the* territories," meant that Israel could forgo a complete withdrawal and negotiate for more defensible borders. However, the Security Council made no such distinction and most members understood the resolution to require a full withdrawal. When the United States took a position on the matter in 1969, Secretary of State William Rogers indicated that minor modifications of the border were possible through negotiation but that border changes should be limited so as not to reflect the "weight of conquest."

73. FRUS, vol. XX, p. 624.

74. Ibid.

75. Ibid., p. 626.

### 3. Nixon and Brezhnev: Cold War and International Terror

1. "The Israelis think that if they continue their present course of military action, Nasser may well fall," Henry Kissinger, the new national security adviser, told President Nixon in a September 25, 1969, memo. "If Nasser falls, his successor will be less dangerous to Western interests." Kissinger added that the Israeli leadership believed that "Israel's very existence prevents total Soviet domination over the region." In this private message to Nixon, perhaps intended by Kissinger to show the president that he held the Israelis at arm's length, Kissinger concluded, "It seems more likely—and some Israelis admit this—that Israel's purpose is to surround itself with weak Arab governments so that it can weather prolonged tension behind its present borders."

2. Neither *The New York Times* nor *The Washington Post* accounts, filed by correspondents who were in Cairo the day of the slaying, mentioned a gunman

kneeling and licking Tal's blood. The three gunmen were said by hotel staff to have fled. They were arrested nearby. See Raymond H. Anderson, "Jordan's Premier Is Slain in Cairo; Three Gunmen Seized," *The New York Times*, November 29, 1971; Jesse W. Lewis Jr., "Jordanian Premier Assassinated by Palestinian Extremist Group," *The Washington Post*, November 29, 1971.

3.  Nixon as de Gaulle is a presidential theme in the private discussions he held with H. R. Haldeman, John Ehrlichman, and others and recorded in H. R. Haldeman, *The Haldeman Diaries: Inside the Nixon White House* (New York: Berkley, 1995), pp. 272, 276.

4.  Eisenhower had expressed doubts about Nixon's leadership qualifications. See Michael Korda, *Ike: An American Hero* (New York: Harper, 2007), p. 688; Ambrose, *Eisenhower*, pp. 400–401.

5.  Melvin R. Laird, Nixon's first secretary of defense, was the most aggressive voice in the new administration urging (in memoranda dated February 27 and March 17, 1969) that a concerted effort be undertaken to stop Israel from developing both nuclear weapons and French-designed strategic ballistic missiles on which to deliver them. Laird warned that Israeli scientists were working at a "rapid pace" and that the Jewish state might complete both systems "this year." Kissinger chaired an interagency group that considered using strong leverage—withholding F-4 Phantom warplanes—to force Israel to foreswear becoming a full-fledged nuclear weapons state. But Kissinger undermined the most forceful recommendations of the group with his own recommendation, which called for nothing stronger than "discussions." Nixon's views were less clear, but he took no step to challenge Israel's entry into the nuclear club.

6.  One unintended benefit for the United States from the closure of the canal was that Soviet cargo ships steaming out of Black Sea ports with arms for North Vietnam were forced to take the long route to Asia around Africa.

7.  Arafat was born in Cairo on August 24, 1929, according to a birth certificate and Cairo University records. He often claimed, however, that he was born in Jerusalem. Tony Walker and Andrew Gowers, *Arafat: The Biography* (London: Virgin Books, 2003), pp. 6–7; Janet Wallach and John Wallach, *Arafat: In the Eyes of the Beholder* (New York: Carol Publishing Group, 1990), p. 26.

8.  Abu Iyad with Eric Rouleau, *My Home, My Land: A Narrative of the Palestinian Struggle* (New York: Times Books, 1981), p. 3.

9.  Eric Pace, "Guerrillas Warn Jordan's Regime," *The New York Times*, September 1, 1970.

10. Iyad, *My Home, My Land*, p. 98.

11. Memorandum of Conversation, Nixon-Meir, March 1, 1973, National Archives, Nixon National Security Files (NNSF).

12. Israeli officials have claimed over the years to possess a voice intercept of Arafat giving the order to execute the diplomats using a code word, but a senior Israeli intelligence official told me such a recording does not exist. During the Reagan administration, a group in Congress called on the Justice Department to indict Arafat for murder. The effort failed, but given the high-profile nature of the Black September assault, and given an earlier plan to attack the American embassy in Jordan, it is likely that Arafat and Abu Iyad were directly involved in giving the orders to the team in Khartoum.

13. David A. Korn, *Assassination in Khartoum* (Bloomington: Indiana University Press, 1993), p. 154.

14. Ibid., pp. 168–71.

15. Patrick Tyler, *A Great Wall: Six Presidents and China* (New York: PublicAffairs, 1999), p. 62.

16. Henry Kissinger, *Years of Upheaval* (New York: Little, Brown, 1982), p. 296; Mahmoud Riad, *The Struggle for Peace in the Middle East* (New York: Quartet Books, 1981), p. 99.

17. Memorandum of Conversation, Kissinger and Ambassador Rabin, 3:30–4:00 p.m., February 27, 1973, NNSF.

18. Memorandum of Conversation, Kissinger and Ardeshir Zahedi, August 13, 1973, NNSF.

19. Memorandum of Conversation; Kissinger–The Shah of Iran, July 24, 1973, 5–6:40 p.m, NNSF.

20. Memorandum for the President's File, From Henry A. Kissinger, re: Meeting with the Shah of Iran, 10:25 a.m.–noon, July 25, 1973, NNSF.

21. The Saudi contingency planning may also have included King Hussein of Jordan, the shah's closest ally among the Arabs and whose Hashemite dynasty had long coveted a return to power on the Arabian Peninsula.

22. Memorandum for Kissinger from King Hussein, May 5, 1973; Memorandum for the President's File From Kissinger, re: Meeting between Nixon and King Hussein of Jordan, 11:35 p.m.–12:45 a.m., February 6, 1973, NNSF.

23. *Sunday Times*, June 15, 1969.

24. Memorandum for the President's Files, June 23 1973, NNSF.

25. Richard M. Nixon, *RN: The Memoirs of Richard Nixon* (New York: Grosset & Dunlap, 1978), p. 885; Anatoly Dobrynin, *In Confidence, Moscow's Ambassador to America's Six Cold War Presidents* (New York: Times Books, 1995), p. 288.

26. Memorandum for the President's File, June 23, 1973, NNSF.

27. Kissinger, *Years of Upheaval*, p. 298.

28. Memorandum of Conversation, Kissinger and Ambassador Rabin, 3:30–4:00 p.m., February 27, 1973, NNSF.

29. Memorandum of Conversation, Kissinger and PFIAB, August 3, 1973, NNSF.

30. *Newsweek*, April 9, 1973, pp. 43–49.

31. Parker, *The October War*, pp. 147–48. Under the headline, "Anwar Sadat's Uncertain Trumpet," *Newsweek* played down Sadat's warning as "verbal overkill," saying Mideast experts were inclined to interpret his "outburst" as "a ploy designed to stifle mounting domestic criticism of his do-nothing regime." Sadat, the magazine said, "was not contemplating anything as suicidal as a full-fledged amphibious attack across the Suez Canal," but perhaps a "limited military gesture," such as a series of commando raids.

32. Mohamed Heikal, *Autumn of Fury: The Assassination of Sadat* (New York: Random House, 1983), pp. 7–11.

### 4. Nixon and Kissinger: Yom Kippur—The October War

1. The Israeli spy, according to authoritative statements by Israeli officials, was Ashraf Marwan, a wealthy Egyptian businessman who was married to the late

President Nasser's daughter, Mona. Until his death, Marwan denied reports that he was the spy who met secretly in Europe with Mossad chief Zvi Zamir on the eve of the Egyptian attack to reiterate a warning that "tomorrow a war will break out." His mysterious death in London in June 2007 was followed by recriminations among Israeli intelligence officials over whether the leaking of Marwan's name to the press had led to his death and compromised the integrity of Israel's intelligence service.

2. Telcon [telephone conversation], Kissinger-Haig, 12:45 p.m., October 6, 1973, National Security Archive, George Washington University.

3. Telcon, Kissinger-Haig, 1:10 p.m., October 6, 1973, National Security Archive.

4. Memorandum of Conversation, Kissinger and Ambassador Huang Chen, 9:10–9:30 p.m., October 6, 1973, NNSF.

5. Heikal, *Road to Ramadan*, p. 41.

6. Memorandum of Conversation, Kissinger-Mordechai Shalev, October 7, 1973, NNSF.

7. Telcon, Kissinger-Nixon, 10:18 a.m., October 7, 1973, National Security Archive.

8. Memorandum of Conversation, Henry Kissinger-Mordechai Shalev, October 7, 1973, NNSF.

9. Author interview with Eitan Haber, November 21, 2005.

10. Telcon, Kissinger-Dinitz, 1:14 p.m., October 8, 1973, National Security Archive.

11. Telcon, Nixon-Kissinger, 7:08 p.m., October 8, 1973, National Security Archive.

12. Ibid.

13. Dayan met with newspaper editors on October 8, 1973. See Raviv and Melman, *Every Spy a Prince*, p. 211. Amos Elon, one of the foremost chroniclers of Israel's first decades and a senior writer at *Haaretz* at the time, told me that "Dayan felt that Israel's existence was at stake. Golda Meir felt the same way." Author interview with Amos Elon, September 26, 2005.

14. Telcon, Haig-Kissinger, 6:05 p.m., October 6, 1973, National Security Archive.

15. Henry Kissinger, *Crisis* (New York: Simon & Schuster, 2003), p. 147. The transcript of the meeting remains classified, but Kissinger has written that "other participants"—he didn't name them—agreed with Schlesinger.

16. A Soviet diplomat in Amman, Jordan, had told King Hussein that morning that the Soviet Union fully supported the Arabs in the conflict with Israel. Moscow, he said, "thought all Arab States should enter battle now." To Kissinger, this was Moscow attempting to broaden the war. He called Dobrynin and expressed indignation, stating that the "King considers this a Soviet request for him to send his army into action." Dobrynin said he knew of no such instruction from Moscow and promised to get back to Kissinger immediately. Soon, a similar report came in from Algeria: A message from Brezhnev to President Houari Boumedienne was published calling on Algerian leaders to "use all means at their disposal and take all the required steps with a view to supporting Syria and Egypt in the difficult struggle imposed by the Israeli aggressor." Most of the Arab states, including Algeria, were supporting Egypt and Syria, by sending either money, troops, or military equipment. Moscow's endorsement of Arab solidarity and assistance were a relatively mi-

nor factor in Egypt's warmaking capacity. But Kissinger interpreted these Soviet blandishments as a sign of superpower intervention that required an American response.

17. Kissinger, *Years of Upheaval*, p. 495.

18. Ibid., p. 493.

19. Kissinger, *Crisis*, p. 153.

20. Memorandum of Conversation, Kissinger and Ambassador Huang Chen, NNSF.

21. Telcon, Kissinger-Dinitz, 7:25 p.m., October 9, 1973, National Security Archive.

22. Bernard Gwertzman, "U.S. Says Moscow Bids Other Arabs Aid Egypt and Syria," *The New York Times*, October 10, 1973.

23. The Israeli bombing of civilian areas of Damascus and Homs prompted a Soviet warning that "Tel Aviv will not be spared if this continues." Kissinger then warned Soviet ambassador Dinitz, "If any Soviet planes are seen over the area . . . there will be direct American involvement." In a telephone call to the Israeli ambassador, Kissinger repeated that the "U.S. will intervene" if Soviet forces deployed to the Middle East. In the course of the conversation, he asserted that he had discussed the situation with the president, though there is no record of this, and on the crucial point of U.S. intervention, he conditioned his remarks by saying, "I have no authority to say this." Telcon, Kissinger-Dinitz, 8:25 p.m., October 12, 1973, National Security Archive.

24. Heikal, *Road to Ramadan*, p. 219.

25. Some historians have suggested that Nixon showed little interest in the details of policy during this period. He was certainly distracted by the change in vice presidents and by Watergate, but a significant declassified record indicates that Nixon was the dominant source of guidance and pressure on Kissinger to use the opportunity of the 1973 war to unlock the diplomatic paralysis that had settled in after the 1967 war and that had plagued William Rogers's Middle East diplomacy during Nixon's first term. See William B. Quandt, *Peace Process: American Diplomacy and the Arab-Israeli Conflict Since 1967* (Washington, D.C.: Brookings Institution Press, 2001), pp. 98–129.

26. Memorandum, William Quandt to Scowcroft, re: Middle East Oil, October 10, 1973, NNSF.

27. Telcon, Kissinger-Schlesinger, October 10, 1973, National Security Archive.

28. Schlesinger has remained somewhat vague about what was in his mind at the time. In an interview, he said he recalls thinking that the United States might deploy an army of occupation to the Arabian Peninsula, landing in the United Arab Emirates, to secure the region's oil supply and presumably to deter any Soviet move into the area. The idea of U.S. forces occupying Saudi Arabia or neighboring oil-producing states was never acted on, but it was a recurring theme later on when both Kissinger and Schlesinger hinted that the United States would not tolerate "strangulation" of the West by OPEC. Given the shah of Iran's secret contingency planning along the same lines, this line of thinking appears to have been more than mere jawboning.

29. On the evening of October 11, 1973, the Defense Intelligence Agency relayed a "spot report," which indicated that Moscow's military headquarters had sent unspecified coded messages to three airborne divisions: Belgrado in the Odessa Military District, Fergana in the Turkestan Military District, and

Kirovabad in the Transcaucasus Military District. DIA could not say whether the messages were "alerts," and noted that there had been no reply or any change in status at the Soviet bases, but DIA inferred nonetheless that the message was preparatory to alert.

30. Telcon, Kissinger-Schlesinger, [11:45 p.m.], October 12, 1973, National Security Archive.

31. Ibid.

32. Telcon, Kissinger-Haig, 11:54 p.m., October 12, 1973, National Security Archive.

33. Telcon, Kissinger-Dinitz, 12:32 p.m., October 13, 1973, National Security Archive.

34. Memorandum of Conversation, Meeting of the Washington Special Actions Group: Kissinger, Kenneth Rush, Joseph Sisco, Ambassador Robert McCloskey, James Schlesinger, William Clements, Admiral Thomas Moorer, William Colby, John Love, Charles DiBonna, Alexander Haig, Brent Scowcroft, Jonathan T. Howe, 9:16–11:00 a.m., October 14, 1973, NNSF.

35. Telcon, Nixon-Kissinger, [9:04 a.m.], October 14, 1973, National Security Archive.

36. Leslie H. Gelb, "Jackson Bids U.S. Speed Israel Aid," *The New York Times*, October 15, 1973.

37. Telcon, Nixon-Kissinger, 9:04 a.m., October 14, 1973, National Security Archive.

38. Ariel Sharon with David Chanoff, *Warrior: An Autobiography* (New York: Simon & Schuster, 1989), p. 316.

39. Transcript, Washington Special Actions Group Meeting, October 17, 1973, NNSF.

40. Memorandum of Conversation, Nixon–WSAG Principals, 4:00 p.m., October 17, 1973, NNSF.

41. Transcript, Washington Special Actions Group Meeting, October 17, 1973.

42. Memorandum of Conversation, Nixon–WSAG Principals, 4:00 p.m., October 17, 1973, NNSF.

43. Kissinger, in a private message to Saudi Arabia's King Faisal on October 14, 1973, asserted that "the Soviets have taken the initiative in launching a massive airlift of arms. They are obviously seeking to exploit the situation to their own advantage in the Arab world . . . In these circumstances, we had no alternative but to begin our own airlift. It is equally important to note that it was only after the Soviet supply effort had reached massive proportions that ours began."

44. Memorandum of Conversation, Nixon–Arab Foreign Ministers, 11:10 a.m., October, 17, 1973, NNSF.

45. Ibid.

46. Nixon, *RN*, p. 928.

47. Daniel Yergin, *The Prize: The Epic Quest for Oil, Money & Power* (New York: Simon & Schuster, 1991), pp. 541–45, 837.

48. Telcon, Scowcroft-Kissinger, 10:45 p.m., October 18, 1973, National Security Archive.

49. Memorandum of Conversation, Kissinger, Schlesinger, Colby, Moorer, and Scowcroft, October 19, 1973, NNSF.

50. Telcon, Haig-Kissinger, 3:20 p.m., October 19, 1973, National Security Archive.

51. Telcon, Haig-Kissinger, 3:20 p.m. October 19, 1973, National Security Archive.

52. Kissinger, *Years of Upheaval*, p. 530.

53. Telegram: Scowcroft to Kissinger, October 20, 1973, NNSF.

54. Kissinger argues in his memoir that it had been "American strategy so far" to "separate the cease-fire from a postwar political settlement and to reduce the Soviet role in the negotiations that would follow the cease-fire." He argued that Nixon's grandiose peace initiative "would involve us in an extensive negotiation whose results we would then have to impose on Israel as the last act of a war fought on the Arab side with Soviet weapons." Kissinger's emphasis on this distorted view of a comprehensive peace reflected how intensely he feared taking any peace proposal to a resistant Israeli leadership.

55. Memorandum of Conversation, Kissinger-Meir, October 22, 1973, NNSF.

56. Dobrynin, *In Confidence*, p. 299.

57. Telcon, Kissinger-Dobrynin, 7:25 p.m., October 24, 1973, National Security Archive.

58. Telcon, Kissinger-Dinitz, 10:00 p.m., October 24, 1973, National Security Archive.

59. Telcon, Kissinger-Haig, 10:20 p.m., October 24, 1973, National Security Archive.

60. Kissinger's transcript of Jackson's call indicates that Jackson did not express any opinion but merely asked if a press report about such a force was true. Kissinger told the senator, "We will under no circumstances agree to it," preempting any consideration by Nixon and his advisers. Kissinger described the situation in a manner that would appeal to Jackson's anti-Soviet and pro-Israeli instincts: "I think we scored a tremendous victory and will not jeopardize it now." In an earlier call with Senator J. William Fulbright, a supporter of détente, Kissinger had described the cease-fire and the pending postwar diplomacy under joint auspices with the Soviets as a triumph of cooperation. Telcon, Kissinger-Jackson, 6:58 p.m., October 24, 1973; Telcon, Kissinger-Fulbright, 8:35 p.m., October 24, 1973, National Security Archive.

61. Telcon, Kissinger-Dinitz, 10:00 p.m., October 24, 1973, National Security Archive.

62. Richard Ned Lebow and Janice Gross Stein, *We All Lost the Cold War* (Princeton: Princeton University Press, 1994), p. 248.

63. Telcon, Kissinger-Dinitz, 7:35 p.m., October 24, 1973, National Security Archive.

64. Telcon, Nixon-Kissinger, 7:10 p.m., October 24, 1973, National Security Archive.

65. At midday on October 24, 1973, Kissinger sent a message to Sadat (via his national security adviser Hafez Ismail) saying, "The Israeli Government was informed that any further offensive operations would lead to a severe deterioration of relations between the Israeli and U.S. Governments." The message also said that President Nixon had "personally intervened with the Prime Minister of Israel to halt the fighting." Given the extensive declassified record to the contrary, these statements appear to be false, and in any case, Kissinger's private communications with the Israeli ambassador throughout the day made no reference to such warnings or demands or to any conversation between Nixon and Meir.

66. Letter, Nixon to Brezhnev, October 25, 1973, NNSF.
67. Telcon, Kissinger-Dinitz, 2:09 a.m., October 25, 1973, National Security Archive.
68. Kissinger did not include any reference to this conversation in his two memoirs of the crisis. The transcript emerged among the more than twenty thousand pages of Kissinger telephone conversations that were declassified by the State Department in Freedom of Information Act litigation brought by the National Security Archive. Some key Kissinger transcripts from the 1973 crisis remain closed.
69. Telcon, Kissinger–Lord Cromer [George Baring], 1:03 a.m., October 25, 1973, National Security Archive.
70. Author interviews with James Schlesinger, August 10, 2005, and Brent Scowcroft, March 16, 2006.
71. Memorandum of Conversation, Kissinger–*Washington Star* journalists, January 25, 1974, NNSF.

## 5. Jimmy Carter: Camp David and the Struggle with Menachem Begin

1. Jehan Sadat, *A Woman of Egypt* (New York: Simon & Schuster, 1987), p. 378.
2. Anwar el-Sadat, *In Search of Identity* (New York: Harper, 1977), p. 309; Sadat, *A Woman of Egypt*, p. 377.
3. David Kimche, *The Last Option: After Nasser, Arafat & Saddam Hussein: The Quest for Peace in the Middle East* (New York: Scribner, 1991), p. 86.
4. Amos Elon, *Jerusalem, City of Mirrors* (New York: Little, Brown, 1989), p. 3.
5. Iyad, *My Home, My Land*, pp. 203–04.
6. For an account of Harriman's and Holbrooke's activities during the Carter transition, see Tyler, *A Great Wall*, pp. 230–35.
7. Kissinger, *Years of Renewal*, p. 428.
8. Ibid., pp. 426, 440.
9. Jimmy Carter, *The Blood of Abraham: Insights into the Middle East* (Boston: Houghton Mifflin, 1985), p. 197.
10. Brzezinski, *Power and Principle*, p. 83.
11. Second presidential debate, October 6, 1976.
12. Harold H. Saunders, Oral History, November 24, 1993, ADST.
13. Author interview with Amos Eiran, November 29, 2005.
14. Ibid.; interview with Eitan Haber.
15. Author interview with Jimmy Carter, April 28, 2006.
16. J. Bowyer Bell, *Terror Out of Zion: The Shock Troops of Israeli Independence* (New York: Avon Books, 1977).
17. Menachem Begin, *The Revolt* (New York: Nash Publishing, 1951), p. xxvi.
18. Ibid., p. 60.
19. Shlomo Gazit, *Trapped Fools* (Portland, OR: Frank Cass, 2003), p. 105.
20. Interview with Jimmy Carter.
21. Jimmy Carter, *Keeping Faith: Memoirs of a President* (New York: Harper, 1982), p. 290.
22. Wolfgang Saxon, "Mideast Peace Plan Attacked by Javits," *New York Times*, June 27, 1977; Steven L. Spiegel, *The Other Arab-Israeli Conflict: Making America's Middle East Policy, from Truman to Reagan* (Chicago: University of Chicago Press, 1985), p. 326; Marvin Kalb, "The New Face of Israel, a Jour-

ney Through a Land of Doubts," *The New York Times Magazine*, July 17, 1977; Bernard Gwertzman, "Carter Offers Jews Assurance on Israel," *The New York Times*, July 7, 1977.

23. Walker and Gowers, *Arafat*, p. 158; Henry Tanner, "Palestinians in Cairo Welcome Carter's Stand on Need for 'Homeland,'" *The New York Times*, March 18, 1977.

24. Bernard Gwertzman, "Secretary Says Saudis Expect Change Soon," *The New York Times*, August 9, 1977.

25. Cyrus Vance, *Hard Choices: Critical Years in America's Foreign Policy* (New York: Simon & Schuster, 1983), p. 189; Walker and Gowers, Arafat, p. 155.

26. Author interview with Hassan Abdul Rahman, September 5, 2005.

27. Department of State Bulletin, "Status of Palestinians in Peace Negotiations," October 10, 1977, p. 463.

28. William B. Quandt, *Camp David: Peacemaking and Politics* (Washington, D.C.: Brookings Institution Press, 1986), p. 102.

29. Hermann Eilts, the American ambassador to Cairo, had heard from Sadat that during the Egyptian leader's travels, he had met and discussed with Jewish financiers in Europe how to undermine Begin's resistance to peace. Their view was that Sadat could go over Begin's head to the Israelis "through direct talks." Hermann Frederick Eilts, Oral History, August 12, 1988, ADST.

30. Moshe Dayan, *Breakthrough: A Personal Account of the Egypt-Israel Peace Negotiations* (New York: Knopf, 1981), p. 47.

31. Reuters, "Israeli Resettlement Chief Envisions a 'Security Belt' Involving 2 Million Jews," September 3, 1977.

32. Brzezinski, *Power and Principle*, p. 105; Dayan, *Breakthrough*, p. 60.

33. Brzezinski, *Power and Principle*, p. 97.

34. Ismail Fahmy, *Negotiating Peace in the Middle East* (Baltimore: Johns Hopkins University Press, 1983), pp. 195–208.

35. Quandt, *Camp David*, p. 123.

36. William Safire, "Selling Out Israel," *The New York Times*, October 7, 1977.

37. Brzezinski, *Power and Principle*, p. 108.

38. Ibid., pp. 108–09; Quandt, *Camp David*, p. 127; Dayan, *Breakthrough*, pp. 66–71.

39. During this critical week at the United Nations, James Angleton, the CIA counterintelligence chief who had been forced into retirement, was working actively and behind the scenes with Mossad, the Israeli intelligence agency, to prove his hypothesis that Yasser Arafat was a KGB agent, a charge that if substantiated would have discredited Arafat and undermined the PLO's claim to represent the Palestinians. It would also have opened the door to King Hussein once again to reassert his suzerainty over the Palestinians, which was the preferred course for Israel. The collaboration between Mossad and Angleton, which reached no firm conclusion, was revealed by Efraim Halevy, a longtime Mossad official, in *Man in the Shadows: Inside the Middle East Crisis with a Man Who Led the Mossad* (New York: St. Martin's Press, 2006), pp. 7–8.

40. Carter, *Keeping Faith*, p. 295.

41. Fahmy, *Negotiating Peace in the Middle East*, p. 260.

42. Herman F. Eilts, Oral History.

43. Fahmy, *Negotiating Peace in the Middle East*, p. 266.

44. In July 1977, Sadat launched a brief border war against Qaddafi after intelligence—passed by Israel's Mossad director to Egypt's military intelligence chief—indicated that Qaddafi was plotting to assassinate Sadat. Egyptian tanks had rampaged through Libyan villages near the border and the Egyptian air force had conducted bombing raids deep into Libyan territory, striking air bases and air defense sites and reportedly killing several Russian technicians. After four days, Sadat announced during an address at Alexandria University that the war was over, and he warned Qaddafi to stop "playing with fire." To the Arab leaders who had expressed concern over the conflict, Sadat said that Qaddafi was "just a child" and that collectively they should "cut him down to size." Arafat was one of the leaders who had shuttled between Cairo and Tripoli in July to bring an end to the fighting. See Heikal, *Autumn of Fury*, p. 95; Marvine Howe, "Sadat Reports Conflict Over; Warns Libyan 'Playing With Fire,'" *New York Times*, July 27, 1977.

45. Fahmy, *Negotiating Peace in the Middle East*, p. 267; Walker and Gowers, *Arafat*, p. 163; Sadat, *A Woman of Egypt*, p. 372.

46. Sadat, *A Woman of Egypt*, p. 367.

47. Brzezinski, *Power and Principle*, pp. 108–09

48. Sadat, *A Woman of Egypt*, p. 367; Eitan Haber, Zeev Schiff, and Ehud Yaari, *Year of the Dove* (New York, Bantam, 1979), p. 24.

49. After Mohammed Riad's resignation, Boutros Boutros-Ghali was named acting foreign minister. He accepted despite warnings from friends that he would be assassinated and that "the airplane will never reach Jerusalem." See Boutros Boutros-Ghali, *Egypt's Road to Jerusalem* (New York: Random House, 1997), p. 16.

50. Ezer Weizman, *The Battle for Peace* (New York: Bantam Books, 1981), p. 58.

51. Quandt, *Camp David*, p. 157; Parker, *The October War*, p. 320.

52. Morris, *Righteous Victims*, p. 461.

53. David Hirst, *Guardian Weekly*, January 8, 1978.

54. Carter, *Blood of Abraham*, pp. 96–97; Carter, *Keeping Faith*, pp. 310–11; interview with Jimmy Carter.

55. James Reston, "Sadness in Jerusalem," *The New York Times*, March 22, 1978.

56. Carter, *Keeping Faith*, p. 312; Dayan, *Breakthrough*, p. 126.

57. Weizman, *Battle for Peace*, p. 316; Haber, Schiff, and Yaari, *Year of the Dove*, pp. 202–03.

58. Haber, Schiff, and Yaari, *Year of the Dove*, p. 206.

59. Brzezinski, *Power and Principle*, p. 238.

60. Dayan, *Breakthrough*, p. 218.

61. Author interview with Gerald Rafshoon, June 12, 2006. Begin kept a photo on his desk of the famous scene of a Jewish boy with his arms raised as he was arrested with women and other children at gunpoint by German soldiers in the Warsaw ghetto. From July to September 1942, hundreds of thousands of Jews were deported from the ghetto to Nazi extermination camps. Author interview with Moshe Arens, June 13, 2006.

62. Carter, *Keeping Faith*, p. 340.

63. Ibid., p. 348.

64. Ibid., p. 355.

65. Ibid., p. 376.

66.   Ibid., p. 398.

67.   Harold H. Saunders, Oral History.

## 6. Carter and the Shah: Khomeini's Revolution

1.    Asadollah Alam, *The Shah and I: The Confidential Diary of Iran's Royal Court, 1969–1977* (New York: St. Martin's Press, 1992), p. 232.

2.    Ibid., p. 21.

3.    Carter, *Keeping Faith*, p. 435.

4.    Farah Pahlavi, *An Enduring Love: My Life with the Shah, a Memoir* (New York: Miramax Books, 2004), pp. 270, 272–73.

5.    James A. Bill, *The Eagle and the Lion: The Tragedy of American-Iranian Relations* (New Haven: Yale University Press, 1988), pp. 234–45; Nikki R. Keddie, *Modern Iran: Roots and Results of Revolution* (New Haven: Yale University Press, 2003), p. 225.

6.    The first time Khomeini's name appeared in *The New York Times* was November 5, 1964, in a three-paragraph story picked up from *The Times* of London saying the state security organization of Iran had announced the ayatollah's exile due to his "instigations against the nation's interests, security, independence and territorial integrity."

      Some critics, such as Henry Precht, head of the State Department's Iran Desk, have asserted that the U.S. embassy in Tehran was tardy in introducing Khomeini as the inspiration for the "troubles" that Iran was experiencing. Henry Precht, Oral History, March 8, 2000, ADST. However, by February 1, 1978, the embassy had dispatched to Washington a survey of the Iranian opposition, describing Khomeini as the "true leader of the Shiite faithful." The cable, drafted by political officer John Stempel, pointed out that in "recent weeks, a more conservative religious opposition has . . . manifested itself publicly" and warned that "dissidence connected with religious beliefs continues to be the most potentially dangerous type of opposition in GOI [Government of Iran] eyes." U.S. State Department Telegram from Ambassador William Sullivan, "The Iranian Opposition," February 1, 1978, National Security Archive, Iran.

7.    "Text of the Declaration of Imam Khomeini," cited in Bill, *The Eagle and the Lion*, pp. 159–60.

8.    Shariatmadari's letter quoted in dispatch from Qom by William Branigin: "Iran's Powerful Moslem Leaders Angry at Government," *The Washington Post*, January 20, 1978.

9.    Shaul Bakhash, *The Reign of the Ayatollahs: Iran and the Islamic Revolution*, (New York: Basic Books, 1984), p. 45.

10.   Bureau of Intelligence and Research, "Iranian Dissidence on the Increase," January 28, 1978, National Security Archive, Iran.

11.   Keddie, *Modern Iran*, p. 226.

12.   Marvin Zonis, *Majestic Failure: The Fall of the Shah* (Chicago: University of Chicago Press, 1991), p. 75.

13.   Nicholas Gage, "Shah of Iran Facing Growing Opposition," *The New York Times*, May 18, 1978.

14.   Zonis, *Majestic Failure*, pp. 66, 205.

15.   William H. Sullivan, *Mission to Iran: The Last U.S. Ambassador* (New York: Norton, 1981), p. 92.

16. Mark Bowden, *Guests of the Ayatollah: The First Battle in America's War with Militant Islam* (New York: Atlantic Monthly Press, 2006), p. 238; author interviews with John Limbert.

17. Carter, *Keeping Faith*, p. 434.

18. Sullivan, *Mission to Iran*, p. 160.

19 Gary Sick, *All Fall Down: America's Tragic Encounter with Iran* (New York: Penguin Books, 1986), p. 58.

20. Bill, *The Eagle and the Lion*, p. 241.

21. Carter, *Keeping Faith*, p. 438.

22. Brzezinski, *Power and Principle*, p. 358.

23. Sick, *All Fall Down*, p. 66.

24. Carter, *Keeping Faith*, p. 439; Brzezinski, *Power and Principle*, p. 359; Sick, *All Fall Down*, p. 4. Only days earlier, on October 27, Sullivan had told the White House that he believed "our destiny is to work with the shah. He has shown surprising flexibility and is, in my judgment, prepared to accept a truly democratic regime here if it can be achieved responsibly." Sullivan had opposed any overture to Khomeini, or any other drastic change in U.S. policy.

25. Brzezinski, *Power and Principle*, p. 365; Sullivan, *Mission to Iran*, p. 171.

26. Sullivan, *Mission to Iran*, p. 172.

27. Anthony Parsons, *The Pride and the Fall: Iran, 1974–1979* (London: Jonathan Cape, 1984), p. 91.

28. Some analysts have asserted that the shah had all the assurance he needed from Washington, and, as one argued, "a phone call from the president's national security adviser *is* confirmation" of American policy. See Kenneth M. Pollack, *The Persian Puzzle: The Conflict between Iran and America* (New York: Random House, 2004), p. 132. Yet, given the well-known struggle between Brzezinski and Vance, the message from Brzezinski was insufficient. Carter's government was having trouble addressing the shah's most critical question: Should he employ his army in a massive crackdown that would steep his regime in the blood of his people, or should he make more concessions to reform or to coalition government? Carter himself could not make up his mind. Worse, he could not pick up the telephone to, at least, talk through the options with an ally. It was a failure of clarity that was not typical of Carter's approach, and it reflected presidential ambivalence toward a critical friend in the Middle East.

29. Brzezinski, *Power and Principle*, p. 363.

30. Ibid., p. 366; Carter, *Keeping Faith*, p. 440; Vance, *Hard Choices*, p. 327.

31. Bakhash, *Reign of the Ayatollahs*, p. 49.

32. Quoted in Nicholas Gage, "Shah puts Military in Control in Iran," *The New York Times*, November 7, 1978; see also Sick, *All Fall Down*, pp. 88–89.

33. Department of State Telegram, William Sullivan, November 9, 1978, National Security Archive, Iran.

34. Sullivan, *Mission to Iran*, p. 189.

35. Brzezinski, *Power and Principle*, p. 368.

36. George W. Ball, "Issues and Implications of the Iranian Crisis," December 12, 1978, National Security Archive, Iran.

37. Quoted in Sick, *All Fall Down*, p. 128.

38. Sullivan, *Mission to Iran*, pp. 211–12.

39. Sick, *All Fall Down*, p. 136.

40. Brzezinski, *Power and Principle*, p. 375.

41. Carter, *Keeping Faith*, p. 443; Brzezinski, *Power and Principle*, pp. 365, 368, 375, 379–81.

42. Letter from Henry Precht to William Sullivan, December 19, 1978, National Security Archive, Iran.

43. Vance, *Hard Choices*, 334–47; Sullivan, *Mission to Iran*, pp. 222–24; Brzezinski, *Power and Principle*, p. 380; Carter, *Keeping Faith*, pp. 444–45.

44. General Robert E. Huyser, *Mission to Tehran: The Fall of the Shah and the Rise of Khomeini* (New York: Harper, 1986), pp. 42–50.

45. Department of State Telegram, William Sullivan to Cyrus Vance, January 10, 1979, National Security Archive, Iran.

46. Sullivan, *Mission to Iran*, p. 226.

47. Ibid., p. 99.

48. Henry Precht, Oral History; Sullivan *Mission to Iran*, pp. 252–53.

49. Sullivan, *Mission to Iran*, p. 258.

50. A tiny U.S. naval presence had existed alongside British forces on Bahrain since World War II. When the British pulled out of the Persian Gulf in 1971, the U.S. navy leased a portion of the former British naval base in Manama, the capital, calling it the Administrative Support Unit, Bahrain. The facility saw little use until the mid-1980s. It was further enlarged to host the U.S. Fifth Fleet under the name Naval Support Activity, Bahrain.

51. Quandt, *Camp David*, p. 295.

52. Christopher S. Wren, "Assurance to Egypt," *The New York Times*, March 11, 1979.

53. Terence Smith, "Carter and Sadat Continue Discussion After Tour on Train," *The New York Times*, March 10, 1979.

54. Carter, *Keeping Faith*, p. 421.

55. Richard Viets, Oral History, April 6, 1990, ADST; Samuel W. Lewis, Oral History, September 7, 1990, ADST.

56. Richard Viets, Oral History.

57. Cited in James Reston, "Politics and Religion," *The New York Times*, March 28, 1979.

58. Much of Kupke's document destruction was for naught. Iranian students captured a breathtaking archive of classified data. They retrieved, from embassy shredders, an additional volume of paper that was painstakingly pieced back together. The embassy's sensitive files were published in a series that ran to more than seventy volumes called, "Documents From the U.S. Espionage Den."

59. Hamilton Jordan, *Crisis: The Last Year of the Carter Presidency* (New York: Putnam, 1982), p. 19.

60. Jimmy Carter, "Crisis of Confidence" speech, July 15, 1979, Miller Center of Public Affairs, Scripps Library and Multimedia Archive.

61. Quoted in Bill, *The Eagle and the Lion*, p. 335.

62. Henry Precht, Oral History.

63. Jordan, *Crisis*, p. 31.

64. Ibid., p. 32.

65. I asked Carter whether he had understood the stakes for Rockefeller's bank-

ing interests. "I didn't understand the financial context in which they were operating," Carter said. Carter had known Rockefeller for many years and respected him. But Carter added that he was not willing to second-guess his decision to admit the shah, whose condition clearly had been life-threatening. Carter also had received a measure of assurance from Bazargan's government that it would do its best to protect the embassy. "The decision was a proper one," Carter said. "It didn't turn out well." And, he added, "as far as my awareness of financial benefit that accrued to Rockefeller primarily and secondarily to Kissinger, the answer is no. I never knew anything about that." Interview with Jimmy Carter.

The details of Chase's actions with regard to Iran's assets are set forth in detail in Mark Hulbert, *Interlock: The Untold Story of American Banks, Oil Interests, the Shah's Money, Debts and the Astounding Connections Between Them* (New York: Richardson & Snyder, 1982), pp. 113–72; Bill, *The Eagle and the Lion*, pp. 319–48. In addition, I interviewed Ibrahim Yazdi in Tehran in 1989 and asked him whether the Bazargan government had intended to withdraw its cash reserves from Chase and then default on the shah's loans, leaving Chase saddled with the shah's debts. Yazdi said that there was a strategy to draw down the cash reserves so that the policy decision could then be made on whether to abandon the shah's loans.

66. Bowden, *Guests of the Ayatollah*, p. 20.
67. For a detailed reconstruction of this brazen attack, see Lawrence Wright, *The Looming Tower: al-Qaeda and the Road to 9/11* (New York: Knopf, 2006), pp. 88–94; also Thomas Hegghammer and Stephane Lacroix, "Rejectionist Islamism in Saudi Arabia: The Story of Juhayman al-'Utaibi Revisited," *International Journal of Middle East Studies* 39, no. 1 (2007): 103–22.
68. Memorandum, Brzezinski to Carter, "NSC Weekly Report #122," December 21, 1979, National Security Archive, Iran.
69. Dobrynin, *In Confidence*, p. 442.
70. George Cave, Oral History Workshop, "History of the Iran-Iraq War," July 19, 2004, Woodrow Wilson International Center for Scholars; National Security Archive.
71. Author interview with Prince Bandar, January 8, 1992.
72. Howard Teicher and Gayle Radley Teicher, *Twin Pillars to Desert Storm* (New York: Morrow, 1993), p. 103.
73. William Safire, "The Ayatollah Votes," *The New York Times*, October 27, 1980.
74. Dobrynin, *In Confidence*, pp. 463–64; 469–71.
75. Carter, *Keeping Faith*, p. 14.

## 7. The Shame of Lebanon: Reagan's Warriors in the Middle East

1. Ian Black and Benny Morris, *Israel's Secret Wars: A History of Israel's Intelligence Services* (New York: Grove Press, 1991), pp. 333–34.
2. Author interview with Samuel Lewis, March 15, 2006.
3. Lewis said he believed that Yitzhak Hofi, the Mossad chief, made a trip to Washington in early 1981 to brief senior officials in the Reagan administration, presumably CIA Director William Casey, about issues of concern to Israel. If Casey was informed of an impending strike, he never admitted it. Richard Allen, Reagan's first national security adviser, has stated publicly that

the White House was completely blindsided and that there had been no warning from the intelligence community. Hofi, speaking in an interview on November 20, 2006, said his memory was hazy, but he supposed that he discussed the Iraq threat in early 1981 as an issue of concern. Hofi was interviewed by Omri Sender, the author's research assistant.

4. Alexander M. Haig, Jr., *Caveat: Realism, Reagan and Foreign Policy* (New York: Macmillan, 1984), p. 183 n.

5. A senior Israeli official told me in early 2008 that he distinctly remembers Haig arriving in Israel after being sworn in as secretary of state and informing Prime Minister Menachem Begin that neither France nor Italy was inclined to cease supplying reactor and nuclear fuel technology to Iraq, a conclusion that would have reinforced an Israeli decision to strike. This official, David Ivry, was at the time the Israeli Air Force commander in charge of planning the Osirak raid. He later served as Israel's ambassador to the United States. If Ivry's recollection is correct, Haig's account of his state of awareness remains incomplete.

6. Reagan noted in his diary, after the fact, that, "We have just learned that Israel & the previous Admin. did communicate about Iraq & the nuclear threat & the U.S. agreed it was a threat. There was never a mention of this to us by the outgoing admin. Amb. Lewis cabled word to us after the Israel attack on Iraq & now we find there was a stack of cables & memos tucked away in St. Dept. files." See Ronald Reagan, *The Reagan Diaries* (New York: Harper, 2007), p. 25.

7. Richard Viets, Oral History. Viets had just arrived in Jordan as the new ambassador and Hussein related this story to him during their first meeting. There have been a number of reports that King Hussein observed the Israeli aircraft, but Efraim Halevy, the Mossad officer who was closer to the Jordanian monarch than any other Israeli official, said in an interview that he seriously doubted that the king reported the imminent attack to Baghdad. Halevy said the king might have claimed to have done so to "cover" himself so as not to be blamed by the Iraqi dictator for possibly colluding with Israel.

8. Alan Cranston, "Condemn Israel? Didn't We Plan to Hit Cuba?" *The New York Times*, June 10, 1981.

9. Reagan, *Reagan Diaries*, pp. 25, 24.

10. Press conference, Jerusalem, June 9, 1981.

11. Robert C. McFarlane, who served as Reagan's Middle East envoy and then national security adviser, asserts that Sharon and Begin "saw the ultimate guarantor of Israel's security as being not the United States, but nuclear power. That, he believed, would be sufficient to safeguard the new geography of the Israeli state." This statement seems to imply that the American relationship, therefore, was not important, as it most certainly was to Begin and to Sharon. The reason is that the Israeli military regarded Congress as its dominant political base and the American defense establishment as its industrial patron for developing Israel's indigenous defense industries and for supplying those high-end weapons systems—most crucially military aircraft—that Israel's industrial base could not manufacture at competitive costs. Robert C. McFarlane, *Special Trust* (New York: Cadell & Davies, 1994), p. 208.

12. Meir, *My Life*, pp. 383–85.

13. Ronald Reagan, *An American Life* (New York: Pocket Books, 1990), p. 408.

14. Iraq was a signatory of the Nuclear Non-Proliferation Treaty and, therefore, its nuclear facilities were subject to inspection by the International Atomic Energy Agency.

15. From text of letter sent by Alexander M. Haig Jr. to Thomas P. O'Neill, speaker of the House, *The New York Times*, June 11, 1981.

16. Teicher and Teicher, *Twin Pillars to Desert Storm*, p. 145.

17. Interview with Prince Bandar.

18. Ibid.

19. Haig, *Caveat*, p. 179.

20. The Senate voted 52–48 in favor of the AWACS sale on November 4, 1981. See George J. Church, "AWACS: He Does It Again," *Time*, November 9, 1981.

21. William E. Farrell, "Israeli Jets Destroy 5 Bridges in Lebanon," *The New York Times*, July 17, 1981.

22. James Reston, "What to Do About Begin?" *The New York Times*, July 19, 1981.

23. Quoted from the Saudi Press Agency in John Kifner, "Saudi Calls for Change in U.S. Mideast Policy," *The New York Times*, August 9, 1981.

24. William E. Farrell, "Sadat, With Anger and Sarcasm, Defends His Crackdown on Foes," *The New York Times*, September 10, 1981.

25. Heikal, *Autumn of Fury*, p. 241.

26. Ibid., p. 255.

27. Henry Precht, Oral History.

28. Nicholas Veliotes, Oral History, January 29, 1990, ADST. In his memoir, Haig never mentioned that he had entertained any thought of allowing Israel to renege on the Camp David Accords, but he recounted that Begin spoke to him about the "difficulties involved in returning the Sinai," which was going to require the uprooting of settlers from Yamit. Haig asserted that he pressed Begin not to renege and that Begin reassured him that he would "meet my commitment or resign." *Caveat*, p. 326.

29. Haig, *Caveat*, p. 328.

30. Interview with Samuel Lewis; Haig, *Caveat*, p. 329.

31. Nir Hefez and Gadi Bloom, *Ariel Sharon: A Life* (New York: Random House, 2006), p. 15.

32. Sharon, *Warrior*, p. 15.

33. Haig, *Caveat*, p. 326; David C. Martin and John Wolcott, *Best Laid Plans: The Inside Story of America's War Against Terrorism* (New York: Harper, 1988), p. 87.

34. Amos Perlmutter, *The Life and Times of Menachem Begin* (Garden City, NY: Doubleday, 1987), pp. 380–81; Zeev Schiff and Ehud Yaari, *Israel's Lebanon War*, trans. Ina Friedman (New York: Simon & Schuster, 1984), p. 42.

35. Schiff and Yaari, *Israel's Lebanon War*, p. 66.

36. Reagan, *Reagan Diairies*, pp. 38, 53–55.

37. Schiff and Yaari, *Israel's Lebanon War*, p. 25; Jonathan C. Randal, *Going All the Way: Christian Warlords, Israeli Adventurers, and the War in Lebanon* (New York: Vintage Books, 1983), p. 2.

38. Casey reportedly took Bashir off the CIA payroll so as not to taint him politically and convinced Reagan to sign an intelligence order to provide $10 million in covert aid to Bashir's Phalange militia, which was also receiving Israeli

support from Sharon and from Mossad. See Bob Woodward, *Veil: The Secret Wars of the CIA, 1981–1987* (New York: Simon & Schuster, 1987), pp. 203–05.

39.  The Arab League was formed in 1945 in Cairo and grew to encompass twenty-two member states, serving as a "pan-Arab" organization that brought together Arab leaders to support the Palestinian cause and render regional policy decisions relating to the Arab-Israeli conflict, Lebanon, and other matters.

40.  Thomas L. Friedman, *From Beirut to Jerusalem* (New York: Farrar, Straus and Giroux, 1989), p. 76; Patrick Seale, *Assad of Syria: The Struggle for the Middle East* (Berkeley: University of California Press, 1988), pp. 332–38; Flynt Leverett, *Inheriting Syria: Bashar's Trial by Fire* (Washington, D.C.: Brookings Institution Press, 2005), pp. 35–36.

41.  Interview with Moshe Arens; Schiff and Yaari, *Israel's Lebanon War*, p. 67; Teicher and Teicher, *Twin Pillars to Desert Storm*, p. 195; Haig, *Caveat*, p. 335.

42.  Israel funded, equipped, and trained a surrogate Lebanese militia force along its border, called the South Lebanon Army under a local commander, Major Saad Haddad, who opposed the PLO presence in Lebanon.

43.  Nicholas Veliotes, Oral History.

44.  Richard V. Allen, a former Nixon aide, had advised the Reagan presidential campaign on foreign policy. He was known for hawkish views and for his advocacy of close ties to both Israel and Taiwan. His resignation followed the discovery of gifts he had apparently accepted from Japanese journalists. Allen asserted that he had never intended to keep the gifts and that their retention in a file cabinet was an oversight.

45.  Reagan, *An American Life*, p. 419. Reagan, unlike Carter, had not been willing to pull the levers of American influence that might have restrained Begin and Sharon. Carter had threatened to go to Congress over Begin's use of American weaponry in offensive operations against Lebanon in 1978. Reagan showed no resolve whatsoever to stop the Lebanon War, reinforcing the view that he, too, supported the concept of destroying the PLO presence to pave the way for a Lebanese-Israeli peace.

46.  Argov recovered from the wound but was paralyzed and disabled. He was fifty-two when he was shot and lived quietly with his wife, Hava, who died in 2002. Argov died the next year at the age of seventy-three.

47.  Lawrence Joffe, "Obituary: Shlomo Argov," *Guardian*, February 25, 2003; Teicher and Teicher, *Twin Pillars to Desert Storm*, pp. 196–97.

48.  Schiff and Yaari, *Israel's Lebanon War*, p. 103.

49.  Ibid., pp. 109–30.

50.  Teicher and Teicher, *Twin Pillars to Desert Storm*, p. 199.

51.  Carter told me he had received a telephone call in 1982 from Ezer Weizman saying that "Sharon got a green light from Al Haig" to go after the PLO. Carter explained: "I had dealt with this same threat while I was still in office and I threatened to withhold all aid," referring to Begin's incursion into Southern Lebanon in 1978. "I was going to have Congress declare that Israel was using American weaponry illegally, because the law says that they can use it only for defensive purposes." Haig publicly denied that he had given a green light to the invasion. The White House sent two NSC staffers to Georgia to explain

to Carter that the administration had been aware of only a limited operation to clear out PLO artillery in a twenty-five-mile zone. Begin also sent word to Carter that he had authorized only the limited operation. Interview with Jimmy Carter.

52. Philip Habib, Oral History, May 24, 1984, ADST.

53. Teicher and Teicher, *Twin Pillars to Desert Storm*, pp. 203–04.

54. Haig, *Caveat*, p. 326; Martin and Wolcott, *Best Laid Plans*, p. 91; Teicher and Teicher, *Twin Pillars to Desert Storm*, pp. 205–206.

55. Reagan, *An American Life*, p. 423.

56. Teicher and Teicher, *Twin Pillars to Desert Storm*, pp. 205.

57. Nicholas Veliotes, Oral History.

58. Interview with Prince Bandar.

59. Zeev Schiff and Ehud Yaari, two of the most seasoned Israeli journalists, wrote credulously that Begin was as surprised as his cabinet when Israeli forces turned up in Beirut. A few sentences later, they argued that Begin was either ignorant of what his army was doing, or trying to conceal the truth. The inability of these two veteran analysts of Israeli military affairs to come to a conclusion, given the record they had assembled and their knowledge of Begin's character, in itself strains credulity. Instead, they settle for a judgment that Begin looked like a fool, but that was hardly the point. Schiff and Yaari, *Israel's Lebanon War*, p. 193.

60. Ibid., p. 196.

61. George P. Shultz, *Turmoil and Triumph* (New York: Scribner's, 1993), p. 87.

62. Author interview with Ed Rollins, August 24, 2005.

63. Teicher and Teicher, *Twin Pillars to Desert Storm*, p. 211.

64. Shultz told his aides, "We must avoid the trap of putting the peace process to one side until Lebanon's problems are solved." Shultz, *Turmoil and Triumph*, p. 86.

65. Ibid., p. 91.

66. Casualty statistics taken from Begin's report to Reagan in early September. Reagan, *An American Life*, pp. 432–33.

67. Robert S. Dillon, Oral History, May 17, 1990, ADST. Shartouni's role was detected because he had telephoned the apartment just before the bomb went off and warned his sister, who had stopped by unexpectedly, to flee.

68. Randal, *Going All the Way*, p. 4.

69. Shultz, *Turmoil and Triumph*, p. 105.

70. Teicher and Teicher, *Twin Pillars to Desert Storm*, pp. 214–15. Teicher's argument seems overstated given that Weinberger had no expectation that Gemayel would be assassinated and therefore that a major revenge attack was conceivable. The marines had protected the Palestinians, but more important, Gemayel was an American client, a recipient of CIA covert funding, and, though his goal was to rid Lebanon of the Palestinian refugee population, he could not expect to succeed in doing so by coercion if he hoped to remain an American ally. His assassination created a spontaneous revenge instinct among his forces. Begin even discussed his own concern about this with Sharon, but Sharon did not inform the cabinet or the prime minister about the decision he had taken that allowed the Phalange to enter the camps.

71. Shultz, *Turmoil and Triumph*, p. 105.

72. Walker and Gowers, *Arafat*, p. 207.

73. Edmund Morris, *Dutch: A Memoir of Ronald Reagan* (New York: Random House, 1999), p. 523.

74. Author interview with Philip A. Dur, December 19, 2005.

75. The War Powers Act of 1973 limits the power of the president to wage war by requiring congressional authorization to dispatch American forces in all but emergency situations: where U.S. forces already are under attack or facing imminent threat of attack. In these cases, congressional approval must be sought soon after deployment.

76. Nicholas Veliotes, Oral History.

77. Reagan, *An American Life*, p. 407.

78. Interview with Philip A. Dur.

79. Carter, *Blood of Abraham*, pp. 148–49; Shlomo Gazit, *Trapped Fools*, p. 117.

80. Robert S. Dillon, Oral History.

81. Robert Baer, *See No Evil: The True Story of a Ground Soldier in the CIA War on Terrorism* (New York: Crown, 2002), pp. 65–67.

82. Schiff and Yaari, *Israel's Lebanon War*, p. 293.

83. Teicher and Teicher, *Twin Pillars to Desert Storm*, p. 229.

84. Clark had the best briefing style for Reagan because he understood how Reagan processed information. Reagan hated to ask dumb questions so Clark would bring in experts and interview them in front of Reagan, who would listen and take notes. Reagan took extensive notes as president in a neat and distinctive cursive.

85. Author interview with Prince Bandar, September 21, 2006.

86. The Lebanese army with its Christian officer corps and ranks filled with Shiite, Sunni, and Druze soldiers had largely disintegrated under factional pressure. Only a small contingent of Muslim soldiers still served with the Christians.

87. Shifting alliances in Lebanon could be baffling. Jumblatt saw advantage in standing with Syria even though it was universally assumed that Syria was behind the murder in 1977 of Jumblatt's charismatic father, Kamal Jumblatt.

88. Teicher and Teicher, *Twin Pillars to Desert Storm*, p. 251.

89. Interview with Philip A. Dur. Walid Jumblatt, the Druze leader, also popularized this description of U.S. firepower. During this period, he frequently complained of the Americans: "They're firing Volkswagens at us!"

90. Martin and Walcott, *Best Laid Plans*, p. 125.

91. "Marine Barracks Bombing," *CNN Presents*, August 5, 2006.

92. McFarlane, *Special Trust*, pp. 263, 267.

93. The CIA was providing satellite imagery to Baghdad. The French were selling Super Étendard jets to the Iraqi air force and these were being used to bomb Iranian oil tankers in the Persian Gulf.

94. McFarlane, *Special Trust*, p. 270.

95. "Marine Barracks Bombing," *CNN Presents*.

96. McFarlane, *Special Trust*, pp. 270–71; "Marine Barracks Bombing"; Teicher and Teicher, *Twin Pillars to Desert Storm*, pp. 265–66; author interview with Howard Teicher, August 15, 2005; interview with Philip A. Dur.

97. McFarlane, *Special Trust*, pp. 270–71; In an interview, Caspar Weinberger feigned a poor memory about the incident. He said he didn't think Reagan's "directive" was "anything as definitive as that." He also said he had been "hor-

rified" by the attack on the marines and "wanted to retaliate, but the retaliation, I felt, had to be specific and focused and based upon very much clearer
information than we had."

98.   Martin and Walcott, *Best Laid Plans*, p. 137.

99.   Teicher and Teicher, *Twin Pillars to Desert Storm*, p. 267.

100.  Talking Points for Rumsfeld from U.S. Interests Section in Baghdad, Decem-
      ber 14, 1983, National Security Archive, Iraq.

101.  Interview with Philip A. Dur.

102.  Department of State Cable, Shultz to U.S. Embassy, Jordan, "Chemical
      Weapons: Meeting with Iraqi Charge," April 6, 1984. The cable described a
      March 29, 1984, meeting between Deputy Assistant Secretary of State James
      Placke and Iraqi Ambassador Nizar Hamdoon. National Security Archive,
      Iraq.

103.  Department of State Cable, Shultz to U.S. Embassy Jordan, and U.S. Inter-
      ests Section Baghdad, "Kittani Call on Undersecretary Eagleburger," March 18,
      1984, National Security Archive, Iraq.

104.  Interview with Ed Rollins.

105.  A last-minute effort among young activists—Teicher on the NSC and Dennis
      Ross in the Office of Net Assessment—to sell a larger marine deployment to
      save the central government in Lebanon failed when Armitage, Weinberger's
      policy enforcer, told Teicher that he should "spend less time thinking about
      what to do with the Marines, and more time thinking about a Lebanon policy
      without the Marines." Teicher and Teicher, *Twin Pillars to Desert Storm*, p. 288.

106.  Judith Miller, "Hussein Rules Out Talks With Israel and Bars U.S. Role," *The
      New York Times*, March 15, 1984.

107.  Reiger was rescued in April by militiamen loyal to Nabih Beri of the Shiite
      Amal Party, which followed a more moderate political line than the Iranian-
      backed Hezbollah.

## 8. The Iran-contra Affair: The Clash of Saudi and Israeli Influence

1.    Interview with Prince Bandar, January 8, 1992.

2.    Author interview with Moshe Arens, October 24, 2006.

3.    Bandar was tutored in American politics by Frederick G. Dutton, and his wife,
      Nancy Dutton, both longtime Democratic activists. Dutton had served in the
      State Department under John Kennedy, and he had run Robert Kennedy's
      presidential campaign before becoming a political consultant and, eventually,
      Prince Bandar's ubiquitous traveling companion and adviser.

4.    Unless otherwise noted, all quotes by Prince Bandar and about King Fahd are
      from interviews with Prince Bandar, January and February 1992.

5.    Roosevelt, just weeks before his death, had outmaneuvered Winston
      Churchill in arranging a summit, aboard the warship the USS *Quincy* in the
      Suez Canal, that clinched relations with the Saudi king. The Saudi oil conces-
      sion—and thus the House of Saud—became a vital national interest for the
      United States.

6.    Steve Coll, *Ghost Wars* (New York: Penguin Press, 2004), p. 89.

7.    The American intelligence community prohibited the transfer of the high-
      resolution satellite photography so as to preserve secrecy about their clarity. A
      staff of intelligence community artists was trained to render these photos as
      highly accurate drawings.

8. On September 20, 1984, a van displaying diplomatic license plates drove up to the U.S. embassy annex in Christian East Beirut and the driver detonated its payload of explosives. Among the fourteen dead were two American military officers. The U.S. ambassador, Reggie Bartholomew, was seriously injured. Again there was a debate whether to retaliate for the attack, which intelligence traced once again to the Hezbollah forces operating with Iranian revolutionary guards in the Bekaa Valley. Satellite intelligence revealed that a mock obstacle course, identical to the cement barriers in front of the embassy in Beirut, had been set up near the Sheikh Abdullah Barracks, presumably so the suicide driver could train for his mission. Again, it was not enough for Weinberger, who led the opposition to a retaliatory strike by pointing out the absence of proof of the terrorists' identity and precise location.

9. Bernard Gwertzman, "Fahd Asks Reagan to Step Up Moves for Mideast Peace," *The New York Times*, February 12, 1985.

10. Reagan's diary all but confirms the conspiracy to evade the law. He said Fred Fielding, his White House counsel, Donald Regan, the chief of staff, and Michael Deaver came in to discuss the "Arabian horses that King Fahd wanted to give me." Reagan stated that he could not accept them as a gift "due to our stupid regulations." He then described, with some satisfaction, how they would circumvent the regulations. "As it stands they are now in Prince Bandar's name & he has asked Bill Clark to take care of them for him. Now what happens 4 years from now is anyone's guess." Reagan, *The Reagan Diaries*, p. 305.

11. White House aides, according to one source close to Reagan's inner circle, convinced Mrs. Reagan that she could not keep the diamonds when her husband left office. It is not known whether they were returned. Mrs. Reagan declined to respond to a query about the matter. A spokesperson for Harry Winston also declined to respond to a query.

12. Author interview with a Reagan aide who was aware of the gifts and the consternation they caused.

13. Prince Bandar, interview by Lowell Bergman, *Frontline*, PBS, November 15, 2001.

14. David Leigh and Rob Evans, "The Secret Whitehall Telegram That Reveals Truth Behind Controversial Saudi Arms Deal," *Guardian*, October 28, 2006. In June 2007, the *Guardian* reported that the British aerospace giant, BAE Systems, had paid more than $1.8 billion in secret commissions to a bank account in Washington controlled by Prince Bandar bin Sultan as part of the 1985 arms deal. Bandar was said to have received checks of $50 million a quarter for ten years. Bandar responded that the allegations were untrue and "grotesque in their absurdity." He said the account in question was a Saudi government account that was audited regularly by the Saudi Finance Ministry.

15. Bandar initiated the secret negotiations with the Chinese for CSS-2 Dongfeng (East Wind) ballistic missiles, whose range is eighteen hundred miles. Bandar's brother, General Khaled bin Sultan, who was chief of Air Defense, completed the arrangements in secret talks with Lieutenant General Cao Gangchuan, the deputy chief of staff of China's People's Liberation Army. Though the missiles were designed to carry nuclear warheads, the Chinese reengineered them to carry a one thousand-pound conventional warhead as far as Tehran or Tel Aviv. HRH General Khaled bin Sultan, *Desert Warrior: A*

*Personal View of the Gulf War by the Joint Forces Commander* (New York: Harper, 1995), pp. 137–39.

16. Stories of Shultz turning away from Arab friends are widespread among Saudi business elites. The two Arab businessmen whose friendships with Shultz ended after he entered office were Suleiman Olayan, chairman of Aramco, the oil consortium in Saudi Arabia that was among Bechtel's largest customers, and Hasib Sabar, a Palestinian businessman whose wife was also very close with Shultz's wife Obie. See William Simpson, *The Prince: The Secret Story of the World's Most Intriguing Royal* (New York: Morrow, 2006), pp. 418–19; author interview with Tareq Shawwaf, September 20, 2006.

17. Nora Boustany, "Beirut Bomb's Legacy Suspicion and Tears," *The Washington Post*, March 6, 1988.

18. Bob Woodward reported that Casey conspired with Prince Bandar to subcontract to Saudi intelligence the assassination of Fadlallah. Bandar, who was interviewed by Woodward, has disputed Woodward's account. In an interview, Bandar told me that there was no question that Casey wanted Fadlallah eliminated and, therefore, might have been tempted to strike at him through proxies. But he denied that Saudi intelligence was involved in fomenting the assassination attempt. Woodward, *Veil*, p. 396.

19. Nicholas Blanford, *Killing Mr. Lebanon: The Assassination of Rafik Hariri* (London: I. B. Tauris, 2006), p. 65.

20. Author interview with Duane R. Clarridge, September 16, 2005.

21. Duane R. Clarridge with Digby Diehl, *A Spy for All Seasons: My Life in the CIA* (New York: Scribner, 1997), p. 13.

22. Ibid., p. 16.

23. Ibid.; interview with Duane R. Clarridge. Abul Abbas, whose real name was Mohammed Zaidan, was captured by American forces in Iraq in April 2003 and was held in custody until his death from natural causes on March 8, 2004. At the time, Clarridge was living in retirement in San Diego, working as a security consultant for corporations and wealthy individuals.

24. Interview with Philip A. Dur.

25. Two former senior DIA officers, Louis Andre and W. Patrick Lang, participated in the internal intelligence community debates with Winfred Joshua. Both described her role as influential because she insisted that the Soviet threat to Iran was intensifying, and she believed Iraq to be under the command of Moscow, an assertion that proved false. Joshua could not be reached for comment.

26. McFarlane, *Special Trust*, p. 19.

27. In McFarlane's account of this conversation, there was no request for arms or quid pro quo for the release of hostages. But Kimche asserted, in his own memoir, "I warned him that, in all probability, we would be faced with a request for some American arms." Kimche, *The Last Option*, p. 211. See also Lawrence E. Walsh, *Firewall: The Iran-Contra Conspiracy and Cover-up* (New York: Norton, 1997), p. 38.

28. A more well-grounded assessment in the intelligence community was that the Soviet buildup in the Far East was directed at China.

29. McFarlane, *Special Trust*, pp. 22–23.

30. Walsh, *Firewall*, p. 38.

31. McFarlane, *Special Trust*, p. 34; see also Walsh, *Firewall*, p. 38.

32. On September 25, PLO gunmen shot and killed three Israelis on a yacht anchored in the port at Larnaca on the coast of Cyprus, claiming they were part of an Israeli spying operation that monitored maritime traffic in the eastern Mediterranean. The Israelis responded harshly, sending F-16s across the Mediterranean to Tunis, where they bombed the relocated PLO headquarters, killing more than seventy people. The United Nations Security Council condemned the attack in a 14–0 vote, with the United States abstaining. The Israeli assault on the Palestinian leadership gave Hezbollah the opportunity to announce Buckley's death. A communiqué said that Buckley had been executed in retaliation for the Israeli raid on Tunis. It was accompanied by a photo of the body. Buckley's remains were recovered in 1991. Ted Gup, *The Book of Honor* (New York: Doubleday, 2000), p. 286.

33. CIA Cable to Casey from McMahon, "Present status in saga regarding the movement of TOW missiles," January 25, 1986, National Security Archive.

34. Walsh, *Firewall*, p. 9.

35. Colonel W. Patrick Lang, Oral History, VMI at War Project, Virginia Military Institute.

36. Howard Teicher alludes to the program. "The United States began providing the Iraqi military with critical intelligence and targeting information, as well as with assistance in planning long-range air attacks against Iran." Teicher and Teicher, *Twin Pillars to Desert Storm*, p. 391.

37. When I reported on this DIA program in 2002, Colin Powell, secretary of state under President George W. Bush, issued a statement saying that my description of the program was "dead wrong." Richard Armitage, who had become Powell's deputy secretary, used an expletive to indicate his denial that the United States had acquiesced in the use of chemical weapons. Carlucci, who had signed the order authorizing the DIA operation, told me, "My understanding is that what was provided" to Iraq "was general order of battle information, not operational intelligence." Patrick E. Tyler, "Officers Say U.S. Aided Iraq in War Despite Use of Gas," *The New York Times*, August 18, 2002. I sought to engage Cheney on this question in 2002, when he was making the case publicly for war against Iraq. He was arguing that the proof of Saddam's danger to the world was his use of chemical weapons on his own people. Cheney's spokeswoman, Mary Matalin, severely criticized my inquiry. Cheney declined to discuss it.

38. Simpson, *The Prince*, pp. 180–81.

39. A senior American official who was in the command center of the Middle East Force described Operation *Praying Mantis* in detail to me immediately after the operation had been completed.

40. Frank Carlucci, Oral History, April 1, 1997, ADST.

41. Robert B. Oakley, Oral History, July 7, 1992, ADST.

42. Walker and Gowers, *Arafat*, p. 256.

43. Interview with Eitan Haber.

44. Quoted in Robert D. McFadden, "Kissinger Urged Ban on TV Reports," *The New York Times*, March 5, 1988.

45. John Kifner, "Israel's Silence Reinforces Belief Its Commandos Killed PLO

Aide," *The New York Times*, April 18, 1988; Walker and Gowers, *Arafat*, p. 266; Raviv and Melman, *Every Spy a Prince*, pp. 396–97.

46. Shultz, *Turmoil and Triumph*, p. 1023.
47. Walker and Gowers, *Arafat*, p. 268.
48. Shultz, *Turmoil and Triumph*, p. 1033.
49. Walker and Gowers, *Arafat*, p. 270.
50. Shultz, *Turmoil and Triumph*, p. 1035.
51. Author interview with Rihab Massoud, July 30, 2005.
52. Shultz, *Turmoil and Triumph*, p. 1035.
53. Walker and Gowers, *Arafat*, p. 276.
54. Ibid., p. 284.
55. Some U.S. intelligence officials believed that Iran actually was behind the attack in retaliation for the downing of the civilian Iran Air jet by the USS *Vincennes* in July 1988 that killed 290 people. Iran was believed, by these intelligence officials, to have "subcontracted" the attack on Pan Am Flight 103 to Libyan intelligence and the Damascus-based Palestinian terrorist group of Ahmed Jibril.

## 9.  Nebuchadnezzar-Land: Saddam Hussein and the Persian Gulf War

1. Patrick E. Tyler, "Saddam Adds to Radical Image; Iraqi Turns to Foreign Conquest to Defuse Domestic Unrest," *The Washington Post*, August 3, 1990.
2. George [H. W.] Bush and Brent Scowcroft, *A World Transformed* (New York: Knopf, 1998), pp. 320–21.
3. King Hussein's great-grandfather, Sherif Hussein, had ruled western Arabia from Mecca until King Abdul Aziz conquered the area, known as the Hejaz, and created the Saudi state in 1932. Chas. W. Freeman, Jr., the American ambassador to Saudi Arabia at the time of the Iraqi invasion, asserted that King Fahd suspected collusion between Iraq and Jordan to return the Hashemite dynasty to power in Arabia. King Hussein's brother, Crown Prince Hassan, had been in touch with prominent families in the Hejaz asking for support in the event that King Hussein returned to Mecca to reclaim his family's realm. Chas. W. Freeman, Jr., Oral History, April 14, 1995, ADST.
4. Bush and Scowcroft, *A World Transformed*, p. 321.
5. Author interview with W. Patrick Lang, September 27, 2005.
6. Saddam's act followed the collective decision of the Gulf Cooperation Council (Bahrain, Kuwait, Qatar, Oman, Saudi Arabia, and the UAR) to form a joint defense-planning committee, the advent of which was taken as a signal that Saudi Arabia would not accept Iraqi hegemony in the Gulf following the defeat of Iran.
7. Andrew Cockburn and Cockburn, *Out of the Ashes: The Resurrection of Saddam Hussein* (New York: Harper, 1999), p. 83; Walker and Gowers, *Arafat*, p. 297.
8. The supergun's inventor, a Canadian engineer named Gerald Bull, was assassinated March 22, 1990, reportedly by the Israeli intelligence agency Mossad, outside his home in Brussels, Belgium. At the time, he was directing Project Babylon to provide the new long-range artillery weapon to the Iraqi army.
9. Interview with Prince Bandar, January 8, 1992.
10. Cockburn and Cockburn, *Out of the Ashes*, p. 82.

11. Youssef M. Ibrahim, "Israel Reports Foiling Speedboat Attack on Beach," *The New York Times*, May 31, 1990; Walker and Gowers, *Arafat*, p. 303; Dennis Ross, *The Missing Peace* (New York: Farrar, Straus and Giroux, 2004), p. 100.

12. Ibrahim, "Israel Reports Foiling Speedboat Attack on Beach."

13. Bush and Scowcroft, *A World Transformed*, pp. 306–307.

14. Transcript of Saddam Hussein–April Glaspie meeting, July 25, 1990, as excerpted in *The New York Times*, September 23, 1990.

15. Glaspie, speaking in a March 2008 interview about her meeting with Saddam, said she had not intended to leave Kuwait "when all this concentraton of troops started," but was persuaded when Saddam interrupted the meeting to take a phone call from Egyptian president Hosni Mubarak. Hussein came back to Glaspie and told her that "he told Mubarak not to worry, that there will be no problem and that he will deal with it without making problems." Glaspie added, "I thought he would not be foolish enough to do it [invade Kuwait] the day he told the most powerful person in the Arab world and the Western world [meaning President Bush through his ambassador, Glaspie] that he was not going to do it. I thought I could take my mother who was ill at home [in Baghdad] and turn around and come back within five days." See: Randa Takieddine, "U.S. Ambassador Top Baghdad Tells Al-Hayat the Story of Her Famous Meeting with the Late Iraqi President," *Dar al-Hayat* [in English], March 15, 2008.

16. April Glaspie's diplomatic career suffered dramatically after this exchange with Saddam was made public. It seemed to serve those in the Bush administration who wished her to take the fall for the failure to perceive Saddam's intentions; but it also was seized on by those who were critical of the Bush administration's failure to forcefully deter Iraq from taking precipitous military action. Glaspie never received another ambassadorial appointment. Her last posting was as consul general in Cape Town, South Africa.

17. Bush and Scowcroft, *A World Transformed*, p. 310.

18. Youssef M. Ibrahim, "A New Gulf Alignment," *The New York Times*, August 3, 1990. A senior Saudi adviser to Prince Saud confirmed to me that he had made this remark, which is not attributed by name in the article.

19. Bush and Scowcroft, *A World Transformed*, p. 317.

20. Michael R. Gordon and General Bernard E. Trainor, *The Generals' War: The Inside Story of the Conflict in the Gulf* (Boston: Little, Brown, 1995), pp. 33–34.

21. Bob Woodward, *The Commanders* (New York: Simon & Schuster, 1991), p. 229.

22. Colin L. Powell, *My American Journey* (New York: Random House, 1995), p. 463.

23. Bush and Scowcroft, *A World Transformed*, p. 319.

24. Ibid., p. 319.

25. Ibid., p. 323.

26. Powell, *My American Journey*, p. 464.

27. Woodward, *The Commanders*, p. 237.

28. Bush and Scowcroft, *A World Transformed*, p. 324.

29. DeYoung, *Soldier*, p. 194; Powell, *My American Journey*, p. 464.

30. According to Scowcroft, he and Cheney "were probably the first ones" among

Bush's advisers who "came to the conclusion that we had to have a conflict" with Iraq. Author interview with Brent Scowcroft, March 16, 2006.

31. Simpson, *The Prince*, p. 204; Bush and Scowcroft, *A World Transformed*, p. 325; Woodward, *The Commanders*, p. 240.

32. Interview with Prince Bandar, January 8, 1992; Simpson, *The Prince*, p. 204.

33. Bush and Scowcroft, *A World Transformed*, p. 326.

34. Interview with Prince Bandar, January 8, 1992; Powell, *My American Journey*, p. 465.

35. Powell, *My American Journey*, p. 465; interview with Prince Bandar, January 8, 1992.

36. Interview with W. Patrick Lang.

37. Bush and Scowcroft, *A World Transformed*, p. 328; Woodward, *The Commanders*, p. 251.

38. Bush and Scowcroft, *A World Transformed*, p. 330.

39. Chas. W. Freeman Jr., Oral History.

40. Woodward, *The Commanders*, p. 267.

41. Chas. W. Freeman Jr., Oral History.

42. Saddam's offer of "money and spoils" to Egypt, Jordan, and Yemen was reported in President Bush's memoir, coauthored with Brent Scowcroft, and was based on information conveyed to Bush in telephone conversations with Mubarak and Canadian premier Brian Mulroney. See: Bush and Scowcroft, *A World Transformed*, p. 339.

43. Bush and Scowcroft, *A World Transformed*, p. 340.

44. Halevy, *Man in the Shadows*, p. 28.

45. Bandar bin Sultan al-Saud, "Facts Are Stubborn, Your Majesty," *The New York Times*, September 26, 1990.

46. Halevy, *Man in the Shadows*, p. 28.

47. Walker and Gowers, *Arafat*, p. 314.

48. Author interview with Prince Bandar, October 2001.

49. Douglas Jehl, "Holy War Lured Saudis as Rulers Looked Away," *The New York Times*, December 27, 2001.

50. Bush and Scowcroft, *A World Transformed*, pp. 396, 445.

51. Ibid., p. 447.

52. Before the war had begun, Yitzhak Shamir had met King Hussein secretly in London and made the argument that since Jordan could not prevent Saddam from firing Scuds over Jordan to hit Israel, Jordan should grant Israel permission to fly its forces over Jordanian territory to reach western Iraq for retaliatory raids. The king had said bluntly that he could not be seen as colluding with Israel and that if Israeli aircraft violated his airspace, he would issue orders to attack any intruders. Halevy, *Man in the Shadows*, p. 32.

53. Bush and Scowcroft, *A World Transformed*, p. 452.

54. Author interview with Moshe Arens, December 10, 2006.

55. Cockburn and Cockburn, *Out of the Ashes*, p. 123.

56. Maureen Dowd, "Bush, Scorning Offer, Suggests Iraqis Topple Hussein," *The New York Times*, February 16, 1991. Brent Scowcroft argued that Bush's "impulsive ad lib" led "unfairly" to charges that he had "encouraged the Iraqi people to rise against Saddam and then failed to come to their aid when they did, at the end of the conflict." Scowcroft said that Bush did hope Saddam

could be toppled, "but we never thought that could be done by anyone outside the military and never tried to incite the general population," an assertion that strains credulity. Scowcroft also fails to acknowledge that Bush had tasked the CIA with finding a way to topple Saddam Hussein. A military revolt with the support of the Iraqi people was precisely the model the CIA was trying to develop. The president's mistake, and it was a costly one for thousands of Iraqis who were encouraged by his words and who revolted, was to speak publicly about this goal without considering the consequences; as it was, the war ended and Saddam was still in command of sufficient military force to brutally put down any rebellion. Bush and Scowcroft, *A World Transformed*, p. 472.

57. Bush and Scowcroft, *A World Transformed*, p. 487.
58. "Transcript of President Bush's Address on End of the Gulf War," *The New York Times*, March 7, 1991.
59. Hans Blix, *Disarming Iraq: The Search for Weapons of Mass Destruction* (New York: Pantheon, 2004), pp. 23–25.
60. Patrick E. Tyler, "Bush Links End of Trading Ban to Hussein Exit," *The New York Times*, May 21, 1991.
61. James A. Baker III with Thomas DeFrank, *The Politics of Diplomacy: Revolution, War & Peace, 1989–1992* (New York: Putnam, 1995), pp. 412–14.
62. Thomas L. Friedman, "Baker, in a Middle East Blueprint, Asks Israel to Reach Out to Arabs," *The New York Times*, May 23, 1989.
63. Joel Brinkley, "Israel, Rebuked on Peace Position, Says U.S. Denied It a Honeymoon," *The New York Times*, June 15, 1990. White House spokesman Marlin Fitzwater reported that six thousand to eight thousand people called the White House through the day and into the night after Baker's testimony to express a range of opinions about Middle East peace. "The switchboard was finally blocked to the point where it just couldn't handle any more," Fitzwater said. "They had to put it on an automatic thank-you tape."
64. Baker, *The Politics of Diplomacy*, p. 546; Clifford Krauss, "White House Rebukes Israeli Envoy," *The New York Times*, February 16, 1991.
65. Ross, *The Missing Peace*, p. 68.
66. Baker, *The Politics of Diplomacy*, p. 419.
67. Ibid., pp.549–53; Adam Clymer, "Pro-Israel Lobby Readies for Fight," *The New York Times*, September 15, 1991.
68. Baker, *The Politics of Diplomacy*, p. 547.
69. Excerpts, Presidential News Conference, *The New York Times*, September 13, 1991.
70. "The Middle East Talks: Excerpts from Speeches in Madrid," *The New York Times*, October 31, 1991.
71. Count Folke Bernadotte, a Swedish diplomat, was shot by a team from the Lehi underground group, also called the Stern Gang, on September 17, 1948. Shamir was among the Lehi triumvirate that ordered the assassination. See: Avi Shlaim, *The Iron Wall: Israel and the Arab World* (New York: W. W. Norton & Company, 2000) p. 37; see also J. Bowyer Bell, *Terror Out of Zion: The Shock Troops of Israeli Independence* (New York: Avon Books, 1977), pp. 422–23.
72. Thomas L. Friedman, "Breakthrough Eludes Mideast Talks," *The New York*

*Times*, September 25, 1992; Youssef M. Ibrahim, "The Middle East Lets Itself Consider Peace," *The New York Times*, September 27, 1992.

73. Clyde Haberman, "Now Is the Moment to Achieve Peace, Rabin Tells Arabs," *The New York Times*, July 14, 1992.

74. Moshe Arens, who had served Begin and then Shamir as defense minister and foreign minister, acknowledged that Likud's policies toward the Palestinians had been flawed. "The greatest mistake of all the governments of Israel since 1967 was the lack of attention paid to the Palestinian population," Arens said after the election. "It goes against all the norms of Israeli society." Clyde Haberman, "Arens Faults Prime Minister's 'Greater Israel' Concept," *The New York Times*, June 29, 1992.

75. Ross, *The Missing Peace*, p. 89.

76. Arafat's jet was caught in a sandstorm and went down near the border of Libya and Sudan. As the plane headed into the dunes, Arafat was said to have cried out, "Abu Jihad, I am coming!" Three crew members died. Walker and Gowers, *Arafat*, p. 346; Ibrahim, "The Middle East Lets Itself Consider Peace."

77. Nathaniel C. Nash, "At Least 6 Die as Blast Destroys Israel's Embassy in Buenos Aires," *The New York Times*, March 18, 1992.

78. This terrorist attack was followed by an even more deadly explosion two years later at the Jewish cultural center in Buenos Aires. The July 18, 1994, blast killed eighty-five people, most of them Jews, and wounded three hundred. Investigation again pointed to Hezbollah's terrorist wing, headed by Imad Mughniyah, the shadowy figure who was believed to be responsible for the 1983 terrorist attacks that killed 241 American marines in Lebanon and, separately, destroyed the U.S. embassy in Beirut, killing sixty people. After evading capture for more than two decades, Mughniyah died on February 12, 2008, in Damascus, when an explosive charge hidden in his car detonated.

79. U.S. Department of State, "Patterns of Global Terrorism: 1992—Latin America Overview," April 30, 1993.

80. Halevy, *Man in the Shadows*, p. 44.

81. Patrick E. Tyler, "U.S. Said to Plan Raids on Baghdad if Access Is Denied," *The New York Times*, August 16, 1992.

82. Walsh, *Firewall*, pp. 451–66.

83. "The Man Who Got Away," interview of Abdul Rahman Yasin by Lesley Stahl, *60 Minutes*, May 31, 2002.

84. Khaled Sheikh Mohammed was captured in Pakistan in 2003 and was held by the CIA at a secret detention facility until late 2006, when he was transferred to the American base at Guantánamo Bay, Cuba. During his interrogation, he was subjected to waterboarding, according to testimony by CIA Director Michael V. Hayden in February 2008. In a partially redacted statement read during a closed military tribunal hearing in March 2007, Sheikh Mohammed said he was responsible for planning the 9/11 attacks "from A to Z." He claimed that he had beheaded Daniel Pearl, the *Wall Street Journal* reporter abducted in Pakistan in 2002. He also claimed to have been involved in planning and assisting the 1993 bombing attack on the World Trade Center carried out by his nephew, Ramzi Yousef. Yousef was arrested in 1995 in Islamabad, Pakistan, and returned to the United States for trial. He, along with others, was convicted in 1997 and sentenced in 1998 to life in prison.

## 10. Bill Clinton: Tilting at Peace, Flailing at Saddam

1. Interview with Prince Bandar, September 21, 2006.
2. Author interview with Nabil Fahmy, December 5, 2005. Nabil was the son of Ismail Fahmy, the late Egyptian foreign minister who resigned over Sadat's decision to visit Jerusalem in 1977.
3. Thomas L. Friedman, "The New Presidency; Clinton Backs Raid but Muses About a New Start," *The New York Times*, January 14, 1993.
4. Mark Parris, who served in senior State Department and White House positions on the Middle East, said that Clinton and Anthony Lake, the national security adviser, showed a distinct lack of interest in the early months of the administration in moving aggressively to confront Saddam Hussein over violations of UN resolutions. As Iraqi violations forced the Clinton administration to bring military and covert pressure on Baghdad, there was always an undercurrent of resistance emanating from the Oval Office. Author interview with Mark R. Parris, September 6, 2007.
5. Uri Savir, *The Process: 1,100 Days That Changed the Middle East* (New York: Random House, 1998), pp.16–17.
6. Interview with Amos Eiran. Eiran explained that Rabin had detested Arafat and had been among the strongest voices opposing any contact with the PLO, but in the course of the post-Madrid negotiations, he observed that all of the local Palestinian politicians looked to Arafat and the PLO for leadership, and so he felt the negotiations were a charade, "like theater." After Oslo, Rabin began to see Arafat as a partner, and that was a genuine transformation of his view.
7. Shlomo Ben-Ami, *Scars of War, Wounds of Peace: The Israeli-Arab Tragedy* (New York: Oxford University Press, 2006), p. 208.
8. Savir, *The Process*, pp. 4–5; author interview with Uri Savir, November 21, 2005.
9. Ross, *The Missing Peace*, p. 119.
10. Yossi Beilin, *The Path to Geneva: The Quest for a Permanent Agreement, 1996–2004* (New York: Akashic Books, 2004), p. 54; Savir, *The Process*, p. 87.
11. The Pentagon had canceled all military assistance programs with Jordan. U.S. warships patrolled the Gulf of Aqaba to enforce the embargo on shipments through Jordan to Iraq. Oslo offered King Hussein a new path out of his fix.
12. Rabin privately informed Warren Christopher that Israel was willing to say— only to the Americans—that Israel would withdraw completely from the Golan Heights in exchange for a full peace treaty with Syria. Full peace would include an exchange of ambassadors, open borders for trade and tourism, and American-staffed early-warning posts and other security measures that would protect Israel's water supply.
13. Dennis Ross, *Statecraft: And How to Restore America's Standing in the World* (New York: Farrar, Straus and Giroux, 2007), p. 200.
14. Ross, *The Missing Peace*, p. 140.
15. Ibid., p. 141.
16. In January 1994, Clinton was absorbed with the appointment of a special prosecutor to investigate charges of financial impropriety regarding a failed real estate venture, the Whitewater Development Corporation, which Bill and Hillary Clinton had participated in along with several Arkansas associates. Then, on February 11, a former Arkansas government employee, Paula Corbin

Jones, stated at a Washington news conference that Bill Clinton had made sexual advances to her at a Little Rock hotel in May 1991.

17.  Gazit, *Trapped Fools*, pp. 314, 321, 337.

18.  Savir, *The Process*, pp. 125–28.

19.  In 1998, the Knesset passed a law prohibiting the establishment of memorials for terrorists, after Goldstein's grave became an attraction for religious extremists. The Israeli army removed much of the shrine around the tomb, which was inscribed with a text saying that he "gave his soul for the people of Israel, his Torah and country."

20.  Savir, *The Process*, pp. 121–23.

21.  Shlomo Gazit, who studied the corrosive effects of the occupation, believed that the fault lay with the "military-security leadership, at the highest level, who was not aware or sensitive to the matter, who did not issue new rules of behavior the day after the Oslo declaration was signed and who did not closely oversee what was happening on the ground." Many young Israelis—about three hundred thousand who had served in the territories—had developed feelings of "superiority and contempt" or just "an intense hate of the Palestinians." Gazit, *Trapped Fools*, pp. 314, 321, 337.

22.  Savir, *The Process*, pp. 132–34.

23.  Clyde Haberman, "PLO's Leader Asks Courage of All Sides," *The New York Times,* July 2, 1994.

24.  Joel Greenberg, "Rabin Takes on Right Wing and Critics of PLO Accord," *The New York Times*, July 4, 1994.

25.  Halevy, *Man in the Shadows*, pp. 84–85.

26.  Ibid., p. 88.

27.  Ibid., p. 93.

28.  Elaine Sciolino, "Quoting Bible and Koran, Two Old Foes Pledge Peace," *The New York Times*, July 27, 1994.

29.  Abba Eban, "Hussein, King of Realpolitik," *The New York Times*, July 20, 1994.

30.  Interview with Prince Bandar, September 21, 2006; interview with Rihab Massoud.

31.  Michael R. Gordon, "U.S. Sends Force as Iraqi Soldiers Threaten Kuwait," *The New York Times*, October 8, 1994.

32.  Interview with Prince Bandar, September 21, 2006.

33.  Savir, *The Process*, p. 152; Ross, *The Missing Peace*, p. 151.

34.  Interview with Prince Bandar, September 21, 2006.

35.  Clinton wrote that he "had been impressed by Fahd's call, in early 1993, asking me to stop the ethnic cleansing of the Bosnian Muslims." Bill Clinton, *My Life* (New York: Knopf, 2004), p. 627.

36.  Richard A. Clarke, *Against All Enemies: Inside America's War on Terror* (New York: Free Press, 2004), p. 87.

37.  On the day that Saddam had begun massing his forces, the CIA's deputy director of operations, Ted Price, and his Near East division chief, Frank Anderson, briefed a high-level interagency committee on the status of CIA efforts to create conditions for a coup d'état through covert action. The group included Peter Tarnoff, the undersecretary of state, George Tenet of the National Security Council, Madeleine Albright, the ambassador to the United Nations, and

Admiral David Jeremiah, chairman of the Joint Chiefs of Staff. The meeting reportedly highlighted the sharp disagreements among the professional intelligence officers over whether any real progress had been made in building a network inside Iraq that was reliable or willing to act. Cockburn and Cockburn, *Out of the Ashes*, pp. 168–69.

38. Interview with Prince Bandar, September 21, 2006; interview with Rihab Massoud.

39. George Tenet, who was on the NSC staff at the time and later moved to the CIA, said he had heard this account from Prince Bandar but had never sought to verify it from American officials after he moved to the agency. Anthony Lake, who traveled with Clinton to Hafr al-Batin, said he did not sit in on the meeting with the king. John Deutch, who was CIA director from May 1995 to December 1996, declined to discuss the covert planning under Clinton. Martin Indyk, the NSC aide in charge of the Middle East at the White House, said he was at Hafr al-Batin but was not in the session with Clinton, King Fahd, and Prince Bandar. Indyk did not dispute the Saudi account but suggested that Clinton's enthusiasm notwithstanding, the CIA appeared to have opted to work with Jordanian intelligence for Saddam's overthrow. The Saudis may have been asked for financial support or other assistance but may not have been in the loop for what followed.

40. George Tenet, referring to the U.S. plots against Saddam Hussein in the mid-1990s, wrote that "some of our potential partners in the region had judged that we were not serious because of the paucity of resources devoted and because we had never committed ourselves to supporting covert action with military force. There was always the possibility that U.S. airpower might come into play once we had validated the feasibility of a potential overthrow of Saddam. In practice, the execution of such a plan was extremely difficult and unlikely." Tenet asserts, however, that the CIA learned how to combine covert action with military power in Afghanistan in 2001, but he doesn't explain why the combination was not employed against Saddam during the Clinton years. Tenet, *At the Center of the Storm*, p. 386.

41. Baker, *The Politics of Diplomacy*, pp. 439–41.

42. Jim Hoagland, "How the CIA's Secret War on Saddam Collapsed; A Retired Intelligence Operative Surfaces with Details and Critique of the U.S. Campaign," *The Washington Post*, June 26, 1997.

43. Author interviews with Ahmad Chalabi, June 2003.

44. Saudi officials assumed that the $50 million they contributed to the CIA after the meeting between Clinton and King Fahd went toward the financing of this operation. Saudi Arabia also contributed a census of tribal names and affiliations in Iraq. It was delivered by Prince Turki, the chief of intelligence, on a compact disc, according to a senior Saudi official.

45. Baer, *See No Evil*, p. 199.

46. Ibid., pp. 177–85; author interview with Lieutenant Colonel (Ret.) Rick Francona, October 31, 2005.

47. Author interviews with Anthony Lake, September 14, 2007; Bruce Riedel, September 20, 2007; Martin Indyk, August 29, 2007; Mark R. Parris, September 5, 2007.

48. Tyler, *A Great Wall*, p. 28.

49. Author interview with Ahmad Chalabi, November 11, 2007.

50. James Risen, "FBI Probed Alleged Plot to Kill Hussein," *Los Angeles Times*, February 15, 1998; Cockburn and Cockburn, *Out of the Ashes*, pp. 183–88.

51. Interview with Martin Indyk.

52. Baer, *See No Evil*, p. 191.

53. *Peshmerga* is a Kurdish word that refers to the region's militia in heroic terms as "those who walk before death."

54. Cockburn and Cockburn, *Out of the Ashes*, p. 187. Baer later asserted that he never promised American air support to the Kurds, but key officials, including Chalabi and Hoshyar Zebari, Barzani's longtime adjutant, insisted that Baer *did* promise air support, which was a pledge that was far beyond his orders.

55. The charges apparently arose from the fact that the National Security Agency had intercepted a number of messages relating to the uprising. The Iranians had reported to Tehran on their contacts with Chalabi. According to Baer, Chalabi told the Iranians that the United States had decided to orchestrate the assassination of Saddam and had dispatched an NSC team to northern Iraq headed by "Robert Pope" to accomplish the mission. There was ample reason in Washington to suspect that "Robert Pope" was an alias for Baer, and the investigation, which lasted a year and resulted in no charges, was part of the recriminations over the March 1995 uprising attempt.

56. Cockburn and Cockburn, *Out of the Ashes*, p. 196.

57. Interview with Mark R. Parris.

58. Charles Enderlin, *Shattered Dreams: The Failure of the Peace Process in the Middle East*, 1995–2002 (New York: Other Press, 2002), p. 12.

59. Savir, *The Process*, pp. 201–04.

60. Interview with Amos Eiran.

61. Savir, *The Process*, pp. 153–54.

62. Ross, *The Missing Peace*, pp. 93, 208.

63. Savir, *The Process*, p. 249.

64. In a 1957 assassination attempt, David Ben-Gurion and Golda Meir suffered minor injuries, and Moshe Shapira, the religious affairs minister, was severely wounded, when a deranged young man threw a hand grenade from the visitors' gallery of the Knesset onto the cabinet table, where it exploded.

65. Interview with Uri Savir.

66. Three days after the funeral, Arafat, on his first known visit to Israel, went to express his condolences to Rabin's widow, Leah. In a sign of respect, he took off his kaffiyeh and entered as an aging and balding man. He told Leah Rabin that her husband had been "a hero of peace, but he was also a personal friend." Mrs. Rabin reportedly replied, "My husband regarded you as his partner in peace." The other Middle Eastern countries represented at the funeral were Morocco, Lebanon, Oman, and Qatar. Not represented were Iran, Iraq, Saudi Arabia, Syria, Libya, Yemen, and Kuwait.

67. Ross, *The Missing Peace*, p. 227.

68. Author interview with Efraim Halevy, July 6, 2007.

69. Steven Erlanger, "As Israeli Peace Team Flies Home, Clinton Calls a Special Meeting," *The New York Times*, March 5, 1996.

70. Serge Schmemann, "Peres Government Vows to Carry 'War' into Palestinian Areas," *The New York Times*, March 5, 1996.

71. Author interview with Stan Moskowitz, August 31, 2005.

72. Author interview with CIA officer who participated in DB/Achilles. A senior Clinton administration official said that Lake initially supported the operation but then raised concerns once it was under way, questioning whether CIA's management had thought through such questions as who would come after Saddam. These high-level queries from the White House, together with a consensus by Clinton's top national security aides that there was no need to increase the pressure on Saddam, may well have prompted John Deutch and CIA's top management to delay giving the command to the infiltration team to go into action, thus leaving it exposed. Other knowledgeable officials, including Ahmad Chalabi, argued that regardless of Washington's vacillation, the operation was penetrated from its early stages and never had a chance. No full report of the episode has ever been made public, more than a decade later.

73. Ibid.

74. Author interview with a senior White House official. See also Tim Weiner, "Iraqi Offensive into Kurdish Zone Disrupts U.S. Plot to Oust Hussein," *The New York Times*, September 7, 1996.

75. Cockburn and Cockburn, *Out of the Ashes*, pp. 218, 220; author interview with a Saudi official.

76. A former senior official of the CIA's Near East division said the White House had been caught by surprise by the rapidity of the infiltration and then began to evince concern about the risks of going forward. Author interview with Rob Richer, June 14, 2007.

77. Richard Perle, who had worked for Senator Henry M. Jackson, was aligned with the right wing of Israeli politics, which promoted muscular American policies in the Middle East in strategic alliance with Israel. Chalabi was popular among these conservatives because he was an Arab nationalist who was willing to discreetly engage the Israelis and their supporters in Congress. Some Israeli leaders believed that Saddam's overthrow was within America's capability. Moreover, if Iraq could be wrested from Baath Party control, Israel would benefit from a new Middle East structure: Iraq would become an oil-rich ally in the Persian Gulf, giving Washington—and Israel—leverage over Saudi Arabia and the other Arab stalwarts.

78. Interview with Ahmad Chalabi. Chalabi, speaking via a Skype connection from Baghdad, said that documents from Iraqi intelligence files gathered by the CIA and other agencies in 2003 contained specific references to the 1996 CIA plot and to the Egyptian courier who was operating as Baghdad's agent inside the operation.

79. George Tenet, the CIA deputy director at the time, said in his memoir, published in 2007, "A combination of Saddam's ruthlessness and our own mistakes had resulted in scores of Iraqis in our employ being killed." He added that "the network was compromised by Saddam's security services" resulting, for al-Shahwani, "in the torture and execution of Shahwani's three sons." Tenet, *At the Center of the Storm*, pp. 385–88.

## 11. Clinton: Flight from Terror; Lost Peace

1. The United States had suffered a horrific truck bomb episode the previous year when Timothy McVeigh blew up the Alfred P. Murrah Federal Building in Oklahoma City, killing 168 people and wounding 850. McVeigh was executed by lethal injection on June 11, 2001.

2.  Steven Erlanger, "Survivors of Saudi Explosion Knew at Once It Was a Bomb," *The New York Times*, June 27, 1996; Louis J. Freeh, *My FBI* (New York: St. Martin's Press, 2005), pp. 1–2; Elsa Walsh, "Annals of Politics—Louis Freeh's Last Case," *The New Yorker*, May 14, 2001; Staff Sergeant Phyllis Duff, "Khobar Towers Changed Air Force Focus on Force Protection," *Air Force Print News*, June 23, 2006.

3.  Department of State, Bureau of Intelligence and Research, "Terrorism/Usama bin Laden: Who's Chasing Whom?" July 18, 1996, released to Judicial Watch, August 2005, pursuant to Freedom of Information Act lawsuit.

4.  Bin Laden initially figured as a possible suspect in the Khobar Towers investigation, but that suspicion faded as the evidence mounted against Iran and Saudi Hezbollah.

5.  Richard A. Clarke, the counterterrorism director in the White House, and FBI director Louis Freeh both point out in their memoirs that the Saudis had failed to tell the United States about the intercepted explosives. Freeh adds that had the United States known about this threat, it might have taken measures to further strengthen security at Khobar Towers. But Clarke indicated elsewhere that U.S. intelligence *had* acquired information about the intercepted carload of plastic explosives from its own sources. He said he had learned of it from a review of top secret reports culled from "thousands on file" the day after the bombing. Though it seems there was negligence in both governments, the failure at Khobar Towers was not a lack of warning: Sergeant Guerrero's watch had received a warning of a possible terrorist strike. The failure, rather, was the vulnerability of Khobar Towers itself to a truck bomb on the perimeter fence. After the 1983 attack that killed 241 marines in Beirut, the billeting of servicemen in a building without blast protection or a physical setback from avenues of approach seems to have been the obvious failure of force protection, as a later review concluded. Freeh, *My FBI*, p. 18; Clarke, *Against All Enemies*, p. 113.

6.  Enderlin, *Shattered Dreams*, p. 33.

7.  Interview with Stan Moskowitz. Also see Melissa Boyle Mahle, "A Political-Security Analysis of the Failed Oslo Process," *Middle East Policy Council Journal*, 12 (Spring 2005). Mahle, a former CIA officer, was among those who worked closely with the Palestinian security forces from 1996 to 2000. In the cited article, she writes, "The CIA put together a massive covert-action program that included training, technical assistance and infrastructure development. As the program evolved, the CIA also played the role of a facilitator, restarting Israeli-Palestinian security cooperation and keeping it going, acting as a monitor to evaluate compliance."

8.  Savir, *The Process*, p. 297.

9.  Wright, *The Looming Tower*, p. 307.

10. Serge Schmemann, "U.S. Helps to Start Negotiations to End the Fighting in Lebanon," *The New York Times*, April 16, 1996.

11. Enderlin, *Shattered Dreams*, p. 38.

12. The status of Jerusalem was perhaps the most volatile of issues in the Arab-Israeli dispute, and though the United States was Israel's staunchest international ally, successive administrations had stood firm on maintaining its embassy in Tel Aviv, thus recognizing the competing claims to Jerusalem as an Israeli and Arab capital.

13. Savir, *The Process*, p. 303.

14. Steven Lee Myers, "U.S. Calls Alert as Iraqis Strike a Kurd Enclave," *The New York Times*, September 1, 1996.

15. Alison Mitchell, "U.S. Continuing Bid to Smash Air Defense," *The New York Times*, September 3, 1996.

16. Elaine Sciolino, "Facing Saddam, Again," *The New York Times*, September 4, 1996.

17. Peter L. Bergen, *The Osama bin Laden I Know: An Oral History of al Qaeda's Leader* (New York: Free Press, 2006), pp. 164, 168–69, 182.

18. Ross, *The Missing Peace*, p. 353.

19. Yossi Melman, "Foreign Sources Say . . . ," *Haaretz*, December 31, 2004.

20. Anton LaGuardia, "Hamas Leader Tells How He Survived Murder Attempt," *Daily Telegraph*, October 4, 1997.

21. Jonathan Broder, "Bibi the Bungler," Salon.com, October 7, 1997; Lisa Beyer, "A Hit Gone Wrong," *Time*, October 13, 1997.

22. Enderlin, *Shattered Dreams*, p. 70.

23. According to Efraim Halevy's account, the king's message to Netanyahu about the proposed truce was treated without any particular urgency by Mossad, which was in the middle of preparing the assassination attempt. Netanyahu saw it only after the Meshal debacle had taken place. A later intelligence assessment discounted the Hamas "trial balloon" as not very serious, but Halevy looked back at the episode and reflected, "We will never know if this method of dealing with [Hamas] was the only valid one, for there was never a discussion of their offer of a truce at the time it could have been operative." Halevy, *Man in the Shadows*, p. 166.

24. Ross, *The Missing Peace*, p. 357.

25. On March 22, 2004, Israeli forces assassinated Sheikh Yassin as he was being wheeled out of a mosque after early morning prayers. He was struck by Hellfire missiles from an American-made Apache helicopter. He was succeeded by Abdel Aziz al-Rantissi, the cofounder of Hamas, who was assassinated less than a month later, also by a missile a strike from an American-made helicopter.

26. Enderlin, *Shattered Dreams*, p. 53.

27. Netanyahu himself made a secret approach to Assad, offering to return the Golan as part of a peace treaty. The negotiations were carried on through businessman Ronald Lauder but reached no conclusion before Netanyahu was voted out of office.

28. From Dore Gold interview in Enderlin, *Shattered Dreams*, p. 49.

29. Ben-Ami, *Scars of War, Wounds of Peace*, p. 218; Itamar Rabinovich, *Waging Peace: Israel and the Arabs, 1948–2003* (Princeton: Princeton University Press, 2003), p. 101.

30. This pledge had been ignored by presidents Carter, Reagan, and Bush when it restricted American flexibility. In early 1978, Carter conspired with Sadat to bring a reluctant Begin into peace talks; Reagan had launched his peace plan in 1982 without consulting Begin; and Bush had launched the Madrid peace conference as an outgrowth of commitments and consultations with Arab leaders. Ross, in his memoir, describes the Kissinger-Ford commitment as an inviolable stricture, yet the record suggested otherwise. Ross, *The Missing Peace*, p. 299.

31. Elon, *Jerusalem*, p. 106.

32. Rabinovich, *Waging Peace*, pp. 99–101.

33. Enderlin, *Shattered Dreams*, p. 56.

34. Interview with Stan Moskowitz.

35. Katharine Q. Seelye, "Changing Tactics, Dole Challenges Clinton's Ethics," *The New York Times*, October 9, 1996.

36. Ross, *The Missing Peace*, p. 267; Enderlin, *Shattered Dreams*, p. 59.

37. Martin Peretz, "Hebron's Deep History," *The New York Times*, October 2, 1996.

38. Netanyahu was accused of appointing Roni Bar-On attorney general in exchange for the support of the Shas Party for the Hebron agreement. The leader of the Shas, Aryeh Deri, was facing corruption charges and sought Netanyahu's pledge that Bar-On, once appointed, would drop the corruption case. Netanyahu was never formally charged in the case.

39. Benny Begin said he believed that Arafat and the Palestinian leadership were still committed to the destruction of Israel and that Arafat had shown he was still "at war" by wearing his uniform to the Oslo signing ceremony on the White House lawn. Author interview with Benny Begin, November 24, 2005.

40. Ross, *The Missing Peace*, p. 339.

41. Beilin, *The Path to Geneva*, pp. 64–65.

42. Boris Yeltsin, *Midnight Diaries* (New York: PublicAffairs, 2000), p. 135.

43. Ross, *The Missing Peace*, p. 369.

44. Neither Martin Indyk nor Bruce Riedel, two other senior American officials staffing the Netanyahu visit, recall the offer that Ross asserted, in his extensive memoir of the Clinton years, the president made. Clinton made no reference to the offer in his own memoir.

45. *The 9/11 Commission Report* (New York: Norton, 2004), p. 109; Tenet, *At the Center of the Storm*, p. 261; Coll, *Ghost Wars*, pp. 391-96.

46. Aimal Kansi was executed by lethal injection by Virginia authorities on November 14, 2002.

47. Coll, *Ghost Wars*, p. 396. Clinton declined to be interviewed for this book and did not mention the May 1998 covert planning in his memoir.

48. *The 9/11 Commission Report*, p. 114.

49. Tenet's explanation of CIA deliberations on the Tarnak Farms proposal does not square with either that of Michael Scheuer, the CIA official running the CIA's bin Laden station—Alec Station—at the time, or that of the 9/11 Commission. Tenet argues that all of Scheuer's superiors recommended against it (Scheuer disputes this), yet Tenet does not explain why, if that were so, the plan was forwarded to the White House. And he is silent on Clinton's view of the plan. Tenet, *At the Center of the Storm*, pp. 109–14.

50. Clinton, *My Life*, p. 789.

51. Tenet also had flown to Riyadh in May 1998 after the CIA had learned that Saudi intelligence had disrupted al-Qaeda cells that were planning to attack American forces. *The 9/11 Commission Report*, p. 115.

52. Clinton, *My Life*, p. 775.

53. Tenet, *At the Center of the Storm*, p. 115.

54. Clarke, *Against All Enemies*, p. 184.

55. Ibid.

56. Tenet's explanation for the poor intelligence lacked precision. He says the

CIA was never able to determine bin Laden's movements that night and, therefore, why he was not where the intelligence had said he would be. He also conceded that placing the pharmaceutical plant on the target list was debatable in light of further examination. Tenet, *At the Center of the Storm*, p. 117.

57. Beilin, *The Path to Geneva*, p. 69.

58. Ross, *The Missing Peace*, p. 394.

59. Tenet, *At the Center of the Storm*, p. 66.

60. Ross, *The Missing Peace*, pp. 443–49.

61. Enderlin, *Shattered Dreams*, pp. 84–96; Swisher, *The Truth About Camp David*, p. 29.

62. Tenet, *At the Center of the Storm*, p. 70.

63. Enderlin, *Shattered Dreams*, p. 99.

64. Beilin, *The Path to Geneva*, p. 82.

65. Ross, *The Missing Peace*, p. 489.

66. Enderlin, *Shattered Dreams*, p. 129.

67. Ross, *The Missing Peace*, pp. 542–43.

68. Barak had also discovered that Netanyahu had carried on an extensive secret negotiation with Assad through Ronald Lauder, an American businessman. Documents pertaining to the negotiation gave the lie to Netanyahu's claim that he had never considered giving up the Golan.

69. Enderlin, *Shattered Dreams*, p. 152.

70. Edward W. Said, *The End of the Peace Process: Oslo and After* (New York: Vintage, 2000), p. xv.

71. Edward W. Said, foreword to Noam Chomsky, *Fateful Triangle: The United States, Israel and the Palestinians* (Cambridge, MA: South End Press, 1999), p. viii.

72. Enderlin, *Shattered Dreams*, p. 150.

73. Ibid., p. 181.

74. Jane Perlez, "Clinton Ends Deadlocked Peace Talks," *The New York Times*, July 26, 2000.

75. Joel Greenberg, "Sharon Touches a Nerve, and Jerusalem Explodes," *The New York Times*, September 29, 2000.

76. The death toll of the Second Intifada climbed to more than 4,000 lives in the period 2000–2005. Of those, more than 3,100 were Palestinians killed by Israeli security forces; 950 were Israelis. B'Tselem, the Israeli Center for Human Rights in the Occupied Territories.

77. Beilin, *The Path to Geneva*, pp. 186–88.

78. Tenet, *At the Center of the Storm*, p. 128.

79. Clinton, *My Life*, p. 1,150.

80. Gilead Sher, *The Israeli-Palestinian Peace Negotiations, 1999–2001*, (New York: Routledge, 2006), pp. 208–09; Enderlin, *Shattered Dreams*, p. 343.

81. Author interview with Hassan Abdul Rahman, September 6, 2005.

82. Interview with Prince Bandar, September 21, 2006.

83. Ibid.

84. Interview with Hassan Abdul Rahman, September 6, 2005.

85. Sher, *The Israeli-Palestinian Peace Negotiations*, p. 209.

86. Rich reportedly denied the remarks attributed to Edward Bennett Williams,

which were recalled by Marvin Davis, the oilman and Williams's friend, in an interview with the journalist Evan Thomas. See: Report of the House Committee on Government Reform, "Justice Undone: Clemency Decisions in the Clinton White House," March 14, 2002, p. 23; see also Evan Thomas, *The Man to See: Edward Bennett Williams: Ultimate Insider; Legendary Trial Lawyer* (New York: Simon & Schuster, 1991), p. 417.

87. A Clinton fund-raiser (for both Bill's and Hillary's campaigns) told me in November 2007 that he believed that Rich was willing to reward handsomely whoever helped to obtain the pardon and that payment would likely have been made outside the country or through a foundation.

88. Report of the House Committee on Government Reform, "Justice Undone: Clemency Decisions in the Clinton White House," March 14, 2002, p. 23.

89. Bill Clinton, *My Life*, p. 944.

## 12. George W. Bush: A World of Trouble

1. Rabin had indicated in his first meeting with Clinton that he was prepared to withdraw from the Golan and to dismantle the Israeli settlements there. Interview with Martin Indyk.

2. Author interview with Colin Powell, August 29, 2005; also, DeYoung, *Soldier*, p. 315.

3. George Tenet, who carried over as Bush's CIA director, concurred in this assessment. Author interview with George Tenet, June 6, 2007.

4. Sheryl Gay Stolberg, "Bush and Israel: Unlike His Father," *The New York Times*, August 2, 2006.

5. Remarks by Ariel Sharon, February 7, 2001, transcript in English by Ministry of Foreign Affairs, Israel.

6. Comment to the author by William Safire, circa 2001.

7. Stolberg, "Bush and Israel: Unlike His Father."

8. DeYoung, *Soldier*, p. 315.

9. Interview with Prince Bandar, September 21, 2006.

10. Bush's remarks are recalled by a person who was present.

11. Thomas L. Friedman, "Bush's First Memo," *The New York Times*, March 27, 2001.

12. Jane Perlez, "Bush Hammers Arafat; Takes a Softer Tone with Israel," *The New York Times*, March 30, 2001.

13. Arafat's accusation outraged Efraim Halevy, then Mossad's director. Halevy, *Man in the Shadows*, p. 123; author interview with Efraim Halevy, November 28, 2005.

14. Author interview with a person who heard the conversation.

15. Author interview with a person who was present during the conversation.

16. Author interview with a person who participated in the conversation.

17. In his June 24, 2002, speech, Bush said, "Yet, at this critical moment, if all parties will break with the past and set out on a new path, we can overcome the darkness with the light of hope. Peace requires a new and different Palestinian leadership, so that a Palestinian state can be born. I call on the Palestinian people to elect new leaders, leaders not compromised by terror. I call upon them to build a practicing democracy, based on tolerance and liberty. If the Palestinian people actively pursue these goals, America and the world will actively support their efforts."

18. Glenn Kessler, *The Confidante: Condoleezza Rice and the Creation of the Bush Legacy* (New York: St. Martin's Press, 2007), p. 124.

19. Robert Draper, *Dead Certain: The Presidency of George W. Bush* (New York: Free Press, 2007), p. 183.

20. Baker, *The Politics of Diplomacy*, pp. 440–41.

21. L. Paul Bremer, "What We Got Right in Iraq—No More Mr. Punching Bag," *The Washington Post*, May 13, 2007.

22. Author interview with John Limbert, June 15, 2007.

23. Bernard Lewis, Irving Kristol Lecture, American Enterprise Institute, Washington, D.C., March 20, 2007.

24. Kessler, *The Confidante*, p. 163.

25. UN Resolution 1559 called for the withdrawal of foreign forces from Lebanon and the "disbanding and disarmament" of militias, Hezbollah's being the largest and most fearsome in the south.

26. Amnesty International's assessment of the damage concluded: "The Israeli Air Force launched more than 7,000 air attacks on about 7,000 targets in Lebanon between 12 July and 14 August, while the Navy conducted an additional 2,500 bombardments. The attacks, though widespread, particularly concentrated on certain areas. In addition to the human toll—an estimated 1,183 fatalities, about one third of whom have been children, 4,054 people injured and 970,000 Lebanese people displaced—the civilian infrastructure was severely damaged. The Lebanese government estimates that 31 'vital points' (such as airports, ports, water and sewage treatment plants, electrical facilities) have been completely or partially destroyed, as have around 80 bridges and 94 roads. More than 25 fuel stations and around 900 commercial enterprises were hit. The number of residential properties, offices and shops completely destroyed exceeds 30,000. Two government hospitals—in Bint Jbeil and in Meis al-Jebel—were completely destroyed in Israeli attacks and three others were seriously damaged. In a country of fewer than four million inhabitants, more than 25 per cent of them took to the roads as displaced persons. An estimated 500,000 people sought shelter in Beirut alone, many of them in parks and public spaces, without water or washing facilities."

27. The 2006 war erupted after a Hezbollah squad crossed the border and attacked two Israeli Humvees, killing three soldiers, injuring two, and seizing two others, Ehud Goldwasser and Eldad Regev. During an Israeli rescue attempt that was staged a short time after the ambush, five more Israeli soldiers were killed. The bodies of Goldwasser and Regev were repatriated in black coffins as part of an exchange of remains (and prisoners) in July 2008.

28. Rice, as secretary of state, believed that *she* had a promise from Bush to back her diplomacy aimed at creating a Palestinian state, yet it was quickly apparent that this promise was not specific enough to commit the president to mobilize the bureaucracy and bring leaders to Washington for negotiations, as Clinton, Bush Sr., and Carter had done.

29. Bush speech to UN General Assembly, September 19, 2006.

# ACKNOWLEDGMENTS

Three excellent research assistants worked on this book during the three years that it was a work in progress.

Joseph Method, a graduate of St. Johns College in Annapolis, Maryland, helped me set up the large-scale chronologies that were the foundation of the research. Joseph's intellect was a great source of inspiration, along with his inquisitiveness and idealism.

Charles Hardage, a graduate of the University of Florida and, soon, Georgetown University Law Center, managed the middle year of endless interview transcriptions and the growth of the chronological record of U.S. diplomacy in the Middle East. His tireless efforts and his scholarly rigor and care were crucial to getting the research in final shape for a long year of writing.

Omri Sender, a law student at Tel Aviv University, was of great assistance in digesting Hebrew books and archives cited in the work, not least Ami Gluska's history of decision making during the Six-Day War, but also Moshe Sharett's diary and other indispensable sources. Omri also helped track down Israeli officials to check critical facts. His keen insights and intellectual rigor were invaluable in reviewing the completed manuscript.

This work is in no small measure a product of their devotion and commitment to a history that would be accessible to a broad audience, informative, and *new* in its reliance on recently opened documents, interviews, and penetrating research.

I conducted dozens of interviews for the book, but it is really the product of thousands of interviews and conversations I have had in twenty-five years of following the Middle East, either as a correspondent living in the region or in Washington, D.C., where I covered the White House, State Department, CIA, Pentagon, and Congress over the years, as the Middle East was becoming an increasingly important region for American policy.

I wish to thank the archivists at the Lyndon B. Johnson Library in Austin, Texas, and at the National Archives in College Park, Maryland. Special appreciation goes to Harold H. Saunders, who collected thousands of pages of raw documents related to the Suez conflict and the Six-Day War and compiled them in a multivolume set at the Johnson Library for future researchers.

I owe a great debt to the National Security Archive at George Washington University, where Tom S. Blanton has made a career out of the single-minded pursuit of openness in government, supported by an able staff, including Malcolm

Byrne, deputy director, and William Burr, one of the most indefatigable inves-
tigative researchers. Many of the declassified collections that I relied on, especially documents from the Nixon, Ford, and Carter administrations, and most
particularly the twenty thousand pages of telephone conversations (Telcons) of
Henry Kissinger, are open as a result of relentless Freedom of Information Act
requests by the archive.

The professional archivists themselves have responded to requests for declas-
sification reviews on many document collections, including the large Nixon collection released in November 2007. This book is the first comprehensive history
of U.S. Middle East policy to take advantage of the combined new releases.

The Woodrow Wilson International Center for Scholars, especially its president, Lee Hamilton (and his deputy, Mike Van Dusen), gave me a wonderful
home during the first half year of writing. The National Security Archive gave me
additional support as a research fellow.

At Farrar, Straus and Giroux, I am most grateful to Jonathan Galassi, the president, who bought my proposal in 2005 and assigned senior editor Paul Elie to
assist brilliantly in shaping the manuscript.

From beginning to end, I was served by one of the most creative and experienced team of agents anyone could have: Robert L. Bernstein and Peter W.
Bernstein, who brought me into their extended family and have supported me
with ideas and introductions in the pursuit of worthy projects that deserve our
collective attention. They are the best. Felicity Bryan, a good friend in the
United Kingdom, inspired the proposal for *A World of Trouble* by showing me,
one day over coffee at the Savoy in 2004, what she described as "the best book
proposal I have ever read." It had nothing to do with the Middle East, but it was
so majestic in its command of its subject (Christianity) that it got me thinking
about a very broad treatment of the American presidency and the Middle East.

I owe immense thanks to Douglas Roberts, a longtime friend and a foreign editor at National Public Radio, who, in our younger days, was a frequent traveling
companion in the press pack that flitted around the Middle East chasing the latest news. He read the manuscript, parts of it more than once, and made excellent suggestions and corrections reflecting his experience and wisdom in a life
devoted to the Middle East. Special thanks also to Nora Boustany of *The Washington Post*, who tutored me on Lebanon over the years and probably saved my
life during a crossing of the Green Line that divided Beirut during the civil war;
also to Jonathan C. Randal, the *Washington Post* veteran who took me out to the
region in 1986 and introduced me around in Arab capitals. I shall never forget
his generosity. My most literate traveling companion over the years, from whom
I am still learning about the Middle East, is Christopher Dickey, the stalwart of
*Newsweek*.

I would never have reached the Middle East had it not been for the support of some of the great editors of our time: Benjamin C. Bradlee at *The Washington Post*, and also Bob Woodward, Jim Hoagland, and Michael Getler. At *The New York Times*, Max Frankel and Joseph Lelyveld, after hiring me in 1990, sent me immediately to Baghdad to witness what in 1991 we thought would be Saddam Hussein's destruction; Howell Raines sent me back to Baghdad in 2003 to witness it again. Howell and I shared a common mentor in Eugene C. Patterson of *The St. Petersburg Times*, and Gene, at a moment like this, would simply say what I feel: I have gloried in my association with all of them.

# INDEX

Page numbers in *italics* refer to illustrations.

Abbas, Mahmoud, 409, 445, 480–81, 550
Abdullah, Ahmed, 488
Abdullah, Crown Prince of Saudi Arabia, 9,
    200, 375, 376, 500, 514, 533, 534–36
Abdullah, King of Jordan, 445, 541, 549,
    558n4
Abrams, Elliott, 11
Abu Abbas, 325–27, 349, 360, 378,
    588n23
Abu Ala, 409, 410, 502
Abu Ghraib, 9, 451
Abu Iyad, *see* Khalaf, Salah
Abu Jihad, *see* Wazir, Khalil al-
Abu Mazen, *see* Abbas, Mahmoud
Abu Nidal organization, 199, 276, 378
Abu Sharif, Bassam, 347
Acheson, Dean, 73, 559n9
*Achille Lauro*, 325, 326, 349, 360
Afghanistan, 199, 200, 380, 399, 426, 487;
    radicalism in, 398; Soviet invasion of, 14,
    243, 246, 257, 261, 314–15, 316, 321,
    330, 348, 397, 459; U.S. invasion of, 538,
    597n40
Agnew, Spiro, 137, 138
Agreement on the Prevention of Nuclear
    War, 122, 129
Agronsky, Martin, 21
Ahern, Thomas, 237
Ahmed Jibril, 590n55
Aidid, Mohamed Farrah, 425
AIPAC, 312, 387, 389, 476
*Al-Ahram*, 50, 199, 263
Alam, Assadollah, 219
al-Aqsa Mosque, 22, 178, 445, 477, 506,
    508, 558n4
Alawi, Ayad, 452, 454, 455
Albert, Carl, 169
Albright, Madeleine, 480, 490, 491, 499,
    526, 596n37
Alec Station, 602
Algeria, 14, 156, 315, 570n16
Algiers, 347
Ali Mosque, 219
Allawi, Iyad, 542–43

Allen, Richard V., 274–75, 580–81n3, 583n44
Alpha Project, 44
al-Qaeda, 7, 9, 400, 459–60, 481, 484, 488,
    511, 530, 537, 540, 557n5
Al Shifa Pharmaceutical factory, 489–90
Amer, Abdel-Hakim, 43, 104
American Israeli Public Affairs Committee,
    *see* AIPAC
Ames, Robert, 291–92
Amichai, Yehuda, 506
Amini, Ali, 227
Amir, Yigal, 443–44
Amit, Meir, 85, 86–87, 93–96, 565n35,
    566n51
Amit, Yona, 86
Amman, 4, 118–19
Amnesty International, 605n26
Anderson, Frank, 596n37
Anderson, John, 257
Anderson, Robert, 98
Anderson, Terry, 324
Andre, Louis, 588n25
Angleton, James J., 94, 575n39
Anglo-Iranian Oil Company, 218
Angola, 315, 316, 348
anthrax attacks, 538
Aoun, Michel, 296
Aqaba, Gulf of, 29, 56, 60, 62, 71, 81, 83,
    84, 85, 87, 89, 94, 97, 249–50, 254, 378,
    595n11
Arab Cooperation Council, 358
Arab-Israeli Control Group, 94
Arab League, 108, 109, 361, 447, 583n39
Arafat, Yasser, 8, 11, 104, 109, 111, 114–15,
    116, 117, 119, 120, 179, 187–88, 192,
    196, 198, 232, 242, 263, 304, 327, 347,
    394, 409, 410, 442–43, 445, 450, 472,
    474, 477, 479–80, 482, 499, 502, 505,
    508, 509, 517, 521–22, 526, 529, 530,
    532, 533–34, 540, 568n12, 575n39,
    576n44, 594n76, 595n6, 602n39; at
    Camp David summit, 503–505, 507;
    Clinton's final proposal and, 513–19;
    Gaza-Jericho Agreement and, 417–18; in

Arafat, Yasser, (*cont.*)
  Geneva, 349–50; on Hebron massacre,
    413, 414–16, 417; intifada and, 343,
    344–45, 346, 349; and Israeli invasion of
    Lebanon, 268, 271, 279, 282, 284; at Oslo
    signing, 402–403, 404, 405–406, *406*, 407,
    477, 502, 517–18; Palestinian statehood
    sought by, 348, 490, 540–41; Saddam
    Hussein and, 378, 388; on tunnel opening,
    478–79; at Wye summit, 491, 492
Aramco, 457
Arbenz, Jacobo, 52
Arens, Moshe, 285, 295, 311, 360–61, 382,
    383, 461, 594*n74*
Argov, Shlomo, 275–76, 583*n46*
Armitage, Richard, 335, 586*n105*, 589*n37*
Arms Export Control Act, 197
Arnett, Peter, 382, 469
Ashrawi, Hanan, 393
Aspin, Les, 433
Assad, Bashar al-, 412, 547
Assad, Basil al-, 412
Assad, Hafez al-, 77, 143, 149, 179, 182,
    188, 193, 257, 272–73, 276, 278, 292,
    293, 294, 305, 377, 389, 411–12, 424,
    446, 448, 470, 498–99, 501, 524, 528,
    601*n27*
Assad, Rifaat al-, 272–73
Associated Press, 157
Aswan Dam, 45, 48, 49, 50, 51, 58, 108,
    195
Atassi, Nureddin, 77
Atherton, Roy, 265
Atlantic Alliance, 59
Atomic Energy Agency, 386
Atoms for Peace program, 561*n38*
Atta, Mohammed, 462
Atwan, Abdel Bari, 467, 469
Avrahami, Yossi, 509
Ayyash, Yehiya, 448, 477
Azhari, Gholam Reza, 226–27, 228
Aziz, Tariq, 327, 361
Azulay, Avner, 520


Baath Party, Iraqi, 6, 251, 326, 427, 452,
    599*n77*
Baath Party, Syrian, 77
Badr Brigade, 435
Baer, Robert, 428–29, 431, 432, 434,
    435–36, 437, 438, 439, 453, 466,
    598*nn54, 55*
Baghdad Pact, 46, 48, 49, 53, 218, 560*n33*,
    561*n48*
Bahrain, 14, 234, 302, 327, 394, 579*n50*
Baker, Howard, 160, 333, 349

Baker, James, III, 16, 281, 311, 357, 369,
    383, 388, 394, 427, 543, 593*n63*; Pales-
    tinians and Israelis and, 389, 390, 407;
    Persian Gulf War and, 377, 386–87
Bakhtiar, Shahpur, 229, 230, 231, 232
Bakr, Ahmed Hassan al-, 251
Bakshi-Doron, Eliyahu, 509
Balfour, Arthur James, 33
Balfour Declaration, 33, 558*n3*
Ball, George W., 228, 229
Bandar bin Sultan, Prince of Saudi Arabia,
    3–5, 8–9, 10–11, 12, 200, 243, 260, 281,
    294, 295, 320, 335, 348, 349, 387,
    421–23, 424, 425, 446, 515, 516–17,
    518, 534–36, 537, 549, 586*n3*, 587*nn10,
    14, 15*, 588*n18*, 597*n39*; on Bir al Abed
    bombing, 323–24; Fahd's U.S. visit and,
    318–19, 320–21; GWB and, 530–32; in
    Iran-contra affair, 311–14, 316; and Iraq's
    invasion of Kuwait, 368–72, 375, 378; at
    Khobar Towers, 459; at Madrid Confer-
    ence, 392; at Oslo signing, 403, 404,
    405–407; Saddam Hussein visited by,
    359; on Saddam's use of gas, 338
Bandung Conference, 46
Banna, Sabri al-, *see* Abu Nidal organization
Barak, Aharon, 206
Barak, Ehud, 155, 411, 447, 497–501, 513,
    514–15, 516, 517, 519, 521–22, 523,
    526–27, 528, 603*n68*; at Camp David
    summit, 502–505, 507
Barak, Fadil, 326–27
Baring, George, 171
Barka, Mehdi Ben, 85
Bar-On, Roni, 602*n38*
Barre, Mohammed Siad, 200
Bartholomew, Reggie, 587*n8*
Barzani, Massoud, 434, 436, 437–39, 465, 466
Barzani, Mustafa, 438
Batin, Hafr al-, 424
Battle, Lucius, 76–77, 83
Bay of Pigs, 433, 436, 452
Baz, Osama el-, 192
Bazargan, Mehdi, 226, 233, 238, 240, 243,
    580*n65*
Bazoft, Farzad, 358, 359
Bechtel, 257, 284–85, 301, 322, 588*n16*
Beckwith, Charles, 244
Begin, Aliza, 290
Begin, Benny, 461, 480, 602*n39*
Begin, Menachem, 35, 36, 70, 81, 103, 113,
    126, 188, 191, 197–98, 236, 262,
    266–67, 269, 271, 274, 282, 346, 476,
    482, 528, 575*n29*, 576*n61*, 582*n28*,
    584*nn59, 70*, 594*n74*, 601*n30*; at Camp
    David summit, 201–208, 221–22, 228,

234–37, 247–48, 318, 372, 410, 503, 601n30; Carter's meetings with, 185–87, 196, 199; Lebanon strikes and, 263, 273, 275, 277, 280, 281, 283–84, 287, 290, 583nn45, 51; and occupied territories, 186; Osirak reactor and, 251, 252, 255, 581n5; and Sadat's visit to Israel, 178, 179, 193, 194–95; Sinai desired by, 250

Beilin, Yossi, 509

Ben-Ami, Shlomo, 409

Ben-Gurion, David, 28–29, 35, 45, 46, 47, 63, 66, 68, 71, 82, 85, 173, 184, 186, 198, 250, 252, 255, 269, 275, 421, 444, 447, 564n19, 598n64; in Suez Crisis, 20, 21, 22–23, 26, 28, 29–31, 56, 60, 62, 315

Bergen, Peter, 469

Berger, Sandy, 421–23, 464, 480, 486, 490, 491, 492, 512, 517, 519

Bergman, Ronen, 565n35

Beri, Nabih, 586n107

Berlin crisis, 88

Berlin Wall, 212, 358, 391, 399

Bernadotte, Folke, 392, 593n71

Bet Shemesh shooting, 481

Bill, James A., 221

bin Laden, Osama, 9, 17, 398, 400, 460, 467, 468, 469, 530, 537, 540, 600n4, 602–603n56; CIA's tracking of, 484, 485, 488–89; Cole bombing and, 511–12; Persian Gulf War and, 379–80; wars declared by, 467, 484, 487

bin Sultan, Khaled, 321, 587nn14, 15

Bir al Abed bombing, 323–24

Black, Eugene, 48

"Black Hawk Down," 425

Black September, 109, 110, 117, 118, 119, 120, 121, 179, 268, 403, 568n12

Blair, Tony, 11, 540, 541, 549, 550

Blix, Hans, 542

Boland Amendment, 310

Bolling, Landrum, 187–88

Borchgrave, Arnaud de, 130, 134

Bosnia, 424–25, 464

Boumedienne, Houari, 570n16

Boutros-Ghali, Boutros, 195, 576n49

Bradlee, Ben, 312

Brady, Nicholas, 364

Brandeis, Louis, 559n9

Bremer, L. Paul, III, 543–44

Brewer, Eleanor, 562n53

Brezhnev, Leonid, 16, 113, 116, 122–23, 126, 127–30, 133, 212, 257, 570n16; and Yom Kippur War, 145, 146, 153, 154, 159, 160–62, 164–68, 170, 171, 172, 464

Brindel, Glenn, 335

Brinn, Paul X., 339

British Petroleum, 25, 26, 214

Brookings Institution, 180

Brown, Harold, 180, 208, 231, 233–34, 242, 253

Brzezinski, Zbigniew, 180–81, 191, 192, 193, 196, 202, 223, 225, 226, 227, 229, 230, 231, 232, 234, 237, 239, 240, 241, 242, 244, 253, 578n28

B'Tselem, 603n76

Buchanan, Patrick, 398

Buckley, William, 295, 307, 322, 324, 332, 589n32

Buenos Aires, 395, 396, 594n78

Bull, Gerald, 590n8

Bundy, McGeorge, 73

Bush, Barbara, 363, 382

Bush, George H. W., 15, 262, 279, 281, 302, 311, 319, 331, 349, 352–53, 362, 365, 394, 401, 411, 424, 427, 513, 527, 530, 591n15; Bandar's friendship with, 3; Gulf War waged by, 16; and Iraq invasion of Kuwait, 353, 354–55, 356, 363–64, 366–74, 376–77; Iraq uprising encouraged by, 433, 545, 592n42, 592–93n56; at Madrid conference, 390–91; Palestinians and Israelis and, 389, 390, 407; Persian Gulf War and, 377, 382, 384–85, 386–87; P.L.O. dialogue suspended by, 361; Saddam Hussein's plot against, 428

Bush, George W., 10, 15, 18, 280, 510, 512, 520, 522, 523, 528, 529, 534–36, 547–48, 551, 589n37, 604n17; Bandar and, 3, 12, 530–32, 535–36, 549; Palestinian statehood and, 535, 536, 540–41, 549–50, 551; Tenet defended by, 7–8; torture sanctioned by, 9–11, 557nn3, 6, 557–58n7; in war on terror, 538–39, 539

Bush, Prescott, 382

Bush (G. W.) administration, 4

Byroade, Henry, 47

Caffery, Jefferson, 42

Cairo, 107–108, 155

Calero, Adolfo, 319

Camp David summit (1978), 201–209, 220, 221–22, 227, 228, 234–35, 249, 263, 264, 266, 274, 284–85, 290, 318, 346, 372, 410, 503, 582n28, 601n30

Camp David summit (2000), 502–505, 507

Carlucci, Frank, 333, 334, 336, 339, 341, 589n37

Carmon, David, 86

Carter, Jimmy, 14, 176, 180, 186, 192, 193, 211, 212, 252, 257, 260, 265, 270, 275, 277, 285, 290, 311, 312, 317, 355, 371,

Carter, Jimmy (*cont.*)
385, 411, 423, 427, 464, 582*n*28, 583*n*45, 583–84*n*51; Begin's meetings with, 186–87, 196, 199; at Camp David summit, 201–209, 220, 221–22, 227, 228, 234–37, 247–48, 266, 318, 372, 503, 601*n*30; Dayan's meeting with, 189–90; Egypt visited by, 235–36; hostage crisis and, 239, 242–44, 245, 246–47, 252, 308; human rights emphasized by, 212–13, 219, 223; Iranian Revolution and, 221–22, 223, 224–29, 233, 579–80*n*65; Middle East rapid deployment force of, 234; on Palestinian homeland, 177, 182, 183, 184, 187; Rabin's meeting with, 183–84; Tehran visited by, 213
Carter, Rosalynn, 187, 213, 235
Carter Doctrine, 243, 245
Casey, William, 8, 258–61, 273, 275, 292, 302–303, 308, 310, 312, 314, 322, 325, 331, 332, 428, 580*n*3, 582*n*38, 588*n*18
Castro, Fidel, 258–59
Catto, Henry, 353, 354
Cave, George, 243, 329
CBS *Special Reports*, 75
Cedar Revolution, 547
Central Intelligence Agency (CIA), 48, 79, 83, 86, 94, 123, 131, 237, 241–42, 259, 270, 275, 336, 419, 427, 431, 450, 465, 467, 551, 562*n*53, 592–93*n*56; Abu Abbas and, 325–27; assassination plots of, 258–39; bin Laden tracked by, 484, 485, 488–89; Bir al Abed bombing and, 323–24; *Cole* bombing and, 511–12; Eisenhower Doctrine rejected by, 59; interrogations by, 9–11; Iranian coup by, 25–26; Iraq and, 6, 7, 428–29, 432, 433–39, 450–56, 461; Israel's nuclear weapons monitored by, 66; Nasser and, 42–43, 76, 80, 101; Near East Division of, 4, 5*n*, 326; Palestinian security force trained by, 461–62; shah funded by, 218; Syrian coup attempted by, 52–53; Yom Kippur War and, 136, 137, 142, 146–47, 149; *see also* Tenet, George
Chad, 13, 245
Chalabi, Ahmed, 429–31, 434, 436–39, 452, 454–55, 456, 465, 466, 467, 542, 598*nn*54, 55, 599*nn*72, 77, 78
Chamberlain, Neville, 49, 410–11
Chamoun, Camille, 53, 63, 271, 288
Chancellor, John, 74
Chase Manhattan Bank, 240, 241, 579–80
Cheney, Dick, 5, 11, 338, 357, 364, 370, 371, 372, 373, 374–76, 382, 398, 526, 530, 534–35, 536, 540, 546, 557*n*3, 589*n*37, 591–92*n*30

China, 24, 30, 66, 111, 112, 139, 223, 314, 321, 322, 328, 357, 444, 458, 529, 554, 588*n*28; nuclear arsenal of, 122–23
Chirac, Jacques, 251
Christian, George, 65, 74, 75, 90
Christopher, Warren, 232, 403–404, 476, 490, 595*n*12
Churchill, Winston, 22, 25, 33–34, 37, 48, 62, 111, 211, 214, 218, 586*n*5
Chuvakin, Dimitri, 79
Clark, Ramsey, 242
Clark, William P., 277, 280, 283, 287, 294, 295, 319, 585*n*84, 587*n*10
Clarke, Richard, 489, 530, 600*n*5
Clarridge, Duane R., 325–27, 428, 588*n*23
Clements, William, 150, 156
Clifford, Clark, 73, 88–89
Clinton, Bill, 15, 17, 399, 400, 401, 407–408, 413, 435, 439, 445, 449–50, 473, 519, 520–24, 525–26, 532, 595–96*n*16, 596*n*35, 602*nn*44, 47, 604*n*1; Bandar's nuclear umbrella request of, 12; bin Laden tracked by, 486–87, 530; at Camp David summit, 502–505, 507; *Cole* bombing and, 511; cruise missile attacks on Iraq by, 466–67, 495–96; empathy of, 424, 425, 522, 524; Fahd's meeting with, 424, 425–27, 432; final peace plan of, 512–19, 526–27, 549; impeachment of, 488, 493; on Khobar Towers bombing, 459; and King Hussein and Rabin's peace, 419–21, 423–24; at Oslo signing, 402–403, 405–406, *406*, 407, 416, 517–18; Palestinian statehood and, 12, 490, 510, 513; Saddam Hussein and, 422, 440, 452, 453, 454, 456, 466–67, 595*n*4, 597*nn*39, *40*, *44*, 599*n*72; scandals of, 416, 482, 483, 484, 486, 487, 488, 491, 595–96*n*16
Clinton, Hillary, 419, 510, 595*n*16
Cogan, Chuck, 312
Cohen, David, 453
Cohen, Eli, 470
Colby, William, 141, 142, 156, 167
Cold War, 13, 123, 124, 212, 256, 280, 289, 352, 356, 357, 362, 381, 385, 457–58
*Cole*, USS, 510–12
Collett, Alec, 324
communism, 25, 26
Conference of Presidents of Major American Jewish Organizations, 191
Conference on Security and Cooperation, 212
Congress, U.S., 11, 17, 28, 50, 88, 581*n*11; Israeli lobby in, 16, 173; Persian Gulf War

resolutions on, 381; *see also* House of
  Representatives, U.S.; Senate, U.S.
Contract with America, 439
contras, 279, 309, 310–14, 316, 325, 333
Cox, Archibald, 137, 157, 159–60, 163,
  168–69
Cranston, Alan, 124
Craxi, Benito, 325
Crocker, Ryan, 287
Cronkite, Walter, 194
Crowe, William J., 339
Cuba, 257, 298, 315
Cuban missile crisis, 66
Czechoslovakia, 48, 259

Dahlan, Mohammed, 448, 492–93, 513
Daoud, Abu, 118–19, 120
Daoud, Muhammad, 199
Darfur crisis, 544
Darman, Richard, 366
Darwish, Zeinab, 323
Dawa, al-, 302
Dayan, Moshe, 36–37, 113, 118, 126, 133,
  186, 191, 194, 199, 201, 412, 507,
  564n29; at Camp David summit, 202,
  206, 207; Carter's meeting with, 189–90;
  at Morocco summit, 188–89; and Sadat's
  visit to Israel, 178, 179; and Six-Day War,
  71, 81, 82, 85–86, 91, 95, 96, 99, 102,
  103, 566n51; in Suez Crisis, 28; in Yom
  Kippur War, 141, 145, 155, 164, 172,
  570n13
DB/Achilles, 431, 599n72
Dean, John, 126–27
Deaver, Michael, 280, 281, 320, 587n10
de-baathification, 543–44
Defense Department, U.S., 149, 181
Defense Intelligence Agency (DIA), 334, 336,
  358, 386, 431, 451, 571–72n29, 589n37
Defense Ministry, Iraqi, 254
Defense Ministry, Israeli, 90
de Gaulle, Charles, 71, 84, 91, 111, 315
Deir Yassin massacre, 35
Delamare, Louis, 291
de Lesseps, Ferdinand, 51
Deri, Aryeh, 602n38
Derian, Patricia M., 212, 223
Desert Fox, 496
d'Estaing, Valéry Giscard, 230
détente, 113, 127, 129, 133, 141, 145, 146,
  148, 152, 153, 154, 168, 181, 357, 573
Deutch, John M., 439, 441, 455, 456, 485,
  597n39, 599n72
DiFranco, Eddie, 297
Dillon, Robert S., 287, 290–91

Dimona complex, 63, 66, 70, 86, 90, 252,
  379, 561n38
Dinitz, Simcha, 140, 141, 150, 151, 164,
  165, 166, 167, 170–71, 571n23
Dobrynin, Anatoly, 122, 129, 138, 147, 165,
  172, 242–43, 246, 570n16
Dole, Bob, 454, 479
Dome of the Rock, 22, 445, 477, 506
Dozoretz, Beth, 520, 521
Draper, Morris, 274
Dreyfus, Alfred, 32
Drudge Report, 482
Druze, 294, 295, 296
Duelfer, Charles, 557n2
Dulles, Allen, 42, 52, 63
Dulles, John Foster, 12, 25, 36, 44, 45, 46,
  47, 48, 49, 50, 63, 71; Eban's meeting
  with, 19–20, 21–22, 23–24, 26–27; in
  Suez Crisis, 19–20, 21–22, 23–24, 26–27,
  28, 37–38, 52, 53, 54, 55, 56–58, 59, 60,
  558n6, 560n33, 562n58
Dur, Philip, 288, 297, 303, 329
Dura, Mohammed al-, 508–509
Dutton, Frederick G., 586n3
Dutton, Nancy, 586n3

Eagleburger, Lawrence, 287, 292, 300, 383
Eban, Abba, 25, 56, 60, 62, 82, 84–85, 87,
  88–89, 91, 95, 101, 102, 134, 142, 287,
  421, 567n64; John Foster Dulles's meeting with, 19–20, 21–22, 23–24, 26–27;
  LBJ's meeting with, 71–72, 89–90
*Economist, The*, 475
Eden, Anthony, 30, 48–49, 51, 52, 54, 55,
  56–58, 62
Egypt, 9, 20, 21, 34, 40–41, 71, 105, 121,
  124, 127, 128, 233, 234, 235, 314, 358,
  363, 376, 377, 397, 410, 505, 564n21,
  566n51, 570n16, 592n42; American aid
  to, 42, 43, 44, 563n9; as British protectorate, 39; Communists in, 26, 41; economy of, 76; Soviet arms purchased by, 30,
  47–48, 49, 50–51, 77, 108, 133, 183; in
  war with Libya, 576n44; *see also* Camp
  David summit; Nasser, Gamal Abdul; Six-
  Day War; Suez Crisis; Yom Kippur War
Ehrlichman, John, 126
Eid, Guy, 121
Eid al-Fitr, 220
Eilts, Hermann, 192, 196, 202, 575n29
Eiran, Amos, 184, 595n6
Eisenhower, Dwight D., 12, 13, 14, 15, 17,
  19, 25, 26, 36, 42, 44–45, 47–48, 66, 68,
  70, 71, 83, 89, 97, 98, 112, 123, 152,
  154, 191, 211, 214, 218, 224–25, 228,

Eisenhower, Dwight D. (*cont.*)
    246, 247, 259, 288–89, 296, 298, 316,
    447, 463, 537, 538, 552, 553, 561*n*38,
    564*n*19; heart attack of, 48, 50; Suez
    crisis and, 16, 21, 24, 27–28, 31, 37–38,
    52, 53–54, 55–56, 58, 61, 62, 84, 98,
    105, 315, 372, 558*n*6, 560*n*33
Eisenhower, Mamie, 48
*Eisenhower*, USS, 299
Eisenhower Doctrine, 53, 59–60
Eitan, Rafael, 262–63, 273, 276, 464
Ekéus, Rolf, 440
Elazar, David, 99
Elephant Grass, 336
Eliot, Theodore, 230
Elon, Amos, 178, 478, 570*n*13
Enlai, Zhou, 46
*Enterprise*, USS, 340
Erbil battle, 465–67
Erekat, Saeb, 392, 505, 522
Ervin, Sam, 160
Eshkol, Levi, 68, 70, 71, 73, 74, 78, 79–82,
    87–88, 90, 91–93, 94, 98, 99, 102, 106,
    108, 173, 271, 565*n*44
Eshkol, Miriam, 71, 87
Ethiopia, 200
Etzion Air Base, 249
Evron, Ephraim, 566*n*51
Exxon, 159

Fadl, Jamal al-, 484
Fadlallah, Mohammed Hussein, 322–24,
    588*n*18
Fahd, Crown Prince of Saudi Arabia, 182,
    187, 200, 244, 260–61, *260*, 261, 263,
    283, 294–95, 311, 324, 348, 359, 361,
    364, 379, 380, 389, 404, 405, 422–23,
    446, 453, 586, 587*n*10, 597*nn*39, 44;
    Clinton's meeting with, 424, 425–27, 432;
    in Iran-contra affair, 312–14; and Iraq's
    invasion of Kuwait, 354–55, 367, 368,
    369, 371–72, 373, 374–76; U.S. visit of,
    316, 317–19, 320–21, 322
Fahmy, Ismail, 123, 179, 190, 192, 193, 406
Fahmy, Nabil, 515, 516, 518
Faisal, King of Iraq, 22
Faisal, King of Saudi Arabia, 4, 69, 104–105,
    147, 159, 314, 316, 354, 572*n*43
Faisal, Prince Saud al-, 187, 363–64, 375,
    459
Faisal, Turki al-, Prince of Saudi Arabia, 379,
    398, 453, 535, 597*n*44
Faisal II, King of Iraq, 22–23, 52, 429–31
Falwell, Jerry, 483
Farah, Empress of Iran, 210, 213

Farouk, King of Egypt, 34, 38, 40, 41, 42,
    114
Fatah, Al-, 104, 114–15, 116, 117, 118–19,
    196–97, 276, 515, 523; Israeli bus hi-
    jacked by, 196–97
Fawzi, Mohamed, 565*n*38
Federal Bureau of Investigation (FBI), 7
Feinberg, Abe, 67, 68, 80, 90, 104,
    562–63*n*4
Feith, Douglas, 11
Fielding, Fred, 557*n*6, 587*n*10
Finance Ministry, Israel, 68
Finance Ministry, Saudi Arabia, 587*n*14
Fitzwater, Marlin, 593*n*63
Ford, Gerald, 169, 174, 180, 182–83, 202,
    212, 265, 353, 601*n*30
Foreign Intelligence Advisory Board, 130
Foreign Ministry, Egyptian, 79, 179
Foreign Office, British, 254
Foreign Service Institute, 120
Fortas, Abe, 67, 75, 88–89, 104
"Framework for the Comprehensive Peace
    Settlement of the Middle East Problem,"
    203
France, 14, 84, 186, 218, 321, 377, 461,
    558*n*9; embassy in Kuwait, 302; in Suez
    Crisis, 27, 29–31, 54–55, 57, 81, 558*n*6,
    559*n*14
Francona, Rick, 336–37, 451–52
Franjieh, Suleiman, 272
Franjieh, Tony, 272
Frankfurter, Felix, 559*n*9
Free China lobby, 49, 51–52
Freeh, Louis, 460, 512, 600*n*5
Freeman, Chas. W., Jr., 375–76, 590*n*3
Front de Libération Nationale (FLN), 30
Fulbright, J. William, 59, 74, 153, 573*n*60
Fuller, Graham, 329

Gage, Nicholas, 216
Gamasy, Mohamed, 192
Gangchuan, Cao, 587*n*15
Gardner, Richard, 180
Garner, Jay, 543
Gast, Philip, 232
Gates, Robert, 374–75, 383, 385, 426
Gaza, 11, 27, 30, 34–35, 37, 40, 46, 53, 60,
    105, 114, 189, 195, 199, 235, 271, 285,
    388, 392, 394, 409, 411, 416, 472, 502,
    505, 507, 510, 527, 532, 550–51; at
    Camp David summit, 203, 205, 247;
    intifada in, 343, 344
Gaza-Jericho Agreement, 417–18
Gazit, Shlomo, 178, 186, 414, 417, 596*n*21
Gemayel, Amin, 289–90, 292–93, 305

Gemayel, Bashir, 262, 271–72, 273, 275, 282, 284, 286, 287, 582, 584n70
Gemayel, Pierre, 271
Geneva, 349–50
Geneva Conference, 188, 192
Geraghty, Timothy, 296, 297, 298
Germany, 32, 39, 77, 461
Gerson, Michael, 541
Ghorbal, Ashraf, 131
Gillon, Carmi, 441–42
Gilmour, Ian, 321
Gingrich, Newt, 433
Ginsburg, David, 67, 80
Giuliani, Rudy, 558
Glaspie, April, 362–63, 364, 591nn15, 16
Glenn, John, 304
Golan Heights, 77, 99, 103, 135, 143, 186, 189, 206, 237, 256, 266, 271, 388, 389, 393, 409, 411, 412, 424, 445, 446, 447, 448, 476, 499–501, 525, 528, 595n12, 601n27, 603n68, 604n1
Gold, Dore, 476
Goldberg, Arthur, 67, 104
Goldstein, Baruch, 413, 415, 416, 596n19
Goldwasser, Ehud, 605n27
González, Felipe, 328
Goodman, Robert, Jr., 304
Gorbachev, Mikhail, 333, 358, 386–87, 390, 424
Gore, Al, 493, 510, 512, 527
Gosaibi, Ghazi, 535
Graham, Billy, 382
Graham, Katherine, 312
Great Britain, 14, 66, 77, 117, 214, 321, 322, 377, 448; in Suez Crisis, 23, 27, 30–31, 51, 54–55, 57, 81, 558nn3, 6, 559n14
Great Society, 67
Grechko, Andrei A., 72, 77, 145, 146
Green, Pincus, 520
Green Zone, 544
Grenada, 298, 301
Gromyko, Andrei, 88, 122
Gruenther, Alfred M., 55
Guadeloupe, 230
Guantánamo Bay, 594n84
Guardian, The, 587n14
Guatemala, 52
Guerrero, Alfredo R., 458, 459, 600n5
Gulf Cooperation Council, 392, 590
Gulf War, see Persian Gulf War
Gur, Mordechai, 141, 178

Haaretz, 93
Haas, Kenneth, 291

Habash, George, 115, 117, 349
Haber, Eitan, 344, 444–45
Habib, Philip, 270, 273, 277, 278, 283, 294
Haddad, Saad, 197, 583n42
Hadden, John, 86–87
Hadley, Steven, 531
Haifa, Princess, 4, 281
Haig, Alexander, 16, 137, 138, 139, 141, 143, 148, 149–50, 157, 159–60, 165–66, 169, 172, 229, 253, 257, 258, 262, 387, 581, 582, 583; and Israeli invasion of Lebanon, 269–71, 273–74, 279, 280–81
Hakim, Mohammed Baqr al-, 435
Halabja massacre, 337–38
Haldeman, H. R., 126
Halevy, Efraim, 86, 378, 398, 419–20, 471, 473, 474–75, 565–66, 575, 581, 601
Hamas, 396, 397, 418, 423, 442, 448, 449–50, 469–70, 472, 477, 491, 494, 502, 523, 534, 550, 601n23
Hamdoon, Nizar, 311
Hamilton, Lee H., 486
Har Homa settlement, 480, 481
Hariri, Rafik, 324, 462, 547
Harman, Avraham, 63, 566n51
Harriman, Averell, 180, 181, 563n9, 574n6
Hashemite kingdom, 29, 63, 109, 354, 560n33, 569n21
Hassan, Crown Prince of Jordan, 472, 590n3
Hassan II, King of Morocco, 85, 188, 240, 480
Hasson, Israel, 478
Hayden, Michael, 557n5, 594n84
Hebron agreement, 479–81, 495, 602n38
Hebron massacre, 413–14, 415–16, 417
Heikal, Mohamed, 50, 132, 145–46, 263, 565n38
Hekmatyar, Gulbuddin, 398
Helms, Richard, 75, 83, 84, 85, 87, 94, 95, 100, 101, 125, 565n35, 566n50
Herter, Christian, 63
Herut, 186
Herzl, Theodor, 32
Herzog, Yaacov, 559
Hezb-i-Islami, 398
Hezbollah, 13, 278, 290, 302, 309, 315, 322–23, 331–32, 394, 395–96, 447, 459, 462, 463, 481, 487, 501, 502, 547, 548, 586n107, 587n8, 589n32, 605nn25, 27; Buenos Aires bombing of, 395, 396, 594n78; charity by, 397; Khobar Towers and, 460, 600n4
Higgins, William R., 396
Hinkley, John W., 256

Hirschfeld, Yair, 409
Hitler, Adolf, 20, 40, 49, 354, 411
Hofi, Yitzhak, 580–81
Holbrooke, Richard, 181
Holocaust, 17, 20, 34, 45, 87, 118, 140,
    178, 182, 202, 251, 391, 564*n19*, 576*n61*
Honduras, 310
House of Representatives, U.S.: Foreign
    Affairs Committee of, 387; Judiciary
    Committee of, 493; *see also* Congress,
    U.S.; Senate, U.S.
Humphrey, Hubert, 98, 111, 124, 150, 168
Hungary, 24, 61, 259
Hurd, Douglas, 547, 548
Hurricane Katrina, 544
Hussein, 215
Hussein, Ahmed, 50, 51
Hussein, King of Jordan, 22, 27, 48, 68, 78,
    95, 105, 109, 115, 116–17, 182, 254,
    268, 290, 306, 347, 353, 358, 364, 366,
    377, 378, 411, 419, 445, 452, 479–80,
    558*n4*, 567*n64*, 569*n21, 22*, 581*n7*,
    592 *n52*, 595*n11*; Mossad's attack on on
    Meshal and, 471, 472–73, 474–75; Ra-
    bin's peace with, 419–21, 423–24,
    439–40, 472
Hussein, Qusai, 431–32
Hussein, Raghad, 440
Hussein, Rina, 440
Hussein, Saddam, 16, 17, 224, 245, 335,
    389, 407–408, 427, 436, 458, 496, 530,
    538, 541–42; Arab summit meeting called
    by, 359–60; Arafat and, 378, 388; capture
    of, 557; Clinton and, 422, 440, 466–67,
    595*n4*, 597*n40*, 599*n72*; Erbil attack by,
    465–67; Glaspie's meeting with, 591*n15*;
    in Iran-Iraq War, 276, 303–304, 308,
    337–39, 362; nuclear reactor of, 250–51,
    252, 255, 256; plot against GHWB by,
    428; WMDs and, 5, 6, 303–304, 336,
    337–38, 350, 355–56, 440, 451, 589*n37*
Hussein, Sherif, 22, 590*n3*
Hussein, Uday, 431–32, 440–41
Husseini, Faisal, 509
Huyser, Robert E., 229, 230, 231

Idris, King of Libya, 77
Imperial Guard, 232
India, 66, 72, 112
Indonesia, 396
Indyk, Martin, 403, 419, 436, 437, 445,
    498, 499, 597*n39*, 602*n44*
Inman, Bobby Ray, 259
International Atomic Energy Agency, 256,
    582*n14*

International Atomic Energy Commission,
    63
intifadas: first, 342–46, 349, 360, 509;
    second, 508–10, 514, 519–20, 521, 528,
    533, 603*n76*
Iran, 12, 14, 15, 71, 112, 124–25, 183,
    210–48, 256, 274, 316–17, 435–36, 464,
    466, 537, 538, 540, 598*nn55, 66*; coup in,
    25–26, 52; economy of, 216–17; hostage
    crisis in, 237–39, 241–44, 245, 246–47,
    252, 308; Khobar Towers and, 460,
    600*n4*; 1963 riots in, 222; nuclear indus-
    try of, 549, 552; oil of, 218, 224, 310;
    political prisoners in, 213; and *Praying
    Mantis*, 339–41; Rabin's warning on, 394;
    revolution in, 13, 219–34, 248, 260, 316,
    328–29; student protests in, 214, 215
Iran-contra affair, 279, 309, 310–14, 316,
    328–31, 399, 482
Iran Freedom Movement, 226
Iranian Revolutionary Guard, 278, 296, 299,
    394, 460
Iran-Iraq War, 13, 245, 276, 302, 303–304,
    308, 310, 313, 315, 324, 335, 336–38,
    341–42, 350, 358, 362, 378, 394, 430,
    451, 585*n93*; chemical weapons in,
    303–304, 336, 337–38, 350, 355–56,
    589*n36*
Iraq, 4, 20, 22, 33, 47, 49, 274, 316,
    598*nn55, 66*; army of, 543; CIA and, 6, 7,
    428–29, 432, 433–39, 450–56, 461;
    Iranian Revolution and, 224; Kuwait
    invaded by, 353, 355–56, 363–64, 366–77,
    591*n16*; nuclear reactor in, 6, 250–56,
    263, 359, 581, 582; oil of, 356, 364, 370,
    419, 434, 438, 466, 599*n77*; sanctions
    against, 6, 386, 422, 467, 510, 537; upris-
    ings in, 429–39, 441, 450–56, 466, 545,
    592–93*n56*; U.S. invasion of, 542–46,
    548–49; *see also* Persian Gulf War
Iraqi Atomic Energy Commission, 251
Iraqi Liberation Act, 496
Iraqi National Accord, 453, 454
Iraqi National Congress, 429, 430–31, 437,
    454, 465, 467
Iraq Survey Group, 5, 6, 557*n2*
Iraq War, 4, 14, 489; cost of, 7; insurgency
    of, 13; prewar intelligence blunders and,
    12; WMDs as pretext for, 5–6, 7
Irgun, 35–36, 65, 184, 290
Islambouli, Khaled el-, 264–65
Islambouli, Mohamed el-, 264
Islamic Amal terrorist wing, 299
Islamic Jihad Organization, 395, 443, 450,
    469, 470, 491, 502
Islamiyya, Gamaat el-, 264

Ismail, Hafez, 573*n65*

Israel, 5, 6, 8, 11, 16, 19, 43, 49, 70–71, 108, 112, 123–24, 130–31, 182, 322, 388–89, 410; American military aid and sales to, 131, 144, 152–53, 156–57, 159, 169, 183, 197, 253, 254, 255, 258, 263, 270, 277, 558*n9*, 562*n3*, 568*n5*; bin Laden's declaration of war against, 467; creation of, 16–17, 32–36, 73; intifada and, 342–46, 349, 360; mobilization for Suez Crisis, 21–22, 23, 26; 1955 Gaza incursion of, 46; nuclear weapons sought and acquired by, 15, 45–46, 47, 63, 66, 86, 93, 105, 106, 141, 173, 183, 195, 199, 203, 558*n9*, 561*n38*, 565*n43*, 568*n5*, 581*nn5, 6, 11*; occupied territories and, 86, 104, 105, 125, 152, 154, 157, 158, 191, 195–96, 198–99, 201, 203–204, 284, 347, 389–90, 450, 475, 480, 481, 493, 502, 522, 528, 550, 567*n72*; Osirak research reactor destroyed by, 6, 250–56, 263, 359, 581*nn5, 6, 7*; Persian Gulf War and, 378–79, 382–83; PLO recognized by, 410; Sadat's visit to, 16, 176–79, 192–93, 194–95, 199, 201; Syria's negotiations with, 500–501; terrorism in, 196–97; threats and attacks against PLO, 263, 267, 269–71, 274, 275, 276–77, 279–80, 282–83, 284, 285, 286, 287, 289, 296; War of Independence of, 20–21, 37, 40, 269, 275; in wars with Lebanon, 13, 16, 113, 197–98, 204, 262–63, 269–71, 273, 277, 278–90, 293–96, 461, 462–64, 507, 529, 548, 583*nn39, 42, 45*, 583–84*n51*, 584*n59*, 605*nn26, 27*; water supply of, 595*n12*; *see also* Camp David summit; Six-Day War; Suez Crisis; Yom Kippur War

Israeli lobby, 16, 49

Ivry, David, 581*n5*

Jabali, Ghazi, 492

Jabotinsky, Vladimir (Ze'ev), 35, 185, 461

Jackson, Henry, 119, 124, 150, 151, 153, 154, 156, 166, 168, 573*n60*, 599*n77*

Jacobsen, David, 324

Jacobson, Eddie, 25

Japan, 39, 119

Jarring, Gunnar, 105

Javits, Jacob, 124, 150, 187

Jenin, 11

Jeremiah, David, 597

Jerusalem, 411, 418, 464, 477–78, 503–504, 505, 506, 507, 509, 510, 513, 515, 600*n12*

Jesus Christ, 178

Jewish Agency, 20, 29

Jewish Defense League, 413, 443

Jewish Temple, 513

Jibril, Ahmed, 590*n55*

John Paul II, Pope, 265

Johnson, Lady Bird, 75

Johnson, Lyndon B., 15, 67, 69, 70, 106, 111, 112, 131, 214, 228, 482, 549; Six-Day War and, 65, 71–75, 79, 80, 82, 83–84, 85, 87, 88–90, 91, 93–94, 95–96, 97–98, 101, 102, 103–104, 142, 563*nn5, 9*; in Suez Crisis, 60, 61

Johnson, Tom, 74

Johnston, Eric, 44, 47

Joint Chiefs of Staff, 94, 286, 525

Joint Logistics Planning Program, 302–303

Jones, Paula, 416, 595–96*n16*

Jordan, 9, 21, 22–23, 27, 29, 33, 34, 47, 48, 52, 68, 77, 86, 95, 105, 109, 114–15, 117, 121, 147, 175, 188, 204, 209, 233, 237, 241, 245, 255, 302–303, 306, 347, 358, 363, 379, 383, 397, 414, 429, 470, 558*nn3, 6*, 592*nn42,52*, 595*n11*

Jordan, Hamilton, 236, 239, 246

Jordan River, 36

*Joseph Strauss*, USS, 341

Joshua, Winfred, 329, 588*n25*

Judea, 441

*Judenstaat, Der* (Herzl), 32

Juhayman el-Utaibi, 264

Jumblatt, Kamal, 585*n87*

Jumblatt, Walid, 294, 585

Justice Department, U.S., 540

Kach organization, 443

Kahan, Yitzhak, 287

Kahan Commission, 290, 292

Kahane, Meir, 413, 443

Kalp, Malcolm, 241–42

Kamal, Muhammad, 201, 207

Kamel, Hussein, 440–41

Kansi, Mir Aimal, 485

Karameh, Battle of, 115, 418

Karbala, Battle of, 215, 219

Kay, David, 5–6, 7, 386

Kean, Thomas H., 486

Kennedy, Edward, 239, 247, 381

Kennedy, John F., 15, 63, 65, 66–67, 70, 105, 111, 112, 123, 181, 225, 228, 252, 380, 456, 553, 562–63*n4*, 586*n3*

Kennedy, Robert, 65, 97, 120, 357, 586*n3*

*Kennedy*, USS, 299

Kent State, 222
Kenya, 487–88
Kerr, Malcolm, 305
Kerry, John, 381
KGB, 63, 79, 562n53, 564n22, 575n39
Khaddam, Abdul Halim, 188, 293
Khalaf, Salah, 114, 117, 119, 179, 343, 348, 568n12
Khalid, King of Saudi Arabia, 200, 279
Khalil, Moustafa, 195
Khalilzad, Zalmay, 543
Khan, Reza, 218
Khartoum, 119–21
Khatami, Mohammed, 512
Khobar Towers, 458–59, 460, 484, 512, 600nn4, 5
Khomeini, Ayatollah, 14, 17, 213, 214, 216, 218–19, 238, 240, 242, 246, 298, 309, 313, 330, 333, 336, 554, 577n6, 578n24; in Iran-Iraq War, 245, 308, 310, 313, 335, 336, 338, 362, 378; in Revolution, 221, 224, 227–28, 230, 231, 232, 233, 329
Khomeini, Mustafa, 215
Kimche, David, 178, 258, 282, 310–11, 330, 331
King David Hotel, 185, 195, 394
Kirkpatrick, Jeane, 280, 289, 292
Kissinger, Henry, 109, 112, 119, 122, 123, 124–25, 127, 129, 130, 174, 180, 182, 183, 202, 210, 211, 223, 226, 240, 241, 246, 257, 270, 279, 294, 301, 328, 357, 432, 438, 456, 476, 543, 558n9, 567n1, 568n5, 579–80n65, 601n30; on intifada, 344; Yom Kippur War and, 16, 137–38, 139, 140, 141, 142, 143, 144–45, 147–48, 149–51, 153–54, 156, 157–61, 162, 164, 165, 166, 168–69, 170–73, 174–75, 179, 570n15, 570–71n16, 571nn23, 25, 28, 572n43, 573nn54, 60, 65, 574n68
Klinghoffer, Leon, 325, 327
Knesset, 56, 90, 93, 184, 192, 193, 194, 207, 282, 393, 410, 498, 500, 552, 596n19, 598n64
Komitehs, 231
Koppel, Andrea, 519
Koran, 397
Korean War, 24, 46
Kosygin, Alexei N., 83, 91, 101, 159
Kraft, Joseph, 160
Krim, Arthur, 65–66, 67, 72, 74, 562n2
Krim, Mathilde, 65–66, 67, 68, 70, 72, 103, 562n2
Krock, Arthur, 63
Kupke, Rick, 238, 579n58

Kurdish Democratic Party (KDP), 434, 466, 467
Kurdish Workers Party, 439
Kurds, 6, 337–38, 384, 428, 429, 432, 434, 436, 437, 438, 451, 456, 545; in battle of Erbil, 465
Kuwait, 13, 16, 156, 302, 335, 394, 423, 424, 428, 541, 546, 598n66; embassy bombings in, 302; Iraq invasion of, 353, 355–56, 363–64, 366–77, 591; oil of, 360, 361, 362, 364, 368, 384; see also Persian Gulf War

Labor Party, Israeli, 82, 173, 184, 185, 186, 315, 346, 387, 388, 419, 463, 475–76, 479, 528
Laingen, Bruce, 238, 243
Laird, Melvin R., 568n5
Lake, Anthony, 421, 425, 432–34, 436–37, 452, 460, 595n4, 597n39, 599n72
Landow, Nathan, 239
Lang, W. Patrick, 334–36, 337, 355, 361, 372, 431–32, 451, 588n25
Larsen, Terje, 408
Lauder, Ronald, 601n27, 603n68
Lavon, Pinhas, 561n37
Lawrence, T. E., 22, 33, 325
Leahy, Patrick, 389
Lebanese National Assembly, 284, 289
Lebanon, 17, 29, 33, 53, 63, 109, 118, 196, 262, 269–70, 302, 305, 315, 316, 372, 394, 412, 414, 500, 505, 529, 538, 558n3, 562nn53, 3, 583nn39, 42, 45, 585n87, 586n105, 598n66; American hostages in, 304, 307, 308–309, 322, 324, 329, 330, 331–32; Bir al Abed bombing, 323–24; civil war in, 14, 262, 271; Israel's wars with, 13, 16, 113, 197–98, 204, 262, 269–71, 273, 277, 278–90, 293–96, 461, 462–64, 507, 529, 548, 583–84, 605nn25, 26; marine barracks bombing in, 297–301, 351, 369, 428, 594n78; refugee camps in, 188, 287, 290, 506; U.S. embassy in, 291–92
Ledeen, Michael, 329–30
Le Duc Tho, 119, 157
Lehi group, 593n71
Le Monde, 510, 538
Levin, Jeremy, 307
Lewinsky, Monica, 483, 486, 488, 491
Lewis, Bernard, 546
Lewis, Samuel, 202, 252, 253, 267, 270, 274, 277, 310, 579–80n3, 581n6
Libby, Lewis "Scooter," 11
Liberty, USS, 99–101, 142

Libya, 13, 77, 119, 235, 245, 256, 257, 270, 317, 378, 576, 594, 598; terrorism by, 316, 328, 360, 590n55, 598n66; U.S. bombing of, 327–28
Libyan Peoples Bureau, 328
Likud, 126, 184, 185, 201, 266, 315, 346, 360–61, 393, 410, 460, 476, 507, 594n74
Limbert, John, 217, 238, 544
Lipkin-Shahak, Amnon, 415, 463
Lippold, Kirk, 510
Lloyd, Selwyn, 31
Lockerbie bombing, 350–51
Lodge, Henry Cabot, 432
*Los Angeles Times*, 483
Lumumba, Patrice, 258
Lyons, James "Ace," 299

Macmillan, Harold, 62
Madrid peace conference, 389, 390–93, 409, 601n30
Magen, Kalman, 164
Mahle, Melissa, 600n7
Majd, Ali Hassan al-, 440
Major, John, 380, 425
Makhluf, Adnan, 412
Malaysia, 396
Malhouk, Abdullah al-, 120, 121
Mansfield, Mike, 83
Mao Zedong, 24, 122–23, 223
Marcos, Ferdinand, 211
Marik, Warren, 428–29, 431
Marwan, Ashraf, 569–70n1
Masood, Ahmad Shah, 398
Massoud, Rihab, 4, 8, 348
Matalin, Mary, 589n37
Matt, Danny, 155
May 17 Accord, 293–94, 295, 306
McCain, John, 557–58n7
McCloskey, Robert, 75
McCone, John, 63
McFarlane, Robert, 258, 294, 295, 296, 297, 298, 299–300, 307, 310–11, 312–13, 316, 318, 319, 328–32, 581n11, 588n27
McGovern, George, 134
McKay, Jim, 118
McLaughlin, John, 5
McMahon, John, 332
McNamara, Robert, 65, 73, 90, 95–96, 567n64
McPherson, Harry, 67, 74, 99, 102
McVeigh, Timothy, 599n1
Meese, Ed, 304, 333
Meir, Golda, 71, 108, *110*, 113, 118, 119, 121, 124, 126, 131, 133, 173, 177, 187, 255, 271, 461, 565n44, 570n13, 598n64;

in Suez Crisis, 56–58; in Yom Kippur War, 137–38, 139, 140, 141, 144, 149, 152, 153, 155, 163, 164, 170, 172, 573n65
Meshad, Yehya al-, 251
Meshal, Khaled, 470–75
Meyerson, Morris, 57
MI6, 562n53
Miller, William, 242
Milner, Alfred, 33
Mitterrand, François, 328, 370
Modai, Yitzhak, 387–88
Mohammed, Khalid Sheikh, 400, 401, 485, 557n5, 594n84
Mohieddin, Zakaria, 98
Mollet, Guy, 23, 28, 29–31, 52
Mondale, Walter, 189–90, 205, 207, 234, 304, 315
Moore, George Curtis, 120
Moore, Sally, 120, 121–22
Moorer, Thomas, 156, 157, 160, 170
Mordecai, Yitzhak, 493
Morocco, 9, 20, 200, 376, 397, 598n66
Morse, Wayne, 50
Moses, 179, 249, 507
Moskowitz, Stan, 450, 478–79, 497
Mossad, 12, 85, 86, 87, 93, 94, 123, 178, 251, 272, 275, 282, 330, 345, 395, 419, 438, 443, 449, 482, 508, 520, 533, 566n51, 575n39, 580n3, 590n8, 601n23; Meshal attacked by, 470–75
Mossadegh, Mohammad, 25–26, 52, 214, 216, 218
Moynihan, Daniel Patrick, 380
Mubarak, Hosni, 192, 193, 265, 353, 356, 361, 364, 366, 377, 400, 460, 516, 591n15, 592n42; Yom Kippur War and, 136
Mughniyah, Imad, 299, 301, 594n78
Mughrabi, Dalal, 196
Muhammad, Prophet, 22, 178, 215, 219, 237, 539
Mulroney, Brian, 592n42
Munich, 49, 51
Munich Massacre, 118–19, 345, 403, 497
Murrow, Edward R., 26
Musawi, Abbas, 395
Musawi, Hussein, 395
Musawi, Hussein al-, 299
Musawi, Siham, 395
Muskie, Edmund, 252, 253
Muslim Brotherhood, 41, 43, 179, 264, 272, 396, 400
Muslim Students Following the Line of the Imam, 239
Mussolini, Benito, 49

Nachumi, Amir, 254
Najibullah, President, 398
Nashiri, Abd al-Rahim al-, 557n5
Nasr, Salah, 79
Nasser, Gamal Abdul, 17, 22, 24, 26, 26, 34,
    36, 39–47, 66–67, 70, 71, 72, 104–105,
    108, 113, 114, 115, 116, 123, 127, 131,
    132–33, 135, 188, 192, 206, 209, 218,
    222, 245, 263, 288, 360, 374, 396, 430,
    463, 537, 563n9, 566n51, 567nn64, 1;
    Gulf of Aqaba blockaded by, 84, 88, 94,
    97; in Six-Day War, 80, 82, 84, 87, 95,
    96–98, 101–102; Soviet arms purchased
    by, 30, 47–48, 49, 50–51, 77, 108; in
Nasser, Gamal Abdul (cont.)
    Suez Crisis, 21, 27, 30, 38–39, 52, 53, 55,
    56, 59–60, 63, 560n33; Yemen invaded by,
    67, 75–76, 77, 82, 563n9
Nasser, Mona, 570
Nassiri, Nematollah, 231
National Front, 226, 229
National Intelligence Estimate, 7
National Religious Party, 480
National Salvation Front, 294
National Security Act, 172
National Security Agency, 9, 64, 370,
    598n55
National Security Council (NSC), 11, 167,
    170, 171, 208, 242, 278, 288, 293, 297,
    310, 329, 343, 364, 372, 486, 530
National Security Planning Group, 258,
    331
NATO, 12, 24, 87, 280, 370, 466
Nazis, 218
Nehru, Jawaharlal, 46
neoconservatives, 5, 7, 11
Netanyahu, Benjamin, 410–11, 441, 450,
    460–61, 462, 465, 469, 471, 476,
    479–80, 482–84, 494, 497, 499, 502,
    507, 522–23, 601nn23, 27, 602nn38, 44,
    603n68; ancient tunnel opened by,
    477–78; Har Homa and, 480, 481; and
    Mossad's attack on Meshal, 472–73, 475;
    Palestinian statehood and, 476, 490–91;
    at Wye summit, 491–93
New Jersey, 297, 306
New Republic, The, 479
Newsom, David, 232
Newsweek, 101, 130, 131, 134, 482, 521,
    569
New York Times, The, 97, 153, 191, 198,
    216, 306, 398, 567–68n2, 577n6
Ngo Dinh Diem, 259
Nicaragua, 310, 315, 348
9/11 Commission Report, 7, 602n49
Nir, Amiram, 329

Nixon, Richard, 14, 15, 17, 63, 106, 109,
    110, 111–13, 116, 119, 120–22, 124,
    125–26, 134, 170, 180, 210, 211, 213,
    236, 257, 259, 265, 279, 281, 284, 301,
    315, 316, 328, 353, 357, 411, 432, 438,
    444, 482, 529, 549, 558n9, 567n1;
    Brezhnev and, 16, 113, 122–23, 126,
    127–30, 161–62, 172, 464; Yom Kippur
    War and, 16, 135–36, 139, 140–41,
    142, 143–44, 146, 148, 149, 150–51,
    153–54, 156–57, 159, 160, 161–62,
    163, 164, 165, 168–69, 464, 573nn54,
    60, 65
Nixon Doctrine, 218
Noble Sanctuary, 509, 513
Noel, Cleo A., Jr., 120–21
Noel, Lucille, 120, 121–22
Nolte, James, 97
Non-Aligned Movement, 46, 72
Noriega, Manuel, 368
North, Oliver, 310, 319, 328
North Korea, 513, 540, 551
North Yemen, 199
Nuclear Non-Proliferation Treaty (1968),
    105, 106, 256, 553, 582n14
Nunn, Sam, 380
Nurzhitz, Vadim, 509

Oakley, Robert, 343
Obeid, Abdel Karim, 396
October War, see Yom Kippur War
Office of Strategic Services, 258, 259
oil, 14, 16, 24, 26, 30, 33, 38, 39, 52, 71,
    105, 112, 125, 133, 156, 157, 162, 174,
    222, 223, 266, 316, 353, 357, 372, 469,
    526, 571n28; Arab embargo of, 146–47,
    152, 158, 159, 314; in Iran, 218, 224,
    310; of Iraq, 356, 364, 370, 419, 434,
    438, 466, 599n77; of Kuwait, 360, 361,
    362, 364, 368, 384; of Saudi Arabia,
    260, 313, 322, 358, 364, 367, 457,
    586n5; from Sinai, 203, 250; see
    also OPEC
Olayan, Suleiman, 588n16
Olmert, Ehud, 346, 477, 547–48, 552
Olympics, 243
Oman, 234, 590n6, 598n66
O'Neill, Thomas P. "Tip," 184
OPEC, 140, 158, 213, 356, 360, 571n28
Operation Ajax, 25–26, 211, 218, 466
Operation Big Pines, 270
Operation Druid Leader, 339, 355, 358
Operation Earnest Will, 335
Operation End Game, 429
Operation Grapes of Wrath, 118, 462–64

Operation Peace for Galilee, 277
Operation Praying Mantis, 339–41, 589n39
Operation Southern Watch, 458
Operation Staunch, 329
Operation Straggle, 52
Organization of African Unity, 460
Osirak research reactor, 6, 250–56, 263,
  359, 581n5, 582n14
Oslo, II, 442
Oslo Accords, 402–404, 405–407, 406,
  408, 410–11, 413, 415, 416–17, 423,
  450, 465, 477, 479, 480, 481, 493,
  495, 497, 498, 502, 503, 509, 517–18,
  523, 529, 595n11, 596n21, 602n39
Osman, Osman Ahmed, 195
Ottoman Empire, 17, 22, 29, 32, 33, 558n3
Owhali, Mohammed al-, 487
Oz, Amos, 499
Özal, Turgut, 370

Pahlavi, Mohammed Reza, 25, 26, 125,
  210–11, 212, 213–14, 215, 216, 218,
  240–41, 244–45, 263, 358, 369,
  385, 563n9, 571n28, 578nn24, 28,
  579–80n65; in revolution, 219–20,
  221–22, 223–24, 225–27, 229, 230, 231,
  233, 235, 310
Pakistan, 242, 314, 560n33, 594n84
Palestine (Ottoman province), 33
Palestine Liberation Organization (PLO),
  105, 109, 114–18, 179–80, 184, 187,
  188, 199, 233, 234, 258, 262, 292, 299,
  304, 306, 327, 378, 392, 394, 492, 502,
  583nn42, 45, 583–84n51, 595n6; intifada
  and, 344, 345; Israeli recognition of, 410;
  Israeli threats and attacks against, 263,
  267, 269–71, 274, 275, 276–77, 279–80,
  282–83, 284, 285, 286, 287, 289n32,
  296; and Oslo Accords, 403, 406, 408;
  Reagan and Bush's dialogue with, 348–50,
  361; Saudi financing of, 314; terrorism by,
  174, 196–97, 361, 589n32; terrorism
  denounced by, 349–50, 360
Palestinian Authority, 411, 417, 418–19,
  424, 442, 472, 479, 484, 490, 498, 503,
  519
Palestinian National Council, 349, 492
Palestinian territories, 11, 12, 23, 35, 36,
  77–78, 188, 191, 194, 195–96, 317, 389,
  418, 563n9, 567n72; Carter on homeland
  for, 177, 182, 183, 184, 187; intifada and,
  342–46, 349, 360; refugees from, 503,
  513; statehood and, 12, 23, 34, 348–49,
  476, 490, 490–91, 510, 513, 535, 536,
  540–41, 549–50, 551

Panama, 368
Panama Canal treaties, 199, 201
Pan Am Flight 103, 590n55
Paris Peace Conference (1919), 33
Parliament, British, 62
Parris, Mark, 595n4
Parsons, Anthony, 225–26, 227
Patriotic Union of Kurdistan (PUK), 434–35,
  466
Pearl, Daniel, 594n84
Pearson, Lester, 56, 88
People's Liberation Army, 587–88n15
Peres, Shimon, 28, 45–46, 82, 191, 262,
  315, 318, 328–30, 345, 347, 387,
  403, 406, 409, 414, 417, 420, 424,
  442, 443, 444, 445, 446–50, 460,
  461, 462, 464–65, 471, 483,
  509
Peretz, Martin, 479
Perle, Richard, 455, 599n77
Perroots, Leonard, 334
Persepolis, 211, 244
Persian Gulf War, 377–88, 399, 406, 422,
  425, 426–27, 545; cease-fire in, 16; UN
  resolutions on, 377, 386, 434, 592n52,
  592–93n56; U.S. Congress resolutions on,
  381; U.S. mobilization for, 377
peshmerga, 437, 598n53
Petraeus, David, 548
Phalange militia, 273, 582–83n38, 584n70
Philby, Kim, 562n53
Philippines, 396
Pickering, Tom, 366
Pinochet, Augusto, 211
Piro, George, 557n2
Podesta, John, 493
Podgorny, Nikolai, 145
Poindexter, John, 328
Pojidaev, Dimitri, 79
Poland, 259, 267, 270
Politburo, 127, 165, 172, 564n22
Pollard, Jonathan, 491–92, 493
Popular Front for the Liberation of Palestine
  (PLFP), 115, 117, 347, 360
Powell, Colin, 6, 8, 11, 13, 286, 333, 334,
  339, 343, 350, 357, 364, 368, 371, 372,
  383, 398, 514, 525–27, 528, 529, 530,
  533, 535–37, 541, 551, 557n3, 558n8,
  589n37
Powell, Jody, 236
Precht, Henry, 229, 240–41, 577n6
Price, Ted, 596
Primakov, Yevgeny, 387
Project Babylon, 590n8
Pundak, Ron, 409
Putin, Vladimir, 549

Qaddafi, Muammar, 192, 245, 257, 325,
    327–28, 350, 389, 576n44
Qatar, 590n6, 598n66
Qom, Iran, 214, 215–16, 219
Quandt, William, 348
Quinn, Sally, 312
Qurei, Ahmed, see Abu Ala


Rabbo, Yasser Abed, 475–76, 510, 521
Rabieh, Mohammed, 348
Rabin, Leah, 184, 446, 598
Rabin, Yitzhak, 108, 123, 130, 140, 182,
    186, 191, 387, 393–94, 406, 407,
    412–13, 418–19, 465, 470, 476, 480,
    483, 497, 498, 499, 501, 507, 522, 525,
Rabin, Yitzhak (cont.)
    595nn6, 12, 604n1; assassination of,
    441–45, 598n66; election of, 173; and
    Hebron massacre, 413, 414, 416, 417;
    intifada and, 342–43, 344–45;
    Netanyahu's criticism of, 410–11; at Oslo
    signing, 404, 410–12, 477; peace made
    with King Hussein, 419–21, 423–24,
    439–40, 472; in Six-Day War, 79–80, 81,
    85, 90, 91, 93, 99; on visit to Carter,
    183–84
Radford, Arthur, 53
Rafi, 82
Rafsanjani, Hashemi, 332
Rafshoon, Gerald, 576n61
Rahman, Hassan Abdul, 514, 519
Rahman, Omar Abdel, 400
Ramadan, 219–20
Ramallah, 11, 540
Rantissi, Abdel Aziz al-, 601n25
Rashid, Mohammed, 513
Rastakhiz, 216
Rather, Dan, 75
Raz, Ze'ev, 254
Reagan, Nancy, 265, 281, 319, 320, 587n11
Reagan, Ronald, 16, 246, 257, 260,
    301–302, 306–307, 311, 316, 326, 356,
    357, 365, 374, 377, 388, 399, 427, 463,
    464, 526, 585n84, 587n10, 601n30;
    Fahd's visit to, 317–19, 320; intifada and,
    346; Iran-contra and, 309, 312, 316, 399;
    Iraq's nuclear reactor and, 252, 253, 255,
    256, 263; and Israel's invasion of
    Lebanon, 270–71, 272, 273, 275, 277,
    279, 280, 281, 283–84, 285, 288, 289,
    297; Libya bombed by, 327–28; and
    marine barracks bombing, 298–301;
    PLO's dialogue with, 348–50; and Praying
    Mantis, 339–40
Reagan Plan, 285, 290, 291, 318

Regan, Donald, 331, 333, 587n10
Regency Council, 229, 230
Regev, Eldad, 605n27
Reid, Harry, 548
Reiger, Frank, 307
Republican Guard, 361, 382, 421–22,
    451
Reston, James, 53, 198
Revava, 390
Revisionist Zionism, 185
Revolt, The (Begin), 185
Reza Shah Pahlavi, 211, 218
Riad, Mohammed, 576n49
Ribicoff, Abraham, 150, 196
Rice, Condoleezza, 530, 533, 536–37, 547,
    548, 557n3, 605n28
Rich, Denise, 520–21
Rich, Marc, 520–21
Richardson, Elliot, 163, 168
Richter, Steve, 453, 455
Rickover, Hyman G., 180
Riedel, Bruce, 436, 602n44
Rifai, Zaid, 117–18
Ritchie, Jim, 361–62
Robertson, Pat, 483
Rockefeller, David, 180, 240, 241, 242,
    579–80n65
Rockefeller, Nelson, 138, 226
Rockefeller family, 223
Rogers, Will C., III, 342
Rogers, William P., 112, 123, 124, 133, 134,
    285, 567n72, 571n25
Rollins, Ed, 304
Rommel, Erwin, 40
Roosevelt, Franklin D., 12, 34, 74, 111, 225,
    228, 256, 313, 374, 424, 553, 586n5
Roosevelt, Kermit, 42, 47, 48, 211
Roosevelt, Theodore, 42
Rosan, Nawaf al-, 276
Rosen, Barry, 237–38
Ross, Dennis, 343, 387, 394, 403, 412, 416,
    419, 443, 445, 446, 448, 464, 473–74,
    483, 484, 490–91, 499, 500, 513, 516,
    519, 526, 532, 586n105, 601n30, 602n44
Rostow, Walt, 64–65, 73, 75, 80, 94, 96,
    565n35, 566n51, 567n64
Rothberg, Ro'i, 36–37
Rubin, Gail, 196
Ruckelshaus, William, 163
Rudeina, Nabil Abu, 519
Rumaila oil field, 360
Rumsfeld, Donald, 303, 305–306, 310, 526,
    530, 544
Rusk, Dean, 65, 70, 71, 73, 83, 88, 89, 97,
    100, 103, 105, 106, 180, 563n9
Russell, Richard, 59

Russell, Steve, 297
Russia, 530
Russian Revolution, 186, 268
Rwanda, 420, 425, 464

Sa'ad, Sheikh, 363
Sabah, Jaber al-, 360, 363
Sabra camp, 287, 290, 506, 529
Sabri, Ali, 133
Sadat, Anwar, 34, 40, 42, 79, 102, 108, 112,
    116, 126, 127, 130–34, 143, *174*, 182,
    188, 190, 192, 196, 198, 200–201, 236,
    245, 262, 263–64, 269, 282, 397, 447,
    569n31, 573n65, 575n29, 576n44; at
    Camp David summit, 201–208, 221–22,
    228, 234, 237, 248, 249, 318, 372, 410,
    503, 601n30; Israel visited by, 16,
    176–79, 192–93, 194–95, 199, 201;
    murder of, 264–65; Yom Kippur War and,
    136, 139, 145–46, 147, 159, 164, 170
Sadat, Atif, 136
Sadat, Jehan, 177, 193
Sadr, Abolhassan Bani, 243
Safire, William, 191, 529
Safran, Nadav, 37
Said, Edward, 502
Said, Hussein Ghassan, 276
Said, Nuri as-, 430
Saif, Mohammed Abu, 471
Salah, Abdullah, 108–109
Saleh, Ali Abdullah, 377
Salman, Prince of Saudi Arabia, 4
Samaria, 441
Samarrai, Wafiq al-, 431–32, 434, 435,
    436–37, 439
*Samuel B. Roberts*, USS, 339, 340
Sanjabi, Karim, 226
San Remo conference, 52
Saturday Night Massacre, 163
Saud, Abdul Aziz al-, King of Saudi Arabia, 4,
    22, 49, 63, 313, 426, 458, 590n3
Saud, King, 63
Saudi Arabia, 3–5, 8–9, 22, 49, 52, 67, 75,
    86, 119–21, 125, 147–48, 156, 179, 183,
    233, 234, 235, 237, 242, 245, 255, 256,
    258, 259–60, 283, 302, 303, 322, 327,
    358, 363, 394, 396–97, 433, 446, 514,
    590n6, 597n44, 598n66; and Iraq's
    invasion of Kuwait, 354–55, 364, 366,
    367–76; oil from, 260, 313, 322, 358,
    364, 367, 457, 586n5; Persian Gulf War
    and, 377–78, 379; U.S. aid and sales to,
    199, 200, 201, 261–62, 311, 312, 316,
    317, 354–55
Saúl Menem, Carlos, 395

Saunders, Harold, 96, 208–209, 566n61
SAVAK, 213, 215, 218, 220, 229
Savimbi, Jonas, 315
Savir, Leo, 408
Savir, Uri, 408, 410, 444, 449, 463, 465,
    502
Scheinerman, Mordechai, 268
Scheinerman, Samuel, 268
Scheinerman, Vera, 268
Scheuer, Michael, 602n49
Schiff, Zeev, 584n59
Schindler, Alexander M., 191
Schlesinger, James, 19, 141–42, 143, 144,
    148, 150, 151, 160, 171, 172, 180, 183,
    570n15, 571n28
Schwarzkopf, Norman, 364, 372, 375–76,
    381, 383, 384
Scowcroft, Brent, 143, 147, 148, 158, 159,
    162, 172, 246, 257, 361, 365, 398, 407,
    426, 433, 591–92n30, 592n42,
    592–93n56; Iraq's invasion of Kuwait and,
    353, 354, 363, 368, 369, 370, 374
Scranton, William, 113
Sea of Galilee, 36
Semenov, Vladimir, 79
Senate, U.S., 168; Armed Services Commit-
    tee of, 6; Foreign Relations Committee of,
    153; Intelligence Committee of, 557n5;
    Intelligence Oversight Committee of, 429;
    *see also* Congress, U.S.; House of Repre-
    sentatives, U.S.
September 11, 2001, terrorist attacks of, 7,
    9, 10, 11, 400, 462, 485, 486, 527, 537,
    538, 539, 594n84
*Seven Letters*, 264
Shafi, Haidar Abdel, 391–92
Shahak, Amnon, 345
Shahwani, Mohammed Abdullah al-, 451–52
Shalikashvili, John, 422–23
Shamir, Yitzhak, 16, 36, 261, 292, 311, 315,
    345, 346, 360–61, 379, 383–84, 387,
    388–89, 390, 391, 392, 394, 476, 482,
    528, 592n52, 593n71, 594n74
Shapira, Moshe Chaim, 85, 598n64
Sharaa, Farouk al-, 392, 393, 499
Sharett, Moshe, 25, 29, 198, 561n37
Shariati, Ali, 217
Shariatmadari, Ayatollah, 215
Sharif, Haram al-, 99
Sharif-Emami, Jafar, 220
Sharm el-Sheikh, 56, 57, 60, 102, 207, 461
Sharon, Ariel, 8, 23, 27, 91, 126, 155, 208,
    262, 266, 267–69, 273, 292, 388, 389,
    390, 394, 421, 461, 475, 480, 491, 494,
    502, 513, 514, 517, 519, 522, 523,
    527–29, 532, 533–34, 540–41, 551,

Sharon, Ariel, (*cont.*)
  584*n70*; on Camp David summit, 503;
  Lebanon strikes and, 262–63, 269–70,
  273–74, 275, 277, 280, 283, 284,
  286–87, 290, 582–83*n38*, 583*n45*,
  583–84*n51*; and Sadat's visit to Israel,
  178, 179; in Suez Crisis, 53, 56, 155;
  Temple Mount climbed by, 506–10; in
  Yom Kippur War, 497
Shartouni, 286
Shas Party, 602*n38*
Shatila camp, 287, 290, 506, 529
Shaw, Bernard, 382
Shazli, Saad el-, 154–55
Shevardnadze, Eduard, 362
Shihabi, Hikmat, 412
Shikaki, Fathi, 443
Shin Bet, 441, 448, 478
Shomron, Dan, 344, 345
Shoval, Zalman, 388
Shultz, George, 283, 284–85, 287, 290, 291,
  292, 293–94, 295, 298, 301–302, 303,
  306, 315, 316, 322, 331, 333, 345,
  346–47, 349, 584*n64*, 588*n16*
Sibai, Yusef al-, 199
Sicherman, Harvey, 387
Sinai Peninsula, 24, 27, 30, 58, 65, 70, 71,
  87, 91, 98, 99, 102, 113, 126, 133, 179,
  186, 191, 249–50, 315; at Camp David
  summit, 203, 205, 208, 234; in Yom
  Kippur War, 145, 146, 147, 152, 154–55,
  497
Sirhan Sirhan, 120
Sisco, Joseph, 138
Six-Day War, 64–65, 71–106, 112, 113, 114,
  123, 142, 185, 186, 188, 206, 316, 344,
  506–507, 563*n9*, 565*nn38, 44*,
  565–66*n48*, 566*n51*, 567*n72*; Egyptian
  mobilization for, 80, 81, 82–84, 87; Israeli
  air strikes in, 64–65; Israeli troop buildup
  preceding, 78–79, 564*n22*; start of, 71,
  567*n64*; Syrian attacks preceding, 78–79
"Six No's," 199
Snow, Tony, 557*n6*
Somalia, 200, 420, 425, 459
Somoza, Anastasio, 211
South Lebanon Army, 197, 501
South Vietnam, 182
South Yemen, 199, 316
Soviet Union, 14, 15, 24, 27, 28, 32, 38, 43,
  48, 54, 59, 68, 77, 91, 111, 182, 189,
  190–91, 200, 214, 254, 260, 266, 321,
  458, 463, 570*n16*; Afghanistan invaded
  by, 14, 243, 246, 257, 261, 314–15, 316,
  321, 330, 348, 397, 459; collapse of, 428;
  Egyptian arms sales of, 30, 47–48, 49,

50–51, 77, 108, 133, 183; Hungary and,
  24, 61; interventions in Africa by, 257;
  Syrian arms sale of, 48, 77; Yom Kippur
  War and, 136, 142, 143, 145, 146, 149,
  151, 153, 154, 159, 160, 161–62,
  164–67, 168
Stalin, Joseph, 218
Starr, Kenneth, 483, 486, 487
Stassen, Harold, 54, 55
State Department, U.S., 25, 42, 67, 83, 90,
  94, 103, 166, 181, 188, 215, 223, 227,
  229, 232, 239, 281, 283, 287, 289, 303,
  318, 350, 460, 466, 533
Status of Forces Agreement, 214, 219
Stempel, John, 577*n6*
Stennis, John, 160
Stern Gang, 36, 392, 593*n71*
Stethem, Robert, 325, 331
Stevenson, Adlai, 24
Stiner, Carl, 296
Studeman, William O., 437
Sudan, 398, 448, 460, 489–90, 544,
  594*n76*, 602–603*n56*
Suez Canal, 14, 104, 113, 128, 133, 135,
  148, 161, 165, 167, 170, 191; building of,
  39, 45; reopening of, 179
Suez Crisis, 16, 19–20, 21–24, 26–31,
  36–39, 51–63, 68, 70, 78, 81, 82, 84, 86,
  98, 105, 277, 315, 372, 559*n13*; canal
  seized in, 38, 51, 56, 58; casualties in, 28;
  Dulles and Eban's meeting in, 19–20,
  21–22, 23–24, 26–27; first shots in, 27;
  Mollet and Ben-Gurion's meeting in,
  29–31
suicide bombings, 418, 423, 424, 448,
  449–50, 461, 469–70, 481, 483, 537,
  538, 540
Suleiman, Omar, 8
Sullivan, William, 217, 220, 224, 225–27,
  228, 229–31, 232, 238, 241, 578*n24*
Sultan, Prince of Saudi Arabia, 200, 321,
  380, 517, 535
Sunni insurgency, 544
Sununu, John, 364
surge, 548
Sutherland, Terry, 324
Swift, Ann, 238
Sykes-Picot Agreement, 558*n3*
Symington, Stuart, 74, 83, 150
Syria, 16, 21, 29, 33, 34, 47, 48, 78, 80, 86,
  95, 99, 101, 103, 105, 108, 109, 127,
  188, 189, 209, 257, 262, 266, 270, 271,
  272, 302, 369, 377, 393, 394, 408,
  411–12, 414, 445–46, 462, 464, 470,
  497, 498, 505, 525, 528, 538, 551–53,
  553, 558*n3*, 564*nn21, 22*, 570–71*n16*,

585*n*87, 595*n*12, 598*n*66; attempted coup in, 52–53, 63; Israel attacked by, 78–79; and Israeli invasion of Lebanon, 270, 273, 274, 277–78, 282, 283, 286, 294, 295, 296; Israel's negotiations with, 500–501; Soviet arms sale to, 48, 77; in Yom Kippur War, 138, 142, 143, 147, 149–50, 154, 167; *see also* Golan Heights

Taiping Rebellion, 325
Tal, Wasfi al-, 108–10, 117, 567–68*n*2
Talabani, Jalal, 434–35, 436, 437, 438, 439, 465, 466
Taliban, 538, 540
Tanzania, 487–88
Tarnak Farms, 485–86, 487, 512, 602*n*48
Tarnoff, Peter, 596*n*37
TASS, 157
Teicher, Howard, 278–79, 287, 293, 299, 310–11, 329, 584*n*70, 586*n*105, 589*n*36
Tel Aviv, 423
Temple Mount, 477, 505–10
Tenet, George, *10*, 482, 492–93, 516, 519, 533, 557*n*1, 596*n*37, 597*nn*39,40, 599*n*79; in Bandar's palace, 3–5, 8, 12–13; bin Laden tracked by, 485–86, 489, 512, 602*nn*49, *51*, 602–603*n*56; Bush's defense of, 7–8; Iraq WMDs and, 7, 557*n*2; prewar intelligence blunders of, *12*, 557*n*3; resignation of, 13, 172; torture and, 9–11, 557–58*n*7; in war on terror, 9
terrorism, 114, 117, 118, 121, 184–86, 196–97, 324–25, 362, 538, 594*nn*78, 84
*Terror Out of Zion* (Bell), 185
Thatcher, Margaret, 321–22, 353, 367, 380, 547
Third Crusade, 506
Third Way, 480
Thompson, Llewellyn, 73
*Time*, 111, 115
*Times, The* (London), 577*n*6
Tiran, Strait of, 57, 60, 71, 83, 90, 93, 94, 127, 206, 207, 566*n*51
Tocqueville, Alexis de, 218
torture: Bush's sanctioning of, 9–11, 557–58*n*7; by Saddam Hussein, 455
Toynbee, Arnold, 559*n*13
Trevelyan, Humphrey, 46
Trilateral Commission, 180
Tripartite Declaration, 28, 53, 548
Truman, Harry S., 12, 24–25, 34, 60, 73, 150, 218, 223, 225, 228, 256, 407, 457–58, 553, 562–63*n*4
Tudeh Party, Iranian, 329

Tuhamy, Hassan, 188
Turkey, 433, 466, 467
Turmos, Ahmed, 323
Turmos, Sobhi, 323
Turmos, Zeinab, 323
Turner, Stansfield, 243
Tuttle, Jerry, 299

United Arab Emirates, 361
United Arab Republic, 63, 78, 362, 564*n*21
United Nations, 20, 21, 24, 56, 57, 60, 61, 67, 70, 72, 76, 78, 138, 191, 198, 269, 304, 346, 357, 383, 425, 427, 461, 463, 536, 541, 548, 549–50, 553, 559*n*14, 589*n*32; Iraq sanctions of, 6, 386, 422, 467, 510, 537; Palestinian statehood and, 23, 34; Persian Gulf War resolutions of, 377, 386; Six-Day War resolution of, 104, 105, 154, 164, 187, 188, 199, 204, 206, 348, 393, 567*n*72; weapons inspectors of, 5, 440, 495; Yom Kippur War and, 139, 144, 147, 163, 168
United Nations Emergency Force, 80
United States, 14, 190–91, 571*n*28, 586*n*5, 589*nn*32, 36, 37, 599*n*1, 600*nn*5, *12*; bin Laden's declaration of war against, 467, 484, 487; Egyptian aid by, 42, 43, 44, 563*n*9; Iranian embassy of, 237–39, 240–44, 245, 246–47, 252, 579*n*58; Iraq invaded by, 542–46, 548–49; Israeli aid from, 131, 144, 151–52, 156–57, 159, 169, 183, 197, 253, 254, 255, 258, 263, 270, 277, 558*n*6, 562*n*3, 568*n*6; Kuwaiti embassy of, 302; Lebanese embassy of, 291–92; Saudi aid and sales from, 199, 200, 201, 261–62, 311, 312, 316, 317, 354–55; in war in Afghanistan, 538, 597*n*40; as world power, 32, 559*n*14
U Thant, 72, 80, 105

Valenti, Jack, 74
Vance, Cyrus, 180, 181, 187, 206, 208, 226, 229, 230–31, 235, 239, 578*n*28
Veliotes, Nicholas, 265–66, 274, 281
Vesey, John W., Jr., 286, 288
Vietnam War, 65–66, 68, 70, 73, 74, 77, 80, 83, 97, 99, 105, 111, 113, 119, 123, 128, 129, 157, 181, 184, 222, 281, 289, 294, 296, 341, 357, 362, 372, 546, 549, 557–58*n*7
Viets, Richard, 236, 581*n*7
*Vincennes*, USS, 342, 590*n*55
Vinogradov, Vladimir, 133–34, 139, 146

*Virginia*, USS, 296–97
Vorontsov, Yuri, 147

Wailing Wall, 515
Waldheim, Kurt, 254
*Wall Street Journal, The*, 594n84
Walsh, Lawrence, 399
Walters, Vernon, 174
Ward, Frederick Townsend, 325
War Powers Act (1973), 288, 585n75
*Washington Post, The*, 6, 132, 312, 324, 336, 353, 483, 567–68n2
waterboarding, 557n5, 594n84
Watergate, 113, 122, 124, 130, 137, 138, 150, 152, 154, 157, 159, 160, 163, 168, 172, 177, 211, 225, 484, 549, 571n25
Watson, Marvin, 74
Wazir, Khalil al-, 344, 345
weapons of mass destruction, 5; as pretext for Iraq invasion, 5–6, 7
Weinberger, Caspar, 257–58, 261, 266, 267, 279, 280, 284, 292, 302, 304, 305, 328, 331, 333–34, 335, 339, 372, 396, 528, 584n70, 585–86n97, 586n105, 587n8; military action in Lebanon opposed by, 285–86, 288, 299–300, 301
Weir, Benjamin T., 307, 331–32
Weizman, Ezer, 81, 85, 93, 96, 194, 195, 197, 200, 201, 203, 208, 236, 424, 583–84n51
Weizmann, Chaim, 29, 33
Weizmann Institute, 70
West Bank, 45, 78, 103, 105, 186, 189, 195, 199, 271, 285, 347, 379, 388, 390, 394, 409, 414, 416, 417, 442, 475, 478, 480, 481, 482–83, 497, 501–502, 505, 507, 510, 513, 515, 527, 528, 532; at Camp David summit, 203, 204, 205, 206, 208, 234, 235, 237, 247
Western Wall, 477, 513, 515
West Iraq Liaison Element, 453
Wheeler, Earle G., 83–84, 88–89
White Revolution, 211, 216
Whitewater Development Corporation, 416, 483, 595–96n16
Will, George, 160
Williams, Edward Bennett, 520
Williams, Pete, 362, 375
Wilson, Harold, 85, 88, 91
Wilson, Joseph, 377
Winston, Harry, 319

Wirthlin, Dick, 348
Wise, Phil, 239
Wolfowitz, Paul, 11, 375
Woodward, Bob, 324, 330, 557n3, 588n18
Woolsey, James, 432, 433
World Bank, 48, 50
World Trade Center: 1993 bombing of, 400–401, 484, 594; *see also* September 11, 2001, terrorist attacks of
World War I, 22, 32
World War II, 14, 17, 31–32, 34, 40, 74, 258, 400
Wye River negotiations, 491–93, 495

Yaakov, Yitzhak, 90, 565n43
Yaari, Ehud, 584n59
Yadin, Yigal, 195
Yadlin, Amos, 254
Yamani, Zaki, 147, 159
Yariv, Aharon, 79, 81, 93
Yasin, Abdul Rahman, 400
Yasin, Musab, 400
Yassin, Ahmed, 442, 473, 474–75, 494, 601n25
Yates, Sidney, 21
Yatom, Danny, 470, 473, 474, 475
Yazdi, Ibrahim, 233, 238, 579–80n65
*Yedioth Aharonoth*, 440
Yeltsin, Boris, 390, 482
Yemen, 20, 67, 75–76, 77, 82, 104, 327, 358, 377, 397, 459, 563n9, 592n42, 598n66
Yom Kippur War, 16, 135–75, 178, 179, 280, 464, 569–70n1, 570n13, 570–71n16, 571nn23, 25, 572n43, 573nn54, 60, 65, 574n68; American airlift in, 151–52, 156–57, 159, 169; casualties in, 155; first wave of attacks in, 136; Israeli intelligence before, 135, 137; Soviet arms in, 142; as threat to Israel, 11, 142; U.S. arms in, 144
Yousef, Ramzi, 399–401, 484–85, 594n84
Yugoslavia, 72

Zahedi, Ardeshir, 210, 225–26
Zaire, 200
Zamir, Zvi, 569–70n1
Zawahiri, Ayman al-, 537
Zebari, Hoshyar, 598n54
Ziegler, Ron, 143
Zionism, 32, 33–34, 35–36, 37, 67–68, 125, 347, 412, 559n9
Zubaida, Abu, 557n5